Teaching Young Children

2nd edition

For Ted and all lifelong learners

Teaching Young Children

Choices in Theory and Practice
2nd edition

GLENDA MAC NAUGHTON & GILLIAN WILLIAMS

Open University Press

Open University Press
McGraw-Hill Education
McGraw-Hill House
Shoppenhangers Road
Maidenhead
Berkshire
England
SL6 2QL

email: enquiries@openup.co.uk
world wide web: www.openup.co.uk

and Two Penn Plaza, New York, NY 10121-2289, USA

Open University Press first edition first published 2004
This edition published 2009

A catalogue record of this book is available from the British Library

ISBN-13: 978 0 335 23592 6   ISBN-10: 0 335 23592 1

Library of Congress Cataloguing-in-Publication Data
CIP data applied for

Printed by Bell and Bain Ltd, Glasgow
www.bell-bain.co.uk

The McGraw·Hill Companies

Contents

Preface

We have been very fortunate in having many forms and sources of support during the process of writing the first, second and now the third editions of this book. Acknowledging them at this point in the book's life is one of the more pleasurable writing tasks.

In writing the first edition of the book we were very lucky to be able to draw on the professional skills of many staff members in the Department of Early Childhood Studies, The University of Melbourne.

The second and third editions drew on additional people from the Centre for Equity and Innovation in Early Childhood (CEIEC) at The University of Melbourne. Kate Alexander provided research assistance that supported us in updating this third edition. She did this in such a calm, organised and careful way that it made the integration of contemporary research a pleasure rather than a task to be accomplished.

Finding good photographs of adults working with children is difficult. We would like to thank children and staff from the Early Learning Centre at The University of Melbourne; Swanston Street Children's Centre; Carlton Child Care Centre; Kew Primary School; the LaTrobe University Occasional Care Centre; Claire, Jude and David; Mimi, Fergus, Eliza and Hannah; and the Davis Street Kindergarten, all of whom allowed Gillian to photograph them at work and at play.

Many thanks to Alison Green at Pearson Education Australia for her commitment to this third edition and to Sandra Goodall for her good and patient guidance throughout the production process.

On a more personal note, Glenda would again like to thank Patrick for his unfailing emotional, political and intellectual support throughout the writing of the book. It was an intense time of writing that brought the third edition to fruition and without that support it would not have seen the light of day. His timely and determined reading and checking of proofs also made it possible for these to be returned to the publisher much more promptly than would otherwise have been possible. Gillian thanks her family: David for his steadfast belief in her abilities, and Amy, Mary, Hannah, Eliza, Mimi, Fergus and Evie for their real-life demonstrations of teaching and learning.

Introduction

It has been our experience that early childhood students and staff are often frustrated by the lack of specific guidance on how to teach young children. There is a plethora of books that can be used to develop early childhood programs and that explore issues in curriculum implementation. Typically, these books explain the theories and principles of early childhood education, present some process for curriculum development and implementation, and contain ideas about how to structure specific learning experiences to enhance children's development. They also contain information about how to incorporate specific discipline-based learning from the arts and the sciences into the curriculum.

While these books provide staff and students with essential knowledge about early childhood education, they provide scant information about the specific teaching techniques they can use to support children's learning. The sparseness of information makes it difficult for staff to evaluate the theory and practice of their own teaching, and to extend and enrich their repertoire of useful and appropriate teaching techniques. The detailed information on teaching techniques is often scattered through journals that are difficult for students and staff to access, or written in very academic and inaccessible language. For these reasons, we felt it was timely to write a book that would present students and staff with an accessible and detailed discussion on the how and why of teaching in early childhood settings. The positive response to the first and second editions of this book, has affirmed our initial decision to develop a book focused on the interaction between adult teaching techniques and young children's learning.

This book presents early childhood students and staff with a broad and diverse range of teaching techniques to support children's learning. We don't want to 'tell' staff what to do but to provide them with options that they can test in practice and integrate into their own teaching repertoire. We examine 18 general teaching techniques commonly mentioned in early childhood texts and 12 specialist techniques that offer diverse theoretical perspectives on teaching. The techniques range from simple methods, such as describing and listening, through to more complex techniques, such as deconstruction and scaffolding.

Each chapter presents one technique. It discusses what the technique is, how staff can use it in their work with children, and when and why they might use it. In thinking about when and why staff might (or might not) opt for a particular technique we have explored current early childhood theory and practice and discussed how this impacts on the goal relevance of the technique and the developmental and equity considerations we consider relevant to the technique. Developmental considerations cover babies, toddlers, preschoolers and children in the early years of school. The specific equity considerations we explore are gender, 'race' and culture, and disability. The word 'race' is in single inverted commas throughout the text to indicate that 'race' is a socially and politically constructed categorisation of people rather than an inherent (biological) fact and to remind readers of the contested nature of this construction. Vignettes and examples show how early childhood staff can use the techniques to support children's learning and help to bring the discussion of each technique to life.

In the final chapter we argue for a strategic approach to selecting teaching techniques which link educational philosophy with choices about specific teaching techniques. We examine the links between the techniques presented in the earlier chapters and specific educational philosophies and goals. To explore this link, we present several approaches to early childhood curriculum highly regarded over some years in the international early childhood field: the Anti-Bias Curriculum, the High/Scope Preschool Curriculum, Montessori Education, the Reggio Emilia Approach, and Steiner and Waldorf Schooling.

The alphabetical organisation of the chapters within each section in this third edition follows the successful formula used in the first two editions. This should make it possible for early childhood students and staff to dip in and out of the book. While the book is not intended to be read sequentially, students and staff will find it easier to understand the specialist techniques in Part 3 if they are familiar with Parts 1 and 2. The final chapter is also more likely to have meaning once readers have explored the earlier parts of the book.

The third edition was written at a time of increasing interest in early childhood education internationally, a rapidly expanding research base about teaching and learning in the field, and shifting and expanding theoretical perspectives about teaching and learning and about childhood. There has been a growing presence of socio-cultural and postmodern perspectives within the field. This has brought a clear recognition of the role of cultural context in mediating learning and development.

The third edition has responded to this dynamic conceptual and research context by significantly updating its research base for each chapter, principally using research from primary sources as it relates to each of the chapters. It draws on several hundred pieces of contemporary research on children's learning and development, the role of new technologies in children's learning and current issues in building more equitable classrooms to highlight current thinking on the what, how and why of each technique. It has been a challenge to source research from countries other than the USA for many of the techniques, but where possible we have sought to include research conducted beyond its borders in recognition of the diverse cultural contexts in which teachers do early childhood work.

In response to the dynamism and diversity within the field (see for example, Keesing-Styles and Hedges 2007; MacNaughton 2005; Anning, Cullen and Fleer 2004) this third edition also highlights at least one contemporary debate or issue as it pertains to a specific teaching technique. We hope this will support readers' critical reflection on specific teaching techniques and their relevance to their own teaching and learning theories and philosophies.

In acknowledgement of the growing interest in children's rights and early childhood education as a socially progressive democratic endeavour (e.g. Kjørholt 2005; MacNaughton 2005; Hughes, MacNaughton and Smith 2007), the third edition also includes two new chapters in the section on Specialist Teaching Techniques: 'Decolonising' and 'Democratising'.

The third edition also provides totally updated further reading and resource lists that include suggested online and multi-media resources relevant to the ideas within the chapter. As a result, the majority of the chapters have been revised and at times extended with additional guidance and examples provided to support exploration of a specific teaching technique.

Analysing teaching in early childhood settings

WHAT IS TEACHING?

> In some respects teaching is like lighting a fire. We bring heat to paper to enable it to start combining with oxygen in its environment. In the classroom our function is similar; we bring to bear various teaching devices with a view to producing a 'flash' between each child and some part of his [and her] environment. (Hughes and Hughes 1937, p. 355)

The daily interactions between staff and children in an early childhood setting provide a myriad of opportunities for such 'flashes'. Skilful staff draw on a wide repertoire of teaching 'devices' during these interactions to maximise children's learning. In this book we will look at how several general and specialist teaching 'devices' can 'light the fire' of children's learning and 'fan its flame'. For ease of access we have grouped the general and specialist 'devices' or, as we prefer, 'techniques' alphabetically.

GENERAL VERBAL AND NON-VERBAL TECHNIQUES

While teaching is a complex, highly interactive process, much of the teaching process involves the continuous use of very simple and subtle verbal interactions that may only last moments. Many of these interactions rely on what we refer to as generic, everyday verbal teaching techniques, such as describing, questioning, recalling and telling. Despite the subtlety and simplicity of such teaching techniques they can be powerful in shaping children's learning. They also form the foundations on which the more complex specialist teaching techniques build.

Non-verbal teaching techniques contribute an important element to the overall tone, texture and meaning within staff's daily interactions with children. For example, listening to children can help contribute to a tone of respect for their ideas and efforts, it can help contribute to a sense of calm within the group and it can help staff to understand more precisely what children are thinking, feeling and learning. Many simple non-verbal teaching techniques such as helping, listening and demonstrating also form the foundation of several of the more complex specialist techniques discussed in this book (for example, scaffolding and task analysis).

The simplicity of many of the non-verbal techniques discussed in this book means that they are easy to learn and easy to use. However, the simplicity of these techniques also means that they can be overlooked or overused. Successful use of these techniques relies on knowing when to use them (timing) and what can be accomplished (or not) by using them.

TIMING

Good teaching relies on good timing. Knowing just when a comment, question or suggestion might be useful can be difficult to judge. So, timing the right moment to intervene in children's learning is hard. Staff need to make judgments by thinking about what will be gained and what will be lost through their intervention. The following questions can help staff decide if the gains from intervening might outweigh the losses.

- Will the children learn more effectively and more enjoyably if I intervene?
- Is the children's learning and enjoyment at risk if I don't intervene?
- Is this the best moment to intervene?

These questions, and the answers to them, often need to be posed and answered in a split second. Careful observation of the children, knowledge of how they learn best and experience of what works best, all combine to help staff judge if and when to intervene.

Choosing the optimum moment and method of intervention is a fundamental art of teaching.

As Edwards (1993, p. 159) writes:

. . . you are always afraid that you are going to miss that hot moment. It's really a balancing act. I believe in intervention, yet personally I tend to wait because I have noticed that children often resolve the problem on their own, and not always in the way that I would have told them to! Children often find solutions that I would never have seen. But sometimes waiting means missing the moment. So it's a decision that you have to make very quickly.

The decision about if, how and when to intervene in children's learning depends on several factors. However, once staff choose to intervene they have another set of choices about how to do so. These choices form the substance of this book.

Choosing the best teaching technique for a specific child or learning experience is complex. Your choice can be affected by many factors. In this book we will consider how your choice of a teaching technique might be influenced by:

- your chosen teaching goals
- a child's developmental age and stage
- research knowledge about how children's learning can best be enhanced
- the desire for equity for boys and girls, children from diverse racial and cultural backgrounds, and children with disabilities.

In the following chapters we consider the relevance of each of these factors in developing excellence in teaching. In this consideration we take an anti-discriminatory (anti-bias) approach to equity issues. This approach rests on the belief that the best way to ensure an excellent education for all children is to actively promote positive acceptance of and respect for diversity. This involves challenging discrimination when it occurs and working to empower children to be active in creating a fair and just world.

Teaching, excellence and respect

All children deserve good teaching. (Hatton 1994, p. xv)

We would argue that all children deserve respectful and excellent teaching. But, how do staff know what excellent teaching is? This book aims to help early childhood staff to think about the best way to teach young children and to become better teachers.

Teaching is a process through which early childhood staff assist and encourage children's learning. It is a highly complex and dynamic process in which staff make decisions about how to respond to children to best support their learning.

To choose the best response for each child, staff need to reflect on:

- what they are going to do
- what they are going to say
- whether they need to do or say anything
- how they will set up the environment.

In early childhood settings excellent teaching involves basing these decisions on knowledge of and understanding about:

- children's differing ways of growing and changing in differing cultural contexts
- individual children's characteristics
- children's rights to have a voice in matters that affect them

- the cultural values of the children's families
- parental desires for their children's learning
- a sense of what is fair, respectful and ethical.

In this book we believe that teaching is a process that aims to respect and foster children's learning and wellbeing. It is an interactive process between child and teacher that is culturally mediated, extremely complex, dynamic and demands that early childhood staff reflect on children's responses to their program and respond in the ways that they believe will most assist children's learning. It is, therefore, a highly value-based process and one that challenges early childhood staff to consider how best to respect children's diverse lives and cultures (MacNaughton and Hughes 2007).

Excellence and intervention: a necessary coalition?

However interested children are in their work, some teaching is necessary. Some skilful teachers apparently give very little teaching. The fact is, however, that they are continuously teaching in many subtle ways . . . (Hughes and Hughes 1937, p. 357)

In the early childhood field there is considerable debate about what is the best way to respond to children to optimise learning. Much of this debate centres on the question of how much and what kind of adult intervention is needed to promote young children's learning. Some people argue for minimal adult intervention and believe that indirect teaching methods are the most appropriate for early childhood settings. Others are convinced that direct, highly interventionist techniques are more appropriate in these settings. As Edwards (1993, p. 152) says, teachers can choose to work 'inside' the group of children or 'just around' them. Several differing views on the level of intervention needed to promote children's learning are reflected in the following quotes.

In interactionist approaches…the role of the adult is critical to children's learning, providing structure and support, with meaning-making the paramount focus. (Makin 1996, p. 76)

The role of the adult is above all one of listening, observing, and understanding the strategy that children use in a learning situation. The teacher has…a role as dispenser of occasions . . . not a judge but a resource. (Edwards 1993, p. 153)

It is the task of the teacher to stand between the known and unknown. The teacher must see where students are and lay the stepping stones to new knowledge surely and safely so that the students come to trust themselves, their teachers and the educational process. (Jonquiere 1990, p. 292)

Adults will observe children interacting with the environment, listen to them, ask questions, demonstrate possible solutions and know when to withdraw and allow the child to make a discovery. (Department of Human Services 1996, p. 6)

I try to stand aside and allow…[the children] to speak for themselves. It is not easy to wait and listen. (Paley 1986, p. xv)

While there are many different views about the precise level and type of intervention that is most likely to optimise children's learning, there seems increasing agreement that some form of adult intervention is necessary. The debate about the optimal nature of this intervention continues with an increase in evidence-based approaches to early education being enacted, tensions between the efficacy of direct instruction and child-directed learning apparent and the move to understand early education as an enactment of democracy evident (see Dahlberg and Moss 2005).

Intervention and reflective teaching

Irrespective of staff beliefs about intervention in children's learning, all staff do and must intervene in the daily actions and decisions of the children in their care. As Spodek (1987, p. 5) reminded us:

> Early childhood education, like all education, is a deliberate intervention in the lives of young children. It results from a belief that children growing up naturally might not come to know all the things we want them to know.

We believe that excellent teaching is most likely to occur when staff make informed choices about their interventions and see excellent teaching as reflective teaching. Engaging with current debates about what young children can know and should know is essential to critical reflection about when, how, where and why to intervene in young children's lives. Reflective teachers think carefully about what they are doing and saying or not saying in the daily interactions with children, and question what children have or have not learnt from these interactions. Reflective teachers are committed to improving their teaching through regular evaluation of their teaching techniques. They question what has or has not worked to enhance children's learning and make changes in their approach accordingly. They ask questions about who benefits from what they do and about the cultural relevance and effects of their work (MacNaughton 2005).

Careful and critical reflection on teaching choices contributes to excellence in teaching in several ways:

- There is considerable evidence that children across different class, gender, ethnic and ability groups experience unequal educational outcomes. Staff, therefore, need to carefully consider how they can best intervene to reduce such inequalities in educational outcomes and to promote greater equality of outcomes for all children in their care.
- Research into teachers' choice of teaching methods suggests that many teachers have a 'fairly narrow and conservative repertoire of teacher behaviours' (Hatton 1994, p. 7) that often mimic those teaching methods they experienced in their own schooling. Access to information about a broad and diverse repertoire of teaching methods can increase the likelihood that staff will choose the best rather than the most familiar way to further children's learning.
- Teaching is full of dilemmas, successes and failures for both experienced and inexperienced staff alike. These dilemmas are increasingly born of tensions between teachers' own beliefs and practices and the practices they believe are required of them through state-mandated curriculum (Adcock and Patton 2001; Oberheumer 2005). Knowledge of a broad and diverse range of teaching methods can help staff reflect on alternative ways to assist children's learning when the more familiar methods fail. It can also assist them to critically engage with state-mandated curriculum practices and the curriculum policy debates that are increasingly evident internationally (Adcock and Patton 2001).

There has been a growing interest in giving teachers a 'voice' in research on teaching and learning (see, for example, Adcock and Patton 2001; Kim 2004; MacNaughton 2005). The argument of those wanting to prioritise teachers' theories of teaching and learning is that the answers to what is meaningful and what works best can be found in real-life settings with real-life teachers and children. In line with this interest, and a commitment in this book to being 'practical', we will draw on early childhood staff's experiences and theories of what works best, not just on formal academic research.

However, we are mindful that written instructions and provocations about what constitutes best teaching practice is just one part of the story of ensuring excellence in teaching for all children. Excellence in teaching relies on early childhood staff making informed decisions about what to do and say, based on their own reflections and analysis of their day-to-day teaching. We strongly support Isenberg's (1990, p. 325) view that:

> Thoughtful teaching is central to professional growth. When teachers reflect upon instruction, they can analyse the result of their decisions on students. Classroom teachers who are active problem-solvers are key agents in school reform . . . Teachers engaged in inquiry about their own practice must become an increasingly important aspect of the continuing development of teachers.

Techniques for Teaching Young Children is not a recipe book to be followed uncritically, but an 'aide-memoir', an 'idea starter' and an 'enricher' to the daily practices and theories of early childhood students and staff. Techniques should be used, modified and/or rejected on the basis of careful evaluation of practice. Excellence in teaching relies on such careful testing and on critical reflection of what best supports young children's learning.

In summary, reflection on teaching involves thinking about what you have said and done (or not said and done) with the children. It also involves thinking about what you can learn from your actions (and inactions) to improve the effectiveness of your teaching for children's learning. We believe that when staff have critically informed access to a diverse range of teaching techniques, children and staff benefit: children are more likely to experience excellent teaching and staff are more likely to find their work satisfying.

Who can teach? The thorny issue of care and education

Education is a process not a place. It can occur within a diverse range of places including child care settings. There is nothing magical about the institutions of kindergartens or schools that gives them the sole prerogative over claiming their work is educational. It is the teaching practices, not the institutions, that make interactions educational. To argue that only people called 'teachers' can teach is misguided, given the particular stage we have reached in training early childhood staff across all service types to deliver flexible, developmentally appropriate services for young children.

We need to move beyond our concern about teaching only happening when people called 'teachers' do it, to a concern with maximising the contribution of all who work in services for young children to fostering excellence and meaning in every interaction they have with young children. In this move we need to ensure that teaching is understood as a deliberate, thoughtful process based on knowledge of how children learn and a set of beliefs about what it is important for them to learn. When this happens we will be optimising learning and possibilities for all children. We hope this book offers a useful contribution to this process.

Conclusion

The principles underpinning the approach to teaching in this section, on which the rest of this book is based, are:

1 All children deserve excellent teaching.
2 Teaching is a highly complex and dynamic decision-making process about how to best respond to children to support their learning.
3 Teaching involves intervention in children's lives.
4 Teaching is value-based.
5 There is no single correct way to respond to children to optimise learning.

6 Careful and critical reflection on teaching choices contributes to excellence in teaching.

7 Choosing the optimum moment and method of intervention is the fundamental art of teaching.

8 Teaching techniques should be relevant to teaching goals.

9 Teaching techniques should be relevant to all children. This means they must be developmentally appropriate, culturally appropriate, acknowledge the different learning styles of girls and boys and of children with disabilities.

10 Teaching techniques should be anti-discriminatory.

11 Education is a process not a place, therefore teaching can occur within a diverse range of settings including those of child care.

12 Drawing on information about best practice from research and from international developments in the early childhood field contributes to excellence in teaching.

Reflecting on the nature of teaching and learning

1 How would you define teaching?

2 How would you define excellent and respectful teaching?

3 Haberman (1994, p. 24) believes that 'good' teaching involves 'drawing out rather than stuffing in'. What do you think this means? Do you agree? How would you define 'good' teaching?

4 What do you see as the relationship between teaching, timing and observation?

5 To what extent do the quotes on pages xii to ix emphasise working 'inside' or 'around' the children? Which of the quotes most closely represent your view of intervention? What factors have influenced your views on intervention? Are there some times or situations in which a higher or lower level of intervention might be appropriate? Does the age group you work with influence how you feel about intervention?

6 What do you think is meant by 'reflecting on teaching'? What do you think can be learned by regular reflection?

7 To what extent do you agree with the following statement?

Teachers need to feel trusted and respected as professionals, free to make choices and decisions (Conzemius, 1999, p. 34).

How might administrators and managers demonstrate 'trust' and 'respect' for teacher choices and decision-making?

FURTHER READING

Adcock, S.G. and Patton, M.M. 2001, 'Voices of effective early childhood educators regarding systematic constraints that affect their teaching', *Journal of Research in Childhood Education*, 15(2), pp. 194–208.

Keesing-Styles, L. and Sumison, J. 2007, 'Connection, dissension and dialogue: the role of the teacher education in promoting social justice', in Keesing-Styles, L. and Hedges, H., eds, *Theorising Early Childhood Practice: Emerging Dialogues* (pp. 211–232), Pademelon Press, Sydney.

Kjørholt, A. 2005, 'The competent child and the "right to be oneself": reflections on children as fellow citizens in an early childhood centre', in A. Clark, A. Kjørholt and P. Moss, eds, *Beyond Listening: Children's Perspectives on Early Childhood Services* (pp. 151–174), Policy Press, London.

MacNaughton, G. 2005, *Doing Foucault in Early Childhood Studies*, Routledge Falmer Press, London, New York and New Delhi [refer to Introduction].

REFERENCES

Adcock, S.G. and Patton, M.M. 2001, 'Voices of effective early childhood educators regarding systematic constraints that affect their teaching', *Journal of Research in Childhood Education*, 15(2), pp. 194–208.

Anning, A., Cullen, J. and Fleer, M. (eds) 2004, *Early Childhood Education: Society and Culture*, Sage Publications, London, Thousand Oaks and New Delhi.

Conzemius, A. 1999, 'Ally in the office', *Journal of Staff Development*, 20, pp. 31–34.

Dahlberg, G. and Moss, P. 2005, *Ethics and Politics in Early Childhood Education*, Routledge Taylor and Francis Group, London and New York.

Department of Human Services 1996, *Babies, Toddlers and Two-Year-Olds: A Curriculum Resource for Developing Child-Centred Programs for Children Under Three*, Government of Victoria, Melbourne.

Edwards, C. 1993, 'Partner, nurturer and guide: the roles of the Reggio teacher in action', in C. Edwards, L. Gandini and G. Foreman, eds, *The Hundred Languages of Children: The Reggio Emilia Approach to Early Childhood Education* (pp. 151–69), Ablex Publishing Company, Norwood, New Jersey.

Haberman, M. 1994, 'The pedagogy of poverty versus good teaching', in E. Hatton, ed., *Understanding Teaching: Curriculum and the Social Context of Schooling* (pp. 17–25), Harcourt Brace, Sydney.

Hatton, E. 1994, *Understanding Teaching: Curriculum and the Social Context of Schooling*, Harcourt Brace, Sydney.

Hughes, A. and Hughes, E. 1937, *Learning and Teaching: An Introduction to Psychology and Education*, Longman, London.

Hughes, P., MacNaughton, G. and Smith, K. 2007, 'The United Nations General Comment (no. 7) on children's rights in their early childhood years: tensions and possibilities', *International Journal of Early Years Education*, 15(2), pp. 161–170.

Isenberg, J. 1990, 'Teachers' Thinking and Beliefs and Classroom Practice', *Childhood Education*, 66(5), pp. 322–327.

Jonquiere, H. 1990, 'My beliefs about teaching', *Childhood Education*, 66(5), pp. 291–293.

Keesing-Styles, L. and Hedges, H. (eds.) 2007, *Theorising Early Childhood Practice: Emerging Dialogues*, Pademelon Press, Sydney.

Kim, M. 2004, 'Teachers' philosophical orientation and practices: a study of novice preschool teachers in South Korea', *Contemporary Issues in Early Childhood,* 5(3), pp. 276–292.

Kjørholt, A. 2005, 'The competent child and the "right to be oneself": reflections on children as fellow citizens in an early childhood centre', in A. Clark, A. Kjørholt and P. Moss (eds.), *Beyond Listening: Children's Perspectives on Early Childhood Services*, Policy Press, London, pp. 151–174.

MacNaughton, G. 2005, *Doing Foucault in Early Childhood Studies,* Routledge Falmer Press, London, New York and New Delhi.

MacNaughton, G. and Hughes, P. 2007, 'Teaching respect for cultural diversity in Australian early childhood programs: a challenge for professional learning', *Journal of Early Childhood Research,* 5, pp. 189–204.

Makin, L. 1996, 'Play and the language profiles and scales', in M. Fleer, (ed.), *Play through the Profiles: Profiles through Play* (pp. 68–84), Australian Early Childhood Association, Watson, ACT.

Oberheumer, P. 2005, 'Conceptualising the early childhood pedagogue: Policy approaches and issues of professionalism', *European Early Childhood Education Journal,* 13(1), pp. 5–16.

Paley, V. 1986, *Mollie is Three: Growing up in School*, University of Chicago Press, Chicago.

Spodek, B. 1987, 'The knowledge base of kindergarten education', in *Five Year Olds in School Conference*, Minnesota, ED280569.

PART ONE

Teaching and the Environment

Chapter 1

Positioning equipment and materials

 Position: the place, situation or location of a person or a thing.
(*Collins Dictionary of the English Language*, p. 1143)

A place for everything and, everything in its place.

(Samuel Smiles [late 19th century],
cited in Cohen and Cohen 1960)

. . . we must expand our thinking beyond the notion of room arrangement. We must ask ourselves what values we want to communicate through learning environments, how we want children to experience their time in our programs.

(Curtis and Carter, 2005, p. 35)

What?

Positioning is the process of placing objects in relation to each other or in relation to people. As a teaching technique, positioning involves placing learning materials to safely and ethically support and enhance children's learning.

Issues and debates

WHOSE RIGHT IS IT TO POSITION EQUIPMENT AND MATERIALS?

There is an increasing move internationally to honour children's rights in early childhood spaces (MacNaughton, Hughes and Smith 2007a; Exley 2005). This has engendered debate about several aspects of how early childhood spaces are organised, including who should position equipment and materials in them. Traditionally, the role of the early childhood professional has been to take the decisions about how equipment and materials are positioned within a specific space.

Now, several early childhood educators are exploring how they might more effectively honour children's rights by giving children a voice and some power in this process (MacNaughton, Hughes and Smith 2007b; Clarke 2007). This involves seeking children's views on what equipment they would like within their learning environment and how it might best be organised. If children have not been used to being involved in these decisions staff can support them to express their ideas through text, conversations and images. While some argue that children are too young to have clear and appropriate ideas about the best ways to position equipment, research is challenging this idea. Clarke (2007) details the strategies successfully used in a project with 28 three- and four-year-old children in the UK to explore children's perspectives on their outside environment. She emphasises the importance of multi-method approaches to gathering children's ideas and the importance of listening carefully to what they are expressing.

How?

Staff need to think about several interrelated facets of the physical organisation of inside and outside space to place materials in such as way as to safely and ethically assist children's learning.

OVERALL PHYSICAL ORGANISATION OF THE LEARNING AREAS

Staff need to decide how to place materials and equipment in the physical learning environment to best assist children's learning. Specifically, they need to decide:

- the equipment, materials and spaces they will make available in the inside and outside play areas
- the balance between the different types of closed and open spaces and materials
- the boundaries between the different areas within the centre
- the ways in which materials will be grouped together
- the ways in which the placement of materials will encourage movement and interaction between children
- the ways in which the placement of materials will allow for quiet moments of reflection
- the ways in which spaces will allow for robust physical exploration of materials.

There can be considerable advantage to having flexible, multi-use spaces that can be quickly adapted to children's changing interests and projects and that allow staff to respond flexibly to what emerges during a day with children. As Curtis and Carter (2005, online) put it:

Creating multilevel spaces inside, as well as on the playground, gives children different ways to explore spatial relationships with their bodies. Modular furniture that can be turned and stacked in different ways will provide more flexibility than when everything is designed for a single use. Offering open-ended materials in a variety of areas will spark children's imaginations and speak to their desire to continually rearrange and combine materials for exploration and inventions.

Staff need to decide with each other or with the children how they will place materials and equipment to facilitate social interaction in the learning environment. For instance, they can make places available for adults and/or children to sit individually, sit in groups, sit on the floor, sit on chairs, stand and move about. They need to decide what equipment will be placed within easy reach of the children, what equipment only adults will be able to access, how possible it will be for children to work in small and large groups, how large the groups will be and what spaces will encourage individual exploration and thinking.

DAILY PLACEMENT OF LEARNING MATERIALS

While staff may have an overall plan for organising the inside and outside learning environments, daily changes enrich and extend children's learning. For instance, placing materials near where a child is working can prompt children's interests and can make their play more elaborate. Staff can consider when and where they will place new materials and how to alter the placement of existing materials to refresh and to excite children's interest in their environment. In the following example staff placed materials to excite children's interest in making things.

In a classroom for five-year-olds, an area is defined for what the children call 'making'. A large table with chairs around it is positioned near several shelves holding tools such as staplers, tape, paste, a hole-puncher, string, pencils, crayons, needles and threads; and resources for creative and engineering work, such as paper of different colours, sizes and textures, boxes, cotton reels, buttons, pieces of plastic and so forth. The children are able to help themselves to anything that they need from the shelves.

Reflective task: Write a list of what could be put in a 'making' area. How could you place these materials so that the children can easily see what is available and use this as they are constructing?

When deciding how to place people and materials, staff should seek to create and maintain a safe, secure, interesting and pleasurable learning environment for children and adults. To do this, staff need to:

- place people to ensure safe supervision of all children and safe work conditions for all
- place equipment to meet children's and their own health and safety needs. For example, a member of staff can make a safety check every day before the first child arrives and a staff member can always be scheduled to be near the climbing equipment to assist children if needed
- place equipment to enhance the aesthetic appeal of the environment, thus maximising children's, parents' and staff's enjoyment of it
- place equipment to ensure that children gain a feeling of security and competence in their learning environment
- place equipment and materials to stimulate children's curiosity and interest by providing elements of surprise and novelty
- place equipment and adults to support equity of access to and participation in the program by all children
- place equipment to stimulate brain development.

In taking the decisions about how to place equipment and materials to support learning, Greenman (2006) emphasised the importance of creating 'working' walls, ceilings and floors that can be used for communication, display, storage and activity space.

The following discussion illustrates how one staff member balanced the need for novelty with the need for security in her approach to placing equipment in a toddlers' room.

A group of teachers are having a discussion at a seminar about environments. Jenny, a new graduate from teachers' college, is in charge of a room with fifteen toddlers. She is enthusiastic and energetic and is keen to try new ideas.

Jenny: 'I'm sick of my room, I have changed all the equipment around three times in two months and the children seem to wander around doing nothing!'

Silvana: 'I used to find that when I changed the environment around too much, the children became unsettled and didn't stay in one area for very long. Now, I keep the main areas the same—that is, the home area, the messy play area, the book corner and so forth—and I add different things to these areas from time to time. Last week I added scarves to the home area with the hats. I put pictures of the children doing finger painting in the "messy area" and I added some vinyl squares to the blocks. I find that the children like the security of everything in its place but they also like the novelty of additions.'

Jenny: 'You've given me food for thought. I can see that the children in my room have become a bit unsettled recently—perhaps I could try your idea and move some things around from time to time, not everything at once!'

Reflection point: Why do you think children need a predictable environment in which to work and play?

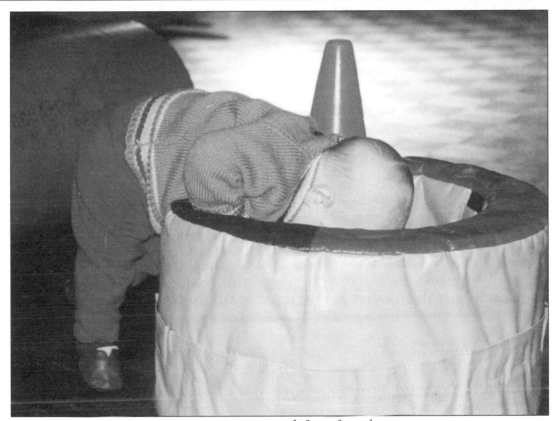

Equipment in easy reach for safe exploration.

Some suggestions to prompt staff to create a safe and satisfying learning environment follow.

PLACING EQUIPMENT TO ENSURE SAFE SUPERVISION OF CHILDREN

Placing equipment to allow for ease of supervision, and in which there are broad visible pathways, gives staff more discretionary time for teaching with individual children. Some strategies that can work are to:

- keep room dividers above adult waist height to a minimum
- when seated, be able to readily scan the inside and outside play areas
- use semi-transparent materials (for example, lace curtains) to create children's secret spaces in which staff can still see the children.

PLACING EQUIPMENT TO ENSURE CHILDREN'S AND STAFF'S HEALTH AND SAFETY

To promote health and safety for everyone in the centre, staff need to ensure that:

- play spaces are well lit
- there are comfortable temperatures and fresh air
- there is room to move around freely (for example, when using a wheelchair or walking frame)
- equipment can be reached easily and safely

- there are no sharp edges that children might knock against
- there is ready access to a space for the recycling of material and to enable the clearing of rubbish from the floor
- there are non-slip surfaces in the 'wet' areas
- there is ready access for staff to all equipment (without straining their muscles)
- dangerous substances are out of children's reach.

Staff should be alert to potential hazards when they are placing equipment. Equipment should be away from:

- electrical hazards such as leads and plugs
- heating appliances on which children can burn themselves
- glass and mirrors that can splinter and break
- things that children might swallow, that are poisonous or that may choke them.

Equipment should also be free from harmful additives or coatings. For instance, copper arsenic treated logs in the outdoor playground, plastics that create static electricity, and vinyl flooring that may have toxic glues (Knackstredt and Wellisch, 2005).

With increasing use of computers in early childhood spaces it is also important to ensure that the placement of computers enables children to sit at the computer to avoid eye and back strain. The *Sesame Street* website shows children and adults how to organise a computer to be ergonomically safe for children. (See <http://www.sesameworkshop.org/parents/solutions/information/article.php?contentId=74305>)

PLACING EQUIPMENT TO ENHANCE AESTHETIC APPEAL AND COMFORT

The lighting, colour, texture, size and density of materials, space, furnishing and equipment contribute to the aesthetics of a space—its sense of beauty—and to its level of comfort. However, people's tastes about what is pleasing are culturally based and, therefore, value-based. In trying to place equipment in a tasteful and pleasing way staff will need to negotiate with children, parents and other staff to develop an aesthetic style that is pleasing to all who use the centre. In general, an aesthetically pleasing space will be one in which:

- equipment and materials are deliberately and carefully placed, and this arrangement is maintained
- the environment evolves over time, with changes reflecting the changing interests of those who work in it
- there are soft areas that encourage people to relax, reflect and rest
- sounds and aromas are placed as carefully as objects—wind-chimes, music and perfumed oils and plants have a place in the program
- texture, shape and colour are used with care and thought to provide enjoyment, stimulation and relaxation
- visual images are hung and treated with care and respect
- there are artefacts, crafts, art and memorabilia that are culturally familiar to the children and adults, and that are displayed with care and respect
- lighting is used to add atmosphere to the room, define areas and mimic natural sunlight.

Staff can develop and maintain an aesthetically pleasing space in many ways. A large preschool in Melbourne is aware of the importance of an aesthetic environment. In order to cater for differences in taste and values, each member of staff is on a two-weekly roster to design and organise the entrance area of the centre so that it is aesthetically appealing to parents and children from different backgrounds. Feedback is sought from the children, parents and staff, and is used to good effect.

Reflective task: What kinds of things would you put in an entrance area so that the space is both aesthetically pleasing and culturally appropriate?

Consider the following descriptions by Gandini (1994) of careful positioning of materials to enhance the aesthetic appeal of a learning area in a school in Reggio Emilia, Italy.

. . . there is in these schools a great deal of attention paid to the beauty and harmony of design. This is evident in both the functional and pleasing furnishings, often invented and built by teachers and parents together. It is also evident in the colours of the walls, the sunlight streaming through large windows, the healthy green plants (p. 140).

When samples of the colourful fall leaves are brought in and pressed, each one's favourites can be placed in small, transparent pockets with other coloured treasures. All these packets are put together and placed on the glass wall to make a large display that catches the light and creates arresting shadows (p. 141).

Source: Edwards, Gandini and Formant (eds), *The Hundred Languages of Children: The Reggio Emilia Approach to Early Childhood Education*, 1994, Ablex Publishing Company, New Jersey. Reproduced by permission of Greenwood Publishing Group.

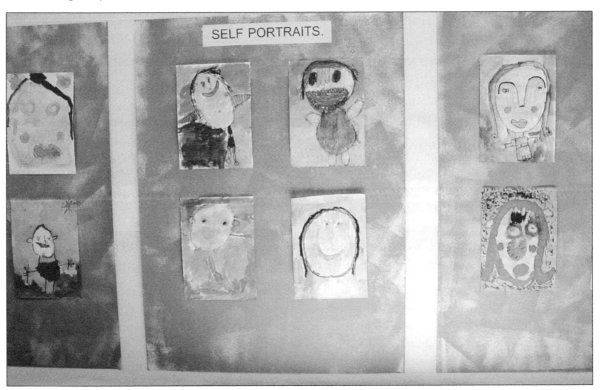

Children's artwork is carefully displayed in the foyer.

Wilson Gillespie (2000) described several changes made to the learning environment in six Head Start centres that explored the implications of Reggio Emilia for their work. For those centres, enhancing the aesthetics of the environment enriched children's play and deepened their involvement in learning. Examples included:

- adding silk flowers and tablecloths to the home-corner area
- replacing all commercially made decorations with those made by the children and staff

- storing materials in clear plastic containers so that they were more visible to the children and so their options were clearer.

PLACING EQUIPMENT TO ENHANCE CHILDREN'S SENSE OF SECURITY AND COMPETENCE

To achieve this staff need to ensure that:

- there are regular major traffic paths in the environment
- children can readily access child-safe cleaning materials and equipment
- everyday materials which children use, such as sticky-tape, glue-sticks, scissors, etc. are readily accessible to the children
- everyday materials are placed to avoid congestion when several children at once want access
- materials used regularly have an obvious home. All containers, shelves and storage bins should be labelled with names or symbols to show children where everything belongs
- children have a personal storage space for their special projects and personal belongings
- children have access to child-sized furniture and equipment when needed
- spaces that promote security and competence are generous in size and allow for child involvement, for children to spread out for moments of peace, and reduce the need to share continuously. (Conn-Powers et al. 2006; Knackstredt and Wellisch, 2005)

PLACING EQUIPMENT AND MATERIALS TO STIMULATE CHILDREN'S CURIOSITY AND WONDER

There are many ways to do this. One simple method is to position some materials 'out of place', such as placing a book in the block corner to stimulate particular types of building, or placing paints near the nature table to suggest painting nature, or using nature in paintings. Another method to stimulate children's curiosity is to place materials with which children may not be familiar in the space. This can prompt experimentation and questioning. A more complex change can also prompt new discoveries and learning.

In spaces that promote curiosity and wonder there is flexibility, open-ended materials, easily moved furniture, nooks and crannies and lots of different levels at which the children can physically work (Curtis and Carter, 2005).

PLACING EQUIPMENT TO SUPPORT EQUITY OF ACCESS AND PARTICIPATION

Staff can create equity of access and participation by ensuring that:

- children of differing physical abilities can move around easily. For example, consider how readily a child using a wheelchair or a walking frame can move around the area
- children of differing physical abilities can participate in a range of experiences
- children of differing abilities, sizes and ages can easily see and touch display areas
- children from differing cultural backgrounds can recognise their own culture in the materials and staff available to them.

PLACING EQUIPMENT TO STIMULATE BRAIN DEVELOPMENT

There is increasing evidence that the early years really do matter to young children's learning and that brain stimulation enhances brain development in very specific ways (Bowman et al. 2001). More broadly, placing equipment to encourage child choice and play and to stimulate children's questions can benefit young children neurologically by fostering new brain growth, and novelty in the environment stimulates brain functioning (Rivkin 2000). Applying some specific findings from neuroscientific understandings of the brain, Schiller (1999) offers the following advice on placing equipment to maximise early brain development:

- Ensure children have access to plenty of water to reduce the likelihood of brain dehydration, which can lead to children being 'bored, listless and drowsy' (p. 49).
- Introduce aromas into the classroom to increase children's learning in several ways. Floral odours can increase 'the ability to learn, create and think . . . Peppermint, basil, lemon, cinnamon, and rosemary are linked to mental alertness. Lavender, chamomile, orange, and rose are used for relaxation and calming' (p. 50).
- Introduce novelty into the environment to increase children's memory. Schiller suggested rotating toys, equipment, books and shelving, and placing things in surprising places.

When and why?

In any early childhood program, staff decisions about how to position materials will be influenced by their vision for the children's learning expressed through their curriculum intentions.

GOAL RELEVANCE

In general, staff can position equipment and materials near someone or something to:

Support thinking and learning
- gain and maintain children's attention during a learning experience. Introducing a 'popular' piece of equipment at the beginning of an experience or adding a new piece of equipment to an experience at a key moment can help gain and maintain children's interest
- increase children's concentration on specific experiences. Placing equipment to allow children to have moments for quiet reflection helps their concentration (Greenman 2005, online).

Promote safety, wellbeing and inclusion
- ensure safe supervision of children's learning. Broadly, staff need to place themselves, furniture and equipment to allow them to see the children. For example, sitting down facing into a room makes scanning the room on a regular basis easy.
- encourage children's participation in a specific experience. For instance, adding a child's favourite toy to a specific area may encourage a reluctant child to participate in a new experience. Adding an object that is culturally familiar to a child may encourage exploration of experiences the child has been avoiding.
- enable children to experience beauty in which the 'aromascape, soundscape, colorscape, texturescape, and lightscape' engage all of children's senses (Greenman 2005, online)
- connect children to nature (Greenman 2005, online).

Build relationships
- encourage social interaction between children. For example, placing several spades in the mud-patch or a very large box in the block area can make it easy and possible for several children to explore the experience. Children challenging adults and creating conflict is lessened when there is sufficient equipment for each child to enjoy a particular experience and when children can have a say in how their environment is organised (MacNaughton, Hughes and Smith 2007b). More specifically, in a digital technology learning area, the use of open-ended software will encourage greater collaboration between children than the use of drill and practice software (Cooper 2005).

- build a sense of community. As Greenman (2005, online) explains:

  Community flows out of an organization and environment that values and sustains relationships. An environment can support gathering together and connecting people with layouts that include meeting places indoors and out and the transparency of design that allows glimpses from place to place through interior windows and open doors. Design can accommodate for moments of needing to be alone or to be with another person, for respite from the group, and for supporting relationships that last over time.

- help children to learn to practise reflective listening. For example, creating a Peace Table as a site in the classroom where conflicts are negotiated through children practising reflective listening and problem-solving with each other. Hintz and Stomfay-Stitz (1999) talk of examples that include the use of a 'decorated felt blanket on the floor' (p. 4) that acts as a site for conflict resolution, and specific tables or desks allocated to the purpose of peace.

DEVELOPMENTAL CONSIDERATIONS

Positioning equipment to encourage interactions between children of mixed abilities can positively affect children's learning. Placing children of mixed age and/or mixed ability in small groups can enhance their learning (Gerard 2005; Halahan 2000) and promote social play (Skinner 2004). Staff should consider the possibility that placing toddlers and babies or toddlers and preschoolers in small groups enhances each child's skills (Cryer, Hurwitz and Wolery 2003).

When babies lie in their cots, in hammocks, or on the floor they spend considerable portions of their time looking at the spaces above them or to the side of them. Their interest, wonder, enjoyment and curiosity about their physical environment can be encouraged by careful positioning of artefacts and materials in these spaces to capture their attention. Their attention can be maintained by choosing items with surfaces that reflect the light, that change as different lights play on them and that enable babies to see the movement of other people. Gandini (1994, p. 143) described how staff from one of the schools in the district of Reggio Emilia in Italy positioned objects and windows to capture and maintain babies' interests:

  None is considered marginal space; for example, the mirrors in the washrooms and bathrooms are cut in different shapes to inspire the children to look in a playful way at their image. The ceilings are used as host to many different types of aerial sculptures or beautiful mobiles all made with transparent, coloured, and unusual material, built by children and set up by teachers. There are glass walls to create a continuity between interior garden and outside gardens; they contribute much natural light and give an occasion for playing with transparencies and reflections.

By three months of age babies can use their hands and feet to touch and move objects near them (Berk 2006). Placing such items within reach will encourage them to physically explore them and begin to teach them about cause and effect and how to make things happen. Once babies show an interest in rolling over, staff can occasionally place toys just out of a baby's reach to encourage stretching and exercise. This helps to strengthen their muscles and increases mobility (Kettman 2005). There are many ways to do this. For example, you can place pillows and large soft animals around the room so that the babies can crawl over them.

Toddlers are active, they move about quickly, they are unpredictable, love exploring how things work and want to do lots of things by themselves. Equipment needs to be positioned carefully to ensure that toddlers' emerging skills are fully supported and their learning is enriched. Toddlers need plenty of space to move around, carry things, push things and then drop them unexpectedly. It is important, therefore, that staff are not too concerned with maintaining clear boundaries between different spaces such as a book area and a block area—some mingling of areas is inevitable with this age group. However, it can be helpful to organise the environment to allow toddlers space by themselves for uninterrupted play so they do not feel crowded by other children. It can also be important to have plenty of opportunities for toddlers to engage in free play with natural materials. This can help to reduce conflicts between toddlers. Researchers in the

Netherlands (Gevers Deynoot-Schaub and Riksen-Walraven 2006) in a study of 70 15-month-old children in child care settings found more negative interaction between toddlers in settings where they had minimal opportunity for pretend play and play with water and sand. As many toddlers are also beginning to establish peer preferences and friendships (Hay, Payne and Chadwick 2004) and are able to interact positively in groups (Ishikawa and Hay 2006) it is important to position equipment so that toddlers have opportunities for social interactions with their friends and their new acquaintances.

Preschoolers are growing in social autonomy and initiative but still need considerable support to manage their social relationships. Placing equipment and materials to promote social interaction between the children can help them to learn the skills such as negotiation and sharing which they need to create and maintain positive peer relationships (Arthur et al. 1996). For instance, placing one wheelbarrow with several shovels in it near the mud-play area means that when several children are involved in digging and moving the mud at the one time, they will have to negotiate over when, how and who can use the wheelbarrow.

In the preschool years children are becoming increasing physically competent. They can run, jump, hop and balance and can co-ordinate a variety of physical movements (large and small) with increasing ease (Berk 2006). In placing equipment and materials it is important to provide children with opportunities to acquire, practise and consolidate a variety of physical skills. Successful use of large and small motor skills helps children to feel a sense of mastery and control over their environment. This in turn promotes a sense of competence and wellbeing that positively supports learning across all domains of development. More specifically, a well-structured physical environment helps build a sense of self-worth and competence in preschool children (Maxwell 2007). Preschoolers need equipment that will support and extend their physical development and that is positioned to allow for consolidation of their existing skills and for challenges which encourage them to develop new skills.

The placement of equipment is also very important in encouraging preschoolers' cognitive development. It encourages children's acquisition of problem-solving skills (see Chapter 27), and helps them to imagine, create and recognise relationships between events and objects in their environment. In the following anecdote, the teacher placed equipment in the outdoor shed in ways that enabled children to make choices and supported their dramatic play.

> The children want to build a cubby house on the platform at the top of the climbing frame. They are discussing how to make the walls. Their teacher reminds them to look in the outdoor shed, which contains different materials and equipment. The children discuss among themselves what they need and choose some old bedspreads and some sheets of masonite.
>
> ---
>
> *Reflective task:* List some materials and equipment that the children could access by themselves from an outdoor storage space.

Children's early numeracy and mathematical thinking can also be supported through the innovative placement of equipment in the classroom. Classrooms in which the placement of equipment encourages children to sort, classify, ask, use simple tools and solve problems positively promotes mathematical thinking (Gallenstein 2005).

For children of all ages, the choice of equipment can be important to their imaginative worlds and the play that they build in them. Natural equipment and environments can encourage children's creativity and concentration and sensory exploration (Knackstredt and Wellisch, 2005). In contrast, research has shown that realistic props, such as plastic food, detailed uniforms, real trucks, etc., can restrict rather than enhance children's imagination and imaginative play. Describing a project designed within a Vygotskian framework, Bodrova and Leong (2001, pp. 17–18) described the importance of non-realistic, minimal props to children's dramatic play:

In the Tools of the Mind project, teachers try to wean children from the need for specific props by introducing games in which children think of different ways to play with ordinary objects. They brainstorm ways in which a wooden block can be used—as a baby, a ship or a chair for a doll. Teachers transition children from using realistic props to using minimal props.

Placing children in nature is very important to the health and wellbeing of children of all ages. Given that green play settings (trees, grass and other plants) have been found to benefit children physically, emotionally and psychologically, it is important to consider their inclusion and placement in the learning environment.

Finally, placing equipment and materials to reduce noise is also important to the health and wellbeing of children of all ages. Chronic exposure to noise can harm children's growing language and discrimination skills (Flynn 2006).

Equity considerations

'RACE' AND CULTURE

The placement of materials can provide children with very important messages about what is valued and how adults understand the relationships between different objects and events. When staff place items of equipment or images next to each other, they should avoid tokenistic placement of images. Tokenism means making a superficial or minimal gesture towards representing and respecting cultural diversity. For instance, having one picture representing Aboriginal Australian families in a display of Australian family diversity would be tokenistic. This is because it would provide children with only a small amount of information about Aboriginal Australian families. One image cannot convey the diversity and complexity of the kinship arrangements of Aboriginal Australian cultures. On the contrary, it can tend to reinforce stereotypes by suggesting that all Aboriginal families live in the way depicted in the picture.

Staff can also use unusual positioning of photographs of activities and people to explore preschoolers' attitudes to cultural diversity. Ramsey (2004) suggested showing people involved in daily tasks (for example, eating using a variety of implements such as chopsticks and knives and forks) to provoke discussion among children about what is 'normal'.

It is important to have places where children who are bilingual can play alongside other children without always needing to use language to interact and have places where they can interact in small groups. This supports a non-threatening environment in which children can learn their second language (Espinosa 2005). Thoughtful positioning of pictorial prompts and cards can support children learning English as a second language to make requests and to participate in decisions about what the group or individuals might do next (Espinosa 2005). Examples could include picture cards of songs, learning experiences or regular requests a child might want to ask for.

GENDER

In groups of four-year-old children it is not unusual for girls and boys to develop boys-only and girls-only play spaces (MacNaughton 2000). Often these spaces are developed in traditionally gender-stereotyped ways, with construction toys such as blocks and Lego in the boys' areas and domestic play areas such as the home corner in the girls' areas (MacNaughton 2000). Disrupting the normal placement of materials in these areas by, for example, placing the dolls in the blocks area, removing physical dividers between the home corner and blocks area or adding Lego to the home corner can encourage more mixed-gender play. Staff need to monitor such changes carefully to ensure that the gender-stereotyped play patterns do not merely transfer to new areas.

Children's understandings of what is normal for males and females to do, think, and feel can also be challenged by careful positioning of images in the centre. Consider placing an image of a man performing caring, nurturing tasks alongside a woman doing these things. Similarly, always place a female involved in physically challenging tasks or traditional male areas of employment alongside any traditional images you have. Children can be stirred to question and discuss gender roles by cutting and pasting images in ways that challenge their understandings about normality. Consider placing a male head on a female body and vice-versa and discussing with children how they know which picture is of a male and which is of a female.

Children's understandings about normality can be challenged by images of non-traditional family lifestyles. Children can be stirred to question and discuss family roles and lifestyles by cutting and pasting images in ways that challenge their understandings about what is a normal family. Consider asking the children to cut and paste families where dad does all the work at home or where there are two mums— one mum is in paid work and the other is at home caring for the children—and discussing how there are lots of different types of families. There are single-parent families, families where people have divorced and mum and dad no longer live in the same house, gay and lesbian families, and families in which grandparents, aunts and uncles and children all live together. Understanding diverse family lifestyles helps children broaden their understanding of gender roles by seeing that there are lots of ways to be dads and lots of ways to be mums.

DISABILITY AND ADDITIONAL NEEDS

The placement of materials and pathways should enable children with disabilities to move about safely and with comfort. Materials and equipment should be positioned to ensure that children with disabilities can participate in the key experiences in the program. The nature and type of each child's disability will determine what this means in practice.

As discussed above, careful positioning of images within the centre can challenge children's understandings of what is normal male and female behaviour. Consider creating similar challenges to children's understandings of disability by placing images of children and adults with different disabilities performing a variety of potentially unexpected tasks alongside images of non-disabled people performing these tasks. An example of this would be using images from the Para Olympics. Staff can use such images to interest the children in people's differing abilities and disabilities and challenge their understandings about what is a normal way to be, think, see, move, hear and feel.

Careful placement of materials can also enhance engagement between children with autism and their environment. McGee et al. (1991) have found that developing a toy rotation play which adds novelty and interest to the materials available helps the integration of children with autism into mainstream early childhood settings. They instigated a fortnightly rotation plan of toys to produce novelty and interest in their classrooms and found that novelty helped increase the engagement of the children with autism with the toys.

Reflecting on positioning techniques

1   Consider the following quote from Gandini (1994, p. 149):

We think that the space has to be a sort of aquarium that mirrors the ideas, values, attitudes and cultures of the people who live in it.

Do the centres you are familiar with position people, objects and artefacts to accomplish these goals? Do you think they should? Why? How could they achieve these goals? How relevant is Gandini's statement to issues of equity and anti-bias in the placement of equipment and materials?

2   How might equipment and materials be positioned to encourage preschoolers' emerging interest in the world of print and the associated skills of reading and writing?

3   How could you use the positioning of equipment and materials to encourage social interaction and conversation between preschool children and babies?

4 What are the key precautions you need to take when positioning equipment to ensure a safe learning environment for all ages?

5 How might your philosophy on adult intervention in children's learning influence the positioning of equipment in the inside learning area?

6 Briggs and Potter (1995) believed that the positioning of space and material can enhance children's learning through:

- encouraging movement and interaction
- encouraging deep involvement
- promoting independence and self-direction
- encouraging the use of specific skills
- increasing or decreasing concentration
- encouraging co-operation between children
- stimulating curiosity and problem-solving.

Use the following table to reflect on how you could position materials in the sand-play area to encourage children to be involved in these processes.

Aim of positioning	Positioning equipment Babies	Positioning equipment Toddlers	Positioning equipment Preschoolers
Movement and interaction Deep involvement Independence and self-direction Skills Concentration Co-operation Curiosity and problem-solving			

Improving teaching in practice

1 Sketch the layout of the inside and outside learning areas in an early childhood centre and take photographs of these areas.

2 How well did placement of equipment support easy supervision of children?

3 How well was equipment placed to support a safe and healthy environment?

- Were play spaces well lit?
- Was there fresh air and were temperatures comfortable?
- Was there room to move around freely (for example, when using a wheelchair, callipers, walking frames, guide dog, etc.)?
- Could equipment be reached easily and safely by children?
- Were sharp edges kept away from areas where children might knock against them?
- Was there ready access to a space for recycling of material and clearing rubbish from the floor?
- Were there non-slip surfaces in the 'wet' areas?
- Could staff readily access all equipment without straining muscles?

4 To what extent did the current placement of equipment enhance the aesthetic appeal of the centre?

- Were equipment and materials deliberately and carefully placed?
- Was the careful placement of materials and equipment maintained?
- Did the environment evolve over time?

- Were there soft areas that encouraged people to relax, reflect and rest?
- Were sounds placed as carefully as objects?
- Were texture, shape and colour used with care and thought to provide enjoyment, stimulation and relaxation?
- Were visual images hung and treated with care and respect?
- Were artefacts, crafts, art and memorabilia culturally familiar to the children and adults?

5   Was equipment placed to enhance children's sense of security and competence?
- Were there regular major traffic paths in the environment?
- Could children readily access child-safe cleaning materials and equipment?
- Were everyday materials children use, such as pencil sharpeners, sticky-tape, glue-sticks, scissors, etc., readily accessible to the children?
- Were everyday materials placed so as to avoid congestion when several children want access at once?
- Did materials used regularly have an obvious home?
- Did children have a personal storage space for their special projects and personal belongings?
- Did children have access to child-sized furniture and equipment for several of their experiences?

6   How was equipment placed to stimulate children's curiosity?
7   Did the placement of equipment and adults support equity of access and participation?
- Could children of different physical abilities move around easily?
- Could children of different physical abilities participate in a range of experiences?
- Could children of different abilities and ages easily see and touch display areas?
- Could all children in the group, irrespective of their cultural background, recognise their own culture in the materials and staff available to them?

8   How and how well were developmental considerations taken into account in the placement of equipment and materials?
9   Did the placement of equipment and materials express the values that were intended?

FURTHER READING

Clarke, A. 2007, 'A hundred ways of listening: gathering children's perspectives of their early childhood environment', *Young Children*, 62(3), pp. 76–81.

Curtis, D. and Carter, M. 2003, *Designs for Living and Learning: Transforming Early Childhood Environments*, Red Leaf Press, St. Paul, MN.

Gandini, L. 1994, 'Educational and caring spaces', in C. Edwards, L. Gandini and G. Forman, eds, *The Hundred Languages of Children: The Reggio Emilia Approach to Early Childhood Education*, Ablex Publishing Corporation, New Jersey [refer to pp. 135–150].

Isbell, R., Exelby, B. and Exelby, G. 2001, *Early Learning Environments That Work*, Gryphon House, Inc., Beltsville, MD.

Strong-Wilson, T. and Ellis, J. 2007, 'Children and place: Reggio Emilia's environment as third teacher', *Theory into Practice*, 46(1), pp. 40–47.

Thompson, D. and Hudson, S. 2003, 'The inside information about safety surfacing', *Young Children*, 58(2), pp. 108–111.

Wein, C.A. 2004, 'From policing to participation: overturning the rules and creating amiable classrooms', *Young Children*, 59(1), pp. 34–40.

ONLINE AND MULTI-MEDIA RESOURCES

Text

Read about designing spaces for children:

White, R. 2004, 'Adults are from earth; children are from the moon. Designing for children: a complex challenge', White Hutchinson Leisure and Learning Group, Kansas City, MO: **http://www.whitehutchinson.com/children/articles/earthmoon.shtml**

NAEYC and J. Greenman, compiled 2005. Resources on environments that support exploring, learning, and living, *Young Children* 60(3), pp. 56, 58, online: **http://journal.naeyc.org/btj/200505**.

The Center for Community Inclusion and Disability Studies, University of Maine has a tip sheet on design for all: **http://www.umaine.edu/cci/ec/growingideas**

Ergonomic guidelines for positioning computers. 'Early connections: health and safety': **http://www.netc.org/earlyconnections/preschool/health.html**

Multi-media

'There's something about a space', 2004, Illinois Facilities Fund, Chicago. Free online access: **http://www.iff.org/resources/video/video02.html** (To watch the video you require a Flash plug-in.)

Hear children's perspectives on their learning environment:

'Schools designed for learning: The Denver School of Science and Technology' and accompanying resource guide. Free online access: **http://www.archfoundation.org**

View diverse approaches to positioning equipment and materials online:

'Explore the Design Share': case studies of innovative learning environments. The 2007 award designs for learning in feature early childhood environments in Turkey, Japan, USA, Australia and China: **http://www.designshare.com/index.php/awards/early-childhood**

Or you can connect to their interactive map to travel the world to view case studies of learning environments from 2000 onwards: **http://www.designshare.com/index.php/maps/awards-projects-firms**

Take a virtual tour of several early childhood learning environments: **http://www.ccia.com/VTWebsite/index.html**

REFERENCES

Arthur, L., Beecher, B., Docket, S., Farmer, S. and Death, E. 1996, *Programming and Planning in Early Childhood Settings*, 2nd edn, Harcourt Brace, Sydney.

Berk, L. 2006, *Child Development*, 7th edn, Pearson/Allyn & Bacon, Boston.

Bodrova, E. and Leong, D. 2001, *Tools of the Mind: A Case Study of Implementing the Vygotskian Approach in American Early Childhood and Primary Classrooms*, International Bureau of Education, Switzerland.

Bowman, B., Donovan, M. and Burns, S. 2001, *Eager to Learn: Educating Our Preschoolers*, National Academy Press, Washington, DC.

Briggs, F. and Potter, G.K. 1995, *Teaching children in the first three years of school*, 2nd edn, Longman Cheshire, Melbourne.

Clarke, A. 2007, 'A hundred ways of listening: gathering children's perspectives of their early childhood environment', *Young Children,* 62(3), pp. 76–81.

Cohen, J. and Cohen, M. 1960, *The Penguin Dictionary of Quotations*, Penguin Books, Middlesex.

Cooper, L.Z. 2005, 'Developmentally appropriate digital environments for young children', *Library Trends*, 54(2), pp. 286–302.

Conn-Powers, M., Frazeur Cross, A., Krider Traub, E. and Hutter-Pishgahi, L. 2006, 'The universal design of early education: moving forward for all children', *Young Children: Journal of the National Association for the Education of Young Children*, September, <http://www.journal.naeyc.org/btj/200609/ConnPowersBTJ.asp> (accessed 17 March 2008).

Cryer, D., Hurwitz, S. and Wolery, M. 2003, 'Continuity of caregiver for infants and toddlers', *ERIC Digest*, EDO-PS-03-17, 4 pp.

Curtis, D. and Carter, M. 2005, 'Rethinking early childhood environments to enhance learning', *Young Children*, 60(3), pp. 34–38.

Espinosa, L. 2005, 'Curriculum and assessment consideration for young children from culturally, linguistically, and economically diverse backgrounds', *Psychology in the Schools*, 42(8), pp. 837–853.

Exley, P. 2005, 'Crafting content, play and space through participation', Paper presented at the J. Paul Getty Museum Symposium, *From Content to Play: Family-Oriented Interactive Spaces in Art and History Museums*, June 4–5.

Flynn, J. 2006, 'First days in school', *School Planning and Management*, 45(2), pp. 30–33.

Gallenstein, N. 2005, 'Engaging young children in science and mathematics', *Journal of Elementary Science Education*, 17(2) pp. 27–42.

Gandini, L. 1994, 'Educational and caring spaces', in C. Edwards, L. Gandini and G. Forman, eds, *The Hundred Languages of Children: The Reggio Emilia Approach to Early Childhood Education* (pp. 135–50), Ablex Publishing Corporation, New Jersey.

Gerard, M. 2005, 'Bridging the gap: towards an understanding of young children's thinking in multiage groups', *Journal of Research in Childhood Education*, 19(3), pp. 243–251.

Gevers Deynoot-Schaub, M. and Riksen-Walraven, M. 2006, 'Peer contacts of 15-month-olds in childcare: links with child temperament, parent-child interaction and quality of childcare', *Social Development* 15(4), pp. 709–729.

Greenman, J. 2005, 'Places for childhood in the twenty-first century: a conceptual framework', *Young Children on the Web*, May, <http://www.journal.naeyc.org/btj/200505> (accessed 17 March 2008).

——2006, Wonderful Walls. *Exchange: The Early Childhood Leaders' Magazine*, 68, p. 62.

Hay, D., Payne, A. and Chadwick, A. 2004, 'Peer relations in childhood', *Journal of Child Psychology and Psychiatry* 45(1), pp. 84–108.

Halahan, A. 2000, 'A comparison of developmental gains for preschool children with disabilities in inclusive and self-contained classrooms', *Topics In Early Childhood Special Education* 20(4), pp. 224–235, <http://www.octf.sa.edu.au/files/links/Carter_Curti_1.doc> (accessed 30 November 2007).

Hintz, B.F. and Stomfay-Stitz, A. 1999, 'Peace education and conflict resolution through expressive arts in early childhood education and teacher education', Paper presented at the *Annual Conference of the Eastern Educational Research Association*, 26 February, Hilton Head, SC, ED433105.

Ishikawa, F. and Hay, D. 2006, 'Triadic interaction among newly acquainted 2-year-olds', *Social Development*, 15(1), pp. 145–168.

Kettman, S. 2005, *The 2000 Best Games and Activities: Using Play to Teach Curiosity, Self-control, Kindness and other Essential Life Skills*, Sourcebook, Inc., Naperville, IL.

Knackstredt, V. and Wellisch, M. 2005, 'Managing challenging behaviour: is the environment a factor?' *Every Child*, 11(1), pp. 30–31.

MacNaughton, G. 2000, *Rethinking Gender in Early Childhood Education*, Allen & Unwin, Sydney, p. 269.

MacNaughton, G., Hughes, P. and Smith, K. 2007a, 'Young children's rights and public policy: practices and possibilities for citizenship in the early years', *Children and Society*, 21(6), pp. 458–469.

——2007b, 'Rethinking approaches to working with children who challenge: action learning for emancipatory practice', *International Journal of Early Childhood*, 39(1), pp. 39–57.

Maxwell, L. 2007, 'Competency in child care settings: the role of the physical environment', *Environment and Behavior*, 39(2), pp. 229–245.

McGee, G., Daly, T., Izeman, S., Mann, L. and Risley, T. 1991, 'Use of classroom materials to promote preschool engagement', *Teaching Exceptional Children*, Summer, pp. 44–47.

Ramsey, P. 2004, *Teaching and Learning in a Diverse World: Multicultural Education for Young Children*, 3rd edn, Teachers' College Press, New York.

Rivkin, M. 2000, 'Outdoor experiences for young children', *ERIC Digest*, December, EDO-RC-00-7, 4 pp.

Schiller, P. 1999, 'Turning knowledge into practice', *Child Care Information Exchange*, March, 126, pp. 49–52.

Skinner, M. 2004, 'Effects of age and developmental status of partners on play of preschoolers with disabilities', *Journal of Early Intervention*, 26(3), pp. 194–203.

Wilkes, G. (ed.) 1979, *Collins Dictionary of the English Language*, Penguin Books, Middlesex.

Wilson Gillespie, C. 2000, 'Six Head Start classrooms begin to explore the Reggio Emilia approach', in *Young Children*, 55(1), pp. 21–27.

Chapter 2

Collecting

 Collect: to gather together.

> *(Collins Dictionary of the English Language, p. 297)*

There are displays of pine cones, shells, or pebbles arranged by size, shape, or color. These displays record events in the children's lives. They contain treasures that children have gathered on special outings or regular walks.

> (Gandini 1993, p. 141)

. . . Digital cameras are easy to find, easy to use, and offer great potential for incorporating technology into your lessons. Project ideas can range from creating collections of objects to identify (e.g., insects, plants, rocks/minerals, and so on) to documenting the signs of the seasons or recording the progress of an investigation and more.

> (Carter, Sumrall and Curry, K. 2006, online)

What?

Collecting is the process of gathering things together. As a teaching technique, collecting is a deliberate process of gathering together objects, information and ideas to help generate children's interest in and learning about their natural and their social and cultural worlds. Collecting can help children learn how to sort, classify, match and organise their world. In doing so, collecting enhances numerous skills across all areas of development.

How?

Collecting can be initiated by staff or by children. It may involve individuals, small groups or the whole group. It may begin simply with something found by a child, for instance a leaf in the garden. When shared with others this prompts them to search for more. Staff can encourage children's enthusiasm for collecting by using their interest in something and simply saying, 'Why don't we see if we can find some more like it? I wonder who would like to help?'. In contrast, staff may begin a collection by introducing something they have found, such as seeds from their own garden, and asking children if they have seen any similar ones at home or on the way to the centre. On some occasions, staff may have something they would like the children or an individual child to explore in more detail. For example, one child's interest in an overseas stamp on a letter that arrives at the centre may prompt staff to ask the children to bring in anything they have from overseas.

All sorts of objects can be collected. Staff can develop collections from things in the natural world or the social and cultural world. Items from the natural world that can be collected include rocks, leaves, plants, shells, seeds, feathers, bones, etc. Items from our social and cultural world that are easily collected include memorabilia and cultural artefacts (photos, diaries, clothes, ornaments, tickets, models) and items from popular culture such as music, records, tapes, books, magazines, comics, toys, etc. Recycled and found objects can also provide lots of ideas about collecting.

The following anecdote shows how one teacher capitalised on the potential of collecting to enhance children's learning.

> The teacher of a class of five-year-olds knows that during the school holidays many of the children will be visiting the beach. She talks to the children about collecting shells and seaweed during their holidays to bring back to school the following term. She reinforces this by sending an informal note to the parents. At the beginning of the next term, the children bring along several kinds of shells and seaweed. These form the basis of a display and promote much discussion, comparing and contrasting, classifying and so forth.
>
> _Reflective task:_ Think about some other things that you could encourage the children to collect at home that they can bring back into the classroom. Write a list of these.

Display—a collection of shells.

Collections do not need to be limited to objects. Interesting collections can also be made from:

- sounds, using tape-recordings or digital files of traffic noises, sounds in the bush, etc.
- jokes. Young children love having fun, and collecting the things they find funny can be developmentally valuable. Children's humour generally derives from what they find incongruous (Kotthoff 2006). This may be a sound that seems odd (ants barking), an action that is incongruous (dogs flying) or word play (Mousey Mick instead of Mickey Mouse). Seeing and understanding such 'mistakes' can assist the development of higher level cognitive skills; as children search for what is funny and try to create their own 'mistakes' they need to problem-solve and create new language
- words and letters collected from newspapers, greeting cards and magazines. These can support children's emergent literacy skills.

Staff can follow some simple principles to ensure that collecting is a positive and productive learning experience for the children. They should:

- set aside a special place for the collected objects to be displayed and investigated by the children
- have reference books and/or online resources available to the children. Children can use the reference books or online resources to label their 'finds' and to compare and contrast different items in the collection. There are several excellent online reference sites that are child-friendly, including several museum sites. Using references (online or hard copy) can enrich their learning by extending their vocabulary and by enabling them to gain more in-depth understandings of how things grow or work
- keep a special box of tools for investigating the objects collected in more detail. This could include a magnifying glass, rulers, simple balance scales, a colour chart and a shape chart
- have some tools handy with which children can record their discoveries. Pencils and paper are obvious, but a camera can be a useful way to record the different ways in which children sort objects and allows several different sortings to be tried. The pros and cons of using different properties such as size or weight to sort objects can then be discussed via the photographs
- display objects with care to encourage children to take care of them
- develop clear rules and limits about who can use the collection and how. If the collection includes things that are rare, expensive, irreplaceable and/or personally precious to people, staff should carefully supervise their use
- take time to think about some of the discoveries that a collection might encourage and how they can use questions and comments to encourage such discoveries
- be available to the children to answer questions, to ask questions and to prompt the children to explore the collection
- ensure that the collection links with or reminds the younger children of real-life experiences
- ensure that all of the objects collected can be handled safely by the children
- avoid collecting flora and fauna which are on the endangered or protected species lists and avoid collecting objects from the natural world that might be home to animals and plants
- avoid collecting becoming a competition about who brings the best or the most of something.

Collecting becomes an enjoyable and worthwhile learning experience when children are encouraged to explore, sort and classify the objects they or the staff have collected. Children can look for a number of properties that differentiate objects from each other or group them together. Shape, sound, size, colour, texture, smell, weight and function can each be used to explore, sort and classify. Asking children to think about how to sort things and what they might call the categories into which they can be sorted can add fun, interest and conceptual challenges to the experience of collecting.

Matthew, a kindergarten director in the outer eastern suburbs of Melbourne, has a passion for woodworking. One day a child came to the kindergarten with an old, hand-made nail (her parents were renovating their house). With Matthew's guidance the children discussed the difference between the old nail and the nails that they had at the kindergarten. This quickly led to an interest in different kinds of nails. The children made a collection of nails that their parents had at home. The nails were categorised as long, short, round-headed, flat-headed, fat, thin, different metals of different weights and different colours. The nails were displayed on an 'interest' table, where the children were able to touch them and to begin to notice differences and to discuss functions.

Reflection point: Why do we want to use the children's interests as starting points in our teaching? Have you observed children bringing things from home to show to their teacher? What were these things? How could these be used as starting points for collections?

You can extend and enrich collecting with children by creating a collection scrapbook—in book or digital form—in which children can draw and comment on their collection, or by making a mini-museum in the classroom or centre. Children can help classify, display and label items. Or, you can lend your collection to another group or centre who can add to it and further the learning through discussion and exploration with others (Ashbrook 2006).

Thinking about different ways to sort and classify collections can stimulate children's thinking. Your collection can be of things that have the same features or attributes (dinosaurs) or things that have a relationship to each other (things that dinosaurs need to live).

Developing a collection of online WebQuests relevant to the children's interests at a given time can also be a productive way to diversify the nature and type of collections that children have access to. A WebQuest is a structured inquiry or exploration using information gained from the web. There are many predesigned WebQuests available online that are organised by grade level and subject area (see <http://webquest.sdsu.edu> or <http://www.kn.pacbell.com/wired/bluewebn>). Some suggested criteria for evaluating WebQuests and ensuring their appropriateness and relevance to young children are:

- ensure they have an engaging beginning
- check that there are clear questions and tasks for the children to explore
- check that the roles provided match the issue/problem being investigated and the resources provided
- check that they encourage higher-order thinking and allow for feedback
- check that they offer suggestions for further learning (Gibson 2004).

Issues and debates

We have not found in the literature specific issues or debates emerging about the effectiveness of collecting as a teaching strategy. However, the content of collections and the ways in which collections are gathered do give rise to specific issues.

COLLECTING FOR DIVERSITY: BEING SENSITIVE TO CULTURAL CONTEXTS AND TRADITIONS

When collections of photographs are used to introduce a homogeneous group of children to diversity, the photo should be carefully chosen. Staff should be careful to ensure that the photos contain contemporary images of each ethnic group and do not reinforce stereotypes prevalent in the centre (Ramsey 2004). Particular care should be taken over the use of photographs of Aboriginal Australians on two counts. Firstly, several Aboriginal groups find it offensive to publicly display images of people who have died. Secondly, many images of Aboriginal people are highly stereotyped and represent a very limited range of Aboriginal lifestyles. The checklist on vetting images in children's books in Chapter 14 can be used when choosing pictures for the collection.

COLLECTING FOR DIVERSITY: WHAT TO DO WITH PROBLEMATIC MATERIALS

Children may bring in images or objects for a collection that staff believe are racist, sexist or in other ways are not respectful of diverse lives and cultures. Staff often face the dilemma of whether or not to exclude these images. If staff decide to exclude them from the collection it is important to tell children why they want to do so. Such images can be used to create a collection of images or objects that can be discussed critically with children. To do this requires considerable thought and care. However, the chapters on deconstructing (Chapter 22) and philosophising (Chapter 26) offer some strategies and suggestions for how to approach this work.

COLLECTING AND ENVIRONMENTAL SUSTAINABILITY

Collecting natural materials needs to be done with care so that teachers do not encourage the collection of endangered or rare flora, fauna or other natural objects, including bark, seed pods and rocks, or of objects that may be habitat for native animals and insects. Checking with your local natural history museum or Parks and Wildlife Officers can alert you and the children to things that should not be collected and why. This can in itself be a point for discussion, reflection and learning in the classroom.

When and why?

Whether collecting begins spontaneously or in a planned way by staff or by children, it may last minutes, hours, days or months. Collections can stimulate socio-dramatic play, scientific discovery or a long-term group project on a specific theme or issue. Collections can help children to develop wonder about their world by encouraging them to sort and to explore the physical or social properties of objects in the world about them. In doing so, children develop new concepts and new language through which to describe and to understand the world about them.

In some parts of Australia, autumn is a wonderful time to collect leaves in and out of the playground. These can be sorted according to colour, size, shape, etc. Leaves can be used to see changes in properties— for example, leaves change in colour and texture as they dry. Leaves can also be used for artwork, collage, pressing between wax paper and then displaying on windows so that the light passes through them.

GOAL RELEVANCE

Collecting develops children's cognitive skills by encouraging children to classify and match objects. For instance, in a study of US kindergarten children Pasnak (2006) found that intensive work on children's classification, seriation and number conservation skills significantly improved their cognitive development. Staff can use open questions to encourage children to think about the similarities and differences between objects. For instance:

- How does this object look like the others we collected?
- What is the difference(s) between these two objects?
- Can you find a picture in the book of an object like this?
- Where could we find more objects like this?

Beaty (1996) argued that collecting natural objects is an important part of inducting children into the scientific mode of inquiry because it helps children to:

- create and maintain a sense of wonder in the world about them
- question and find out about their world
- learn to take care of the things in the world about them.

Collections to stimulate scientific thinking can be real or digital. For instance, Carter, Sumrall and Curry (2006) explored the properties of trees with children using digital technology and resources. Collecting can also develop children's socio-symbolic competencies. Staff can use 'Jackdaws' to develop and extend children's understandings of particular stories and enrich the children's socio-dramatic play. A 'Jackdaw' is:

> . . . a collection of reproductions of primary source documents, gathered together on a single topic. Its name comes from the crow like bird who makes a habit of collecting objects to bring back to its nest. Jackdaws are usually on history topics, though some have been made for science, literature, and biographical topics as well. (Hartman 2007, online)

You can build 'Jackdaws' from a story or items that might be found in a place or time in which the story is set. You can place the 'Jackdaw' in a special place (in a box or on an interest table) so that the children can explore it alone or in small groups. This exploration can extend children's understandings of the story, enhance their vocabulary and lead to individual or group project work related to the story.

Collecting can be a group activity that promotes social competence through providing children with the opportunity to share discoveries, to help others to find things, to feel the enjoyment of working with a group towards a common goal and to practise contributing to group projects. Collecting can create a real sense of excitement within the group as each child finds something to add to the collection and the children make discoveries about the properties of each item.

Collections also contribute to specific curriculum domains such as mathematics and literacy. For instance,

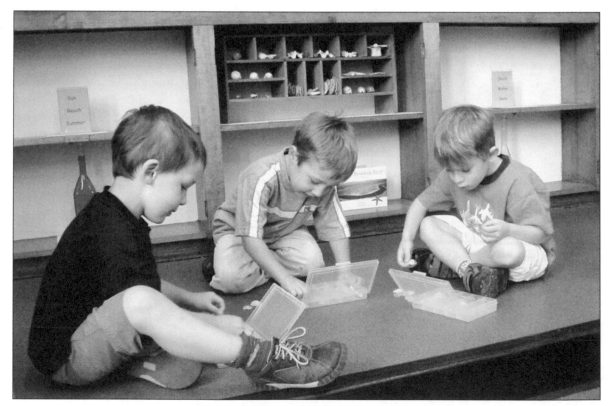

Classifying is engaging for these boys.

collections from the natural world of similar objects (seeds, stones, shells, leaves) that are of different sizes can assist in building children's knowledge of and skills in seriation:

> Laura also brought to the classroom her own collection of 17 pinecones—from giant Sequoia cones from California to very tiny pinecones. They enjoyed putting them in order from the smallest to the biggest and vice versa . . . The inclusion of vocabulary like first, second, third and so forth helped the children to develop representational knowledge of seriation. (Kirova and Bhargava 2002, p. 12)

A collection can also be used to build children's counting skills. Willis (1999) noted that not all children will necessarily use items in a collection in the same way to achieve specific mathematical outcomes. She discussed how many Indigenous Australian children, and some non-Indigenous children, particularly from working-class backgrounds, could count just by looking at a collection of objects. It is therefore important to be flexible in how collections are used to teach specific skills to specific children.

Collections of books or bookmarked websites that represent different perspectives on a topic, experience, feeling or way of being can help build children's critical literacy skills. Swindler Boutte (2002, p. 148) suggests collecting books that:

- represent various ethnic groups, genders, religions, ages, lives, family structures
- represent historical and contemporary depictions of different people
- describe different holidays and cultural rituals and traditions
- share fairytales from different cultures
- show different gender roles being performed by men and women, boys and girls
- are written in different languages and different dialects.

These books or bookmarked websites can be used to discuss with children the different ways in which people think and act at different points in history and in different cultural groups. Having a diverse range of books and/or bookmarked websites enables comparisons to be made, stereotypes to be critically discussed and simplistic and tokenistic views of who we are to be explored through comparisons and contrasts offered within the books or the websites.

DEVELOPMENTAL CONSIDERATIONS

Collecting is a useful teaching technique for all age groups. However, the younger the child, the more the collecting needs to be done by the staff for the children. The children's developmental stage is likely to influence the types of objects of interest they collect themselves or have others collect for them. A good rule of thumb is to collect diverse objects that introduce young children to different sensory experiences. Some possibilities would be:

- different smells from a collection of aromatherapy oils, herbs and spices
- different textures from objects in the constructed and natural worlds
- objects with different plays of light on them, such as glass pebbles, mirrors and mobiles
- objects with sounds from the natural and constructed worlds including audio-tapes, CDs and DVDs.

Toddlers are interested in themselves and what they can do; have a great interest in the here and now; are grappling with object permanence so enjoy things that appear and disappear; want to learn the names of the things about them; and are fascinated by how things work. Collections that are likely to interest toddlers include:

- personal items such as 'my toys' or 'my bed-time things'
- items in the natural world that they can readily name (for example, insects, rocks and shells)

- things that appear and disappear (jack-in-the-box toys, pop-up books or cards)
- simple mechanical items that have clear workings (hole punchers, hand-held flour sieves)
- things that can be taken apart and put together again easily (torches, watering cans with removable nozzles, large padlocks and keys, pairs of shells, large seed pods, fasteners, zippers, 'nests' of things such as Russian dolls, measuring spoons and jars).

Clarissa is a staff member in a child care centre in a small country town in Victoria. She encouraged the parents of the children in the toddler room to bring several types of padlocks to the centre so she could develop a padlock collection for the children to play with. The children enjoyed undoing the locks. Clarissa was able to use this time with the children to enhance their language development and to foster their social skills. She talked about the different shapes and sizes of the padlocks and how they were made of different types of metal. The children were encouraged to take turns at opening and closing the locks and to watch others practising their skills.

Reflection point: When working with toddlers, what do you need to take into consideration when using collections?

Toddlers have a few basic characteristics that may influence the success of collecting:

- Their understandings of right and wrong are just beginning to evolve, so staff should not expect them to follow complex rules about how to use and care for items in the collection.
- They often enjoy finding out how things work and what things can and cannot do. This means they explore objects in somewhat enthusiastic and unconventional ways. Keeping collections of objects they can 'handle' is one way forward. However, it is also important for toddlers to learn how to care for precious things. If there are items in the collection that could be easily damaged or broken there should always be an adult present to reinforce simple rules about how to care for these items.
- They can sometimes find it difficult to share. When collections are built from objects that toddlers have collected themselves, they will need help to share these with the group.
- They generally find out about how things work by, among other things, putting them in their mouths. Adult supervision should be constant around such objects that could be dangerous if swallowed or tasted.

Preschool children are becoming increasingly adept in all areas of development. They are gaining more control over their fine motor skills so they can handle a variety of objects with care and will enjoy objects that they can explore using their fine motor skills. Collections of things that can be taken apart and put together such as nuts and bolts and keys and padlocks can offer preschoolers the opportunity to practise and consolidate their fine motor skills.

By four and five years of age children's moral development has reached a point where they can understand the differences between what is fair or not fair, and between what is kind or unkind in everyday situations (MacNaughton 2005; Ramsey 2004). Consequently, collections of objects can be used to help children share and to negotiate use of the objects in the collection. It also becomes more possible to collect objects and images that develop critical thinking about stereotypes (see below) and which can encourage children to think about what is fair and unfair, kind and unkind.

Beginning readers can benefit from access to a vibrant collection of Big Books. When teachers read aloud to beginning readers from Big Books, children's interest in the relationship between print and language increases, their enjoyment in reading times improves and they generally more vividly recall words and storylines from the book (Renck Jalongo 2007). Children can also help to make their own Big Books to add to the collection. In addition to buying commercially published Big Books, teachers and children can use new or old technologies to make their own books from events in the classroom that combine children's artwork with teacher and/or child print. Teachers need to ensure that their collection of Big Books includes lots of stories that have repetitive phrases or are written in rhyme so that beginning readers can readily recall the words and begin to associate them with the text within the books.

Collecting and organising information is also an important dimension of building young children's mathematical thinking and knowledge in the early years of school (Charlesworth 2005), and simple computer programs can support this work in the classroom when they form part of a broader mathematical program (Starkey, Klein and Wakeley 2004).

Equity considerations

'RACE' AND CULTURE

Collecting cultural artefacts and memorabilia can help children to share their own culture and to learn about cultures of other children in their group. Everyday objects express many aspects of a group's culture, including what it celebrates, how it celebrates, its art and craft traditions, its folk mythology, its language, its family structures and its ways of valuing others. Collections of photos, ornaments, clothes and household items can all stimulate discussions about many aspects of the different cultural lifestyles of children in the group.

If children have things from their culture on display in a centre this can help build a sense of belonging and a sense that they are being valued. Seeing things from other people's daily lives can help increase children's understandings of the similarities with and differences between their own cultural background and that of other people. However, such collections should not be 'one-off' events that reinforce what Derman-Sparks (1989) called a 'tourist approach' to cultural diversity. Such approaches invite children to 'visit' a culture for a day or a week by looking at clothes, food, etc. of cultures different to their own. This can make the other cultures seem exotic destinations to be visited rather than an important and everyday part of living in a multicultural society.

Collecting and sharing children's family histories and current traditions can build respect and acceptance of diversity within the group. However, this should be done with care and thought. It should always be discussed with *all* children's parents before starting such a project. While some parents may feel comfortable sharing their family history within the group, others may not. Sharing family history can raise painful memories such as the violent death of loved ones in war-torn countries or enforced migration to Australia. Some refugee families may have lost much of the record of their lives and have little in the way of memorabilia. For children of these families, being unable to 'bring in' things to share may result in them feeling isolated and marginalised. They may also feel confused when requests for them brings sadness to their family. Families may have many complex reasons for not participating in such projects. Staff need to remember all families have a right to privacy.

Some Aboriginal Australian children may find that collections of family memorabilia help them build relationships more quickly within the group. By encouraging the group to share personal history and interests, such collections can in part reflect what happens in their own communities when people who don't know each other meet. Such processes of getting to know each other should be reciprocal: staff should be prepared to share who they are with the Aboriginal children. This will help build positive relationships more quickly.

Collections of photographs of people can be a particularly positive way of representing and talking about ethnic diversity. Children can become familiar with and comfortable about physical diversity by looking at and comparing the facial characteristics and expressions of the people in the photographs. There is some evidence that children will make less stereotyped comments about photographs than they will about other images of ethnic diversity (Ramsey 2004).

GENDER

Collecting popular culture icons and images can be a useful technique for teaching preschool children about gender-role stereotyping and sexism and helping them to think critically about these issues. Askew and Ross (1988) used collecting as a way of helping six-year-old boys to think critically about traditional forms of masculinity and violence. They asked the boys to collect images from television, comics and magazines about heroes. Once the boys had a collection of images of heroes, they thought about what it means to be a hero and decided that to be a hero you had to be brave. Askew and Ross (1988) then asked the boys to use their collection of images to find out what it meant to be brave. The boys found that lots of 'brave' heroes were violent and involved in hurting others. Staff and children then discussed whether or not this was a 'good' way to be a hero and what other things you could do to be a hero. The online Gender Equality Bookshop (see the 'Online and multimedia resources' section at the end of this chapter) offers some excellent guidance on how to use non-sexist and feminist books with boys and with girls.

Staff can use such a process to explore a broad range of stereotypes with young children. For instance, staff could ask children to collect images of girls being heroines, men being caring, the jobs that women do, etc. to begin discussions with the children about male and female roles and the pros and cons of these. Staff can also talk about why it is hard to find images of particular things—for example, women being 'brave'.

DISABILITY AND ADDITIONAL NEEDS

Collecting and collections need to be accessible to children in the group with disabilities. It is also important that staff offer sufficient variability in the objects collected, the ways they can be collected and how they are displayed to enable children with disabilities to find a personally appropriate way of exploring the collection. To ensure that all children can collect and explore the collection staff need to provide a safe environment. Children with physical disabilities often require more floor space for freedom of movement and this should be taken into account when collecting in the centre and when displaying the collection. In addition, floor placement of the collection can facilitate easy access for those children who have difficulty with balance and bending. Consider collecting things that will demonstrate the special abilities of children with visual or hearing impairment. Anastasia's work shows how this might be done.

Anastasia is working with visually impaired children in a special setting. Most of the children have little or no sight. She encouraged the children to bring their soft toys from home. Eventually they formed a collection of these toys. Anastasia taped open shoe boxes together and put them on a low table. Into each of the boxes she put one soft toy. The children were encouraged to pick up each toy, to notice the texture of the material, the shape, the smell, how hard and soft the toys were, and to notice similarities and differences. A good deal of learning took place, their expressive language was increased and they had many opportunities for social interaction.

Reflective task: Think of other collections that you could use with visually impaired or blind children. List some collections that emphasise shape, texture and smell.

Developing collections of visual aids and props that can help staff to talk easily with children about a variety of disabilities is a positive way to use collecting to enhance anti-discriminatory attitudes in the group. Involving the children in collecting images that represent people with disabilities can heighten children's awareness of, interest in and understanding of disability. Sorting images broadly into major areas of disability, such as people with visual impairment, or people with mobility impairment, can encourage children to explore the similarities and differences between these people. They can learn that not all people who are blind look the same, and begin to talk about different degrees of sight. Some people who are blind use guide dogs to help them see, some use a white stick, some need very strong glasses, etc. Children can also be encouraged to think about how they find images of people with less obvious disabilities such as hearing impairment or epilepsy. For instance, 'What does a person with epilepsy look like?', 'Can you tell from a picture that a person has epilepsy?'. The availability of new technologies in the classroom can enable teachers and children to access images and information about the diverse ways in which people with different disabilities can look and act using WebQuests.

Reflecting on collecting techniques

1 Define collecting.
2 What are the key factors that contribute to successful teaching through collecting with young children?
3 What are 10 recycled objects that you could collect and use with babies?
4 What sorts of objects might preschoolers like to collect and why?
5 What everyday objects express your group's culture?
6 Make a list of the items you could collect when you first work with a group of children to ensure that your area creates a sense of belonging for all children in the group.
7 What cultural artefacts or memorabilia do you have in your home that represent your personal history and current traditions? Which of these could be used to begin a collection with young children? Would they be suitable to use with all age groups of children?
8 What sort of images could you collect that you could use to challenge traditional gender-role stereotypes with three-year-old children?
9 What are the key factors you would need to consider when involving a four-year-old child with hearing impairment in a group collecting project?

Improving teaching in practice

1 Develop a list of the types of visual aids and props you could collect that could be used to talk with children easily about a variety of disabilities.
2 Start a collection of images that you could use to promote positive attitudes to cultural and 'racial' diversity with children.
3 Choose one storybook you could use with two-year-old children and one storybook you could use with four-year-old children. Begin a 'Jackdaw' collection for each of the books.
4 Visit an early childhood centre and evaluate its approach to collecting. Did it:
   • set aside a special place for the collected objects to be displayed and investigated by the children?
   • have reference books available to the children?
   • keep a special box of 'tools' for investigating the objects collected in more detail?
   • have some 'tools' handy to help children record their discoveries?
   • display objects with care to encourage children to take care of them?
   • develop clear rules and limits about use of the collection?
   • have staff available to the children to answer questions, to ask questions and to prompt their exploration?
   • ensure that all of the objects collected were safe for the children to handle?
   • avoid collecting flora and fauna on endangered or protected species lists and avoid collecting objects from the natural world that might be home to animals and plants?
   • avoid turning collecting into a competition about who brings the best or the most of something?

FURTHER READING

Ashbrook, P. 2006, 'Communicating about collections', *Science and Children*, 44(3), pp. 18–20.

Jared, L. and Thwaites, A. 2005, 'What is your favourite color?', in J. Anghileri, ed., *Mathematical Thinking in the Primary Years: Perspectives on Young Children's Thinking* (Chapter 7, pp. 110–123), Continuum International Publishing Group Inc., London.

Haugland, S. 2005, 'Selecting or upgrading software and web sites in the classroom', *Early Childhood Education Journal*, 32(5), pp. 329–340.

Wick, W. 2004, 'Can you see what I see?', *Cool Collections: Pictures Puzzles To Search And Solve*, Scholastic, New York, <http://www.walterwick.com/cys_cc_cars.htm>

ONLINE AND MULTI-MEDIA RESOURCES

Text

Ideas for collections of everyday objects to promote scientific explorations: **http://www.kindergarten-lessons.com/science-center-materials.html**

Sorting and classifying games with young children: **http://www.kindergarten-lessons.com/kindergarten-sorting-games.html**

Children collecting and sharing cultural artefacts, 'Kids collect': **http://www.museumca.org/exhibit/exhi_kids_collect.htm**l

Developing and managing a classroom museum: http://www.campaignformuseums.org.uk/miclass/html/mi_class/classroom.htm

The online Gender Equality Bookstore offers collections of books to foster gender equity and multiculturalism for boys and girls. They also have free study guides for use of these books with adults and children: **http://www.genderequalbooks.com**

Multi-media

'Science and social studies in the multiage classroom: collecting seeds', Apple Learning Interchange. Shares a teaching and learning experience in which students collect seeds, display, organise and document their observations. Free access video clip: **http://edcommunity.apple.com/ali/story.php?itemID=620&version=360&pageID=1574**

REFERENCES

Ashbrook, P. 2006, 'Communicating about collections', *Science and Children*, 44(3), pp. 18–20.

Askew, S. and Ross, C. 1988, *Boys Don't Cry*, Open University Press, Milton Keynes.

Beaty, J. 1996, *Preschool appropriate practices*, 2nd edn, Harcourt Brace, New York.

Carter, L., Sumrall, W. and Curry, K. 2006, 'Say cheese! Digital Collections in the classroom', *Science and Children*, 43(8), pp. 19–23.

Charlesworth, R. 2005, 'Prekindergarten mathematics: connecting with national standards', *Childhood Education Journal*, 32(4), pp, 229–236.

Derman-Sparks, L. and the Anti-Bias Task Force 1989, *The Anti-Bias Curriculum*, National Association for the Education of Young Children, Washington, DC.

Gandini, L. 1993, 'Educational caring spaces', in C. Edwards, L. Gandini and G. Foreman, eds, *The Hundred Languages of Children: The Reggio Emilia Approach to Early Childhood Education* (pp. 135–149), Ablex Publishing Company, New Jersey.

Gibson, S. 2004, 'How can social studies teachers best use the internet with young learners?', *Canadian Social Studies*, 39(1), <http://www.quasar.ualberta.ca/css/Css_39_1/index39_1/ARgibson_SSteachers_internet_young_learners.htm>.

Kirova, A. and Bhargava, A. 2002, 'Learning to guide preschool children's mathematical understandings: a teacher's professional growth', *Early Childhood Research and Practice*, 4(1), pp. 1–20.

Kotthoff, H. 2006, 'Let's have a joke! Children's joking and humour—some age and intercultural differences', *10 RESEARCH 19/2006 E*, <http://www.br-online.de/jugend/izi/english/publication/televizion/19_2006_E/19_2006_E.htm>.

MacNaughton, G. 2005, *Doing Foucault in early childhood studies*, Routledge, London.

Pasnak, R. 2006, 'Acceleration of cognitive development of kindergartners', *Psychology and Schools*, 24(4), pp. 358–363.

Ramsey, P. 2004, *Teaching and Learning in a Diverse World: Multicultural Education for Young Children*, 3rd edn, Teachers College Press, New York.

Renck Jalongo, M. 2007, *Early Childhood Language Arts*, 4th edn, Allyn & Bacon, Canada.

Starkey, P., Klein, A. and Wakeley, A. 2004, 'Enhancing young children's mathematical knowledge through a kindergarten mathematics intervention', *Early Childhood Research Quarterly*, 19(1), pp. 99–120.

Swindler Boutte, G. 2002, 'The critical literacy process: guidelines for examining books', *Childhood Education*, 78(3), pp. 147–52.

Wilkes, G. (ed.) 1979, *Collins Dictionary of the English Language*, Penguin Books, Middlesex.

Willis, S. 1999, 'Numeracy and outcomes in the early years', *Every Child*, 5(1), pp. 8–9.

Chapter 3

Scheduling

 Schedule: a plan of procedure for a project, allotting the work to be done and time for it.

(*Collins Dictionary of the English Language*, p. 1304)

Children of all ages, like adults, typically enjoy taking breaks in the course of a demanding school, and work, day.

(Holmes, Pelligrini and Schmidt, 2006, p. 735)

Time is a technology of discipline.

(Germeten 2000, p. 1)

What?

Scheduling, as a teaching technique, involves taking decisions about how to organise the tempo and duration of current and future interactions between children, between children and adults, and between people and materials. The aim is to organise the day to ensure there is a balanced, productive and pleasing momentum to these interactions, and that children's learning is enhanced through careful use of time. This means that staff need to consider how to plan time for key events such as arrivals, departures, transitions and meals, and how this time meshes with the remainder of the day.

While a centre schedule should be planned in advance, it should also be flexible. For example, on a hot day the children may need to go to sleep earlier than usual because they may be more tired; on a rainy day the indoor playtime may be extended if the children have had long periods of 'inside time'.

Issues and debates

FLEXIBILITY VERSUS SCHEDULES

There is a long history of debate about the best ways to schedule children's learning in early childhood services. Some argue for tight scheduling of the day, others for more flexible and open-ended scheduling of children's time. Introduction of specific times for specific forms of learning, such as the Literacy Hour in the

UK (Whitehead 2004), has its advocates and its opponents (see Campbell 1998; Fisher 2004; Burkard 2005). The debates about how best to schedule young children's learning generally rest on different theoretical perspectives on how young children learn (see MacNaughton 2003 for an overview).

FULL DAY PROGRAMS VERSUS SESSIONAL EXPERIENCES

Debates have also centred on how much time young children should have in early childhood programs. For instance, the pros and cons of sessional kindergarten versus full day programs engender considerable debate in several countries (e.g. Boardman 2003; Davis and MacNaughton 1999). In a review of 27 years of research exploring the pros and cons of full day versus sessional kindergartens in the USA, Elicker (2000) concluded:

> . . . full-day students consistently progress further academically during the kindergarten year compared to half- or alternate-day students. There is tentative evidence that full-day kindergarten has stronger, longer-lasting academic benefits for children from low-income families. There is no current, strong evidence that academic achievement gains of full-day kindergarten persist beyond first grade. There is no evidence of detrimental effects of full-day kindergarten (p. 1).

In this section we focus on three very different issues that staff can explore to reflect on how best to schedule time within their own programs.

NEW MATERIALS AND EXPERIENCES DISRUPTING THE EBB AND FLOW OF THE DAY

As computers and new technologies increasingly enter the early childhood learning space, some researchers have suggested that the introduction of computers into an early childhood space can interrupt the 'ebb and flow' of the day's rhythm (Labbo et al. 2000) as children and adults work out how best to use the computer within their specific space. Locating a computer centrally can help with the process of integrating the computer and its use into the day's rhythm. It will be important when computers and other new technologies are first introduced into a group that teachers plan time to help children learn the basic skills that they need to ensure their meaningful use in children's learning.

GIVING EQUAL IMPORTANCE TO THE CELEBRATIONS OF DIVERSE CULTURAL GROUPS

There is debate in Australian early childhood centres and elsewhere about whether or not they should set aside time in their yearly schedule to celebrate special festivals and events, long recognised as important by the dominant Anglo-cultural groups, such as Christmas and Easter (see Dau and Jones 2004). Celebrating only the holidays of the dominant cultural groups in a given community marginalises the children of minority groups. While it can be challenging to give equal importance to all holidays and festivals for all cultural groups, choosing those that are most relevant to the specific communities in a service is one way forward.

REFLECTING ON THE POLITICS OF REGULATING YOUNG CHILDREN

For Foucault, the institutional organisation of time is a disciplinary technology that is designed to produce docile bodies. The institutional organisation achieves this through the timetable. Timetables in specific institutions 'establish rhythms, impose particular occupations, regulate the cycle of repetition' (Foucault 1980, p. 149). Modern timetables aim to cram as much into time as possible and act as a disciplinary technology by deeply affecting how we act and think within them. In early childhood services the production of time as a scarce resource is being intensified by work intensification—increased regulation and accountability (Hughes and MacNaughton 2007). These ideas challenge educators to think about the extent to which their scheduling of children's learning is producing docile children and to ask how they might work against this. Foucault's ideas on time also challenge us to think about how the way we organise time might enable us to establish power over children and work against their rights to have a say in their daily lives. For Foucault, one's relation to disciplinary time marks one's rank in a hierarchy: '. . . each individual is caught up in a temporal series which specifically defines his level or his rank' (Foucault 1980, p. 159). This idea is further taken up by Sterne and Raine (2003), who argue that time orchestrates and shapes relationships:

> Time often seems like a technical matter outside the conduct of social life, but the keeping of time is a crucial aspect of governance. It orchestrates individual and collective activity and shapes relations between individuals and institutions, between institutions, and within networks of individuals. (<http://www.firstmonday.org/issues/special11_9/sterne/index.html>)

These ideas challenge staff to consider how their orchestration of time is shaping relationships in their services and the possibilities for children's rights to be honoured during their time in early childhood services.

How?

Staff need to consider several, interrelated dimensions of how they and the children use time if they are to produce a productive and pleasing learning environment.

ORGANISATION OF TIME DURING THE DAY: THE TIMETABLE

Staff need to develop a plan for how they can best use their time to enrich and extend children's learning. To do this they need to organise time to:

- maximise enjoyment and a sense of wellbeing in the children, parents and staff
- ensure that children gain a feeling of security and competence in their learning environment
- support children's differing learning styles and patterns
- support equity of access to and participation in the program for all children.

The following discussion at a staff meeting shows how scheduling can help children feel secure in a new environment.

A new group of three-year-olds is about to start the kindergarten year and the staff are discussing ways in which they can help the children to settle in.

Dean: 'Let's decide on a timetable for the day and keep this for the first weeks of the term.'

Andrea: 'That's a good idea. It'll help the children, and it'll help me, too, because I don't have to think too much about what we're going to do next. I'm always so busy with the children at the start of a new term—they seem to need so much individual attention!'

Dean: 'I think that inside time is best done first; that way the children get used to the room.'

Reflection point: Why is it important, in this instance, to stick to the same timetable each day?

ORGANISING TIME FOR CHILDREN'S AND STAFF'S SENSE OF ENJOYMENT AND WELLBEING

Staff can achieve a sense of enjoyment and wellbeing for both children and staff in the centre by:

- organising time flexibly to cater for their own and the children's changing interests and levels of concentration and energy during the day. For instance, US researchers (Holmes, Pelligrini and Schmidt 2007) replicated previous research that has studied the effects of outside play on young children's learning. They found, like previous researchers, that preschool children's concentration increased after periods of outside play of between 10 and 20 minutes

- organising time to create a relaxed, unhurried, non-regimented tempo to the day and allow specific time for children to relax. German researchers (e.g. Stueck and Gloeckner 2005) have found that structured time for relaxation can reduce young children's stress levels and improve their sense of wellbeing within and without the classroom
- organising time to allow staff to have in-depth conversations with children and to actively explore things with them and build meaningful learning (Glassman and Whalley 2000)
- organising time to allow staff to become actively involved with the children as well as doing 'housekeeping' tasks
- planning quiet times for rest and recovery in between, or after more intense and active experiences for staff and children (Holmes, Pelligrini and Schmidt 2006)
- planning time to allow for the unhurried transition between one experience or part of the day and another
- organising time so children can just 'be' and have some time to dream and wonder. This can help children's wellbeing.

ORGANISING TIME FOR CHILDREN'S SENSE OF SECURITY AND COMPETENCE

Staff can help children by ensuring that:

- there is a regular pattern to the children's day, providing them with predictability. Visual supports, such as an illustrated daily timetable kept at the children's eye level, can help children to understand the daily sequence and, in doing so, 'allay fears and uncertainties, and allow the child to participate more fully throughout the day' (CDPP 2007, p. 1)
- there are blocks of time for children to improve their competence through practising new and old skills.

ORGANISING TIME TO SUPPORT CHILDREN'S DIFFERING LEARNING STYLES AND PATTERNS

Children's learning styles can be supported by staff who organise time to:

- take account of children's differing levels of concentration
- enable children to finish activities in their own time rather than in pre-set time periods
- allow time to offer challenging extensions to children's experiences (Briggs and Potter 1995)
- allow children to follow their interests at length and in depth (Lally 1991)
- enable children to make their own decisions about when to have snacks, when to rest and when to be involved in inside or outside activities (Lally 1991)
- meet the changing needs of the children as the year progresses
- meet the demands and challenges of changing weather patterns during the year by, for example, taking account of children's and their own differing energy levels in hot and cold weather
- allow ample opportunities for children to make choices during the day.

At the Little People Centre, staff have a schedule that allows the children to finish their projects and to work in their own time without the pressure that is often imposed by having to 'pack up' at pre-arranged times.

They have an informal snack time in the morning and in the afternoon. The snack—fruit or biscuits and drink— is set out on a table and the children help themselves over a period of about 45 minutes. A staff member sits at the table during this time to cut up the fruit, help the children pour drinks and encourage social interaction. This arrangement allows the children to decide for themselves if they are hungry and thirsty at this time of the day.

Reflection point: In the vignette above the staff are aware that children should be allowed to self regulate. What other things could be incorporated into the program to help children to make their own decisions?

ORGANISING TIME TO SUPPORT EQUITY OF ACCESS AND PARTICIPATION

Staff can ensure that:

- children of differing physical abilities have the time to move around easily
- children of differing physical abilities have the time to participate in a range of experiences
- children of differing abilities have similar amounts of quality time with them
- children of differing abilities and ages can explore experiences and materials for lengths of time commensurate with their differing levels of concentration
- children in the group, irrespective of their cultural background, have time with them
- boys and girls have similar amounts of quality time with them.

When and why?

Staff's approach to curriculum and their specific teaching and learning goals for the children will influence their scheduling decisions.

GOAL RELEVANCE

In general, staff can use scheduling to ensure that children have time to:

- explore a balanced variety of experiences from within the arts and the sciences
- develop and practise skills and dispositions across a broad range of developmental domains
- experience personal control over their learning
- wonder and just 'be'
- satisfy their routine needs for eating, drinking, resting and toileting.

DEVELOPMENTAL CONSIDERATIONS

Understanding that infants go through different states of being during a day can help you to tune into their needs and support their wellbeing and learning proactively and calmly. According to Honig (2006) there are three states of being of being for infants that it is important to consider in timing your interactions with them:

- the sleepy state
- the calm/alert state
- the active/alert state.

During their first 12 months of life, babies have widely differing patterns of sleeping, eating and toileting, and the daily timetable must take account of this. Staff will face considerable difficulties if they try to ensure that all babies in a group eat, sleep and have their nappies changed at the same time! Babies can react with anger, distress and fussiness or irritability if they are forced into a routine that does not suit their own individual rhythms (Honig 2006). On the other hand, when the daily timetable takes account of the differing rituals and routines of individual children then positive attachments between babies and staff can grow (Sims and Hutchins 1999). Positive attachments between babies and early childhood staff are critical to a baby's wellbeing.

Scheduling time for one-on-one interactions between individual staff and individual babies is also critical to a baby's wellbeing. If individual staff have time to actively and positively respond to a specific baby's cues and 'know them well enough to be able to respond in ways that work for them' (Rolfe 2002, p. 10) then babies will feel secure and cared for. Hence, building time to be caring into a day working with babies is critical.

Toddler characteristics vary across cultures because there are different assumptions in different communities about when and how they should learn to follow rules and acknowledge others' needs (Rogoff 2003). So getting in 'sync' with the specific individual and cultural expectations prevalent in the communities that staff are working with is important. In many Anglo communities, toddlers will dislike being hurried as they are only just beginning to master the skills needed to be independent in routines and play experiences. Thus, there should be sufficient time in a toddler program for each of the daily routines and for each of the learning experiences. Transition from one experience or routine to another will be easier if staff warn toddlers that they will soon need to bring their activity or routine to a close. In addition, staff should organise sufficient time for toddlers to watch others and to contemplate what is happening. This helps them make sense of their daily world. Using photographic or picture prompts that give toddlers concrete, visual cues of the scheduled activities and routines can help them to understand what is about to happen and what will happen during a specific routine.

However, as the following example indicates, creating such flexibility in toddler settings often means innovative use of staff time.

> A child care centre attached to a factory in the outer eastern suburbs of Adelaide decided that their toddler program could best meet the children's developmental needs by employing an extra member of staff to be present during routines and transition times. This would enable the children to take their time eating, dressing and going to sleep. The addition of a further member of staff would allow the children to finish activities at their own pace, to dress and undress themselves with help and to eat more slowly or quickly. The director approached the committee with well-thought-out arguments and obtained funding for an extra three hours of staff time per day.
>
> *Reflection point:* What difference would an additional staff member make to a centre you work in or are familiar with?

Staff also need to plan for continuity from one day to the next. Children as young as two and three years of age can work in-depth over several months on projects of interest to them (New 2000).

There are many different approaches to organising timetables for preschool children. Irrespective of how staff approach scheduling for preschoolers, they should plan for their increased competence and concentration. Time for in-depth and focused work is essential to create learning challenges for this age group.

A similar balance is also important for children in the early years of schooling. However, children's ability and desire to concentrate on the same project for a considerable period of time can grow as their cognitive skills grow. Children in the early years of schooling also benefit from time for in-depth work on projects that offer learning challenges for them. For example, their ability to invent increasingly complex games and follow rules is best supported by scheduling that allows them to work on their inventions over several days (Castle 1990). This principle applies to many other areas of project work with children of this age. There is evidence from the USA that whole-day programs that give children more extended time to focus on their learning than half-day programs produce gains in learning across several curriculum areas (e.g. Nielsen and Cooper-Martin 2002).

Children in the early years of schooling can also benefit from recall time being planned into each day. This can be a time in which children 'explain and describe to other children what they have done and/or learnt in the course of an activity' (Fisher 1998, p. 40) and this can assist teachers to assess their learning. It can also offer children practice in sharing their experiences and ideas with others.

All children can benefit from time during which they experience control over their own learning and direct it. Research suggests that lack of personal control over learning can lead to anxiety in children in the early years of schooling (Broadhead 2001). The timetable can be used to counter the development of anxiety in young children by providing them with extended periods of time in which they direct their own learning activities and initiate and follow through on social relationships with each other.

Snack time—a time to be together.

A timetable that also allows time for children and teachers to experience pleasure in learning and in classroom relationships is important. Too often, haste to move through routine times, such as meal times, can lead to coercive relationships in which the adult's power over the child dominates and the experience of pleasurable relationships between child and adult is diminished (Phelen 1997). Allowing time to deviate from the normal routine of the day can free children and adults to experience greater power over their lives with each other, to 'win back children's—as well as their own—rights to their bodies and desires' (Leavitt and Bauman Power 1997, p. 71).

For children of all ages the rhythm of the day can be established using simple rituals such as a repeated song, rhyme, game or movement. This can help to remind children what is coming next or what they need to do now (Ostrosky et al. 2003).

Equity considerations

'RACE' AND CULTURE

Adults' use of time sends clear messages to children about who is most valued in the group. Consequently, staff should monitor how much time they are spending with each child. If there are children with whom they tend to spend superficial or minimal time, staff need to ask themselves, 'Who are these children?'. For example, staff decisions about how they spend their time can unintentionally reinforce racism: when staff spend only token amounts of time with particular children or on their specific interests, those children can believe that they are less valued than other children in the group. Staff need to monitor their interactions with all children in the group to avoid such tokenism. Consider the following scenario.

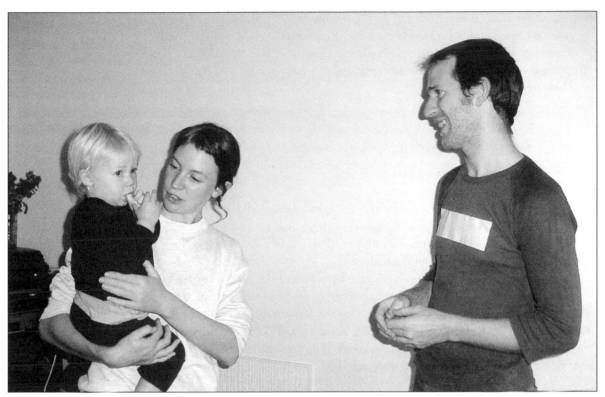

David talks to Jude's mother when she picks him up.

The Greenfields child care centre in an outer suburban area had a small number of Aboriginal Australian children. The staff wanted the Aboriginal children to feel included in the group and decided that one way to do this was to make time to say something to each Aboriginal child each day. However, as they reflected on this idea, they felt that it was tokenistic. It would not give the Aboriginal children in-depth time with staff and it could result in staff spending only small amounts of time with Aboriginal children, indicating that these children were not valued as highly as other children in the centre.

When there are ethnic and cultural differences between children and staff it is especially important to reflect on how best to organise staff time to support the growth of respectful relationships. More specifically, if there are broader 'racial' and ethnic tensions between specific ethnic and cultural groups within the wider community, this can influence how well children from those ethnic groups who face discrimination and racism fare in child care. Howes and Shivers (2006) studied 200 ethnically diverse US toddlers who were new to childcare. They concluded that if the ethnic differences between children and their caregivers:

> . . . are mirrored by dominant/minority culture discrimination and racism, the children may fare better in childcare if there are adults in childcare who share the children's cultural communities . . . (p. 577) [because] . . . the children who shared an ethnic/racial heritage with their caregivers were able to form more secure child–caregiver attachment relationships than the children who did not share a heritage (p. 597).

To build respectful and responsive relationships in services where staff may be working with families who have experienced war-driven dislocation and refugee-related trauma, it is particularly important to allow time for children and families to settle into new routines and expectations without experiencing hurrying or stress. If staff and families do not speak the same language then bilingual support workers can be helpful in building understandings and relationships. However, they should not be suddenly withdrawn from children and families. Instead there should be a carefully planned transition in which early childhood staff take increasing responsibility for building relationships with the child and the family.

Cultural marginalisation can lead to a different sense of time and to different priorities in using time. Consider Treppte's comments (1994, p. 19) about planned meeting times in an early childhood project involving German and Lebanese women:

> [The] . . . Lebanese women . . . proposed that each week, one of them should be phoned by the teacher on the morning of the day that they were expected to come. They argued that in the situation they live in— . . . with nothing to do and nowhere to go—they find it difficult to remember the day of the week. . . . Of course, we take it for granted that our way of organising and defining sequences of time is rational and the only possible way to do so. Yet, it is not.

Treppte (1994) argued that while the Lebanese women did not have a different sense of time to the German teachers in the project, they were so marginalised in German society that time had a different meaning to them. For similar reasons, staff need to consider if time might have a different meaning for some families in their specific early childhood setting.

It takes regular amounts of in-depth time to make anti-discriminatory perspectives work, and staff should recognise this when timetabling specific work to learn about and respect cultural and 'racial' diversity. Further, it takes support and time to develop the knowledge and skills to work in critically reflective anti-discriminatory ways (MacNaughton 2005). Thus, as staff plan regular time for the children to learn about cultural and 'racial' diversity and to work with them against any biases they may have, they should ensure that this work develops slowly and with care.

GENDER

Research over time has consistently shown that boys and girls spend their time differently in early childhood spaces. Girls tend to remain longer than boys with single items of equipment; boys tend to spend more time than girls in high levels of physical activity and in less-stable social groupings (Davies and Bremner 1994); boys often demand and get more staff time than girls (MacNaughton 2001); and they can be more aggressive towards their peers (Gevers Deynoot-Schaub and Riksen-Walraven (2006). Staff can alter these gendered patterns of involvement in the early childhood program by spending time with boys to extend and enhance their concentration and with girls to enhance their interest in higher levels of physical activity (Davies and Bremner 1994). In such work it is important for staff to monitor the amount of time they are spending in these tasks with boys and girls. Recently, a Dutch study of 70 toddlers attending child care (Gevers Deynoot-Schaub and Riksen-Walraven 2006) found two factors directly related to scheduling that made a difference to boys' levels of aggression. First, boys were less aggressive towards their peers in centres where there was more opportunity for pretend play, sand play and water play. Secondly, they were less aggressive when staff were engaged in more social interaction with them.

Some early childhood staff have organised the timetabling of specific activities to ensure equal access to and involvement in them by boys and girls. Some teachers have 'everybody plays with blocks' day, a 'girls-only' block time once a week and a 'boys-only' sewing time or art time. Research (for example, MacNaughton 2001) has shown that such techniques will lead to girls being more involved with blocks, but organising children's time in this way can also create difficulties. MacNaughton (2001) identified two difficulties. First, once girls-only time was stopped, the children reverted to their 'old' patterns. Second, during girls-only times, groups of boys tried to disrupt the play through what one practitioner described as 'seek and destroy' missions. This involved boys making very swift forays into the girls' play and disrupting it through the use of loud voices, or aggressive actions. Often, this occurred when staff were otherwise occupied. Hence, staff need to carefully monitor such techniques to ensure that they achieve the planned gender equity outcomes for all children.

DISABILITY AND ADDITIONAL NEEDS

Children with disabilities may need special equipment or care. Planning time so that sta specifically and individually to these needs is complex but important because it leads to i effective teaching for children with disabilities (Grisham-Brown and Pretti-Frontczak 2003). to have a positive attitude to the time and effort needed to give special care to children with d to support use of any special equipment or resources that they may need. Staff who resent teach children with disabilities that they are not valued and will teach children without disabilities to devalue those with disabilities.

Alongside the need to plan time for any special care and attention needed by specific children with disabilities, it is also important to plan time in which children without disabilities in the group can become familiar with any special care and equipment needs of children who have disabilities in the group. Routine activities such as group or circle time can provide an important platform for those children with disabilities that need to practise social skills to do so. Macy and Bricker (2007) found that embedding social skill development into the routines of an early childhood classroom increased the social competency of the children with disabilities that they worked with. The use of visual supports that depict the day in chronological sequence and show key steps during routine times can also help children with autism to feel more secure and comfortable in the preschool setting (CDPP 2007).

Reflecting on scheduling techniques

1 Define scheduling.
2 Consider the following quote from Lally (1991, p. 78):

The routine in a nursery class should be more concerned with the establishment of flexible daily patterns rather than with set times for whole group activity. A whole class approach is clearly not consistent with a developmental approach where individual needs are of paramount concern . . .

3 Do the centres you are familiar with organise time for a whole group approach? Do you think that they should? Why? How could they achieve these goals?
4 How might time be organised to encourage toddlers to practise independent decision-making?
5 How could you use the organisation of staff time to encourage social interaction and conversation between preschool children and babies?
6 How might your philosophy on adult intervention in children's learning influence how you organise your daily timetable?
7 Beaty (1996) believed that there are three keys to the productive organisation of time within an early childhood centre. These are:
- providing an orderly sequence of events
- ensuring that children experience a minimum of waiting
- ensuring that children have a maximum amount of time for doing what they want to do.

Use the following table to reflect on one thing you could do to accomplish these tasks during a long day-care program for children of different ages.

Keys to good timing	Babies	Toddlers	Preschoolers
Provide an orderly sequence of events. Ensure children experience a minimum of waiting. Ensure children have a maximum of time for doing what they want to do.			

Improving teaching in practice

1 Note the daily and weekly timetables of an early childhood centre.
2 How well does the centre's organisation of time enable children to develop their own learning styles and patterns?
3 To what extent does the current organisation of time enhance a sense of enjoyment and wellbeing for staff and children?
4 Note the times when children are required to wait.
5 Was equipment used to enhance children's sense of security and competence?
6 Did the organisation of adult time support equity of access and participation?
7 How and how well were developmental considerations taken into account in the way staff organised their time?
8 To what extent was there time for pleasure in the day?

FURTHER READING

Dau, E. and Jones, K. 2004, *Revisiting Celebrations with Young Children*, Australian Early Childhood Association, Watson, ACT.

Holmes, R., Pelligrini, A. and Schmidt, S. 2006, 'The effects of different recess timing regimens on preschoolers' classroom attention', *Early Childhood Development and Care*, 176(7), pp. 735–743.

Honig, A. 2006, 'How to calm and comfort children', *Scholastic Early Childhood Today*, 21(1), pp. 27–28.

Leavitt, R. and Bauman Power, M. 1997, 'Civilizing bodies: children in day care', in J. Tobin, ed., *Making a Place for Pleasure in Early Childhood Education* (pp. 40–75), Yale University Press, New Haven and London.

Winters, D.L., Saylor, C.H. and Phillips, C.Y. 2003, 'Full-day kindergarten: a story of successful adoption and initial implementation', *Young Children*, 58(6), pp. 54–58.

ONLINE AND MULTI-MEDIA RESOURCES

Text

Tips and ideas for making visuals to support young children: **http://www.vanderbilt.edu/csefel/modules/module3b/handout2.pdf**

Beneke, S. 2000, 'Implementing the project approach in parttime early childhood education programs', *Early Childhood Research into Practice*, 2(1): **http://www.ecrp.uiuc.edu/v2n1/beneke.html**

Brewster, C. and Railsback, J. 2002, 'Full-day kindergarten: exploring an option for extended learning', *By Request Series*, December 2002, Northwest Regional Educational Laboratory (NWREL), Portland, OR: **http://www.nwrel.org/request/dec2002/kindergarten.pdf**

Ostrosky, M.M., Jung, E.Y., Hemmeter, M.L. and Thomas, D. 2003, 'Helping children make routines and schedules', Center on the Social and Emotional Foundations for Early Learning: **http://www.csefel.uiuc.edu/what works.html** (accessed 6 September 2005).

——2003, 'Helping children understand transitions between activities', Center on the Social and Emotional Foundations for Early Learning: **http://www.csefel.uiuc.edu/what works.html** (accessed 6 September 2005).

Multi-media

Daily routines—multi-media resources: **http://www.pbs.org/wholechild/providers/little.html**

Scheduling for student independence in a primary school multi-age classroom. Free access video and text: **http://edcommunity. apple.com/ali/story.php?itemID=620&version=360&pageID=1577**

REFERENCES

Beaty, J. 1996, *Preschool appropriate practices*, 2nd edn, Harcourt Brace, New York.

Boardman, M. 2003, 'Half-days or full days of kindergarten? How and why parents decide', *Australian Journal of Early Childhood*, 30(1), pp. 36–43.

Briggs, F., & Potter, G. K. 1995, *Teaching children in the first three years of school*, 2nd edn, Longman Cheshire, Melbourne.

Broadhead, P. 2001, 'Investigating sociability and cooperation in four- and five-year-olds in reception class settings', *International Journal of Early Years Education*, 9(1), pp. 23–36.

Burkard, T. 2005, *After the Literacy Hour: May the Best Plan Win!*, Centre for Policy Studies, London.

Campbell, R. 1998, 'A literacy hour is only part of the story', *Literacy*, 32(1), pp. 21–23.

Castle, K. 1990, 'The second year: 12–24 months', in E. Surbeck and M. Kelly, eds, *Personalizing Care with Infants, Toddlers and Families* (pp. 23–32), Association for Childhood Education International, Wheaton, MD.

CDPP 2007, 'Using visual supports in the preschool environment: timetables and schedules', *ACT-NOW Fact Sheet 32*, Monash University, <http://www.med.monash.edu.au/spppm/research/devpsych/actnow>

Dau, E. and Jones, K. 2004, *Revisiting Celebrations with Young Children*, Australian Early Childhood Association, Watson, ACT.

Davies, J. and Bremner, I. 1994, 'Morning and afternoon nursery sessions: can they be equally effective in giving children a positive start to school?', *International Journal of Early Years Education*, 2(2), pp. 43–53.

Davis, K. and MacNaughton, G. 1999, 'Early childhood review', Structural issues research paper, University of Melbourne.

Elicker, J. 2000, 'Full-day kindergarten: exploring the research. From inquiry to practice', *Eric Digest*, ED463885.

Fisher, J. 1998, 'The relationship between planning and assessment', in I. Siraj-Blatchford, ed., *A Curriculum Handbook for Early Childhood Educators*, pp. 15–44, Trentham Books, London.

Fisher, R. 2004, 'Embedding the literacy strategy: snapshots of change', *Literacy*, 38(3), pp. 134–140.

Foucault, M. 1980, *Discipline and Punish*, Pantheon Books, New York.

Germeten, S. 2000, 'Early childhood education in Norway: time as an indication for pedagogical space?', Paper presented at *10th European Conference on Quality in Early Childhood Education (EECERA)*, 29 August – 1 September, London.

Gevers Deynoot-Schaub, M. and Riksen-Walraven, J. 2006, 'Peer contacts of 15-month-olds in childcare: links with child temperament, parent-child interaction and quality of childcare', *Social Development*, 15(4), pp. 709–729.

Glassman, M. and Whalley, K. 2000, 'Dynamic aims: the use of long-term projects in early childhood classrooms in light of Dewey's educational philosophy', *Early Childhood Research and Practice*, 2(1), <http://ecrp.uiuc.edu/v2n1/glassman.html>.

Grisham-Brown, J. and Pretti-Frontczak, K. 2003, 'Using planning time to individualize instruction for preschoolers with special needs', *Journal of Early Intervention*, 26(3), pp. 31–46.

Holmes, R., Pelligrini, A. and Schmidt, S. 2006, 'The effects of different recess timing regimens on preschoolers' classroom attention', *Early Childhood Development and Care*, 176(7), pp. 735–743.

Honig, A. 2006, 'How to calm and comfort children', *Scholastic Early Childhood Today*, 21(1), pp. 27–28.

Howes, C. and Shivers, E. 2006, 'New child-caregiver attachment relationships: entering childcare when the caregiver is and is not an ethnic match', *Social Development*, 15(4), pp. 574–590.

Hughes, P. and MacNaughton, G. 2007, 'Space, time and regulation: the politics of everyday staff-parent relationships', Paper presented at *Honoring the Child, Honoring Equity 7* conference, 15–17 November, Melbourne.

Labbo, L., Sprague, L., Montero, M. and Font, G. 2000, 'Connecting a computer center to themes, literature and kindergarteners' literacy needs', *Reading Online*, 4(1), <http://www.readingonline.org/electronic/labbo/index.html> (accessed 7 June 2007).

Lally, M. 1991, *The Nursery Teacher in Action*, Paul Chapman Publishing, London.

Leavitt, R. and Bauman Power, M. 1997, 'Civilizing bodies: children in day care', in J. Tobin, ed., *Making a Place for Pleasure in Early Childhood Education*, (pp. 40–75), Yale University Press, New Haven and London.

New, R. 2000, 'Reggio Emilia: catalyst for change and conversation', *ERIC Digest*, ED447971.

MacNaughton, G. 2001, *Rethinking Gender in Early Childhood*, Allen & Unwin, Sydney.

MacNaughton, G. 2003, *Shaping Early Childhood: Learners, Curriculum and Contexts*, Open University Press, Milton Keynes.

MacNaughton, G. 2005, *Doing Foucault in early childhood studies*, Routledge, London.

Macy, M.G. and Bricker, D.D. 2007, 'Embedding individualized social goals into routine activities in inclusive early childhood classrooms', *Early Child Development and Care*, 177(2), pp. 107–120.

Nielsen, J. and Cooper-Martin, E. 2002, 'Evaluation of the Montgomery County Public Schools Assessment Program: kindergarten and grade 1 reading report', Montgomery Public Schools, Office of Shared Accountability, Rockville, MD, <http://www.mcps.k12.md.us/departments/dea/pdf/Kinder2002.pdf> (accessed 24 October 2007).

Ostrosky, M.M., Jung, E.Y., Hemmeter, M.L., Thomas, D. 2003, 'Helping children make transitions between activities', Center on the Social and Emotional Foundations for Early Learning, <http://www.csefel.uiuc.edu/what works.html> (accessed 6 September 2005).

Phelen, A. 1997, 'Classroom management and the erasure of teacher desire', in J. Tobin, ed., *Making Place for Pleasure in Early Childhood Education*, (pp. 76–100), Yale University Press, New Haven and London.

Rogoff, B. 2003, *The Cultural Nature of Human Development*, Oxford University Press, Oxford.

Rolfe, S. 2002, *Promoting Resilience in Children*, Australian Early Childhood Association, Watson, ACT.

Sims, M. and Hutchins, T. 1999, 'Positive transitions', *Australian Journal of Early Childhood*, 24(3), pp. 12–16.

Sterne, J. and Raine, E. 2006, 'Command tones: Digitization and sounded time', *First Monday Journal*, <http://www.firstmonday.org/issues/special11_9/sterne/index.html>, accessed 2 Dec 2007.

Stueck, M. and Gloeckner, N. 2005, 'Yoga for children in the mirror of science: working spectrum and practice fields of the Training of Relaxation with Elements of Yoga for children', *Early Childhood Development and Care*, 175(4), pp. 371–377.

Treppte, C. 1994, 'Multicultural approaches in education: a German experience', *International Journal of Early Childhood*, 2(2), pp. 5–30.

Whitehead, M. 2004, *Language and Literacy in the Early Years*, 3rd edn, Sage, London.

PART TWO

General Teaching Techniques

Chapter 4

Demonstrating

 Demonstrate: *to show.*

(Collins Dictionary of the English Language, p. 395)

Watching a skilled movement being made helps a learner to acquire skill . . . by deliberately imitating other people, they get the feel of the movement and the learning process is accelerated.

(Hughes and Hughes 1937, p. 221)

Teacher demonstration is an important method used to teach both reading and writing.

(Oppenheimer 2007, online)

What?

To demonstrate something is to show how it is done. As a teaching technique, demonstrating can help children's learning by showing them how to use materials and special tools or how to accomplish a particular task. Simply moving in and showing a child how to approach a task can be a very effective way of reminding a child how to do something that they may have forgotten or of teaching them a new skill. It can also help children to learn alternative and more effective ways of approaching a problem.

Issues and debates

There is little debate or concern within the literature about the effectiveness and use of demonstration as a teaching technique when it is used as part of a teacher's repertoire. However, it is important not to rely on demonstration as the main way of teaching young children as this can reduce their capacity to innovate and to discover things for themselves.

Later in this chapter (see the section considering 'race' and culture) we have identified the importance of using competent and knowing demonstrators when you are demonstrating the use of specific cultural artefacts or traditions to young children.

How?

Demonstrating will most effectively support children's learning when staff:

- use clear, unambiguous verbal instructions to support their demonstration
- break a skill or task into small, sequential steps. This is particularly important when staff are demonstrating complex techniques to children. Task analysis (see Chapter 30) will assist in this
- allow time for the children to intently observe and 'listen in' to what you hope for them to learn through the demonstration (Rogoff et al. 2003)
- are familiar with the steps involved in the skill or technique they are demonstrating so they do not confuse children. For instance, if staff can turn on a new hose-nozzle with ease, their demonstrations are likely to effectively teach children the technique
- review with children what they have learnt so that additional demonstrations can be planned if necessary (Benelli and Yongue 1995)
- provide the children with lots of opportunities to practise the skill or technique being demonstrated (Benelli and Yongue 1995).

Staff may also find it helpful to support their demonstration of key skills or techniques with visual aids, such as picture cards or picture sequences. At a later date, children can refer to the visual aids to refresh their memory of the sequence involved in a particular task. Chris has found this useful in supporting children's learning in the woodworking area:

> Chris has brought a new piece of equipment—a vice—to the centre's woodworking area. She is aware that the children have never used a vice before, so she demonstrates how to use it in several small steps: first put the wood in the vice; then turn the screw to tighten it; finally saw the wood. Next to the woodworking area, Chris places a three-step diagram of how to use the vice, so that the children can look at the pictures and remind themselves how to use it properly.
>
> *Reflective task:* Draw a three-step diagram to help the children in this situation.

When and why?

Demonstrating will be most appropriately used as a teaching technique when:

- children are keen to learn the skill or technique
- children have the necessary competence to learn the new technique or skill with minimal adult support and with a minimum of frustration
- children's own creativity and experimentation with skills and techniques are not be hampered by an adult direction. Hughes's and Hughes's caution of almost 70 years ago is still pertinent:

    The moment when a child is absorbed in creative work that is giving him intense satisfaction is obviously not an occasion for attempting to teach him technique. (Hughes and Hughes 1937, p. 224)

GOAL RELEVANCE

There are many occasions when simply showing children how to do something can be the most effective way to assist their learning. In general, demonstration can be used to teach children how to do something that requires specific skills or techniques that they lack. Here are some examples of such occasions:

- When children need help with a task or technique but staff cannot talk to them at that precise moment because they are talking with another child or an adult. Here, a quick demonstration of how to approach the task or technique can provide a child with the information and attention they need to proceed.
- When children have reached a point in doing something or using something when support or encouragement will assist with success or perseverance.
- When children are exploring new equipment or materials that require skills or techniques that are new to them. For instance, if the hose for the sandpit has a new hose-nozzle that requires a special technique for releasing water, it will be helpful to demonstrate how the hose works. Or, when children's dramatic play might benefit from seeing how a specific task or job is done. Parents can be used sometimes to demonstrate specialist jobs or tasks to children (Youngquist 2004).
- When children's learning will benefit from knowing the most effective and safe way to use a tool such as a hammer or a saw. Some techniques will be more effective and less dangerous than others.
- When children want to learn a new skill or technique to help complete a task or solve a problem. For instance, if staff demonstrate the most effective way to hold scissors or to use sticky-tape, children at the collage table can concentrate on when to use them and not become frustrated by learning how to use them.
- When children need reminding about how to do something. For instance, children may need reminding that the stapler works best if it is placed on the table and the top is pressed down firmly.
- When adults want to increase children's technical competence in a particular area. For instance, Edwards (1993, p. 164) described how Paola Notari, a teacher in the Reggio Emilia district, used demonstration to increase children's skill at working clay:

> Finishing the new slab [of clay], she takes it over to the girl needing it. Seeing her first piece, Paola comments, 'Look at that marvel! Now you have to think about what else you want to do. You could put the same marks in it [the new slab] you did before. Or you could place these pieces folded, or standing up.' She demonstrates, using little strips of clay.

Maria Montessori believed that demonstration was a particularly useful technique for helping children to learn basic daily living skills, such as preparing food and setting the table. In addition, she believed that learning these skills nurtured the young child's need to constantly improve their daily living skills (Oriti and Kahn 1994). (Refer to Chapter 31 for additional information on Montessori's approach to early childhood education.) Demonstration is also seen as a useful technique for teaching children to respect the environment. When staff demonstrate to the children their enjoyment of nature, children learn to respect the environment. For instance, teachers can demonstrate how to save energy by turning out lights whenever the sun provides adequate light indoors or how to conserve water by running only a trickle of water then turning it off when they are washing their hands (Lewin-Benham 2006).

Research has shown that demonstration can be important in developing young children's scientific literacy if it is combined with questions that probe children's understandings of what has been demonstrated (Klein et al. 2000). However, the researchers highlighted that not all children learn equally well with a strongly teacher-directed approach to science and that using diverse teaching techniques adapted to individual children is important.

Children's emergent literacy skills are also helped through demonstration in specific contexts. For instance, when adults demonstrate how to use text and other visual resources within dramatic play, children's knowledge of text and its uses is enhanced (Arthur and Makin 2001). When teachers physically guide children's early writing attempts, it can also support children in building their writing skills. Demonstration has also been identified by beginning writers as helpful to them (Martello 1999); however, this should not be the only technique used.

'This is how you do it!'

Demonstrations can also support children's artistic development as adults show children how to use specific art tools, skills and techniques (Bae 2004). As creativity grows from innovating on what we are familiar with, this supports the development of creativity in young children. As Rogoff (1990, p. 198) puts it, 'a creative idea is in some sense a reformulation of existing ideas . . . that forge a new connection between ideas and tools that are already familiar'. In this way, demonstration can support the growth of young children's artistic development.

Increasingly, computers are being used as 'demonstrators' of specific skills, especially literacy and numeracy skills, in the early-years classroom. Westwood (2006), in reviewing research on computer demonstration in the classroom, notes that this can be a time-effective way to allow children to process information when processes demonstrated are well sequenced and organised. Specific Information and Communication Technologies (ICT) developments such as 'talking' word processors can demonstrate ways to use and sound out words and allow children the time to respond and practise their responses.

DEVELOPMENTAL CONSIDERATIONS

Babies constantly try to make sense of the world about them by acting on it. When babies begin to explore objects physically by hitting, banging, sucking and grasping them, they can also begin to intentionally imitate people (Berk 2006). From this point in a baby's development, staff can use simple demonstrations of how to do things to help develop a baby's concentration on an experience. Staff can show babies how to hold, push and pull objects to make interesting sounds, sights and events, thus extending the babies' interest in the experience. Puna often uses simple demonstrations to support the learning of the babies in her room:

> Puna sits on the floor with Aisha, who is seven months old. Aisha is between Puna's legs to give her extra support as she is presented with different equipment to enjoy. Puna presents Aisha with a toy that has a large button on the top. As she demonstrates how to press the button to make the toy squeak, she says, 'Look Aisha, you press the button like this'. The baby imitates her action, the toy squeaks and Aisha gurgles with delight.
>
> _Reflection point:_ What have you seen babies imitate?

New Zealand research (Barr and Hayne 2003) has shown that babies also learn by watching older siblings. This suggests that older children may also be effective demonstrators for babies, helping them to acquire new behaviours and skills. However, the focus should be on allowing child-initiated learning in this way (Lally and Mangione 2006).

There is some evidence that demonstration may be more effective with children between 14–18 months of age than with those under 12 months of age. Goubet et al. (2006) found that 14–18-month-olds solved physical problems that they encountered (e.g. opening a suitcase or picking up a toy) more effectively than nine-month-old children after watching adults demonstrating how to solve the problem.

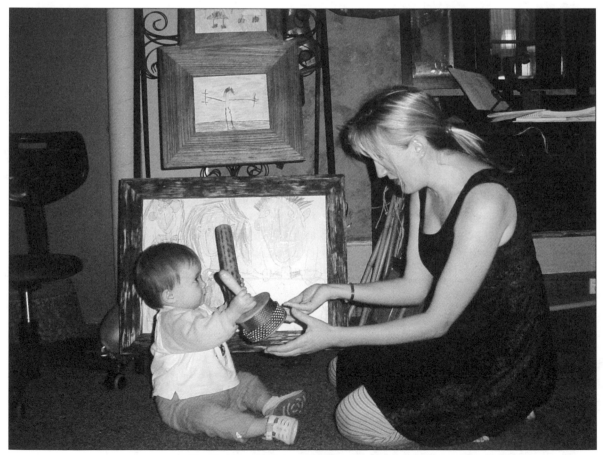

'Look what happens when you shake it.'

Toddlers often like to do things that adults do, using the objects that they have seen adults use (Rogoff 2003). For this reason, demonstration can be an effective way of teaching toddlers how to use objects in their local environment.

Toddlers are also keen to gain greater control over themselves and their bodies. They are also keen to use their increasing physical competence to help them explore their environment. With so much to do and so much to learn, toddlers often forget how to do something they learnt just recently. For instance, they may forget how to make the blocks balance or how to open the door of the oven in the imaginative play area. Toddlers' active exploration of their environment also means that they often meet situations that require a skill or a technique that they have not tried before. For instance, they may decide to fill a screw-top container with water and be unsure as to how to screw the top on.

Toddlers' ability to imitate the actions of others means that by demonstrating a new or momentarily forgotten skill or technique, staff can easily provide the support toddlers need to succeed or to maintain their efforts. However, toddlers generally cannot remember a complex sequence of events, so staff should keep the demonstration short and simple. In addition, toddlers have ever-changing needs and interests and quickly move on to new challenges, so demonstrating a new skill or technique will be most effective if it happens at the moment the toddler needs it. Molly is alert to the importance of this in her work:

An old child care centre in the middle of Melbourne has had a face lift and the children's bathrooms now have taps with handles which swing to the side rather than turn. Molly is in the bathroom to make sure that the four-year-old children, who are using the bathroom for the first time, become familiar with the new environment. As the children come to wash their hands after toileting, Molly demonstrates to each one how to use the new taps. She then asks each child to do it by themselves so that she can check if they are able to turn them on and off.

Reflection point: As Molly is demonstrating to the children she also talks about what she is doing. Why does she do this?

Preschoolers gain increasing competence in using their fine motor skills by doing a wide range of activities such as drawing, pasting, painting, sewing, cutting, joining and using computer keyboards. In the preschool years, children need many of these skills to complete tasks or solve problems. For instance, children involved in dramatic play in which they have decided to set up a real estate office might want to use a saw to cut a piece of wood to make a 'For Sale' sign. They may also want to join two pieces of wood together to make their sign stand up by itself and they may want to write 'For Sale' on the sign. If staff demonstrate the most effective way to saw the wood and to join it, the children can concentrate on developing their dramatic play rather than having to work out for themselves how to saw and join the wood. Having said this, it is often appropriate that staff allow children the time and opportunity to solve such problems for themselves. Therefore, the time staff save by demonstrating how to do things needs to be balanced against the need for children to solve problems for themselves.

Gaining new technical skills can enhance children's work on a particular project and as children become older there is a wider range of techniques they can use to express their meanings to others. It is also important to teach children the technical skills of 'getting on' with each other, such as how to handle conflicts, problem-solve and develop relationships, as the children's capacity to get on with each other grows (Joseph and Strain 2003). Teacher demonstration of these skills is an important part of how children can learn them. Children learn these skills best when you explain the skill, demonstrate it, allow children to practise it and then give them positive feedback on their progress (Fox et al. 2003).

Equity considerations

'RACE' AND CULTURE

In a program based on strong multicultural perspectives, children are likely to encounter tools and utensils from a wide variety of cultures. Just some of the tools and utensils that may be seen in early childhood programs are chopsticks, a wok, bamboo steamers, a tortilla press, spatulas, a coffee pot, tongs, a *tava* (griddle), a *degchi* (large cooking pot), a *karai* (wok), *thali* plates, a coconut grater, a soufflé dish, a *chatty* (claypot), a mortar and pestle (*nuoc cham* in Vietnamese), *wajan* (Indonesian wok), boomerangs, hammers and clap sticks.

Children should learn how to use these tools and utensils appropriately for two reasons. First, understanding how a tool or utensil is used within a culture avoids children learning negative values of supremacy. Values of supremacy develop when children believe that they are superior to others (MacNaughton 2005). When children are unfamiliar with correct ways to use a tool from another culture they may use it incorrectly, fail to make it work and learn to see the tool and the culture it is from as 'silly'. Demonstrating correct uses of the tool can prevent this from happening.

Second, understanding how a tool or utensil is used within a culture builds respect for that culture and helps to counter stereotypes about it. Staff should not include in their program a range of tools from a culture other than their own without knowing what the tools are for and how to use them. It implies that they don't care about other cultures or are not prepared to take the time to learn about them. If staff demonstrate to the children how to use the tools or utensils correctly, they also demonstrate interest and respect for diversity.

When staff introduce tools and utensils from a particular culture into a centre, they can use children who are familiar with the items to help demonstrate to the group how to use them correctly. Using children's specialist knowledge and skill in this way can help build their self-esteem. However, it is important that staff do not stereotype children and assume, for example, that all children from a Chinese background know how to use chopsticks with confidence or that all children from an Indonesian background have a *wajan* (flat metal cooking pot like a wok) in their home. To avoid such stereotyping, staff should check with children and/or their parents what children use within their own homes. Maybe an Anglo-Australian child has a *wajan* in their home because their parents love Indonesian food and bought one on their recent trip to Indonesia.

There is evidence that children from many different cultural groups and cultural contexts use intent observation of adult ways of doing and being as a basis for their own, so demonstration may be appropriate as a teaching technique for a wide range of cultural groups in diverse contexts (Rogoff 2003).

GENDER

Gender differences often exist in children's technical competence in using tools and utensils. Many four- and five-year-old boys may be very competent in using tools such as spades and hammers, while many girls of the same age find these tools difficult to use. Conversely, girls may be more competent than boys in the fine and detailed cutting of materials. These differences are the result of the often-different expectations, opportunities and experiences that boys and girls have, rather than any genetic differences between them. In many cultures, boys are often expected to be good with spades and hammers but rarely expected to be good at sewing. The opposite is often true for girls.

Consequently, children can often lack confidence when using tools that are normally associated with the other gender. Boys can lack confidence when sewing and girls can lack confidence when hammering. This lack of confidence sometimes combines with a belief that boys don't sew or girls don't hammer. The result is a 'learned helplessness' around tasks traditionally associated with the other gender based on boys' views 'that's for girls' and girls' views 'that's for boys'. Staff can support and encourage boys and girls to test out tools traditionally associated with the other gender by demonstrating the most effective way to hold and use the tool. Such demonstrations can reduce the possibility that children will not achieve what they hoped to because they used the tool inappropriately. If a girl successfully uses a spade to dig a hole, she is more likely to return to the activity another time. However, if her attempts to dig a hole flounder because she has used the spade inappropriately, she may not feel confident to try again.

There is considerable evidence (MacNaughton 2006) that boys and girls try to undermine each other when they move into areas traditionally associated with the other gender. Boys will often tease girls when they begin to use tools such as hammers and spades and girls will tease boys as they learn to sew and cook. Using same-gender groups to demonstrate the use of tools can avoid this possibility to a large extent. For instance, staff may find it helpful to demonstrate how to use spades in girls-only groups and how to use a needle and thread in boys-only groups. Once the children become confident and competent users within their same-gender group, they can apply their new skills and techniques in play with the other gender. However, it is important that the adults monitor the cross-gender play for any resistance the 'other' gender may display.

DISABILITY AND ADDITIONAL NEEDS

Demonstration is one way to enhance children's skills, but the skills that most children focus intently on observing are those that they observe within their specific cultural context (Rogoff 2003). For this reason, it is important to ask:

- Is the skill or activity valued by the child's parents and by society in general?
- Does the skill or activity contribute to the child's positive interactions with their peers?
- Is the skill or activity appropriate for the child's age?
- Does the child have an interest in, or preference for, the skill or activity?
- Is it likely that the child will acquire the skill or activity, given reasonable time and resources?
- Are there opportunities to practise the skill or activity?
- Will the skill or activity enhance the child's physical wellbeing?
- Will the skill or activity be required in the child's later life?

When working with children with additional needs it is important to consider what opportunities and capacities they have for intent observation and focus strongly on those skills where this will be possible.

Once staff feel confident that it is worthwhile to teach a particular skill to a child with disabilities and that demonstration is a useful technique for such teaching, it is important to demonstrate the skill or technique in small, manageable parts. Task analysis (see Chapter 30) can assist in this process.

Reflecting on demonstrating techniques

1 Define demonstration.
2 To what extent do you think that Hughes's and Hughes's caution of almost 70 years ago (see quote below) is still pertinent when thinking about when and how to demonstrate a skill or a technique to a child?

The moment when a child is absorbed in creative work that is giving him intense satisfaction is obviously not an occasion for attempting to teach him technique. (Hughes and Hughes 1937, p. 224)

3 How could demonstrating be used to help a three-year-old child learn to use a magnifying glass? What would be the pros and cons of using this technique?
4 Would demonstrating be appropriate to help a toddler learn how to construct a tall block tower? Why?
5 Which of the following goals for children's learning could be supported through adult demonstration? Why?

- Goal 1—for the children to learn how to put blocks away.
- Goal 2—for the children to practise co-operation with each other.
- Goal 3—for the children to learn how to mix colours.
- Goal 4—for the children to express their ideas through movement.

6 How could you use demonstrating to overcome a five-year-old boy's 'learned helplessness' at bathing a baby?

7 The following extract presents a teaching episode with preschool children. How has the teacher used demonstrating to support children's learning in this episode? Do you believe this was an appropriate technique to use? Why?

Some children were building haphazard piles of blocks and knocking them down. I sat alongside them on the floor and silently began to sort through a container of plastic animals, putting them in identical pairs to form a long queue. The children stopped what they were doing and joined in my play. (Skinner 1996, p. 62)

8 Read Paley (1986, pp. 8–9). To what extent is the use of demonstration to show Mollie how to make green successful? Was demonstration an appropriate teaching technique in this instance? Why?

9 How might you use demonstration to help the children in Christopher's group learn to communicate with him?

We do a lot of massage on each other's hands and feet, and this gives the children an awareness of their bodies and body parts. This is particularly important for Christopher because he tends to stiffen up because of his disability. His hands just close tight. (DEET 1994, p. 33)

Improving teaching in practice

1 Videotape the teaching interactions you have with children during a five-minute teaching period on several different occasions.
2 When using demonstration to support children's learning did you:
   - use clear, unambiguous verbal instructions to support the demonstration?
   - break the skills or tasks into small, sequential steps?
   - ensure that you were familiar with the steps involved in the skill or technique you were demonstrating?
3 How and how well did you take account of developmental considerations in how you demonstrated skills and techniques to the children?
4 Did your demonstrations support equity of access and participation in the program?
5 What are your strengths and weaknesses in using demonstrating to promote children's learning?
6 How can you work to improve your demonstrating techniques in practice?

FURTHER READING

Edwards, C. 1993, 'Partner, nurturer and guide: the roles of the Reggio teacher in action', in C. Edwards, L. Gandini and G. Forman, eds, *The Hundred Languages of Children: The Reggio Emilia Approach to Early Childhood Education*, (pp. 151–169), Ablex Publishing Company, Norwood, NJ.

ONLINE AND MULTI-MEDIA RESOURCES

Text

US Department of Education, 'Ideas that work—literacy rich environments': **http://www.osepideasthatwork.org/ParentKit/literacy.asp**.

Multi-media

'Letters and sounds'. A teacher demonstrating sounds to children. Free access video streaming or podcast: **http://www.readingrockets.org/podcasts/classroom#sounds**

Inclusive Technology is a site that gives a good overview of current software programs for young children that demonstrate specific skills and knowledge that they can acquire: **http://www.inclusive.co.uk/early_learning/index.shtml**

REFERENCES

Arthur, L. and Makin, L. 2001, 'High quality literacy programs', *Australian Journal of Early Childhood*, 26(2), pp. 14–19.

Bae, J. 2004, 'Learning to teach visual arts in an early childhood classroom: the teacher's role as a guide', *Early Childhood Education Journal*, 31(4), pp. 247–254.

Barr, R. and Hayne, H. 2003, 'It's not what you know, it's who you know: older siblings facilitate imitation during infancy', *International Journal of Early Years Education*, 11(1), pp. 8–21.

Benelli, C. and Yongue, B. 1995, 'Supporting young children's motor skill development', *Childhood Education*, 71(4), pp. 217–220.

Berk, L. 2006, *Child development*, Pearson/Allyn & Bacon, Boston.

Department of Employment, Education and Training (DEET) 1994, *Like Any Child: Planning for Children with Disabilities*, DEET and the Brotherhood of St Lawrence, Melbourne.

Edwards, C. 1993, 'Partner, nurturer and guide: the roles of the Reggio teacher in action', in C. Edwards, L. Gandini and G. Forman, eds, *The Hundred Languages of Children: The Reggio Emilia Approach to Early Childhood Education*, (pp. 151–60), Ablex Publishing Company, Norwood, NJ.

Fox, L., Dunlap, G., Hemmeter, M., Joseph, G. and Strain, P. 2003, 'The teaching pyramid: a model for supporting social competence and preventing challenging behavior in young children', *Young Children*, 58(4), pp. 48–52.

Goubet, N., Rochat, P., Marie-Leblond, C. and Poss, S. 2006, 'Learning from others in 9-18-month-old infants', *Infant and Child Development*, 15, pp. 161–177.

Hughes, A. and Hughes, E. 1937, *Learning and Teaching: An Introduction to Psychology and Education*, Longman, London.

Joseph, G. and Strain, P. 2003, 'Comprehensive evidence-based social-emotional curriculum for young children', *Topics in Early Childhood Special Education*, 23(2), pp. 65–76.

Klein, E.R., Hammrich, P., Bloom, S. and Ragins, A. 2000, 'Language development and science inquiry: a child-initiated and teacher-facilitated program', Paper presented at the *Annual Meeting of the American Education Research Association*, April, New Orleans, ED440756.

Lally, J.R. and Mangione, P. 2006, 'The uniqueness of infancy demands a responsive approach to care', *Young Children*, 61(4), pp. 14–20.

Lewin-Benham, A. 2006, 'One Teacher, 20 preschoolers, and a goldfish: environmental awareness, emergent curriculum, and documentation', *Young Children: Beyond the Journal*, <http://www.journal.naeyc.org/btj/200603/LewinBTJ.asp>.

MacNaughton, G. 2005, *Doing Foucault in early childhood studies*, Routledge, London.

——2006, 'Constructing gender in early years education', in C. Skelton, B. Francis and L. Smulyan, eds, *The Sage Handbook of Gender and Education*, pp. 127–128. Sage Publications, London, New Delhi and Thousand Oaks.

Martello, J. 1999, 'In their own words: children's perceptions of learning to write', *Australian Journal of Early Childhood*, 24(3), pp. 32–7.

Oppenheimer, L. 2007, *Kindergarten curriculum*, The Center for Young Children, The University of Maryland: <http://www.education.umd.edu/CYC/kindergarten_curriculum.htm>.

Oriti, P. and Kahn, D. (eds.) 1994, *At Home with Montessori*, North American Montessori Teachers Association, Cleveland Heights, OH.

Rogoff, B. 1990, *Apprenticeship in thinking: cognitive development in social contexts*, Oxford University Press, New York.

Rogoff, B., Ruth Paradise, R., Mejía Arauz, R., Correa-Chávez, M. and Angelillo, C. 2003, 'Firsthand learning through intent participation', *Annual Review of Psychology*, 54, pp. 175–203.

Skinner, P. 1996, 'Play and the mathematics profile', in M. Fleer, ed., *Play through the Profiles: Profiles through Play*, (pp. 57–66), Australian Early Childhood Association, Canberra.

Westwood, P. 2006, *Teaching and Learning Difficulties: Cross-Curricular Perspectives*, Australian Council for Educational Research, Melbourne.

Youngquist, J. 2004, 'From medicine to microbes: a project investigation of health', *Young Children*, 59(2), pp. 28–32.

Chapter 5

Describing

 Describe: to give an account or representation in words.
(*Collins Dictionary of the English Language*, p. 401)

The purpose and problems of describing as a teaching procedure are quite unlike those of casual description.

(Hogg and Foster 1973, p. 218)

. . . the effectiveness of narration and description depends very largely on a child's previous knowledge and on the way in which the new knowledge is connected with it.

(Hughes and Hughes 1937, p. 368)

What?

When we describe something to someone we try to paint a word-picture of how something or someone feels, looks, sounds, tastes or moves. We do this by recalling the key features or characteristics of the event, object or feeling. As Hogg and Foster (1973, p. 218) stated:

It [describing] is a process of using language to convey an idea or image of an object, event, or the properties of objects or events being described, from one person to a second person, in such a way that the second person can recognise what is being described.

A person knows they have successfully described something when it is recognised by the person to whom they are describing it.

The purpose of using description as a teaching technique is to help children to see increasingly finer and more complex distinctions between events, people and things in their daily world. Good descriptions help children to expand their understandings of the world. Good descriptions draw children's attention to the features, properties or characteristics of events, people and things that they may not have noticed or that they themselves may lack the language to describe.

Issues and debates

MONITORING CULTURALLY RESPECTFUL LANGUAGE

A concern when using description as a teaching technique is that descriptions of ourselves and of other people provide children with the vocabulary to describe themselves and other people. Using culturally relevant, respectful and non-biased language to describe social diversity to young children is an important aspect of implementing an anti-bias approach to teaching and learning. How to do this is discussed further in the latter sections of this chapter.

It is also important to allow children time to describe what is happening for themselves. Listening to children (Chapter 10) before we describe what we want them to know or to focus on is important in building respectful and meaning dialogue in learning communities with young children.

How?

Staff can have their powers of description tested regularly by children's interest in the world about them and their disposition from an early age to ask, 'Why?'. A staff member's descriptive powers can be challenged by children's questions, such as: 'What is a flood?', 'What happens when dogs die?', 'How does that man get out of his wheelchair into bed?'.

Staff can increase the effectiveness of their descriptive powers with young children by:

- ensuring that they are familiar with what is to be described
- thinking about the key features to be described
- trying not to describe every single feature or property of something. Staff need to focus on the main characteristics of what they are describing: a lot of detail at once can confuse young children
- thinking about what is unique or specific to what they are describing and what will help the children to recognise what is being described
- using language as clearly and precisely as possible. A description is only useful if the children understand what is being said
- keeping sentences short, especially when working with children who are learning the teacher's language as their second or third language. Tsybina et al. (2006) found that Canadian teachers working with preschool children who are learning English as their second language frequently use sentences three times longer than those of the children. This can impair rather than strengthen the children's second language learning
- being prepared to rephrase a description if children do not understand it. Children may not immediately recognise what is being described because they have focused on different features to those that staff have focused on. It may also be that they have not understood the description
- checking with the children that they have understood the description
- remembering that people do not always 'see' things in the same way. Two people can describe the same event, person or object, but their descriptions can be very different because each person focuses on features that are of importance to them
- ensuring that description is used as part of conversations in which children have a chance to interact with and respond to adults.

Yvonne and Sasha are two early childhood staff who are trying to improve their powers of description:

Yvonne was working on a project about sound with her five-year-old students. That day, she went home and studied how people hear and how the ear works, anticipating that the next day the children would ask questions about listening and hearing.

Sasha asks David, a four-year-old, to tell her what he has understood about magnets. She then paraphrases and builds on what he has already described to her.

Reflection point: Being prepared for students' questions is important when you are teaching. In what ways could you practise describing different things?

Young children's capacity to describe events in their lives, such as what they did during their day in an early childhood centre, is enhanced when they have photographs of those events; their descriptions are more detailed and rich (DeMarie and Ethridge 2006). Using picture books with sparse text can also prompt children to engage in rich and elaborate descriptions of images and ideas in the book (Ghiso and McGuire 2007).

When and why?

Describing something to children only begins their process of understanding it (Allen and Hart 1984). By itself, an adult's description is rarely sufficient to create total understanding of an event or person by the young child. It is a teaching technique that must be supplemented by opportunities for children to explore in a practical and concrete way the things being described.

GOAL RELEVANCE

As a teaching technique, description can be used to:

- heighten children's awareness of the characteristics of particular things. Describing what children are doing or looking at can be a useful technique for developing their competence in using descriptive language and word learning (Aukrust 2007). Talking about what is happening and what children are doing can help them to become more specific and precise in their own use of descriptive language. Often such descriptions will be very simple:

I can see Clara sliding to the violin music. Now she is stamping to the drum music.

A group of three-year-olds is playing in the sand with water. Neil, their teacher, is sitting with them. His aim is to encourage the children to use descriptive language by using the language for them: 'Look what happens when the water is mixed with the sand—the sand becomes darker in colour!'

Reflective task: Write 10 descriptive words to describe qualities of water.

- extend children's vocabulary. Staff can do this by using appropriate adjectives and by encouraging children to use words to describe their world. Access to a wide range of descriptive words and phrases increases our ability to convey our meanings to others. When staff use descriptive words and phrases, they can increase children's awareness of and familiarity with an increasingly large descriptive vocabulary. Describing what children are doing as they are doing it provides them with concrete experiences of how new words can be used, meaningfully extending their vocabulary. While there is evidence that the frequency with which children hear words increases their vocabulary, hearing rare and unusual words can also increase vocabulary (Aukrust 2007). As Susan realises below, staff need to develop a wide range of descriptive words and phrases:

Susan, a student teacher, is working in a prep class during her teaching rounds. She is aware that her own descriptive vocabulary is limited and decides to broaden it and to use it with the children. She asks her supervising teacher to give her specific feedback on this each day.

Reflective task: Practise descriptive words by using them in your everyday interactions with other people.

- enable children to share their knowledge and understandings with others. When children are asked to describe an event or an object with which they are familiar, they have an opportunity to share with others what they know and to gain a sense of competence and of belonging within the group
- build children's listening skills. Teacher talk at story time was found to support children's engaged listening (Cooper 2004). Guessing games in which staff describe the key features of an event or an object can also build children's ability to listen. Children's analytical listening skills can be supported by games that require them to assess the information provided and to make judgments about what is being described.

DEVELOPMENTAL CONSIDERATIONS

There are many challenges in a baby's daily world. One of the early challenges is how to match spoken words with objects (Berk 2006). Chatting with babies and describing what is being touched, played with and looked at can help them to match words and objects. Staff can sing or chant descriptions that accompany babies' actions as part of incidental and reciprocal daily interactions with individual babies. In those interactions it is important to remember that repetition is a cornerstone of how babies learn new skills, including language skills. It is also important to remember that repetition best promotes a baby's learning and wellbeing when it arises naturally from playful interactions in which the adult and baby are in rhythm with each other (Charlesworth 2003).

As adults describe events in the babies' world to them, babies begin to learn that language can be used to give and receive information (Thompson 2001). Such learning is most effectively supported if descriptive talk is part of a responsive and caring relationship between adult and baby. If a baby is interested by an adult's descriptions of things or events around them or of what they are seeing and feeling, the adult should respond by repeating the description and elaborating on it. This helps babies to learn that language is an important part of how people interact. It also helps introduce babies to the sounds of new words. Research shows that babies enjoy novelty and that new sounds will help build their capacity to remember, understand cause and effect and make sense of their world (Thompson 2001).

In several cultures, a key developmental task for children in their first three years of life is to develop a sense of themselves as autonomous, capable and independent people (Thompson 2000, 2001). Successful accomplishment of this task means that they can tell other people what is happening and can understand other people's descriptions. By two and a half years of age, children can begin to use words to describe mental and personal properties. They can talk about favourite things, wishes, being careful, scared, worried, glad, happy and better, and about thinking, liking and being disliked and what's fair and unfair (MacNaughton et al. 2005). Adding these words to the descriptive language to which toddlers are exposed can strengthen their ability to describe their thinking and feelings. This, in turn, strengthens their ability to express themselves. For example, toddlers can learn to tell others how they feel rather than relying on others to do so for them:

Justine, two years old, was feeling sad because her mother had gone away for a few days. The staff at the centre were aware of this and were able to encourage Justine to express how she felt by asking her questions and paraphrasing what she said. They listened to her words and gave her new descriptive words to express how she was feeling. They talked with her about feeling sad and unhappy, and how when you are unhappy it feels like crying inside.

Reflective task: Write down five other ways you can describe feeling sad to a two-year-old.

However, it is important to remember that description relies on words and is based on symbolic thinking. It involves the ability to substitute words for objects and still understand what is being talked about. As such, it is a teaching technique that gains additional power when children begin to think symbolically. Preschool children are becoming increasingly adept at symbolic thought, as demonstrated by the increasing complexity of their socio-dramatic play. In this play, they regularly substitute one object for another, substitute objects for ideas and use increasingly complex language structures. This means that descriptions can become more intricate, varied and less repetitive than with the toddler age group.

In the preschool years, descriptions can also begin to cover a wider range of concrete and less concrete events in children's lives. They are most likely to engage preschoolers' interests when they are relevant to their interests (Thompson 2001). Those interests are as diverse as are children and they will differ in different cultural contexts. Faced with a diverse range of interests, the challenge for staff using description as a teaching technique is two-fold: to use description appropriately and to use description incidentally in response to children's queries.

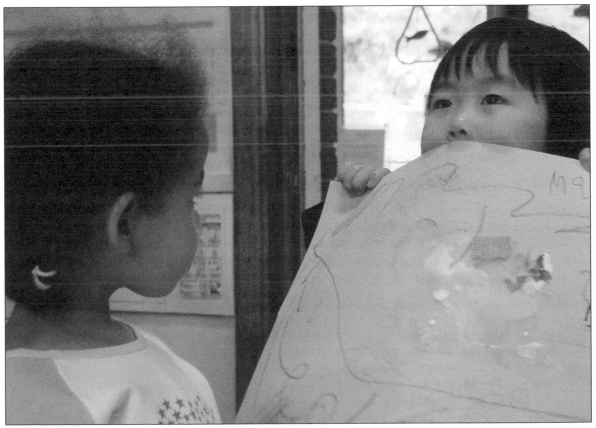

Showing and discussing at work.

Teacher talk generally supports children's learning within the primary classroom (Myhill, Jones and Hopper 2006). It can specifically support children's literacy skills when used to describe the books teachers read them (Ghiso and McGuire 2007). Such descriptions strengthen several areas of literacy development, including vocabulary, format literacy, visual literacy and verbal literacy. Descriptions of how the book is presented, how the images relate to the text and how the book presentation helps give it meaning, aid children's critical awareness of the relationships between text and meaning. Teachers can initiate such descriptions and then involve the children in developing their own descriptions of the books they read or listen to.

Equity considerations

'RACE' AND CULTURE

When describing people's cultural and 'racial' backgrounds, it is important that adults provide children with accurate terms with which to describe physical and cultural diversity, and that the language they use with children is non-culturally biased and non-racist. This means that staff must learn to avoid reinforcing tokenism, inaccuracies and stereotypes in their descriptions of cultural and 'racial' difference. Some basic principles that can help staff develop an anti-bias approach to description are:

- Staff can learn from parents the correct cultural and language group names of children attending their centre.
- Staff can learn from parents the correct cultural descriptors for the clothes, hairstyles, skin tones, dialects, country of origin, celebrations, etc. of the children attending their centre, and can learn how to describe these simply and accurately to the children in their group.
- Staff can learn from parents the correct words for all aspects of a culture they are describing to children, including its traditions, rituals, symbolic forms, norms and values.
- Staff can ask people from cultural and 'racial' groups other than their own what features of their particular culture should be shared and how best to do so. This helps staff to learn the correct words to use in their descriptions to children.
- Staff can ensure that they are describing the contemporary life of cultural groups and that they are not assuming all people within the group live identical lives.
- When a word that describes an idea, musical instrument or tradition is not easily translated into English, staff can learn its correct pronunciation and spelling and teach this to the children.

As staff apply these principles to their cultural and 'racial' descriptions, they can use the following pointers to judge their success. Anti-discriminatory descriptions will:

- enhance all children's understanding of cultural and 'racial' diversity
- reinforce children's self-esteem and their pride in their cultural and 'racial' identity
- present positive messages about cultural and 'racial' diversity. Staff should describe diversity to children in ways that focus on the strengths, joys and richness of living with diversity. For example, staff can focus on the benefits of living in a country with cultural and 'racial' diversity by describing what they like about such diversity and by encouraging the children to talk about what they like about it
- be accessible to all the children in the group. For example, when English-speaking staff are using words to describe something to children from a non-English-speaking background, their descriptions may help to extend the children's vocabulary. Rich verbal descriptions and extensive teacher talk in a study in Norwegian preschools was found to assist Turkish children to acquire better word definition skills in English as a second language (Aukrust 2007)
- encourage children to value each other's backgrounds. For example, it is important that staff do not present one particular lifestyle as more important or more interesting than another by giving it more

time or by describing it in more detail. Staff can research children's backgrounds so that they can teach children the words and ideas that describe each other's lifestyles

- encourage children to empathise with each other. For example, when talking with children about physical differences, staff can also focus on the similarities in what makes us happy or sad
- avoid words and ideas that are offensive to particular cultural and 'racial' groups. By three years of age children can match, label and identify people by 'racial' groupings, so it is important that they are provided with inoffensive descriptive language with which to do so. Terms to describe different 'racial' groups are extremely problematic: distinctions between people on the basis of physical traits have been the basis and justification of a number of discriminatory practices.

Ramsey (2004) pointed to the difficulties that arise from the following ways of describing 'racial' diversity. Words such as 'black', 'white', 'coloured', 'brown' and 'yellow' do not accurately describe people's skin tone and they ignore the other physical characteristics such as hair and facial features that contribute to our physical diversity. Despite this, some groups choose to use such words to describe 'racial' diversity. As Brown (1995, p. 10) explained:

We use the term 'black' in an oversimplified way to refer not only to those people of African, Caribbean, or South Asian origins who are most immediately perceived as 'black' by most white people, but also to those of Chinese, Cypriot, Arab, Malaysian or Latin American backgrounds who also experience differential treatment as a result of being perceived as so-called 'non-white'. It is important to acknowledge that this usage is not acceptable to all such groups themselves. Difference of culture both within and between different ethnic groups must not be overlooked just because of their common experience of discrimination in Britain.

Many groups prefer words that refer to their continent of origin, such as 'Asian', 'Australian', 'African' and 'American'. However, they do not accurately describe the origins of many people whose immigration history does not neatly fit into such 'boxes'. Nor do they accurately describe children and immigrants who are from 'racially mixed' backgrounds.

Avoid	Term preferred	Reasons for preferred term
Slang names such as 'wop', 'spic', 'nigger', 'wog' and 'dago' (all are offensive)	Use country of origin labels such as 'Italian heritage', 'Anglo-Greek' and 'Vietnamese Australian'.	Is more objective, descriptive and less subjective and offensively value-laden.
Terms such as 'coloured' (offensive).	Use colour label terms 'black' or 'white', or 'people of colour'.	Whites have historically used 'coloured' to describe 'other than-white' and the term is offensive to many black people. It was prevalent during the slavery era in America.
Terms such as 'part-Aborigine', 'quarter-Aborigine' (misleading and outdated).	'Person of Aboriginal or Torres Strait Islander descent.'	Being Aboriginal is a cultural, social and historical self-identification that involves more than blood relationships.
The term 'migrant' once a person has settled in Australia. This should only be used to describe a person in a state of transition from one country to another.	'Greek Australian', 'Vietnamese Australian', etc.	'Migrant' is inaccurate once a person has settled and it gives the impression that they do not really belong in their new country.

In several countries, indigenous people have specific words to describe who they are, and these are often different from the labels they have been given historically. It is important to find out what these are to avoid causing offence. For example, the term 'native' is no longer acceptable to Indigenous peoples in Australia. They prefer to be called Aboriginal Australians or to be identified through reference to their specific language group. 'Indian' is no longer acceptable to the indigenous peoples of North America. They may prefer to be called 'Native Americans', 'American Indians' or 'People of the First Nations' (Ramsey 2004). The following extract highlights some of the complexities of using labels to describe people:

> I am sometimes asked, 'Are you Indians? Native Americans? What do you prefer to be called?' . . . By race, I am an American Indian; by citizenship, I am an American citizen. (I have also been told that by treaty with the Sioux nations and Canada, I'm also a Canadian citizen.) By nationality, I am an enrolled member of the Oglala Sioux nation. I am also a hereditary member of the Cheyenne and Arapaho nations in Okalahoma. (GossMan 1992, p. 146)

When in doubt about which descriptors they should use, staff should always ask others who can advise them. These may be parents, other staff, or advisory staff from specialist resource services such as a multicultural resource agency.

GENDER

Description relies on language and language is not neutral. The language we use has many in-built assumptions and values that shape our understandings of the world about us. Among other things, our language shapes our understandings of ourselves as male and female, and our understandings of gender relations. Much of the language we use on a daily basis has gender-stereotyped assumptions and values built into it. Consider the following statements and their related gender assumptions:

Statement: 'Last night politicians and their wives attended . . .'
Assumption: All politicians are men.
Statement: 'Last night politicians and their husbands attended . . .'
Assumption: All politicians are women.

Which statement is more common?

As young children learn about their own gender and other people's, it is important that staff use language that broadens children's views of themselves rather than narrowing them. Words, phrases and meanings that stereotype and denigrate must be avoided. When describing people, the things they do, how they feel and what they think, staff should use gender-inclusive language, using descriptions that will:

- expand children's views of masculinity and femininity
- reinforce boys' and girls' self-esteem and pride in their own gender identity. This is particularly important for girls and for those boys who adopt non-traditional ways of being masculine. Traditionally, masculine boys are already likely to have a strong sense of self-esteem and pride in their gender identity
- present positive messages about different ways of being masculine and feminine. The descriptions of gender diversity that staff use with children should focus on the strengths, joys and richness of being with different sorts of boys and girls. For example, preschoolers can learn that some boys like dancing, some boys like pink or some girls like climbing. We do not all have to be the same. It's more interesting if we are different
- encourage boys and girls to empathise with each other
- avoid unnecessary gender suffixes or modifiers which demean and belittle women and girls, such as 'the little woman', 'the lady doctor', 'the fair sex' or 'the weaker sex'
- avoid words and ideas that denigrate or restrict girls' and women's capabilities. The table below offers some guidance on how to do this.

Avoid	Term preferred	Reasons for preferred term
'Policeman', 'fireman', 'ambulanceman'.	'Police officer', 'firefighter', 'paramedic'.	Provides children with the message that men and women can do all types of work.
'Lady doctor', 'woman lawyer'.	'Doctor', 'lawyer'.	Provides children with the message that men and women can do all types of work.

DISABILITY AND ADDITIONAL NEEDS

Children with disabilities may have their ability to hear, see, move, think, touch or feel impaired in some way, and staff may not be able to rely as much on oral language to describe the world to these children. For example, to describe what is happening to a child with a hearing disability, staff may need to rely more on visual language and gesture. Similarly, they may need to emphasise touch and sound when describing something to a child with a visual disability.

Staff who are trying to develop an anti-discriminatory approach to people with disabilities in their centres can use descriptions of similarities and differences between people to provide children with appropriate language and ideas about human diversity. When describing people with disabilities, staff should provide positive messages about disability which are acceptable to such people. Some examples of preferred terms to describe people with disabilities include:

Avoid	Term preferred	Reasons for preferred term
Abnormal, subnormal, defective or deformed.	Specify the disability.	Less negatively value-laden.
Afflicted with . . .	The person has . . . (a disability). Uses a wheelchair.	Affliction is a very negative word. A wheelchair provides mobility not restriction.
Mongol.	Person with Down's syndrome.	More specific and less offensive to Mongolian people.
Spastic.	Person with cerebral palsy.	Less negatively value-laden and places the person at the centre.

Reflecting on describing techniques

1 Define describing.
2 What does research suggest are the keys to using describing to optimise children's learning?
3 When do you think description should be used in your teaching?
4 Are there any times when you think that the use of description is inappropriate with young children?
5 How could descriptions be used to promote communicative competence with infants? What sort of descriptions could you use to achieve this aim?
6 What items do you think toddlers would enjoy having descriptions of?
7 What are the most interesting descriptions that you have heard other adults provide for four-year-old children?
8 Imagine you were working with a group of three-year-olds who were going to visit an art gallery for the first time. What words could you use to describe the gallery to the children?
9 Develop a plan for a learning experience for four- to five-year-old children in which you wanted to increase their descriptive vocabulary in relation to feelings. How could you use description as a teaching technique to do this?
10 Imagine you were working in a mixed group of two- to five-year-old children. One of the three-year-olds had just returned from overseas and you were discussing the journey with the group. One of the

four-year-old children asked what the inside of an aeroplane looked like. What words could you use to describe the inside of an aeroplane that the children might be familiar with? What new language might you need to use and explain in your description?

Improving teaching in practice

1 Record (using a tape-recorder or written notes) the descriptions you provided during several half-hour teaching periods.
2 What is your current style of describing? Do you:
   - ensure you are familiar with whatever you describe to the children?
   - think in advance about the key features you would describe?
   - focus on the main characteristics?
   - identify what is unique or specific to what you describe?
   - use clear and precise language?
   - rephrase your description when children don't understand?
   - check with the children that they understand the description provided?
3 How and how well did you take account of developmental and equity considerations?
4 What are your strengths and weaknesses in using description to promote children's learning?
5 How can you work to improve your description techniques in practice?
6 Make a list of the words you could use to describe anger, happiness, joy, sadness.

FURTHER READING

Diffily, D. and Sassman, C. 2006, *Positive Teacher Talk for Better Classroom Management: Grades K-2.* Scholastic, New York.

Garhart Mooney, C. 2006, *Use Your Words: How Teacher Talk Helps Children Learn*, Redleaf Press, USA.

Klein, E.R., Hammrich, P., Bloom, S. and Ragins, A. 2000, 'Language development and science inquiry: a child-initiated and teacher-facilitated program', Paper presented at the Annual Meeting of the American Education Research Association, April, New Orleans, ED440756.

Ramsey, P. 2004, *Teaching and Learning in a Diverse World: Multicultural Education for Young Children*, 3rd edn, Teachers' College Press, New York [refer to pp. 15–35].

REFERENCES

Allen, K. and Hart, B. 1984, *The Early Years: Arrangements for Learning*, Prentice Hall Inc., New Jersey.

Aukrust, V. 2007, 'Young children acquiring second language vocabulary in preschool group-time: does amount, diversity, and discourse complexity of teacher talk matter?', *Journal of Research in Childhood Education*, 22(1), pp. 17–37.

Berk, L. 2006, *Child development*, Pearson/Allyn & Bacon, Boston.

Brown, B. 1995, *All Our Children: A Guide for Those who Care*, 3rd edn, British Broadcasting Commission Education, London.

Charlesworth, R. 2003, *Understanding Child Development: For Adults who Work with Children*, 7th edn, Delmar Publishing, New York.

Cooper, H. 2004, 'Teacher talk: promoting literacy development through response to story', *Journal of Research in Childhood Education*, 19(2), pp. 115–129.

DeMarie, D. and Ethridge, E.A. 2006, 'Children's images of preschool: the power of photography', *Young Children*, 61(1), pp. 101–104.

Ghiso, M. and McGuire, C. 2007, '"I talk them through it": teacher mediation of picturebooks with sparse verbal text during whole-class readalouds', *Reading research and Instruction*, 46(4), pp. 341–361.

GossMan, H. 1992, 'Meeting the needs of all children: an Indian perspective', in B. Neugebauer, ed., *Alike and Different: Exploring our Humanity with Young Children*, (pp. 146–51), National Association for the Education of Young Children, Washington, DC.

Hogg, A. and Foster, J. 1973, *Understanding Teaching Procedures*, Cassell Australia, Sydney.

Hughes, A. and Hughes, E. 1937, *Learning and Teaching: An Introduction to Psychology and Education*, Longman, London.

MacNaughton, G. and Smith, K. 2005, 'Exploring ethics and difference: the choices and challenges of researching with children', in A. Farrell (ed.) *Exploring ethical research with children*, Open University Press, Buckingham, pp. 112–123.

Myhill, D., Jones, S. and Hopper, R. 2006, *Talking, Listening, Learning : Effective Talk In The Primary Classroom*, Open University Press, McGraw-Hill, Maidenhead, UK.

Ramsey, P. 2004, *Teaching and Learning in a Diverse World: Multicultural Education for Young Children*, 2nd edn, Teachers College Press, New York.

Thompson, R. 2000, 'The legacy of early attachments', *Child Development*, 71, pp. 141–52.

—— 2001, 'Development in the first years of life', *The Future of Children*, 11(1), pp. 21–33.

Tsybina, I., Girolametto, L., Weitzman, E. and Greenberg, J. 2006, *Early Childhood Education Journal*, 34(2), pp. 177–185.

Chapter 6

Encouraging, praising and helping

  Help: to assist or aid (someone to do something).

(Collins Dictionary of the English Language, p. 682)

Praise: the act of expressing commendation, admiration, etc.

(Collins Dictionary of the English Language, p. 1151)

Encourage: to inspire (someone) with the courage or confidence (to do something).

(Collins Dictionary of the English Language, p. 482)

Encouragement is to 'give heart' to someone.

(Huang 2007, p. 14)

While some teachers may like this use of praise because it works, the cost is unrecognized children who feel unworthy of praise and resentful that the teacher has favorites.

(Gartrell 2007, online)

What?

To encourage someone means to reassure and to support them when they are having difficulty with a task or experience. This reassurance and support might be verbal or non-verbal. Staff use encouragement as a teaching technique to reassure and support children attempting new or difficult activities. The aim of such encouragement is to help children persevere with the task and to learn new skills or dispositions.

VERBAL ENCOURAGEMENT AND PRAISE

To praise someone means to show that you approve of what they have done and that their act deserves acclaim. As a teaching process, praise shows children that they deserve recognition, acclaim and approval.

Some early childhood texts confuse 'praise' and 'encouragement' and often use them interchangeably. However, in terms of children's learning, there are very significant differences between the two terms. Encouragement is given while a child is doing something to support them to continue it and to show appreciation of their efforts. Praise is given after a child has completed part or all of a task to show them that their achievement is worthy of your approval.

Over time the research literature has indicated that children's learning is best supported through encouragement rather than praise (e.g. Hitz and Driscoll 1988; Sigler and Aamidor 2005). A recent study in the USA of 50 preschool teachers' interactions with children who misbehave found that praise was rarely used in teacher interactions with those children, irrespective of whether or not they were misbehaving (Dobbs, Arnold and Doctoroff 2004).

NON-VERBAL ENCOURAGEMENT AND HELPING

To physically help someone is to assist them, to aid and contribute to what they are doing. Help can take many forms and may last for moments or for much longer. Physically helping a child with a task may involve holding their hand as they enter a situation about which they feel apprehension, or helping them to use a piece of equipment by holding it steady. Such help can encourage children to continue with their task and can assist them to achieve success. Non-verbal forms of encouragement such as holding a child's hands can be just as valuable in supporting children's learning as verbal encouragement. The following example shows how simple such non-verbal support can be:

> To make Jaya feel safe as he jumps, Miklosh holds Jaya's hands on the jumping board.

Issues and debates

CREATING PRAISE JUNKIES?

There is considerable debate about the effectiveness of praise with young children. Kohn (1999) and Grille (2005, online) believe that praise creates 'praise junkies' who cannot think independently and rely on others for their sense of self-worth and self-esteem. Opponents of praise share views similar to those expressed by Grille:

> Rewards and praise condition children to seek approval; they end up doing things to impress, instead of doing things for themselves. This can hold back the development of self-motivation and makes them dependent on outside opinion. When children get used to getting goodies for 'performing', they become pleasers, over-reliant on positive strokes. Rewards and praise can create a kind of addictive behavior: children can get addicted to recognition, and thus lose touch with the simple joy of doing what they love.

Three additional issues emerge in discussions about the use of encouragement, helping and praise. Each is discussed in turn below.

PRAISE CAN BECOME MEANINGLESS AND IRRITATING

Staff can prevent their praise becoming meaningless or irritating by drawing on the following guidance offered:

- Use praise sparingly and focus on specific efforts or achievements of the child. Several studies have shown over time that general and non-targeted praise can reduce children's ability to judge their own work and can create anxiety in the children about whether their efforts will meet with staff approval. It can also encourage them to focus on external rather than intrinsic rewards. (Schiller 1999; Henderlong and Lepper 2002; Bronson 2007)
- Avoid social comparison praise. Comparing children when praising can reduce children's motivation. (Henderlong and Lepper 2002)
- Praise children equitably. Research (Briggs and Potter 1995) suggests that teachers tend to praise only

those children who they think are high achievers, yet overpraising these children for their general competence can have negative effects in the long term. They can feel increasingly anxious about their capacity to consistently perform at a high level and take failure very badly. (Henderlong and Lepper 2002)

- Praise children only for new achievements or consistent effort. Praising children for accomplishing tasks that require little effort can encourage them to try less difficult tasks. (Bronson 2007)

UNDERSTANDINGS OF PRAISE ARE CULTURALLY SPECIFIC

However, yet again caution needs to be applied to the use of praise. Children's response to praise is culturally mediated. Some researchers have found that children from more collectivist cultures (specifically, China and Japan) valued praise more highly when they were praised for effort rather than ability and outcome (Henderlong and Lepper 2002). It is important for staff to not assume that praise and encouragement have identical effects for all children and therefore they need to monitor the effects of their use within their specific community of families and children. For staff working in culturally diverse communities, this means being especially alert to what might be most valued and effective for specific children within the community.

HELPING IS NOT TAKING OVER

It is important for staff to remember that helping is about doing something with someone, not doing it for them. Helping involves doing a task with a child, not taking over the task from the child and completing it for them:

> Lois, a volunteer from the local secondary school, is sitting with some children at the drawing table. The children are three-year-olds and are at different levels of ability and skill. Damien asks Lois to draw him a person. Lois obliges and draws a 'stick figure'. At the end of the session with the children, Andrew, the teacher has a discussion with Lois about drawing for them. He explains how Lois can help the children to draw their own pictures so that they need not rely on adults to do it for them. Andrew gives her some suggestions on how to encourage them to do their own work, including phrases such as, 'Can you show me how you would draw a person?', or 'Let's think about what you need to have in a drawing of a person', and 'I think you could draw a very interesting person if you try. I'll come and look when you've finished.'
>
> _Reflection point:_ Can you remember a time when someone took over a task from you. How did that feel?

How?

VERBAL ENCOURAGEMENT

Verbal encouragement can act as a positive motivator for children's learning if some basic rules are followed. Staff need to ensure that their encouragement is very specific and that it focuses on how a child is undertaking a specific task. This is best done when the child and the adult are alone, rather than part of a large group, because this prevents the adult's comments embarrassing the child in front of other children (Hitz and Driscoll 1988).

Words of encouragement should extend children's learning rather than reduce it. Schwartz (1995, p. 400) argued that '. . . emphasizing the process of thinking, rather than the product, extends the thinking'. For example, a comment such as, 'Great job!' focuses on the product and does not extend the child's thinking.

In contrast, a comment such as, 'I wonder how we could make that happen again, it looked really interesting' not only tells the child that what they have done is worthy of interest and comment, but also encourages them to think about how to extend what has happened. This specific form of praising is most likely to increase children's motivation over time (Henderlong and Lepper 2002).

NON-VERBAL ENCOURAGEMENT AND PHYSICAL HELP

There are several simple non-verbal ways of offering encouragement and physical help to a child. These include:

- moving a toy closer to a child
- moving yourself closer to a child
- offering a helping hand
- finding a special tool or item that will enrich a child's play
- handing a child a toy that is out of reach
- sitting by a child to offer support when needed
- smiling at the right moment.

Staff can support children's learning through non-verbal encouragement and physical help if they:

- ask the child if they would like assistance
- provide help appropriate to the level of difficulty a child is having. For example, if a child needs help to complete a puzzle, merely placing one piece of the puzzle correctly might be sufficient to help the child complete the task themselves. On the other hand, if a child is trying to construct a large and complex collage, staff may need to help at several points in the process
- ask the child if they would like any additional assistance
- encourage children to help each other by providing positive models of helping behaviour and by commenting positively on children's helping behaviours.

These guidelines have helped Jemma to provide just the right amount of verbal and non-verbal encouragement to Ursula:

Jemma is sitting at the collage table with five four-year-old preschoolers. The children are all busily constructing their own creations. They are talking with each other and with Jemma as they work. Jemma notices that Ursula is having trouble with the tape. She offers assistance: 'Can I help you, Ursula? That tape looks hard to get off.' Ursula responds that she would like help. Jemma moves around to hold the tape dispenser for Ursula and says: 'I'll hold it and then it will be easier for you to break a piece off.'

Reflection point: How else could Ursula encourage Jemma's collage work?

When and why?

GOAL RELEVANCE

There are many moments during a child's day when a small amount of encouragement by an adult can make the difference between an enjoyable and satisfying learning outcome for the child or a frustrating and disappointing one. For example, encouragement by an adult would be essential to a toddler who had climbed to the top of a climbing frame but was becoming upset because she could not find her way down again. In these circumstances, withholding help could be dangerous both to the toddler's safety and to their emotional wellbeing.

Staff can use physical help and verbal encouragement as a teaching strategy to:

- increase the likelihood that children will behave in pro-social ways, such as helping each other to tidy up or sharing materials with each other (Warner and Lynch 2002/03; Henderlong and Lepper 2002)
- extend children's thinking about an event, an idea or a material (Schwartz 1995)
- help children practise complex skills and techniques (Schwartz 1995)
- support children's expression of their ideas through movement and music, visual arts, etc.
- provide children with positive attention to accentuate children's positive behaviours within the group (Warner and Lynch 2002/03).
- reassure and reduce the anxiety levels of children who may be anxious about their learning capacities or a particular experience. In a study of 33 primary school children in the USA researchers (LaBillois and Lagacé-Séguin 2007) found that high levels of teacher encouragement that focus on the success of a student can help reduce anxiety in children who struggle with it.

When offering non-verbal encouragement and physical help, staff need to strike a balance between allowing children to solve problems for themselves and by themselves, and helping them to do so. Physical help should always be provided when children's safety and wellbeing is at risk, but beyond this, staff's individual philosophy on adult intervention in children's learning will guide when and how often help is provided:

> At the weekly staff meeting at the Little Geese Children's Centre, the director, Heather, expresses some concerns about staff members' styles of helping. Staff have fallen into the habit of doing things for the children rather than helping them or encouraging them to do things for themselves. Heather gives several examples: dressing the

Angela uses verbal and non-verbal encouragement as Nam moves across the monkey bars.

children, putting things away, completing puzzles when the children have abandoned them, pushing children on the wheel toys rather than encouraging them to use their feet to move themselves along. She encourages the staff to discuss what they want for the children and gently reminds them of the centre's mission statement, which states that, 'The centre aims to help the children to become autonomous'. She then facilitates a discussion about useful techniques through which staff can help the children to do things for themselves. She also gives the staff some practical advice.

Reflective task: Make a list of the different things that preschool children could do autonomously during a day in an early childhood setting.

Information and Communication Technologies (ICT) can also offer children encouragement as they build their language and literacy skills. Van Scoter and Boss (2002) describe a number of specific ways that ICT can encourage children to express themselves through oral and written language. These include the use of digital photos of children's daily activities that encourage them to describe to others orally or through written short stories or captions what has happened during their day, or the use of email and online projects in which children communicate with a real audience.

DEVELOPMENTAL CONSIDERATIONS

There are many non-verbal ways through which staff can encourage babies to actively explore their environment. Many of these are examined in Chapters 1 and 12. Verbal encouragement is an effective way of supporting the emerging communicative competence of babies in their first 12 months. Honig (1990) believed that one key skill to encourage is that of combining vowels and consonants in sounds such as 'mu-mu' and 'ba-ba', because it enables babies to develop their own language through which to express their needs. Babies can learn to use 'mu-mu' to ask for milk or 'ba-ba' to ask for their bottle. If adults respond with similar sounds whenever babies produce them, babies are strongly encouraged to repeat their sounds and to experiment with new vowel–consonant combinations.

During their second year of life, young children become increasingly sensitive to the reactions of the adults around them. Adult praise and encouragement has also been found to support toddlers' need to explore and learn from their world. One Israeli study of 299 toddlers in day care settings (Frank, Stolarski and Scher 2006) found that toddlers cried less in those centres in which there were high levels of staff to mediate the toddler's interactions with their social and physical world. Mediation strategies including encouragement and praise help children to explore and learn more effectively from the world around them.

The preschool years are a time of considerable growth in the complexity of children's imaginative play, and children rapidly build their social and communication skills through this play. During sequences of socio-dramatic play, staff can use verbal encouragement to increase children's '. . . social interaction, make-believe, role-playing and verbal communication . . .' (Ward 1994, p. 9). For example, if a group of children is preparing to have a party but is unclear about what to do next, staff could comment on how well their preparations are going and extend the play through posing a question such as, 'I wonder what would happen if you did…?'. Ward (1994, p. 12) argued that such intervention in children's play is essential for children to develop into what she called 'master players'. However, there is some evidence to suggest that praise can lead preschool children to do the opposite of what is intended. They may come to dislike a situation or experience that they have received frequent praise for participating in (Henderlong and Lepper 2002). So again, it is important to not overuse praise as a key teaching technique.

Binh sings with Oliver.

Staff can develop their own skills in using verbal encouragement through sharing ideas with each other:

At a children's centre in Hobart there is a list in the staff tearoom on which the staff write down examples of how to verbally encourage children. In this way the staff share different ways of speaking to the children and increase their own 'encouraging' vocabulary and behaviours. The list includes: focus comments on the child's process of learning, not their products; comment on how children are achieving success; ask questions that show interest in how children could extend their achievements; use words that show children you have confidence in their abilities to problem-solve, achieve and extend themselves.

Reflection point: Could you add to this list?

Children who are learning to write need lots of technical practice at writing. They need practice at forming letters on paper and at choosing the correct letters and putting them in the correct order. The experience can be frustrating and children will generally know when they have 'got it wrong' or 'messed it up'. A well-placed word of encouragement can help children persevere with the acquisition of their technical writing skills. The more they can be encouraged to refine these skills through repetition the more pleasure they will derive from them. More specifically, praise can improve the reading performance of children with learning difficulties in this area of literacy (Woolley 2004).

Computers can also give children praise with some effect. Children have been shown to change behaviours when praised by a computer in a similar way and with similar effect as they do when they receive praise from a person (Campanella Bracken and Lombard 2004). New technologies can also be a strong 'encourager' for children in other ways—they can encourage children to use and practise their literacy skills. As Van Scoter and Boss (2002, p. 24) note:

> Seeing text on the screen encourages students to read their own and others' writing as they work at the computer, and the amount of time children choose to read and have opportunities to read strongly correlates with reading proficiency.

Equity considerations

'RACE' AND CULTURE

Children gain a sense of their 'racial' and cultural identity through interacting with others. Also, children develop a strong and positive 'racial' and cultural identity and feel good about who they are if there are strong and positive images of their own 'racial' and cultural group around them. Children who lack such positive images can quickly develop a poor sense of identity and low self-esteem. There is a strong risk of this happening for children from 'racial' and cultural groups who experience racism in the wider society (Ramsey 2004), as they will regularly confront negative images of their own group. In Australia, such children would be those with Aboriginal or Torres Strait Islander backgrounds and children of parents whose background is from countries in the Middle East, Southeast Asia, Africa and the Pacific Islands.

Low self-esteem can damage children's thirst for learning in a number of ways, so staff encouragement may be particularly important when children with black and ethnic minority backgrounds explore new experiences, practise existing skills and do things for themselves. Support and reassurance can make the difference between persevering and feeling good about their efforts or giving up and feeling bad about what they have not done. When staff help children with black and ethnic minority backgrounds to feel good about their own efforts, they also help them to:

- counter the racist images and messages they have experienced in the wider society
- develop a positive 'racial' and cultural identity during their time in the centre
- build self-esteem with which to counter a negative attitude towards their 'racial' and cultural identity.

As with any child, the encouragement of children of black and ethnic minority groups will be most effective when it is specific to the task or skill. This helps the children to learn that they are being encouraged for effort, rather than for who they are.

Encouragement also needs to extend children's learning rather than reduce it, making it more likely that the children will want to take on new challenges. Talking with parents to ensure that staff efforts at encouragement and praise are culturally relevant and sensitive will support the skill development of children (McCay and Keyes 2001/02).

New technologies can be particularly effective as a tool for encouraging English Language Learners (ELL) to take control of their language learning. As Van Scoter and Boss (2002, p. 21) explained:

> Technology offers special promise for ELL students because it allows them to learn at their own pace in a non-threatening environment, gives students flexibility and choice, and empowers them to make learning decisions and to be successful.

New technologies can also encourage the strengthening of children's first language by giving them access to ways to record and share their personal and community experiences within their communities. For instance, children can use tape-recorders and video-recorders to interview members of their own communities in their community languages and then translate what they learn into English for sharing beyond their communities. Experiences of settling into a new country, migration and important cultural events and traditions can be shared in this way and affirm connections between the children and their communities (Van Scoter and Boss 2002). In New Zealand new technologies have been used to co-author multi-media learning stories with children and their communities to encourage English and Māori language use in early childhood services (Han 2004).

GENDER

Gender can make a difference to how teachers distribute praise and encouragement to children. Teachers in one US study of 50 preschool teachers and 153 children (Dobbs, Arnold and Doctoroff 2004) found that boys misbehaved more often than girls and that teachers generally used commands to control their behaviour. Encouragement was more evident in teacher interactions with the girls. There is also evidence over time to suggest that within the early childhood environment, boys and girls are encouraged to do different things and take on different challenges (Ebbeck 1985; Dunn and Morgan 1987; Alloway 1995; Henderlong and Lepper 2002). For example, boys are often verbally encouraged to become actively involved in a variety of gross motor activities such as running, jumping and climbing. Girls, on the other hand, are often verbally encouraged to become actively involved in the quieter and more passive fine motor activities such as making collage, solving puzzles, drawing and painting. Staff who want gender equity in their program will need to carefully monitor their interactions with the children to ensure that they are encouraging both boys and girls to fully explore all aspects of the program. Again, research over time (Dweck, Davidson, Nelson and Enna 1978; Ebbeck 1985; Dunn and Morgan 1987; Alloway 1995) consistently suggests that staff should guard against:

- encouraging girls but not boys to help with packing away. For example, staff may comment on how well the girls have helped with the task but not comment on the boys' involvement or lack of involvement
- encouraging boys but not girls to extend their climbing skills. For example, staff may move over to the boys when they are being active on the climbing frame and comment on their skill in climbing so high, but not when girls accomplish similar feats
- encouraging girls in their domestic play but not similarly encouraging boys in this play. For example, staff may positively comment on how well the girls have worked together to bake a cake but not when boys successfully work together in domestic play
- encouraging boys but not girls to engage in messy mud play. For example, staff may comment on how deep a hole the boys have dug but not comment on girls' achievement in the digging area
- encouraging girls but not boys to be involved in quiet, table activities. For example, staff may comment on how quiet the girls have been while they completed a puzzle but not comment on similar success by boys
- praising girls for neatness while praising boys for intellectual ability.

Staff need to ensure that they expend equal effort on girls and boys as part of the process of encouraging them to try different activities. Some time ago West (1992) noted that in some centres staff made great efforts to encourage boys to explore non-traditional roles but not the girls.

Gender also appears to affect how children respond to praise (Henderlong and Lepper 2002), with boys more responsive to praise that focuses on achievement and provides clear information about those achievements.

DISABILITY AND ADDITIONAL NEEDS

Children without disabilities can develop misconceptions about the abilities of children with disabilities as they interact with them (Brown 1995; Diamond and Innes 2001; Diamond and Kensinger 2002), but positive experiences of inclusive education can encourage children to build rich and nuanced understandings of diverse disabilities (Magiati, Dockrell and Logotheti 2002). More specifically, teacher encouragement for children to play with each other can help promote positive play and interaction between children with disabilities and those who do not have a disability (Diamond and Huang 2005).

As part of the process of developing an anti-bias approach to disability, staff should counter these misconceptions with accurate information about people with disabilities. However, staff cannot counter misconceptions unless they are aware of them, and a good way to bring misconceptions into the open is to encourage children without disabilities to ask questions about children with disabilities. Staff can encourage open discussion by responding to children's questions with comments that extend their interests in each other rather than closing them off. For example, if a child asks why another child has to wear glasses, by responding that 'It's rude to ask such questions' staff would close their interest and allow misconceptions to develop. In contrast, responding with comments such as, 'I'm glad you asked that question. It shows that you have been thinking about Tim. How could we find out if he can see very far without his glasses?' is likely to encourage further interest in Tim and what makes him special.

Children with severe disabilities often face considerably greater challenges than other children in acquiring the basic skills required in daily living. Children with severe disabilities who can understand verbal feedback can be powerfully supported via verbal encouragement in their efforts and successes to acquire these basic skills. In addition, it is important for staff to encourage children with disabilities to become as independent as possible in the classroom, ensuring that there is the time and opportunity for the children to build the skills required for independent classroom learning. This includes specifically assigning children tasks, allowing them choices and providing time for independent exploration (McCay and Keyes 2001/02).

Encouragement can be a powerful strategy to support children with cognitive disabilities who demonstrate challenging behaviours in the classroom (for example, biting, kicking and screaming) by helping them adapt to build pro-social behaviours. For example, a synthesis of 100 research studies of children with cognitive disabilities has shown that frequent encouragement and reinforcement of positive behaviours and redirection of anti-social behaviours can help to build pro-social behaviours in these children (Warger 1999).

Reflecting on techniques for encouraging children

1 Define encouragement.
2 What are the differences between verbal and non-verbal encouragement?
3 What does research suggest are the keys to encouraging and optimising children's learning?
4 When do you think encouragement should be used in your teaching?
5 Are there any times when you think that the use of encouragement is inappropriate with young children?
6 How would you explain the differences between praise and encouragement?
7 When do you think it is appropriate to praise young children?
8 Imagine you are working with a group of three-year-olds who are just beginning to share their toys with each other. What forms of encouragement would you use to support their sharing behaviours?
9 Develop a plan for a learning experience for four- to five-year-old children in which you wanted to increase their balancing skills. How would you use encouragement as a teaching strategy to do this?
10 Which of the phrases below represent encouragement and which represent praise?
   • Sally, thank you for your help today, it made it much easier for us to pack away before lunchtime.
   • Anu, you are such a tidy girl.
   • Good boy, Richard.
   • Calamity, I can see that you are working really hard on that collage. It must have been difficult to make the boxes stick together.

Improving teaching in practice

1   Record (using a tape-recorder or written notes) the encouragement you provide to children during several half-hour teaching periods.

2   What is your current style of verbal encouragement? Do you:
   - ensure your encouragement is very specific?
   - ensure your encouragement focuses on how a child is undertaking a specific task?
   - encourage children individually or in group settings?
   - ensure that your encouragement extends children's learning rather than reduces it?
   - use praise sparingly?
   - praise children equitably?
   - praise children only for new achievements or consistent effort?

3   What is your current style of physical encouragement and help?

4   How and how well did you take account of developmental and equity considerations?

5   What are your areas of strength and weakness in using encouragement to promote children's learning?

6   How can you work to improve your encouragement techniques in practice?

7   What do you see as the hardest part of improving your encouragement techniques?

FURTHER READING

Henderlong, J. and Lepper, M. 2002, 'The effects of praise on children's intrinsic motivation: a review and synthesis', *Psychological Bulletin*, 12(5), pp. 774–795.

Kostelnik, M., Whiren, A., Soderman, A. and Gregory, K. 2006, *Guiding Children's Social Development: Theory to Practice*, Thomson/Delmar Learning, Clifton Park, NY

Schwartz, S. 1995, 'Hidden messages in teacher talk: praise and empowerment', *Teaching Children Mathematics*, (March), pp. 396–401.

Sigler, E. and Aamidor, S. 2005, 'From positive reinforcement to positive behaviors: an everyday guide for the practitioners', *Early Childhood Education Journal*, 32(4), pp. 249–253.

ONLINE AND MULTI-MEDIA RESOURCES

Text

Kohn, A. 2001, 'Five reasons to stop saying "Good job"': **http://www.alfiekohn.org/parenting/gj.htm** (full text available in English and Spanish).

Multi-media

'Invented spelling'. A teacher uses a variety of encouragement and support strategies to support a child to build their spelling skills. A free access video clip: **http://www.readingrockets.org/podcasts/classroom#text**

Devereux Early Childhood Initiative (DECI) and Video Active Productions in partnership with NAEYC, 2007, *Facing the Challenge: Working with Children who Use Challenging Behaviors* (video series, disc one: 65 min; disc two: 75 min.), DECI, Villanova, PA. Available from NAEYC.

REFERENCES

Alloway, N. 1995, *Foundation Stones: The Construction of Gender in Early Childhood*, Curriculum Corporation, Melbourne.

Briggs, F. and Potter, G. 1995, *Teaching Children in the First Three Years of School*, Longman, Melbourne.

Bronson, P. 2007, 'How not to talk to your kids: the inverse power of praise', *Parenting Methods*, 40(16), pp. 24–31.

Brown, B. 1995, *All Our Children: A Guide for Those Who Care*, 3rd edn, British Broadcasting Commission Education, London.

Campanella Bracken, C. and Lombard, M. 2004, *Social Presence and Children: Praise, Intrinsic Motivation, and Learning with Computers*, International Communication Association.

Diamond, K. and Huang, H. 2005, 'Preschoolers' ideas about disabilities', *Infants & Young Children: An Interdisciplinary Journal of Special Care Practices*, 18(1), pp. 37–46.

Diamond, K. and Innes, F. 2001, 'The origins of young children's attitudes toward peers with disabilities', in M. Guralnick, ed., *Early Childhood Inclusion: Focus on Change*, Paul H. Brookes, Baltimore, MD, p. 159–177.

Diamond, K.E. and Kensinger, K. 2002, 'Vignettes from *Sesame Street*: preschooler's ideas about children with Down syndrome and physical disability', *Early Education and Development*, 13, pp. 409–421.

Dobbs, J., Arnold, D. and Doctoroff, G. 2004, 'Attention in the preschool classroom: the relationships among child gender, child misbehavior, and types of teacher attention', *Early Child Development and Care*, 174(3), pp. 281–295.

Dunn, S. and Morgan, V. 1987, 'Nursery and infant school play patterns: sex-related differences', *British Educational Research Journal*, 13(3), pp. 271–281.

Dweck, C.S., Davidson, W., Nelson, S. and Enna, B. 1978, 'Sex differences in learned helplessness: II. The contingencies of evaluative feedback in the classroom and III. An experimental analysis', *Developmental Psychology*, 14, pp. 268–276.

Ebbeck, M. 1985, 'Pre-school teachers' interactions with boys as compared with girls: a report of an observation study', *Australian Journal of Early Childhood*, 10(2), pp. 26–30.

Frank, I., Stolarski, E. and Scher, A. 2006, 'Caregivers' mediation and toddlers' emotional responses in the child care context', *Early Child Development and Care*, 176(3), pp. 239–251.

Gartrell, D. 2007, 'Guidance matters. "You really worked hard on your picture!" Guiding with Encouragement', *Young Children on the Web—Beyond the Journal*, May. <http://www.journal.naeyc.org/btj/200705/BTJGuidance.asp> (accessed May 2007).

Grille, R. 2005, 'Rewards and praise: the poisoned carrot. "You really worked hard on your picture!" Guiding with encouragement', *Young Children on the Web—Beyond the Journal*, <http://www.journal.naeyc.org/btj/200705/BTJGuidance.asp> (accessed May 2007).

Han, W. 2004, 'Nonstandard work schedules and child care choices: Evidence from the NICHD Study of Early Child Care', *Early Childhood Research Quarterly*, 19(2), pp. 231–256.

Henderlong, J. and Lepper, M. 2002, 'The effects of praise on children's intrinsic motivation: a review and synthesis', *Psychological Bulletin*, 12(5), pp. 774–795.

Hitz, R. and Driscoll, A. 1988, 'Praise or encouragement? New insights into praise: implications for early childhood teachers', *Young Children*, July, pp. 6–13.

Honig, A. 1990, 'The baby—birth to twelve months', in E. Surbeck and M. Kelley, eds, *Personalizing Care with Infants, Toddlers and Families* (pp. 10–22), Association for Childhood Education International, Wheaton, MD.

Huang, W. 2007, 'Encouragement: giving "heart" to our learners in a competency-based education model', *Family Medicine*, 39(1), pp. 13–15.

Kohn, A. 1999, *Punished by Rewards—The Trouble with Gold Stars, Incentive Plans, A's, Praise, and other Bribes*, Mariner Books, New York.

LaBillois, J. and Lagacé-Séguin, D. 2007, 'Does a good fit matter? Exploring teaching styles, emotion regulation, and child anxiety in the classroom', *Early Child Development and Care*, 177 (1), pp. 1–14.

Magiati, I., Dockrell, J. and Logotheti, A. 2002, 'Young children's understanding of disabilities: the influence of development, context, and cognition', *Journal of Applied Developmental Psychology*, 23(4), pp. 409–430.

McCay, L. and Keyes, D. 2001/02, 'Developing social competence in the primary schools', *Childhood Education*, 78(2), pp. 70–8.

Ramsey, P. 2004, *Teaching and Learning in a Diverse World: Multicultural Education for Young Children*, 2nd edn, Teachers College Press, New York.

Schiller, P. 1999, 'Turning knowledge into practice', *Child Care Information Exchange*, March, 142, pp. 49–52.

Schwartz, S. 1995, 'Hidden messages in teacher talk: praise and empowerment', *Teaching Children Mathematics*, March, pp. 396–401.

Sigler, E.A. and Aamidor, S. 2005, 'From positive reinforcement to positive behaviours: an everyday guide for the practitioner,' *Early Childhood Education Journal*, 32(4), pp. 349–253.

Van Scoter, J. and Boss, S. 2002, 'Learners, language and technology: making connections that support literacy', Northwest Regional Educational Laboratory, <http://www.netc.org/earlyconnections/pub/index.html> (accessed 30 October 2004).

Ward, C. 1994, 'Adult intervention: appropriate strategies for enriching the quality of children's play', Paper presented at the *Annual Conference of the Southern Early Childhood Association*, 11–16 April, New Orleans.

Warger, C. 1999, 'Positive behaviour support and functional assessment', *ERIC Digest*, ED0-99-8.

Warner, L. and Lynch, S. 2002/03, 'Classroom problems that don't go away', *Childhood Education*, 79(2), pp. 97–100.

West, B. 1992, 'Children are caught—between home and school, culture and school', in B. Neugebauer, ed., *Alike and Different: Exploring our Humanity with Young Children*, (pp. 127–39), National Association for the Education of Young Children, Washington, DC.

Woolley, G. 2004, 'The use of praise and academic feedback to students with reading difficulties', in B. Bartlett, F. Bryer and D. Roebuck, eds, *Educating: Weaving Research into Practice*, (pp. 255–265), School of Cognition, Language and Special Education, Griffith University, Qld.

facilitating

Chapter 7

acilitating

easier: to assist the progress of.
(*Collins Dictionary of the English Language*, p. 521)

ht in a flexible but well-planned, well-organized environment
where curriculum ideas are generated by children as well as

(Catron and Allen 1993, p. 39)

fective facilitation is a key to making them work. By facilitation
te a strategy.

(Jablon and Wilkinson 2006, online)

ng fers to the process of making children's learning easier. Facilitation, therefore, re all ng aff do to make children's learning more possible, such as scheduling, selecting materials, c ng , and interacting verbally and non-verbally with them. In other words, it concerns the majority of the te ng techniques discussed in this book! However, facilitating is also about careful observation and thoughtful timing to ensure that learning is appropriate to the children's needs and interests.

Issues and debates

IS FACILITATION DIRECTIVE ENOUGH?

Facilitation can be understood as a very non-directive and low-intervention teaching technique through which the adult establishes a learning environment and then intervenes and interacts with children only when it is seen as absolutely necessary. When teachers rely strongly on facilitating learning in this way, building strong and respectful communities of learners can be problematic as research has shown low-intervention techniques can be implicated in sexist and racist relationships between peers (MacNaughton 2000; 2007; MacNaughton and Davis 2001). Young children often see cross-gendered behaviour as highly problematic and thus work to keep gender stereotypes in place unless teachers actively intervene in their play and learning to challenge this (Blakemore 2003). Boys in particular can be highly resistant to changing their traditional gender roles in preschool settings. This means teachers need to be proactive in how they work with boys to challenge such resistances.

How?

Facilitating children's learning can take many forms. Jablon and Wilkinson (2006) note it involves deliberative teacher action to engage children in learning, using strategies such as:

- having a clearly stated purpose for what children are asked to do
- giving children explicit directions
- providing children with the materials needed
- guiding students through their tasks by asking questions, answering questions and providing them with clear feedback.

Facilitation supports children's learning by paying attention to what materials they are offered, how space is used, how their time is organised and how people are used. Staff can facilitate specific children's learning on specific occasions through regularly:

- observing how children approach a specific task and identifying the elements of the task with which they have difficulties. Providing tasks that support children to 'go to the next' challenge can be important. In Yuzawaa et al.'s (2005) study of the mathematical understandings of 69 three- to six-year-old Japanese children they found that young children's mathematical learning is supported by teachers giving them tasks that push them to the next level in their understandings
- reflecting on how they can make a task easier for the child but with minimal intervention. Specifically, staff need to think about what changes to the use of people, space, time and materials might make a task easier for the child. Such changes might include ensuring that distractions, such as loud noises or other children, are kept to a minimum by redirecting the other children to alternative tasks, placing a tool nearby that might make the task easier, expanding the space available for the activity by moving furniture and joining two tables together, or moving another adult nearby to assist with a particularly tricky negotiation between the children. The following anecdote shows how simply this can be done:

Randolf has started to play with his puzzle on the floor outside the bathroom. However, he is having difficulties concentrating on it because he is distracted by children walking around him as they go to the bathroom. His teacher suggests that he may be able to do a better job if he moves himself to the quiet corner set aside for this type of work. She carefully helps him to carry his puzzle over to the quiet area and stays with him for a moment until he is absorbed in his task.

Reflection point: How else could the teacher facilitate his learning?

- waiting a few seconds after they have made changes in the organisation of space, time, materials and people to see if additional changes are needed; then monitoring at regular intervals.

Facilitating children's learning also involves constantly assessing the environment to see if more significant changes are needed in the positioning of people (Chapter 12), the positioning of equipment and materials (Chapter 1), or the scheduling of the day (Chapter 3). In other words, facilitating learning can involve a strategic use of a combination of teaching techniques to support specific forms of learning. For instance, Reutzel and Smith (2004), in a review of expert opinion on facilitating young children's learning to read, identified general principles for facilitating children to read that included teachers modelling and scaffolding reading, teachers keeping children on task, teachers providing access to diverse reading materials and providing a print rich classroom, and teacher encouragement and support for silent reading.

When and why?

GOAL RELEVANCE

Staff can facilitate children's learning through using equipment, time, materials, space and people, and through being intentional in their interactions with children. Staff can do this when they are encouraging children to be independent learners and to learn through self-discovery. A supportive and helpful learning environment will make it more likely that these goals will be achieved and that children will be self-motivated learners. However, this environment will look different in different contexts. Reflecting on cultural traditions and expectations in how an early childhood space can and should look to facilitate children's learning is important to explore and debate (Li 2006). Staff can also use the organisation of space and time to facilitate learning to:

- increase the complexity of children's fantasy play through ensuring that they spend lots of time in the outdoor play space. In particular, boys' fantasy play tends to be more complex in the outdoor play area than in the inside play area (Pelligrini and Boyd 1993)
- increase children's social play with each other through ensuring that they have lots of time in the outdoor play space. Children's play outdoors is generally rich, often open-ended and allows for problem solving skills to be built. As they often prefer to be outdoors playing, it offers an important space for learning (Greenfield 2004)
- increase children's sense of belonging and place. Inviting and welcoming spaces that include familiar features facilitate children's sense of belonging in the space (Read 2007)

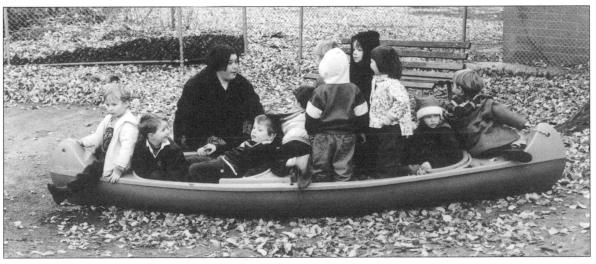

Sarah facilitates fantasy play outside by adding a new boat and spending time with the children in it.

- increase children's pretend play by ensuring diverse and flexible props are available for their play. High quality pretend play enhances cognitive development through facilitating children's experience of perspective-taking and use of symbolic and abstract thought (Bergen 2002)
- increase children's co-operative play through participating in it and using language to model to children how to extend their play and negotiate and share roles (Hintz and Stomfay-Stitz 1999)
- increase children's use of Information and Communication Technologies (ICT) by preparing network connections for specific webpages or loading a specific CD-ROM in advance. In a small study of the use of ICT in Hong Kong, two early childhood classrooms (Han 2003) found that this preparation was an effective strategy to facilitate children's use of ICT by reducing the time they needed to wait before using the technology. Several studies also indicate that if adults make themselves available to support children as needed then children show more interest in computer use (Bolstad 2004)
- increase children's sense of autonomy through ensuring that they can make choices about when, where, with whom and with what they play:

At a meeting in a bayside suburb of Melbourne, teachers are discussing how to help children in their centres to become more autonomous. Susie has some concerns. She feels that she has not been able to facilitate the children's transition from being told what to do throughout the session at the beginning of the year, to choosing their own activities now, six months later.

Susie: 'I have not let them become independent. After two terms, they still rely on me to tell them what to do. Now I think it's too late for them to be any other way.'

Shaun: 'How about starting off by giving them choices about what they might do and then progress to giving them complete freedom of choice, so that they can cope with small changes at a time? You could ask them if they want to play inside or outside and then progress to informing them that they can play where they like.'

Susie: 'That sounds like a good idea! That way, we can all get used to the change gradually.'

- increase the confidence of children learning English as a second language through ensuring that there are opportunities for solitary fantasy play. Research has shown that solitary fantasy play provides a safe space for children learning English as a second language to practise their new language (Novick 2002):

In a kindergarten in one of the outer suburbs of Brisbane where there is a large proportion of NESB families, Greta makes sure that she provides plenty of opportunities each day for the children to engage in solitary dramatic play. An area of the room is set up for this purpose. Greta presents such things as a sandbox with small animals and people in it, a collection of interesting objects with stimulus pictures or some magnets. She regularly talks with parents to ensure that the objects she uses are of particular interest to the children learning English.

- increase peer interactions between children by providing toys that encourage social interaction—for instance, large toys that require children to work together to move them and use them (Bovey and Strain 2003)
- reduce children's stress. Increased space per child in a play space decreases children's stress levels (Legendre 2003)
- increase children's language competency. When teachers respond to children's utterances and intentions with spoken language they can facilitate children's language development by helping them to understand the rules of social interaction such as joint attention, responsiveness and turn-taking (Girolametto, Weitzman and Greenberg 2006)

- support young children's science literacy development by providing an environment that enables them to explore and create and by 'relating experiences and answering personal questions when appropriate' (Klein et al. 2000, p. 12). When techniques of facilitation are combined with explicit teaching of scientific knowledge, children's science literacy is enhanced significantly (Klein et al. 2000)
- encourage children to share ideas while using computers by placing computers side by side (Bowman et al. 2001), especially between children with and without disabilities (Lau, Higgins, Gelfer, Hong and Miller, 2005)
- support children's aesthetic development by staying with children during art activities and engaging in conversation with them about their artwork (Bae, 2004).

Additional goals that can be achieved through facilitation are discussed in the chapters on organising the environment (Chapters 1 to 3).

DEVELOPMENTAL CONSIDERATIONS

Babies are more likely to pay attention to adult faces and sounds when they are calm and rested than when they are excited, tired or distracted. Paying attention to adult faces and sounds helps a baby learn to communicate with others. Through watching an adult's face and listening to the sounds they make, a baby learns that the things they can do, such as cooing, can attract an adult's attention and that adults will respond with coos or smiles. This is the beginning of babies learning that communication is a two-way process with a logic and a sequence. To facilitate this early form of two-way communication in an early childhood setting, staff need to spend time with babies when the babies are calm and rested. Staff also need to organise space and equipment to create places and spaces in which staff and babies can attend to each other without distraction. Staff at the Tiny Tots Children's Centre in north-western Sydney have made sure that part of the floor in the babies' room is set aside for a member of staff to simply sit and be available to the children for unplanned verbal and physical interaction.

Toddlers are generally becoming more physically competent, learning to gain control over their bodies and to use this control to become more independent. However, they are only just gaining many motor skills that help them to use objects in their daily lives. The objects that they learn to use will differ in different cultural contexts, but could include kicking and throwing balls or other objects, building with small blocks or other objects, turning handles, rolling and squeezing play dough or clay, and wrapping and unwrapping things (Douville-Watson, Watson and LaVisa 2002). To acquire these skills, toddlers need lots of practice. Staff can facilitate this by providing plenty of space for toddlers to practise their gross motor skills, lots of time for them to try their skills out over and over again, and lots of culturally relevant equipment and objects that allow them to use their developing skills:

> Peta, a teacher education student, was set the task of encouraging the toddlers to use their gross motor skills. Each day she set up the area in new and exciting ways. Peta was given some feedback from her supervising teacher about this. Her teacher explained that the children do not necessarily need novel equipment each day. It was more important that they had her support and the time to practise their skills over and over.

A study of Italian and US children found that children do best in the transition from preschool to school when they are engaged in 'priming events' (Corsaro and Molinari 2000). These events prepare children for transition by preparing them for what it might look and feel like. For instance, visits to children's prospective schools can give children information that helps them to imagine and build pictures of where they are going.

Preschool children are able to make and maintain relatively stable friendships over a long period of time (Ladd, Herald and Andrews 2006). Staff can facilitate the development of friendships among children through careful selection of materials and experiences that promote quality peer interaction. Dramatic play experiences are more likely to promote social interaction than experiences such as painting and playing with sand and water.

Broadly, free play which involves children in problem-solving is more likely to promote social interaction than highly structured adult-led activities (Burdette and Whitaker 2005).

In the early years of schooling, children are increasingly being exposed to computers in the classroom. The following suggestions facilitate children's acquisition of computer skills in ways that support rather than hinder learning:

- Use visually rich and stimulating software packages. In a small study of Australian primary school children, Vincent (2001) found that students' writing increased and became more complex when they could use rich visual and animation features of software when writing stories.
- Organise software and hardware so that children can use it with minimal adult support (Han 2003).
- Provide lots of support and guidance when children first use new software (Han 2003).
- Encourage group use and co-operative problem-solving over time (Van Scoter and Boss 2002).
- Ensure that all children get a fair go with using the equipment by implementing simple rules about sharing, helping each other and taking turns (Bolstad 2004).
- Use computers as a means of learning new things (Bolstad 2004).

Explanations of how to approach new situations or unfamiliar problems can also facilitate successful problem-solving and generalisation skills with children in the early years of schooling (Crowley and Steigler 1999).

Computers themselves can act as facilitators of children's learning, supporting the development of literacy skills. Vincent (2001) reports on research with five older children in Australia using Microworlds that shows its effectiveness in facilitating language and literacy skills in children who prefer to learn visually.

Equity considerations

'RACE' AND CULTURE

Children with a positive sense of self-worth and confidence engage in early childhood programs with enthusiasm and confidence. Developing a positive sense of self can be difficult for children who have experienced negative reactions to their skin colour and physical characteristics. This is particularly likely to be the case for black children. In some cultures children's self-worth is enhanced as they learn to be competent decision-makers and to be independent learners. In other cultures children's self-worth is linked to their capacity to contribute to a group. Facilitating opportunities for black children to make decisions and to become powerful learners can be one important way to build their sense of self-worth and confidence. This work should be linked strongly to the cultural values of their communities and what is valued within those communities for building a strong sense of self-worth and group belonging.

Staff can facilitate children's acceptance of cultural and 'racial' diversity by creating an environment in which children can notice and talk about such diversity. If there is 'racial' diversity within a group of children, they will notice and talk about it as they learn about each other. However, in a predominantly white group of children, staff will need to facilitate other opportunities for them to notice, reflect on and to talk about 'racial' diversity. Having posters, dolls, books, puzzles and pictures that represent the full 'racial' diversity of a specific country is a simple but effective way to do this. Using web-based and other multi-media resources can also facilitate children's engagement with cultural and 'racial' diversity (see some suggested beginnings in the 'Online and multi-media resources' section of this chapter).

More specific information on how to organise the environment to facilitate positive attitudes to 'racial' diversity is provided in Chapters 1 and 2.

In culturally diverse classrooms teachers can facilitate a sense of welcome and safety for all children if they ensure the images, symbols, sounds and languages of the children's cultural background are infused throughout the classroom. When children can recognise their identities reflected within the classroom it affirms who they are and their culture (Adler Matoba 2001).

GENDER

Children's fantasy play is influenced by the gender composition of playgroups and by the props available to them. When preschool boys and girls play together using stereotypically masculine props or gender-neutral props, boys tend to choose the masculine fantasy play storylines (MacNaughton 1997, 2000). Staff can facilitate girls' ability to choose diverse fantasy play storylines by encouraging girls-only groups when they want to play with stereotypically masculine or gender-neutral props, and by encouraging the use of stereotypically feminine props in mixed group play. For example, adding lots of dolls to the block area makes it more likely that the girls may be able to choose the storyline when they are playing with the boys in this area.

To facilitate boys in cross-gender play appears to be more challenging. Research over time has shown boys often have less knowledge than girls about cross-gender play (Green, Bigler and Catherwood 2004). It is also likely that traditionally gendered boys will be less willing to publicly play with what they consider to be 'girls' toys' than will girls. Recent studies of 296 US children aged between four and 12 years (Gee and Heyman 2007) found that children as young as four years of age believed that boys are less likely to reveal that they like to play with dolls than girls when social norms suggest that boys don't play with dolls. Teachers will need to facilitate boys' cross-gender play more proactively by providing safe spaces in which they can transgress what they perceive to be gender norms.

Choosing software that challenges gender stereotypes is another way to facilitate gender exploration and diversity in the preschool years. Again this can be a challenging yet important task. A content analysis of educational software for preschool children showed that it often contains gender stereotyping and there is greater visibility of male characters than female characters (Sheldon 2004). This is important because cultivation media theorists argue that the more children are exposed to media messages, for instance about conceptions of masculinity and femininity, the more likely it is that they will hold similar views to those media messages (Sheldon 2004).

Staff can facilitate a more equitable gender climate in their classrooms in the early years of schooling by ensuring that girls receive recognition for their achievements, by taking care to remember the girls' names and to use them, and by regularly sitting with the girls to support their work. More specifically, teacher presence in the computer areas can facilitate greater use and social interaction (Medvin, Reed, Behr and Spargo 2003); it can be particularly important for teachers to position themselves in this area of their classroom to facilitate girls' use of new technologies. Girls' use of new technologies can also be facilitated if they are given the opportunity to use the computer as a tool to accomplish the things that matter to them (Yelland, Rubin and McWilliam 2002).

DISABILITY AND ADDITIONAL NEEDS

Developing a positive sense of self is as important for children with disabilities as it is for other children. However, developing a positive sense of self can be difficult for children who have experienced negative reactions to their disabilities. This is particularly likely to be the case for children who have visible disabilities.

Facilitating opportunities for children with disabilities to make decisions and to become independent learners can be one important way to build their self-esteem. This can be difficult to do when staff feel uncertain about a child's specific strengths and abilities. Staff need to talk with parents and learn about the special abilities of children with disabilities. Providing lots of open-ended materials that have no inherently right or wrong way to use them can be a useful way forward. Sometimes a simple adaptation to the physical environment is all that is needed to facilitate a child's successful involvement in an experience:

One of the modifications we made for him was to create a sand tray which was elevated from the ground. Instead of him going down to the sand, we brought the sand up to him. (Department of Employment, Education and Training 1994, p. 28)

Increasingly, new technologies can facilitate learning for children with diverse special needs or characteristics. Assistive or adaptive technologies that make something accessible that would not have been accessible otherwise include screen magnifiers, voice recognition software and modified keyboards including touch screens or a modified mouse, trackball or electronic pointing devices (Bray, Brown and Green 2004). Children's own perspectives on how technologies can best assist their learning can also be sought. Light, Page, Curran and Pitkin (2007) researched the ideas of six young children with disabilities about how best to design assistive technologies for children with complex communication needs. They found that children 'characterized the systems as companions and utilized innovative names, bright colors, lights, transformable shapes, popular themes, humor, and amazing accomplishments to capture interest, enhance appeal, build self-esteem, and establish a positive social image' (p. 274). (See the 'Online and multi-media resources' section of this chapter for information on assistive and adaptive technologies for children and their role in facilitating learning for young children with disabilities.)

Recent research (Lau, Higgins, Gelfer, Hong and Miller 2005) has also shown that computer activities with teacher facilitation can promote greater social interaction between children with disabilities and those without disabilities in inclusive classrooms.

Staff can facilitate children's acceptance of diverse abilities and needs by creating an environment in which children can notice and talk about their own abilities and disabilities. When there are children within the group who have visible disabilities, the children will notice and talk about diversity as they learn about each other. However, in a group of predominantly able-bodied children, staff will need to facilitate other opportunities for children to notice and talk about disability and diversity. Having posters, dolls, books, puzzles and pictures that represent a range of visible disabilities is a simple but effective way to do this. It is especially important for children to have the opportunity to interact with each other with positive adult support and facilitation (Diamond and Huang 2005).

More specific information on how to organise the environment to facilitate positive attitudes to people's diverse abilities is provided in Chapters 1 and 2. Ways of talking with children about the differences between them are detailed in Chapters 5 and 14.

Reflecting on facilitation techniques

1 Briefly define facilitating.
2 What do you think is the major difference between helping and facilitating?
3 List 10 non-verbal ways of facilitating children's learning. Would each of these processes be suitable for use with babies?
4 What are most successful ways that you have seen other adults help toddlers build self-esteem through facilitation?
5 What are three ways in which you could facilitate children's social play?
6 What are three ways in which you could facilitate girls' ability to choose the storylines for their fantasy play?
7 Observe a child in an early childhood setting who has a visible disability. How and how well have staff facilitated the child's learning?
8 Observe a group setting for babies. How and how well does the organisation of space, time, materials and people facilitate two-way communication between the babies and the staff?

Improving teaching in practice

1 Videotape the non-verbal teaching interactions you have with children during several five-minute teaching periods.
2 How and how well did you facilitate children's learning? Did you:
   - observe how the children were approaching a specific task and identify the elements of the task they were having difficulties with?
   - focus on what you could do to make the task easier for the children with minimal intervention?
   - wait a few seconds after you had made changes in the organisation of space, time, materials and people to see if additional changes were needed?
   - monitor the need for additional facilitation at regular intervals?
3 What are your areas of strength and weakness in using facilitation as a teaching technique to promote children's learning?
4 How can you work to improve your facilitation techniques?

FURTHER READING

Bae, H. 2004, 'Learning to teach visual arts in an early childhood classroom: the teacher's role as a guide', *Early Childhood Education Journal*, 31(4), pp. 247–254.

Carlson, B., Samels, S., Goldberg, P. and Goldberg, M. 1997, 'Kids included through technology are enriched: a guidebook for teachers of young children and project KITE', *Young Children and Technology*, PACER Center, Inc., Minneapolis, MN.

Doctoroff, S. 2001, 'Adapting the physical environment to meet the needs of all young children for play', *Early Childhood Education Journal*, 29(2), pp. 105–109.

Haigh, K., Rodriguez, D. and Schroeder, G. 2002, 'A study of hands: Chicago Commons explores Reggio Emilia', *Child Care Information Exchange*, 144(3), pp. 42–45.

Lennox, M. 2004, 'Storytelling for young children in a multicultural world', *Early Childhood Education Journal*, 28(2), pp. 97–103.

ONLINE AND MULTI-MEDIA RESOURCES

Text

Ball, J. 2006, 'Talking points: exploring needs and concepts for Aboriginal early childhood language facilitation and supports', Concept discussion paper prepared for the Public Health Agency of Canada, Aboriginal Head Start in Urban and Northern Communities. PDF download at: **http://www.ecdip.org/earlylanguage/index.htm**

'Early Intervention Assistive Technology Resource Chart'. Pdf download at: **http://www.jeffline.jefferson.edu/cfsrp/products/presentations/WhatdoweknowaboutATStatePresentationDEC2005.pdf**

Multi-media

'Early messages: facilitating language development and communication' (video), The Program for Infant/Toddler Caregivers, WestEd, Center for Child and Family Studies, California Department of Education, Child Development Division. Free access 3 minute segment available at: **http://clas.uiuc.edu/fulltext/cl03011/cl03011.html**

Diversity resources for children

Multiverse (UK based). Excellent links to sites exploring cultural and 'racial' diversity in UK and Europe including links to Key Learning Areas guidelines: **http://www.multiverse.ac.uk**

Teaching tolerance (US based). Activities for children and adults: **http://teachingtolerance.org**

Exploring diversity (US based). Links for teachers to explore diversity with children: **http://www.ilovemath.net/exploring_diversity.htm**

Website for facilitating learning with ICT for children with and without disabilities
Cyberstart: **http://www.cyberstartpa.info/resources/techandyoung.php**

REFERENCES

Adler Matoba, S. 2001, 'Racial and ethnic mirrors: reflections on identity from an Asian American educator', in S. Grieshaber and G. Cannella, eds, *Embracing Identities in Early Childhood Education: Diversity and Possibilities* (pp. 148–57), Teachers College Press, New York.

Bae, H. 2004, 'Learning to teach visual arts in an early childhood classroom: the teacher's role as a guide', *Early Childhood Education Journal*, 31(4), pp. 247–254.

Bergen, D. 2002, 'The role of pretend play in children's cognitive development', *Early Childhood Research and Practice*, 4(1), <http://www.ecrp.uiuc.edu/v4n1/bergen.thml>

Blakemore, J. 2003, 'Children's beliefs about violating gender norms: boys shouldn't look like girls, and girls shouldn't act like boys', *Sex Roles*, 48(9/10), pp. 411–419.

Bolstad, R. 2004, *The Role and Potential of ICT in Early Childhood Education: A Review of New Zealand and International Literature*, Ministry of Education, Wellington, NZ.

Bovey, T. and Strain, P. 2003, 'Using environmental strategies to promote positive social interactions', *What Works Briefs*, ED481994.

Bowman, B., Donovan, M. and Burns, S. 2001, *Eager to Learn: Educating Our Preschoolers*, National Academy Press, Washington, DC.

Bray, M., Brown, M. and Green, T. 2004, *Technology and the Diverse Learner: A Guide to Classroom Practice*, Corwin Press, Thousand Oaks, CA.

Burdette, H. and Whitaker, R. 2005, 'Resurrecting free play in young children. Looking beyond fitness and fatness to attention, affiliation, and affect', *Archive Pediatric Adolescent Medicine*, 159, pp. 46–50.

Catron, C. and Allen, J. 1993, *Early Childhood Curriculum*, Macmillan Publishing Company, New York.

Corsaro, W. and Molinari, L. 2000, 'Priming events and Italian children's transition from preschool to elementary school: representations and action', *Social Psychology Quarterly*, March, 63(1) pp. 16–33.

Crowley, K. and Steigler, R.S. 1999, 'Explanation and generalisation in young children's learning strategy', *Child Development*, 70(2), pp. 304–316.

Department of Employment, Education and Training 1994, *Like Any Child: Planning for Children with Disabilities*, DEET and the Brotherhood of St Lawrence, Melbourne.

Diamond, K. and Huang, H. 2005, 'Preschoolers' ideas about disabilities', *Infants & Young Children: An Interdisciplinary Journal of Special Care Practices*, 18(1), pp. 37–46.

Douville-Watson, L., Watson, M. and LaVisa, C. 2002, *Infants & Toddlers: Curriculum and Teaching*, 5th edn, Delmar Publishers, Albany, New York.

Gee, C. and Heyman, G. 2007, 'Children's evaluation of other people's self-descriptions', *Social Development*, 16(4), pp. 800–818.

Girolametto, L., Weitzman, E. and Greenberg, J. 2006, 'Facilitating language skills: inservice education for early childhood educators and preschool teachers', *Infants & Young Children*, 19(1), pp. 36–46.

Green, V., Bigler, R. and Catherwood, D. 2004, 'The variability and flexibility of gender-typed toy play: a close look at children's behavioral responses to counterstereotypic models', *Sex Roles*, 51(7/8), pp. 371–386.

Greenfield, C. 2004, '"Can run, play on bikes, jump the zoom slide, and play on the swings". Exploring the value of outdoor play', *Australian Journal of Early Childhood*, 29(2), pp. 1–5.

Han, C. 2003, 'Challenges of using ICT in Hong Kong early childhood settings', Paper presented at the *Young Children and Learning Technologies* conference, Australian Computer Society IFIP Working Group 3–5, July, Parramatta, NSW.

Hintz, B.F. and Stomfay-Stitz, A. 1999, 'Peace education and conflict resolution through expressive arts in early childhood education and teacher education', Paper presented at the *Annual Conference of the Eastern Educational Research Association*, 26 February, Hilton Head, SC, ED433105.

Jablon, J. and Wilkinson, M. 2006, 'Using engagement strategies to facilitate children's learning and success', <http://www. journal.naeyc.org/btj/200603/JablonBTJ.asp>

Klein, E.R., Hammrich, P., Bloom, S. and Ragins, A. 2000, 'Language development and science inquiry: a child-initiated and teacher-facilitated program', Paper presented at the *Annual Meeting of the American Education Research Association*, April, New Orleans, ED440756.

Ladd, G., Herald, S. and Andrews, R. 2006, 'Children's peer relations and social competence', in B. Spodek and O. Saracho, eds, *Handbook of Research on the Education of Young Children*, Lawrence Erlbaum Associates, New Jersey.

Lau, C., Higgins, K., Gelfer, J., Hong, E. and Miller, S. 2005, 'The effects of teacher facilitation on the social interactions of young children during computer activities', *Topics in Early Childhood Special Education*, 25(4): pp. 208–217.

Legendre, A. 2003, 'Environmental features influencing toddlers bioemotional reactions in day care centers', *Environment and Behavior*, July, 35, pp. 523–549.

Li, Y. 2006, 'Classroom organization: understanding the context in which children are expected to learn', *Early Childhood Education Journal*, 34(1), pp. 37–43.

Light, J., Page, R., Curran, J. and Pitkin, L. 2007, 'Children's ideas for the design of AAC assistive technologies for young children with complex communication needs', *Augmentative and Alternative Communication*, 23(4), pp. 274–287.

MacNaughton, G. 1997, 'Who's got the power? Rethinking gender equity strategies in early childhood', *International Journal of Early Years Education*, 5(1), pp. 57–66.

——2000, *Rethinking Gender in Early Childhood*, Allen & Unwin, Sydney; Sage Publications, New York.

——2007, 'Constructing gender in early years education', in C. Skelton, B. Francis and L. Smulyan, eds, *Sage Handbook: Gender and Education*, Sage Publications, New York, London and New Delhi, pp. 127–138.

MacNaughton, G. and Davis, K. 2001, 'Beyond "othering": rethinking approaches to teaching young Anglo-Australian children about Indigenous Australians', *Contemporary Issues in Early Childhood*, 2(1), pp. 83–93.

Medvin, M., Reed, D., Behr, D. and Spargo, E. 2003, 'Using technology to encourage social problem solving in preschoolers', in G. Marshall and Y. Katz, eds, *Learning in School, Home And Community. ICT for Early and Elementary Education* (pp. 13–20), Kluwer Academic Publishers, Boston.

Novick, R. 2002, 'Many paths to literacy: language, literature, and learning in the primary classroom', NWERL, Portland, OR.

Pelligrini, A. and Boyd, B. 1993, 'The role of play in early childhood development and education: issues in definition and function', in B. Spodek, ed., *Handbook of Research on the Education of Young Children* (pp. 105–21), Macmillan Publishing Company, New York.

Read, M. 2007, 'Sense of place in child care environments', *Early Childhood Education Journal*, 34(6), pp. 387–391.

Reutzel, D.R. and Smith, J.A. 2004, 'Accelerating struggling readers' progress: a comparative analysis of expert opinion and current research recommendations', *Reading and Writing Quarterly*, 20(1), pp. 63–89.

Sheldon, J. 2004, 'Gender stereotypes in educational software for young children', *Sex Roles*, 51, pp. 433–444.

Skinner, P. 1996, 'Play and the mathematics profile', in M. Fleer, ed., *Play through Profiles: Profiles through Play* (pp. 57–66), Australian Early Childhood Association, Canberra.

Van Scoter, J. and Boss, S. 2002, 'Learners, language and technology: making connections that support literacy', Northwest Regional Educational Laboratory, <http://www.netc.org/earlyconnections/pub/index.html> (accessed 30 October 2004).

Vincent, J. 2001, 'The role of visually rich technology in facilitating children's writing', *Journal of Computer Assisted Learning*, 17, pp. 242–250.

Wieder, S. and Greenspan, S. 1993, 'The emotional basis of learning', in B. Spodek, ed., *Handbook of Research on the Education of Young Children* (pp. 77–87), Macmillan Publishing Company, New York.

Wilde, M. and Sage, R. 2007, 'Developing the communicative competence and narrative thinking of four and five-year-olds in educational settings', *Early Child Development and Care*, 177(6), pp. 679–693.

Wilkes, G. (ed.) 1979, *Collins Dictionary of the English Language*, Penguin Books, Middlesex.

Yelland, N., Rubin, A. and McWilliam, E. (eds) 2002, *Ghosts in the Machine: Women's Voices in Research with Technology*, Peter Lang Publishing, New York.

Yuzawaa, M., Bartb, M., Yuzawac, M. and Junkod, I. 2005, 'Young children's knowledge and strategies for comparing sizes', *Early Childhood Research Quarterly*, 20(2), pp. 239–253.

Chapter 8

Feedback

 Feedback: to offer or suggest (information, ideas, etc.) in reaction to an inquiry, experiment, etc.

(Collins Dictionary of the English Language, p. 533)

. . . a teacher's positive feedback to children is the basis for the effectiveness of all the other teaching strategies.

(Allen and Hart 1984, p. 261)

Children learn a broad range of information, ideas, values, attitudes and skills from others . . . It occurs daily through interaction, observation, practice, and feedback from others.

(Robison and Schwartz 1982, p. 107)

What?

Feedback is the provision of information before, during and after an experience. This feedback may be verbal, such as a comment on how a child has approached a task; or it may be non-verbal, such as a smile that shows a child that you have appreciated their efforts during a task. Staff assist children's learning by using verbal and non-verbal feedback to give children explicit information about what they have done. Feedback can give children information that clarifies what they are doing and evaluates their actions (Seefeldt 1980). Feedback supports children's learning most effectively if it gives them clear and specific information so that they think about what to do next.

Generally, children gain more useful information from verbal feedback than from non-verbal feedback, as verbal feedback can be more explicit. For example, a child can find it harder to identify the precise action or event to which non-verbal feedback refers.

Consider the following example of a child who has successfully put the final pieces in a puzzle after several attempts. She was finally successful because she decided to match the colours on one side of the puzzle piece with the colours in the puzzle. Staff could give feedback on her success through a smile or through comments such as, 'You must be pleased to have found how the piece fits after so many tries. It seemed to work when you put the same colours together.' Words are more likely to help the child learn from her experience because a smile cannot tell her why she was successful, and so it does not help her to build strategies that can help her when she next tries to do a puzzle. For this reason we will concentrate mainly on verbal feedback.

Issues and debates

COMPUTERS AS AGENTS OF FEEDBACK

Feedback has traditionally been seen as something that teachers use to support children's learning. More recently, researchers have found that computers can also act as an agent of feedback in young children's learning. Drawing on the idea that computers are social actors, researchers have explored the extent to which humans interact socially with computers. In an experimental study with 42 eight- to ten-year-olds researchers found that children of this age responded to computer feedback as they would to a person and that this response impacted positively on their learning, and on their recall and recognition capacities (Campanella Bracken and Lombard 2004). More specifically, positive feedback from the computer on a memory recognition and recall task increased children's overall performance on the task better than neutral feedback from the computer. Children who received positive computer feedback as they were completing the task also rated their own ability more highly than did those children who received neutral feedback from the computer.

Computer feedback has also been found to assist children in the USA who are struggling with learning to read in their first years of schooling. When a computer program offers children the opportunity for self-paced activities, linked to their specific reading needs, and provides them with immediate feedback, they can progress their reading skills more quickly than children not provided with this opportunity (Macaruso, Hook and McCabe 2006).

While researchers argue that young children can and do have intense and positive learning relationships with computers they also caution against creating a teaching and learning environment for young children in which computers 'replace' teaching and learning relationships between children and adults (Campanella Bracken and Lombard 2004). The existing research base on children and their social relationships with computers does not give a clear indication of the extent to which positive feedback from computers has positive effects over time.

Young children can also be powerful teachers capable of providing feedback to their peers and siblings. A study of Maya children (Central/South America) between three and 11 years of age (Maynard 2002) found that by four years of age children were teaching their younger siblings using verbal feedback, demonstrations, explanations and physical guidance. This teaching increased the participation of younger children in culturally important tasks.

How?

Feedback should be appropriate to a child's learning style and abilities. Some children's learning will be supported through verbal feedback while for others non-verbal feedback will be more effective. If staff are familiar with the learning styles and abilities of each child in their group they can judge which form of feedback is most appropriate.

Verbal feedback is most successful when it:

- is explicit and describes specific events, relationships, features of a task, interactions or behaviours
- is given in context
- describes what the child is doing rather than places a value judgment on it:

Oskar (a four-year-old) is using indoor blocks to construct a large building. Kylie, his teacher, sits close to him. After a period of observation she remarks, 'I like the way you have used the long blocks at the bottom. This has made your building stronger. You have been working here for a long time this morning and I can see that you have been concentrating hard.'

Reflection point: Why might this feedback be successful?

- is given soon after the actions to which it refers. Consider the following discussion among teachers about giving feedback to children:

Christie: 'I always give positive feedback when the children are concentrating well. I hope that this encourages them to stay at one activity for more than a minute and a half!'

Carol: 'That's right. I always give feedback when I think the children are making an effort to do something they haven't tried before.'

Anne: 'I guess that I always give feedback when the children are showing any kind of prosocial behaviour like helping another child, or sharing or taking turns. But when I look at it, I'm not really describing what it is they've done right, I'm just praising them for doing it.'

Christie: 'I see what you mean, yes. I'm going to put more description into my feedback from now on. Instead of saying, "I like the way you finished the puzzle, Jack", I will say something like, "I like the way you looked carefully at each piece before you put it into the puzzle". I can see that this will be more useful to him because he will know what he did right.'

Reflection point: What style of feedback do you use?

(Adapted from Seefeldt 1980; Dunlap, Lewis and McCart 2006; Honomichl and Chen 2006.)

More detailed information on feedback and its specific role in reinforcing and scaffolding can be found in Chapters 28 and 29.

When and why?

GOAL RELEVANCE

Verbal feedback is a way to actively respond to children's efforts to learn something new (Rimm-Kaufman et al. 2007) and to improve their capacity to learn from their environment (Frank, Stolarski and Scher 2006). Feedback actively and explicitly responds to children's actions in order to positively reinforce them and to mediate their learning. Feedback as a positive reinforcer supports:

Children's wellbeing
- Feedback enables children to learn the likelihood that what they're doing will be successful (Wieder and Greenspan 1993). For example, the comment, 'Tina, I think the cart will make it up the hill this time if you keep pushing it with both hands' tells Tina that her current approach to pushing the cart should achieve her goal. The feedback will, hopefully, encourage Tina to keep trying.
- Feedback allows children to learn that staff take an interest in their achievements and are responsive to their learning efforts. For example, the comment, 'Sandy, I was interested to see how you used the really long nails to join those two pieces of wood together for your boat' tells Sandy that her hard work

was appreciated by the adult. The feedback will, hopefully, encourage Sandy to try different ways to join wood.

- Verbal feedback supports the development of self-concept in preschool children (Penn 2000).
- Staff can also use verbal feedback to check their own understandings of what is happening to a child. For example, staff could ask, 'Ashley, I thought you looked very sad after Bill left today. Was that how you felt?'. The feedback will, hopefully, provide the staff member with accurate information about Ashley's feelings. This form of feedback can enrich children's vocabulary for describing mental states and, in doing so, improve their understanding of the mental states of others (Harris, de Rosnay and Pons 2005).

Building growth and success in learning

- Responsive feedback builds the young child's communication skills and allows children to learn about their progress in developing their skill or interactions with people or materials (Matthews, Lieven and Tomasello 2007). For example, the comment, 'Sipho, sharing that towel with Tim was really helpful. It meant he could dry his doll as well' tells Sipho that his actions were appreciated and welcomed. The feedback will, hopefully, encourage Sipho to share again.
- Feedback supports the development of the internal motivation to succeed in young children's exploration of their world (Klein et al. 2000).
- Staff could use verbal feedback as a teaching technique when children will benefit from their support and reassurance in tackling a task or becoming involved in a particular experience:

> Lettie is new to the children's centre. She appears shy and withdrawn and is hesitant to try the activities that the staff have put out for the children. Griselda has been allocated to help Lettie to feel more comfortable as she settles in. She deliberately uses verbal feedback to help Lettie to become more involved. For example, she says, 'Lettie, you've tried painting and playing with the puzzles this morning, I'm happy to see you experimenting with new things. Well done!'.
>
> *Reflection point:* How might you use feedback to reassure a younger child?

- Staff can also use feedback to provide children with explicit information on their learning strategies. This form of feedback can expand the ways in which children learn and support the development of independent learning (Hendy and Whitebread 2000).

Specific areas of children's learning

- Children's early mathematics and reading skills are supported by staff feedback on how their writing is progressing (Rimm-Kaufman et al. 2007). A study of effective mathematical teaching in China found that Chinese teachers give immediate feedback to children in mathematical question and answer sections (Zhang and Zhou 2003). As discussed above, computer feedback can also assist in building the reading skills of young children struggling with reading in their early years of schooling (Macaruso, Hook and McCabe 2006).
- Feedback encourages children's scientific theory-making when teachers use feedback to validate children's theories and elaborate on children's experimentation (McWilliams 1999).
- The development of preschool children's social and language development is supported when staff use clear verbal feedback to facilitate peer interactions between children (Girolametto and Weitzman 2007).

DEVELOPMENTAL CONSIDERATIONS

Some researchers (Tomasello, Carpenter and Liszkowski 2007) believe that when babies point, this is a social act and a form of pre-linguistic communication. Being responsive to infant pointing through giving infants verbal and non-verbal feedback when they point offers one important way in which to help infants to learn that others are interested in their early efforts to communicate and to influence the actions of adults. Babies in the US have been found to use eye contact to establish social contact with others and have demonstrated their capacity to follow the gaze and gestures of adults (Mundy et al. 2007). When babies demonstrate this capacity, adults can use gesture and gaze as a form of responsive feedback to babies to let them know that their efforts to initiate social contact with adults have been successful.

Children feel good about themselves when they know that they can make things happen. Staff can help infants and toddlers to feel good about themselves by giving non-verbal feedback—for example, by using mirrors. Marshall (1989, p. 47) suggested that:

> When infants can see both themselves and their image moving at the same time, they can learn about the effects of their own actions and their ability to control their world.

Toddlers are able to read both positive and negative non-verbal feedback. They can tell if a gesture or look is one of approval or disapproval, and are developing a memory for what has happened to them emotionally in the past as well as beginning to strategically control their own emotions (Brownhill and Kopp 2007). When toddlers demonstrate this capacity staff can provide them with positive feedback about their

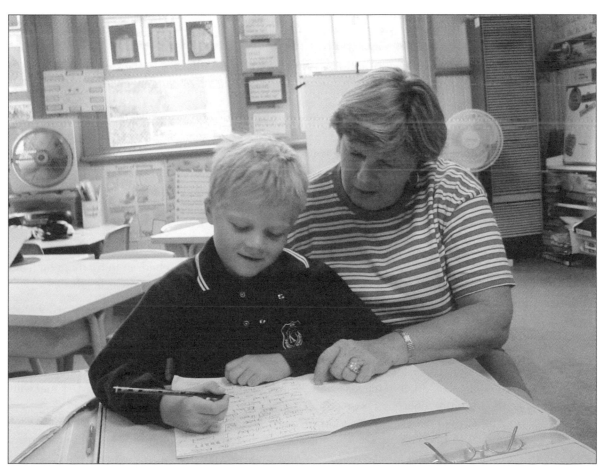

Di gives Sam verbal feedback about his writing.

accomplishments. For example, during a story time a staff member might say, 'You have made a big space on the carpet for the other children to sit with us'.

Preschool children are just developing the ability to predict whether or not they might succeed at a cognitive task, so their predictions are often overstated (Shin, Bjorklund and Beck 2007). Staff can support the development of more accurate predictions through giving children feedback on their efforts. For example, when a staff member observes a block building getting higher and higher, they could say, 'This building has been built with strong foundations, so I'm sure it will stand up'. This feedback should be reliable and accurate, as three- and four-year-old children in the USA have been found to trust information from those who have provided accurate information in the past and to distrust those whose information has proved to be unreliable (Harris 2007).

Feedback is also helpful for older children who are trying to refine their writing and other literacy skills. The most effective literacy teachers use explicit skill-based feedback deliberately and regularly as part of their teaching repertoire. This feedback should be timely—linked to the specific incident or skill on which the teacher is giving feedback (Louden et al. 2005). For instance, feedback on where commas might go or how exclamation marks might help the children give emphasis to their statement should be given at the time when children need to use them in a specific composition or piece of writing that they are doing.

Equity considerations

'RACE' AND CULTURE

Toddlers can notice differences between people such as hair colour and texture, skin colour and facial characteristics. They notice that some people have darker skin than others, some people have curlier hair than others, some have flat noses and some people have long noses. When toddlers notice these physical differences, staff can help them to understand and enjoy diversity by giving clear, accurate, descriptive feedback about what they have seen. If staff describe to toddlers the differences they are seeing in simple words, they can reduce the possibility that they will develop fear or discomfort about people who are different to themselves.

For example, when a toddler from an Anglo-Australian background stares at a black child from northern Africa, staff can give verbal feedback such as: 'Sally, you have just seen Sasha. She has very dark skin. Sometimes people are born with light skin like yours, sometimes they are born with dark skin like Sasha's.' Associating such observations with simple stories and games to familiarise children with differences between people, and discussions, consolidate their understandings of physical diversity. Giving feedback to children during these experiences is an important part of such consolidation.

York (1991) listed a wide range of activities that help children learn about 'racial' differences and similarities that still offer some good beginning points for staff. They included:

- collecting nylon stockings in lots of different shades and encouraging children to try them on hands and feet till they find a shade that matches their skin tones. Staff's descriptive feedback can give children words to help them name and talk about skin tone. For example, 'Timmy, you're wearing a coffee-coloured stocking, but your skin looks much more like a caramel colour to me. What do you think? Can you find a stocking that is more like caramel?'
- mixing batches of play dough in different colours and encouraging children to mix the colours until they create colours that match their skin tones. Staff's descriptive feedback can give children words to help them name and talk about skin tone. For example, 'Jessie, your dough looks dark and shiny just like the colour of molasses. Do you think your skin is as dark and shiny as molasses?'
- collecting pictures of people from a variety of 'racial' groups and encouraging children to find people like themselves in the pictures. Once again, staff's descriptive feedback can give children words to help them name and talk about skin tone. For example, 'This person in the picture has skin like golden wheat. Does anyone here have skin like golden wheat?'.

These activities can be an especially good way to begin to talk about the similarities and differences between children in 'mixed-race' groups. However, in mono-'racial' groups, children will also be likely to discover differences in their skin tones and can learn words that help them to name their own specific skin tone. Researchers in the USA (Brownell, Zerwas and Ramani 2007) found that children's capacity to accurately reflect on and represent their bodies grows over time but that children as young as 18 months old can reflect on and represent aspects of their bodies. This suggests that children as young as 18 months of age are likely to benefit from accurate descriptive feedback on their bodies and the bodies of others.

GENDER

Adults and girls may underestimate the capacity of girls to do mathematics in the early years of school, but they do not follow this pattern with girls' literacy skills. In a study of 300 children in their early years of school, US researchers (Herbert and Stipek 2005) found that both girls and the girls' parents underestimated the girls' capacity to do mathematics and overestimated the capacity of boys to do mathematics. There were no

'What colour is your hand?'

foundations for these inaccurate estimations of children's abilities based on their gender. Teachers should be alert to the possibility that gender may influence how girls see their capacities and explore the extent to which this is so in their particular context. If specific girls are underestimating their abilities in specific tasks or areas of learning, the use of positive feedback may help to mediate this and build the confidence of the girls.

Adults with traditional views about gender roles may give feedback to girls about their appearance and feedback to boys about their physical achievements. Staff who want to expand girls' and boys' understanding of what it is possible to do as a boy and as a girl should be alert to these tendencies. They should look for opportunities to give feedback to girls on their accomplishments rather than their appearance and to give feedback to boys about their moments of caring for others as well as their physical achievements.

However, staff should be very careful about when and how they give feedback to girls on their achievements. Past research (Browne and Ross 1991) suggested that girls learn that they need to do very little in non-traditionally female play areas such as Lego and blocks to receive positive feedback. Staff eager to support girls' exploration of construction materials can inadvertently encourage underachievement by giving girls positive feedback for merely putting a couple of pieces of Lego together. If girls are to increase their confidence in the mathematics, science and technology areas of the curriculum, they need specific and direct positive feedback on their hard work and problem-solving attempts.

DISABILITY AND ADDITIONAL NEEDS

Toddlers notice differences between people with visible disabilities and those without them. They notice that some people use wheelchairs, some people have one arm shorter than the other, some people wear very thick glasses and some people have had their windpipe removed (tracheotomy). When toddlers notice these differences, staff can help them to '. . . develop a comfortable awareness of others' (Derman-Sparks et al. 1989, p. 22) by providing them with immediate and '. . . simple feedback that supports their observations and helps sort out what is happening' (Derman-Sparks et al. 1989, p. 23). If staff can use simple words to describe to the toddler what they have seen, they can reduce the possibility that toddlers will develop fear or discomfort about people with disabilities.

For example, when a toddler stares at someone who has no fingers on one hand, staff can give verbal feedback such as, 'Suzy, you have just seen a person who has no fingers on one of her hands. Sometimes people are born with no fingers on their hands, sometimes they have no fingers because they have had an accident.'

However, providing descriptive verbal feedback to toddlers when they notice people with visible disabilities should be just the beginning of helping them to feel comfortable with diversity. Simple stories and discussions can consolidate children's early understandings of ability and diversity.

Reflecting on feedback techniques

1 Define feedback.
2 What are the keys to using feedback to optimise children's learning?
3 When do you think feedback should be used in your teaching?
4 Are there any times when you think the use of feedback is inappropriate with young children?
5 How could feedback be used to promote communicative competence with infants? What sort of feedback could you use to achieve this aim?
6 What things do you think toddlers would enjoy having feedback about?
7 What are most meaningful forms of verbal feedback that you have heard other adults provide to four-year-old children?
8 Develop a plan for a learning experience for four- to five-year-old children in which your goal is to increase children's problem-solving skills. How could you use feedback as a teaching technique to do this?

9 What words could you use to give a toddler feedback when she first observes a person in a wheelchair?

10 Observe staff working with babies. To what extent do they use verbal and non-verbal feedback to encourage babies' two-way communication competence?

Improving teaching in practice

1 Record (using a tape-recorder or written notes) the verbal feedback you give children during several half-hour teaching periods.

2 What is your current style of giving feedback? Do you:
   - describe what the child is doing rather than place a value judgment on it?
   - describe specific events, interactions and behaviours?
   - provide feedback close to the time the child is doing the act?

3 How and how well did you take account of developmental and equity considerations?

4 What are your areas of strength and weakness in using verbal feedback to promote children's learning?

5 How can you work to improve your feedback techniques in practice?

FURTHER READING

Honomichl, R. and Chen, Z. 2006, 'Learning to align relations: the effects of feedback and self-explanation', *Journal of Cognition and Development*, 7(4), pp. 527–550.

ONLINE AND MULTI-MEDIA RESOURCES

Text

Bo-Linn, C. 2003, 'Effectively using informal early feedback', Centre for Teaching Excellence, University of Illinois at Urbana-Champaign: **http://www.cte.uiuc.edu/Did/Resources/Illini%20Instructor/informalearlyfeedback.htm**

Multi-media

'Making plans with individual children'. A teacher in a multi-age primary classroom provides feedback to a child on his learning progress during the week. Free access video clip, 2 min. 49 sec.: **http://edcommunity.apple.com/ali/story.php?itemID=620&version=360&pageID=1577**

Reading and literacy learning: free access podcasts and video streaming. Phonemic awareness: 'Helping struggling' shows teacher feedback in action. **http://www.readingrockets.org/podcasts/classroom#sounds**

REFERENCES

Allen, K. and Hart, B. 1984, *The Early Years: Arrangements for Learning*, Prentice Hall Inc., New Jersey.

Browne, N. and Ross, C. 1991, '"Girls' stuff, boys' stuff": young children talking and playing', in N. Browne, ed., *Science and Technology in the Early Years* (pp. 37–51), Open University Press, Milton Keynes.

Brownell, C., Zerwas, S. and Ramani, G. 2007, '"So big": the development of body self-awareness in toddlers', *Child Development*, 78(5), pp. 1426–1440.

Brownhill, C. and Kopp, C. 2007, *Socioemotional Development in the Toddler Years: Transitions and Transformations*, Guildford Press, New York.

Campanella Bracken, C. and Lombard, M. 2004, 'Social presence and children: praise, intrinsic motivation, and learning with computers', *Journal of Communication*, 54(1), pp. 22–37.

Derman-Sparks, L. and the Anti-Bias Task Force 1989, *The Anti-Bias Curriculum*, National Association for the Education of Young Children, Washington, DC.

Dunlap, G., Lewis, T. and McCart, A. 2006, 'Program-wide positive behavior support for young children', *Newsletter*, Technical Assistance Center on Positive Behavioral Interventions and Supports, 3(3), <http://www.pbis.org/news/New/Newsletters/Newsletter3.aspx>

Frank, I., Stolarski, E. and Scher, A. 2006, 'Caregivers' mediation and toddlers' emotional responses in the child care context', *Early Child Development and Care*, 176(3), pp. 239–251.

Girolametto, L. and Weitzman, E. 2007, 'Promoting peer interaction skills: professional development for early childhood educators', *Topics in Language Disorders. Social Communication Problems and Peer Interactions*, 27(2), pp. 93–110.

Harris, P. 2007, 'Trust', *Developmental Science*, 10(1), pp. 135–138.

Harris, P., de Rosnay, M. and Pons, F. 2005, 'Language and children's understanding of mental states', *Current Directions in Psychological Science*, 14(2), pp. 69–73.

Hendy, L. and Whitebread, D. 2000, 'Interpretations of independent learning in the early years', *International Journal of Early Years Education*, 8(3), pp. 245–254.

Herbert, J. and Stipek, D. 2005, 'The emergence of gender differences in children's perceptions of their academic competence', *Journal of Applied Developmental Psychology*, 26(3), pp. 276–295.

Honomichl, R. and Chen, Z. 2006, 'Learning to align relations: the effects of feedback and self-explanation', *Journal of Cognition and Development*, 7(4), pp. 527–550.

Klein, E.R., Hammrich, P., Bloom, S. and Ragins, A. 2000, 'Language development and science inquiry: a child-initiated and teacher-facilitated program', Paper presented at the *Annual Meeting of the American Education Research Association*, April, New Orleans, ED440756.

Louden, W., Rohl, M., Barratt-Pugh, C. 2005, *In teachers' hands: effective eliteracy teaching practices in the early years of schooling*, DEST, Canberra.

Macaruso, P., Hook, P. and McCabe, R. 2006, 'The efficacy of computer-based supplementary phonics programs for advancing reading skills in at-risk elementary students', *Journal of Research in Reading*, 29(2), pp. 162–172.

Marshall, H. 1989, 'The development of self-concept', *Young Children*, 44(5), pp. 44–51.

Matthews, D., Lieven, E. and Tomasello, M. 2007, 'How toddlers and preschoolers learn to uniquely identify referents for others: a training study', *Child Development*, 78(6), pp. 1744–1759.

Maynard, A. 2002, 'Cultural teaching: the development of teaching skills in Maya sibling interactions', *Child Development*, 73(3), pp. 969–982.

McWilliams, M. 1999, 'Fostering wonder in young children', Paper presented at the *Annual Meeting of the National Association for Research in Science Teaching*, 28–31 March, Boston, MA, ED444833.

Mundy, P., Block, J., Delgado, C., Pomares, Y., Vaughan van Hecke, A. and Venezia Parlade, M. 2007, 'Individual differences and the development of joint attention in infancy', *Child Development*, 78(3), pp. 938–954.

Penn, C. 2000, 'An evaluation of the impact of attributional feedback on the self-concept of children aged four to six years of age', EDD, Queensland University of Technology.

Rimm-Kaufman, S., Fana, X., Chiua, Y-J. and Youa, W. 2007, 'The contribution of the Responsive Classroom Approach on children's academic achievement: results from a three year longitudinal study', *Journal of School Psychology*, 45(4), pp. 401–421.

Robison, H. and Schwartz, S. 1982, *Designing Curriculum for Early Childhood*, Allyn & Bacon Inc., Boston.

Seefeldt, C. 1980, *Teaching Young Children*, Prentice Hall Inc., New Jersey.

Shin, H., Bjorklund, D. and Beck, E. 2007, 'The adaptive nature of children's overestimation in a strategic memory task', *Cognitive Development*, 22(2), pp. 197–212.

Tomasello, M., Carpenter, M. and Liszkowski, U. 2007, 'A new look at infant pointing', *Child Development*, 78(3), pp. 705–722.

Wieder, S. and Greenspan, S. 1993, 'The emotional basis of learning', in B. Spodek, ed., *Handbook of Research on the Education of Young Children* (pp. 77–87), Macmillan Publishing Company, New York.

Wilkes, G. (ed.) 1979, *Collins Dictionary of the English Language*, Penguin Books, Middlesex.

York, S. 1991, *Roots and Wings: Affirming Culture in Early Childhood Programs*, Toys'n Things Press, Minnesota.

Zhang, H. and Zhou, Y. 2003, 'The teaching of mathematics in Chinese elementary schools', *International Journal of Psychology*, 38(5), pp. 286–298.

Chapter 9

Grouping

Grouping: a number of persons or things located close together, or considered or classed together.

(*The Concise Oxford Dictionary of Current English*, p. 522)

A social group is simply a number of people who interact with each other on a regular basis.

(Giddens 1989, p. 275)

The study of groups and of individuals in groups, as well as the study of individuals by themselves, is necessary for a full understanding of the arts of learning and teaching.

(Hughes and Hughes 1959, p. 2)

Erickson and Shultz (1992) report research from the anthropology and history of education. In traditional societies, they note, individual rather than group instruction is often the norm.

(cited in Pinar et al. 1995, p. 783)

What?

Grouping, as a teaching technique, involves taking decisions about how and when to organise and bring children together to assist their learning.

Groups may be informal or formal. They may be curriculum-based, age-based or project-based. They may be temporary or fixed for a period of time. As most early childhood staff work with more than one child they have to actively decide how to group children, when to do so and why. If staff know what can be accomplished through different types of grouping, they can proactively match their approach to grouping children with their teaching and learning intent.

Issues and debates

There is considerable debate about the ways in which grouping children affects their learning. In this section we focus on three issues within current debates about grouping children.

SIZE MATTERS

Several studies have shown that how children are grouped affects children's learning. For instance, smaller group sizes are associated with: 'more opportunities for teachers to work on extending language, mediating children's social interactions, and encouraging and supporting problem-solving' (Bowman et al. 2001, p. 145); cognitive gains on IQ tests when there is also a high staff–child ratio (Bowman et al. 2001); and improved performance for ethnic minority children in reading and for girls in mathematics (Nye, Hedges and Konstantopoulos 2004). However, in many contexts overall group size or classroom size is not within the control of the teacher. Given this, it may be important for teachers to consider how they can organise their day to spend some time in small groups with children, despite the overall size of their class or group.

DIFFERENCE AND DIVERSITY OF CHILDREN MATTERS

Working in heterogeneous groups is often seen as a key strategy for reducing bias and prejudice between specific groups of children. However, it is important to note the caution on grouping for equity offered by Sleeter and Grant (1999, p. 96):

> Depending on how a teacher structures group work, it can be either very successful or disastrous. Some teachers mistakenly believe that contact by itself among members of different groups is beneficial. Actually, contact by itself can encourage stereotyping, prejudice, and social rejection.

To avoid group work reinforcing bias and rejection it is critical that staff have clear protocols in place for building a co-operative approach to being in groups. These include developing listening skills, conflict management and sharing ideas (refer to the ideas in Chapter 6 for working effectively to promote co-operative learning).

TEACHER DIVERSITY MATTERS

It is also important to be aware of the role that the 'race' of the teacher might play in children's attitudes to their own 'racial' identity and that of other children. A study of children's peer preferences in 58 'mixed-race' classrooms in the USA (Jackson et al. 2006) found that children's preferences were influenced by the 'race' of their teacher. The children were asked who they 'like most', 'like least', and who were 'leaders' and 'fighters'. Black children's 'like most' ratings increased as their presence in the classroom increased. They also received higher ratings as 'leaders' when the teacher was also black. The 'race' of the teacher made no change to the white children's ratings as 'leaders'. It's important that teachers reflect on how their own identity might work for and against the position of children in their groups or classes and their social relationships and then explore ways to strengthen the identities of all children in diverse classrooms.

How?

Informal and formal groups can support productive and pleasing learning relationships, thus maximising children's wellbeing and learning. Informal groups are those that arise spontaneously. Formal groups are those that are deliberately constructed by staff to meet specific teaching and learning goals. They can include age grouping, multi-age grouping, ability grouping, mixed-ability grouping, small task-based groups, whole groups and project groups.

INFORMAL GROUPING

Informal groups may form and reform during a specific learning experience or project, and membership of the group will be flexible and determined by the children rather than by the staff. Allowing time for children to create and maintain informal groups is important for their learning. Membership of informal groups can:

- support literacy learning when children are involved in dramatic play that is rich with literacy resources (Arthur and Makin 2001)
- help children to build close relationships and a sense of community as children share stories with each other (Phillips 2000).

MULTI-AGE GROUPING

Multi-age groups are formed when children of different ages are brought together in the same room or classroom. The children are generally at least one year apart in age. Multi-age groups are also referred to as vertical groupings (Wardle 2005), cross-age groupings, mixed-age groupings or family groupings, and in school settings may be called ungraded, non-graded or composite classrooms (Goldstein 1997). They are generally characterised by older children mentoring younger children and by collaborative learning. As Goldstein explained:

> Multi-age groupings give children the opportunity to be both a younger and an older in the same classroom; they provide opportunities for cross-age tutoring; and they are developmentally appropriate, fostering flexibility and responsiveness to the individual needs of the particular students. (Goldstein 1997, p. 40)

Research exploring peer interactions in preschool children's fantasy play has shown that multi-age grouping can benefit preschool children because 'more capable peers do scaffold activity in play in such a way that learning and development take place' (Fimreite et al. 1999, p. 9). Studies have also consistently found that multi-age groupings can improve children's social skills, reduce discipline problems, increase co-operative problem-solving between children and improve literacy outcomes (Ong et al. 2000).

Effective multi-age grouping requires teachers to support:

- peer tutoring
- cognitive scaffolding
- co-operative learning
- heterogeneous grouping
- emphasis on socio-emotional goals (Ong et al. 2000).

ABILITY GROUPING

Ability grouping sorts children according to their perceived abilities. Individual staff may track children's abilities over time to produce specific ability groups or schools may track student performance over time to formally group children into ability groups. Ability grouping is not without controversy because teachers can form lower expectations for those students in what are considered to be lower ability groups. However, some research suggests that ability groups can enhance the kindergarten children's literacy performance (McCoach et al. 2006).

MIXED-ABILITY OR MIXED CULTURE AND GENDER GROUPING AND INCLUSIVE CLASSROOMS

Mixed grouping (or heterogeneous grouping):

- supports the development of 'multi-racial' knowledge if there is an active multicultural curriculum (Perkins and Mebert 2005)
- enhances literacy learning. For instance, 'using mixed groups of children that include children without language delay may provide additional modelling opportunities for children with language delay' (Lonigan et al. 1999, p. 318). Specifically, in shared reading sessions with children of mixed reading abilities there were positive gains in children's oral language skills, print knowledge and phonological sensitivity for children considered at risk (Lonigan et al. 1999)

- facilitates the development of positive interactions between peers with and without disabilities if staff actively model pro-social behaviours for children (Dietrich 2005)
- supports the improved performance of students considered to be of 'lower ability' (McCoach et al. 2006).

One model of group investigation widely adapted for use in heterogeneous classrooms described by Joyce and Weil (1972) still has considerable currency for supporting learning within heterogeneous groups. Children are required to complete a task or produce a product together, drawing on the different skills within the group.

- Phase 1—encounter puzzling situation (planned or unplanned).
- Phase 2—explore reactions to the situation.
- Phase 3—formulate study task and organise for study (problem definition, role, assignments, etc.).
- Phase 4—independent and group study.
- Phase 5—analyse progress and process.
- Phase 6—recycle activity. (Joyce and Weil 1972, pp. 237–8)

Sleeter and Grant (1999) described two other models for group investigation in heterogeneous groupings: a jigsaw model and team games. In a jigsaw model two groups are required to complete a task. Each group is given different aspects of the task to enable them to become experts in complementary but separate aspects of the task. The two groups then rejoin, each as experts on different aspects of the task and share their learning. Commenting on this model Sleeter and Grant (1999, p. 97) wrote:

> Many teachers like this particular model of cooperative learning because when students get to their second group, everyone has an important piece to contribute that the rest of the group members need. Even the lowest academic achievers have some expertise to share.

In team games children in different groups compete. Each member of the group supports each other to learn as much as possible before the teams meet and compete against each other.

Strategies that help support children's learning in mixed-ability groups include:

- encouraging children to give and receive explanations about what is working or not, how to approach a task or what to do next (Lou et al. 2001)
- encouraging children to focus on learning and how to complete tasks rather than on comparing themselves favourably and unfavourably with other children (Klein et al. 2000).

ISSUE RESPONSE GROUPS

A specific issue or experience in a classroom or centre room may best be explored in a small group. Some examples of this include:

- helping children to cope with a traumatic event such as the experience of war, forced migration, violence and/or abuse. When children have the opportunity to share their ideas and feelings with each other it can reduce the fears and anxieties that are often associated with trauma (Alat 2002)
- working on building peaceful ways to resolve conflicts. Small group drama and socio-dramatic play can help children learn how to work with others in small teams and to co-operate in the execution of a task (Hintz and Stomfay-Stitz 1999).

A specific form of an issue response group is the classroom meeting (also known as circle time or group time) when the whole of the class comes together to discuss events of the day, issues and challenges, and to share concerns and problem-solve. This is a regular event at the Crossley Heath primary school in the reception class:

Some of the children in the class have complained to the teacher (Malcolm) that they are not getting a fair go at the computer learning centre in the classroom. The teacher decides to open their daily classroom meeting with a question that will enable children to share their concerns with the whole class, and so asks the whole group the question, 'How is work going at the computer learning centre?'. There is silence. He asks the question in a different way, 'I wondered if everyone was happy with how work is going at the computer learning centre?'. One of the children who complained to him about it earlier wriggles and then quietly says, 'I like the computers but it's hard to get to play there'. At this point, other children contribute their views and Malcolm continues asking children how they feel and what they think they might do. The discussion brings the group to a consensus about the way forward.

Reflection point: Can you think of other questions that the teacher could have asked the children at the beginning of the meeting?

The group discussions that structure a classroom meeting can help children to reflect on what is happening in the group and why, and build a sense of belonging to a group for children over time (Miller and Nunn 2001). These meetings need to be planned in advance and develop a strong ethic of respect among the group. Joyce and Weil's (1972) description of the phases in a classroom meeting with social problem-solving aims is comprehensive and still helpful for teachers beginning to work on these issues with young children:

The Classroom Meeting Model for social problem-solving includes six phases: (1) establishing a climate of involvement; (2) exposing the problem for discussion; (3) making a personal value judgement; (4) identifying alternative courses of action; (5) making a commitment; and (6) behavioural follow-up. These phases may take place during one or more meetings or they may be quickly accomplished in a single meeting, even for several problems. (p. 209)

Staff can adapt these phases of involvement to construct their approach to group meetings and as a point of reflection on how effectively they led the group meeting. For instance, each of the six phases can be used to produce the following questions for staff to use in developing group discussions:

- How will I or how did I establish a climate of involvement for each of the children?
- How will I or how did I expose the problem for discussion? What are the comments I will or did make? What are the questions I led or will lead with? Will I or did I use a story, image or piece of writing to begin the discussion?
- What is it I value here? How will I or how did I explain that to the children?
- How will I or how did I identify alternative courses of action? What do I see these as being? Will I or did I generate these with the children?
- How will I or how did I make a commitment to act as a result of the discussion? Is a commitment to act necessary?
- How will I or how did I follow up with the children on what we agreed as an action?

SAME-AGE GROUPINGS

While same-age groupings are quite common in many early childhood institutions internationally, Rogoff (2003) has argued that this approach to organising children's learning is a relatively new phenomenon that has been 'prompted by the growth of bureaucracies and reductions in family size' (Rogoff, 2003, p. 125).

The organisation of children into groups of the same age (such as baby, toddler and preschool groups) assumes that children of the same age have similar developmental needs, interests and learning capacities. This assumption is not, however, borne out by research (Ong et al. 2000).

At the Strahan Park Community Child Care Centre the co-ordinator, Pieta, wants to change from same-age groupings to mixed-age groupings in the centre. Some staff are not feeling comfortable with the move:

> **Shira:** 'I think the babies will have a really hard time having their needs met in a mixed-age group. I don't know how we will keep track of their individual needs.'
>
> **Benny:** 'I agree. How are we going to set up our rooms in ways that are developmentally relevant for babies, toddlers and the preschoolers? They each have such different interests.'
>
> **Paula:** 'I have similar concerns but I think we will just have to be creative. The preschool children in my group have different interests now and different capacities developmentally. I have to plan for diverse children now anyway. I am not sure this will be so different.'
>
> **Pieta:** 'I think it could give us more flexibility in how we use each room in the centre. We could have a room just for art and one just for natural materials if we don't have to cater for all the children in one room. Children could move from space to space irrespective of their age.'
>
> **Shira:** 'I like that idea, but how will we keep track of individual children?'
>
> **Paula:** 'That's going to be really important. We could invite staff from one of the other centres locally who have moved to mixed-age groups to talk with us about what they have done.'
>
> _____
>
> *Reflection point:* How might you answer Shira's question about keeping track of individual children?

In all small group work where children are being asked to work together it is important that they have a clear sense of their roles and responsibilities. Staff can support successful group work if they explain what the group is going to do, who is going to do what (roles), set limits and take responsibility for debriefing the group (Hintz and Stomfay-Stitz 1999).

When and why?

Staff members' approaches to curriculum and their specific teaching and learning goals for the children will influence how they group children. For instance, multi-ability grouping can be of most benefit to children's learning when the task is complex and children can bring their joint skills, knowledge and resources to bear on the task (Lou et al. 2001).

GOAL RELEVANCE

In general, staff can use grouping to support children's learning in several ways:

Children's wellbeing
- Early childhood programs can serve as a bridge for children between home and school by providing exposure to the varied interaction styles (large group, small group, one-on-one learning) that the children will encounter in school (Bowman et al. 2001, p. 179).
- The self-esteem and independence of children with disabilities in inclusive classrooms can be enhanced if there is an emphasis on the goals of interdependence and collaboration through small group work (Okagaki and Diamond 2000).
- Older children gain self-esteem and self-confidence when they tutor younger children in cross-age or multi-age groups (Wood and Frid 2005).
- Sharing memories and stories in small groups can help children construct a positive sense of themselves and enable children to integrate the different parts of their lives (Grey 2002).

Specific areas of learning and skill learning in small groups

- Studies show that children's learning using computers is positively enhanced when they are learning in small groups compared to learning as individuals (Lou et al. 2001). Computer use may also support their co-operative play. In one US study of 84 white, middle-income four-year-old children, co-operative play at the computers was greater than when they using manipulative equipment but the same as when they were engaged in block and domestic play (Anderson, Hilton and Wouden-Miller 2003).
- Children's cognitive development can be enhanced when they work in small groups where there is group discussion and collaboration. Although it should be noted that one study (Murphy and Messer 2000) found that children between five and seven years of age, when working alone on a task, were more able to transfer the learning from that task to a similar task.
- Large group instruction in mathematical learning can hide the specific skills and needs of individual children, so individual and small group work is recommended (Sarmana and Clements 2004).

Specific areas of learning in multi-age, multi-ability groups

- Multi-age grouping can increase children's capacity to take responsibility for their own learning (Wood and Frid 2005).
- Children's social skills can grow through grouping less socially competent children with those who are more socially competent (Bovey and Strain 2003).

DEVELOPMENTAL CONSIDERATIONS

Children can benefit developmentally from mixed-age and same-age grouping (Avgitidou 2001) at all ages. Babies can learn from watching each other when they are in small groups and when they have sensitive, responsive and reciprocal relationships with the key carers in their lives. It is important for staff to remember that one-to-one interaction benefits babies by helping them build secure and caring relationships with key people in their lives. When babies are in groups it is important these key adults are with them, can support their interactions and respond to any signs of distress or discomfort a baby experiences in a group setting.

Toddlers learn from each other even when they cannot talk to each other. They learn through watching each other, listening to each other's sounds and focusing on each other's body language. They also teach each other using the same strategies (Pratt 1999). Therefore it is important that toddlers have the opportunity to be in small groups with each other for some part of their day and to have the chance to meet with the minds of others (Rayna 2001, p. 114). If the group size is small it is possible for staff to readily support toddlers as they attempt to interact with each other and in the moments when conflicts arise. Small groups also help toddlers to form friendships and gain from the wellbeing and confidence that being friends with someone brings (Bleiker 1999).

Some action research undertaken by teachers with 31 children between two and five years of age found that multi-age grouping reduced negative behaviours within their group as follows:

> . . . dominance behaviors (hitting, kicking, spitting, taking or demanding objects, etc.) were significantly less prevalent in multiage groupings than in classrooms of same-age peers. The children in the multiage groups also demonstrated higher rates of language exchange—talking to each other and imitating speech—than children with same-age peers. (Logue 2006, p. 70)

Preschoolers take a lively interest in their peers and interacting with them is crucial to their learning. Building informal groups and friendships is critical to their learning. Children can experience learning difficulties in schooling and their academic achievement can be disrupted if they lack friends and positive social interactions with their peers (Coplan et al. 2001). Dramatic play offers staff a powerful vehicle to create opportunities for preschool children to interact socially with their peers. It should be noted that a study in the UK found that dramatic play involved more complex and richer peer relations when it occurred in the outside play area where less structured play materials were available and less adult intervention occurred (Shim et al. 2001).

In the early years of schooling children begin to gain a stronger sense of what is needed to create and maintain a social group. They can see and make sense of more subtle and complex cues from their peers and begin to problem-solve in groups more effectively (Broadhead 2001). However, they will benefit by staff supporting them to learn different ways to enter group play, select and act in different roles in the group and in building a shared sense of direction for the group with others. Older children can also strengthen their own mathematical skill development by taking on an 'advisory' or 'tutoring' role with younger children in the school setting (Wood and Frid 2005) or by working in study groups (Sloane 2007).

Children who are struggling to read do better in dynamic and flexible ability groupings rather than static ones. For instance, students with similar abilities benefit from being with readers of a similar ability in reading aloud sessions. However, if they do literacy work only with children of the same ability they can build a poor self-image and their achievement overall in reading is compromised (Reutzel and Smith 2004).

Equity considerations

'RACE' AND CULTURE

Cultural assumptions can be made by staff about how best to group children to support their learning. Furthermore, a child's cultural background can affect the extent to which they will be encouraged to learn in groups or to learn independently of others. Some cultural groups value independence and self-reliance, while others value collective and collaborative learning. A study of young children in child care settings explored the effects of cultural expectations on children's conflict resolution skills and group behaviour. It compared how children from the Netherlands and Andalusia (Spain) negotiated conflict and found cultural differences in the extent to which children were prepared to disrupt the group to maintain their own point of view (Sanchez Medina et al. 2001). The researchers concluded that cultural values determined the extent to which children focused on maintaining group harmony in their interactions with other children. Taking note of this research, staff need to be alert to how the children they are working with may understand their role in groups and the goals they may prioritise in their group interactions.

Research suggests that not all children learn equally well in groups and that specific forms of grouping benefit some groups of children more than others. For instance, in the USA multi-age grouping was found to benefit the mathematics and literacy learning of non-Hispanic school-age children more than Hispanic children (Ong et al. 2000). Children whose first language is not English can be supported to learn first language through the use of flexible and dynamic ability groupings (Reutzel and Smith 2004). There is particularly strong evidence, from a five-year follow up and an analysis of randomised controlled trials in the USA on class sizes, that minority students' reading skills and performance benefit from small group sizes (Nye, Hedges and Konstantopoulos 2004).

As with all teaching techniques, it is important that staff reflect on the effects of their grouping decisions. Questions to assist in that reflection could include:

- Which children are actively engaged in this group?
- Are there different levels of engagement for children from different ethnic and 'racial' backgrounds?
- Which children have their ideas listened to by other children?
- Which children take a leadership role? Is this role always taken by the same children?

GENDER

There is considerable discussion about the extent to which different forms of grouping children benefit one gender over the other. For instance, differences in the mathematics and literacy achievement of girls and boys remained constant in both multi-age and single-age groups in a study of primary school children's achievement (Ong et al. 2000). However, given that in one extensive US study of class sizes girls did best at mathematics when they were in small classes (Nye, Hedges and Konstantopoulos 2004), size of group may be more important for girls' mathematical success than the nature of the group. In contrast, girls may benefit from multi-age and multi-ability play groupings more than boys do. In one study (Sluss and Stremmel 2004) preschool girls who had complex play skills assumed leadership roles and became even more complex in their play with less-skilled girls. This was not the case for boys.

Same-sex play groupings can influence how teachers and children see girls and boys. In a US study of 60 middle-class preschool children, boys and girls preferred children who engaged in same-sex fantasy play. Boys were liked more by their peers when they engaged in rough and tumble play with other boys than when they did this with girls. Teachers rated the boys and girls who engaged in same-sex fantasy play as more competent (Colwell and Lindsey 2005). It is important for teachers to reflect on the extent to which these dynamics are at play in their particular settings.

Teachers should also remember that in cross-gendered groupings boys as young as two years of age can be more negative towards their peers than girls (Gevers Deynoot-Schaub and Riksen-Walraven 2006). The extent to which this is happening within a specific context should be carefully monitored and challenged where it occurs.

Some research evidence indicates that adults call on boys more than girls to answer questions in small group discussions. It is important for staff to reflect on their interactions with children in small group discussions and small group work and work against any gender biases that they see occurring in their own behaviours (Marshall et al. 1999).

Classroom meetings can be adapted to explore gender dynamics and perspectives within the classroom, as the following extract discussing a study of teaching for gender equity highlights:

Isabel often was observed using workshare, a classroom ritual where students' work is highlighted and discussed in a public forum, to bring gender issues to the foreground of the curriculum . . . Not only did Isabel encourage students to talk about their individual understandings of gender, but she also worked dialectically with students, drawing from her own and others' experiences, to further challenge gender norms. By manipulating and orchestrating workshare to include competing, and often biased, understandings about gender, Isabel encouraged students to question and confront narrow assumptions of gender. (Ryan et al. 2001, p. 53)

Questions which can assist staff to reflect on the gender dynamics of grouping in their classroom include:

- Which children are actively engaged in this group?
- Are there different levels of engagement for boys and girls? Is there any pattern to which girls and boys seem differently engaged?
- Which children have their ideas listened to by other children?
- Which children take a leadership role? Is this role always taken by the same children?
- How do I avoid gender biases in whose voice I invite to be heard in group discussions?

DISABILITY AND ADDITIONAL NEEDS

There is evidence that many children with disabilities in inclusive classrooms may be accepted by their peers, but they may not. In a study of 16 inclusive settings in the USA, Odom et al. (2006) found approximately 50 per cent of children with disabilities in inclusive classrooms were rejected by their peers. In multi-ability grouping, staff need to be alert to this possibility and to the power relations in the play between children of different abilities. Differential power relations have been found between children with disabilities and other children in some studies.

> When sighted children and children who are visually impaired are playing with each other it can be difficult for the latter children to have their ideas taken up in the play; their ideas tend to be ignored by the sighted children. This can lead to the child who is visually impaired withdrawing and playing alone. However, sighted children do respond positively to requests for help by children who are blind. (Janson 2001)

It is also important for staff to take account of the different capacities of young children with disabilities to engage in group activities and co-operative learning. Roe (2001, p. 11) explains in relation to children with Autism Spectrum Disorder:

> In a group situation they are often the 'loners' who stay outside the group or move to a table by themselves. Some children just appear to ignore other children altogether . . . The child with a milder Autism Spectrum Disorder may be able to play co-operatively for short periods, but finds it very difficult when others wish to play something they have not chosen or cannot control.

In these instances it will be important for staff to work with children to help them understand social cues and practise social skills through drama, cartoons and rehearsing behaviours they may need in social situations (Roe 2001).

Questions which can assist staff to reflect on the disability dynamics of grouping in their classroom include:

- Which children are actively engaged in this group?
- Are there different levels of engagement for children with and without disabilities?
- Which children have their ideas listened to by other children?
- Which children take a leadership role? Is this role always taken by the same children?

Reflecting on grouping techniques

1   Define grouping.
2   Consider the following quote from Goldstein (1997, p. 40):

> Ungraded classrooms . . . deal honestly with the vicissitudes of child development, allowing children to learn and grow at their own pace.

To what extent do you agree with this statement?

3   Do the centres you are familiar with organise time for small group learning? Do you think they should? Why?
4   How might groups be organised to encourage toddlers to practise friendship building?
5   How could you use mixed-age grouping to encourage social interaction and conversation between preschool children and babies? What might the benefits of this be? What might the challenges be?
6   How might your philosophy on adult intervention in children's learning influence how you group children and when you group them for learning?
7   Review the extract by Ryan et al. (2001) earlier in this chapter, in the section on gender. To what extent do you think Isabel's use of workshare would contribute to gender equity in the classroom? How might you group children to support your efforts to work for gender equity with young children?

Improving teaching in practice

1 Note the grouping strategies of an early childhood centre, and if and/or how they change during a day or during a week.

2 Discuss with staff the pros and cons of their approach to grouping for individual children within the service.

3 How does the grouping of children support equity of access and participation?
- How and how well were developmental considerations taken into account in how staff organised their groupings of children for learning?
- To what extent were there opportunities for children to have time by themselves?
- To what extent did you see positive social interaction between the children? How did the nature of the grouping link to this?

FURTHER READING

McCoach, B., O'Connell, A. and Levitt, H. 2006, 'Ability grouping across kindergarten using an early childhood longitudinal study', *The Journal of Educational Research*, 99(6), pp. 339–346.

Sleeter, C. and Grant, C. 1999, *Making Choices for Multicultural Education: Five Approaches to Race, Class and Gender*, 3rd edn, Merrill Prentice Hall, New Jersey [refer to pp. 95–107].

Steer, B. and Smith, M. 2005, 'Cross-age learning', *Teacher*, October, pp. 32–33, Australian Council for Educational Research.

ONLINE AND MULTI-MEDIA RESOURCES

Text

Cross-age tutoring research: **http://www.ncjrs.org/html/youthbulletin/9907-2/cross-3.html**

Bovey, T. and Strain, P. (no date), 'Environmental strategies to promote positive social interactions', *What works? Brief 6*, Centre on the Emotional and Social Foundations for Early Learning: **http://www.vanderbilt.edu/csefel/briefs/wwb6.html** (accessed 1 October 2007).

Multi-media

Burchfield, D. 1992, 'An interview', North Central Regional Educational Laboratory. A first grade teacher in Virginia, USA discusses how he groups children to promote learning in his classroom. You can download an audio file or a text transcript: **http://www.ncrel.org/sdrs/areas/issues/students/earlycld/ea100.htm** (accessed 1 October 2007).

'Enhancing learning through multiage grouping', North Central Regional Educational Laboratory. Text, html links and free audio downloads of interviews with teachers in multi-age classrooms: **http://www.ncrel.org/sdrs/areas/issues/methods/instrctn/in500.htm** (accessed 1 October 2007).

'The magic of multi-age', Apple Learning Interchange. Free access text and video clips of the steps a primary school took to implement a multi-age program in the USA: **http://edcommunity.apple.com/ali/story.php?itemID=620**

'Small group teaching', National Board for Professional Teaching Standards. Free access text and video clips on teaching in small groups: **http://newali.apple.com/ali_sites/deli/exhibits/1000348/Small_Group_Instruction.html**

REFERENCES

Alat, K. 2002, 'Traumatic events and children: how early childhood educators can help', *Childhood Education*, 79(1), pp. 2–7.

Allen, R. (ed.), 1990, *The Concise Oxford Dictionary of Current English*, Clarendon Press, Oxford.

Anderson, G., Hilton, S. and Wouden-Miller, M. 2003, 'A gender comparison of the cooperation of 4-year-old children in classroom activity centers', *Early Education and Development*, 14(4), pp. 441–452.

Arthur, L. and Makin, L. 2001, 'High quality early literacy programs', *Australian Journal of Early Childhood*, 26(2), pp. 14–19.

Avgitidou, S. 2001, 'Peer cultural and friendship relationships as contexts for the development of young children's pro-social behaviour', *International Journal of Early Years Education*, 9(2), pp. 145–152.

Bleiker, C. 1999, 'Toddler friendship: the case of Hiro and John', *Young Children*, 54(6), pp. 18–23.

Bovey, T. and Strain, P. 2003, 'Using environmental strategies to promote positive social interactions', *What Works Briefs*, Centre on Social and Emotional Foundations for Early Learning, University of Illinois at Urbana Champaign, Champaign, IL.

Bowman, B., Donovan, M. and Burns, S. 2001, *Eager to Learn: Educating Our Preschoolers*, National Academy Press, Washington, DC.

Broadhead, P. 2001, 'Investigating sociability and cooperation in four and five year olds in reception class settings', *International Journal of Early Years Education*, 9(1), pp. 23–36.

Colwell, M.J. and Lindsey, E.W. 2005, 'Preschool Children's Pretend and Physical Play and Sex of Peer Play Partner', *Sex Roles*, 52, pp. 497–509.

Coplan, R., Wichmann, C. and Lagace-Seguin, D. 2001, 'Solitary-active play behaviour: a marker variable for maladjustment in preschool?', *Journal of Research in Childhood Education*, 15(2), pp. 164–172.

Dietrich, S. 2005, 'A look at friendships between preschool-aged children with and without disabilities in two inclusive classrooms', *Journal of Early Childhood Research*, 3(2), pp. 193–215.

Fimreite, H., Flem, A. and Gudmundsdottir, S. 1999, 'Peer interactions among preschool children in play', Paper presented at *The 8th European Conference for Research on Learning and Instruction*, 24–28 August, Goteborg, Sweden.

Gevers Deynoot-Schaub, M. and Riksen-Walraven, J. 2006, 'Childcare links with child temperament, parent-child interaction and quality care', *Social Development*, 15(4), pp. 710–729.

Giddens, A. 1989, *Sociology*, Polity Press, London.

Goldstein, L. 1997, *Teaching With Love: A Feminist Approach to Early Childhood Education*, Peter Lang Publishing, New York.

Grey, A. 2002, 'Children's earliest memories: a narrative study', *Australian Journal of Early Childhood*, 27(4), pp. 1–5.

Hewitt, V.M. 1999, 'A case study of an inclusive early childhood setting', *Early Education and Development*, 10(4), pp. 532–549.

Hintz, B.F. and Stomfay-Stitz, A. 1999, 'Peace education and conflict resolution through expressive arts in early childhood education and teacher education', Paper presented at the *Annual Conference of the Eastern Educational Research Association*, 26 February, Hilton Head, SC.

Hughes, A. and Hughes, E. 1959, *Learning and Teaching*, 3rd edn, Longman, London.

Jackson, M., Barth, J., Powell, N. and Lochman, J. 2006, 'Classroom contextual effects of race on children's peer nominations', *Child Development*, 77(5), pp. 1325–1337.

Janson, U. 2001, 'Togetherness and diversity in preschool play', *International Journal of Early Years Education*, 9(2), pp. 135–144.

Joyce, B. and Weil, M. 1972, *Models of Teaching*, 3rd edn, Prentice Hall International, New Jersey.

Klein, E.R., Hammrich, P., Bloom, S. and Ragins, A. 2000, 'Language development and science inquiry: a child-initiated and teacher-facilitated program', Paper presented at the *Annual Meeting of the American Education Research Association*, April, New Orleans, ED440756.

Logue, M. 2006, 'Teachers observe to learn: differences in social behavior of toddlers and preschoolers in same-age and multiage groupings', *Young Children*, 61(3), pp. 70–76.

Lonigan, C., Anthony, J., Bloomfield, B., Dyer, S. and Samwel, C. 1999, 'Effects of two shared reading interventions on emergent literacy skills of at-risk preschoolers', *Journal of Early Intervention*, 22(4), pp. 306–322.

Lou, Y., Abrami, P. and d'Apollonia, S. 2001, 'Small group and individual learning with technology: a meta-analysis', *Review of Educational Research*, 71(3), pp. 449–521.

Marshall, N., Robeson, W. and Keefe, N. 1999, 'Gender equity in early childhood education', *Young Children*, 54(4), pp. 9–13.

McCoach, D., O'Connell, A., Reis, S. and Levitt, H. 2006, 'Growing readers: a hierarchical linear model of children', *Journal of Educational Psychology*, 98(1), pp. 14–28.

Miller, M. and Nunn, G. 2001, 'Using group discussions to improve social problem-solving and learning', *Education*, Spring, <http://findarticles.com/p/articles/mi_qa3673/is_200104/ai_n8952854>

Murphy, N. and Messer, D. 2000, 'Differential benefits from scaffolding and children working alone', *Educational Psychology*, 20(1), pp. 17–31.

Nye, B., Hedges, L. and Konstantopoulos, S. 2004, 'Do minorities experience larger lasting benefits from small classes?' *The Journal of Educational Research*, 98(2), pp. 94–100.

Odom, S., Li, S., Sandell, S., Zercher, C., Marquart, J. and Brown, W. 2006, 'Social acceptance and rejection of preschool children with disabilities: a mixed-method analysis', *Journal of Educational Psychology*, 98(4), pp. 807–823.

Okagaki, L. and Diamond, K. 2000, 'Responding to cultural and linguistic differences in the beliefs and practices of families with young children', *Young Children*, 55(3), pp. 74–80.

Ong, W., Allison, J. and Haladyna, T. 2000, 'Student achievement of 3rd graders in comparable single-age and multiage classrooms', *Journal of Research in Childhood Education*, 14(2), pp. 205–215.

Perkins, D. and Mebert, C. 2005, 'Efficacy of multicultural education for preschool children: a domain-specific approach', *Journal of Cross-Cultural Psychology*, 36(4), pp. 497–512.

Phillips, L. 2000, 'Storytelling: the seeds of children's creativity', *Australian Journal of Early Childhood*, 25(3), pp. 1–5.

Pinar, W., Reynolds, W., Slattery, P. and Taubman, P. 1995, *Understanding Curriculum*, Peter Lang Publishing, New York.

Pratt, M. 1999, 'The importance of infant/toddler interactions', *Young Children*, 54(4), pp. 26–27.

Rayna, S. 2001, 'The very beginnings of togetherness in shared play among young children', *International Journal of Early Years Education*, 9(2), pp. 109–116.

Reutzel, D.R. and Smith, J.A. 2004, 'Accelerating struggling readers' progress: a comparative analysis of expert opinion and current recommendations', *Reading and Writing Quarterly*, 20, pp. 63–80.

Roe, D. 2001, *Autism Spectrum Disorder and Young Children*, Australian Early Childhood Association, Watson, ACT.

Rogoff, B. 2003, *The Cultural Nature Of Human Development*, Oxford University Press, Oxford.

Ryan, S., Oschner, M. and Genishi, C. 2001, 'Miss Nelson is missing! Teacher sightings in research on teaching', in S. Grieshaber and G. Cannella, eds, *Embracing Identities in Early Childhood Education: Diversity and Possibilities* (pp. 45–59), Teachers College Press, New York.

Sanchez Medina, J., Lozono, V. and Goudena, P. 2001, 'Conflict management in preschoolers: a cross cultural perspective', *International Journal of Early Years Education*, 9(2), pp. 153–160.

Sarmana, J. and Clements, D. 2004, 'Building blocks for early childhood mathematics', *Early Childhood Research Quarterly*, 19, pp. 181–189.

Shim, S., Herwig, J. and Shelley, M. 2001, 'Preschooler's play behaviours with peers in classroom and playground settings', *Journal of Research in Childhood Education*, 15(2), pp. 149–163.

Sleeter, C. and Grant, C. 1999, *Making Choices for Multicultural Education: Five Approaches to Race, Class and Gender*, 3rd edn, Merrill Prentice Hall, New Jersey.

Sloane, M.W. 2007, 'First grade study groups deepen math learning', *Young Children* 62(4), pp. 78–82.

Sluss, D. and Stremmel, A. 2004, 'A sociocultural investigation of the effects of peer interaction on play', *Journal of Research in Childhood Education*, 18(4), pp. 293–305.

Wardle, F. 2005, 'Rethinking early childhood practices', *Early Childhood News*, 17(1), pp. 12–19.

Wood, K. and Frid, S. 2005, 'Early childhood literacy in a multiage setting', *Mathematics Education Research Journal*, 16(3), pp. 80–99.

Chapter 10

Listening

Listening: to take heed, to pay attention (to concentrate on hearing something).

(Collins Dictionary of the English Language, p. 858)

When teachers listen to children, they are, first of all, building a climate of acceptance of the children and their ideas.

(Seefeldt 1980, p. 148)

. . . listening can be understood as more than just a tool or instrument: it can also be understood as an ethic, a way of being that permeates all practice and relationships.

(Moss 2005, p. 5)

What?

When you listen to someone you attend to them. You concentrate on what is said and what is not said; you note what they are saying and not saying and think about it carefully. When staff use listening as a teaching strategy, they try to understand what children are saying and, through doing so, try to better understand them and to become sensitive to their ideas (Rinaldi 2005). Listening is a process of reciprocity in which we attend to what is said and meant to build an ethic of care and respect (Moss 2005). It is the foundation of respectful learning relationships with children and it helps us to enter their ways of thinking and being in the world (Rinaldi 2005). It helps us to attend to children's thought.

Lerner et al. (1987) identified six interrelated phases to everyday listening: hearing, focusing on what is heard, identifying what is heard, translating this into meaning, interpreting it and then remembering it. When staff listen to children in this way, they feel valued and included. This can increase their sense of inclusion, self-esteem and confidence.

Issues and debates

TAKING CHILDREN SERIOUSLY—MAKING TIME TO LISTEN

Many adults are poor listeners who are '. . . preoccupied, distracted and forgetful nearly 75 per cent of the time' (Renck Jalongo 1995). So if staff want children to become thoughtful and active listeners they will need to guard against such tendencies in themselves. Sometimes staff don't have sufficient time to listen to what a particular child has to say because they are needed elsewhere in the play area or are in the midst of another conversation. On such occasions, staff can still let children know that they value what they have to say by suggesting they tell staff about it in some other way. Renck Jalongo (1995, pp. 14–15) suggested children could be encouraged to write or draw what they want to say:

> We can still let the children know that we are listening by channeling the child's enthusiasm into other means of self-expression, such as drawing or writing.

LISTENING AS AN ETHICAL PEDAGOGY—WELCOMING THE 'OTHER'

Drawing from the work and thinking in the Reggio Emilia pre-primary schools in Italy (Dahlberg and Moss 2005) there is a growing interest in the idea of a pedagogy of listening as a driving ethic for the practice of relationships with children in early childhood spaces. Listening is seen as an ethical and political encounter with children that opens us up to 'otherness and difference, connectedness and relationships' (p. 15) as we struggle to make meaning of what is said and thought, leaving behind our preconceptions of what should or can be said by children. Rinaldi (2005), talking of the pre-primary schools of Reggio Emilia, described how listening is embedded into the fabric of the programs, and the challenges in this, as follows:

> Learning how to listen is a difficult undertaking; how you open yourself to others, and we all need this. Competent listening creates a deep opening and predisposition toward change. Listening is a premise of every learning relationship. (p. 114)

If we take this view of listening, then making the time for listening to children is a core ethical responsibility of early childhood educators.

LISTENING AS AN ETHIC AND PRACTICE OF CHILDREN'S RIGHTS

There is also growing interest in the place that listening has as a practice for honouring young children's right to participate in decision-making about matters that affect them. This interest in listening as a practice of participation that enacts children's rights extends across several fields including environmental planning (Roe 2006), disability support services (Naylor and Prescott 2004) and local government policy (MacNaughton, Hughes and Smith 2007). From within this perspective, being listened to is a right that children have. The challenges that this brings teachers are several. First, they have to reflect on how they will respond to what children say. Secondly, they need to consider the extent to which what children tell them will influence their decision-making. Thirdly, the idea of children as citizens with the right to have a say in matters that affect them unsettles traditional power relationships between adults and children, and teachers need to reflect on if and how they will share their power in early childhood spaces with young children. This often involves rethinking their image of the child and seeing the child as a knowing, competent meaning-maker within their world (MacNaughton, Hughes and Smith 2007).

How?

Staff can improve their listening skills by:

Building a climate of respect for listening
- ensuring children know that adults believe that they are 'worthy of being listened to' (Fraser 2007, p. 18)
- trying to think carefully about what important things the children are saying to staff and to each other and practice 'listening for thought' (Dahlberg and Moss, p. 15)

- being open and sensitive to what young children would like to share or say (Clark, Moss and Kjørholt 2005)
- welcoming what children have to say to us in all its diversity
- modelling active listening skills to help children learn to listen to others
- responding to children's comments with care and thought. For further information on this issue, readers should refer to the ways of developing discussions with children in Chapter 5, and to Chapter 8 about giving children feedback.

Strategically planning for listening in the group
- ensuring children have access to different ways to speak and share their ideas that could include talking, writing, drawing, dramatising, painting, photographing, building, singing and acting (Clark, Moss and Kjørholt 2005)
- acting as a scribe for what children say when they ask for help. Ideas for documenting children's work can be found in Chapter 24

A class of six-year-olds have been on an excursion to Scienceworks (a science museum for children in Melbourne). Their teachers have set aside time for the children to recall their experiences. One teacher is sitting at a table with the children as they draw pictures of the various exhibits and chat about what they have seen. He listens carefully to what they are saying and offers to be a scribe for two of the children while the other children make their own notes on their drawings. One older child sings a song about her visit.

Reflection point: How might digital technology help you be a scribe for children?

- using visual aids and props to links help link words and meanings (Fraser 2007)
- using group meetings to help older children practise listening to each other. The teacher can model turn-taking in the early meetings until the children become familiar with this process (Fraser 2007). The more dialogic (two-way) the conversations, the more effective they will be in building children's capacities for speaking and listening more broadly (Jones 2007)
- using interactive new technologies that encourage children to learn through listening as well as by doing. In Europe an interactive musical system (the Continuator) has been shown to work well to engage three- to five-year-old children in musical listening and doing (Addessi and Pachet 2005)
- teaching children about listening skills so they can build their own skills in listening and learning language through which to express themselves (Morris and Leavey 2006)
- using new technologies that support children to construct stories. US researchers found that the Story Listening System (SLS) was helpful in this regard (Cassell 2004)
- using new technologies that broaden our sense of what listening is. Students can listen to digital books, re-listen to key ideas and moments through the replay and pause facilities in the digital environment, and record what they would like to listen and re-listen to (Rose and Dalton 2007). For preschool children it is important that these allow for repetition of favoured stories and sounds. German researchers found that preschool children enjoyed novel stories with repetition, and characters who had music or other attention-seeking devices attached to them (Vorderer et al. 2006).

When and why?

GOAL RELEVANCE
Staff listen to and understand what children are telling them when they are trying to:

- encourage children to share a thought or an experience. It is important for staff to listen so the children learn that what they say is important to others. They need to know that their thoughts and comments on the world matter:

> Jack brings his excitement about a car crash that he's seen to the kindergarten. Arthur, his teacher, allows Jack to tell his story and listens attentively. Later on, Arthur makes sure he gives Jack more time to talk about what he saw.
>
> _Reflection point:_ How else could Arthur listen to Jack's story so he better understands what it meant for Jack?

- help children explain their ideas to others. If staff listen to children, they can learn more about what children understand and thus make their teaching more relevant to the children's growing interests and developmental abilities. Vivienne Paley, in a now classic book on teaching and learning with young children (1986, p. 94), suggested that listening is often the best way to learn:

> And I, outsider to three-year-old thinking, am learning to listen at the doll corner doorway for the sounds of reality.

- decide if and when to intervene in children's play. Staff will have a better sense of when children's play needs adult guidance, support or control if they listen carefully to children's exchanges with themselves and with others
- learn about and contribute to the children's language development:

> Cathy notices that Mitzu, who is 20 months old, has just begun to join more than one word together. She hears 'me up' and 'shoes on'. This tells Cathy that Mitzu has moved to another level in her language development, and is able to ask for what she wants more easily.

- show children that their play and their ideas about the world are valued (Clark, Moss and Kjørholt 2005):

> Dina is talking to her Year 1 class about how they might use their 'free play' time in the afternoon. 'I saw William making tunnels in the digging patch yesterday; he was channelling the water in three different directions. He has thought about how to do this very carefully, I wonder who would like to work some more on William's project?'
>
> _Reflection point:_ In what other ways could Dina show the children that their ideas are valued?

- develop an emergent and democratic curriculum based on children's interests and curiosities. If staff are listening carefully to children they will have a strong sense of what children's current interests are and thus be in a strong position to respond to and extend their interests (Clark, Moss and Kjørholt 2005)
- allow children to express their questions, fears and worries after they have experienced a traumatic event. As increasing numbers of young children experience or see traumatic events, such as those associated with the attacks of September 11, 2001 in New York and Washington, DC, it is important that they have the opportunity to have their questions, fears and worries heard and responded to by adults around them. Listening to children's feelings can validate them and help children learn from each other about fears and feelings (Alat 2002).

DEVELOPMENTAL CONSIDERATIONS

Young children's wellbeing is strongly influenced by their interactions with staff in early childhood settings. For instance, a study of caregiver relationships with babies in the Netherlands found that babies are more emotionally positive when staff interactions are co-operative and sensitive (Esther, Riksen-Walraven and de Weertha 2007). High-quality interactions with babies are responsive, respectful and attentive, and an important ingredient in such interactions is listening. When staff take time to listen to a baby's babbles and coos, they show the baby they care about her or his efforts to communicate (Honig 2007). Babies need to experience such care and attention to thrive.

Staff can learn about a baby's likes and dislikes by listening to her gurgles, chuckles, coos, grunts, giggles, babbles or cries. Each baby will communicate through a range of sounds and a range of tones within those sounds. For example, some babies grunt when they actively enjoy the effort of stretching their limbs, trying to crawl or pushing themselves up, while other babies might gurgle during such movements. Learning each baby's repertoire of sounds and the meanings of those sounds can help staff make judgments about when that baby needs further support and encouragement. It can also help staff to recognise when a baby is tired, hungry, unwell, excited, frustrated, fascinated or rested. Staff can then judge how best to be with a baby. Sometimes cuddles will be appropriate and at other times new challenges will be more appropriate. What is critical for a baby's wellbeing is that staff respond to her efforts to communicate her needs and interests. Responsive, sensitive and co-operative caregiving is at the heart of best practice with babies and toddlers (Benson McMullen 1999; Thompson 2001; Esther, Riksen-Walraven and de Weertha 2007).

Listening to toddlers as they struggle to verbally express themselves is also a sign that you care about them and respect them (Winter 2004). If staff take time to find out what is being expressed, children learn that it is worth sharing their ideas and thoughts with staff. If, however, staff pretend to have heard what was said or give up on what was said, children learn that the adults don't care about what they have to say. At 20 months of age, Jo is learning that his thoughts are important to his caregiver:

> Jo is 'talking' animatedly with his caregiver as she hangs out the bibs. He is playing with the pegs and looking up at the clothes line. Jo uses intonation and patterns that are very like 'real' speech. He uses sentence-like structures. After about one minute of this type of verbalising, he looks expectantly up at his caregiver. The caregiver tries to guess what Jo has been talking about. She uses all the clues available to her, drawing on the immediate environment and her knowledge of Jo. 'Yes, Jo', she responds, 'It is windy today and the clothes are blowing about a lot in the wind'.
>
> _____
>
> *Reflection point:* In what other ways could Jo's caregiver listen to what toddlers say?

However, sometimes it can be hard for staff to hear what toddlers might be trying to tell them. When they are in a rush to express their wishes, their words can be garbled or muddled. On such occasions, staff can ask the child to repeat themselves slowly and listen carefully to what the child says. Slowing a toddler down improves staff's chances of understanding what they are being told. Slowing a toddler's speech is likely to improve the clarity of their key word and will change their tone of voice to a lower, less excited pitch. Changes in '. . . the tone of voice, the rate of the utterance, [and] keywords' (Partington and McCudden 1992, p. 139) can all improve staff's ability to understand what is being said.

Confusion over meaning can arise when toddlers begin to use two- and three-word sentences such as, 'Me toilet', 'Go water' or 'Me bike home'. These sentences generally consist of a noun or verb, or a noun and a verb together, and are known as telegraphic sentences because they rely on a few words to express their meaning. Telegraphic sentences are an important phase in children's expressive language development. However, sometimes a toddler's sentences are so 'telegraphic' that their meaning is unclear. For example, 'Me blocks' could mean, 'I would like to play with the blocks' or it could mean, 'Come and see the block

Kylie and Isobel listen to Tristan.

building I have just made'. In such instances, staff can help clarify the meaning by asking a toddler to show them what they want or to take them where they want to go. Staff can also turn a sentence into a question and clarify the intended meaning through a toddler's response. For example, if a toddler says, 'Me toilet', staff could ask, 'Would you like to go to the toilet?' or 'Have you just been to the toilet?'. The toddler's response will probably reveal their intended meaning. Once again, staff should take the time to listen to the toddler's response, rather than give up or assume that they know what was intended. Toddlers need to learn that their communication matters.

Listening is also important for toddlers' language learning. Toddlers can learn new words by listening to others. Researchers in the USA have shown that toddlers can learn new and novel words through overhearing them and listening to other people's conversations (Floor and Akhtar 2006).

Preschoolers' language skills increase rapidly and they constantly use language during the day to express their ideas and feelings to themselves and to others. Children between three and four years of age will have an average vocabulary of between 1500–2000 words and they can readily relate their experiences and feelings (Buckley 2003). Staff can learn a great deal about preschool children's social, emotional and cognitive developmental interests and needs by listening to what they say. Listening can, therefore, provide staff with valuable information about how to best support the preschool child's learning across various developmental areas. For example, preschoolers will often talk to themselves for long periods of time when they are concentrating on an activity or when they are involved in imaginative play:

> Hannah plays in a corner of the room that is set up like a home environment. She is playing with her favourite doll, bathing her, dressing and feeding her, and putting her to bed. 'I'm gonna take the towel, yeah, the towel, and rub your head, rub, rub, rub, you gotta rub to make clean . . . not too hard 'cos it hurts, like that, yeah . . . like that. Now, finish, get clothes . . . where put them . . . can't find them . . . nothing here. Stop wriggling, doll. Bad to wriggle. Now, where . . . where is nappy? Up botty, now put on nappy. Oops! Powder first . . . that's right, powder. Sit up now, that's right, good girl, that's good, good girl for mummy, mummy loves you . . . good girl.'
>
> *Reflection point:* How could you extend the ways that you listen to preschoolers?

A child's monologues can tell staff a good deal. For example, staff listening to the above monologue could learn that Hannah is familiar with a baby's bathing and dressing routine. She remembers the sequence of the routine and goes through it much as she must have seen an adult go through it. She imitates an adult in her play and talks to the doll much as an adult might talk to a child. She uses language to monitor her play.

Vygotsky referred to this language as 'private speech' and believed that it is important to children's ability to develop new cognitive skills and abilities. More detailed information on the role of private speech in children's cognitive development can be found in Chapter 29.

Listening to children can also provide staff with important information about children's social relationships. Children can use speech to share, negotiate and maintain positive social relationships with each other. They can also use it to demand, command, threaten, exaggerate, boast, tease, tell tales and name-call (Buckley 2003). By listening to how children use speech, staff can judge how and when to support children in their social relationships and how and when to help children learn positive ways of relating to each other.

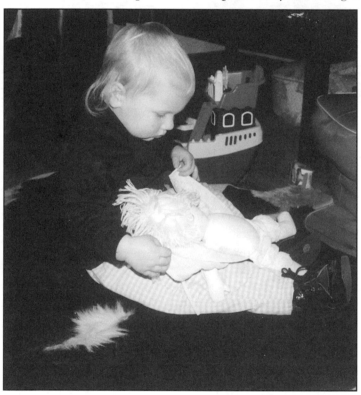

Hannah talks to herself as she undresses a doll.

Children's ability to tell simple stories is an important pre-reading skill. Storytelling helps children develop an understanding of narrative and helps them build their own language fluency (Phillips 2000). Listening to children's stories encourages them to tell more stories as they learn that staff take their stories seriously. In addition, listening to children's stories can also help teachers assess children's understanding of narrative and their current level of language fluency. Teachers can then target their questions and comments on the story to prompt children to fill the gaps in their narrative and to help children clarify their story so that others can understand it (Soundy and Humadi Genisio 1994). By about the age of five, children can begin to include feelings and reasons for doing things in their stories. Staff can use this development to help build on children's vocabulary for talking about emotions and moral behaviour.

Young children's stories will often be about events in their daily lives. Children will often enthusiastically share their story of what happened the night before when the electricity went off and no-one could remember where the candles were, or what dad did when the new dog fouled the carpet. Staff need to listen to these stories with respect and show acceptance of the children's diverse family values and lifestyles. There is much diversity that staff will encounter. Some children will be leading very complex lives, for example living with their dad and his new partner on the weekend and their mum during the week. Other children will have a parent who is not in any permanent relationship but has lots of friends visiting. Still other children will have gay or lesbian parents who may or may not lead a very traditional lifestyle. If children are to share their stories with staff they will need to know that their family lifestyle is accepted and respected. They will learn about staff's attitudes to their family lifestyle by how staff listen to their stories. Staff who raise eyebrows, snicker or ask questions in disbelief when children tell their stories of daily family life will quickly silence such stories. Such silencing means a lost opportunity for assisting children's acquisition of language and pre-reading skills.

Staff can also learn a lot about preschool children by listening to their play narratives. In their pretend play children often construct a well-structured narrative that can tell adults much about what children feel, know and wish to explore further. In a study of 30 Turkish preschool children, researchers found a clear narrative structure to their pretend play and found that children's stories are more clearly structured when they can 'play' them than when they are asked to tell them (Ilgaz and Aksu-Koç 2005).

Listening to children's comments and questions is an important strategy in building children's interest and sense of wonder in the world about them (Jacobs and Crowley 2006). For instance, teachers can support the growth of wonder in children when they listen attentively to children's theories, comments and questions about the world and demonstrate interest and respect for them by commenting and sometimes extending on the child's questions and comments.

Peer-tutoring, in which one child listens to another and supports another child's learning, can be an effective way to build children's oral fluency in the early years of school. A study of 27 peer tutors and tutees in the USA found increased oral fluency in those students who participated in the program (Wright and Cleary 2006).

Equity considerations

'RACE' AND CULTURE

As mentioned above, children's expressive language is influenced by their age and stage of development. However, it is also influenced by the context in which they try to express themselves. Children are more likely to want to express themselves in an environment where their ideas are valued and are not subject to bias. They will feel that their ideas are valued when staff take the time to listen to them. Staff need to ensure that they listen for equal time and with equal attention to each child in the group, irrespective of 'race' or cultural background.

There is some evidence to suggest that staff distribute their listening time unevenly between children from different cultural and 'racial' backgrounds. Ebbeck (1991) pointed to staff's tendency to spend more time with 'talkative' children than with 'quiet' children. This can result in staff spending less time with children learning English as a second language (ESL) than with English-speaking children because many children learning ESL go through a 'silent period' in which they do not communicate verbally (Clarke 1992). Once children with an ESL background are through their 'silent period', staff should take time to listen to their responses to questions. Partington and McCudden (1992, p. 139) argued that:

> The second language learner needs time to process what is said. It may involve receiving the English, translating it into the first language, arriving at a response and translating it into English and them giving it in a form understood by the teacher.

Staff need to provide time for such processing, translating and replying to occur. When staff wait for a response they are supporting and respecting the child's efforts to learn a second language. Some recent research suggests that allowing a response time for children learning English as second language is important to their successful learning of letter names (Gilbertson and Bluck 2006). Listening to children's responses to teaching in this way helps the ESL child to develop their second language competence.

Young babies in the first six months of life prefer to hear their native language spoken rather than other languages (Valji and Polka 2004). This preference suggests that it is important for staff to ensure that babies in early childhood settings have the opportunity to listen to their native language during the day. The opportunity for children to listen to their own language provides them with a sense that their language is valued. As English is the dominant language spoken in most early childhood centres in Australia, children whose language is other than English may have few opportunities to listen to their first language and, thus, to maintain and enrich their competence in it. Its important that children can speak their first language in the preschool setting as this not only enhances their sense of belonging but proficiency in their first language builds gains for children across the curriculum more broadly. Some ways to support first language proficiency include:

- employing appropriate bilingual staff in their centres
- encouraging parents and/or community members who speak a child's first language to participate in their program
- including resources and learning materials in the child's first language as a matter of course within the program.

Children whose first language is not English will clearly benefit from hearing their own language spoken in the early childhood centre, but so will the whole group. Each child can benefit by experiencing the richness and diversity of sounds and meanings from a language other than their own, and staff can take the opportunity to model respect for and enjoyment in diversity of language. Stories and folk tales have been found to be an effective way to help learning a second language. When there are images associated with words in this way it helps children to reconstruct the storyline and the language that goes with it (Verdugo, Belmonte and Alonso 2007). Using a pre-test, post-test research design, Spanish researchers found that digital stories offered an important way to support second language learning for 220 six-year-old Spanish children. The researchers tested children's listening and recall as part of the study and found the digital storytelling environment supported the growth of children's comprehension skills.

Children who are second language learners in primary school may also benefit from some direct instruction in listening. A small study in Singapore showed that direct teacher instruction in listening gave students a deeper understanding of how listening works, increased confidence in listening-based classroom tasks and used better strategies for making sense of language learning tasks (Goh and Taib 2006).

It is also important that staff listen closely to children's comments and conversations with each other so they can be alert to biased or racist comments and respond to them proactively. Chapter 26 on philosophising and Chapter 22 on deconstructing have some specific suggestions about how best to approach this work.

GENDER

Staff can learn a lot about children's gender relationships through listening to how children speak to each other. Staff can hear if boys and girls are speaking in ways that show respect for the other or not. They can note if children are using speech pro-socially to share, negotiate and maintain positive social relationships with each other. They can also note who is using speech anti-socially to demand, command, threaten, exaggerate, boast, tease, tell tales and name-call. Noting the gender balance in use of pro-social and anti-social speech gives staff important information about if and how children's play is gender-biased, and can alert them to the need to intervene immediately in children's play to stop or challenge what is happening. For example, a staff member who is listening to a group of boys and a girl playing and hears the boys teasing the girl could immediately intervene to stop the teasing. However, they could also use the experience to plan how to reduce gender bias in the future by, for example, teaching the girl concerned how to stand up to the boys in the future and where to go for support whenever it happens.

It is particularly important to listen to girls' and boys' pretend play when they cross traditional gender boundaries in it—for example, when girls move into the blocks areas when boys are present or when boys play with dolls when girls are present. In these situations, gender-based teasing, verbal threatening and name-calling between girls and boys can occur. Girls can also have their ideas and suggestions ignored by boys in these situations. If staff are listening carefully to the play that occurs when girls do cross the gender boundaries in their play then they can actively intervene to support positive joint interactions and to ensure that girls are supported to express their ideas and have them heard by their peers.

DISABILITY AND ADDITIONAL NEEDS

Listening to children with disabilities is an important way to understand how inclusive educational practices are working or not working for them. A researcher found that children with disabilities who face marginalisation in inclusive primary schools in Cyprus could talk about their marginalisation and how they felt about it and thus shed important light on the complex ways in which they were affected by their marginalisation (Kyriaki 2006).

The successful integration of children with disabilities into an early childhood program depends on building positive and respectful attitudes towards people with disabilities. Listening to children's discussions with each other can help staff to assess the extent to which children are developing positive and respectful attitudes towards people with disabilities. Staff need to be alert to the disrespectful ways in which children without disabilities can speak to those with disabilities, including teasing, name-calling or verbally threatening. If this occurs, staff must swiftly counter the effect of such disrespect on the child at whom it is targeted and help the children to understand why such language is unacceptable.

Listening to children's questions about people with disabilities can also help staff to assess how far children have developed positive and respectful attitudes towards people with disabilities. From children's questions, staff can learn about children's understandings of the lifestyle, feelings, needs and interests of people with disabilities and about their misconceptions, fears or prejudices concerning disabilities. Staff can also judge the extent to which children without disabilities feel positively or negatively about people with disabilities. Staff can use this information to plan how to correct and enrich what the children know about disabilities. Questions such as, 'Why won't Sammy climb to the top of the slide by himself?' offer staff opportunities to explain that Sammy's arms and legs are not strong enough for him to climb the slide without help.

Reflecting on listening techniques

1 Briefly define active listening.
2 What do you think is the major difference between listening and hearing?
3 What might you learn about a three-year-old child's cognitive skills through listening to their private speech as they complete a puzzle?
4 What are the main reasons you might listen to a baby's sounds when they are playing with a mobile above their cot?
5 List three ways you could show a four-year-old child you were interested in their ideas if you did not have the time to listen to them.
6 What are three characteristics that you need to be an effective listener?
7 Record the sounds and movements made by a baby under 12 months of age during a 15-minute observation period. How did the baby express pleasure? How did it express displeasure? Would listening to the baby be sufficient to tell you when it needed your attention?
8 Record the monologue of a three-year-old child. What can you learn about the child's developmental interests and needs from this monologue?
9 Observe a small group of five-year-old boys and girls engaged in play with each other. How often did they use language to develop positive social relationships? How often did they use language to develop negative social relationships? Were there any gender differences in the use of pro-social and anti-social speech?
10 Observe a small group session between an early childhood worker and a group of four-year-old children. What factors made it easy and what factors made it difficult for the worker to:

- make time to listen to children?
- wait a few seconds before responding?
- model active listening skills?
- respond to children's comments with care and thought?

Improving teaching in practice

1 Videotape the conversations you have with children during several five-minute teaching periods.
2 How well did you:
- make time to listen to children?
- wait a few seconds before responding?
- model active listening skills?
- respond to children's comments with care and thought?
3 How and how well did you take account of equity considerations as you listened to the children?
4 What are your areas of strength and weakness in listening to promote children's learning?
5 How can you work to improve your listening techniques in practice?

FURTHER READING

Deans, J., Brown, R. and Dikes, H. 2005, 'A place for sound: raising children's awareness of their sonic environment', *Australian Journal of Early Childhood*, 30(4), pp. 43–47.

Fleer, M. and Cahill, A. 2001, *I Want to Know: Learning about Science*, Australian Early Childhood Association, Watson, ACT [refer to pp. 3–12].

Fraser, S. 2007, 'Play in other languages', *Theory into Practice*, 46(1), pp. 14–22.

Rinaldi, C. 2006, *In Dialogue with Reggio Emilia: Listening, Researching and Learning* Routledge Falmer, Oxon, pp. 65–68.

Winter, P. 2004, 'Respectful relationships: listening to the voices of infants and toddlers in care', *Every Child*, 10(2), pp. 24–25.

ONLINE AND MULTI-MEDIA RESOURCES

Text

'Tips for listening', *The Poetry Archive*. Full text: **http://www.poetryarchive.org/poetryarchive/teachersTips.do**

Betrand, J. 'Teaching speaking and listening skills', British Council: **http://www.britishcouncil.org/languageassistant-teaching-listening-and-speaking.htm**

Multi-media

'Early years workshop—listening and questioning', *Teachers' TV* (accessed 21 October 2007). Free access download: **http://www.teachers.tv/video/3437**

REFERENCES

Addessi, A. and Pachet, F. 2005, 'Experiments with a musical machine: musical style replication in 3–5 year old children', *British Journal of Music Education*, 22, pp. 21–46.

Alat, K. 2002, 'Traumatic events and children: how early childhood educators can help', *Childhood Education*, 79(1), pp. 1–8.

Benson McMullen, M. 1999, 'Achieving best practices in infant and toddler care and education', *Young Children*, 54(4), pp. 69–77.

Buckley, B. 2003, *Children's Communication Skills: From Birth to Five Years*, Routledge, New York.

Cassell, J. 2004, 'Towards a model of technology and literacy development: story listening systems', *Journal of Applied Development Psychology*, 25(1), pp. 75–105.

Clark, A., Kjørholt, A. and Moss, P. 2005, *Beyond Listening: Children's Perspectives on Early Childhood Services*, Paul Chapman Publishing, London.

Clarke, P. 1992, *English as a 2nd Language in Early Childhood*, FKA Multicultural Resource Centre, Melbourne.

Dahlberg, G. and Moss, P. 2005, *Ethics and politics in early childhood education*, Routledge Falmer, Oxfordshire.

Ebbeck, M. 1991, *Early Childhood Education*, Longman Cheshire, Melbourne.

Esther, M., Riksen-Walraven, J. and de Weertha, C. 2007, 'Infants' interactions with professional caregivers at 3 and 6 months of age: a longitudinal study', *Infant Behavior and Development*, 30(4), pp. 631–640.

Floor, P. and Akhtar, N. 2006, 'Listening', *Infancy*, 9(3), pp. 327–339.

Fraser, S. 2007, 'Play in other languages', *Theory into Practice*, 46(1), pp. 14–22.

Gilbertson, D. and Bluck, J. 2006, 'Improving responsiveness to intervention for English-Language learners: a comparison of instruction pace on letter naming rates', *Journal of Behavioural Education*, 15(3), pp. 131–147.

Goh, C. and Taib, Y. 2006, 'Metacognitive instruction in listening for young learners', *ELT Journal*, 60(3), pp. 222–232.

Honig, A. 2007, 'Oral language development', *Early Child Development and Care*, 177(6 & 7), pp. 581–613.

Ilgaz, H. and Ayhan Aksu-Koç, A. 2005, 'Episodic development in preschool children's play-prompted and direct-elicited narratives', *Cognitive Development*, 20(4), pp. 526–544.

Jacobs, G. and Crowley, K. 2006, *Play Projects and Preschool Standards: Nurturing Children's Sense of Wonder and Joy in Learning*, Redleaf Press, St. Paul, MN.

Jones, D. 2007, 'Speaking, listening, planning and assessing: the teacher's role in developing metacognitive awareness', *Early Child Development and Care*, 177(6/7), pp. 569–579.

Kyriaki, M. 2006, 'Conversations with children: making sense of marginalization in primary school settings', *European Journal of Special Needs Education*, 21(1), pp. 39–54.

Lerner, J., Mardell-Czudnowski, C. and Goldenberg, D. 1987, *Special Education for the Early Childhood Years*, 2nd edn, Prentice Hall Inc., New Jersey.

MacNaughton, G., Hughes, P. and Smith, K. 2007, 'Rethinking approaches to working with children who challenge', *International Journal of Early Childhood*, 39(1), pp. 39–58.

Morris, T. and Leavey, G. 2006, 'Promoting phonological awareness in nursery-aged children through a Sure Start Early Listening programme', *International Journal of Early Years Education*, 14(2), pp. 155–168.

Moss, P., Clarke, A. and Kjørholt, A. (eds) 2005, *Beyond Listening: Children's Perspectives on Early Childhood Services*, The Policy Press, Bristol, UK.

Naylor, A. and Prescott, P. 2004, 'Invisible children? The need for support groups for siblings of disabled children', *British Journal of Special Education*, 31(4), pp. 199–206.

Paley, V. 1986, *Mollie is Three: Growing up in School*, University of Chicago Press, Chicago.

Partington, G. and McCudden, V. 1992, *Ethnicity and Education*, Social Science Press, Sydney.

Phillips, L. 2000, 'Storytelling: the seeds of children's creativity', *Australian Journal of Early Childhood*, 25(3), pp. 1–5.

Renck Jalongo, M. 1995, 'Promoting active listening in the classroom', *Childhood Education*, 72(1), pp. 13–18.

Rinaldi, C. 2005, *In Dialogue with Reggio Emilia: Listening, Researching and Learning*, Routledge Falmer, London.

Roe, M. 2006, '"Making a wish": children and the local landscape', *Local Environment*, 11(2), pp. 163–182.

Rose, D. and Dalton, B. 2007, 'Plato revisited: learning through listening in the digital world', Paper published by *Recording for the Blind and Dyslexic*, 9 January.

Seefeldt, C. 1980, *Teaching Young Children*, Prentice Hall Inc., New Jersey.

Soundy, C. and Humadi Genisio, M. 1994, 'Asking young children to tell the story', *Childhood Education*, 71(1), pp. 20–23.

Thompson, R.A. 2001, 'Development in the first years of life', *The Future of Children*, 11(1), 21–33.

Valji, A. and Polka, A. 2004, 'Language preference in monolingual and bilingual infants', *The Journal of the Acoustical Society of America*, 115(5), pp. 2435–2510.

Verdugo, D., Ramirez, V. and Alonso, I. 2007, 'Using digital stories to improve listening comprehension with Spanish young learners of English', *Language, Learning and Technology*, 11(1), pp. 87–101.

Vorderer, P., Böcking, S., Klimmt, C. and Ritterfeld, U. 2006, 'What makes preschoolers listen to narrative audio tapes?', *Zeitsschrift für Medienpsychologie*, 18(1), pp. 9–18.

Wilkes, G. (ed.) 1979, *Collins Dictionary of the English Language*, Penguin Books, Middlesex.

Winter, P. 2004, 'Respectful relationships: listening to the voices of infants and toddlers in care', *Every Child*, 10(2), pp. 24–25.

Wright, J. and Cleary, K. 2006, 'Kids in the tutor seat: building schools' capacity to help struggling readers through a cross-age peer-tutoring program', *Psychology in the Schools*, 42(1), pp. 99–107.

Chapter 11

Modelling

 Model: a representation.

(Collins Dictionary of the English Language, p. 947)

The ways that you communicate, solve problems, and relate to others form a powerful model for how children and others . . . will behave. Children tend to do what adults do regardless of what adults say.

(Feeney et al. 1991, p. 15)

There are several reasons why modeling influences are heavily favoured in promoting everyday learning. Under circumstances in which mistakes are costly or dangerous, skilful performances can be established without needless errors by providing competent models who demonstrate the required activities.

(Bandura 2006, p. 3)

What?

Modelling is a process through which children learn how to behave by copying (modelling) the behaviour of others. Staff can teach children how to behave 'appropriately' through presenting them with examples (models) of the dispositions, attitudes and values that the adults around them consider to be appropriate behaviour. Modelling occurs when children copy these behaviours.

New technologies, such as video or DVDs, can also act as models for young children to learn from (see Bellini, Akullian and Hopf 2007).

Issues and debates

BEYOND THE PERSONAL: TECHNOLOGIES AS MODELS

New technologies have brought an increasing number of symbolic models for children on TV and through the new digital technologies. Toddlers and babies can learn from watching models on TV or video screens (Huang and Charman 2005). However, there is some evidence that toddlers find it easier to model other people that they watch in 'real life' than they do people they watch on video. When toddlers were told where to find a hidden toy face-to-face and by a person on a video they were more likely to find the toy when told face-to-face (Troseth, Saylor and Archer 2006). However, there is also some evidence that toddlers learn words through modelling computers equally well as through modelling people (Boelens et al. 2007). With this increase in new technologies as a source for children's models comes a debate about the extent to which this is a positive advance and a concern about the content of what is being modelled, especially violence (e.g. Hausemann et al. 2003).

BEYOND THE DEVELOPMENTAL IN MODELLING

A child's capacity to imitate behaviours is fundamental to learning through modelling. There is some emerging evidence that individual differences in a children's ability to imitate behaviour is not necessarily a developmental phenomenon. Fenstermacher and Saudino (2006) argue that recent studies on children's capacity to imitate behaviour 'challenge early cognitive developmental theories' proposal of an adherence of the capacity to imitate to a fixed progression of developmental stages' (p. 346). They argue that genetics could explain individual differences in children's capacity to model what others do or say.

How?

Modelling is a low-intervention teaching technique. Staff do not intervene directly in children's learning but teach by example. For example, if staff want children to share materials with other children then they need to create circumstances in which they can model sharing materials with the children.

Children may model themselves on the adults around them even when the adults are not deliberately teaching through example. Thus, staff should try to demonstrate only those behaviours that they want children to emulate! The following points offer guidance on how to successfully use modelling as a deliberate teaching technique.

PLAN WHAT AND HOW YOU WILL MODEL

- Decide which behaviours, skills and dispositions you want the children to learn:

> The Shotby child care centre does this at its regular monthly meeting for the staff. There is always an agenda item concerning the behaviours, attitudes and dispositions on which the staff will concentrate with the children for the month.

- Identify the smaller steps and components involved in achieving these behaviours, attitudes and dispositions (Robison and Schwartz 1982).
- Plan specific occasions that offer opportunities to provide children with a model of the desired skill.
- Be alert to incidental and unplanned opportunities to model the desired skills.
- Be prepared to model behaviours over time. Children are more likely to learn through example if they have lots of examples to follow (Robison and Schwartz 1982; Marion 1987).

BE AWARE OF WHAT WORKS FOR CHILDREN

It used to be understood that modelling is successful when children incorporate the behaviours the adults (or peers) have modelled into their own behavioural repertoire (Seefeldt 1980). However, more recent research suggests some more complex factors at play. Children tend to model more precisely when they do not understand the overall reason for what an adult is demonstrating to them. When they do understand they are more likely to add their own flourishes to what they reproduce (Williamson and Markman 2006). In addition, it is worth noting the following advice about what works for young children:

- Remember that peers, siblings, adults, popular culture heroes and characters in books and stories and on TV can be used to model desired skills (Allen and Hart 1984; Linebarger and Walker 2005). However, popular culture models should be chosen with care. Linebarger and Walker (2005) found that different TV programs and different content have different effects on babies and toddlers, with specific programs increasing children's expressive language and other programs increasing a child's vocabulary. Those programs that did both include *Dora the Explorer*, *Blues' Clues* and *Dragon*.
- Recognise that children are more likely to model a particular behaviour if they see the person modelling it being rewarded for the behaviour (Seefeldt 1980).
- Recognise that children are more likely to continue to model a particular behaviour if they are rewarded when they display that behaviour (Seefeldt 1980).
- Remember that children are more likely to model the people whom they regard as powerful and nurturing in their environment (Marion 1987).
- Remember that children will watch the verbal and non-verbal actions and reactions of the social models around them, including television and video models (Linebarger and Walker 2005).

Carmel is a teacher who is very alert to the social model she provides. She has strong views about taking care of the environment and being careful about the earth's resources. She has set up recycling areas in the kindergarten and the children and adults are encouraged to sort out any waste material. The centre also has a worm farm with which to recycle food scraps and the children regularly clean this out, putting the worm casts on the garden to fertilise the plants. Carmel takes care to model respect for the environment inside and out.

Reflective task: Consider what specific things Carmel could do to model respect for the environment. Make a list and seek suggestions from colleagues.

When and why?

Modelling can be used when staff want children to learn new 'chunks' of behaviour through observing and imitating the social models around them.

GOAL RELEVANCE

Modelling can be used to teach verbal and non-verbal skills to children of all ages (Robison and Schwartz 1982). For example, adult role modelling can be a successful teaching technique when staff want to:

Build children's wellbeing and learning

- extend or enrich children's play (Arthur et al. 1996):

Nikki is keen to enrich imaginative play. She is sitting on the floor with three toddlers. She has provided some dress-ups, lots of hats and a mirror for them to look into. Liam, who is one of the more reticent toddlers, is watching the other children as they try on hats and vests. Nikki puts on a hat and says to Liam, 'Look at me, I've got a hat on'. Liam takes a hat and puts it on.

Reflection point: What could Nikki do to model different ways of using the hats and mirror for other children?

- help children learn to play co-operatively (Feeney et al. 1991; Hintz and Stomfay-Stitz 1999)
- increase children's desire to eat healthy foods (Feeney et al. 1991):

> At a child care centre in inner Melbourne, the staff always eat with the children because they can model enjoyment of wholesome food to them.

- build socially inclusive classrooms (McCay and Keyes 2001/02)
- discourage and change bullying behaviour in the classroom (Rigby 2003).

Build specific skills
- improve children's reasoning ability and mathematical thinking (Diezmann et al. 2002)
- encourage children to enter dramatic play (Rybczynski and Troy 1995)
- promote children's ability to actively listen to others (Renck Jalongo 1995)
- encourage children to tell their own stories (Hough et al. 1987)
- help children learn to solve problems. Children who have observed adults solving problems perform better on these tasks than children who have not had this experience (Feeney et al. 1991)
- build children's capacity to think aloud to support their thinking (Dorl 2007)
- build children's interest in reading and writing for themselves (Feeney et al. 1991; Gray 1995; Cress 2000) and build their writing skills (Mayer 2007)
- enhance the development of intimacy and enjoyment in close relationships (Roland and Lawhon 1994)
- increase children's pro-social behaviours, such as sharing and being socially competent (Lerner et al. 1987; McCay and Keyes 2001/02). There is evidence from a UK study of over 5000 children that encouraging imitation may foster socially insightful behaviour in toddlers (McEwen et al. 2007). This capacity could be drawn on in building prosocial behaviours in which children understand their and other people's behaviours.

DEVELOPMENTAL CONSIDERATIONS

At all stages of their development, children can imitate adult models. Research by van Kleeck et al. (1996) showed that babies as young as six months of age can learn about thinking from adults who model giving and receiving information, and that they can learn to imitate actions from videos as well as live demonstrations (Huang and Charman 2005). They can model simple behaviours such as answering their own questions, underlining text in a book with a finger when the text is spoken, repeating statements for emphasis and speaking for the baby:

> Quentin is sitting on a large bean bag with two 11-month-old babies. He is showing them a book and as he looks at each page he points to the pictures, labels them and shows interest in the babies' responses.
>
> *Reflection point:* In what other ways could Quentin model reading to babies?

However, it is important to remember that children's ability to imitate specific behaviours will be limited by their cognitive, emotional, social and physical ability to reproduce the skills or dispositions they observe. Consider the following example:

> A very young child who had observed an adult express affection to a dog by a multiple set of actions such as patting, kissing and hugging, in that order, copied only one behaviour, the patting action. Having little sense of the intensity of the patting, and limited motor ability to control it, the child hit the dog repeatedly, provoking a snapping reaction from the dog (Robison and Schwartz 1982, p. 109).

Angela models actions during creative movement.

According to Cole and Chan (1990), modelling requires the child to have the following abilities:

- to be able to grasp what adults want them to reproduce
- to be able to remember the key elements of what adults want them to reproduce
- to be able to represent what is to be reproduced in symbolic form
- to be able to convert the symbolic information into action.

However, more recent Australian research on toddlers' modelling behaviours suggests that modelling is more complex than this. The nature of the model's behaviours makes a difference to what a child will model. The more social a model is, the more likely it is that children at 18 months of age will model the action of the model, and at 24 months of age the more likely it is that a child will model the actions of the model and produce the modelled outcome (Nielsen 2006). This is in line with research from the mid-1990s that indicated children are more motivated to model adult behaviours when they have a close bond with the adult concerned (Roland and Lawhon 1994). However, children will also model the skills and dispositions of children more competent than themselves (Arthur et al. 1996; Allen and Hart 1984). This suggests that mixed-age and mixed-ability groupings can encourage children to 'try' more complex skills.

Access to same-age peers as models can be particularly important to toddlers. Toddlers add to their rapidly expanding repertoire of social and cognitive skills and behaviours through modelling each other (Castle 1990). They try out what other toddlers are doing and, in doing so, solve social and cognitive problems they may not have confronted before. This means that it is very important for staff to provide time, space and opportunity for toddlers to watch and imitate each other. Toddlers are also growing in their capacity to distinguish the pretend world from the real world (Ma and Lillard 2006), so it is important for adults to be clear about this when modelling—toddlers will know when they are pretending.

Teachers who model communication with preschool children have been shown to positively support children's cognitive development (Bowman et al. 2001).

In the early years of schooling children are becoming increasingly competent language users. They have a strong enough understanding of the structure and meaning of language to be able to play with words and sentence structures and create funny alternatives to what should normally be said or written (Arthur et al. 1996). Teachers can build on this tendency to enhance their creative language use through modelling enjoyment in language games and sharing funny words and word games with the children.

Modelling was also shown to be an effective component of a literacy program with children in the early years of school when children with and without disabilities were paired to tutor each other in reading. Each member of the pair took on the role of coach and/or reader and acted as tutors for each other in learning to read. Teachers used modelling to introduce the whole class to the different roles taken by children in their literacy pairs and to show what these roles looked like in practice (Fuchs et al. 2001).

Research has shown that young children learn many early literacy skills and behaviours through modelling and that many early writers have observed their parents regularly engaged in reading and writing activities (Cress 2000). This points to the need for teachers to proactively model literacy behaviours to beginning writers. Teachers can also effectively use modelling to help children develop skills in critically choosing books for reading and deciding whether or not a book would be too difficult for them. Research has shown that when teachers modelled these behaviours the children used them more effectively than when didactic teaching methods were used (Kragler 2000).

Equity considerations

'RACE' AND CULTURE

A positive self-identity is the basis for confident involvement in the world. Racism can mar the development of a positive self-identity for many black and ethnic minority children. These children develop a positive self-identity partly by having access to positive role models from within their own ethnic and 'racial' group. Over 20 years ago, Perry and Furkawa (1980, cited in Cole and Chan 1990) showed that models that are similar in 'race' to the child will enhance the acquisition of desired behaviours and dispositions. Studies from the USA also showed that 'own-race' models can be important for minority student learning. They increased student achievement in mathematics and reading for black and white students. However, providing positive role models for children from different 'racial' and ethnic backgrounds presents a major challenge for early childhood staff in some contexts, such as Australia, because the majority of early childhood workers are 'white, female, middle-class people with Western practices, beliefs, values and attitudes' (Fleer 1996, p. 7).

There is clearly a need to work for greater ethnic diversity within the staff group, but there are some other ways in which staff can offer children positive ethnic role models. Adler Matoba explains the reasons for this powerfully within the context of the USA:

> European American teachers, particularly in the Midwest, may view their Asian American students through cultural lenses formed by their own limited experiences with people of color, stereotypes like the 'model minority' . . . and a color-blind perspective, which focuses on overlooking racial differences. (Adler Matoba 2001, p. 151)

Within an Australian context it is extremely important that Indigenous Australian children are exposed to positive Indigenous role models with which to develop a positive self-identity and to counter the effects of racism against Indigenous Australians. This need is as pertinent now as it was in the mid-1990s when Colbung and Glover wrote the following:

> The availability of cultural role models will, to a large degree, affect children's achievements. Role models show children that they do not have to sacrifice their Aboriginality in order to succeed in mainstream institutions . . . (Colbung and Glover 1996, p. 38).

Staff can introduce Indigenous children to positive Indigenous role models by bringing local Indigenous 'identities' into the centre and by inviting Indigenous performers and artists to visit it. Local Indigenous adults can advise staff how best to do this. Staff can do similar things to offer positive adult role models to children whose ethnic and 'racial' background differs from that of the staff group. However, it is important in this endeavour to avoid doing it only occasionally—that is, tokenistically.

Children who have prejudiced behaviours and beliefs modelled at home can reject these and so it is important that staff proactively model for all children anti-racist ways of thinking and acting at all times. As Sleeter and Grant (1999, p. 85) explained:

> Teachers who are 'real' with students—who talk honestly with them about real issues—can serve as influential role models and can prod students to think about their beliefs.

GENDER

Much of the daily content of early childhood programs provides children with clear representations of how males and females should behave, think and act. Research (for example, MacNaughton 2007) indicates that many of the gender role models that children see in early childhood settings are gender-stereotyped. In addition, many stories, posters, games, puzzles, poems and songs contain mainly male role models. It is, therefore, important that staff include resources in their program that present girls and boys with positive, non-stereotypical female role models. One way to expand the gender role models available to young girls is to invite to the centre women who have jobs from which they have traditionally been excluded, such as fire-fighting and truck driving.

Female staff can expand girls' involvement in curriculum areas and experiences that they often avoid, such as those traditionally associated with the sciences and mathematics, by modelling an active interest in them. Similarly, male staff can expand boys' involvement in curriculum areas and experiences which they often avoid, such as those traditionally associated with the arts, the caring professions and the world of daily domestic life, by modelling an active interest in them. However, it is important for staff to remember that modelling alone is unlikely to change well-entrenched gender role differences in young children (MacNaughton 2007). Modelling should be combined with more proactive teaching techniques to produce changes in gender expectations and participation in the early years.

Research over time has found that children as young as two years of age recognise gender stereotypes and can and do discriminate between what is considered to be behaviour consistent and inconsistent with those stereotypes. US researchers found that two-year-old children focused more intensely on adults modelling gender-inconsistent activities than they did those performing gender-consistent activities (Hill and Flom 2007). This may offer a window of opportunity for teachers to model non-stereotypical gender behaviours with some effect at this age.

Similarity in gender between adult models and the child is important, as this has been shown to enhance the child's acquisition of desired behaviours from the adult model (Cole and Chan 1990). The opportunities to do this are likely to be greater when there is a mix of male and female staff in a centre:

At a meeting in an early learning centre in Sydney's southern suburbs, the staff are discussing how they might help boys and girls to experience less gender-stereotyped play.

Albert: 'We have two male teachers and three female teachers at the centre and I can't help but notice that we are all falling thoughtlessly into particular roles. For example, I'm the one who always teaches and supervises the carpentry and Jannette always takes the children for cooking activities.'

Jannette: 'That's because I love cooking and you don't enjoy it much!'

> **John:** 'What about if I do cooking sometimes and perhaps Sally, Dia and Jannette could do some of the more physical activities like the outside block play, gardening and digging? In this way, the children won't get the idea that only men do some things and women others.'
>
> _Reflection point:_ What non-traditional role modelling do you do in your work with children?

However, caution should be given about the link between modelling and gendered behaviours. In a study of 283 single-parent families and 6420 nuclear families, no difference was found between gender-role behaviours in the children of father-present and father-absent families. This suggests that children are learning their gender-role behaviours in complex ways (Stevens, Golombok and Beveridge 2002).

DISABILITY AND ADDITIONAL NEEDS

Meeting a child with a disability in an early childhood setting may be the first encounter many able-bodied children have with disability. Adults can provide clear signs to able-bodied children about how to respectfully handle this encounter through modelling respect and acceptance themselves (Winter 1994/95). Crary (1992, pp. 12–14) suggested that staff should model the following behaviours:

- Greet people with disabilities directly and with respect by, for example, making eye contact as staff would with other people. Many people with disabilities report that they can feel invisible because other people speak to whoever they are with rather than directly to them.
- Respect the personal space of people with disabilities by not touching them in ways that would be inappropriate with others and by not leaning on or touching their special equipment (for example, wheelchairs) unless given permission to do so.
- Allow time for people with disabilities to be independent in their movements or speech, and model patience in waiting for them.

If children with disabilities have learned to see themselves as 'odd' or 'different', staff should provide children with positive role models of living with a disability by, for example, inviting people with disabilities to the centre to talk about their achievements, and by using posters, books, poems and puzzles that include positive models of being a person with a disability. However, staff should ensure that such sessions aren't one-off, tokenistic sessions. (For more information in this area refer to Chapter 3.)

Modelling can be a very effective in teaching a wide variety of skills, including social skills, to children with a wide range of disabilities (Lowenthal 1996; Fuchs et al. 2001; McCay and Keyes 2001/02). More recently, video modelling and video self-modelling techniques in which children are shown footage of themselves performing desired behaviours were found to increase the social engagement of preschool children with autism spectrum disorders (Bellini, Akullian and Hopf 2007; Bellini and Akullian 2007). Video modelling using an animated toilet training video for teaching daytime urinary control was also shown to be effective in toilet training young boys with autism (Keen, Brannigan and Cuskelly 2007).

Cole and Chan (1990) and McCay and Keyes (2001/02) discuss how modelling may be used to teach social and other skills to children with disabilities. However, modelling alone may not be sufficient to teach social competence to children with disabilities. McCay and Keyes (2001/02, p. 77) concluded:

> The key then becomes providing multiple skill exposure and practice for children with low cognitive functioning, while offering new and varying learning opportunities for children without such disabilities . . . the teacher should actively choose to teach social competence, using his or her professional knowledge of many perspectives to select from a wide repertoire of strategies.

Marg shows Eliza how to use a spade.

Reflecting on modelling techniques

1 Define modelling.
2 What does research suggest are the keys to using modelling to optimise children's learning?
3 When do you think modelling should be deliberately used in your teaching?
4 Are there any times when you think that the use of modelling is inappropriate with young children?
5 How could modelling be used to promote communicative competence with infants? What sort of modelling could you use to achieve this aim?
6 What things do you think could be successfully taught to toddlers through modelling?
7 What dispositions do you think you could successfully teach through modelling to four-year-old children?
8 List three behaviours that you would like to model with a mixed-age group of children. Identify five ways you could actively model these behaviours to them. Identify five difficulties you could encounter in trying to model these behaviours. How could you overcome these difficulties? Would you need to draw on any other teaching techniques to assist you in this work?
9 List the types of visual aids and props you could collect to provide positive role models for children with disabilities.

10 Choose one storybook you could use with two-year-old children to provide them with a positive role model of being black.

11 Find one poem you could use with four-year-old children to provide a positive role model of girls being adventurous.

Improving teaching in practice

Visit an early childhood centre and discuss with the adults what behaviours and dispositions they are trying to teach the children through modelling. How are they trying to teach them? To what extent did the staff:

- decide in advance what they wanted the children to learn?
- take a logical, step-by-step approach to modelling?
- analyse each child's current level of ability to acquire the desired behaviour?
- show awareness of what children might learn from verbal and non-verbal behaviours being modelled?
- plan specific times to model for the children?
- use incidental opportunities for modelling?
- model over an extended period of time?
- involve other people and resources in the modelling process?
- reward the children when they reproduced the desired behaviour?

FURTHER READING

Cole, P. and Chan, L. 1990, *Methods and Strategies for Special Education*, Prentice Hall Inc., New Jersey [refer to Chapter 7].

Crary, E. 1992, 'Talking about differences children notice', in B. Neugebauer, ed., *Alike and Different: Exploring our Humanity with Young Children* (pp. 11–15), National Association for the Education of Young Children, Washington, DC.

Hunter, T. 2000, 'Modeling possibilities', *Young Children* 55(5), p. 40.

Kean, J. 1991, 'Socialization of affect display in young children: a review', *Australian Journal of Early Childhood*, 16(2), pp. 15–19.

Marion, M. 1987, *Guidance of Young Children*, 2nd edn, Merrill, USA [refer to pp. 192–195].

Parker, M. and Hurry, J. 2007, 'Teachers' use of questioning and modelling comprehension skills in primary classroom', *Educational Review* 59(3), pp. 299–314.

ONLINE AND MULTI-MEDIA RESOURCES

Text

Gallacher, L., 'Video and young learners 1 and 2', British Council and BBC Teaching English explores the pros and cons of using video as a model in the classroom, criteria for selecting video to use, the types of video that can be helpful and techniques for using video in the classroom: **http://www.teachingenglish.org.uk/think/resources/video_young1.shtml**

Multi-media

'Literacy is priceless: a blog for reading teachers'. A site with YouTube videos of teachers teaching reading. 'Word Families' is a video-clip showing a teacher modelling word sounds to children: **http://literacyispriceless.wordpress.com** (accessed and published 26 October 2007).

REFERENCES

Adler Matoba, S. 2001, 'Racial and ethnic mirrors: reflections on identity from an Asian American educator', in S. Grieshaber and G. Cannella, eds, *Embracing Identities in Early Childhood Education: Diversity and Possibilities* (pp. 148–157), Teachers College Press, New York.

Allen, K. and Hart, B. 1984, *The Early Years: Arrangements for Learning*, Prentice Hall Inc., New Jersey.

Arthur, L., Beecher, B., Dockett, S., Farmer, S. and Death, E. 1996, *Programming and Planning in Early Childhood Settings*, 2nd edn, Harcourt Brace and Company, Sydney.

Bandura, A. and Walters, R. 2006, *Social Learning and Personality Development*, Holt, Rinehart and Winston, New York.

Bellini, S. and Akullian, J. 2007, 'A meta-analysis of video modeling and video self-modeling interventions for children and adolescents with autism spectrum disorders', *Exceptional Children*, 73, pp. 261–284.

Bellini, S., Akullian, J. and Hopf, A. 2007, 'Increasing social engagement in young children with autism spectrum disorders using video self-modeling', *School Psychology Review*, 36, pp. 80–90.

Boelens, H., Hoffman, B., Tamoddoni, T. and Eenink, K. 2007, 'Specific effect of modeling on young children's work productions', *Psychological Record*, 57(1), pp. 145–167.

Bowman, B., Donovan, M. and Burns, S. 2001, *Eager to Learn: Educating Our Preschoolers*, National Academy Press, Washington, DC.

Castle, K. 1990, 'The second year: 12–24 months', in E. Surbeck and M. Kelly, eds, *Personalizing Care with Infants, Toddlers and Families* (pp. 23–32), Association for Childhood Education International, Wheaton, MD.

Colbung, M. and Glover, A. 1996, 'In partnership with Aboriginal children', in M. Fleer, ed., *Conversations about Teaching and Learning in Early Childhood Settings* (pp. 33–40), Australian Early Childhood Association, Canberra.

Cole, P. and Chan, L. 1990, *Methods and Strategies for Special Education*, Prentice Hall Inc., New Jersey.

Crary, E. 1992, 'Talking about differences children notice', in B. Neugebauer, ed., *Alike and Different: Exploring our Humanity with Young Children* (pp. 11–15), National Association for the Education of Young Children, Washington, DC.

Cress, S. 2000, 'A focus on literacy in home day care', *Australian Journal of Early Childhood*, 25(3), pp. 6–11.

Diezmann, C., Watters, J. and English, L. 2002, 'Teacher behaviours that influence young children's reasoning', in A.D. Cockburn and E. Nardi, eds, *Proceedings 27th Annual Conference of the International Group for the Psychology of Mathematics Education 2* (pp. 289–206), Norwich, UK.

Dorl, J. 2007, 'Think aloud! Increase your teaching power', *Young Children*, 62(4), pp. 101–105.

Feeney, S., Christensen, D. and Moravcik, E. 1991, *Who am I in the Lives of Children? An Introduction to Teaching Young Children*, 5th edn, Macmillan Publishing Company, New York.

Fenstermacher, S. and Saudino, K. 2006, 'Understanding individual differences in young children's imitative behaviours', *Developmental Review*, 26(3), pp. 346–364.

Fleer, M. 1996, 'Talking about teaching and learning', in M. Fleer, ed., *Conversations about Teaching and Learning in Early Childhood Settings* (pp. 1–8), Australian Early Childhood Association, Watson, ACT.

Fuchs, D., Fuchs, L., Al Otaiba, S., Thompson, A., Yen, L., McMaster, K., Svenson, K. and Yang, N. 2001, 'K-Pals: helping kindergartners with reading readiness: teachers and researchers in partnerships', *Teaching Exceptional Children*, March/April, pp. 76–80.

Gray, L. 1995, 'Taking from books by asking questions', *Journal of Research in Childhood Education*, 10(1), pp. 23–28.

Hausemann, L., Moise-Titus, J., Podolski, C. and Eron, L. 2003, 'Longitudinal relations between children's exposure to TV violence and their aggressive and violent behaviour in young adulthood 1977–1992', *Developmental Psychology*, 39(2), pp. 201–221.

Hill, S. and Flom, R. 2007, '18- and 24-month-olds' discrimination of gender-consistent and inconsistent activities', *Infant Behaviour and Development*, 30(1), pp. 168–173.

Hintz, B. F. and Stomfay-Stitz, A. 1999, 'Peace education and conflict resolution through expressive arts in early childhood education and teacher education', Paper presented at the *Annual Conference of the Eastern Educational Research Association*, 26 February, Hilton Head, SC, ED433105.

Hough, R., Nurss, J. and Wood, D. 1987, 'Tell me a story: making opportunities for elaborated language in early childhood classrooms', *Young Children*, November, pp. 6–12.

Huang, C-T. and Charman, T. 2005, 'Gradations of emulation learning in infants' imitation of actions on objects', *Journal of Experimental Child Psychology*, 92(3), pp. 276–302.

Keen, D., Brannigan, K. and Cuskelly, M. 2007, 'Toilet training for children with autism: the effects of video', *Journal of Developmental and Physical Disabilities*, 19(4), pp. 291–303.

Kragler, S. 2000, 'Choosing books for reading: an analysis for three types of readers', *Journal of Research in Childhood Education*, 14(2), pp. 133–141.

Lerner, J., Mardell-Czudnowski, C. and Goldenberg, D. 1987, *Special Education for the Early Childhood Years*, 2nd edn, Prentice Hall Inc., New Jersey.

Linebarger, D. and Walker, D. 2005, 'Infants' and toddlers' television viewing and language outcomes', *American Behavioural Scientist*, 48(5), pp. 624–645.

Lowenthal, B. 1996, 'Teaching social skills to preschoolers with special needs', *Childhood Education*, 72(3), pp. 137–140.

Ma, L. and Lillard, A. 2006, 'Where is the real cheese? Young children's ability to discriminate between real and pretend actions', *Child Development*, 77(6), pp. 1762–1777.

MacNaughton, G. 2007, 'Constructing gender in early years education', in C. Skelton, B. Francis and L. Syulyan, eds, *The Sage Handbook of Gender and Education* (pp. 127–138), Sage Publications, London, Thousand Oaks and New Delhi.

Marion, M. 1987, *Guidance of Young Children*, 2nd edn, Merrill, USA.

Mayer, K. 2007, 'Research in review. Emerging knowledge about emergent writing', *Young Children*, 62(1), pp. 34–40.

McCay, L. and Keyes, D. 2001/02, 'Developing social competence in the primary schools', *Childhood Education*, 78(2), pp. 70–78.

McEwen, F., Happé, F., Bolton, P., Rijsdijk, F., Ronald, A., Dworzynski, K. and Pomin, R. 2007, 'Origins of individual differences in imitation, links with language, pretend play, and socially insightful behaviour in two-year-old twins', *Child Development*, 78(2), pp. 474–492.

Nielsen, M. 2006, 'Copying actions and copying outcomes: social learning through the second year', *Developmental Psychology*, 42(3), pp. 555–565.

Renck Jalongo, A. 1995, 'Promoting active listening in the classroom', *Childhood Education*, 72(1), pp. 13–18.

Rigby, K. 2003, *Bullying Among Young Children: A Guide For Teachers And Carers*, Australian Government Attorney-General's Department, Canberra.

Robison, H. and Schwartz, S. 1982, *Designing Curriculum for Early Childhood*, Allyn & Bacon Inc., Boston.

Roland, S. and Lawhon, T. 1994, 'How do I love thee: enhancing intimacy in children', *Childhood Education*, 71(1), pp. 38–41.

Rybcyznski, M. and Troy, A. 1995, 'Literacy-enriched play centres: trying them out in "the real world"', *Childhood Education*, 72(1), pp. 7–12.

Seefeldt, C. 1980, *Teaching Young Children*, Prentice Hall Inc., New Jersey.

Sleeter, C. and Grant, C. 1999, *Making Choices for Multicultural Education: Five Approaches to Race, Class and Gender*, 3rd edn, Merrill Prentice Hall, New Jersey.

Stevens, M., Golombok, S. and Beveridge, M. 2002, Does father absence influence children's gender development? Findings from a general population study of preschool children', *Parenting*, 2(1) pp. 47–60.

Troseth, G., Saylor, M. and Archer, A. 2006, 'Young children's use of video as a source of socially relevant information', *Child Development*, 77(3), pp. 786–799.

van Kleeck, A., Imholz Alexander, E., Vigil, A. and Templeton, K. 1996, 'Verbally modeling thinking for infants: middle-class mothers' presentation of information structures during book sharing', *Journal of Research in Childhood Education*, 10(2), pp. 101–113.

Wilkes, G. (ed.) 1979, *Collins Dictionary of the English Language*, Penguin Books, Middlesex.

Williamson, R. and Markman, E. 2006, 'Precision of imitation as a function of preschoolers' understanding of the demonstration', *Developmental Psychology*, 42(4), pp. 723–731.

Winter, S. 1994/95, 'Diversity, a program for all children', *Childhood Education*, 71(2), pp. 91–95.

Chapter 12

Positioning people

 Position: the place, situation or timing of a person or thing.
(Collins Dictionary of the English Language, p. 1143)

The experienced teacher, even when she is working with one child, will be in a position to observe at a glance what the other children are doing—alert to the total situation.

(Read et al. 1993, p. 101)

If given appropriate access and connectivity, groups of children can learn to operate and use computers and the internet with no or minimal intervention from adults.

(Dangwal et al. 2006, p. 44)

What?

Positioning is the process of placing oneself near other individuals, groups or objects in ways that support children's learning and that maintain children's safety. Careful positioning of people can enrich children's planned and unplanned learning experiences.

Issues and debates

HOW NECESSARY IS ADULT PROXIMITY FOR CHILDREN TO LEARN?

Much of the research that this chapter draws on supports the idea that the teacher proximity has an overall positive effect on young children's learning. Teacher involvement in young children's learning has been characterised often as a sign of quality preschool provision. For instance, direct teaching and sustained thinking and interaction between staff and children were associated strongly with high quality curriculum in two major studies in the UK ('The Effective Provision of Pre-School Education' study and the 'Researching Effective Pedagogy in the Early Years' study) (Sylva et al. 2007).

However, researchers in India have been exploring ways of supporting children's learning when the teacher is absent. Mitra and Rana (2001) characterise this as 'Minimally Invasive Education' and link it directly to constructivist theories of learning and teaching (Dangwal et al. 2006). In Minimally Invasive

Education the teacher sets up the environment and then is absent. To date it has focused on children's acquisition of computer skills in disadvantaged communities where children may have no access to formal schooling. The researchers have established computer kiosks in public areas where children may be and then tracked what children learn with no adult assistance. They have found that diverse groups of children can acquire computer literacy without any formal instruction from adults:

> The results of this experiment indicate that groups of children can learn to use computers irrespective of who or where they are. In spite of their diversity in terms of ethnicity, language, gender, and socio-economic status, they all acquired computing skills on their own. (Dangwal et al. 2006, p. 56)

This research sits alongside research in other contexts that shows staff proximity to computers in the classroom enables them to mediate children's learning in this area and supports children's skill building in use of Information and Communication Technologies (ICT) (Plowman and Stephen 2007). However, there is also research that suggests it is important that children have control of the activity if their engagement is to be sustained. Research on children's engagement with computers indicates that boys' attention and engagement in particular is greatest when they have control of the program rather than when they watch an adult control it for them (Calvert, Strong and Gallagher 2005).

Against this background, it is important for teachers to think about the extent to which adult proximity to children is necessary to children's learning and to reflect on what is gained and lost through teacher proximity to children in early-years settings.

How?

Staff can best assist children's learning by thinking about several interrelated levels of organisation:

- overall social organisation of the learning areas
- daily timetabling of staff–child interactions
- daily placement of adults
- safe placement of people
- placing people for security and for competence
- positioning staff for meaning-making with children.

OVERALL SOCIAL ORGANISATION OF THE LEARNING AREAS

In placing materials and equipment within the learning environment in ways which facilitate social interaction, staff need to think about the following issues:

- that there are places for adults and/or children to stand and sit individually and in groups on the floor and on chairs
- that equipment is placed within easy reach of the children
- that some equipment is accessible only to adults
- that children are able to work in groups of different sizes
- that there are spaces to encourage individual learning
- that placement of staff reflects these considerations.

DAILY TIMETABLING OF STAFF–CHILD INTERACTIONS

Staff need to reflect on the placement of children and adults throughout each day. They have many choices about how to do this. Staff can place themselves near a learning experience when it begins to help capture children's interest in that experience. Once a learning experience has begun, staff can join in to maintain children's interest in it and to support their explorations of it. Staff can join a learning experience after some time to extend children's interests and to prompt their exploration of alternative solutions to problems. This array of choices requires staff to consider when timetabling if they will:

- sit near a particular child or group of children
- place themselves inside or outside of the group
- place themselves near a particular learning experience or move about
- stand, kneel or sit.

The Millicent child care centre is in an inner urban area under some housing commission flats. The staff are keen to help the children to develop curiosity and enthusiasm for learning. Each day before the children arrive, the staff have a five-minute meeting to discuss which staff will be where in the room and which will be outside in the playground. In this way, they make sure that they cover all areas and thus ensure that the children are safe and that staff are available to help stimulate children's interest and curiosity.

Reflection point: Positioning adults is important for safety reasons as well as for extending children's learning. What are some key areas in a learning environment where it is important to have adults close by?

DAILY PLACEMENT OF ADULTS

Staff may have an overall plan for organising their responsibilities during the day, but some daily changes can enrich and extend children's learning. For example, placing a visitor such as a parent or student near where a child is playing can prompt the child's interests and make their play more elaborate. Staff need to think about when and where they will place adults to encourage children's active involvement in the program.

Lynne, a kindergarten teacher in a country town in Victoria, has spent a lot of time and energy trying to include the parents and members of the community in her program. She has a strong belief that children's learning is enhanced by having adults around who can stimulate curiosity and develop children's learning. She has advertised in the local newspaper for volunteers and she has made personal contact with each family to ask for their time. She keeps a list of extra adults who will be at the kindergarten each day. At the beginning of each session, Lynne talks with each adult and gives them suggestions as to where they should position themselves in relation to the children.

Reflection point: Lynne could also give the adult volunteers in her programs examples of things to say and do with the children in order to extend their learning. What are some of the things that Lynne might say to the volunteers in this instance?

In deciding how to place people, staff should ensure that their decisions create and maintain a safe, secure, interesting and pleasurable learning environment for children and adults. To do this staff need to ensure that:

- children's and staff's health and safety needs are met
- children gain a feeling of security and competence in their learning environment.

PLACING PEOPLE FOR SAFETY

Staff can ensure that they can supervise children's learning by placing themselves where they can easily see the children. Staff should always sit in places from where they can easily scan the room on a regular basis. Careful staff positioning is particularly important near high-risk activities, to ensure children's safety while allowing them new and challenging experiences. High-risk activities include those in which:

- there is water in containers on the ground near young children. Babies and toddlers might drown if they land face-down in the water
- there are sharp tools, such as in the digging patch, gardening area, clay modelling, collage or woodworking areas. Children might damage themselves or others through awkward or careless use of these tools
- children might overreach or over-balance and fall—these are part of the new challenges with climbing equipment
- children have access to animals that might sting, bite or scratch them
- children are near heat sources such as stoves and heaters
- children are handling very hot or very cold materials (liquids or solids)
- there are very small items that children could swallow if left unsupervised.

These experiences should only be attempted if close, constant and careful adult supervision can be guaranteed. Staff should also have a clear understanding of the children's particular skills and limitations. Each child's particular physical, emotional, social and cognitive stage of development will create different potential hazards.

Some questions to prompt staff reflection on how to place themselves and others to promote a safe learning environment include:

- Do staff know who will be available when, and to supervise which areas?
- Can staff readily scan the inside and outside play area when sitting?
- Can staff move quickly to all areas they are supervising?
- Are staff positioned near all high-risk activities?
- Have staff assessed children's developmental abilities before offering high-risk activities?

POSITIONING FOR SECURITY AND COMPETENCE

Children need to feel secure and competent in their daily environment in order to build positive relationships with adults. By sitting near children or alongside them staff can easily promote an atmosphere of warmth and caring through simple gestures such as eye-to-eye contact, cuddles and smiles and by engaging in meaningful conversations with children. Strong social relationships between adults and children support young children's literacy learning, especially those children who are struggling to learn to read and write (Ostrosky, Gaffney and Thomas 2006).

Being near children also enables staff to provide them with a sense of security and to easily remind children of the safety rules in the group as necessary. For example, by sitting near children in the sand play area, a staff member can more easily remind children that throwing sand is unacceptable because it can get into other children's eyes. Also, sitting or standing between children who are about to interfere with each other, or between whom tension is mounting, may defuse these tensions or threats of intrusion.

POSITIONING FOR MEANING-MAKING

There is increasing interest in generating early childhood curriculum through the lived experiences of young children and the teacher in their daily classroom life together. Curriculum is generated through teachable moments, responsiveness to individual children's interests and shared decision-making between children and teachers (Burton 2001; Hyun 2001). Central to this approach to curriculum is the capacity of the teacher to actively engage in meaning-making with children. This can happen only if the teacher is positioned within the classroom in ways that make close interaction with children possible. Staff need to consciously plan how they will position themselves in ways that link them with children's activities and learning, and enable them to actively engage with children's meaning-making through listening, commenting, questioning and enriching conversations with children.

Some questions to prompt staff reflection on how to place themselves and others to engage proactively with children's meaning-making include:

- Do staff know who will be available when, and to engage with children in which areas?
- Will staff be able to have periods of time with individuals and small groups of children?
- Are staff positioned near enough to children to be able to engage in conversation with them?

When and why?

In any early childhood program, decisions about how to position staff will be influenced by the staff's approach to curriculum and by their specific teaching and learning goals for the children.

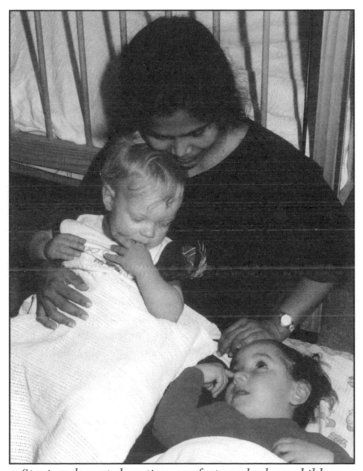

Staying close at sleep time comforts and relaxes children.

GOAL RELEVANCE

In general, staff can position themselves or others near someone or something for the following reasons, supporting learning and engagement broadly by:

- increasing children's engagement in specific experiences. If staff place themselves near children who have trouble concentrating, they can use simple verbal or non-verbal techniques to increase such children's concentration

- encouraging children's participation in a specific experience. For example, including a child's favourite adult in a specific area may encourage a reluctant child to participate in a new experience. Similarly, placing a person from a child's own cultural background may encourage them to explore experiences they have avoided
- extending or enriching a particular experience. Lally (1991, p. 13) describes how this can happen:

In one class, the children had been observed making police and fire service vehicles with the large, hollow, wooden block, and had been using these in dramatic play. They were using small, rectangular blocks as 'walkie talkie' radios. The teacher, remembering that she had two unwanted, broken pocket radios at home, brought these into school the next day and added them to the block play areas. These added a new dimension to the play as the children learned where the on/off switch was, how to change the frequency and how to put the aerial up and down.

DEVELOPMENTAL CONSIDERATIONS

Positioning adults to encourage interactions between children of mixed language abilities can have positive effects on children's learning (Schechter and Bye 2007). This is also the case for reading (McCoach, O'Connell and Levitt 2006). This suggests that placing children of mixed ages and/or mixed abilities in small groups could enhance children's learning. For example, placing toddlers and babies or toddlers and preschoolers in small groups could enhance each child's skill development.

Babies benefit from much close and caring attention from adults. By placing comfortable adult chairs in areas where babies will be, staff can create space in which babies, other children and adults can sit quietly and comfortably together, and can cuddle and be involved in playful games with each other. Pillows, bean-bags and soft-carpeted surfaces can make it more likely that adults will be comfortable placing themselves with babies on the floor and can make the floor a comfortable and safe space from which babies can explore the world around them.

Babies also need responsive and close communication with adults to grow emotionally strong and learn how to communicate their needs to others. They need adults who can 'tune into the infant's emotional signals and actively try to understand them' (Fleer and Linke 2002, p. 6). To do this, adults need to be positioned near enough to babies to pick up on their cries, noises, movements and expressions that tell others how a baby is feeling. Finding time to hold babies, sit them on your lap and be positioned so you can see baby and they can see you is critical to building 'responsive communication with infants' (Fleer and Linke 2002, p. 7). One study used an approach of 'Watch, wait and wonder' to help build stronger and more responsive relationships between mothers and their babies (Rance 2005). While this approach was targeted at mothers and babies, it offers a way for staff to think about how they can respectfully observe and come to know the individual strengths of the babies they work with.

Toddlers sometimes find sharing difficult and so it can be useful for staff to position themselves near toddlers who are practising sharing and co-operation. Such positioning enables staff to quickly add another toy to the experience so that each toddler has their own, or to avoid conflict by simple redirection. Adults also need to be close enough to toddlers to guard against accidents, yet far enough away to enable toddlers to feel independent in exploring the world about them.

Planning the learning environment so toddlers can spend time talking with each other is also important. Toddlers' talk with peers is an important way in which they create and maintain their relationships with each other. Building toddlers' language skills is important to building their relationships with each other (Katz 2004).

Preschoolers are often extremely mobile, often social and highly inquisitive people who can often enter social and physical situations without the skills with which to engage in them safely and enjoyably. It is, therefore, important that staff are vigilant in supervising all areas of preschoolers' activity. In addition, preschoolers are just beginning to form complex and changing friendships and adults need to position themselves far enough away from small groups of children to allow them independence and social exploration, but close enough to ensure fair play and to ensure that difficulties are resolved readily. With each age group this is a balancing act in which experience with a particular child or group of children will often guide how best to reach the balance.

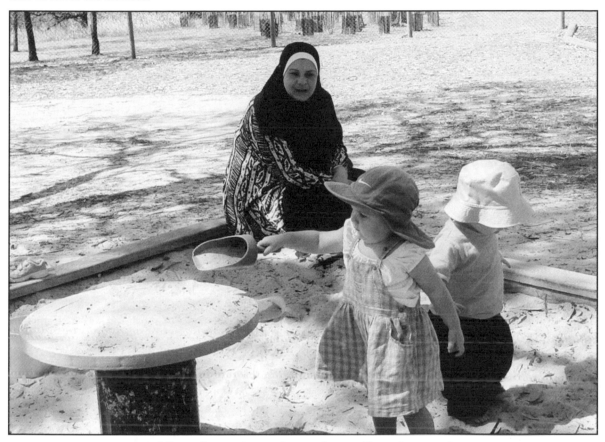

Toddlers play in the sandpit with a staff member nearby.

Children in the early years of school are able to work independently of adults for considerable periods of time. Many teachers draw on this ability to organise small group project work. While children learn lots through peer interactions in small group projects they also benefit considerably from adult involvement. Children's acquisition of literacy and numeracy skills is greatly enhanced through high quality teacher interactions that involve open-ended questioning, modelling and making connections for children (Hass Dyson and Genishi 1993; Moyles 1989; Flynn 2007). This is particularly important when children are using electronic media to support their acquisition of literacy and numeracy. Staff need to strongly supervise children's use of new programs and be available for ongoing mediation of their use. Staff alert to the learning potential that arises from children talking about how and what they are learning need to maximise their opportunities for such talk with children.

For many children, but especially young children, sharing interactions with adults in which adults are attentive to the interests and expressions of a child is important. Positioning teachers so that respectful episodes of 'joint attention' in which they 'focus, follow and talk' with children (Cain, Rudd and Saxon 2007, p. 159) are possible is important for many aspects of a child's growth and wellbeing, including their emotional wellbeing and the successful acquisition of language. Smith (1999) studied joint attention episodes in New

Zealand early childhood centres and concluded that 'about a third of the children in the study (35%) did not experience any joint attention episodes with caregivers' (p. 94). This is a reminder of the importance of actively planning where and how teachers are positioned within a room so that they can actively create and participate in moments of shared attention with young children.

Equity considerations

'RACE' AND CULTURE

People have different levels of comfort about what is an acceptable physical distance between one person and another. Staff who work with children and adults from a different cultural background to their own should familiarise themselves with each person's personal space comfort zones. Staff can demonstrate respect for others by taking note of each person's comfort zone and using it in their daily interactions with children and other adults.

Staff working with younger children should also reflect on the effects on those children who do not share an ethnic heritage with adults in the centre, especially when a child is from a minority ethnic group and staff are from a majority ethnic group. Researchers have found that when this occurs young children find it harder to form attachments with staff. It is important that children from a minority ethnic group have as much as opportunity as possible to interact with adults from their ethnic group while in early childhood services (Howes and Shivers 2006).

When children are learning English as an additional language staff need to be alert to their relationships with those children if they themselves do not speak the child's first language. Researchers in the UK found that early childhood teachers' relationships with children learning English as a second language were not as close at the beginning of the year as they were with children who spoke English as their first language (Fumoto, Hargreaves and Maxwell 2007). Language can be a key way in which staff and children share ideas and experiences and build relationships. Again, this research can act as a point of reflection for staff on how they position themselves within their group to build strong relationships with all children. Supporting the potential of children with English as an additional language is an important responsibility for all staff. This responsibility is formalised in the curriculum policies of several countries, including the UK where *The Curriculum Guidance for the Foundation Stage* emphasises the importance of staff recognising the benefits to children of speaking more than one language (Qualifications and Curriculum Authority 2000).

Positive relationships between staff and children are important for all children but especially for those children considered 'at-risk'. For instance, improving relationships between at-risk African-American children and their teachers in the USA increased the students' engagement with learning and improved their academic outcomes (Decker, Dona and Christenson 2007).

GENDER

Adults can have a strong influence on the nature of play between boys and girls in preschools. Boys' play with other boys tends to be more active and forceful the further away from adults that they are. Boys and girls play more together when they are near adults (Fabes, Martin and Hanish 2003). Staff can explore the extent to which these dynamics operate within their groups and use the strategy of positioning themselves to encourage cross-gender play.

Research over time has shown that boys receive more attention from teachers than do girls in US preschool classrooms. Generally, boys receive attention because of their misbehaviour, and when they are not misbehaving tend to receive more commands from their teachers than do girls. Overall, girls receive more positive interactions from their preschool teachers than do boys (Dobbs, Arnold and Doctoroff 2004). This research can act as a prompt for staff to explore if and how gender influences their patterns of interaction with young children and to reflect on how best to direct attention to children within their specific contexts.

Gender can also influence children's patterns of interaction and friendship choices. A US study of 40 preschool girls and 35 preschool boys found that the girls tended to choose girls with low activity levels as their friends. On the other hand, boys tended to choose boys with high activity levels (Gleason et al. 2005). If staff are alert to the influences of gender on children's friendship patterns in their specific context they can explore ways to extend cross-gender friendships within their groups. Adults' position in the early childhood centre gives children strong messages about what and who the adults value. For example, some adults who work with toddlers position themselves more actively alongside boys who are building with blocks than they do when girls build with blocks (Leipzig 1992). Also, adults' positions influence children's play choices. Girls are more likely to become involved in activities traditionally associated with boys if a female staff member is nearby; and boys are more likely to become involved in activities traditionally associated with girls if a male staff member is nearby (Browne and Ross 1991; MacNaughton 2000). Staff can use this knowledge to encourage boys and girls to explore areas of the program that they have avoided.

Staff should consider placing children in girls-only and boys-only groups sometimes. Girls perform less well when they are involved in discussion and problem-solving sessions that are mixed gender than when the sessions are individual or girls-only (Parkin 1991). Placing girls and boys in separate groups can also lead them to appreciate the accomplishments of the other group. Epstein (1995) found that girls-only building times changed some boys' opinions of the girls' ability to build. As one boy said:

> I used to think girls don't do bricks. Then we made a girls' time for bricks. They made really good houses, specially Clare. Now I like to play with Clare in the bricks. We make lots of good buildings. (Epstein 1995, p. 65)

There can be gender differences in how male and female early years teachers see pro-social behaviour between children and how they see inclusion and exclusion within peer relations. Researchers in the USA (Ostrov, Crick and Keating 2005) found that males were less accurate in identifying relational aggression (inclusion and exclusion) and pro-social behaviour between peers than were females. Again, this research offers a point of reflection for staff on how they position themselves within the classroom and how their gender might influence what they look for and what they see in the children's relationships.

DISABILITY AND ADDITIONAL NEEDS

Staff should monitor their position in relation to children with additional needs in the group to ensure that they do not 'hover over' children with disabilities as they struggle, as all children do, to become independent. These children should have the opportunity to build the skills that will enable them to become independent learners (Palmer 1995), but staff should be nearby to help when needed. Close proximity will make it easier to offer verbal and physical support to children. Circle (or group) time has been used effectively to individualise goals for some children with disabilities in inclusive early childhood classrooms (Macy and Bricker 2007). This strategy helps to balance teacher proximity for support with child independence.

As mentioned above, adults' positioning in an early childhood centre gives strong messages to children about who and what the adults value. Staff can use this knowledge to actively model enjoyment in the acceptance of children with disabilities. They can ensure that they regularly work alongside children with disabilities in activities that show adult and child positively responding to each other. Staff can also use this knowledge to give children messages that they trust children with disabilities to be in charge of their own learning.

Reflecting on positioning techniques

1 Define positioning.
2 Robison and Schwartz (1982) believed that there were five main teaching roles for early childhood staff. These were:
   - nurturer—this involves offering children positive support and encouragement
   - reinforcer—this involves ensuring that desired forms of behaviour increase and undesired forms decrease
   - information giver—this involves telling children about particular facts or ideas
   - challenger—this involves creating novel and puzzling environments for children
   - tutor—this involves actively instructing a child how to do something.
   To what extent do you think that positioning can be used to assist you in each of these roles?
3 Visit an early childhood centre. Sketch the inside and outside learning areas. Note the strategic places to position yourself to ensure safe and wide supervision of children's learning. Note any areas that are potentially hazardous for children's learning.

Improving teaching in practice

1 Record the different ways in which you positioned yourself in relation to children and staff during several half-hour periods during the day. Note how long you stayed in each place and why you moved from one position to another.
2 How often did you use positioning to:
   - gain and maintain children's attention during a specific learning experience?
   - increase children's concentration on specific experiences?
   - ensure safe supervision of children's learning?
   - extend or enrich a particular experience?
   - encourage children's participation in a specific experience?
   - encourage social interaction between children?
3 How and how well did you take account of developmental considerations when positioning yourself?
4 How and how well did you take account of equity and anti-bias considerations when positioning yourself?

FURTHER READING

Brown, J. 2007, 'Time, space and gender: understanding "problem" behaviour in young children', *Children and Society*, 21(2), pp. 98–110.

Fleer, M. and Linke, P. 2002, *Babies: Good Beginnings Last Forever*, Australian Early Childhood Association, Watson, ACT.

Gandini, L. 1994, 'Educational and caring spaces', in C. Edwards, L. Gandini and G. Foreman, eds, *The Hundred Languages of Children: The Reggio Emilia Approach to Early Childhood Education* (pp. 135–50), Ablex Publishing Corporation, New Jersey.

Ostrosky, M., Gaffney, J. and Thomas, D. 2006, 'The interplay between literacy and relationships in early childhood settings', *Reading and Writing Quarterly*, 22(2), pp. 173–191.

ONLINE AND MULTI-MEDIA RESOURCES

Text

Barbuto, L., Swaminathan, S., Trawick-Smith, J. and Wright, J. 2003, 'The role of the teacher in scaffolding children's interactions in a technological environment: how a technology project is transforming preschool teacher practices in urban schools': **http://crpit.com/confpapers/CRPITV34Barbuto.pdf**

Sumison, J. and Olsen, A. 2000, 'Teacher play interaction styles and their impact on children's oral language and literacy: An ecobehavioural analysis of early childhood classrooms', Paper presented at the *Annual Conference of the Australian Association for Research in Education*, December, Sydney: **http://www.aare.edu.au/00pap/ols00513.htm**

Multi-media

Magna Systems 1995/2002, 'Teacher child interaction', *Early Childhood Training Series*, available from Marcom Projects at **http://www.marcom.com.au**

Magna Systems 2002, 'Exploring and learning', *Curriculum for Infants and Toddlers Series*, available from Marcom Projects at **http://www.marcom.com.au**

REFERENCES

Browne, N. and Ross, C. 1991, '"Girls' stuff, boys' stuff": young children talking and playing', in N. Browne, ed., *Science and Technology in the Early Years* (pp. 37–51), Open University Press, Milton Keynes.

Burton, L. 2001, 'Children's mathematical narratives as learning stories', Keynote address presented at the *European Conference on Quality in Early Childhood Education (EECERA)*, 29 August–1 September, Alkmaar, Netherlands, ED462135.

Cain, D., Rudd, L. and Saxon, T. 2007, 'Effects of professional development training on joint attention engagement in low-quality childcare centres', *Early Childhood Development and Care*, 177(2), pp. 150–185.

Calvert, S., Strong, B. and Gallagher, L. 2005, 'Control as an engagement feature for young children's attention to and learning of computer content', *American Behavioural Scientist*, 48(5), pp. 578–589.

Dangwal, R., Jha, S., Chatterjee, S. and Mitra, S. 2006, 'Research report: a model of how children acquire computing skills from hole-in-the-wall computers in public places', *The Information Technologies and International Development*, 2(4), pp. 41–60.

Decker, M., Dona, D. and Christenson, S. 2007, 'Behaviourally at-risk African American students: the importance of student-teacher relationships for student outcomes', *Journal of Social Psychology*, 45(1), pp. 83–109.

Dobbs, J., Arnold, D. and Doctoroff, G. 2004, 'Attention in the preschool classroom: the relationships among child gender, child misbehaviour, and types of teacher attention', *Early Child Development and Care*, 174(3), pp. 281–295.

Epstein, D. 1995, '"Girls don't do bricks": gender and sexuality in the primary classroom', in J. Siraj-Blatchford and I. Siraj-Blatchford, eds, *Educating the Whole Child: Cross-Curriculum Skills, Themes and Dimensions* (pp. 56–69), Open University Press, Milton Keynes.

Fabes, R., Martin, C. and Hanish, L. 2003, 'Young children's play qualities in same-, other-, and mixed-sex peer groups', *Child Development*, 74(3), pp. 921–932.

Fleer, M. and Linke, P. 2002, *Babies: Good Beginnings Last Forever*, Australian Early Childhood Association, Watson, ACT.

Flynn, N. 2007, 'What do effective teachers of literacy do? Subject knowledge and pedagogical choices for literacy', *Literacy*, 41(3), pp. 137–146.

Fumoto, H., Hargreaves, D. and Maxwell, S. 2007, 'Teachers' perceptions of their relationships with children who speak English as an additional language in early childhood settings', *Journal of Early Childhood Research*, 5(2), pp. 135–157.

Gleason, T., Gower, A., Hohmann, L. and Gleason, T. 2005, 'Temperament and friendship in preschool-aged children', *International Journal of Behavioural Development*, 29(4), pp. 336–344.

Hass Dyson, A. and Genishi, C. 1993, 'Visions of children as language users: language and language education in early childhood', in B. Spodek, ed., *Handbook of Research on the Education of Young Children* (pp. 122–36), Macmillan Publishing Company, New York.

Howes, C. and Eva Marie Shivers, M. 2006, 'New child-caregiver attachment relationships: entering childcare when the caregiver is and is not an ethnic match', *Social Development*, 15(4), pp. 574–590.

Hyun, E. 2001, 'Cultural complexity that affects young children's contemporary growth, change and learning', Paper presented at the *Annual Meeting of the Educational Research Association*, 10–14 April, Seattle, WA, ED451941.

Katz, J. 2004, 'Building peer relationships in talk: toddlers' peer conversations in childcare', *Discourse Studies*, 6(3), pp. 329–346.

Lally, M. 1991, *The Nursery Teacher in Action*, Paul Chapman Publishing, London.

Leipzig, J. 1992, 'Helping whole children grow: non-sexist childrearing for infants and toddlers', in B. Neugebauer, ed., *Alike and Different: Exploring our Humanity with Young Children* (pp. 32–41), National Association for the Education of Young Children, Washington, DC.

Macy, M. and Bricker, D. 2007, 'Embedding individualized social goals into routine activities in inclusive early childhood classrooms', *Early Childhood Development and Care*, 177(2), pp. 107–120.

MacNaughton, G. 2000, *Rethinking Gender in Early Childhood Education*, Allen & Unwin, Sydney.

McCoach, B., O'Connell, A. and Levitt, H. 2006, 'Ability grouping across kindergarten using an early childhood longitudinal study', *The Journal of Educational Research*, 99(6), pp. 339–346.

Mitra, S. and Rana, V. 2001, 'Children and the Internet: experiments with minimally invasive education in India', British *Journal of Educational Technology*, 32(2), pp. 221–232.

Moyles, J. 1989, *Just Playing: The Role and Status of Play in Early Childhood Education*, Open University Press, Milton Keynes.

Ostrosky, M., Gaffney, J. and Thomas, D. 2006, 'The interplay between literacy and relationships in early childhood settings', *Reading and Writing Quarterly*, 22(2), pp. 173–191.

Ostrov, J., Crick, N. and Keating, C. 2005, 'Gender-biased perceptions of preschoolers' behavior: how much is aggression and prosocial behaviour in the eye of the beholder?', *Sex Roles*, 52(5/6), pp. 393–398.

Palmer, A. 1995, 'Responding to special needs', in B. Creaser and E. Dau, eds, *The Anti-Bias Approach in Early Childhood* (pp. 71–84), Harper Educational, Sydney.

Parkin, R. 1991, 'Fair play: children's mathematical experiences in the infant classroom', in N. Browne, ed., *Science and Technology in the Early Years* (pp. 52–64), Open University Press, Milton Keynes.

Plowman, L. and Stephen, C. 2007, 'Guided interaction in pre-school settings', *Journal of Computer Assisted Learning*, 23(1), pp. 14–26.

Qualifications and Curriculum Authority 2000, *Curriculum Guidance for the Foundation Stage*, London.

Rance, S. 2005, 'Attending to early relationships difficulties: applying the "Watch, Wait and Wonder" approach in a pilot project for babies and parents', *Infant Observation*, 8(2), pp. 125–138.

Read, K., Gardner, P. and Mahler, B. 1993, *Early Childhood Programs: Human Relationships and Learning*, 9th edn, Holt, Rinehart and Winston Inc., Fort Worth, TX.

Robison, H. and Schwartz, S. 1982, *Designing Curriculum for Early Childhood*, Allyn & Bacon Inc., Boston.

Schechter, C. and Bye, B. 2007, 'Preliminary evidence for the impact of mixed-income preschools on low-income children's language growth', *Early Childhood Research Quarterly*, 22(1), pp. 137–146.

Smith, A. 1999, 'Quality care and joint attention', *International Journal of Early Years Education*, 7(1), pp. 85–98.

Sylva, K., Taggart, B., Siraj-Blatchford, I., Totsika, V., Ereky-Stevens, K., Gilden, R. and Bell, D. 2007, 'Circular quality and day-to-day learning activities in preschool', *International Journal of Early Years Education*, 15(1), pp. 49–65.

Wilkes, G. (ed.) 1979, *Collins Dictionary of the English Language*, Penguin Books, Middlesex.

Chapter 13

Questioning

 Questioning: a form of words addressed to a person in order to elicit information or evoke a response.

(*Collins Dictionary of the English Language*, p. 1197)

. . . the art of questioning remains an important teaching technique, and many rules laid down in method books of the last century are still useful.

(Hughes and Hughes 1937, p. 392)

Asking questions to children provides them with an opportunity to think and to use language in a functional manner by allowing them to report observations, describe experiences, and make predictions.

(Ramsey and Fowler 2004, p. 33)

What?

A question is 'a sentence worded or expressed to seek information' (Allen 1990, p. 981). When we ask questions about someone or something, we are trying to find out about them or it. We use questions to gain new information, to increase our understanding of something or to compare our own understandings with those of other people.

Issues and debates

OPEN-ENDED AND CLOSED-ENDED QUESTIONING

Staff can use two main types of questions to gain information from children: open questions and closed questions. Each type of question makes different demands on children's cognitive skills, their language skills and their need to go beyond what they already know.

A closed question limits the answer that is possible to give—it 'closes off' the options a person has in answering it. Often, a closed question is a request for factual information and the answer to it is clear and known to the questioner. Closed questions often require only a short answer, so they can be used to find out what a person knows about something or what they recall of a particular event. In early childhood settings, closed questions can be used to find out if children know the names of particular animals or what the rules of the centre are.

Closed questions generally require children to recall what they have been told or experienced. Here are some examples:

Recalling facts
'What is your cat's name?'; 'Do you have a brother?'; 'How many cups are on the table?'; 'What colour are your eyes?'.

Recalling experiences
'What was the name of our visitor yesterday?'; 'What did you do after milk and fruit today?'; 'Which colour swing did you play on today, Kwong?'.

Research over time has found (for example, Turney 1985; Tizard and Hughes 1984; Parker and Hurry 2007) that some teachers rely heavily on closed-ended questioning for the very limited purposes of checking:

- what facts children know and, therefore, what they need to be taught. For example, do children know their colours, the correct names for animals or road safety rules?
- what children have remembered of what they have been taught. For example, do they remember how to count to 10 or what the words of a particular song are?

Children find such closed questions boring and quickly learn to ignore them. Research (Parker and Hurry 2007) into teacher questioning to teach reading comprehension, in 51 primary school classrooms in the UK, showed that while teachers do use a variety of questioning techniques, two-thirds of the questions that teachers asked children were closed-ended. The researchers concluded that:

> The prevalent form of questioning in the classroom is shown to be a 'recitation script'. This type of directive questioning tends to produce predictable correct answers, and only occasionally are teachers' questions used to assist pupils to develop more elaborated ideas. The range of the teachers' questions is wide and appropriate but, importantly we think, this places the pupil in too passive a role.

Despite the fact that some teachers rely on closed-ended questioning, it does not have a powerful impact on children's learning. In contrast, the power of skilful open-ended questioning to promote children's learning across diverse domains of being and thinking is now well-established (e.g. Ramsey and Fowler 2004; Parker and Hurry 2007; Taylor et al. 2003; Wegerif 2005). Skilful open-ended questioning encourages children to explore possibilities, imagine and create rather than checking what children already know, feel and imagine.

Open questions assume that there is no right or wrong answer. There are many possible answers to an open question—there are many 'openings' for the person answering the question to express what they know, think, feel or believe. Open questions are often used to find out how others are thinking about and making sense of the social and natural world about them. For example, they can encourage children to hypothesise about how the natural world works, create new storylines in their imaginative play, or predict outcomes around specific events. Seefeldt (1980, p. 150) called open questions 'thought questions'.

Open questions generally inquire into the child's thought processes and require the child to share their theories, understandings, imaginings and feelings with adults or other children. They can be used to interest the child in an event, person or object, and to provoke thought and puzzlement over it. They also encourage the growth of children's problem-solving skills (Klein et al. 2000), science and mathematical learning (Ramsey and Fowler 2004). Here are some illustrations:

Sharing theories and understandings
'How do you think it works?'; 'Is this part important? Why?'; 'How could we find out more about it?'; 'Why do you think Sulu did that?'; 'What do you notice about this?'

Sharing feelings
'How did it make you feel when Craig knocked over your blocks?'; 'How do you feel when Sarah is crying?'

Sharing imaginings and provoking thoughts
'What do you think would happen if . . .?'; 'How could we end the story differently?'; 'What would we call an animal that was half elephant and half cat?'

QUESTIONING TECHNIQUES TO AVOID

Turney (1985) argued that there are four questioning techniques that should be avoided:

- repeating the same question until children answer it
- repeating children's answers
- answering one's own questions
- encouraging chorus answers.

Each reduces the effectiveness of questioning as a teaching technique because it can lead to children losing interest in what is being said and ignoring questions from staff on future occasions.

How?

Learning to ask questions that prompt children's learning takes time (Sook Lim and Cole 2002). As with any teaching technique, questioning will be most effective if staff have established a positive relationship with children, have good classroom guidance in place, and have appropriate staff–child ratios that allow for relaxed and meaningful conversations between staff and children (Ramsey and Fowler 2004).

From this base, staff can become skilful questioners of children by drawing on research that has grown over time that suggests the following:

Types of questions
- asking children how, when, where, what or why and ensuring that their questions have a simple and direct sentence structure. The younger the child, the more important this becomes. Young children will find it easier to follow a direct question such as, 'What is the name of your brother?' than an indirect question such as, 'The name of your brother is . . .' Good 'how' questions to support the development of mathematical and scientific thinking include: 'How are they alike?', 'How are they different?' and 'How do you know?' (Ramsey and Fowler 2004)

> William has just arrived from America and joined the Year 2 class. The teacher, to help William settle into his new class, is careful to include him in the group at 'sharing time' by asking him questions that he is able to answer easily: 'Do you have any brothers and sisters?'; 'Did you fly to Australia or did you come by sea?'

- focusing questions on a single task, thought or event. Young children can be confused by 'double-barrelled' questions (Turney 1985) such as, 'How many meals do you have a day and what do we call the last meal of the day?'. 'Double-barrelled' questions should be divided in two and the second should only be asked once the child has responded to the first

- using short sentences. Young children are more likely to readily comprehend these than long, wordy sentences, and they are more effective in arousing children's interest (Hogg and Foster 1973).

Style and rhythm of questioning

- asking one question at a time. Asking two or more questions at once can confuse young children:

> At lunchtime Anna is careful to ask the toddlers one question at a time about their food preferences: 'Would you like some rice?' 'Shall I give you some peas?'

- asking questions in a logical order to avoid misunderstandings and confusion (Briggs and Potter 1995)
- allowing children time to answer questions. Teachers can wait longer for children whom they believe to be more capable of answering questions than they do for those they believe to be less capable (McAllister 1990). This can reinforce some children's sense that their ideas and their abilities are valued less than other children's
- responding to children's answers with interest and warmth, as this shows children that their answers are valued and builds a responsive and respectful climate for child–teacher talk (Hyson 2003)
- using prompting techniques to encourage children's thinking and perseverance. For example, rephrasing or simplifying the question or summarising what the children have said to date can prompt children to respond further to the questions (Turney 1985)
- Reversing children's questions when they are directed at you to prompt their creative thinking. For example, when a child asks what to do next a teacher could ask 'What ideas do you have?'. This helps to prompt what Burnard et al. call 'possibility thinking' (2006, p. 252).

To summarise, when questioning: ask meaningful questions which are simple and direct; ask how, when, where, what and why; and use short sentences. Ask one question at a time, be logical, limit group questions and allow time for answers. Respond warmly and prompt children to encourage perseverance, and use questioning prudently.

When and why?

GOAL RELEVANCE

Questioning is such a valuable and pervasive teaching technique that it is relevant to most learning experiences for young children. Questioning builds learning across diverse domains, skills and areas of learning, including mathematical and science learning (Ramsey and Fowler 2004) and literacy learning (Hansen 2004). It can be used to:

- direct children's attention to a particular issue, event or phenomenon:

> Carla is keen for the six-year-old children in her class to learn how to observe differences between several rabbits they have in the classroom. Carla is encouraging them to look carefully at the physical properties of the animals and uses questions to direct their attention to some of the key differences between the rabbits.
>
> 'Can you see the length of the fur?'; 'What colour is it?'; 'Can you see the different shapes of their ears?'; 'What words could you use to talk about the differences?'
>
> _____
>
> *Reflection point:* Can you think of other questions Carla could ask?

- excite children's interest and curiosity about events, information or feelings
- help children reflect on information, feelings or events
- involve children in active learning through discussion
- identify children's difficulties in understanding
- encourage children to question themselves, others and their social and natural environments
- involve children in using a variety of cognitive abilities including their problem-solving capacities
- extend and enrich children's imaginative and socio-dramatic competencies
- develop children's curiosity and wonderment
- extend children's communication and language skills, including their ability to create their own stories
- encourage children to empathise with other children's feelings:

> Stephanie is a kindergarten teacher who uses questions to support the development of empathy between children. She is helping her small group to understand how Solonge (a new child) feels. She asks 'open' questions:
> 'How would you feel if you went to a new kindergarten and you didn't know any of the other children?'; 'How can we all help Solonge to feel comfortable about being here?'
>
> _Reflection point:_ Write down three additional questions you could ask to help the children think about Solonge's feelings.

The following discussion provides staff with some pointers on how to vary their questioning and thus the ways in which children engage with and learn from an experience. For example, it shows how staff can use one style of questioning to help children learn through looking and another for helping children learn through reflection.

Direct attention to a particular issue, event or phenomenon
One of the easiest ways to direct young children's attention to something is to ask them a question about it. Questions should be short and simple, and should be asked in a tone of voice that conveys the questioner's own interest in the subject. For example: 'Why is the fire engine in such a hurry?'; 'How did Lee get the dolls inside his block building?'; 'Do you know what I've found?'; 'Why have all the daffodils fallen over?'

Excite interest and curiosity about events, information or feelings
Questioning is an important technique through which to excite children's interest in something and, thus, to initiate their learning about it. A learning experience which begins with a question is valuable because it invites the children to discover something for themselves. Staff can also use questions to sustain interest in a particular learning experience. For example, 'Sam, can you guess what happens next?'; 'Tilly, how are you going to decorate the cake?'; 'Joshua, where could we find some clean clothes for the baby?'; 'Babette, what else could we use to help us fight the fire?'

Help children reflect on information, feelings or events
Reflection is the process of thinking about something. It involves taking time to ponder. Reflection is an important part of the process of making sense of our daily world and of building a sense of what we understand about it. Questions that encourage children to reflect on what they know need not always require answers: staff may use them to help children begin to reflect on what they have been learning. Children can be prompted to reflect by being asked to think about what they have learned or what they think they know about something. Such questions are useful when children assert that something is true. For example: 'How do you know that all cats meow?'; 'Is there anything else you need to have before you build your hospital?'; 'Do you know what astronauts do when they go to the moon?'

Involve children actively in learning through discussion
Learning is a highly active process in which children seek to make sense of their world and become competent in it across all domains of development: social, emotional, cognitive, communicative and physical. High-quality diaiologic teaching—that is, teaching in which adults ask children reflective questions about their experiences—prompts children to learn at a higher level than they might otherwise have done (Fisher 2007).

Encourage children to question themselves, others and their social and natural environments
Raising questions with children about the natural world can be an effective way to involve them in scientific learning. Scientific inquiry asks 'How?' about a variety of 'happenings' in the natural world and it reflects a constructivist view of learning where children make meaning through their own investigations and discoveries. Asking a question is the starting point for such inquiry. As Gallenstein (2005, p. 32) explains, actively constructing scientific knowledge involves:

- asking a question about objects, organisms, and events in the environment
- planning and conducting a simple investigation
- employing simple equipment and tools to gather data and extend the sense
- using data to construct a reasonable explanation
- communicating investigations and explanations.

Involve children in using a variety of cognitive abilities
Questions can be used to actively promote children's thinking and to develop a broad range of cognitive skills (Huber and Lenhoff 2006) and metacognitive skills (Annevirta and Vauras 2006). They can encourage children to:

- organise, use, compare and evaluate information
- articulate their reasoning
- problem-solve
- co-construct knowledge with others (see Chapter 19)
- explore creative and novel ideas.

Questions vary considerably in the intellectual operations they demand of the child and some types of questions are better than others in assisting children's cognitive development. Davis and Tinsley (1986) identified the following types of questions that positively assist the development of a child's higher order thinking skills:

- Interpretative questions require the child to describe the relationships between particular types of information—to interpret how one thing relates to another.
  For example: 'What happened when we added soap to the water?'; 'How did you make the slippery material stay on the paper?'; 'Why did Sally close the windows in the play-room when it rained?'
- Translation questions require the child to change information from one form to another (for example, visual information in a picture can be changed to a three-dimensional representation of it or to a verbal description). The child needs to translate understandings from one form of representation to another.
  For example: 'Can you draw a picture of your block building?'; 'Can you build a model of the car you have just painted?'; 'Can you tell me how feeling happy looks?'
- Application questions require the child to use knowledge and skills to solve a real-life problem. The child has to apply her understandings or skills.
  For example: 'How can we use the blocks to make the bed big enough for Sam?'; 'What other tools could we use to make holes in the paper?'; 'What musical instruments could we use to make a sound like thunder?'

- Synthesising questions require the child to combine a variety of knowledge and skills in order to wonder about or create a solution to problems they might not have encountered before. Children have to synthesise (combine) what they know to solve a problem.

    For example: 'We have a new child, Jansen, starting at the centre next week who cannot hear very well. How could we make Jansen feel welcome?'; 'How could we make sure that everyone has a fair go at playing with our new water-wheel?'; 'What could we do to invite all the parents to our end-of-year party?'

- Evaluative questions require the child to make judgments about what should happen, what might work and what could be done differently.

    For example: 'Why do you think the bridge fell down?'; 'How do you know if Sarah's happy with playing in her tent?'; 'What do you think we could do next time to make sure everyone has a piece of pineapple?'; 'Why do you think that we can't dig deep enough to find the treasure?'

Deepen children's aesthetic awareness

Questions can be used to challenge children to use all of their senses and perceptions in producing and appreciating art and to develop musical skills in young children. Questions that deepen musical awareness encourage children to make observations and comparisons (Cooper and Grimm-Anderson 2007). For example, questions that encourage musical observations and comparisons might be as simple as, 'Have you heard a sound like this before?', 'What else do you know that sounds like this?' or 'What other songs are as fast as this one?'

Extend and enrich children's imaginative and socio-dramatic competencies

There are many different ways to encourage children's imagination, and questioning is important in several of them. Questions can prompt children to create new storylines for their socio-dramatic play and to practise their own story-telling skills. For example, introducing the children to props such as puppets, dolls or pictures and then inviting them to tell a story based on those props is a simple and effective way to encourage them to develop their imaginations. Soundy and Humadi Genisio (1994, p. 21) believed that once a prop has been introduced, simple follow-up questions would often initiate children's stories:

> . . . the teacher could begin by displaying a skunk puppet and suggesting the class make up a story about another uninvited visitor to the campsite. Two or three follow-up questions could help initiate the story-telling: 'What name shall we give the skunk?', 'What kind of trouble might this skunk create?' and 'What do you think scares a skunk?'.

Questions can also challenge children to imagine beyond what they know and to play around with the fantastic. Children can be asked to imagine new words, to create new animals or to think in new ways about everyday events. For example: 'What would a name be for an animal that is part cockatoo and part kangaroo?'; 'How might a rainbow sound?'; 'What might the movement of butterfly wings look like on paper?'; 'What could be a different ending for this story?'; 'What would we call someone who lived on the moon?'

Questions can encourage children to have fun playing with sounds, movements, words, ideas and events, and can also encourage them to create new ways of thinking about them. Questions can also encourage children to tell their own stories and to build their story-telling skills (Hough et al. 1987).

Develop dispositions of curiosity and wonderment

Katz (1989) argued that to be curious and full of wonder is the key to successful learning. Questioning is an important process through which staff can convey their own sense of curiosity and wonderment about the world to children and can encourage children to be curious about the world around them. Curiosity and wonderment can be fostered by asking children:

- how to find out more about things that interest them
- how and why things work
- how they can make things happen
- how they can make their thoughts visible to others.

Questions that invite wonder need to invoke a sense of 'paradox or puzzlement, not knowing' (McWilliams 1999, p. 9). Such questions include:

- Why is this so?
- How is this so?
- I wonder what would happen if . . . what do you think?

Some examples of questions that children generated when a teacher asked them to wonder about the moon included:

- Is the moon made of cheese?
- If you touch the moon will it move?
- Is the moon bumpy? (McWilliams 1999, p. 9).

Extend children's communication and language skills
In the first few years of life, children's language and communication skills are building rapidly. Modelling good questioning styles and using questions to build conversational patterns with children of all ages are important to the development of these skills in young children. 'Open' questions that require the children to think carefully can develop more complex language-use in children from three years of age, can encourage them to form sentences and to ask questions of each other and of adults, and can help them to become confident when responding to questions from others (Beaty 1996). Questions that encourage children to think about alternatives and move them beyond fact and recall increase children's language and communication skills (Girolametto and Weitzman 2002). These questions include follow-up or take-up questions; high-level, open-ended questions; and questions that the teacher does not already know the answer to (McIntyre 2007).

Encourage children to empathise with other children's feelings
The success of children's learning is influenced by its social and emotional context and responsiveness of adults to children (Abbott and Rodger 1994; Hyson 2003). Questioning can be an important technique through which to build positive relationships between peers and thus to develop a supportive and co-operative learning environment. From two to three years of age, children can talk about their relationships with other children and with adults. Staff can help them to empathise with others' feelings by asking children to think about the consequences for others of their or somebody else's actions. Questions commonly used in this process include: 'How do you think that made Shona feel?'; 'What could we do to make Gerald feel happier?'; 'How do you feel when someone hurts you? Do you think Marci feels that way too?' Staff can also use questions to encourage children to think about how to be kind and fair to others. For example: 'What do you think "kindness" means?'; 'How would you know if someone was being fair to you?'; 'Do they think that kindness is a good thing?' (Smith 1982).

DEVELOPMENTAL CONSIDERATIONS

From an early age, children use questions as an important way to communicate with each other and with adults. Therefore, adults should use questioning to promote learning through dialogue with children. Young children's communicative and cognitive competence clearly influences the nature and type of questions that adults can usefully ask them. As a general guideline, the younger the child, the simpler, more concrete and more focused on the here and now the question should be. For example, asking toddlers about a cat they have just seen is more likely to generate responses than asking them why cats are called cats.

Staff can judge the likely influence of children's developmental competence on the type of questions they ask by observing the questions asked by children of differing ages or stages. Staff can then use this knowledge to 'pitch' their questions at appropriate levels. For example:

- Pre-verbal children ask questions using body language such as pointing or gesturing, or using a particular intonation. Verbalising such questions plays an important role in developing their communicative competence.
- Children under two generally use single words to ask questions. They can, therefore, understand simple questions adults ask of them. Children as young as two use questions to gain information with which to make sense of their world. Often these questions are very concrete about the here and now. Therefore, questions about the here and now are likely to interest children at this age.
- Children between two and five are extremely persistent questioners, one of their favourite questions being 'Why?'. More complex questions about how and why things happen can be introduced at this stage.

Children's age provides a guide for the staff's nature and style of questioning, but staff should 'experiment' with asking children of all ages a variety of concrete and abstract questions. Research and experience shows that from a very early age, children are capable of reflecting on and answering quite abstract questions about the past, present and future. Some two-year-olds may be quite fascinated by a question about why cats are called cats, and many four-year-olds need and enjoy questions about the immediate, concrete, here and now. Such questions can often lead children to give quite complex and abstract answers. However, the

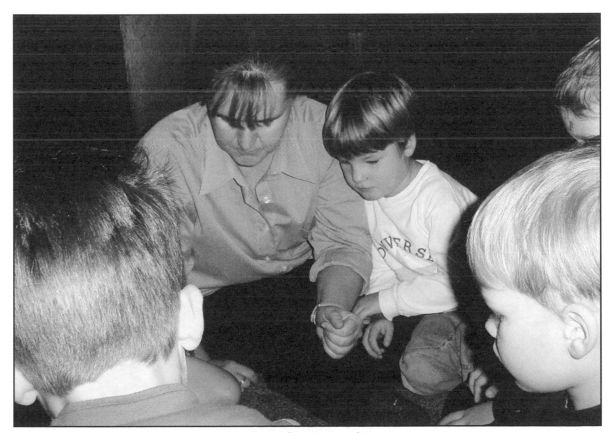

'How does it move?'

type of questions staff ask and the level of children's responses can vary with age. Canadian research in 13 preschools and 13 child care centres showed that preschool children respond more frequently to teachers' questions than do toddlers and that preschool children respond more extensively to open-ended questions than they do closed-questions (de Rivera et al. 2005).

Staff will not know what questions children can answer until they ask them, as in the following conversation between an adult and a four-year-old child:

> **Adult:** 'I've noticed that you are often the only girl playing with the boys. Why is that Chloe?'
>
> **Chloe:** 'Well, you see, it's like this. In all the movies, there's only one girl playing with the boys. That's why.'

The 'movies' to which Chloe referred included *Ninja Turtles* and *Ghostbusters*. At four years of age, Chloe had made a very complex and sophisticated observation about sexism within the media and had used this observation to make sense of her own and her peer group's play patterns.

Questions are also an effective way to build the literacy skills of children in their early years of schooling. By about seven years of age children can answer questions about meanings in written and spoken language, and can begin to question the structure of their own written and spoken language (Roop 1990). However, the most effective questions to promote literacy skills are higher order questions that go beyond fact and recall (Taylor et al. 2003) and that are open-ended (Flynn 2007).

Staff can use questions to encourage children in the early years of schooling to reflect on their own language use and to help them understand that they can improve their writing skills through such reflection. Roop (1990, p. 283) suggested that questions such as the following are useful to promote such reflection:

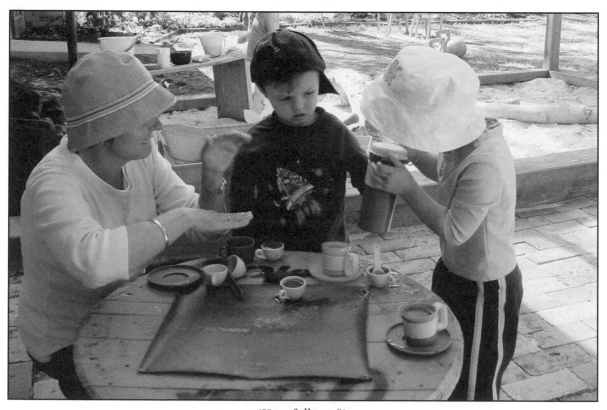

'How full is it?'

Does this sentence make sense? Does this part move the story forward? Is this really the way my character would react . . .? Can I shorten this paragraph and say the same thing in a better way?

Children's reading skills can be enhanced through the use of questions (Flynn 2007). Beck and McKeown (2001, p. 14) described a read-aloud program with children in the early years of school that used two types of questions that can be used to help children construct meaning from texts during reading aloud sessions. They were:

- initial questions—interspersed open questions which require children to describe and explain text ideas, rather than recall and retrieve words from text
- follow-up questions—questions which scaffold students' thinking by using their initial responses to form questions that encourage elaboration and development of initial ideas.

Questions can also be an important part of building children's metacognitive skills as they make sense of the sense world around them. Staff can alert children to their own ways of thinking through using questions that guide them to 'imagine, think, verbalize and reflect' (Doverborg and Pramling Samuelsson 1999, p. 100). With older children, asking 'not' questions can help extend children's metacognitive skills (Buckleitner 2007). The 'not' questions are those that ask, 'What animal does not bark?' or 'What do crocodiles not do?'

Equity considerations

'RACE' AND CULTURE

Most questions require answers and in Anglo-Australian culture there is a strong sense of turn-taking associated with questioning—one person asks a question and then waits for an answer. However, staff in multicultural settings should remember that each culture has its own rules associated with social discourse and turn-taking, and that these can lead to 'different speakers being accused of rudeness, even though they are operating within a set of culturally accepted rules: but they are the rules of another culture' (Partington and McCudden 1992, p. 221). To avoid misunderstandings, it is important for staff to familiarise themselves with the patterns of social discourse used by children in their group who have cultural backgrounds different from their own.

Aboriginal children may have learned within their communities that periods of silence in conversations are quite acceptable and they may decide to remain silent or to ignore questions. This does not mean they do not know the answers to the questions posed or are being disrespectful. In some cultures silence can also be seen as a polite and non-offensive way of responding to a question when a child believes the answer may offend the questioner (Carlin 2003).

Silence also plays an important social role in the language interactions of many people from a variety of Asian backgrounds. Lynch and Hanson (1992, p. 233) explained:

On the one hand, maintaining silence in a conversation may serve as an expression of interest and respect. On the other hand, if silence follows consistent verbal responses . . . it may indicate disagreement or negative reactions such as anger . . .

It is, therefore, very important that early childhood staff develop an awareness of and sensitivity to how the children in their care may respond to questions. They should avoid simplistic, stereotyped understandings about how 'Asians', 'Aborigines' or any other group of children respond to questions. There are differences both within and between cultures. Staff can learn about these by drawing on the advice and expertise of staff in relevant advice agencies in their state.

A structured conversation with young children can be an effective tool to gain an understanding of what children do and do not understand about the diversity in the world around them and what their attitudes to 'racial' and ethnic diversity are. To build positive attitudes towards 'racial' and ethnic diversity, questions should help children to restructure their understandings of diversity, rather than just describe what they know (Bernstein et al. 2000). It is also important to allow children's questions to surface during discussions about diversity.

GENDER

From as early as two years of age, many boys and many girls begin to decide in traditional, gender-stereotypical ways about where to play, what to play with and how to play with each other, and these choices solidify as the children develop (Green, Bigler and Catherwood 2004). Questioning can help children to think about how they might make less gender-stereotyped choices in their play. For example, Epstein (1995) described a discussion circle in which she asked boys to explain why they were excluding girls from block play and asked the girls to explain why they wanted to play in block play. She used this as a basis from which to develop some 'rules' about 'fair' play in the block area.

Research on gender in education over time has consistently found that gender plays a strong role in how teachers attend to and engage with children, and the issues have remained very similar over time (Beaman, Wheldall and Kemp 2006). Some time ago Leipzig (1992) found that early childhood staff interrupt infants' and toddlers' explorations more frequently if they are girls than if they are boys. Leipzig (1992) suggested that this may make girls feel less able to complete tasks by themselves than boys. While this is now some time ago, it offers a point of reflection for staff on how gender may influence their approach to questioning young children. Staff could consider the impact of questioning on a specific girl in their particular context if this might enable her to complete a task by herself.

DISABILITY AND ADDITIONAL NEEDS

When staff question children with additional needs they should take into account individual children's particular developmental levels and abilities, as they do with all children, and adjust their questioning accordingly. In addition, staff may need to specifically modify their questioning techniques to take account of a child's specific disability. For example, as staff speak to children with hearing impairments, they may need to stand face-to-face with them.

Asking children with disabilities if they need and want staff's help to do things is an important way in which staff can show respect. If children can understand and respond to questions, staff should ask them if they would like help, rather than automatically assuming that they would. Helping the children without asking them first 'tells' them that staff do not believe they are capable of doing things for themselves and that they have no rights to decide for themselves when help is appropriate.

Asking questions that children might have about children with disabilities in the group is an important technique for helping children feel comfortable about diversity. It provides staff with an avenue through which to clarify children's misconceptions and answer any fears or concerns they may have.

Reflecting on questioning techniques

1 Define questioning.
2 What does research suggest are the keys to using questioning to optimise children's learning?
3 When do you think closed questions should be used in your teaching?
4 Are there any times when you think that the use of open questions is inappropriate with young children?
5 'A questions curriculum empowers both teachers and students' (Wing 1992, p. 81). To what extent do you agree with Wing? Why? Why not?
6 How could questions be used to promote communicative competence with infants? What sort of questions could you use to achieve this aim?

7 What things do you think toddlers would enjoy having questions asked about?

8 What are the most interesting questions you have heard adults ask four-year-old children?

9 What do you know about the role of questions in cultures different to your own?

10 What differences have you noticed in how boys and girls respond to questions?

11 How could you use questions to promote self-esteem for children with disabilities?

12 Imagine you were working with a group of three-year-olds who were visiting a city farm. Try to develop at least two questions that would achieve the following aims:
   - direct attention to a particular issue, event or phenomenon
   - excite interest and curiosity about events, information or feelings
   - help children to reflect on information, feelings or events
   - involve children actively in learning through discussion
   - encourage children to become questioners of themselves, others and their social and natural environments
   - involve children in using a variety of cognitive abilities
   - extend and enrich children's imaginative and socio-dramatic competencies
   - encourage children to develop dispositions of curiosity and wonderment
   - extend children's communication and language skills
   - encourage children to empathise with other children's feelings.

13 Questions that develop higher order thinking skills in young children need to help them interpret, translate, apply, synthesise and evaluate information. Develop a plan for a learning experience for four- to five-year-old children in which you have examples of questions that achieve each of the above aims.

14 Imagine you are working in a mixed group of two- to five-year-old children. One of the five-year-old children has brought their pet turtle to the centre to share with the other children. Would you use closed or open questions to provoke and enrich the group's interest in the turtle? Write some examples of the questions you might use to assist the development of children's creativity and imagination as they learn about the turtle.

Improving teaching in practice

1 Record (using a tape-recorder or written notes) the questions you ask children during several half-hour teaching periods.

2 What is your current style of questioning?
   - What balance did you have between open and closed questions?
   - Was your use of open and closed questions appropriate?
   - How repetitive was your questioning?
   - How did children respond to your questioning?
   - Did your questioning encourage children to expand their understandings of the world about them?

3 How and how well did you take account of:
   - developmental considerations?
   - equity and anti-bias considerations of culture, 'race', gender and disability?

4 What are your areas of strength and weakness in using questions to promote children's learning?

5 How can you work to improve your questioning techniques in practice?

FURTHER READING

Briggs, F. and Potter, G. 1995, *Teaching Children in the First Three Years of School*, 2nd edn, Longman, Sydney [refer to pp. 268–273].

Heausler Adams, N. 1994, 'Ask, don't tell', Paper presented at the *Annual Conference of the Association for Childhood Education International*, ED372867.

Paley, V. 1990, *The Boy Who Wanted to be a Helicopter*, Harvard University Press, Cambridge, MA [refer to pp. 151–63].

Parker, M. and Hurry, J. 2007, 'Teachers' use of questioning and modelling comprehension skills in a primary classroom', *Educational Review* 59(3), pp. 299–314.

Wasserman, S. 1991, 'The art of the question', *Childhood Education*, 67(4), pp. 257–259.

Wing, L. 1992, 'The interesting questions approach to learning', *Childhood Education*, 69(2), pp. 78–85.

Wragg, E. and Brown, G. 2001, *Questioning in the Primary School* (Successful Teaching Series), Routledge Falmer, London.

Yoon, J. and Onchwari, A. 2006, 'Teaching young children science: three key points', *Early Childhood Education Journal*, 33(6), pp. 419–423.

ONLINE AND MULTI-MEDIA RESOURCES

Text

'Classroom questioning'. A useful overview of research on teacher questioning—what works, what doesn't: **http://www.nwrel.org/scpd/sirs/3/cu5.html**

Multi-media

Bleiker, C. 2005, 'Early Childhood Settings and Approaches' (DVD). A free access segment from the DVD on Reggio Emilia provides a good example of teacher questioning in action in an early childhood setting: **http://www.prenhall.com/merrillmedia/media/bleiker.mov**

MacNaughton, G., Campbell, S., Smith, K. and Lawrence, H. 2002, *Equity Adventures in Early Childhood*, Centre for Equity and Innovation in Early Childhood, University of Melbourne (CD). Strand on stories shows different approaches to questioning children during and after stories: **http://www.edfac.unimelb.edu.au/CEIEC/resources**

'Early years workshop—listening and questioning', *Teachers' TV*. Free access download: **http://www.teachers.tv/video/3437** (accessed 21 October 2007).

REFERENCES

Abbott, L. and Rodger, R. 1994, *Quality Education in the Early Years*, Open University Press, Milton Keynes,

Allen, R. (ed.) 1990, *The Concise Oxford Dictionary of Current English*, Clarendon Press, Oxford.

Annevirta, T. and Vauras, M. 2006, 'Developmental changes of metacognitive skill in elementary school children', *Journal of Experimental Education*, 74(3), pp. 195–226.

Beaty, J. 1996, *Skills for Preschool Teachers*, 5th edn, Prentice Hall Inc., New Jersey.

Beaman, R., Wheldall, K. and Kemp, C. 2006, 'Differential teacher attention to boys and girls in the classroom', *Educational Review*, 58(3), pp. 339–366.

Beck, I. and McKeown, M. 2001, 'Text talk: capturing the benefits of read-aloud experiences for young children', *The Reading Teacher*, 55(1), pp. 10–20.

Bernstein, J., Schindler Zimmerman, T., Werner-Wilson, R. and Vosburg, J. 2000, 'Preschool children's classification skills and a multicultural education intervention to promote acceptance of cultural diversity', *Journal of Research in Childhood Education*, 14(2), pp. 181–192.

Briggs, F. and Potter, G. 1995, *Teaching Children in the First Three Years of School*, 2nd edn, Longman, Sydney.

Buckleitner, W. 2007, 'Helping young children find and use information: how to create an "information friendly" environment in your classroom', *Early Childhood Today*, April, 2007, <http://content.scholastic.com/browse/article.jsp?id=3746207> (accessed 16 July 2007).

Burnard, P., Craft, A. and Cremin, T. with Duffy, B., Hanson, R., Keene, J., Haynes, L. and Burns, D. 2006, 'Documenting "possibility" thinking: a journey of collaborative enquiry', *International Journal of Early Years Education*, 14(30), pp. 243–262.

Carlin, A. 2003, 'On owning silence: talk, texts, and the semiotics of bibliographies', *Semiotica*, 146, pp. 117–138.

Cooper, S. and Grimm-Anderson, S. 2007, 'Structured English Immersion (SEI) in the music classroom: music instruction for crossing borders', *General Music Today*, 20(2), pp. 20–24.

Davis, O. and Tinsley, D. 1986, 'Cognitive objectives revealed by classroom questions asked by social studies student teachers', in M. Hammersley, ed., *Case Studies in Classroom Research* (pp. 63–69), Open University Press, Milton Keynes.

de Rivera, C., Girolametto, L., Greenberg, J. and Weitzman, E. 2005, 'Children's responses to educators' questions in preschool and child care play groups', *American Journal of Speech-Language Pathology*, 14, pp. 14–26.

Doverborg, E. and Pramling Samuelsson, I. 1999, 'Apple cutting and creativity as a mathematical beginning', *Kindergarten Education: Theory, Research and Practice*, 4(2), pp. 87–103.

Epstein, D. 1995, 'Girls don't do bricks', in J. Siraj-Blatchford and I. Siraj-Blatchford, eds, *Educating the Whole Child: Cross-curricula Skills, Themes and Dimensions* (pp. 56–69), Open University Press, Milton Keynes.

Fisher, R. 2007, 'Dialogic teaching: developing thinking and metacognition through philosophical discussion', *Early Child Development and Care*, 177(6/7), pp. 615–663.

Flynn, N. 2007, 'What do effective teachers of literacy do? Subject knowledge and pedagogical choices for literacy', *Literacy*, 41(3), pp. 137–146.

Gallenstein, N. 2005, 'Engaging young children in science and mathematics', *Journal of Elementary Science Education*, 17(2), pp. 27–41.

Girolametto, L. and Weitzman, E. 2002, 'Responsiveness of child care providers in interactions with toddlers and preschoolers', *Language, Speech, and Hearing Services in Schools*, 33, pp. 268–281.

Green, V., Bigler, R. and Catherwood, D. 2004, 'The variability and flexibility of gender-typed play: a closer look at children's behavioural responses to counterstereotypic models', *Sex Roles*, 51(7/8), pp. 371–387.

Hansen, C. 2004, 'Teacher talk, promoting literacy development through response to story', *Journal of Research in Childhood Education*, 19(1/2), pp. 115–129.

Hildebrand, V. 1991, *Introduction to Early Childhood Education*, 5th edn, Macmillan Publishing Company, New York.

Hogg, A. and Foster, J. 1973, *Understanding Teaching Procedures*, Cassell Australia, Sydney.

Hough, R., Nurss, J. and Wood, D. 1987, 'Tell me a story: making opportunities for elaborated language in early childhood classrooms', *Young Children*, November, pp. 6–12.

Huber, L. and Lenhoff, R. 2006, 'Mathematical concepts come alive in pre-k and kindergarten classrooms', *Teaching Children Mathematics*, 13(4), pp. 226–232.

Hughes, A. and Hughes, E. 1937, *Learning and Teaching: An Introduction to Psychology and Education*, Longman, London.

Hyson, M. 2003, *The Emotional Development of Young Children: Building an Emotion-Centered Curriculum*, Teachers College Press, New York.

Katz, L. 1989, 'Children as learners: a developmental approach', in *Weaving Webs: A Collaborative Approach to Teaching and Learning in the Early Childhood Curriculum*, 11–13 July, Melbourne.

Klein, E.R., Hammrich, P., Bloom, S. and Ragins, A. 2000, 'Language development and science inquiry: a child-initiated and teacher-facilitated program', Paper presented at the *Annual Meeting of the American Education Research Association*, April, New Orleans, ED440756.

Leipzig, J. 1992, 'Helping whole children grow: non-sexist childrearing for infants and toddlers', in B. Neugebauer, ed., *Alike and Different: Exploring our Humanity with Young Children* (pp. 32–41), National Association for the Education of Young Children, Washington, DC.

Lynch, E. and Hanson, M. 1992, *Developing Cross-Cultural Competence*, Paul H. Brookes, Baltimore.

McAllister, E. 1990, 'Anatomy of a crushed spirit', *Childhood Education*, 66(4), pp. 204–205.

McIntyre, E. 2007, 'Story discussion in the primary grades: balancing authenticity and explicit teaching', *The Reading Teacher*, 60(11), pp. 610–621.

McWilliams, S. 1999, 'Fostering wonder in young children', Paper presented at the *Annual Meeting of the National Association for Research in Science Teaching*, 28–31 March, Boston, MA, ED444833.

Parker, M. and Hurry, J. 2007, 'Teachers' use of questioning and modelling comprehension skills in a primary classroom', *Educational Review*, 59(3), pp. 299–314.

Partington, G. and McCudden, V. 1992, *Ethnicity and Education*, Social Science Press, Sydney.

Ramsey, J. and Fowler, M. 2004, '"What do you notice?" Using posters containing questions and general instructions to guide preschoolers' science and mathematics learning', *Early Child Development and Care*, 174(1), pp. 31–45.

Roop, P. 1990, 'The magic of writing: how a writer teaches writing', *Childhood Education*, 66(5), pp. 281–284.

Seefeldt, C. 1980, *Teaching Young Children*, Prentice Hall Inc., New York.

Smith, C. 1982, *Promoting the Social Development of Young Children*, Mayfield Publishing Company, Kansas.

Sook Lim, Y. and Cole, K. 2002, 'Facilitating first language development in Korean children through parent training in picture book interactions', *Bilingual Research Journal*, 26(2), pp. 213–227.

Soundy, C. and Humadi Genisio, M. 1994, 'Asking young children to tell the story', *Childhood Education*, 71(1), pp. 20–23.

Taylor, B., Pearson, D., Peterson, D. and Rodriguez, M. 2003, 'Reading growth in high-poverty classrooms: the influence of teacher practices that encourage cognitive engagement in literacy learning', *The Elementary School Journal*, 104(1), pp. 3–28.

Tizard, B. and Hughes, M. 1984, *Young Children Learning: Talking and Thinking at Home and at School*, Fontana, London.

Turney, C. 1985, *Anatomy of Teaching*, Novak Publishing, Sydney.

Wegerif, R. 2005, 'Reason and creativity in classroom dialogues', *Language and Education*, 19(3), pp. 223–237.

Wilkes, G. (ed.) 1979, *Collins Dictionary of the English Language*, Penguin Books, Middlesex.

Wing, L. 1992, 'The interesting questions approach to learning', *Childhood Education*, 69(2), pp. 78–85.

Chapter 14

Reading

Read: to comprehend the meaning of (something written or printed) by looking at and interpreting the written or printed characters.

(*Collins Dictionary of the English Language*, p. 1215)

Reading is an act of thinking and understanding, and learning to read is a constructive problem-solving process.

(Spodek and Saracho 1994, p. 337)

When we read to [children] . . . we expose them to the beauty of the literary language and a wider variety of language forms than they hear in other situations.

(Robison and Schwartz 1982, p. 245)

What?

Reading is the recognition and interpretation of the meaning(s) of a printed word or symbol and of groups of words or symbols. Reading is about making meaning(s) from print. When we read a road sign we recognise the word or symbol on the sign and then try to interpret its meaning(s). When we read books we recognise groups of printed words and images in the book and then try to interpret their meaning(s). We read for many reasons. It enables us to do diverse things, such as follow signs, find out a person's name, order food in a restaurant, pass exams and experience stories. We read to gain information and for enjoyment. Reading to someone involves us speaking the written word, the other person hearing the sounds we make and then interpreting them. Therefore, as we read or are read to, we are involved in a process of constructing meaning from printed words or symbols.

As a teaching technique, reading helps children to construct meanings about the world around them. For the purposes of this chapter, we will focus on primarily on reading for enjoyment. Reading books and stories is one of the most common ways in which early childhood staff read to or with children, because it is often a very pleasurable experience for those involved.

> The story method of reading is really a form of word and picture play and is an immediately pleasurable activity for children and adults alike. (Moyles 1989, p. 52)

This chapter will focus on how reading to or with children can support their learning and wellbeing.

Issues and debates

DOES THE READER MATTER?

The opportunity for children to read digital stories and to be 'read to' by a computer in a web-based environment is a 21st century phenomenon. Young children can now access websites such as the International Children's Digital Library where they can be read to and read stories in many different languages, create stories and link with other children to ask and answer questions about stories.

There is considerable interest in, and research into, exploring the ways to use this form of literature to positively enhance children's learning. There is evidence that an e-literature environment entices children to read more and expands the diversity of what they read. For instance, researchers have found that children using the International Children's Digital Library enjoy engaging with children from other parts of the world even when they do not share the same language as each other (Komlodia et al. 2007). They have also found that use of the library increased children's motivation for reading. In a four-year case study of 12 children living in Germany, Honduras, New Zealand and the United States researchers found that children using the International Children's Digital Library increased the diversity of stories they read, increased their motivation for reading stories and increased their interest in other cultures. Interestingly, children still used local libraries and enjoyed the social interaction involved in reading in libraries (Druin et al. 2007).

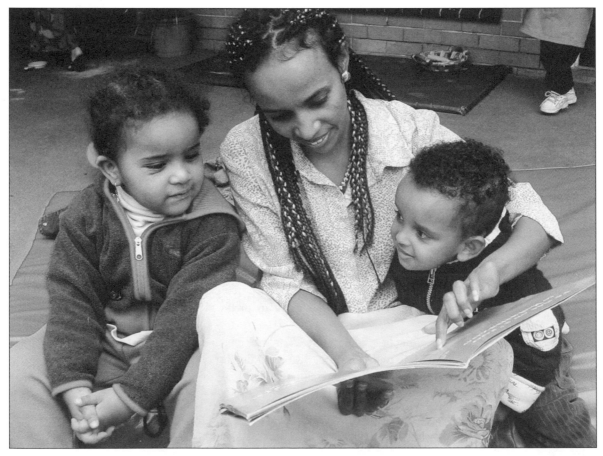

Nasta reads with the children.

The development of and increased access to e-literature for young children is also generating some concerns. There is a concern to ensure that within the e-literature environment children are supported to critically engage with what they are reading and to ensure that the limitations of e-literature are recognised:

> They have the potential to promote passivity, putting readers into a sort of 'spectator stance' in which they let the computer do the 'work' of reading rather than becoming actively engaged in the reading process. (Lefever-Davis and Pearman 2005, p. 246)

How?

There are strong opinions in the early childhood field about the best way to read books to or with young children. Staff will need to develop their own list of do's and don'ts, but the following suggestions can provide a starting point for reflecting on how best to share books with children. Points to consider include ensuring that the books:

- are in good repair with no torn or missing pages and with covers intact
- match and/or enrich the children's interests and ways of thinking about the world
- do not frighten the children
- are culturally respectful and meaningful
- are read to children in ways that enable the children to readily see any pictures related to the words being read.

Children concentrate best when they are comfortable. They may be comfortable sitting on an adult's knee, cuddling up by someone in a big, soft chair or resting against large, soft floor cushions. Choosing a relaxed and comfortable environment for reading will help both adults and children to feel more relaxed and comfortable:

> Sandy, a Year 2 teacher, regularly takes the children outside to read under the large gum tree in the yard. They take a rug from the classroom so that they can be comfortable. The children sit and lie on the rug as they become engrossed in the stories which Sandy reads.
>
> _Reflection point:_ Where could you take children for story times in your centre?

When staff show enthusiasm for reading and enjoyment in using books for fun and learning, children will develop a love of books and reading. When thinking about how children can get the most from being read to, staff may find that the following research findings act as useful pointers:

- Showing pleasure in reading the story (Strommen and Mates 2004).
- Re-reading stories which children enjoy and that are predictable help children to build their vocabulary (Linse 2007). This also helps children with early literacy skills as they '. . . acquire an understanding of the functions of print, of how print is used, and of what people are doing when they are reading' (Spodek and Saracho 1994, p. 352).
- Allowing children opportunities to ask questions about what is being read to them and hearing answers helps children's understandings and knowledge to grow (Soundy 1993; Whitehurst et al. 1998). More recent research found that USA preschool children's novel word acquisition was greatest when they asked questions during storybook reading (Walsh and Blewitt 2006). Allowing children to ask questions can also help children to develop critical thinking skills (Lehr 1990).

- Engaging in conversation with the children about the story encourages them to share their own observations about it and to develop their own interpretations. This can increase children's interest in a story and their understanding of narrative. It also helps build their vocabulary (Walsh and Blewitt 2006).
- Retelling stories with props can increase children's understandings of words, plots and characters (Soundy 1993; Smyth 2005).
- Picture books can be an effective tool for generating verbal interactions between adults and children (Natsiopoulou, Souliotis and Kyridis 2006).

When and why?

GOAL RELEVANCE

Reading can enhance children's learning in many ways. It is particularly helpful in achieving the following goals:

Language and literacy skills
- Developing a sense of wonderment in children about the social, cultural and physical world (St Amour 2003; Rowcliffe 2004; Witt and Kimble 2006). Children's sense of wonderment in the world is encouraged when adults read stories to them with enthusiasm and excitement (Haiman 1991).
- Developing children's language skills. Reading stories to children can help them to learn the meanings of words as they hear them being used in a variety of ways (Moyles 1989; Sook Lim and Cole 2002) and expose the children to grammar and the sounds of their language (Ezell and Justice 2005). Stories about feelings, thoughts and values help children develop metacognitive language—that is, language through which they can talk about what they know, how they think and what they remember. Fairy stories seem to be particularly rich in ideas that develop metacognitive language (Hinchcliffe 1996).
- Supporting children's early literacy development by reading stories to children and reading with them using a variety of print materials—for example, books, newspapers and signs (Gaskins and Labbo 2007). Children who have been read to early in their life learn to read at an early age (McCarthy 1995).
- Supporting children's oral language development. Reading and telling stories to children develops their oral language skills (Isbell et al. 2004).
- Increasing children's understanding of narrative forms (Ezell and Justice 2005). Reading stories to children can help them to understand that experiences have beginnings, middles and endings (a narrative form). This helps children to recall key ideas and events in stories and in their own lives (Lehr 1990; Beck and McKeown 2002).
- Building children's early mathematical vocabulary and concepts such as size, shape and length. Reading to children stories about size or shape can help them to learn mathematical language and reinforce concepts being explored through other more concrete experiences. It can also help to support mathematical problem-solving skills (Kersh and Mercer Young 2004). Wilburne at al. (2007) suggest that this should be planned to address specific mathematical concepts and that it is important to ask different problem-posing mathematical questions of children each time you read a specific book.
- Stimulating children's thinking and concept development. Reading to children stories that are humorous and that use '. . . exaggeration and physical incongruity' (Klein 1992, p. 215) helps children to think about everyday events and concepts.
- Reading to children from birth also helps their language comprehension and vocabulary development.

Children who are read to regularly also show, by the time they are two, greater language comprehension and larger vocabularies than their peers (Raikes et al. 2006).

- Reducing children's stress and distress. Reading to children stories about the events and experiences that cause stress in their daily lives, such as nightmares and separating from their parents, can help children to cope with these events. If the stories are humorous, the laughter they generate helps the children to relax (Klein 1992).

DEVELOPMENTAL CONSIDERATIONS

Once babies can sit on an adult's lap, they generally enjoy looking at simple picture books and listening to adults read to them. This helps babies to associate sound symbols (words) with images. The ability to use symbols such as words to think and to understand is an important part of becoming a competent language user. Reading to babies also helps to develop a sense of sharing and closeness between the baby and the adult as it provides an opportunity for one-to-one communication and a time to enjoy each other's company:

> In the corner of the babies' room is a large armchair in which the staff can sit comfortably holding the children as they look at books. Each day, time is set aside for this to happen. The staff enjoy this quiet time with the babies and use it as an opportunity to relax with them.
>
> _Reflection point:_ In what other ways can you listen to babies in a child care setting?

Toddlers often imitate the humour of those around them, so reading humorous stories to toddlers is a good way to encourage their sense of humour. There is good evidence that a shared sense of humour is important to the development of friendships for young children (Bergen 2007).

Nichols and Sears (1987) suggested that stories to be read to toddlers should:

- have simple plots
- be based on events and experiences with which the toddlers are familiar
- have a small number of characters
- have some repetition in what the characters do or say
- be read enthusiastically by the adult.

Even taking these factors into account cannot guarantee a toddler's interest in a story or book. Sometimes they will be happy to read the same story repeatedly for long periods of time. Sometimes they will lose interest in a story that has been a favourite. Sometimes they will want to listen to stories being read and sometimes they won't. Reading to toddlers in small, informal groups allows individual toddlers to come, stay and go as their interest dictates, and creates story times which both children and staff find relaxed and enjoyable.

Toddlers can also engage successfully with stories read to them in a digital environment (Smith 2005). Irrespective of the source of stories, babies and toddlers benefit from stories read to them that:

- help them to acquire and strengthen their first language
- have positive images of people from different cultural and 'racial' backgrounds involved successfully in everyday tasks and in building relationships.

Reading regularly to children from birth also supports their language and cognitive learning. A study of 2531 US children living in low-income families who were read to regularly (at least once daily) in their first two years of life found that they had more developed language comprehension, and greater vocabulary and cognitive skills than their peers (Raikes et al. 2006).

Preschool children can make connections between the stories they hear, real-life events and their own personal lives. Staff can use this ability to help teach children specific ideas and concepts:

. . . when one of the children . . . heard a story about a lost giraffe, the mother used the story as an opportunity to underscore the value of not wandering off. The child responded by recalling a time that he had gotten lost. (Lehr 1990 p. 39)

Preschool children's emergent literacy skills can be supported through story-telling as it enhances their grammar, vocabulary, utterance length, and sentence formation (McGrath, Taylor and Kamen 2004). Their emergent literacy skills can also be supported through staff reading other forms of print to them. These forms can include lists of favourite toys or songs, labels on toys, signs around the centre, and stories that the children tell (Strickland and Riley-Ayers 2006). Reading each form of print to children helps them to associate meaning with printed words and symbols, and helps them to learn that reading can be used for many purposes. An environment which features a rich variety of forms of print and in which adults explain the meanings within the print will help children to 'learn a great deal about the processes involved in reading and writing' (Sumison 1991, p. 16). Such indirect teaching supports children's own reading skills much more effectively than direct reading tuition (Strickland and Riley-Ayers 2006).

Reading to preschool children who are bilingual strongly supports their development of oral language, increasing how long they speak for, how often they speak and the range of words they use when they speak (Sook Lim and Cole 2002).

In the early years of schooling, children are developing the ability to write about their own lives for themselves. Stories about things children do in their local community, places they visit outside their community and the daily events that make up their lives in school are all good sources of inspiration for the children's own writing. Through having such stories read to them they learn that people's daily lives, including their own, are worthy of writing about. In using story-reading to support young children's language comprehension and vocabulary development it is important that 'a teacher intersperses reading with open questions and discussion, and follows each story with explicit attention to vocabulary' (Beck and McKeown 2002, p. 18). Beck and McKeown discuss the need for teachers to focus, monitor and scaffold children's language learning during story-reading sessions.

Shared reading activities can also help develop young children's oral language skills and other emergent literacy skills, such as listening, comprehension and the development of vocabulary. For instance, a study of 95 children from low-income families considered to be at risk showed that 19 sessions of 10–15 minutes of shared reading activities significantly increased oral language and emergent literacy skills for these children (Lonigan et al. 1999). Conversely, the more limited a child's experiences with language and literacy through activities such as shared reading with adults, the more likely that a child will struggle in learning to read for themselves (Strickland and Riley-Ayers 2006).

Story-telling has also been used to support the growth of young children's mathematical skills using problem-solving adventure stories (Kersh and Mercer Young 2004).

Beck and McKeown (2002) detailed the criteria they used to choose books that supported children's capacity to construct meaning in the early years of school. Such books needed to:

- be intellectually challenging in that they required children to explore ideas and to use language to explain the ideas that were in the text
- be more reliant on language than image to convey meaning
- have a structure that was event based.

Equity considerations

Children identify with characters who are like themselves, characters who share their lifestyle, their cultural and 'racial' background, their gender and their ability levels. For this reason, it is very important that staff read to children stories that represent children in all their diversity. Stories should present them with a diverse range of characters from a diverse range of backgrounds who are powerful and competent and who feel like 'real' people.

Some specific points to consider when choosing stories to reflect children's 'racial', cultural, gender and ability interests are detailed below.

'RACE' AND CULTURE

When choosing a book with which to challenge traditional 'racial' and cultural stereotypes, staff need to be alert to the following elements:

- Physical features. Are the skin tones and facial features of people from black and ethnic minority backgrounds portrayed accurately? Are colours lifelike or are black people a grey colour? Do black and ethnic minority people look like white people who have been coloured in as an afterthought? Do black and ethnic minority characters appear identical in appearance, with one variety of hair, skin tone and similar facial features?

- Setting. Are black and ethnic minority characters shown in a variety of settings? Books in which black and ethnic minority characters are mainly in less affluent settings reinforce the idea that all black and ethnic minority people are poor and to be pitied. In Australia, it is especially important to show Aboriginal people in a variety of rural and urban settings. Books in which Aboriginal people appear only in tribal, rural settings reinforce the stereotype that all Aborigines still live traditional lifestyles. Are the stories set in Australia? It is important that children from black and ethnic minority backgrounds have stories about their own lives and lifestyles here in Australia.

- Characters. Are all the characters in the book decision-making and self-respecting? Do black and ethnic minority characters have the power to decide what happens to them and others? Do black and ethnic minority characters get involved in a wide variety of tasks and activities, including every-day tasks? Books in which black and ethnic minority characters are mainly involved in special celebrations or events reinforce the idea that their lifestyle is different and exotic.

Kim and the children enjoy a story.

- Language. Is the language respectful of all groups of people? Is offensive language avoided? Is dialect used in ways that demean or caricature a character?
- Storylines. Are there storylines in which black and ethnic minority children can identify with self-confident characters who have interesting and exciting adventures? Are there storylines in which black and ethnic minority children can identify with characters who are caring and who desire to co-operate with other people? Do the storylines reinforce feelings of superiority that white children may have? Do storylines show black and white people working and living together co-operatively?

GENDER

When choosing a book with which to challenge traditional gender-role stereotypes, staff need to be alert to the following elements:

- Clothing. Do women, girls, men and boys wear lots of different sorts of clothes? Books in which women appear dressed in pretty, frilly, pink dresses reinforce the idea that women's and girls' clothing should always be feminine rather than functional and that women's and girls' clothing is for looking good in, rather than for doing active things in. Books in which men are always dressed in sombre colours and work clothes reinforce the ideas that men's and boys' clothing should always be functional.
- Setting. Do women, girls, men and boys appear in a variety of settings? Books in which women and girls appear mainly in indoor, domestic settings reinforce the idea that this is their main area of responsibility and competence. Books in which men and boys appear mainly in outdoor, adventure and work settings reinforce the idea that this is their main area of responsibility and competence.
- Characters. Are all the characters in the book decision-making and self-respecting? Do women and girls have the power to decide what happens to themselves and others? Are women, girls, men and boys involved in a wide variety of tasks and activities? Books in which women and girls are shown mainly involved in indoor domestic tasks reinforce the idea that this is their main area of responsibility and competence. Books in which men and boys are mainly involved in outdoor, adventure and work tasks reinforce the idea that this is their main area of responsibility and competence.
- Language. Is gender-inclusive language used to describe objects, animals and jobs? Books in which all objects and animals are described by the male pronouns (he and him) reinforce the idea that the male is the most important gender in our society. Books in which only the cute, soft, cuddly, silly or gentle objects and animals are described by the female pronouns (she and her) reinforce the idea that the female is the more vulnerable and less serious gender in our society. Books in which all occupations are described by the male gender, such as 'policeman' or 'postman' reinforce the idea that these jobs are best done and only done by men.
- Storylines. Are there storylines in which girls can identify with self-confident characters who have interesting and exciting adventures? Are there storylines in which boys can identify with characters who are caring and who have a desire to co-operate with other people?

Choosing the right book is only half the battle. Davies (2003) showed that boys and girls will often resist storylines that challenge their own gender stereotypes and can read non-traditional storylines in very traditional ways. Staff need to deconstruct (see Chapter 22) children's gender role stereotypes as part of the process of reading stories to and with them.

DISABILITY AND ADDITIONAL NEEDS

Books offer lots of opportunities to present positive images and ideas about the interests and abilities of children with disabilities. Books convey very powerful messages about people and about the ways in which they are or aren't valued. Staff working within an anti-discriminatory approach to disability should read children stories in which the heroine has a disability and in which a disability is not presented as an overwhelming handicap. Staff should avoid books containing negative messages about disabilities. Several children's books contain powerful negative images of people with disabilities and present people with disabilities as naughty or frightening—for example, the nasty one-handed pirate, Captain Hook. The following checklist can help early childhood practitioners to use an anti-discriminatory perspective to critically evaluate the disability content of books:

- Faces. Are people with disabilities portrayed in ways that show they have lots of different emotions? Books in which people with disabilities are portrayed in ways which invoke sadness or pity reinforce the idea that people with disabilities should be pitied.
- Setting. Do people with disabilities appear in a variety of settings and surroundings? Books in which they appear mainly in settings reflecting able-bodied people's needs reinforce the view that people with disabilities don't require special adaptations to be made to their environment. Books in which people with disabilities are in a variety of indoor, outdoor, adventure and work situations reinforce the idea that they can be independent and competent in a variety of settings.
- Characters. Are all the characters with disabilities in the book decision-making and self-respecting? Do people with disabilities have the power to decide what happens to them and others? Do people with disabilities get involved in a wide variety of tasks and activities? Books in which people with disabilities are shown as passive and mainly dependent on able-bodied people reinforce the idea that people with disabilities cannot do things for themselves. Do people with disabilities have distinct characters or are they portrayed just in terms of their disability?
- Language. Is the disability of a character described accurately? Are the characters presented through stereotypical images? Are there value-laden terms such as 'Stand on your own two feet' and 'As blind as a bat'?
- Storylines. Are there storylines in which children with disabilities can identify with self-confident characters who have interesting and exciting adventures? Are children with disabilities the heroes and heroines? Are there storylines in which children with disabilities can identify with characters who are caring and who have a desire to co-operate with other people? What does the storyline say about relations between people with disabilities and people without disabilities?

Reflecting on reading techniques

1 Briefly define reading.
2 Find three books that you could read to toddlers to support their exploration of the natural world around them. Choose at least one that is a digital book by visiting the International Children's Digital Library (<http://www.icdlbooks.org>).
3 Find four books that you could read to preschoolers to support their mathematical learning in relation to classifying and comparing size, shape and number. Choose at least one that is a digital book by visiting the International Children's Digital Library (<http://www.icdlbooks.org>).
4 Review three humorous books written for very young children. Choose at least one that is a digital book by visiting the International Children's Digital Library (<http://www.icdlbooks.org>).To what extent do you think they would help stimulate children's thinking about the world about them? In what ways could they do this?
5 Collect your five favourite books for young children. Use the equity and anti-bias checklists above to review the books. How and how well did your favourite books support equity and diversity considerations?
6 Watch a story-reading session on a children's television program. How and how well did the presenter use voice to interest children in the story?

7   Observe an early childhood staff member reading a book to a group of children. How and how well did the staff member:
   • stress clearly important words?
   • allow children opportunities to ask questions about what was being read to them?
   • engage in conversation with the children about the story?
8   Engage a toddler or preschooler in a digital story reading session by visiting Story Place (<http://www.storyplace.org>). How did the toddler or preschooler respond to the session? What did you see as the pros and cons of a digital story reading session?

Improving teaching in practice

1   Record (using a tape-recorder or written notes) yourself reading a story to a small group of preschool children, a baby and a toddler.
2   How and how well did you:
   • choose a story that linked to children's current levels of understanding?
   • use your voice to gain children's interest and attention?
   • acknowledge children's questions about the story?
   • talk with the children about the story?
3   What are your strengths and weaknesses in reading to young children?
4   How can you improve your reading techniques?

FURTHER READING

Beck, I. and McKeown, M. 2001, 'Text talk: capturing the benefits of read-aloud experiences for young children', *The Reading Teacher*, 55(1), pp. 10–20.

Fletcher, K. and Reese, E. 2005, 'Picture book reading with young children: a conceptual framework', *Developmental Review*, 25(1), pp. 64–103.

Klein, A. 1992, 'Storybook humor and early development', *Childhood Education*, 68(4), pp. 213–217.

Nichols, J. and Sears, L. 1987, *Storytimes for Two-Year-Olds*, American Library Association, Chicago and London.

Smyth, J. 2005, *Storytelling with Young Children* (Research in Practice Series), 12(1), Early Childhood Australia, Watson, ACT.

Soundy, C. 1993, 'Let the story begin! Open the box and set out the props', *Childhood Education*, 69(3), pp. 146–149.

The Australian journal *Every Child* and the US journal *Childhood Education* each have a regular section which describes and reviews books for young children. They are an excellent resource for ideas about appropriate books to read to and with young children.

ONLINE AND MULTI-MEDIA RESOURCES

Text

'Storytelling'. A website with a myriad of links to support telling stories to children: **http://www.courses.unt.edu/efiga/STORYTELLING/StorytellingWebsites.htm**

Strickland, D. and Riley-Ayers, S. 2006, *Early Literacy: Policy and Practice in the Preschool Years*, National Institute for Early Education Research (NIEER), Rutgers University. Full text available at: **http://www.readingrockets.org/article/11375** (accessed 25 October 2007).

Multi-media

Building Early Literacy Competencies in Early Childhood (video), 2000, Educational Media, Australia.

Haas, M. and Hass, J. 2005, 'Storytelling: When! Why! How!' International Reading Association, no. 9207, available from: **http://www.reading.org/publications/bbv/videos/v9207**

International Children's Digital Library: A Library for the World's Children. Free access to children's digital books in many different languages. Excellent search facility and easy interface. **http://www.icdlbooks.org**

MacNaughton, G., Campbell, S., Smith, K. and Lawrence, H. 2002, *Equity Adventures in Early Childhood*, Centre for Equity and Innovation in Early Childhood, University of Melbourne. Strand on stories: **http://www.edfac.unimelb.edu.au/CEIEC/ resources**

Reading and literacy learning with toddlers (Reading Rockets). Free access podcast and video streaming. Print awareness: becoming aware of print: **http://www.readingrockets.org/podcasts/classroom#sounds**

REFERENCES

Beck, I., McKeown, M. and Kucan, L. 2002, *Bringing Words to Life: Robust Vocabulary Instruction*, Guilford Press, New York.

Bergen, D. 2007, 'Humor as a facilitator of social competence in early childhood', in D. Bergen, ed., *Contemporary Perspectives on Socialization and Social Development*, Information Age Publishing, Charlotte, NC, pp. 19–38.

Davies, B. 2003, *Frogs and Snails and Feminist Tales: Preschool Children and Gender*, revised edition, Cresskill Hampton Press, New Jersey.

Druin, A., Weeks, A., Massey, S. and Bederson, B. 2007, 'Children's interests and concerns when using the International Children's Digital Library: a four country case study', *Proceedings of the international conference on digital libraries*, Vancouver, pp. 167–176.

Ezell, H. and Justice, L. 2005, *Shared Storybook Reading: Building Young Children's Language and Emergent Literacy Skills*, Paul H. Brookes Publishing Co, Baltimore, MD.

Gaskins, I.W. and Labbo, L.D. 2007, 'Diverse perspectives on helping young children build important foundational language and print skills', *Reading Research Quarterly*, 42(3), pp. 438–451.

Haiman, P. 1991, 'Developing a sense of wonder in children', *Young Children*, 46(6), pp. 52–53.

Hawthorne, W. 1992, 'Young children and mathematics', *Australian Early Childhood Resource Booklets* (1), Canberra, ACT.

Hinchcliffe, V. 1996, 'Fairy stories and children's developing theories of the mind', *International Journal of Early Years Education*, 4(1), pp. 35–46.

Isbell, R., Sobol, J., Lindauer, L. and Lowrance, A. 2004, 'The effects of storytelling and story reading on the oral language complexity and story comprehension of young children', *Early Childhood Education Journal*, 32(3), pp. 157–163.

Kersh, J. and Mercer Young, J. 2004, 'Storytelling sagas: an effective medium for teaching early childhood mathematics', *Early Childhood Research Quarterly*, 19(1), pp. 167–172.

Klein, A. 1992, 'Storybook humor and early development', *Childhood Education*, 68(4), pp. 213–217.

Komlodia, A., Houb, W., Preeceb, J., Druinb, A., Golubb, E., Alburob, J., Liaob, S., Elkissb, A. and Resnikb, P. 2007, 'Evaluating a cross-cultural children's online book community: lessons learned for sociability, usability, and cultural exchange', *Interacting with Computers*, 19(4), pp. 494–511.

Lefever-Davis, S. and Pearman, C. 2005, 'Early readers and electronic texts: CD-ROM storybook features that influence reading behaviors', *The Reading Teacher*, 58(5), pp. 446–454.

Lehr, S. 1990, 'Literature and the construction of meaning: the preschool child's developing sense of theme', *Journal of Research in Childhood Education*, 5(1), pp. 37–46.

Linse, C. 2007, 'Predictable books in the children's EFL classroom', *ELT Journal*, 61(1), pp. 46–54.

Lonigan, C., Anthony, J., Bloomfield, C., Dyer, S. and Samwel, C. 1999, 'Effects of two shared reading interventions on emergent literacy skills of at-risk preschoolers', *Journal of Early Intervention*, 22(4), pp. 306–322.

McCarthy, R. 1995, 'The importance of storybook reading to emergent literacy: a review of the research', *Eric Digest*, ED396235.

McGrath, K., Taylor, D. and Kamen, R. 2004, 'Storytelling: enhancing language acquisition in young children', *Education*, 125(1), pp. 3–14.

Moyles, J. 1989, *Just Playing: The Role and Status of Play in Early Childhood Education*, Open University Press, Milton Keynes.

Natsiopoulou, T., Souliotis D., Kyridis, A. and Hatzisavvides, S. 2006, 'Reading children's books to the preschool children in Greek families', *International Journal of Early Childhood*, 38(2), pp. 69–79.

Nichols, J. and Sears, L. 1987, *Storytimes for Two-Year-Olds*, American Library Association, Chicago and London.

Raikes, H., Pan, B.A., Luze, G.J., Tamis-LeMonda, C.S., Brooks-Gunn, J., Constantine, J., Tarullo, L.B., Raikes, H.A. and Rodriguez, E. 2006, 'Mother-child bookreading in low-income families: correlates and outcomes during the first three years of life', *Child Development*, 77(4), pp. 924–953.

Read, K., Gardner, P. and Mahler, B. 1993, *Early Childhood Programs: Human Relationships and Learning*, 9th edn, Holt, Rinehart and Winston Inc., Fort Worth, TX.

Robison, H. and Schwartz, S. 1982, *Designing Curriculum for Early Childhood*, Allyn & Bacon Inc., Boston.

Rowcliffe, S. 2004, 'Storytelling in science', *School Science Review*, 86(314), pp. 121–126.

Smith, C. 2005, 'The CD-ROM game. A toddler engaged in computer-based dramatic play', in J. Marsh, ed., *Popular Culture, New Media and Digital Literacy in Early Childhood*, Routledge, London, pp. 108–125.

Smyth, J. 2005, *Storytelling with Young Children* (Research in Practice Series), 12(1), Early Childhood Australia, Watson, ACT.

Sook Lim, Y. and Cole, K. 2002, 'Facilitating first language development in young Korean children through parent training in picture book interactions', *Bilingual Research Journal*, 26(2), pp. 213–227.

Soundy, C. 1993, 'Let the story begin! Open the box and set out the props', *Childhood Education*, 69(3), pp. 146–149.

Spodek, B. and Saracho, O. 1994, *Right from the Start: Teaching Children Ages Three to Eight*, Allyn & Bacon, Boston.

St. Amour, M. 2003, 'Connecting children's stories to children's literature: meeting diversity needs', *Early Childhood Education Journal*, 31(1), pp. 47–51.

Strickland, D. and Riley-Ayers, S. 2006, *Early Literacy: Policy and Practice in the Preschool Years*, National Institute for Early Education Research (NIEER), Rutgers University, New York.

Strommen, L. and Mates, B. 2004, 'Learning to love reading: interviews with older children and teens', *Journal of Adolescent & Adult Literacy*, 48(3), pp. 188–200.

Sumison, J. 1991, 'Playing with print', *Australian Early Childhood Association Resource Book Series* (4), pp. 1–16.

Walsh, B. and Blewitt, P. 2006, 'The effect of questioning style during storybook reading on novel vocabulary acquisition of preschoolers', *Early Childhood Education Journal*, 33(4), pp. 273–278.

Whitehurst, G., Falco, C.J., Lonigan, J.E., Fischel, M., DeBaryshe, B., Valdez-Menchaca, M. and Caulfield, M. 1998, 'Accelerating language development through picture book reading', *Developmental Psychology*, 24(4), pp. 552–559.

Wilburne, J., Napoli, M., Keat, B., Dile, K., Trout, M. and Decker, S. 2007, 'Journeying into mathematics through storybooks: a kindergarten story', *Teaching Children Mathematics*, 8 (27), pp. 232–237.

Wilkes, G. (ed.) 1979, *Collins Dictionary of the English Language*, Penguin Books, Middlesex.

Willert, M. and Kamii, C. 1985, 'Reading in kindergarten: direct vs. indirect teaching', *Young Children*, May, pp. 3–8.

Witt, S. and Kimble, L. 2006, 'How does your garden grow? Teaching preschool children about the environment', *Early Childhood Development and Care*, 178(1), pp. 41–48.

Chapter 15

Recalling

 Recall: to bring back, to recollect, to remember.
(*Collins Dictionary of the English Language*, p. 1218)

Remember: to become aware of something (forgotten), to bring back
to one's consciousness, to recall.
(*Collins Dictionary of the English Language*, p. 1234)

*Recalling and remembering involve making associations. Children enjoy recalling what they did
once or what they saw when they were on a walk or a trip.*
(Read et al. 1993, p. 305)

Purpose is a most important factor in determining what we recall.
(Hughes and Hughes 1937, p. 164)

What?

To recall something is to recollect or to remember it. We can recall feelings, sights, sounds, images, texts, people, fragrances and textures. The ability to recall something relies on our ability to remember things that we have previously known or experienced. We cannot recall things that we have not known or experienced or that we have not remembered. For example, we can only recall the fragrance of a rose if we have had the experience of smelling a rose and have remembered the fragrance we smelled. Hence, experience and memory are each critical to our ability to recall.

Issues and debates

While there are no major debates about recall as a teaching strategy with young children that we uncovered in the literature, there is debate about what it is children are invited to recall and by whom and the extent to which very young children can recall.

TELEVISION AS A TEACHER AND BRAND RECALL

Dutch researchers, Valkenburg and Buijzen (2005), found that children between two and eight years of age demonstrated commercial brand awareness. They studied the relative impact of various environmental factors, including television, peers and parents, on the children's capacity to recall brands. They found that children as young as two years of age could recognise more brands than they could recall the name of, and that television was a key environmental factor in teaching brand recognition. Greater exposure to television was related directly to greater brand recognition.

WHEN MEMORIES BEGIN, WHEN RECALL BECOMES POSSIBLE

There is considerable debate within the literature on memory in childhood about when memories begin. Some researchers believe that memories begin *in utero*, others that memories of past lives carry into present lives and influence behaviours (Howe and Courage 2004). In a review of research on children and memory, Courage and Howe (2004, p. 6) concluded that the:

> . . . basic processes needed to encode, store, and retrieve information are present very early in life and that although significant developmental advances take place across early childhood, many of the processes that govern memory in preverbal children are common with those of verbal children and adults.

How?

Several factors influence children's ability to recall, including:

- the relevance of what is being recalled to their own goals. Children are more likely to recall something if it is relevant to what they are doing or what they want to do (Arthur et al. 1996)
- the extent to which adults prompt recall through reminiscence. Research with New Zealand children at two years of age found that the more that mothers reminisced with their children over the subsequent year, the more that the children at three years of age produced accurate memories themselves and the more self-aware that they were (Reese and Newcombe 2007)
- their capacity to put their ideas into words or images. Like adults, children cannot always find the right words or images to express their ideas and memories (Moyles 1989). The fact that a child cannot verbally or pictorially recall an event or an idea does not necessarily mean that they do not have an accurate mental picture of it
- their level of familiarity with what is being recalled. The more concrete and familiar the experience, the more likely it is that children will recall it with ease and interest (Denham 1991)
- an adult's involvement in their play. Children are more likely to recall what they did in their play when an adult is involved as a 'parallel player' (Moyles 1989, p. 141) or when adults engage in elaborative talk during an event. Australian researchers found that five- and six-year-old children's verbal and non-verbal recall was influenced strongly by the extent to which teachers elaborated on the event while it was happening (McGuigan and Salmon 2006)
- the reality of the event. Preschool children and children in the early years of schooling are more likely to accurately recall a real life event than an event they have viewed on a video, DVD or television (Theirry and Spence 2004)
- their attention to what is being recalled. Children are more likely to recall something to which they paid close attention when first experiencing it. Memory games and sorting-and-matching games are good ways to develop children's skills in noticing detail:

Teachers may introduce games that depend on paying attention and remembering, such as a game where the child first looks carefully at objects placed in front of her, then closes her eyes while one of these is removed and, when she looks again, tries to remember the missing object. (Read et al. 1993)

Generally, children's success in recalling will be maximised if they are asked to recall in the following circumstances:

- When recall will help them to meet their own goals. For example, if children want to reproduce something they have done before, such as building a cubby house, the staff member might say, 'Remember the cubby you built last week under the climbing frame? You used the blankets and the corrugated fibreglass sheet for the roof.'
- When they have a high level of interest in what they are being asked to recall. For example, if a child was very interested in a current project, such as dinosaurs, they will probably recall details of each different dinosaur.
- When they enjoyed what they are being asked to recall. For example, if they have enjoyed an excursion to the zoo, they will probably recall each animal they saw there.
- When they can remember what they are being asked to recall. For example, a staff member may invite toddlers to recall what they played with outside the previous day.
- When they are reasonably familiar with what they are being asked to recall. For example, a staff member may ask a group of three-year-olds, 'What do we do after pack-up time?', knowing that the children are familiar enough with the routines to be able to answer correctly.
- When what they are being asked to recall occurred relatively recently. For example, a staff member who is helping a four-year-old child to use a complicated construction toy might ask, 'How did you get the other one to stay in? That's right—you twisted it.'
- When they can physically move and hand gesture during the recall (Stevanoni and Salmon 2005).

Other techniques staff can use to help children practise their verbal recall skills include rehearsing information with children, playing memory games and sorting-and-matching games, and elaborating on what is to be recalled through singing songs or telling a story about it (Arthur et al 1996). Children can be encouraged to practise their non-verbal recall skills through making pictures, posters and models of events and experiences that are meaningful to them. For example, after an excursion to the zoo, staff could sing songs about the animals and make a poster of them to help the children remember them. Digital technology can make this process quick and easy, and digital books of children's photos and daily lives in an early childhood setting can help children's recall and extend and deepen their experiences (Nilson 2004).

Questions which are 'open' and process-oriented (see Chapter 13) can effectively encourage children's recall (Schwartz 1996). Some examples of such questions are:

- What happened when you tried that?
- How did that happen?
- What do you remember about . . .?
- How did that work?

Using Bloom's taxonomy of thinking, researchers (Klein et al. 2000) exploring children's scientific literacy skills in the early years of schooling used the following questions to invite children to recall specific science demonstrations in the classroom. They offer some simple starters for engaging children in recall. They were:

- Tell what—for example, what happened when we . . .?
- Tell when—for example, when did X happen?
- Tell where—for example, where were you when it happened?

- Tell who or whose—whose actions made it happen?
- Tell which—which X made it happen?
- Tell how—how did it happen?
- Tell how many—how many times did it happen?

Generally, the most effective questions for prompting children's recall of specific events are open ended and ask children to recall what they remember seeing and hearing (Elischberger and Roebers 2001).

When and why?

GOAL RELEVANCE

The ability to recall is critical to many facets of learning: we can learn spoken language effectively only if we can recall words. To know that the word 'dog' is associated with a particular animal requires the ability to recall the word and associate it with the animal. Learning language involves constantly recalling such associations. Similarly, the ability to recall is central to the ability to solve problems. If a child wants to build a block building that looks like the fire station near his home, then part of solving the problem of how to do this will involve the child recalling what the fire station looks like.

> Year 1 children are recalling their visit to a supermarket. Their teacher asks each one to recall what they saw there—for example, the number of aisles, the position of the checkout counters and how the food was presented.
>
> ---
>
> *Reflection point:* Write a list of questions that the teacher might ask here to help the children recall their visit.

Kylie writes on Sam's painting as he recalls the excursion.

Children's ability to recall is associated with their abilities to remember and to attend, and it is critical to later cognitive development. Specifically, asking children to recall things can help them to:

- reinforce their ideas, concepts and knowledge
- review their own learning
- express their understandings and develop a sense of self (Howe, Courage and Edison 2004)

- practise sharing ideas and information with other people
- document their work. Recollection is an important part of the process of developing, running and documenting projects based on the Reggio Emilia multi-symbolic approach to children's learning. Forman et al. (1994, p. 235) explained the role of recollection in the 'City in the Snow' project at the Marks Meadow Elementary School in Massachusetts, New England:

> Children discuss the recollections of snow, how it changes the playground, how it affects walking, what you can do in the snow, and how the city handles huge quantities of snow . . .
>
> From this discussion, children developed some initial drawings of snow scenes, simulated a snowfall and eventually moved to a point of drawing clouds and machines that make snow. Children's ability to recall snow was the foundation for all that emerged throughout the project.

(Additional information about the role of recall in documentation of children's learning and about the Reggio Emilia schools can be found in Chapters 23 and 31.)

DEVELOPMENTAL CONSIDERATIONS

The ability to recall is related to the ability to remember. Therefore, fostering children's skills in recalling is an important part of fostering their memory skills. However, practising recalling with young children will not immediately lead to obvious gains in their learning. Research into children's infant cognition suggests that practising recalling for some time benefits later cognitive development in their preschool years (Tsybina et al. 2006).

Very young children from at least 12 months of age have recall memory that enables them to imitate others (Rose, Feldman and Jankowski 2005). Babies' abilities to remember events and objects can be developed through simple games in which they can practise their recalling skills. Games such as peek-a-boo and jack-in-the-box encourage listening and watching, and involve clear sight and sound pictures that help babies practise their recall skills. Toddlers' abilities to remember events and objects can be developed through find-and-seek games and through simple guessing games. As children become more able to remember several events or objects at once, the games can become more elaborate. For example, a ball may be hidden where the child has looked for it before, then it may be hidden in a place where the toddler has not looked yet. Verbal clues may be given at first to help the child to remember.

Developing children's abilities to recall lays the foundation for encouraging them to transfer information from their short-term to their long-term memory. This cognitive technique is an important component of children's learning across all developmental domains (Seifert 1993) and is influenced by a sense of self (Prudhomme 2005). However, children's ability to recall will be influenced by their ability to represent ideas and images to others.

Toddlers are increasingly able to express themselves through language, but they are also likely to rely on non-verbal ways of recalling an experience such as painting or drawing it. When toddlers recall experiences in this way they are more likely to represent the experience on paper through movement and gesture than pictorially, as Fasoli (1988, p. 60) explained:

> An example of this would be a child zooming the crayon all over the page as a way to represent a car.

Staff can encourage toddlers to build their capacity to recall in non-verbal as well as verbal ways. A toddler who has just seen a cat run up a tree is very keen to tell other children about it but will have difficulty recalling the event verbally. Staff could encourage the child to recall the event through drawing it for others. Physical props and prompts can also be effective in encouraging toddler recall (Morrs and Baker-Ward 2007). Encouraging children to experiment with diverse ways of representing their experiences provides an important foundation for learning how to use mathematical symbols such as numbers (Hawthorne 1992).

Research over time shows that toddlers can also be encouraged to recall events that occurred when they were pre-verbal (Morrs and Baker-Ward 2007) or that happened some time ago. For instance:

Two-year-olds can often remember the locations of novel objects seen only once, many months earlier, for example, the drawer where a rarely visited grandparent kept a deck of cards on a previous visit. (Seifert 1993, p. 12)

Three-year-olds can have some difficulty recalling a belief they held once they learn that their belief is false. They quickly replace their false belief with their new understandings and can accurately recall this (Freeman 1995).

As early literacy skills depend on a child's memory, staff can support the growth of early literacy in preschool children by encouraging them to recall events and experiences.

Preschool children tend to recall events and experiences more easily when they have *talked with* an adult about them as they are occurring than when the adult *talks to* the child about the event (Seifert 1993). In other words, when preschool children have conversations with adults during experiences, they are more likely to recall the experiences later. This likelihood is increased if adults reminisce during these conversations about past experiences that are connected in some way to the current experience. Staff can begin these conversations with phrases like, 'Do you remember when . . .?' Research has shown that adults can help preschoolers' ability to recall a museum experience by talking to them about related experiences (Seifert 1993). For instance, the children were more able to recall a visit to a museum when the adults talked about a visit to the zoo in which children had seen the same animals as those in the museum.

Preschool children are also more likely to be able to recall when they have had lots of practice at recalling. Practice builds children's capacity to recall. Greek preschool children's spontaneous recall was found to be greater when they had been read a fictional book than when they had been read a factual book. The researchers suggest that this '. . . recall marks their need to re-experience the pleasure they felt when listening to the story by retelling it' (Moschovaki and Meadows 2005, online).

Children in the early years of school are often able to recall events in great detail because of their increasing memory capacity and their increasing ability to develop strategies which help them to remember, such as rehearsing information, developing a story about what has happened, asking people to remind them about what they want to remember and writing things that they want to remember (Arthur et al. 1996). Talking with the children about how they have tried to remember things and what strategies have been successful helps to build their recalling skills (Teale and Yokota 2000, Almasi 2003).

Overall, some researchers argue that children's capacity to explicitly recall events and information follows a linear developmental trajectory—they remember more, more accurately with age (Jordan et al. 2008).

German researchers (Schneider, Kron, Hünnerkopf and Krajewski 2004) have also shown that when children use multiple strategies to sort and organise information they have better recall than when children use a single or no strategy to sort and organise information. Other researchers have found that six-year-old children's capacity to recall events after a six month period is improved when the adult reminds the child of the context in which the event occurred (La Rooy, Pipe and Murray 2006), while Australian researchers found that six-year-old children's recall was improved when they were allowed to use hand gestures as they recalled events (Stevanoni and Salmon 2005).

Recall can be used to increase teacher understanding of children's scientific literacy and problem-solving skills in children in the early years of schooling. A stepped process where the teacher asks a child to recall factual information about science demonstrations, comment on what has changed, make generalisations, and analyse and make judgments about what has happened provides teachers with insights into children's scientific understandings (Klein et al. 2000).

Equity considerations

'RACE' AND CULTURE

Empathy is an important foundation on which to build a positive attitude towards 'racial' and cultural diversity with young children (Whaley and Swadener 1990). Empathy enables children to '. . . sustain stable and meaningful relationships . . .' with people from a diverse range of backgrounds (Brown 1995, p. 14) and to understand that racism is hurtful.

Children who develop empathy can respond to other people's emotions (Strayer 1986), but to respond to other people's emotions, children need to accurately recognise a range of human emotions. For instance, children need to be able to recognise feelings of hurt if they are to empathise with someone who has been hurt by a racist comment or image and to respond with concern. Children learn to accurately recognise other people's emotions by expressing and experiencing a broad range of emotions in themselves and in others (Whaley and Swadener 1990). However, they also need to be able to name and remember these feelings if they are to develop empathy (Strayer 1986). Staff need to provide children with names or labels for their emotions and encourage the children to remember these labels if empathy is to grow.

Recalling can help staff in this process. Children are able to recall events and experiences more easily when they have talked with an adult during an experience or event (Seifert 1993). Hence, talking with children about their own feelings and the feelings of others will help children to recall the labels for those feelings more readily. If these conversations with children involve reminiscences about their own feelings, their capacity for accurately naming them should be enhanced. Staff could, therefore, begin conversations about feelings with phrases like, 'Do you remember how sad you felt when you lost your pink teddy bear? Well, that's a little like Nathan feels now.' Preschool children are able to recall their emotional reactions to events as well as the events themselves very accurately (Liwag and Stein 1995).

However, it is equally important to explain to the children why someone is unhappy so that they learn that negative comments about physical appearance and lifestyle can hurt. In the previous example it would be important to add, 'Nathan is very sad because Kelly said his skin looks yucky'.

A specific form of recall—recasting children's words and phrases in a more accurate grammatical way—may be an important strategy for educators to use with children learning English as a second language. It may strengthen their language acquisition when it occurs naturally as part of small group conversation between children and teachers (Tysbina et al. 2006).

New technologies can also support the learning of second languages. One way to do this is to use the computer and web for story-telling in a child's second language. Researchers in Taiwan designed a story-telling website which included a story composition model and a replay module, and tested it in the classroom. They found that this strategy significantly enhanced student recall in their second language (Tsou, Wang and Tzeng 2004).

GENDER

There is strong evidence from research in Canada that children as young as two years of age can recall gender stereotypes in familiar daily activities such as housework and care for the self (e.g. shaving and sleeping) (Poulin et al. 2002) and know when behaviour is consistent or inconsistent with those stereotypes (Hill and Flom 2007). This suggests that staff can work with children from an early age to build non-stereotypical ways of thinking and acting and encourage children to recall these in their daily interactions with adults in early childhood services.

There is evidence that girls' ability to learn mathematics may be inhibited by the fact that they have '. . . less well-developed three-dimensional, spatial visualisation skills than boys . . .' (Hawthorne 1992, p. 13). Staff can help to maximise girls' chances of developing their three-dimensional, spatial visualisation skills by providing girls with access to a variety of concrete, three-dimensional experiences. When girls have access to these experiences, their skills can be improved by encouraging them to recall three-dimensional objects such as buildings. Staff can help girls to recall three-dimensional objects visually through encouraging them to make models or draw pictures of them and to recall these objects verbally through dialogue.

DISABILITY AND ADDITIONAL NEEDS

Developing empathy is an important part of building positive and accepting relationships between children with different abilities. The majority of able-bodied children may have their first close experience of a child with a disability in an early childhood setting. Early in this experience, the able-bodied children and the child with a disability may be curious or fearful about each other. Staff can use recall to help build empathetic relationships between the children at this early stage in their relationships with each other.

This is particularly important when a child with a disability is introduced into a settled group of children. Staff can help children to think about how they might make friends with their new group member by talking about how it feels to have friends and people who like them, and how it feels when no-one plays with them. Children can be encouraged to recall moments when they were new in the centre and didn't know people and to recall the moments when they knew they had friends. Such recalling can act as a basis for talking about how they might make friends with their new group member. Staff will need to help children think of non-verbal ways of showing that they would like to be friends with a new group member with language and communication disabilities (Brown 1995).

Reflecting on recalling techniques

1   Briefly define recalling.
2   What do you think is the relationship between remembering and recalling?
3   List 10 ways of using recalling to support children's learning. Would each of these processes be suitable for use with babies?
4   To what extent do you agree with the statement that 'Purpose is a most important factor in determining what we recall' (Hughes and Hughes 1937, p. 164)?
5   What factors influence your own ability to recall experiences, events and people? How many of these factors could influence a preschooler's ability to recall experiences, events and people?
6   Paying attention to an experience is an important factor in successfully recalling the experience. Design two games you could play with toddlers that require them to pay attention to something and then to recall it.
7   What changes would be needed to make these games suitable for preschoolers?
8   How could you use recall to help a toddler new to your group to learn the daily routine of the centre? Would recall be the most appropriate technique to use? Why? Why not?
9   Observe a small group discussion between an adult and a group of four-year-old children. How was recall used to promote children's learning?

Improving teaching in practice

1   Videotape the teaching interactions you have with children during several five-minute teaching periods.
2   How and how well did you use recall to support children's learning? Did you ask children to recall when:
   •   you wanted to support them in achieving their own goals?
   •   they were clearly interested in what was being talked about?
   •   you knew they had enjoyed and were still interested in a specific experience, event or person?
   •   you knew they had some recent memories of note?

3   What are your areas of strength and weakness in using recall as a teaching technique to promote children's learning?

4   How can you improve your recall techniques in practice?

FURTHER READING

Catron, C. and Allen, J. 1993, *Early Childhood Curriculum*, Macmillan Publishing Company, New York [refer to pp. 231–235 for games to promote children's recall skills].

Denham, S. 1991, 'Teaching thinking skills: the "what" and the "how" of young children's thinking', *Early Childhood Development and Care*, 71, pp. 35–44.

Read, K., Gardner, P. and Mahler, B. 1993, *Early Childhood Programs: Human Relationships and Learning*, 9th edn, Holt, Rinehart and Winston Inc., Fort Worth, TX [refer to pp. 303–306].

ONLINE AND MULTI-MEDIA RESOURCES

Multi-media

'Teaching Math: Grades K-2: communication'. Focuses on the role of teacher questioning and student recall in mathematics learning in a primary classroom. There is also a free access video download: **http://www.learner.org/channel/courses/teachingmath/gradesk_2/session_02/section_03_c.html**

'Explaining the learning centers', Apple Learning Exchange. A teacher uses open-ended questions to prompt a student to recall her learning during the past week. Free access video clip: **http://edcommunity.apple.com/ali/story.php?itemID=620&version=360&pageID=1576**

High/Scope 1997, *How Adults Support Children at Recall Time*. A video 'visit' to High/Scope's Demonstration Preschool. **http://www.earlychilded.delmar.com/video**

REFERENCES

Almasi, J. 2003, *Teaching Strategic Processes in Reading*, Guildford Publications, New York.

Arthur, L., Beecher, B., Dockett, S., Farmer, S. and Death, E. 1996, *Programming and Planning in Early Childhood Settings*, 2nd edn, Harcourt Brace and Company, Sydney.

Brown, B. 1995, *All Our Children: A Guide for Those Who Care*, 3rd edn, British Broadcasting Commission Education, London.

Courage, M. and Howe, M. 2004, 'Early memory development research: insights about the dark side', *Developmental Review*, 24(1), pp. 6–32.

Denham, S. 1991, 'Teaching thinking skills: The "what" and the "how" of young children's thinking', *Early Childhood Development and Care*, 71, pp. 35–44.

Elischberger, H. and Roebers, C. 2001, 'Improving young children's free narratives about an observed event: the effects of nonspecific verbal prompts', *International Journal of Behavioral Development*, 25, pp. 97–104.

Fasoli, L. 1988, 'Nurturing creativity', in A. Stonehouse, ed., *Trusting Toddlers: Programming for One to Three Year Olds in Child Care Centres* (pp. 54–64), Australian Early Childhood Association, Watson, ACT.

Forman, G., Lee, M., Wrisley, L. and Langley, J. 1994, 'The city in the snow: applying the multisymbolic approach in Massachusetts', in C. Edwards, L. Gandini and G. Forman, eds, *The Hundred Languages of Children: The Reggio Emilia Approach to Early Childhood Education* (pp. 233–50), Ablex, New Jersey.

Freeman, N. 1995, 'Cued-recall approach to three-year-olds' memory for an honest mistake', *Journal of Experimental Child Psychology*, 60(1), pp. 102–115.

Hawthorne, W. 1992, 'Young children and mathematics', *Australian Early Childhood Resource Booklets* (1), Australian Early Childhood Association, Watson, ACT.

Hill, S. and Flom, R. 2007, '18-month and 24-month-olds' discrimination of gender-consistent and inconsistent activities', *Infant Behavior and Development*, 30(1), pp. 168–173.

Howe, M. and Courage, M. 2004, 'Demystifying the beginnings of memory', *Developmental Review*, 24(1), pp. 1–5.

Howe, M., Courage, M. and Edison, S. 2004, 'When autobiographical memory begins', *Developmental Review*, 23(4), pp. 471–494.

Hughes, A. and Hughes, E. 1937, *Learning and Teaching: An Introduction to Psychology and Education*, Longman, London.

Jordan, C., Johnson, A., Hughes, S. and Shapiro, E. 2008, 'The Color Object Association Test (COAT): the development of a measure of declarative memory for 18- to 36-month-old toddlers', *Child Neuropsychology*, 14(1), DOI: 10.1080/09297040601100430.

Klein, E.R., Hammrich, P., Bloom, S. and Ragins, A. 2000, 'Language development and science inquiry: a child-initiated and teacher-facilitated program', Paper presented at the *Annual Meeting of the American Education Research Association*, April, New Orleans, ED440756.

La Rooy, D., Pipe, M. and Murray, J. 2006, 'Enhancing children's event recall after long delays', *Applied Cognitive Psychology*, 21(1), pp. 1–17.

Liwag, M. and Stein, N. 1995, 'Children's memory for emotional events: the importance of emotion-related retrieval cues', *Journal of Experimental Child Psychology*, 60(1), pp. 2–31.

McGuigan, F. and Salmon, K. 2006, 'The influence of talking on showing and telling: adult-child talk and children's verbal and non-verbal event recall', *Applied Cognitive Psychology*, 20(3), pp. 365–381.

Morrs, G. and Baker-Ward, L. 2007, 'Fragile but real: children's capacity to use newly acquired words to convey preverbal memories', *Child Development* 78(2), pp. 448–458.

Moschovaki, E. and Meadows, S. 2005, 'Young children's spontaneous participation during classroom book reading: differences according to various types of books', *Early Childhood Research and Practice*, 7(1), <http://www.ecrp.uiuc.edu/v7n2/moschovaki.html>.

Moyles, J. 1989, *Just Playing: The Role and Status of Play in Early Childhood Education*, Open University Press, Milton Keynes.

Nilson, B. 2004, *Week by Week: Documenting the Development of Young Children*, Thompson Delmar Learning, Australia; Clifton Park, New York.

Poulin, D., Serbin, L., Eichstedt, J., Sen, M. and Beissel, C. 2002, 'Men don't put on make-up: toddlers' knowledge of the gender stereotyping of household activities', *Social Development*, 11(20), pp. 161–181.

Prudhomme, N. 2005, 'Early declarative memory and self-concept', *Infant Behaviour and Development*, 28(2), pp. 132–144.

Read, K., Gardner, P. and Mahler, B. 1993, *Early Childhood Programs: Human Relationships and Learning*, 9th edn, Holt, Rinehart and Winston Inc., Fort Worth, TX.

Reese, I. and Newcombe, R. 2007, 'Training mothers in elaborative reminiscing enhances children's autobiographical memory and narrative', *Child Development*, 78(4), pp. 1153–1170.

Rose, S., Feldman, J. and Jankowski, M. 2005, 'Recall memory in the first three years of life: a longitudinal study', *Developmental Medicine and Child Neurology*, 47, pp. 653–659.

Schneider, W., Kron, V., Hünnerkopf, M. and Krajewski, K. 2004, 'The development of young children's memory strategies: first findings from the Würzburg Longitudinal Memory Study', *Journal of Experimental Child Psychology*, 88(2), pp. 193–209.

Schwartz, S. 1996, 'Hidden messages in teacher talk: praise and empowerment', *Teaching Children Mathematics* (March), pp. 396–401.

Seifert, K. 1993, 'Cognitive development and early childhood education', in B. Spodek, ed., *Handbook of Research on the Education of Young Children* (pp. 9–23), Macmillan Publishing Company, New York.

Stevanoni, E. and Salmon, K. 2005, 'Giving memory a hand: instructing children to gesture enhances their event recall', *Journal of Nonverbal Behavior*, 29(4), pp. 217–233.

Strayer, J. 1986, 'Current research in affective development', *Journal of Children in Contemporary Society*, 17(4), pp. 27–55.

Teale, W. and Yokota, J. 2000, 'Beginning reading and writing: perspectives on instruction', in D.S. Strickland and

L.M. Morrow, eds, *Beginning Reading and Writing: Language and Literacy Series* (pp. 3–21), International Reading Association, Newark, DE.

Theirry, K. and Spence, M. 2004, 'A real life event enhances the accuracy of preschoolers' recall', *Applied Cognitive Psychology*, 18, pp. 297–309.

Tsou, W., Wang, W. and Tzeng, Y. 2004, 'Applying a multimedia storytelling website in a foreign language learning', *Computers and Education*, 47, pp. 17–28.

Tsybina, I., Girolametto, L., Weitzman, E. and Greenberg, J. 2006, 'Recasts used with preschoolers learning English as their second language', *Early Childhood Education Journal*, 34(2), pp. 177–185.

Valkenburg, P. and Buijzen, M. 2005, 'Identifying determinants of young children's brand awareness: television, parents and peers', *Journal of Applied Development Psychology*, 26(4), pp. 456–468.

Webb, S. 2007, 'Recognition memory: brain-behaviour relations from 0–5', in D. Coch, K. Fischer and G. Dawson, eds., *Human Behavior, Learning, and the Developing Brain: Typical Development*, Psychological Assessments Australia, Jannali, NSW.

Whaley, K. and Swadener, B. 1990, 'Multicultural education in infant and toddler settings', *Childhood Education*, 66(4), pp. 238–420.

Wilkes, G. (ed.) 1979, *Collins Dictionary of the English Language*, Penguin Books, Middlesex.

Chapter 16

Singing

 Sing: to produce or articulate (sounds, words, etc.) with definite and usually specific musical intonation.

(*Collins Dictionary of the English Language*, p. 1358)

Singing is present in every culture. It provides a sense of community and belonging. Music is a component of cultural identity, and singing is the most basic musical expression. Singing—like all music—can be a source of joy, comfort, and emotional sensation. It is the birthright of every child with a normal speaking voice. It is also a teachable skill.

(Smith 2006, p. 28)

. . . children's singing interconnects with a complex network of language, movement, dance, drawing and playing with toys.

(Young 2006, p. 276)

What?

When people sing, they use their voice to make musical sounds. People may sing songs or chants for a number of reasons. As a teaching technique, staff may sing songs or chants with or for children to enhance their learning across all developmental domains during formal small and large group times and during informal moments throughout the day.

Issues and debates

WHOSE SINGING DO WE VALUE?

Young (2006) believes that young children's daily singing improvisations are under-researched and often go unnoticed in Western early childhood classrooms. She sees that this is in part because of a preference in white Anglo-British groups to focus on spoken language and to be fearful of emotional expression through voice that is not controlled. Reviewing approaches to singing and music for young children, Young argues that our definitions of singing in Western art music education are extremely narrow and focus on the accuracy of vocal expression and timbre to the detriment of our understandings of the pleasures and meanings children give to their own singing. Young studied children's improvised singing in early childhood settings in South East London and concluded that their singing 'interconnects with a complex network of language, movement, dance, drawing and playing with toys' (p. 276) that is creative, meaningful and strengthens social bonds. Young challenges adults to take seriously children's improvised and playful singing and to not limit our views of singing to those formalised in traditional Western music education.

How?

Singing comes more easily to some people than to others. Staff who find singing difficult could:

- focus on singing very simple songs which they put to the melody of nursery rhymes with which they are familiar (Honig 1995; Booth Church 2006)
- listen to lots of children's music and sing along in private till they feel they can manage without the record or tape (Honig 1995)
- clap as they sing the song to children to keep to a simple rhythm when singing (Booth Church 2006).

Irrespective of staff's singing competence, the following suggestions can help to maximise children's wellbeing, enjoyment and learning through singing:

- Children often sing if they are having fun and are able to move in rhythm to the singing. Janet often combines song with movement:

It is a windy day and Janet, a teacher of a prep class, is outside with the children. She watches the children as they run around and begins to sing a 'windy day' song with them. She then extends this song into verses about what the wind can do. The children translate each verse into different movements. They move to show how they can blow, be tossed about, swirl around and land on the ground.

Reflection point: What other situations inside and outside could be a vehicle for singing with children?

- The more opportunity children have to sing, the more that they will sing (Smith 2006).
- Many of the songs that children make up and sing to themselves are low-pitched and in a minor key. Singing similarly pitched songs with the children will make singing fun rather than challenging (Read et al. 1993).
- From an early age children love a diversity of music types and styles (Roulston 2006) so it is important for staff to ensure that they sing songs with young children that are from diverse musical genres. Many young children love songs about, '. . . animals, themselves or their friends, and some nonsense rhymes and jingles . . .' (Brewer 1992, p. 332) but children's tastes can differ from one cultural context to another.
- Children learn songs best when they hear the whole song first and then hear it repeated whole several times till they have learnt it (Booth Church 2006).
- Children can practice singing as part of their informal social interaction in the preschool setting (Gruhn 2005).

Singing together.

When and why?

GOAL RELEVANCE

Singing can enhance children's learning, especially when staff wish to:

Support children's wellbeing

- encourage children's own singing efforts. Respecting and celebrating children's different ways of singing will encourage them to use singing as a form of creative and meaningful self-expression (Young 2006). For instance, a staff member may pick up on a song that a child is singing and extend it or repeat it to '. . . awaken a love of poetry and imagery . . .' (Honig 1995)
- help children play with words and develop a sense of humour (Honig 2007). For instance, a staff member may sing some new, funny words to a familiar tune
- help children to reveal and express their feelings and understandings (Patterson 2004). It can be especially powerful if children have experienced trauma and/or disaster (Ahmed and Siddiqi 2006) or a family member is absent, such as on military deployment (Allen and Staley 2007). Favourite songs can reassure and support children in these contexts.

Some research suggests that musical activities, including singing, can support the learning of children who 'find it difficult to learn from a strictly verbal presentation' (Strickland 2001/02, p. 103), but that it is important that the music selected is enjoyed by those children.

Build children's specific skills and knowledge

- help children to learn daily routines, as there is neuroscientific evidence that music triggers memories (Molnar-Szakacs and Overy 2006). With this in mind, a song may be used to cue children into various routines, such as pack-up time, story time or time for meals
- familiarise children with basic musical concepts such as melody, rhythm, tempo, pitch and tone
- provide opportunities for children to solve problems as they negotiate roles and tasks in musical experiences together (St John 2006)—for instance, thinking about actions they can do to songs or by thinking about new words they could sing together to a familiar tune
- support children's acquisition of language. Singing simple songs in which the words of the song match the children's actions helps them to learn the meaning of words. This can be a particularly effective way to build toddlers' language competence (Olsson 1988) and to help with the acquisition of English as a second language (Huy Lê 1999). It can also help children to learn the alphabet (Ringgenberg 2003)
- support the acquisition of reading skills in four- and five-year-old children (Anvarie, Trainor, Woodside and Levy 2002)
- support children's cognitive learning. For instance, research with Japanese five-year-old children suggests that including music that is culturally familiar to children enhances their concentration and involvement in tasks, thus supporting their cognitive development (Schellenberg et al. 2007)
- give children's instructions or directions during the day (Booth Church 2006).

Ann, Chris and Anouk each incorporate singing into their program on a regular basis:

Ann, a child care worker in the three-year-old group, always uses singing when there is a transition time—for instance, at pack-up time, at lunchtime and at going outside time.

Chris loves to make up songs about the children and their activities. At the end of each kindergarten session he sings a song to the children about what he has seen them doing during the morning or the afternoon. Sometimes Chris uses tunes that the children already know and sometimes he invents new tunes.

Anouk sings simple repetitive songs to her group of one-year-old children. As they play outside, she sings about what the children are doing. For instance, she sings to Sarah in the sand pit, 'digging, digging, in the sand,' or to Tran on the swing, 'Tran is swinging, swinging, swinging'.

Reflective task: Research two songs with repetition that you could use in the outside area with younger children.

DEVELOPMENTAL CONSIDERATIONS

By six months of age, babies seem particularly sensitive to singing in some cultures. They will engage in more sustained attention on singing than on speech (Nakata and Trehub 2004). Babies' attentiveness to singing can help staff to soothe and calm them in moments of stress (for example, when separating from a parent) by singing soft, gentle songs such as lullabies or to calm an exuberant baby in preparation for rest times. A study of 70 US babies between six and nine months of age suggested that recorded music is less likely to be as effective as a 'real' human voice. Babies' physical responses to recorded music were more negative than they were to the sounds of a person singing (de l'Etolle 2006).

US researchers have found also that babies can recognise the difference between different rhythms and melodic structures from as young as seven months of age (Hannon and Johnson 2004). Research also shows that babies can and do respond to different types of music from birth and that they can be calmed, excited or distressed by music. In general, very young babies (under four months of age) tend to find quiet, gentle music calming and lively music exciting.

Working with babies and toddlers involves lots of daily care routines such as rest times, nappy changing times and meal times. These can be made more enjoyable and enriching for children and adults through song. Simple songs and chants can help to de-stress staff and quieten children, as they can provide something for them to focus on other than the routine itself and help them to feel cared for (Honig 1995; Linke and Fleer 2002). These songs and chants can be made up by the staff on the spot. The more that staff practise impromptu 'made up' songs, the easier it becomes. Singing to babies and playing rhyming games with them can also support emergent literacy skills and knowledge (Cress 2000) through expanding their vocabulary and enhancing their sense of connection between language and actions.

> Toddlers have reached the stage in their musical development where they can 'dance' to music and enjoy doing so. Action songs, such as 'Hokey Pokey', are likely to interest toddlers at this stage of their development.
>
> The toddler now attempts to 'dance' to music by bending his [her] knees in a bounding motion, turning circles, swaying, swinging his [her] arms, and nodding his [her] head. He [she] especially likes a marked rhythm, so band music, nursery songs, or catchy TV jingles may be favorites. (Bayless and Ramsey 1991, cited in Brewer 1992, p. 336)

With this in mind, staff can increase toddlers' enjoyment of song by providing lots of space and opportunities for 'dancing' to song. Toddlers generally love it when the staff join in with their dancing.

Preschoolers increasingly enjoy using song to express their ideas. They can create their own songs or use familiar songs to accompany their play (Brewer 1992). Staff can encourage these developments through singing with the children. During their preschool years, children's interest in and understanding of song lyrics increases (Welch 2006) and staff can use this as an opportunity to expand children's vocabulary and introduce them to new ideas. Children are not only able to understand songs but also to produce their own if they are afforded the opportunity to do so. Encouraging children to produce their own songs acknowledges that they have the capacity to be music-makers and offers the staff opportunity to scaffold this music-making (Whiteman 2001).

Songs and chants are particularly powerful ways to introduce children to the alphabet. Songs and chants that are fun and that emphasise the sounds and names of letters help children remember the alphabet (Reutzel 1992). Children in the early years of school will enjoy puns and humour in their songs, and the more they enjoy the songs the more effective the learning will be. The television program *Sesame Street* has used this knowledge to good effect! Songs can also be helpful in introducing children to new languages and, alongside other methods, enhance their learning of a new language (Omari 2001).

Children's capacity to 'sing in tune' grows over time as does the range of their vocal pitch (Welch 2006). Staff should not be concerned if younger children do not 'sing in tune'; it is more important that they enjoy the process of singing and have fun with it. However, preschool children's capacity for and interest in listening to music for extended periods of time varies widely, with some younger children listening to music for longer periods than older children and longer than might be expected for their age (Sims 2005). It is important that teachers take account of this variance when singing with children, individually or in groups.

New technologies can be used in the early years of school to enable children to create and share their own songs. Swedish researchers invited eight-year-old children to compose musical pictures using a synthesiser and computer. They found that the children were able to create—and enjoyed creating—music that has form and structure (Nilsson and Folkestad 2005). This offers teachers in the early years of school the opportunity to work with children to compose their own songs in ways that can be shared with others and that support the strengthening of children's technological thinking and skills.

Equity considerations

'RACE' AND CULTURE

Song is an important means of expression in many cultures. It can be a way to share joys and sadness. It can also be a way to record the history of a cultural group and to share that history with others. Many cultures have a rich and diverse bank of songs known by different groups who use them for a wide variety of purposes. From lullabies to work songs, singing is an expression of cultural meanings and values.

Children's enjoyment of specific music grows through regular exposure to it. There is some evidence that babies are more open to the music of other cultures than adults (Stewart and Walsh 2005). Teachers can use babies' openness to the music of diverse cultures to share with children the songs they enjoy from a diverse range of cultures, developing children's enjoyment in and respect for diverse music forms. If children enjoy songs from a diverse range of cultures they can:

- learn about similarities and differences within and between different cultural groups and build more positive attitudes towards people from other cultures (Hafeck 2007)
- discover cultural diversity. Learning about music from different cultures can be an enjoyable and effective way to learn about cultural diversity. Children often enjoy the folk songs and the work songs of different cultures because of their repetitive lyrics and strong rhythms (Ramsey 2004)
- share their own cultural heritage with others. Children can help to teach songs from their own culture to other children in the group. This helps enrich the group's sense of community and children build a sense of worth from contributing to this repertoire (Purnell et al. 2007). Researchers in the USA found that the self-esteem of 138 primary school age immigrant and refugee children was improved through their participation in creative expression workshops that included singing, as the workshops emphasised the children's strength and resilience (Rousseau et al. 2005)

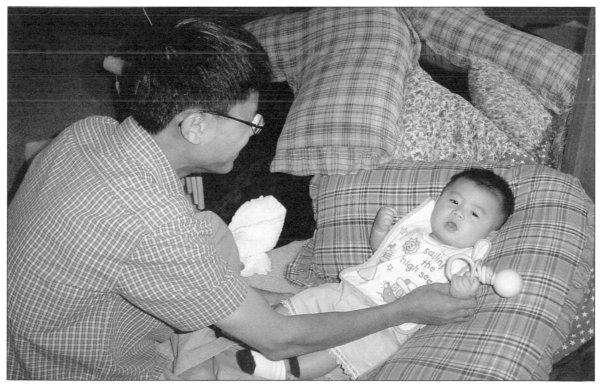

Showing enjoyment in vocalisations encourages language development.

- learn a second language. Simple songs with repetitive lyrics can help children to learn to say 'Hello', 'Good-bye', 'Welcome', etc. in their local community languages. Songs can also help children to learn English as a second language (Multilingual Children's Association, 2004).

Acceptance of and respect for cultural diversity can increase when staff share songs that:

- represent the languages and lifestyles of all the children in the group. Babies learn their first language through being constantly surrounded by its sounds. Their first language acquisition will best be supported by being able to listen to and communicate with staff who share their first language. When staff do not share a baby's first language, they can help to support language acquisition by learning simple songs and lullabies in the baby's first language. This not only supports that specific baby's language acquisition but also enriches the diversity of languages available to all babies in the centre
- increase children's awareness of cultural diversity within the wider community. When children spend time in primarily mono-cultural groups, staff should make a special effort to familiarise them with the multicultural nature of their local world. Songs can be a fun part of this process
- reflect the songs and chants that are sung by people from particular cultural groups. This prevents the children learning stereotyped ideas about what is sung within a particular cultural group. For instance, not all Spanish people will necessarily sing 'La Bamba'!
- draw on the diversity of song within a culture. Children can enjoy and learn from all song genres in a culture, including traditional, contemporary, folk and classical genres of song and chant
- encourage empathy and identification with people from diverse cultural backgrounds (Ramsey 2004). Young children can recognise emotion in song, and songs about people's joys and sadnesses can help children to empathise with others. For example, researchers found that Japanese children were sensitive to the emotions of joy, anger and sadness in both the music they were culturally familiar with and the music that was not culturally familiar to them (Balkwill, Forde Thompson and Matsunaga 2004)
- counter stereotypes. Song lyrics should not make fun of or demean a particular cultural group or present them as frightening or silly. For instance, the song, 'We are Siamese' from the musical, *The King and I* presents Siamese (now Thai) people as silly. The song, 'Ten Little Indians' reinforces the stereotype that Native Americans all have bows and arrows and live in tepees
- are integrated in a consistent and meaningful way in the life of the centre. Children will learn to enjoy and respect diversity when it is a daily part of their lives. Learning only one song from a culture for a special occasion is tokenistic.

Staff can also teach children songs that '. . . encourage differences, acceptance, and cooperation' (York 1991, p. 60). For example, 'What is your name? My name's Amy', or 'I wonder what your name is. I really ought to know. My name is Amy, hello, hello', etc.

GENDER

UK researchers (Leighton and Lamont 2006) have found gender differences in boys' and girls' preferences for group singing in the early years of school. In a two-year longitudinal study of 28 children (17 boys and 11 girls) between five and seven years of age, the boys generally preferred singing alone and the girls generally preferred singing in groups. Furthermore, when boys did sing in groups their pitch was not as accurate as when singing alone, especially when learning new songs in groups. Teachers could use this research to reflect on the extent to which its findings might be relevant for the children in their contexts. It may be that informal one-to-one singing with boys may be important in building their skills and enjoyment in singing in the early years of school, especially when they are learning new songs.

The songs selected for use with preschool children should be so much fun to sing that it's okay that there's a message in there. (Neugebauer 1992, p. 64)

If children enjoy songs, they are more likely to learn the messages contained within them, including messages of gender equality. They can:

- learn about similarities and differences within and between men and women, boys and girls. Preschool children often have very gender-stereotyped views about men's and women's range of feelings and behaviours (Alloway 1995). They can find it hard to believe that women can carry heavy weights, can be adventurous, can be leaders and can do jobs traditionally done by men. They can also find it hard to believe that men can be caring and gentle, can change nappies and do the dishes and can do jobs traditionally done by women. Staff can challenge children's gender stereotypes by sharing songs with the children that celebrate the non-traditional ways of being male and female. Staff may need to make up songs and rhymes if they can't find any

- discover gender diversity. Many songs and rhymes for young children are very sexist. They tell of girls (Polly) putting kettles on and boys (Johnny) working with hammers. One way to increase children's awareness of gender role diversity is to substitute boy's/girl's names in the songs and rhymes. 'Polly put the kettle on' can become, 'Johnny put the kettle on'; and 'Johnny works with one hammer' can become 'Polly works with one hammer'. If the children are familiar with the song, they will often tell staff that they have got the words 'wrong'. Staff can use this assertion as a way of talking to the children about gender stereotypes and of beginning to deconstruct gender stereotypes with the children (for further information on this, refer to Chapter 22)

- share their achievements with others. Staff can make up songs to sing to the children about the things they do each day that challenge traditional gender stereotypes. Singing about 'The big block building the girls made', or 'How the boys helped with tidying up the home corner' can help to celebrate gender-role diversity in the group. However, staff need to be alert to the possibility that many girls may be less confident than many boys about singing about their achievements. Boys tend to be louder and more confident in mixed-gender groups than girls

- learn new concepts. Song can be a fun way to introduce children to a variety of pre-number concepts. Songs such as 'Five Little Ducks' help children to learn to count to five, to subtract and to count backwards. There is some evidence that structured music programs might be a particularly effective way to teach pre-number concepts to girls:

    . . . a formal Kodaly program can increase a preschooler's understanding of prenumber concepts of comparison, order, classification, and pattern—but only for girls. (Craig Peery 1993, p. 214)

If song is to increase children's acceptance of and respect for gender diversity, staff need to ensure that their songs and chants:

- represent the gender styles of all the children in the group
- increase children's awareness of gender role diversity within the wider community
- encourage empathy and identification between diverse gender styles
- counter stereotypes—the lyrics in songs should not make fun of a particular gender or make it seem frightening or silly.

However, staff need to be alert to the fact that preschool children will often resist messages that challenge their gender-role stereotypes (Davies 2003; MacNaughton 2004). To challenge children's gender-stereotyped beliefs, staff need to do more than change a few words in a few songs. They need to combine this work with an ongoing program in which they use a variety of techniques such as questioning, deconstruction and empowerment to help children grow free from gender stereotyping that restricts their development.

DISABILITY AND ADDITIONAL NEEDS

Using music to encourage children to listen to and interact with others can build empathy (Craig Peery 1993). Empathy between children of diverse needs and abilities can be supported when songs help children:

- learn about similarities and differences within and between people of varying abilities. Children can be introduced via song to the idea that different people's bodies work in different ways. Singing songs about the different ways we can move our bodies, such as crawling, waving, walking, etc. can be an easy place to start. These songs can help children to think about the similarities and differences between how people with mobility and motor disabilities move their bodies and how people without those disabilities move theirs
- share their achievements with others. Staff can make up songs to sing to the children about the special things they do each day. This can encourage the children to make up their own songs to celebrate their own achievements and those of their friends
- learn new concepts and words. Hearing children can be taught to 'sign' simple songs as a way of expanding their understanding of language and communication. Children can learn that signs they make with their hands have the same meanings as sounds they make or words they write.

Songs should not reinforce the continued invisibility or inaudibility of people with disabilities. Simple changes to the words of familiar and oft-used songs can help in this process. Such changes include:

- changing 'The Wheels of the Bus' to 'The Wheels of the Wheelchair' when a child with a wheelchair is in the group
- changing the 'finger' play, 'Ten Little Fingers' to 'Two Big Arms' when a child with an arm with no fingers is in the group.

If song is to increase acceptance of and respect for people of diverse abilities, staff need to choose songs that:

- represent the abilities of all the children in the group. Songs about all the children's bodies and experiences need to be included
- increase children's awareness of people with diverse abilities within the wider community. Songs that celebrate the skills and abilities of people with disabilities need to be included
- encourage empathy and identification between people with diverse abilities
- counter stereotypes—the lyrics in songs should not make fun of a particular disability or additional need a child has, or make the child seem frightening or silly.

For some children with special education needs there is good evidence to suggest that music more broadly may calm and focus children and therefore enhance their learning (Črnčec, Wilson and Prior 2006). Teachers should get to know the specific children in their context with special learning needs to clarify the extent to which this might be the case for them.

Reflecting on singing techniques

1 Briefly define singing.
2 How could singing be used to help toddlers learn how to wash their hands after toileting? What would be the pros and cons of using singing to achieve this aim?
3 Find three simple songs you could use to help introduce new vocabulary to a three-year-old child just beginning to learn English as a second language.
4 Find three simple songs you could use to help children improve their memory skills.
5 Make up a simple song you could use to help children learn about taking turns.

6 Write down the words of five of your favourite songs for children. Would your songs need adapting in any way to make them more inclusive of gender or disability? To what extent would the songs extend children's awareness of songs from a diverse range of cultures?

7 View an episode of *Sesame Street*. How was singing used to assist children's learning?

8 Which of the songs and rhymes used in the program would be suitable to sing to a group of toddlers? Why?

9 How and how well do the singers on *Sesame Street*:
- encourage children to have fun by moving in rhythm to what they are singing?
- show enjoyment in singing?
- sing to children in a low-pitched minor key?
- sing about subjects children enjoy such as themselves, their friends or familiar events?

Improving teaching in practice

1 Record (using a tape-recorder or written notes) several occasions during which you used singing as an incidental teaching technique.

2 How and how well did you encourage fun and enjoyment in the experience through modelling enjoyment and choosing songs and actions of interest to the children?

3 What are your areas of strength and weakness in using singing as a teaching technique to promote children's learning?

4 How can you work to improve your singing techniques in practice?

FURTHER READING

Baker, B. 1993, 'Strengthening language experiences for children through fingerplays', *Eric Digest*, ED360094.

Booth Church, E. 2006, 'Singing songs with children', *Scholastic Early Childhood Today*, 21(1), p. 4.

Burton, L.H. and Kudo, T. 2000, *SoundPlay: Understanding Music through Creative Movement* (book and CD set, available from NAEYC), National Association for Music Education, Reston, VA.

Clarke, P. 1992, *English as a Second Language in Early Childhood*, FKA Multicultural Resource Centre, Melbourne [refer to pp. 39–41].

Levin-Gelb Communications 2002, 'Getting in tune: the powerful influence of music on young children's development' (brochure, available in English and Spanish), Zero to Three, Washington, DC.

Neelly, L.P. 2002, 'Practical ways to improve singing in early childhood classrooms', *Young Children*, 57(4), pp. 80–81.

Ringgenberg, S. 2003, 'Using music as a teaching tool: creating story songs', *Young Children* 58(5), pp. 76–79.

Smith, W. 2003, 'Learning about music' (no. 3 of the *Learning at Home* series), Early Childhood Australia, Watson, ACT.

Suthers, L. 2004, 'Music experiences for toddlers in day care centres', *Australian Journal of Early Childhood*, 29(4), pp. 45–49.

ONLINE AND MULTI-MEDIA RESOURCES

Text

'The Children's Music Web' has information for teachers on music in the curriculum and classroom songs. It links to other music education resources and provides children with links to child-friendly music websites: **http://www.childrensmusic.org**

Custodero, L. (ed.) 2002, 'Special issue, "Musical lives of babies and families"', *Zero to Three*, 23(1), National Center for Infants, Toddlers, and Families, USA: **http://www.zerotothree.org**

Lee, P. 2006, 'Singing in tune': **http://www.teachingexpertise.com/articles/singing-in-tune-1431**

'Music for young children'. Website of Music Teacher International: **http://www.musicteachermag.com/articles/article.asp?a=136**

Multi-media

Multicultural Lullabies Around the World (CD): **http://www.songsforteaching.com/store/Multicultural-Lullabies-Around-the-World-CD-p-1412.html**

'Music—Singing for teachers: Strategies in the classroom', *Teachers' TV*. Video download of how primary school teachers use warm-ups, chants and songs with children: **http://www.teachers.tv/video/2550**

REFERENCES

Ahmed, S. and Siddiqi, M. 2006, 'Healing through art therapy in disaster settings', *The Lancet*, 368, pp. S28–S29.

Allen, M. and Staley, L. 2007, 'Helping young children cope when a loved one is on military deployment', *Young Children on the Web*, <http://journal.naeyc.org/btj/200701/pdf/BTJAllen.pdf>

Alloway, N. 1995, *Foundation Stones: The Construction of Gender in Early Childhood*, Curriculum Corporation, Melbourne.

Anvarie, S., Trainor, L., Woodside, J. and Levy, B. 2002, 'Relations among musical skills, phonological processing, and reading ability in preschool children', *Journal of Experimental Child Psychology*, 83(2), pp. 111–130.

Balkwill, L., Forde Thompson, W. and Matsunaga, R. 2004, 'Recognition of emotion in Japanese, Western, and Hindustani music by Japanese listeners', *Japanese Psychological Research*, 46(4), pp. 337–349.

Booth Church, E. 2006, 'Group time: enlivening literature with music and movement', *Early Childhood Today* (3), 20(6) pp. 44–45.

Brewer, J. 1992, *Introduction to Early Childhood Education: Preschool through Primary Grades*, Allyn & Bacon, Boston.

Clarke, P. 1992, *English as a Second Language in Early Childhood*, FKA Multicultural Resource Centre, Melbourne.

Craig Peery, J. 1993, 'Music in early childhood education', in B. Spodek, ed., *Handbook of Research on the Education of Young Children* (pp. 207–24), Macmillan, New York.

Cress, S. 2000, 'A focus on literacy in home day care', *Australian Journal of Early Childhood*, 25(3), pp. 6–12.

Črnčec, R., Wilson, S. and Prior, M. 2006, 'The cognitive and academic benefits of music to children: facts and fiction', *Educational Psychology*, 26(4), pp. 579–594.

Davies, B. 2003, *Frogs and Snails and Feminist Tales: Preschool Children and Gender*, Hampton Press, New Jersey.

de l'Etolle, S. 2006, 'Infant behavioural responses to infant-directed singing and other maternal interactions', *Infant Behaviour and Development*, 29(3), pp. 465–470.

Derman-Sparks, L. and the Anti-Bias Task Force 1989, *The Anti-Bias Curriculum*, National Association for the Education of Young Children, Washington, DC.

Gruhn, W. 2005, 'Children need music', *International Society for Music Education*, 23(2), pp. 99–101.

Hafeck, L. 2007, 'Contextual analyses of children's responses to an integrated Chinese musical experience', *Music Education Research*, 9(3), pp. 337–353.

Hannon, E. and Johnson, S. 2004, 'Infants use meter to categorize rhythms and melodies: implications for structure learning', *Cognitive Psychology*, 50(4), pp. 354–377.

Honig, A. 1995, 'Singing with infants and toddlers', *Young Children*, July, pp. 72–78.

——2006, 'Infants & toddlers: how to calm an exuberant baby,' *Early Childhood Today*, 20(6), pp. 22–23.

——2007, 'Oral language development', *Early Child Development and Care*, 177(6/7), pp. 581–613.

Huy Lê, M. 1999, 'The role of music in second language learning: a Vietnamese perspective', Presentation at *Combined 1999 Conference of the Australian Association for Research in Education and the New Zealand Association for Research in Education*, <http://www.aare.edu.au/99pap/le99034.htm>.

Leighton, G. and Lamont, A. 2006, 'Children's singing development: do experiences in early schooling help or hinder?', *Music Education Research*, 8(3), pp. 311–330.

Linke, P. and Fleer, M. 2002, *Babies: Good Beginnings Last Forever*, Australian Early Childhood Association, Watson, ACT.

MacNaughton, G. 2004, *Respect for Diversity in Early Childhood: A Theory and Research Map*, Bernard van Leer Foundation, The Hague, The Netherlands.

Molnar-Szakacs, I. and Overy, K. 2006, 'Music and mirror neurons: from motion to 'e'motion', *Social Cognitive and Affective Neuroscience*, 1(3), pp. 235–241.

Multilingual Children's Association 2004, '10 Tips for Boosting the Minority Language', <http://www.multilingualchildren.org/tips/ideas.html>

Nakata, T. and Trehub, S. 2004, 'Infants' responsiveness to maternal speech and singing', *Infant Behaviour and Development*, 27(4), pp. 455–464.

Neugebauer, B. (ed.) 1992, *Alike and Different: Exploring our Humanity with Young Children*, National Association for the Education of Young Children, Washington, DC.

Nilsson, B. and Folkestad, G. 2005, 'Children's practice of computer-based composition', *Music Education Research*, 7(1), pp. 21–37.

Olsson, B. 1988, 'Experiences for toddlers: some practical suggestions', in A. Stonehouse, ed., *Trusting Toddlers: Programming for One- to Three-Year-Olds in Child Care Centres* (pp. 132–9), Australian Early Childhood Association, Watson, ACT.

Omari, D. 2001, 'A comparison of foreign language teaching methods: total physical response versus song/chants with kindergarteners', *Eric Digest*, ED461987.

Patterson, C. 2004, 'Play based curriculum: a strong foundation for future learning', in R. Clements and L. Fiorentino, eds, *The Child's Right to Play: A Global Approach*, Greenwood Publishing Group, Westport, CT, pp. 111–118.

Purnell, P., Ali, P., Begum, N. and Carter, M. 2007, 'Windows, bridges and mirrors: building culturally responsive early childhood classrooms through the integration of literacy and the arts', *Early Childhood Education Journal*, 34(6), pp. 419–424.

Ramsey, P. 2004, *Teaching and Learning in a Diverse World: Multicultural Education for Young Children*, 2nd edn, Teachers College Press, New York.

Read, K., Gardner, P. and Mahler, B. 1993, *Early Childhood Programs: Human Relationships and Learning*, 9th edn, Holt, Rinehart and Winston Inc., Fort Worth, TX.

Reutzel, R. 1992, 'Breaking the letter-a-week tradition', *Childhood Education*, 69(1), pp. 20–23.

Ringgenberg, S. 2003, 'Using music as a teaching tool: creating story songs', *Young Children*, 58(5), pp. 76–79.

Robison, H. and Schwartz, S. 1982, *Designing Curriculum for Early Childhood*, Allyn & Bacon, Boston.

Roulston, K. 2006, 'Investigation of young children's music preferences', *International Journal of Education and the Arts*, 7(9), pp. 1–23.

Rousseau, C., Drapeau, A., Lacroix, L., Déogratias Bagilishya, L. and Heusch, N. 2005, 'Evaluation of a classroom program of creative expression workshops for refugee and immigrant children', *Journal of Child Psychology and Psychiatry*, 46(2), pp. 180–185.

Schellenberg, E.G., Nakata, T., Hunter, P.G. and Tamoto, S. 2007, 'Exposure to music and cognitive performance: tests of children and adults', *Psychology of Music*, 35, pp. 5–19.

Sims, W. 2005, 'Effects of free versus directed listening on duration of individual music listening by prekindergarten children', *Journal of Research in Music Education*, 53(1), pp. 78–86.

Smith, J. 2006, 'Every child a singer: techniques for assisting developing singers—all children can sing if you take the time to teach them', *Music Educators Journal*, 93(2), pp. 28–35.

Spodek, B. and Saracho, O. 1994, *Right from the Start: Teaching Children Ages Three to Eight*, Allyn & Bacon, Boston.

St John, P. 2006, 'Finding and making meaning: young children as musical collaborators', *Psychology of Music*, 34(2), pp. 238–261.

Stewart, M. and Walsh, V. 2005, 'Infant learning: music and the brain', *Current Biology*, 15(2), pp. R882–R884.

Strickland, S. 2001/02, 'Music and the brain in childhood development', *Childhood Education*, 78(2), pp. 100–103.

Welch, G. 2006, 'Singing and vocal development', in G.E. McPherson, ed., *The Child as Musician: A Handbook of Musical Development*, Oxford University Press, New York, pp. 311–329.

Whiteman, P. 2001, 'How the bananas got their pyjamas: a study of the metamorphosis of preschoolers' spontaneous singing as viewed through Vygotsky's Zone of Proximal Development', Doctoral thesis, University of New South Wales.

Wilkes, G. (ed.) 1979, *Collins Dictionary of the English Language*, Penguin Books, Middlesex.

York, S. 1991, *Roots and Wings: Affirming Culture in Early Childhood Programs*, Toys 'n Things Press, Minnesota.

Young, S. 2006, 'Seen but not heard: young children, improvised singing and educational practice', *Contemporary Issues in Early Childhood*, 7(3), pp. 270–280.

Chapter 17

Suggesting

 Suggest: to put forward (an idea, plan etc.) for consideration.

(Collins Dictionary of the English Language, p. 1453)

In addition to serving as models for appropriate emotional expression, teachers need to give children concrete suggestions for dealing with feelings.

(Ahn 2005, p. 55)

The suggestibility of children gives teachers great power, and the use of suggestion in the classroom entails a great responsibility . . .

(Hughes and Hughes 1937, p. 366)

What?

A suggestion is an offer of advice, ideas or recommendations about what to do next. People make suggestions because they believe there is a better, more interesting or more effective way to do things.

Issues and debates

We did not identify any specific debates in the literature on the use of suggestion as a teaching technique. In this section we alert staff to two issues to be alert to when using suggestion as a teaching technique.

GETTING THE BALANCE RIGHT BETWEEN ADULT SUGGESTION AND CHILD EXPLORATION

Suggestions are a direct form of adult involvement in children's learning in which the adult attempts to direct a child's learning. Getting the balance right between teacher suggestion and child exploration and meaning-making is important. Swedish researchers (Emilson and Folkesson 2006) studying the relationships between teacher control and toddler participation in their learning found too much teacher direction and framing of learning restricted toddler participation. In contrast, UK researchers (Plowman and Stephen 2007) studying Information and Communication Technologies (ICT) in the preschool classroom found that teachers were minimally involved in supporting children's learning about and use of ICT. This meant that ICT was often poorly used by children. They point to the way in which simple teacher guidance and suggestion can enhance meaningful and extended use of ICT by preschool children.

UNDERSTANDING THAT SUGGESTIONS OFFER CHILDREN A CHOICE

When staff use suggestion they are offering children a choice. For example, 'Rowan, you could use the green blanket in the home corner for your tent', is a suggestion. Rowan can decide whether to use the green blanket or not. As children can ignore or modify suggestions, staff should offer suggestions only when they are prepared for children to ignore or modify them. As there is good evidence that children are more co-operative and engaged when they are offered choices (McCormick, Jolivette and Ridgley 2003), suggestion can be an effective strategy for gaining children's co-operation. If staff need or want the children to follow their advice, ideas or recommendations then they should tell (refer to Chapter 18) the children what is to be done rather than suggest it. To illustrate this using the previous example, if the staff member wanted Rowan to use the green blanket because it was the only blanket she was prepared to have Rowan use, then Rowan should have been told this: 'Rowan, if you want to use a blanket for your tent you will need to use the green blanket in the home corner. It is the only blanket we can wash easily if it gets dirty.'

How?

Allen and Hart (1984) believed that most teaching techniques act as a form of suggestion. By way of illustration, questions about what a child intends to do next can act as a suggestion by prompting the child to test out a new idea. Questions such as 'Have you thought about doing it this way?', 'Have you tried using the bigger trolley to carry the blocks?' or 'Do you think it would be easier if one person pushed and the other person pulled?' can all suggest alternative ways of approaching a task to a child. Verbal feedback can also act as a suggestion by prompting a child to try an alternative way of doing things. Comments such as: 'Have you thought about . . .' or 'I wonder what would happen if . . .' can also suggest to a child alternative ways of approaching a task.

Many suggestions will start with phrases such as:

- 'You could try it this way . . .'
- 'If you do this . . . then . . . x might happen'
- 'Why don't you try this?'
- 'How about we try it this way?'
- 'It might help if you did that . . .'
- 'Try doing this . . .'
- 'This might help . . .'
- 'Maybe you could try this . . .'

While children may choose to ignore staff's suggestions, the following guidance will reduce this possibility.

Suggestions are more likely to be followed if they are positive. Positive suggestions tell the child what they might do, rather than telling them what not do to. The suggestion sounds constructive rather than negative and restricting (Marion 2002). For example, 'If you walk while you're holding that jug of juice it will not spill'. Suggestions will also work best if staff:

- avoid flooding children with more than one suggestion at a time
- allow children time to test suggestions out in practice
- accept that children may not use your suggestions. If they do not have a choice about what to do next, make it clear that you are not suggesting what to do but telling them what to do
- keep suggestions personal to the child and specific to their needs.

Jenny suggests ways to use the climbing equipment.

Suggestions can be direct or indirect. Direct suggestions might start with 'Let's try it this way'. Less direct suggestions might start with 'What would happen if you did it a different way?' The more direct the suggestion, the more likely it is that the children will follow it. The younger the child, the more specific and direct the suggestions need to be.

Staff can also use gestures as a form of suggestion or as a way to strengthen their verbal suggestions, as these can orient children to the most salient features of the suggestion (Roth 2001).

When and why?

GOAL RELEVANCE

Suggestions can be used to enhance many areas of children's learning, including the following:

Thinking, discovery and learning
- to increase children's engagement in learning. US research (Cole and Levinson 2002) with preschool children suggests that giving children choice allows them to feel more power over their environment, which in turn motivates their participation in an experience and they remain engaged in it for longer
- to prompt children to make an independent discovery by trying out a new method or approach to a problem they are encountering. Children are more thoughtful when staff make suggestions

about how to use objects in science programs, such as magnets (Howe 1993). Suggestions can also help build mathematical knowledge. Staff can help children build generalisations by suggesting they revisit experiences (Schwartz 1996). For example, 'Perhaps if you want to make another road of the same length you may need to find five more blocks this long. I wonder if it would work if you did that?'

- to redirect children's attention from one task to another. Suggesting that a child play with a toy or get involved in an experience similar to the one they are in can help redirect children's attention (Ahn 2005). For example, 'You might want to take that dolly over to the basin and wash her'. If this is accompanied by gestures that reinforce where the basin is it will strengthen the suggestion (Roth 2001)
- to direct children's attention to the salient features of a particular problem—for example, 'Take a good look at this machine, can you notice the wheels and the cogs?'
- to help children remember. Suggesting children respond to stories through drawing can help children's memory (Soundy, Guha and Qiu 2007).

Creativity

- to enrich children's storylines in dramatic play. Staff interaction with children here can increase the children's interest in this form of play if staff suggestions extend rather than redirect the play (Dempsey and Frost 1993).

Relationships

- to help children resolve a social dispute (Fox and Harper 2006). When children both want the same toy, staff can suggest ways that each can have a turn. Children can then work through how to solve their own dispute
- to increase children's pro-social behaviour. US research (Kohler et al. 2001) has shown that the pro-social behaviour of preschool children in Head Start Centres and those children who are withdrawn, or have autism, conduct problems or emotional disturbance can be increased through teacher suggestions about how to interact with each other (sometimes referred to as priming)
- to give children 'knowing how to interact' information that can help grow their social understandings by helping them to understand other people's views and feelings (Porath 2007).

Wellbeing

- to help children relax. For example, staff can help children relax through teaching them to take slow, deep breaths. To do this, staff can suggest different ways of slowing down their breathing and taking deeper breaths. According to Roe (1996, p. 8), the following suggestions help: '. . . suggesting children puff their breath in and out like a train, suggesting children try to breathe like an elephant who is asleep and suggesting children pretend to be a fish and breathe with their mouth open'
- to help children deal constructively with emotion (Ahn 2005)
- to increase children's perseverance and to reduce their frustration with a task they are finding difficult. A suggestion about what shape puzzle piece to look for might help a child maintain interest in a puzzle that the child is finding difficult to complete.

DEVELOPMENTAL CONSIDERATIONS

Staff need to adapt their suggestions to the children's language capacities and thought, moving from more to less direct suggestions as they get older.

Suggestion is a verbal teaching technique. As such, it is most appropriately used with children once they have the language competence to understand what is being suggested. Young children's language capacities influence the extent to which they will follow a suggestion (Roebersa and Schneiderb 2005). However, talking with babies as they babble is an important way in which they learn about how language works as a form of communication (Honig 2007). Staff can find it difficult to find things to talk about with babies. Suggestions can often be a good starting point to a conversation with a baby. When staff combine actions with conversation phrases such as: 'How about we try it this way?', 'Try doing this . . .', 'This might help . . .' or 'Maybe you could try this . . .' it can help babies learn that words and actions have some correspondence. As staff wait for a baby's response to their physical and verbal suggestion they are helping babies learn about the pattern of two-way communication—speech and or action by one person, and the expected response by another.

Babies and toddlers often have a strong interest in musical sounds (Illari 2002) and have an understanding of rhythm from an early age (Derri at al. 2001). Providing babies and toddlers with lots of opportunities to listen to different musical tones, pitch and rhythm can help develop their cognition (Illari 2002). It has also been found some time ago to help develop toddlers' problem-solving abilities. As they encounter the problems, such as how to make sounds louder and softer, how to use their hands or mouth to make sounds, and how to stop sounds once they begin, staff suggestions can help them become more thoughtful about how to solve the problems they encounter (Howe 1993).

A staff member at the Emu Children's Centre collected old pots and pans from opportunity shops, and also collected a series of wooden spoons. She put these on the floor for the toddlers in her group to experiment with. She modelled different ways to bang the pots: 'Inside makes a different sound from outside'; 'The lids make yet another sound when you bang them'. She then allowed the toddlers to experiment with making different sounds.

Reflection point: What simple song could you sing to engage the toddlers further in enjoying this experience?

Toddlers have insights about social behaviours and their reasons from as young as two years of age (Porath 2007). However, they can often find it difficult to resolve their own disputes over who should play with a particular toy or whose turn it is. Staff can help toddlers gain the social knowledge they need to resolve their own disputes through direct suggestion—for example, by suggesting another toy that a toddler might play with while he awaits a turn with the desired toy. Suggesting constructive ways for toddlers to express their emotions, such as using their words to resolve disputes, is effective in helping toddlers to build constructive social relationships (Ahn 2005). For instance, if one toddler takes another toddler's favourite hat, the teacher might say, 'Why don't you tell her that you want it back, rather than cry?' Specific direct suggestions are important if toddlers are to find them helpful, given they are just beginning to learn to use terms whose meaning is context specific (known as deictic terms). As Honig (2007) explains:

Deictic terms are too difficult for toddlers. Using terms such as 'this one' and 'that one' requires that the speaker becomes the point of reference from which the terms can be understood. Thus, when speaking with young children, an adult needs to use specific terms. Saying 'put these blocks over there and those blocks over here' is frustrating for the child. Labelling long versus short blocks and specifying the exact shelf on which to store the blocks will be very helpful in gaining children's cooperation at clean-up time. (pp. 585–586)

Preschoolers can empathise with each other's feelings and so they are often able to successfully negotiate a conclusion to their own disputes (Ladd and Coleman 1993). However, sometimes their negotiations 'get stuck'. Staff can use these occasions to help build preschoolers' capacity for fair dispute resolution by suggesting ways forward. Questions can often form the basis of this process:

> A dispute over who should use the computer next is occurring between two four-year-olds. They seem unable to come to any resolution so the teacher intervenes, saying, 'You don't seem to be able to solve this problem. Would your problem be solved if we tossed a coin to see who should go next? Would that be fair?'.

The older the child the less specific and less direct the suggestions need to be. Staff can use broad suggestions in the form of comments or questions to help expand older children's use of writing as a method of communication. Staff can suggest different ways and different occasions that children can use writing to communicate with others, including:

- letters and thank you notes to each other, to visitors who contribute to classroom life and to people involved in places they might visit
- letters or email notes to ask other people for information
- letters or notices to tell people about what is happening in their classroom
- letters to newspapers or public figures to express their reactions to current events.

Children's writing skills can also be supported through the use of journals or folders. As staff read these they can make suggestions about how a story might evolve or where a child might go to next in their writing. Suggestions can show the children that their writing is being taken seriously and is being valued.

Sometimes suggestions can be very helpful for primary school children—for instance, when they are attempting to resolve conflicts outside of the classroom. If staff suggest specific games that children can play that are acceptable it can help children to 'work things out during recess' (McDermott 1999, p. 82). It may be necessary when there are difficulties between children at recess time to be with them as they begin their games and make specific suggestions about how to progress them until children can successfully play the game themselves (McDermott 1999).

For children of all ages there is evidence that children's gestures offer an important insight into their levels of cognitive competence on difficult tasks. Research indicates that 'gestures provide cognitive support when children attempt to talk about difficult tasks' (Roth 2001, p. 373). For some children gestures also provide a more accurate sense of what they are understanding than do their words. Some children can 'gesturally express correct conceptual understanding, whereas their speech still expresses incorrect conceptual understanding' (Roth 2001, p. 373). If teachers are alert to these phenomena then they can target their suggestions about how to complete difficult tasks or understand new concepts more precisely.

Equity considerations

'RACE' AND CULTURE

Young children can act and think in racially prejudiced ways by the time they are preschoolers (MacNaughton 2005; Connelly 2007). They can also act and think in anti-discriminatory ways and learn to stand up against unfairness towards themselves and others (Connelly 2007). However, young children need considerable staff support to stand up for themselves and for others when they encounter racial prejudice. With support they can learn how to stop racial name-calling and teasing between children.

Staff can use suggestion to support children's attempts to stand up against unfairness in several ways. They can suggest ways for children to let other people know that they are upset. This might involve suggesting some words the children can use to tell others that they feel angry or hurt. It also involves teaching children how to ensure that others know they mean what they say. Staff can offer suggestions about this. With practical suggestions and encouragement children can learn respect for diversity. This respect can then be consolidated in the early years of schooling by staff suggesting new words and new ways children can express their feelings of hurt to others. This might include writing them a note, telling a story about their feelings to other children or composing a song to share with the group.

GENDER

Children's dramatic play is influenced by the gender mix of the playgroups. The storylines the boys choose often give them a powerful leadership role and the girls a passive and submissive role (MacNaughton 2001). Staff can help create greater gender equity in mixed-gender playgroups by suggesting alternative storylines in which girls and boys can alternate and share decision-making and leadership. Lots of domestic, rural and adventure storylines lend themselves to this. For example, introducing the idea of co-pilots in spacecraft, shared child care at home or rounding up sheep means that more than one child can experience taking control of the spacecraft, the child (and the play) or the sheep. Staff can suggest to children the advantages of sharing, such as being able to rest when they're tired and to call on help in emergencies.

As children are likely to be less familiar with these storylines, staff may need to take an active role initially in 'play tutoring', as it has been found to increase socio-dramatic play (Linden 2001). Play tutoring involves staying with the children as they play and providing direct and indirect suggestions about how the play might proceed, and how differences of opinion might be resolved. If children were 'rounding up the sheep' staff could make suggestions about how many dogs might be needed, what to use to build the sheep pens, who might be in control of the gate, who might be in control of the dogs, or how a ute might be able to help. As staff make suggestions it is important they try to ensure that girls have active, leadership roles in the play and that all the fun jobs are not done by the boys—staff would need to guard against the girls being the sheep and the boys being the dogs, gatekeeper and the ute driver.

DISABILITY AND ADDITIONAL NEEDS

Toddlers are very curious about the physical differences and similarities between people. When toddlers first notice and think about these differences, staff have a chance to help them learn to enjoy and value people's diversity.

For this to occur staff need to provide toddlers with active support for understanding the physical differences and similarities between the people they see around them. Simple feedback (refer to Chapter 8) about what they have seen provides critical support. The opportunity to read stories about people's diversity and to play with dolls that reflect different abilities and disabilities all help in this process. However, despite staff's best efforts toddlers may feel fearful and uncomfortable when confronted by disability. If this occurs, staff can combine doll play with suggestions to help toddlers feel more comfortable with physical disability (Dare and O'Donovan 2002). This play can continue on several different occasions until the child feels comfortable with the diversity.

Reflecting on suggesting techniques

1   Briefly define suggesting.
2   What is the difference between direct and indirect suggestion? Provide an example of each.
3   Which of the following suggestions are direct and which are indirect?
    ● 'You could have a go at doing this . . .'
    ● 'If you try this . . . then it might work better'
    ● 'Why don't you put this one here?'
    ● 'How about we see what happens when . . .?'
    ● 'It might be easier if you did that . . .'
    ● 'Try pushing like this . . .'
    ● 'This tool might be more useful . . .'
    ● 'Maybe you could take another approach . . .'
4   List 10 ways of using suggesting to support children's learning in a mixed-age group setting. Would each of these processes be suitable for use with babies?

5 To what extent do you agree with the statement that 'Most of the other teaching strategies teachers use also serve as suggestions to children' (Allen and Hart 1984, p. 259)? Provide examples of how each of the following techniques could act as a suggestion: recalling, reading, singing, describing, demonstrating and modelling.

6 Observe staff working with toddlers. How and how well did they use suggestion to help toddlers learn the daily routine of the centre? Was suggestion the most appropriate technique to use? Why? Why not?

7 Observe a group discussion between an adult and a group of four-year-old children. How was suggestion used to promote children's learning?

8 Observe a dispute between a group of three- to five-year-old children. How could adult suggestion be used to help children resolve the dispute?

Improving teaching in practice

1 Videotape the teaching interactions you have with children during several five-minute teaching periods.

2 How and how well did you use suggestion to support children's learning? Did you:
   - tend to use direct or indirect suggestions?
   - adjust the specificity of your suggestions according to the children's age?
   - pace your suggestions so that children could absorb what was being said and test them out for themselves?
   - allow children to reject or ignore your suggestions?
   - ensure your suggestions were relevant to each child's particular needs?

3 What are your areas of strength and weakness in using suggestion as a teaching technique to promote children's learning?

4 How can you improve your suggestion techniques in practice?

FURTHER READING

Cadwell, L. 2003, *Bringing Learning to Life: The Reggio Approach to Early Childhood Education*, Teachers College Press, New York.

Fleer, M., Edwards, S., Hammer, M., Kennedy, A., Ridgway, A., Robbins, J. and Surman, L. 2006, *Early Childhood Learning Communities: Sociocultural Research in Practice,* Pearson Education Australia, French's Forest, NSW.

Harada, V., Lum, D. and Souza, K. 2002/03, 'Building a learning community: students and adults as inquirers', *Childhood Education*, 79(2), pp. 66–71.

Lubeck, S. and Post, J. 2000, 'Creating a Head Start community of practice', in L. Diaz Soto, ed., *The Politics of Early Childhood Education* (pp. 33–58), Peter Lang Publishing, New York.

Read, K., Gardner, P. and Mahler, B. 1993, *Early Childhood Programs: Human Relationships and Learning*, 9th edn, Holt, Rinehart and Winston Inc. Fort Worth, TX, [refer to pp. 89–99].

Watson, M. and Battistich, V. 2006, 'Creating and sustaining caring communities', in C. Evertson and C. Weinstein, eds, *Handbook of Classroom Management: Research, Practice and Contemporary Issues*, Lawrence Erlbaum Associates, New Jersey, pp. 253–280.

ONLINE AND MULTI-MEDIA RESOURCES

Bovey, T. and Strain, P. 2005, *Strategies for Increasing Peer Social Interactions: Prompting and Acknowledgment*, Center on the Social and Emotional Foundations for Early Learning: **http://www.vanderbilt.edu/csefel/briefs/wwb17.html**

'Cooperative and collaborative learning in early childhood classrooms'. Early Childhood Australia webportal: **http://www.earlychildhoodaustralia.org.au/.../program_approaches/collaborative_cooperative_learning.html**

Multi-media
Supporting Children's Active Learning: Teaching Strategies for Diverse Settings (Video), The High Scope Press, 1992.

'Writing'. A short free access video clip of one teacher's approach to building children's writing skills. She uses 'suggesting' as a key technique to build these skills: **http://www.readingrockets.org/podcasts/classroom#sounds** (accessed 19 October 2007).

Intercultural Development Research Association podcasts featuring Josie Danini Cortez, M.A., Dr Juanita García and Aurelio Montemayor, M.Ed. *Professional Learning Communities in Schools*: **http://www.idra.org/Podcasts**

REFERENCES

Ahn, H. 2005, 'Child care teachers' strategies in children's socialization of emotion', *Early Child Development and Care*, 175(1), pp. 49–61

Allen, K. and Hart, B. 1984, *The Early Years: Arrangements for Learning*, Prentice Hall Inc., New Jersey.

Cole, C.L. and Levinson, T.R. 2002, 'Effects of within-activity choices on the challenging behavior of children with severe developmental disabilities', *Journal of Behavior Interventions* 4(1), pp. 29–37.

Connelly, P. 2007, 'The role of research: promoting positive attitudes towards ethnic diversity', *Early Childhood Matters*, June, pp. 50–55.

Dare, A. and O'Donovan, M. 2002, *Good Practice in Caring for Young Children With Special Needs*, Nelson Thornes Publishers, Cheltenham, UK.

Dempsey, J. and Frost, J. 1993, 'Play environments in early childhood education', in B. Spodek (ed.), *Handbook of Research on the Education of Young Children*, Macmillan Publishing, New York, pp. 306–21.

Derri, V., Tsapakidou, A., Zachopoulou, E. and Gini, V. 2001, 'Complexity of rhythmic ability as measured in preschool children', *Perceptual and Motor Skills*, 92, pp. 777–785.

Emilson, A. and Folkesson, A. 2006, 'Children's participation and teacher control', *Early Child Development and Care*, 176 (3/4), pp. 219–238.

Fox, L. and Harper, R. 2006, '"You got it!" Teaching social and emotional skills', *Young Children: Beyond the Journal*, November, <http://www.journal.naeyc.org/btj/200611/BTJFoxLentini.asp>

Honig, A. 2007, 'Oral language development', *Early Child Development and Care*, 177 (6/7), pp. 581–613.

Howe, A. 1993, 'Science in early childhood education', in B. Spodek, ed., *Handbook of Research on the Education of Young Children* (pp. 225–235), Macmillan, New York.

Hughes, A. and Hughes, E. 1937, *Learning and Teaching: An Introduction to Psychology and Education*, Longman, London.

Illari, B. 2002, 'Music perception and cognition in the first year of life', *Early Child Development and Care*, 172(3), pp. 311–322.

Kohler, F.W., Anthony, L.J., Steighner, S.A. and Hoyson, M. 2001, 'Teaching social interaction skills in the integrated preschool: an examination of naturalistic tactics', *Topics in Early Childhood Special Education*, 21(2), pp. 93–103.

Ladd, G. and Coleman, C. 1993, 'Young children's peer relationships: forms, features and functions', in B. Spodek (ed.), *Handbook of Research on the Education of Young Children*, Macmillan Publishing, New York, pp. 57–76.

Linden, J. 2001, *Understand children's play*, Nelson Thornes Publishers, Cheltenham, UK.

Marion, M. 2002, *Guidance of Young Children*, 6th edn, Prentice Hall, New Jersey.

MacNaughton, G. 2001, *Rethinking Gender in Early Childhood Education*, Allen & Unwin, Sydney.

—— 2005, *Doing Foucault in early childhood studies*, Routledge, London.

McCormick, K.M., Jolivette, K. and Ridgley, R. 2003, 'Choice making as an intervention strategy for young children,' *Young Exceptional Children*, 6(2), pp. 3–10.

McDermott, K. 1999, 'Helping primary school children work things out during recess', *Young Children*, 54(4), pp. 82–84.

Plowman, L. and Stephen, C. 2007, 'Guided interaction in pre-school settings', *Journal of Computer Assisted Learning*, 23(1), pp. 14–26.

Porath, M. 2007, 'Fostering social expertise in early childhood', *Early Child Development and Care*, 9999(1), pp. 1–16, DOI: 10.1080/03004430600989098.

Roe, D. 1996, 'Young children and stress: how can we help?', *Australian Early Childhood Association Resource Book Series*, 3(4), pp. 1–14.

Roebersa, C. and Schneiderb, W. 2005, 'Individual differences in young children's suggestibility: relations to event memory, language abilities, working memory, and executive functioning', *Cognitive Development*, 20(3), pp. 427–447.

Roth, M.W. 2001, 'Gestures: their role in teaching and learning', *Review of Educational Research*, 71(3), pp. 365–392.

Schwartz, S. 1996, 'Hidden messages in teacher talk: praise and empowerment', *Teaching Children Mathematics* (March), pp. 396–401.

Soundy, C.S., Guha, S. and Qiu, Y. 2007, 'Picture power: placing artistry and literacy on the same page', *Young Children*, 62(3), pp. 82–88.

Wilkes, G. (ed.) 1979, *Collins Dictionary of the English Language*, Penguin Books, Middlesex.

Chapter 18

Telling and instructing

 Instruct: to direct to do something, to teach (someone) how to do (something).

(*Collins Dictionary of the English Language*, p. 758)

Tell: to let know or notify, to order or instruct.

(*Collins Dictionary of the English Language*, p. 1494)

Instruction: telling the pupil what to do, and/or imparting information

(Fisher 2007, p. 618)

We tell so that children can hear, but we do not always tell so that they can understand . . .

(Hughes and Hughes 1937, p. 368)

What?

When you tell a person something you describe it, generally providing some verbal account of what is happening or should happen. Telling children is a conventional teaching technique in which someone with information or knowledge (often the adult) passes that information on to someone (often the child) who does not have it. It is often associated with 'chalk and talk' approaches to teaching, and associated with direct instruction of children. Staff can tell children about events, experiences, ideas, opinions, concepts and reasons for doing things, or tell children to do things (instructing).

Issues and debates

TELLING, DIRECTING AND VOICING

Direct instruction is a very specific form of telling. When you instruct someone you tell them how to do something. Direct instruction as a key technique for teaching young children has engendered significant debate over the years. Its opponents argue it discourages children's social and emotional development, love of learning and creativity. Its proponents argue that it improves academic achievement and children's school-readiness (see Banks 2001). It is often characterised by one-sided teacher talk where the teacher as expert leads and shapes classroom dialogue (Fisher 2007).

However, telling can also be an important part of classroom dialogue and of building a dialogic community (see Chapter 26 on philosophising and Chapter 20 on community building) that empowers children to think, understand and reflect. Telling can become part of 'talk for thinking' (Fisher 2007, p. 619) as teachers and children listen to what the other is telling them, ask questions of it and reflect on its meaning. In other words, the context within which 'telling' is used and how it is balanced against other ways of sharing meanings determine its value in a teacher's teaching repertoire.

How?

Telling children about things and telling children to do things is one way of providing them with the information staff want them to have. Telling is also a way of sharing information, dreams, ideas and feelings. If it forms part of a dialogue between teachers and children it can enrich thinking and learning in the classroom (Fisher 2007).

However, if telling is always teacher-led and is the main form of teacher talk, the opposite can happen. Telling as a one-way form of communication allows very little opportunity for children's participation in making meaning. If it dominates classroom talk, children may become passive learners, quickly bored and disinterested in listening to adults. To avoid this, children need to be instructed in the rules of dialogue and learn how to question, reflect on, extend and explore what they are told and what they tell others. When telling forms part of a cognitively challenging dialogue, learning happens. As Fisher explained:

> Speaking and listening does not necessarily lead to learning. Classroom research shows that children talking together does not often evidence what Habermas (1991) called 'communicative rationality' or cognitive challenge (Fisher 2003, 2005a, 2005b). There is therefore a need to identify the elements of effective dialogue and other kinds of talk used in school if the potential for speaking and listening to promote and accelerate children's learning is to be fully realised. (2007, p. 617)

Telling may be necessary to instruct children in safety or other important classroom rules. In this instance, telling is likely to be most effective when it is accompanied by actions and/or objects, when simple, clear sentences are used, and when children are familiar with the words being used:

The teacher in Year 1 at the Merrivale Primary School tells the children the rules about playground behaviour: children must play fairly, they must not hurt each other, they must wear hats on sunny days and they must put any rubbish they have in the nearby bins. She states the rules in clear, unambiguous terms so that the children are all clear on how to behave when they go out to play.

Reflection point: What do you need to tell the children that you work with?

However, setting social rules by telling children how to behave socially (for example, to always share) is unlikely to be a successful teaching technique by itself as it does not deal with 'why' children might behave otherwise or challenge social norms within a group:

Gabrielle, a new graduate working in a kindergarten in the outer western suburbs of Adelaide, has brought a problem to the local kindergarten teachers' group for discussion.

Gabrielle: 'My problem is that the children fight all the time and won't share the equipment, especially outside. I seem to spend my time "putting out fires", going from one dispute to the next and sorting out the children's arguments. What techniques can I use other than telling them what to do and acting as a referee?'

Carlene: 'At the beginning of the year I make all the rules clear to the children. I tell them what the rules are and then I remind them again and again. I mean rules like walking inside, only four people at the clay table, keep the sand in the sandpit; and I also mean rules of behaviour towards others—that is, sharing, not taking others' equipment, using voices not fists and so on. When the children do something that doesn't fit in with the rules I remind them and help them. If two children are fighting over a wheelbarrow outside, I'll remind them that sharing outside is desirable, and that they need to work this out verbally. At the beginning of the year they don't know how to do this, so I model for them and give them suggestions and techniques for working out turn-taking. They soon get the hang of it and after a few weeks they start to use words instead of physically fighting.'

Gabrielle: 'Is it too late for me to do this? I can see they've got into the habit of me telling them what to do.'

Carlene: 'You should start right away! It's never to late to learn!'

Reflection point: What habits of telling do you have?

Moreover, there is a growing movement (based on a children's rights approach to teaching and learning) to have children participate in the making of classroom rules. Not only is this seen as their right as members of the classroom community but also as an important way in which to build that community and collective ownership of the rules (see Chapter 23 on democratising and Chapter 20 on community building).

If staff do decide that telling children about or to do something (instructing) will support children's learning, Garhart Mooney's (2005) advice on encouraging children to listen to adults may be helpful:

- Get children's attention before you begin to tell them something.
- Use clear, uncluttered language that avoids words that may be unfamiliar to the children.
- Give children practical examples to illustrate the points being made.
- Emphasise the key points or items through tone of voice and gesture.
- Gain feedback from the children to ensure that they've understood what's been said.

Picture prompts can also be used to 'instruct' children. Ramsey and Fowler (2004) used posters with instructions to children and families on how to interact scientifically and mathematically with everyday objects and events in their environment. This process increased the number of scientific and mathematical activities that children engaged in inside and outside of the three US preschool classrooms that they studied.

Some research suggests that young children are more likely to learn to do things through story-telling than through direct instruction. As Seifert (1993, p. 14) so simply put it some years ago:

They may learn to zipper jackets more easily if the task is represented as a story ('A bird flying out of its nest').

Story-telling is a very special form of telling children about things and it is very different to story-reading.

- Story-telling depends on the *spoken word* to connect a story-teller and listener so that a story is created in the imagination.
- Story-reading depends on a *focus on print* (words and/or illustrations) for the understanding and appreciation of a story (Smyth 1996, p. 2).

Smyth's (1996) advice on successful story-telling with young children is still pertinent. She suggests:

- telling stories that have a clear theme. Themes that work well are those that derive from the children's own experiences and do not confuse or frighten them
- telling stories that move along quickly and have a plot and a sequence
- telling stories in which staff have enjoyment and interest
- telling stories in settings where children will not be distracted by light, noise and other children.

However, as story-telling traditions vary in different cultures it is useful to explore those traditions that are relevant to your specific context. See the 'Online and multi-media resources' section of this chapter for useful links to follow.

When and why?

GOAL RELEVANCE

Sometimes it is important for children to learn something by being told about it rather than discovering it for themselves. Giving children information rather than waiting for them to discover it for themselves is particularly relevant when:

Learning safety and social rules
- Children may need to know something to be safe. For example, children need to know about road rules, rules about how to use hammers and rules about using matches. They may need to be told: 'You stop when traffic lights are red'; 'You never put your thumb under a hammer'; 'Hot water will burn you if you touch it'; 'It is dangerous to cross the road without an adult'.
- It can be difficult for children to find some things out for themselves. If children need to know about social rules and conventions, reading from left to right in English, or not to masturbate in public, then direct instruction is important. Research about children with autism (Brookes 2007) indicates that directly instructing children in the use of social phrases and rules improves the children's social relationships and social acceptability in preschool settings.

Gaining new knowledge and skills
- Children may experience considerable frustration or embarrassment trying to discover something for themselves (for example, where the toilet is).
- Children may want to use a new tool or gain a new skill to help with their independence. For example, if a new tool, such as a drill, is introduced into the woodworking area, the children must be instructed on how to use it.
- Children may need to know what to do next. For example, in a movement and dance class, instructions can be used to tell children when to stop, or move to exploring the next movement or dance. It can help children understand and respond to transitions during the session (Clark 2007). The teacher may tell the children, 'When I clap and say "pause", you will stop your dance' or 'When I tap the drum come close and listen to me'. Instruction can also support the development of children's musical skills and abilities. For instance, specific piano keyboard instruction was found not only to improve young Greek children's keyboard skills but also to improve their cognitive skills development (Zafranas 2004).
- Children can learn specific literacy skills, such as reading comprehension, through direct, explicit instruction on what, when, where and how to read. This can increase children's knowledge and metacognitive awareness of what they read (Courtney and Montano 2006).

DEVELOPMENTAL CONSIDERATIONS

It is possible to 'tell' people things through spoken language, gesture or sign language. So, although telling is primarily understood as a verbal teaching technique, it can be used with pre-verbal babies to promote their cognitive and language learning. This is because babies enjoy listening to the human voice. Research over time has shown that newborn babies find listening to the human voice preferable to sounds such as music, and babies by six weeks of age find looking at faces that are speaking preferable to those that are not speaking (Rookes and Willson 2000; Gross 2003).

One way in which staff can capitalise on the interest babies have in the human voice is by telling them simple stories about daily events. Staff can tell babies about what is happening around them, what might happen to them and what has happened previously. For example, a caregiver may say to a baby, 'I'm going to change your nappy now, then we're going to have lunch. You're going to sit in your special chair, your blue chair, remember? The one you sat in yesterday.'

This simple story-telling provides opportunities for babies to:

- react and respond to sounds
- begin to learn basic language concepts
- listen to speech
- attach meaning to speech
- learn to recognise verbal sequences
- begin to visualise the meanings of sounds
- associate sound with actions and events.

The opportunity to practise these skills and gain these meanings helps the child learn to engage in reciprocal communication with adults. Such participation is the key for a child to become a competent member of a social group, and the precursor of oral and written literacy.

By two years of age, children are able to use words and simple sentences to communicate their ideas and needs to other people, and they are able to follow simple adult instructions. It is, therefore, possible for toddlers to learn how to do things through being told how or being told about them. However, many toddlers in diverse contexts are very active people who most enjoy learning about the world though their own exploration of it (Charlesworth 2003). They often like to move rapidly from one new adventure to another and spend much of their time trying out solutions to the many problems they encounter. They want to know how to make things happen. How to make a block balance on another block, how to turn a tap off or how to make a sandcastle may be just some of the problems faced by a toddler who is busy exploring their world. Telling a toddler how to do these things will generally be inappropriate. The point for toddlers is to discover this for themselves. Telling is probably only useful when:

- they need to be told how to do something for safety reasons—showing a toddler how to do something is as important as telling them how to do it. A simple, 'Let's do it this way . . .' accompanied by a demonstration will give the words more meaning
- they have asked to be told the name of something or someone. Toddlers often communicate in simple sentences that rely on nouns and verbs to convey meaning. Telling toddlers the name of things or actions when they show an interest in them or when they ask, 'What's that?' helps expand their vocabulary and shows that you are taking their questions seriously
- they are experiencing considerable frustration trying to discover something for themselves. Toddlers' enthusiasm for exploration and finding out how things work is often not matched by their physical and cognitive problem-solving abilities. This can create considerable frustration. If they are trying to find out how to make one block balance on another and they cannot figure it out, it can be frustrating. Staff can reduce the frustration toddlers feel by telling them how to do it. However, as indicated

above, showing a toddler how to do something can be as important as telling them how to do it. Once again, a simple, 'Let's try it this way . . .' accompanied by a demonstration will give the words more meaning:

> Narelle is sitting on the floor with Lorenzo as he plays with the Duplo. He is having trouble putting the small person on to the long block. Narelle says: 'Put it on top, Lorenzo'. She then demonstrates for him how the person fits on the top of the block.
>
> *Reflection point:* Would you use 'telling' in this situation? Why? Why not?

Toddlers begin to tell their own stories and follow simple adult stories. Staff can use these emerging abilities to support many aspects of toddlers' learning through story-telling. This form of telling can be far more meaningful than simple instructions. Research indicates that narrative (stories) and metaphor are well understood by young children. Telling toddlers stories about things that have happened to them can be a very powerful way of helping them learn from their own experiences. As Smyth (1996, p. 4) argued:

> When we put the familiar into story form we offer a new interpretation—we help children to structure the events of their own lives.

Preschoolers begin to use language to talk with other children, express their feelings, think about why and how things work, and to share their experiences with others. In many cultures they are also increasingly asking questions about how the world works and why. The question, 'Why?' is one of their most frequently asked questions (Fiske, Schacter and Kazdin 2005). If staff know the answer to the question, 'Why?' they can tell preschoolers the answer. However, telling them the answers may not help their learning. Children may quickly forget the answer or become dependent on adults to answer their questions. Staff can encourage children to seek the answers for themselves through open-ended questioning (Chapter 13), problem-solving (Chapter 27) and empowering (Chapter 25). This can help children become independent learners.

Children's mathematical understandings in the early years of schooling has been found to grow through direct instruction with young children when material is new or difficult and when specific children are struggling to learn specific mathematical concepts (van de Grift 2007). The specific dimensions of direct instruction that support mathematical learning are as follows:

> . . . beginning the lesson with a short statement of goals, reviewing previous learning, presenting new material in small steps, allowing pupils practice time after each step, giving clear and detailed instructions/explanations, providing active and ample practice, asking questions, checking for understanding and obtaining responses from all pupils, providing guided practice and explicit instruction. (van de Grift 2007, p. 133)

Telling children what to do in early science learning may also be helpful for some children. UK researchers (Pell and Jarvis 2001), in a study of 800 primary school children's attitudes to school, have found that young children prefer the teacher telling them what to do in science lessons.

Children telling stories to each other can also support struggling readers and the development of co-operative learning skills for children in the early years of school (Whitehead 2007). Hintz and Stomfay-Stitz (1999) described a program in which an early-years teacher in Toronto integrated children's story-telling into a Peacemaking program, and in doing so children who had been struggling with reading improved their reading skills considerably. Children were invited to choose their favourite books and then in small groups they told the stories to each other:

> In the beginning, her voice was the loudest, and children joined it in their own pace. She enabled her students to progress by providing a 'safety net' of strategies learned through Peacemaking, such as avoiding derogatory remarks or laughing at those whose pace was slower. (Hintz and Stomfay-Stitz 1999, p. 5)

Information and communication technologies can also support children's literacy learning through story-telling and retelling in the preschool and early years of school. Several programs exist to support this work. Sam is one such specific program that has been designed to do this and it has been shown to improve children's abilities to tell stories to each through modelling story-telling for children (Ryokai, Vaucelle and Cassell 2003). A number of interfaces such as multiple mice have also been developed to help young children to collaboratively tell and retell their stories.

Whitehead (2007) suggests allowing bilingual children to act as language tutors to each other by sharing stories as part of building their oral language skills and confidence in talking with each other using different languages.

Equity considerations

'RACE' AND CULTURE

As indicated earlier in this chapter, staff may need to tell children things to keep them physically safe. However, children also need to feel emotionally safe. Prejudice and racism can make early childhood settings emotionally unsafe for children from black and ethnic minority backgrounds. Comments such as, 'My mum hates darkies and so do I!' will be very hurtful to a black child and will make the centre feel unsafe. Children need to know that staff have rules about treating each other fairly and with respect. They will not know about these rules unless they are told and reminded about them.

Telling is also an appropriate technique for giving children information that is important to have but difficult to find for themselves. For example, by three years of age children are aware of differences in skin colour and they become interested in how and why such differences occur. It is difficult for young children to discover for themselves why these differences exist. Yet it is important that they have an accurate answer as this prevents misunderstandings developing. Children can think differences exist because people with light skin tones wash themselves harder than people with dark skin tones or because people with dark skin tones eat lots of chocolate.

To find the answer to how and why skin tones differ, children need to be told the answer in ways that they can understand:

> We get our skin colour in three different ways: from our parents and from relatives who lived long ago, called ancestors; from the sun; and from something called melanin . . . You can't see the tiny melanin grains but everyone has melanin in their skin. If you have dark skin, the melanin in your body is very active. If you have light skin, the melanin in your body is not very busy. (Kissinger 1994, pp. 11–13)

Children may also need to be told how to use a tool or implement from a culture different from their own. If staff are adding cooking implements from a particular culture into the program it is important that children are told the correct name and correct use of the implements. Once again, this helps avoid misunderstandings that could be offensive or hurtful to other children and adults in the group.

Story-telling can be an especially powerful tool to explore issues of diversity and 'race' with young children (Araujo and Strasser 2003; Whitehead 2007). Rutter (2003) suggests telling children folk stories from refugees' countries of origin to help children talk to each other about issues such as moving, fear, justice, ethnic differences and being new to a country.

GENDER

Children are gender-knowing from a young age (Keddie 2003), part of which is knowing about biological differences between males and females. Telling can be an appropriate technique for giving children information about biological sex differences between people. For example, by three years of age children might become interested in why boys have penises and where girls' penises are. As with differences in skin tone, it is difficult for young children to discover for themselves why these differences exist. It is equally important that they have an accurate answer to prevent misunderstandings. The following conversation highlights how three-year-old children can misunderstand anatomical differences between males and females, and how telling children the facts can overcome such misunderstandings:

> 'My mom doesn't have a penis; she has hair'. The teacher, overhearing the remarks, comments also matter-of-factly, 'Yes, and she has a vagina too. Women have vaginas, men have penises. That's what makes them a woman or a man'. (Derman-Sparks et al. 1989, p. 50)

Understanding that it is anatomical differences that make us male or female helps children learn that what you do doesn't change your biological sex. You will still be a girl if you wear trousers or play with the trucks and you will still be a boy if you wear a skirt and play with dolls. This understanding can help children to begin to think critically about gender stereotypes. They can learn that having or not having a penis should not make any difference to your ability to climb, use blocks, dress up in 'sparkly' clothes or play with dolls. Brown and Brown (2000) also offer some useful advice on how to tell children about biological differences.

DISABILITY AND ADDITIONAL NEEDS

Children without disabilities are often curious about children with visible disabilities. They might ask questions about why a child has a particular prosthesis, if it hurts or not and what they can or cannot do with the prosthesis. Once again, letting children find their own answers to such questions allows misconceptions to develop. Misconceptions and misunderstandings are the basis for prejudice towards people with disabilities.

Misconceptions can be avoided by staff telling children the answers to their questions using simple and non-emotive language. Again, the following anecdote from the now classic Dermon-Sparks et al. (1989, p. 41) book on anti-bias curriculum shows how simple explanations can be. Misha is three years old and has had a tracheotomy. On her first day in the centre, at group time the teacher allows children to raise any questions they want to ask about Misha, and explains the tracheotomy as follows:

> . . . Misha sings and talks. She gets air for singing and talking through a special tube in her throat.

Derman-Sparks et al. (1989) also suggest that staff check with the parents of children with disabilities to find out what they want staff to tell other children about their child. This can ensure that you use words with the children without disabilities that are meaningful to the child that has a disability.

Direct instruction has also proved over time to be an effective way to teach young children with disabilities specific pro-social skills (Vaughn et al. 2003). For example, researchers in the USA (Kroeger, Schultz and Newsom 2007) working with 24 preschool children with autism found that direct instruction in social skills over a five-week period was more effective than a free play program in increasing children's pro-social skills.

Reflecting on telling and instructing techniques

1 Briefly explain the differences between 'telling about' and 'telling what to do'.
2 How could telling be used as a technique to help toddlers learn how to wash their hands after toileting? What words would be best employed to achieve this aim?
3 Is telling an appropriate teaching technique to use with babies?
4 To what extent do you believe that telling is an appropriate technique to use in early childhood settings?
5 List five occasions on which you think it would be important for children to learn something by being told about it rather than discovering it for themselves.

6 What words might you use to tell a child why people have different skin tones?

7 What words might you use to tell a child why another child had one arm shorter than the other and had no fingers on the hand of this arm?

8 What words might you use to tell a child what a vagina is?

9 Research suggests that young children are more likely to do things when staff use story-telling or metaphors rather than through direct instruction. How might you tell a child what he needs to do on the following occasions through a short story or metaphor?
   - tying shoelaces
   - rubbing hands with soap to get them clean
   - putting away blocks on the shelf.

10 Observe an early childhood staff member during a routine time with toddlers. How and how often did she tell the children about the routine in order to help them learn about it? How did the children respond to this? Would it have been possible to tell the children what they needed to do through a short story or metaphor?

11 Observe an early childhood staff member as he works with a small group of preschool children. How and how often did he tell the children about the group experience and group rules in order to help them learn about both? How did the children respond to this? Would it have been possible to tell the children what they needed to do through a short story or metaphor?

Improving teaching in practice

1 Record (using a tape-recorder or written notes) the verbal teaching interactions you had with children during several half-hour teaching periods.

2 How often did you:
   - tell the children how to do things?
   - tell the children about things?

3 When telling children, did you:
   - use your tone of voice and gesture to emphasise what you were saying?
   - ensure that they understood what you were telling them by using clear, simple, descriptive language?

4 Tell a group of toddlers a simple story about an event that has recently happened in the centre. What did the toddlers learn from the story?

5 Tell a baby a simple story. Did the baby listen to and learn about how language is patterned and how meaning is associated with language?

6 What are your areas of strength and weakness in using telling and instructing as teaching techniques to promote children's learning?

7 How can you improve your teaching techniques in practice?

FURTHER READING

Courtney, A.M. and Montano, M.A. 2006, 'Teaching comprehension from the start: one first grade classroom', *Young Children* 61(2), pp. 68–74.

Isbell, R.T. 2002, 'Telling and retelling stories: learning language and literacy', *Young Children* 57(2), pp. 26–30.

Lennox, M. 2000, 'Storytelling for young children in a multicultural world', *Early Childhood Education Journal*, 28(2), pp. 97–103.

Olfman, S. 2003, *All Work and No Play: How Educational Reforms Are Harming Our Preschoolers*, Greenwood Press, New Jersey.

ONLINE AND MULTI-MEDIA RESOURCES

Text

Banks, J. 2001, *The Early Childhood Education Curriculum Debate: Direct Instruction vs. Child-Initiated Learning* (last updated June 2004), The Clearinghouse on Early Education and Parenting Digest. Detailed references and extensive links to research and professional debate on the topic: **http://ceep.crc.uiuc.edu/poptopics/preschoolcurr.html**

'Direct instruction and special education fact sheet'. Reviews research on direct instruction for children with disabilities: **http://www.baltimorecp.org/docs/DI_Special_Ed_Facts.pdf**

Multi-media

'Explaining the Schedule and Learning Ticket'. In this free access video clip a teacher uses 'telling' to explain to a child how the Learning Ticket works in a primary school multi-age classroom: **http://edcommunity.apple.com/ali/story.php?itemID =620&version=360&pageID=1577**

REFERENCES

Araujo, L. and Strasser, J. 2003, 'Confronting prejudice in the early childhood classroom', *Kappa Delta Pi Record*, Summer, <http://findarticles.com/p/articles/mi_qa4009/is_200307/ai_n9258251/pg_5>

Banks, J. 2001, 'The early childhood education curriculum debate: direct instruction vs. child-initiated learning' (last updated June 2004), The Clearinghouse on Early Education and Parenting, <http://www.ceep.crc.uiuc.edu/poptopics/preschoolcurr.html>

Brookes, P.H. McGee, G.G. and Daly, T. 2007, 'Incidental teaching of age-appropriate social phrases to children with autism', *Research and Practice for Persons with Severe Disabilities*, 32(2), pp. 112–123.

Brown, L., and Brown, M. 2000, *What's the Big Secret?: Talking About Sex With Girls & Boys*, Little, Brown and Company, Boston.

Castle, K. 1990, 'The second year: 12–24 months', in E. Surbeck and M. Kelly, eds, *Personalizing Care with Infants, Toddlers and Families* (pp. 23–32), Association for Childhood Education International, Wheaton, MD.

Charlesworth, R. 2003, *Understanding Child Development: For Adults Who Work with Young Children*, Thompson Delmar Publishing, USA.

Clark, D. 2007, 'Classroom management challenges in the dance class', *Journal of Physical Education, Recreation & Dance*, 78(2), pp. 19–25.

Courtney, A.M. and Montano, M.A. 2006, 'Teaching comprehension from the start: one first grade classroom', *Young Children* 61(2): 68–74.

Derman-Sparks, L. and the Anti-Bias Task Force 1989, *The Anti-Bias Curriculum*, National Association for the Education of Young Children, Washington, DC.

Fisher, R. 2007, 'Dialogic teaching: developing thinking and metacognition through philosophical discussion', *Early Child Development and Care*, 177(6/7), pp. 615–663.

Fiske, S., Schacter, D. and Kazdin, A. (eds.) 2005, *Annual Review of Psychology*, 58, Palo Alto, California.

Garhart Mooney, C. 2005, *When Adults Speak, Children Listen*, Redleaf Press, California.

Gross, R. 2003, *Key Studies in Psychology*, Oxford University Press, Oxford.

Hintz, B.F. and Stomfay-Stitz, A. 1999, 'Peace education and conflict resolution through expressive arts in early childhood education and teacher education', Paper presented at the *Annual Conference of the Eastern Educational Research Association*, 26 February, Hilton Head, SC, ED433105.

Hughes, A. and Hughes, E. 1937, *Learning and Teaching: An Introduction to Psychology and Education*, Longman, London.

Keddie, A. 2003, 'Little boys: tomorrow's macho lads', *Discourse: Studies in the Cultural Politics of Education*, 24(3), pp. 289–306.

Kissinger, K. 1994, *All the Colours We Are*, Redleaf Press, St. Paul, MN.

Kroeger, K., Schultz, J. and Newsom, C. 2007, 'A comparison of two group-delivered social skills programs for young children with autism', *Behavioural Science*, 37(5), pp. 808–817.

Pell, T. and Jarvis, T. 2001, 'Developing attitude to science scales for use with children of ages from five to eleven years', *International Journal of Science Education*, 23(8), pp. 847–862.

Ramsey, J.L. and Fowler, M.L. 2004, '"What do you notice?" Using posters containing questions and general instructions to guide preschoolers' science and mathematics learning', *Early Child Development and Care*, 174(1), pp. 31–45.

Rookes, P. and Willson, J. 2000, *Perception: Theory, Development and Organisation*, Routledge, New York and London.

Rutter, J. 2003, *Supporting Refugee Children in 21st Century Britain*, Trentham Books, London.

Ryokai, K., Vaucelle, C. and Cassell, J. 2003, 'Virtual peers as partners in storytelling and literacy learning', *Journal of Computer Assisted Learning*, 19(2), pp. 195–208.

Seifert, K. 1993, 'Cognitive development and early childhood education', in B. Spodek, ed., *Handbook of Research on the Education of Young Children* (pp. 9–23), Macmillan Publishing Company, New York.

Smyth, J. 1996, 'Let's tell stories: sharing stories with young children', *Australian Early Childhood Association Resource Book Series*, 3(3), pp. 1–14.

van de Grift, W. 2007, 'Quality of teaching in four European countries: a review of the literature and application of an assessment instrument', *Educational Research*, 49(2), pp. 127–152.

Vaughn, S., Kim, A., Sloan, C.V., Tejero Hughes, M., Elbaum, B. and Sridhar, D. 2003, 'Social skills interventions for young children with disabilities: a synthesis of group design studies', *Remedial and Special Education*, 24(1), pp. 2–26.

Whitehead, M. 2007, *Developing Language and Literacy with Young Children*, Paul Chapman Publishers, London, UK.

Wilkes, G. (ed.) 1979, *Collins Dictionary of the English Language*, Penguin Books, Middlesex.

Zafranas, N. 2004, 'Piano keyboard training and the spatial-temporal development of young children attending kindergarten classes in Greece', *Early Child Development and Care*, 174(2), pp. 199–211.

PART THREE

Specialist Teaching Techniques

Chapter 19

Co-constructing

Construct: to put together substances or parts, assemble.
(*Collins Dictionary of the English Language*, p. 323)

Co: prefix together, joint or jointly, mutual or mutually.
(*Collins Dictionary of the English Language*, p. 289)

The key to construction of knowledge is interaction.

(Williams 1994, p. 158)

Co-construction views learning as occurring through complex and dynamic exchanges between children and their actions to make sense of the world and the social and cultural processes in everyday activities.

(Hedges and Cullen 2005, p. 72)

What?

In everyday language to construct something is to form or build 'it'. To co-construct is to form with others. As a teaching strategy, co-construction refers to staff and children forming meaning and building knowledge about the world with each other.

Issues and debates

CAN WE SPEAK THROUGH SILENCE?

The co-construction of meaning is often presented as a way to bring young children's voices and perspectives more powerfully into the curriculum (for example, Harris 2000). To that extent it relies strongly on children's active expression of their understandings, feelings and experiences. In considering the power of this for building more equitable curriculum with young children it is also important to note the equity alerts associated with adults seeking children's voice as a source of curriculum. Those alerts arise from diverse sources (for example, MacNaughton 2003; Viruru and Cannella 2000) but they raise similar points that staff may wish to reflect on as they attempt to co-construct meaning with young children. The privileging of voice as a curriculum goal assumes that silence is less valued and valid. Yet silence may not always mean a child is not being heard or is feeling ignored. Silence may be a strategy used by children to resist adults and a strategy for learning. Consider the comments by Viruru and Cannella (2001, pp. 167–168) as you reflect on the equity considerations in co-constructing meaning with young children:

> Are there ways to hear the voices of children, to regard them as human beings, without imposing our voices, expectations or our agenda on them? Do we have the right to question, observe, and interpret them? How do our methods create those who are younger as objects of colonising power? What of silence? Do we place too much emphasis on oral and behaviour expression? Even when we have the best of intentions, how do our attempts to hear children serve as colonisation? Are there ways that those of us who want to work with other human beings can learn to know each other without inadvertently working as colonisers? (Refer to Chapter 21 on decolonising.)

THEORETICAL BACKGROUND

CONSTRUCTIVISM, SOCIAL CONSTRUCTIVISM AND CO-CONSTRUCTION

The strategy of co-constructing derives from the constructivist philosophical tradition in which it is believed that '...to understand this world of meaning one must interpret it...' (Schwandt 1994, p. 118). This philosophical tradition has led early childhood education to two approaches to understanding children's cognition: constructivism and social constructivism. Constructivism is evident in the work of Piaget and social constructivism in the work of Vygotsky. The difference between these approaches lies in the emphasis each one places on the role of the social and cultural world in children's construction of meaning.

Constructivists, building on Piaget's work, believe that children learn through active engagement with their physical environment. In particular, they believe that concrete activities which encourage children to explore and search for meaning help them to form their own knowledge about the world (Morrison 1995). As children interact with the concrete world around them and make sense of this interaction they form (construct) their own '...personal understandings and knowledge...' (Arthur et al. 1996, p. 88). Children create their knowledge about the world through direct physical experience of it.

Social constructivists, building on Vygotsky's work, also believe that children are active in constructing (forming) their own knowledge about the world and that this occurs as children interact with their physical world. However, social constructionists see social interaction in a historical and cultural context as the critical element in young children's meaningful construction (Amin and Valsiner 2004). They believe that '...all knowledge emerges in the process of self- and social construction' (Rinaldi 1993, p. 105). Vygotsky sought to study what distinguished humans from animals rather than what was similar (Daniels 2005).

This theory holds that children become knowledgeable and are able to give meaning to their world by negotiating meaning with others. The difference between the two theoretical traditions is summarised succinctly by Morrison (1995, p. 74) as follows:

> Vygotsky believed that children's mental, language, and social development is supported and enhanced by others through social interaction. This view is the opposite from the Piagetian perspective in which children are much more solitary developers of their own intelligence and language.

Wertsch (2001, p. 1) also discussed a key difference between Piaget and Vygotsky:

> ...their views concerning the importance of culture, in particular, the role of mediation of action through artifacts, on the development of the mind. Piaget emphasised the role of artifacts, Vygotsky emphasised the role of social interaction in the construction of meaning. It should be noted that other writers argue that the two thinkers had very similar and complementary understandings of child development by the early 1930s (Shayer 2003; Amin and Valsiner 2004).

However, it is the broad belief in the collaborative nature of learning derived from social constructivism that underpins the belief in co-construction as an effective teaching strategy.

How?

Staff can co-construct knowledge with young children through emphasising the study of meaning rather than the acquisition of facts. Meaning is how we make sense of, understand, interpret or give significance to our world. To study meaning involves studying this process. To acquire facts involves gathering descriptions, information, data and figures about our world.

For example, an adult studying the meaning of sound with children would study how children understand sound, how children interpret different sounds and which sounds children see as significant. To do this, the adult needs to encourage the children to share what they think and know. The adult could encourage children to talk about which sounds they like, which sounds make them feel happy and which sounds make them feel sad. Talking with children would be one way for the adult to study the meanings children give to sound. However, adults could also study the meaning children give to sound by asking children to express being happy through voice-sounds or by making musical and non-musical sounds. Additionally, the meaning children give to sound could be studied by encouraging children to draw or mime a sound. Irrespective of how the adult chooses to study this, it would be necessary for him or her to access and reflect on the child's meanings.

On the other hand, a person wanting children to acquire facts about sound would encourage them to gather descriptions, data, information and figures. To do this, the adult would need to teach the child to listen to and recall the sounds the child experienced and made. This could involve encouraging a child to learn the names of sounds, to describe a particular sound or to react in particular ways to specific sounds. For an adult to teach a child the facts about sound requires the child to observe, listen and remember what they are told by the adult.

In summary, the study of meaning involves uncovering, expressing and sharing meaning, and the acquisition of facts involves observing, listening and remembering. Staff can help children study meaning by encouraging them to:

- uncover, express and share their meanings with others
- uncover, read and acknowledge the meanings of others (refer to Chapter 26 on philosophising for further discussion of studying meanings with children).

The study of meaning becomes the co-construction of meaning when children's and adults' understandings, interpretations and sense of significance are developed in negotiation with each other and come to reflect the other. As Forman (1996a, p. 1) explained:

In this co-constructivist curriculum the teachers form a community of learners with the children and with the parents and other teachers . . . They discuss the social and symbolic processes by which meanings are negotiated toward some level of shared understanding. Co-construction is supported through a negotiated curriculum based on design, documentation and discourse.

Forman (1996a) defined these three elements of a negotiated curriculum as follows:

Design refers to any activity in which children make records of their plans or intended solutions. (p. 2)

Discourse connotes a deep desire to understand each others' words . . . a struggle to understand, where speakers constructively confront each other, experience conflict, and seek footing in a constant shift of perspectives. (p. 3)

Documentation refers to any activity that renders a performance record with sufficient detail to help others understand the behaviour recorded. (p. 3)

Design and documentation enable children to uncover, express and share their ideas with others. They also enable children to see and acknowledge other people's ideas. Discourse is the process through which meaning is expressed, shared and negotiated with others as they struggle to understand each other's designs and documentation of a problem, issue or phenomenon. Discourse, in this sense of the word, is talk with children about meaning. Staff need to look for and discuss children's theories, assumptions, contradictions and misunderstandings about what is being studied to ensure that their talk supports the children's study of meaning rather than their acquisition of facts. For this reason, documenting (Chapter 24) is an important part of the process of co-constructing meaning with young children. It allows staff to examine in detail children's discourse and their own. Hughes (2002, p. 139) details the importance of documentation to the processes of co-constructing a meaningful curriculum with children in the early years of school:

> Written transcripts and drawings of the children's experiences allow teachers to examine their teaching practices. In addition, teachers can review their questions and comments, and study the ways their responses influence the children's actions or thinking.

As staff review children's discourse and their own they can begin to map the exchange of ideas and triggers and barriers to the development of shared understandings between themselves and children. They can then reach deeper insights about how meanings were negotiated with children to build shared understandings, and draw on those insights in their future teaching with young children.

During the process of negotiating meaning with children, staff need to remember that children co-construct meaningful knowledge with each other when they share an interest in a particular phenomenon or issue (Hill 1994) and when they have the time to work together on it in some depth (Forman 1996b).

Harris (2000) studied a toddler and preschool children's art exhibition in which the images and constructions of children between 17 months and six years of age were exhibited. She described how this exhibition was used to facilitate a process of co-construction with the children and early childhood

Co-constructing knowledge about sand properties.

student-teachers. She described four phases in the study that highlight the process of co-construction in action:

- Phase 1—Children's responses to, and interactions with, the three-dimensional artworks at the exhibition.
- Phase 2—Student teachers' exploration of symbolic representation within the context of the exhibition.
- Phase 3—Student teachers' extension of the children's representations (i.e. art, stories and enactments) through a process of sharing their own symbolic representations with children.
- Phase 4—Children/student teacher exchanges of creative works within their respective contexts (Harris 2000, p. 188).

While these phases describe a research process they also offer a process of co-construction that can be used by staff within early childhood services to proactively engage in co-construction with young children.

When and why?

Co-constructing meaning with adults and peers helps children to learn how to create new meanings, problem-pose and problem-solve with others. Hence, co-constructing is a relevant teaching technique for extending children's current level of understanding and expression in any area of development. It is particularly pertinent when staff want to challenge children to predict and explain their world through a variety of symbolic media and to build shared understandings about their world.

GOAL RELEVANCE

When staff and children or children and children co-construct meaning, children can learn that:

- meanings are socially shared and negotiated
- there are many ways to explore the one problem, issue or phenomenon and learn through the ideas of others
- children can be meaning-makers
- learning from others is valuable
- we can change each other through sharing ideas
- ideas can be transformed and extended through interaction and exchange with others (Emde, Wolf and Oppenheim 2003; Harris 2000; Forman 1996a).

DEVELOPMENTAL CONSIDERATIONS

The co-construction of meaning is possible whenever children are struggling to give meaning to their world. Research suggests that babies are actively engaged in doing this in many ways and that success in co-constructing meanings influences later development. For instance, early co-constructions between mothers and babies influence a baby's capacity to act with intention and communicate with others (Harding et al. 1997). To co-construct meaning, children need to be given a wide range of media through which to express their understandings of the world and through which to share these understandings with others. They also need to have access to adults who listen for, watch and interact with them as they struggle to represent their meanings to others.

The forms of expression children can use to represent and discuss their meanings will vary from child to child and within each child as they grow and develop. A baby cannot dance, tell stories and make models in the ways that older children can. However, babies can express themselves through gesture, movement and sound. Staff need to offer children media for self-expression that are relevant to the current and emerging capacities of the child for self-expression. Pointers for staff on how to do this include:

- Babies are exploring the world via their senses and they can best share and express the meanings they give to their explorations via sensory play (DeRue-Durkin and Davey 1996). An environment which allows babies to touch, smell, move, listen, feel and taste will enable staff to listen for, watch and interact with them as they struggle to represent their meanings to others. The following extract describes how one centre approached the challenge of offering a rich and safe sensory environment for babies to explore:

  A shallow plastic wading pool was filled with scented water, pink camellias floating on the surface. Wind chimes hung from the ceiling above mountains of fat cushions covered by fluffy old bedspreads. Here the infants could venture across a landscape of satisfying textures and big soft bumps. There were fruit fingers and sorbet to satisfy the youngest palate. (DeRue-Durkin and Davey 1996, p. 68)

- Toddlers are rapidly acquiring the ability to explore and express their meanings through language, images, models and constructions. They have a wide range of gestures they use to help them express their meanings and discoveries to others, and are beginning to be able to use the symbolic languages of music, drama, story, image-making and movement to discover other people's meanings and to share their own. The following extract shows how staff can draw on these abilities to study and negotiate meaning with toddlers:

  The farm in the storm and the zoo under the rainbow . . . it was rainbows which had captured their further interest. One of the books we had been using illustrated medieval ideas about the structure of rainbows, and Simon and Jesse chose to illustrate these. However, a dilemma faced them. They both wished to use brown and black, and Phoebe, pink, but wherever they looked in the books they could not find evidence of these colours in rainbows. Each would take a turn, flipping through the pages, as if not trusting the other to have looked hard enough . . . Their drawings were sophisticated, showing that they understood the schema of rainbows and the spectrum. (Kolbe and Robertson 1996, p. 154)

- Preschool children's capacity for meaning-making and meaning-negotiation becomes increasingly complex and well-developed. They develop a growing competence in using the symbolic languages of music, drama, story, image-making and movement to discover other people's meanings and to share their own. The following extract shows how staff can draw on these abilities to study and negotiate meaning with preschool children:

Trees and forests

This investigation which ultimately involved five boys (and on one occasion one girl) for several weeks, was initially prompted by one child's spontaneously-made vertical structure which he identified as a tree. A second child seemed fascinated by the challenge of making a similar vertical structure . . . and was inspired to make two more trees. From then on, various further versions were made . . . As each new version was created the innovations were duly acknowledged by the group and often emulated and incorporated within the shared vocabulary of tree-making. Staff encouraged and extended this interest by discussing the discoveries with the children, displaying and photographing the clay trees, as well as encouraging the investigation and drawing of trees in the bush outside the centre . . . in terms of developing shared understandings about building vertical structures, and in developing each other's skills in communication, their knowledge about the appearance of trees through clay and graphic media . . . I was delighted with the progress made. (Kolbe and Robertson 1996, p. 164)

Sharing meaning with others enables children to reconstruct their own meanings. Through this co-construction and subsequent reconstruction, children can enrich their understandings of how to represent the world for themselves and to others. Gardner (1993a; 1993b) proposed that children have seven intelligences through which they can make and express meaning. They are: logical–mathematical, linguistic, musical, spatial, bodily-kinaesthetic, interpersonal and intrapersonal. Gardner defines them as follows:

- Logical–mathematical intelligence '. . . began as sheer pattern ability in infancy and developed through symbolic mastery of early childhood education and the notations of the school years'.
- Linguistic intelligence is about sensitivity to word order and meaning, sounds, rhythms and inflections, and to the different ways in which language can be used.
- Musical intelligence is the ability to enjoy and replicate music.
- Spatial intelligence is the ability to '. . . perceive the visual world accurately, to perform transformations and modifications…and to be able to re-create aspects of one's visual experience'.
- Bodily-kinaesthetic intelligence is the ability to use and control the body to express meaning.
- Interpersonal intelligence is the ability to '. . . understand and work with others'.
- Intrapersonal intelligence is the ability to '. . . understand and work with oneself'.

Gardner's idea that children have multiple intelligences can be used to expose children to an enormous variety of opportunities for making, sharing and negotiating meaning. His work suggests that children of all ages have diverse forms of intelligence they can use to symbolise their world and thus make, share and negotiate meaning. They can do this on a specific topic using the categories listed above. Staff can encourage children to see and understand a specific issue or phenomenon through one or several of these intelligences.

As children explore meaning through several forms of intelligence they confront different ways of knowing and, therefore, different meanings (Forman 1996b). For example, exploring trees musically might involve trying to replicate the sounds made by them. Exploring trees spatially might involve looking at how to build a model of a tree. Each form of intelligence about trees brings forth different understandings of them. As children confront different ways of knowing about trees they revisit their original concepts and reform them. As children share this changing understanding with others they engage in the co-construction of meaning:

> Children in the bayside Doandale Kindergarten have been co-constructing their knowledge of the sea. The project has progressed over several weeks and the children are now representing their knowledge in different ways. In dance they explore the movements of the tides, in modelling they make models of sea creatures with clay, and in painting they explore how to represent the colours they have observed in the water. At each stage of the project they have shared their representations of the sea with each other and their teacher.
>
> _Reflection point:_ What other strategies and materials could be used by teacher and children to construct their knowledge of the sea?

Children's ability to uncover, represent, share and negotiate meaning will increase as they progress through childhood. In the early years of schooling, children are more able to understand the perspectives and feelings of others and use words to help them in their negotiation of meaning. However, children in the early years of school should still be provided with lots of opportunities to explore the diverse forms of intelligence they can use to symbolise their world and negotiate meaning. Experiences such as dance and music, which allow them to express and negotiate meaning spatially and kinaesthetically, can be powerful in contributing to their learning and in enriching their capacity to construct meaning.

A key issue in constructing meaning with children in their early years of schooling is managing conflict in small group situations (Vermette, Harper and Dimillo 2004). Researchers have shown than conflicts arise at least six times an hour between younger students in primary school classrooms. This can be managed by teaching children simple conflict resolution skills (Stevahn et al. 2000).

Equity considerations

'RACE' AND CULTURE

Children's 'racial' identities are forming and reforming from an early age. Research shows consistently that young black children and white children in the USA demonstrate pro-white, anti-black attitudes (e.g. Baron and Banaji 2006). There are similar findings from other countries including Australia (MacNaughton 2004) and Japan (Dunham, Baron and Banaji 2006). This has significant implications for how young black children form a sense of self and identity. Children's 'racial' identity can influence their desire to co-construct meaning with others. To contribute to group meaning-making, children need to have positive self-esteem and a belief that their contributions will be taken seriously by others. This is difficult for many black children who live in situations where they experience marginalisation and discrimination (Lesane-Brown 2006). Children who have experienced racism may have poor self-esteem and believe that their contributions will be dismissed or ignored by the group (Sleeter and Grant 2003). Children who have to negotiate their sense of self within two cultural groups are particularly vulnerable to low self-esteem when they double their capacity to be successful members of their community (Ramsey 2004). Two aspects of co-construction support the development of positive self-esteem for these children. Children are more likely to develop positive self-esteem when they can construct meanings rather than learn facts and when adults show interest in their ideas. However, staff should be alert to the fact that children may not feel comfortable to express their experiences of and feelings about racism towards them if they are working with staff who have not had similar experiences themselves.

Positive attitudes to 'racial' diversity develop from a willingness to understand and respect other people's points of view. To do this children need an awareness of difference in others, the ability to notice other people's point of view, experience working with others and positive social interactions with others (Ramsey 2004). Co-construction supports these experiences in very active ways because it teaches children how to uncover, express, share and negotiate meaning. Children can be encouraged to engage in such meaning-making in relation to 'race'. They can be encouraged to uncover their understandings of 'race', express these through a variety of media, share them with others and to negotiate new meanings if and when they represent racist understandings

GENDER

Research on gender differences and how young children deal with disagreements and differences has consistently shown that boys are generally more physically aggressive than girls and use physical aggression to solve problems (Ostrov et al. 2004). This tendency develops early and is well-established by the time boys are eight years old. For example, by two years of age boys are often more unco-operative, non-compliant and aggressive than girls (Sanson et al. 1993). In contrast, young girls tend to solve the social problems they encounter through verbal reasoning and negotiation.

Young boys' tendencies towards violent social problem-solving strategies have implications for staff encouraging children to co-construct knowledge with each other and with staff. First, in mixed-gender groups girls may feel inhibited in expressing, sharing and negotiating meanings with boys. When girls fear that a difference of opinion may be resolved physically rather than verbally they become silent or move away from the conflict (MacNaughton 2000). Girls' meanings may be silenced or marginalised as a result. This turns co-construction of meaning into male-only meaning-construction. Staff can guard against this by allowing girls to work in girls-only groups or by actively seeking and supporting girls' meaning-making in mixed-gender groups. Second, staff may be able to reduce boys' tendencies to use violent problem-solving strategies by improving their verbal reasoning skills (Sanson et al. 1993). Staff can work with young boys on ways to uncover, express, share and negotiate meaning verbally. This may be in boys-only groups until boys have gained the skills necessary to negotiate meaning with girls in less aggressive ways.

DISABILITY AND ADDITIONAL NEEDS

Co-constructing meaning in a group of children with diverse abilities can be made exciting and enriching for all children if staff ensure children have a diverse range of media through which to discover, represent, share and negotiate meanings. Staff need to honour diverse ways of representing the world and encourage children to do the same. Talking with the children about how differently each person sees and understands the world helps build respect for diversity. It is through active involvement with each other's struggles to make meaning that children can learn to communicate with each other in innovative ways. Children can learn to listen to and read meaning in a wide variety of ways as they become familiar with the meanings in each other's images, sounds, gestures and computer messages. Consider the richness of meaning-making in the following scenario in which children of diverse abilities struggled to co-construct meaning:

> Children were trying to understand the night and its darkness. Several had been talking about what they could see at night and how it differed from what they could see during the day. In the group there was a child (Tanya) whose vision impairment resulted in reduced acuity (ability to see detail) and reduced colour vision. She could only see shades of grey. Staff encouraged children to paint the night and the day and to then explore what was similar and different about their images. Tanya's images of the night and the day were full of lots of colour. For the remainder of children in the group their pictures of night were full of lots of grey and black. This led to lots of discussion about why Tanya's night looked different. The children struggled to understand each other. Tanya struggled to understand how what she saw as grey others saw as colour. The rest of the children struggled to understand how, if Tanya's world was grey, she painted it in colour. However, as the children started to talk about the content of their paintings they learned about what understandings of night they shared in common. Many, including Tanya, had painted bedtime. They started to see that night means more than colour.

Children with disabilities who have difficulty communicating via spoken language should be encouraged to find other ways of uncovering and representing their meanings to others. In a small study of interactions between a child care worker and a child with multiple disabilities, researchers found that they each used multiple strategies to co-create meaning (Olsson 2004). Children should have the opportunity to experiment with many media to find which ways of symbolising their meanings work best. For some children, clay, paint, chalk, blocks, movement, dance or music might be relevant. For other children, computer-enhanced communication might be best. The challenge for staff who want to co-construct meaning with children who cannot speak is to find another language through which the child can communicate. Doing so is important, as opportunities to co-construct meaning with others positively influence the outcomes for children with disabilities in inclusive classrooms (Nind and Wearmouth 2006).

Reflecting on co-constructing techniques

1   Define co-construction.
2   How does co-construction differ from construction?
3   What is the study of meaning?
4   How does the study of meaning differ from the acquisition of facts?
5   Identify five ways in which you could encourage children to uncover their understandings about shade and light. Would these be appropriate for children of all ages?
6   What do you see as the main gender equity issues in co-constructing knowledge with children?
7   What do you see as the main 'race' equality issues in co-constructing knowledge with children?
8   How might co-construction be used to support anti-discriminatory perspectives on disability?
9   To what extent do you believe that co-construction relies too heavily on forms of expression that devalue a child's silence?

Improving teaching in practice

1 Record (using a tape-recorder or written notes) several occasions on which you co-construct meaning with a small group of children.
2 What was your current style of co-construction? How and how well did you encourage children to:
- uncover, express and share their meanings with others?
- uncover, read and acknowledge the meanings of others?
- negotiate their meanings with others?
3 How and how well did you take account of developmental and equity considerations?
4 What are your areas of strength and weakness in using co-construction to promote children's learning?
5 How can you improve your co-construction techniques in practice?
6 What do you see as the hardest part of improving your co-construction techniques?

FURTHER READING

Ebbeck, M. 1996, 'Children constructing their own knowledge', *International Journal of Early Years Education*, 4(2), pp. 5–27.

Forman, G. 1996a, 'Design, documentation and discourse: cornerstones of negotiated curriculum', Paper presented at the *Weaving Webs: Collaborative Teaching and Learning in the Early Years Curriculum Conference*, July, Melbourne,

——1996b, 'A child constructs an understanding of a water wheel in five media', *Childhood Education*, 72(5), pp. 269–273.

Harris, V. 2000, 'A unique pedagogical project contextualised within a children's art exhibition', *Contemporary Issues in Early Childhood*, 1(2), pp. 153–170.

Hughes, E. 2002, 'Planning meaningful curriculum: a mini story of children and teachers learning together', *Childhood Education*, 78(2), pp. 134–139.

ONLINE AND MULTI-MEDIA RESOURCES

Text

Cole, M. and Wertsch, J., 'Beyond the individual–social antimony in discussions of Piaget and Vygotsky', pp. 1–7: **http://www.massey.ac.nz/~Alock/virtual/colevyg.htm**

Department of Psychology, Massey University, has an introduction to Vygotsky's work by Trish Nicoll at: **http://www. massey.ac.nz/~Alock/virtual/trishvyg.htm**

There is an excellent source of resources on Vygotsky's work at: **http://www.kolar.org/vygotsky**

Multi-media

Forman, G. and Gandini, L. 1994, *The Amusement Park for Birds*, (video) Performanetics Press, Amherst, MA.

Magna Systems 1997, *Theories of Development*. Studies of the child video, available from Marcom Projects at: **http://www.marcom.com.au** [refer to the section on Vygotsky's theories of development].

REFERENCES

Amin, T. and Valsiner, J. 2004, 'Coordinating operative and figurative knowledge: Piaget, Vygotsky and beyond', in I. Jeremy, ed., *Social Interaction and the Development of Knowledge*, Lawrence Erlbaum Associates, New Jersey, pp. 87–110.

Arthur, L., Beecher, B., Dockett, S., Farmer, S. and Death, E. 1996, *Programming and Planning in Early Childhood Settings*, 2nd edn, Harcourt Brace and Company, Sydney.

Baron, A. and Banaji, M. 2006, 'The development of implicit attitudes. Evidence of race evaluations from ages 6 and 10 and adulthood', *Psychological Science*, 17(1), pp. 53–58.

Daniels, H. (ed.) 2005, *An Introduction to Vygotsky*, Routledge, London and New York.

DeRue-Durkin, Y. and Davey, A. 1996, 'Empowering infants', Paper presented at *Weaving Webs: Collaborative Teaching and Learning in the Early Years Curriculum Conference*, July, Melbourne, pp. 65–76.

Dunham, Y., Baron, A. and Banaji, M. 2006, 'From American city to Japanese village: a cross-cultural investigation of implicit race attitudes,' *Child Development*, 77(5), pp. 1268–1281.

Emde, R., Wolf, D. and Oppenheim, D. 2003, *Revealing the Inner Worlds of Young Children: The MacArthur Story*, Oxford University Press, Oxford.

Forman, G. 1996a, 'Design, documentation and discourse: cornerstones of negotiated curriculum', Paper presented at the *Weaving Webs: Collaborative Teaching and Learning in the Early Years Curriculum Conference*, Melbourne, July.

——1996b, 'A child constructs an understanding of a water wheel in five media', *Childhood Education*, 72(5), pp. 269–273.

Gardner, H. 1993a, *Frames of Mind: The Theory of Multiple Intelligences*, Basic Books, New York.

——1993b, *Multiple Intelligences: The Theory in Practice*, Basic Books, New York.

Harding, C.G., Weissman, L., Kromelow, S. and Stilson, S.R. 1997, 'Shared minds: how mothers and infants co-construct early patterns of choice within intentional communication partnerships', *Infant Mental Health Journal*, 18(1), pp. 24–39.

Harris, V. 2000, 'A unique pedagogical project contextualised within a children's art exhibition', *Contemporary Issues in Early Childhood*, 1(2), pp. 153–170.

Hedges, H. and Cullen, J. 2005, 'Subject knowledge in early childhood curriculum and pedagogy: beliefs and practices', *Contemporary Issues in Early Childhood*, 6(1), pp. 66–79.

Hill, S. 1994, 'Co-operative communities in early childhood', *Australian Journal of Early Childhood*, 19(4), pp. 44–47.

Hughes, E. 2002, 'Planning meaningful curriculum: a mini story of children and teachers learning together', *Childhood Education*, 78(2), pp. 134–139.

Kolbe, U. and Robertson, J. 1996, 'The farm in the storm and other stories from Mia-Mia: children's collaborative learning', Paper presented at *Weaving Webs: Collaborative Teaching and Learning in the Early Years Curriculum Conference*, July, Melbourne.

Lesane-Brown, C. 2006, 'A review of race socialization within Black families', *Developmental Review*, 26(4), pp. 400–426.

MacNaughton, G. 2000, *Rethinking Gender in Early Childhood*, Allen & Unwin, Sydney; Sage Publications, New York; Paul Chapman Publishing, London.

——2003, 'Eclipsing voice in research with young children', *Australian Journal of Early Childhood*, 28(1) pp. 36–43.

—— 2004, 'Learning from young children about social diversity: challenges for our equity practices in the classroom', in A. van Keulen, ed., *Young Children Aren't Biased, Are They?* (pp. 65–76), B.V. Uitgeverij SWP, Amsterdam.

Morrison, G. 1995, *Early Childhood Education Today*, 6th edn, Merrill, New Jersey.

Nind, M. and Wearmouth, J. 2006, 'Including children with special educational needs in mainstream classrooms: implications for pedagogy from a systematic review', *Journal of Research in Special Educational Needs*, 6(3), pp. 116–124.

Olsson, C. 2004, 'Dyadic interaction with a child with multiple disabilities: a system theory perspective on communication', *Augmentative and Alternative Communication*, 20(4), pp. 228–242.

Ostrov, J., Woods, K., Jansen, E., Casas, J. and Crick, N. 2004, 'An observational study of delivered and received aggression, gender and social psychological adjustment in preschool: "This white crayon doesn't work"', *Early Childhood Research Quarterly*, 19(2), pp. 355–371.

Ramsey, P. 2004, *Teaching and Learning in a Diverse World: Multicultural Education for Young Children*, 3rd edn, Teachers College Press, New York.

Rinaldi, C. 1993, 'The emergent curriculum and social constructivism: an interview with Lella Gandini', in C. Edwards., L. Gandini and G. Forman, eds, *The Hundred Languages of Children: The Reggio Emilia Approach to Early Childhood Education* (pp. 101–111), Ablex, New York.

Sanson, A., Prior, M., Smart, D. and Oberklaid, F. 1993, 'Gender differences in aggression in childhood: implications for a peaceful world', *Australian Psychologist*, 28(2), pp. 86–92.

Schwandt, T. 1994, 'Constructivist, interpretivist approaches to human inquiry', in N. Denzin and Y. Lincoln, eds, *Handbook of Qualitative Research* (pp. 118–137), Sage Press, Thousand Oaks, CA.

Shayer, M. 2003, 'Not just Piaget, not just Vygotsky, and certainly not Vygotsky as an alternative to Piaget', *Learning and Instruction*, 13(5), pp. 465–485.

Sleeter, C. and Grant, C. 2003, *Making Choices for Multicultural Education: Five Approaches to Race, Class, and Gender*, 4th edn. John Wiley & Sons, New York.

Stevahn, L., Johnson, D.W., Johnson, R.T., Oberle, K. and Wahl, L. 2000, 'Effects of conflict resolution training integrated into a kindergarten curriculum', *Child Development*, 71(3), pp. 772–784.

Vermette, P., Harper, L. and Dimillo, S. 2004, 'Cooperative & collaborative learning...with 4–8 year olds: how does research support teachers' practice?', *Journal of Instructional Psychology*, 1(20), pp. 130–134.

Viruru, R. and Cannella, G. 2001, 'Postcolonial ethnography, young children and voice', in S. Grieshaber and G. Cannella, eds, *Embracing Identities in Early Childhood Education: Diversity and Possibilities* (pp. 158–172), Teachers College Press, New York.

Wertsch, J. 2001, 'Beyond the individual-social in discussions with Piaget and Vygotsky', <http://bion.psy.ed.ac.uk/lorenzo/Docs>

Wilkes, G. (ed.) 1979, *Collins Dictionary of the English Language*, Penguin Books, Middlesex.

Williams, L. 1994, 'Developmentally appropriate practice and cultural values', in B. Mallory and R. New, eds, *Diversity and Developmentally Appropriate Practice: Challenges for Early Childhood Education* (pp. 155–165), Teachers College Press, New York.

Chapter 20

Community building

 Community: a feeling of belongingness within a group.

(Osterman 2000, p. 323)

[T]he community is the site of the mediating structures that intervene between the domain of the everyday life of individuals and the larger social, political and economic context…The word community conveys a sense of connectedness between people and their [our emphasis] organisations . . . The community is a social space, a sector made up of informal and relatively unmanaged associations.

(Casswell 2001, pp. 3–4)

What?

A community can 'refer to a territorial or geographic unit' (Osterman 2000, p. 323) or 'the quality or character of human relationships' (Osterman 2000, p. 323). Building is the process of putting something together to create a new object. Community building is, however, a slippery term to define. The literature concerning community building and early childhood education is marked by the absence of a shared definition of 'community', and a shared understanding of how to build one.

There are two possible reasons for this. First, the multitude of socially, culturally and geographically based groups referred to as 'communities' is so broad and the social processes of building them are so complex that they may just defy definition. Second, 'community' is in such widespread use that it may preclude the need for definition—why consciously define a term that appears everywhere and is used by anyone to mean anything?

There is also a range of different ways in which community building is linked to learning. Terms such as 'learning communities' and 'communities of learners' populate the literature on building communities in educational settings.

'Learning community' describes a collection of individuals, groups and organisations—a community— that is evolving or developing through learning, rather as a living organism does (Graves 1992). 'Communities of learners' describes collections of individuals who are learners. Jilk (1999, pp. 2–3) distinguished communities of learners from learning communities thus:

> A community of learners…is a community that is a good place to live, work and play, and where everyone is engaged in lifelong learning…A learning community…is continually expanding its capacity to create its future; the community itself is a learner; and it is a community that responds to needs much faster than others.

For example, 'learning communities' could be used to refer to an early childhood centre where parent involvement is embedded in their children's learning and in the life of the centre, rather than being just an add-on. By contrast, 'communities of learners' is often applied to programs around early childhood centres that seek to involve parents as learners. Fidler (1995, p. 4) described a learning community in terms of the relationships within it:

> A group of colleagues who come together in a spirit of mutual respect, authenticity, learning and shared responsibility to continually explore and articulate an expanding awareness and base of knowledge. The process of a learning community includes inquiring about each other's assumptions and biases, experimenting, risking and openly assessing the results.

In this chapter we focus on building learning communities in early childhood services and how this work might be approached to enhance young children's learning.

Issues and debates

PEOPLE IN COMMUNITIES ARE NOT ALL THE SAME

Building communities with young children does not mean that staff should attempt to create learning spaces in which children all share the same views and visions of the task at hand. Instead, they need to create spaces for learning in which diversity is possible in what is thought, how a topic is approached, what skills are used and what knowledge is valued within the group. Exploring cultural and 'racial' differences and commonalities is an important part of building communities in early childhood settings. A community does not mean we are all the same but that we know how to be respectful of our differences. As Mattai (2002, p. 27) put it:

> The teacher should become culturally synchronized with students so that they understand the cultural repertoire of their classroom and work to expand their own cultural horizons.

A community of learners will also be a safe space within which to express differences. Within this, staff need to be watchful of whose ideas come to the fore by asking the questions, 'Whose ideas are dominant within this community?', 'Whose ideas are silenced?', 'Whose ideas are marginalised?'. Such questions can help staff to reflect on the potential for one cultural group's ideas to dominate and they can alert them to moments when racist views emerge that may silence the voices of children from economically, socially, culturally, 'racially' and linguistically diverse backgrounds. Learning to 'listen to, rather than talk about or speak for, those who are at the margins of the culture of power' (Swadner Blue 2000, p. 127) is a critical task for staff wishing to build equitable learning communities.

How?

Shared work and common purpose are the basic elements that form the cornerstone of community (Balaban 2003, p. 87).

Building a learning community is a multifaceted teaching technique that draws on many of the other teaching techniques in this book, including:

- encouragement (of co-operative learning)
- grouping (for co-operative and small group learning)
- co-operative problem-solving
- questioning to develop and excite curiosity and wonder
- collecting diverse resources to support flexible and open-ended learning

- facilitating learning rather than telling children the answers.

The first step in community building is to make a conscious commitment to it (Pascarella 1998). Campbell et al. (2002) provide an example of how one children's service has expressed this commitment:

Our philosophy

We are all people with unique historical, cultural and economic backgrounds living in a social world of shared and unshared meanings. We believe that access to knowledge and power is important in ensuring equity for everyone. Therefore, the service is committed to creating a critically reflective and collaborative learning environment by:

- providing an environment in which all participants have equal access to knowledge, space and time regardless of gender, culture, 'race', class and sexuality
- collaborating with parents, children and teachers in implementing a critical curriculum
- actively challenging bias and inequity in language, practices and relationships
- using different theories of learning as a curriculum frame that acknowledges the multiplicity of people within the service. These include: developmental psychology, critical theory, post-structuralism, feminist post-structuralism and post-colonialism.

Once a commitment is made, staff can develop a set of principles to guide their work with children and with each other. Identifying the critical features of learning communities offers the basis for developing a set of guidelines to guide staff's community building with young children. The following features of learning communities are taken from Harada et al. (2002/03, pp. 66–67):

- The focus is on the process of learning, rather than on mastering isolated skills.
- Learning is viewed as a social experience, with opportunities for co-operative problem-solving.
- Engagement involves wrestling with real-life problems.
- Learning is a demonstrated performance . . . through such acts as explaining, creating analogies, and generalising.
- Students have access to diverse resources. The environment is open and flexible. . .
- Assessment is continuous and in context. Time for reflection is an integral part of the process.
- Roles for instructors shift back and forth . . . Adults still ask questions, but they are doing so to arouse curiosity or to stretch children's thinking.

Within these broad principles for organising teaching and learning in a specific centre or classroom it is also important that staff build a strong sense of belongingness for each child within the group. Research suggests that specific classroom practices can be used to enhance children's sense of belongingness. These include:

- emphasising co-operative learning rather than competition in learning. For instance, grouping older children (see Chapter 9) so that they are regularly interacting with each other and relying on each other to complete tasks, helping each other and caring about each other's learning (Anderman and Maehr 1994)
- using dialogue as a tool for learning and as a way for children to learn about different ideas and feelings within the group (Osterman 2000) and build empathy within and across the group (Schertz 2007). This can occur face-to-face but also through online discussions. Such discussions are often respectful and can be used to help children with theory building and sharing diverse ideas (Kim et al. 2007)
- allowing children time to engage in discussions about difficult issues and about what is right and what is wrong (Hong 2004)
- building adult–child and child–child relationships that are caring and supportive (Osterman 2000)

and that allow children to problem-solve how to be more caring of and generous to each other (Gross 2005)

- taking care to include each child in positive social exchanges, as peer rejection leads to loneliness and a sense of not belonging (Osterman 2000)
- building meaningful and reciprocal relationships with children's parents that involves them actively in learning (Konzal 2001). For instance, the recognition that parents have their own learning needs as well as being invaluable to their children's learning is regarded by Whalley et al. (2001) as central to the success of one of the Early Excellence Centres in the UK—the Pen Green Centre in Corby:

Over 17 years we had been able to develop a comprehensive parent partnership programme. More than 6,000 local parents had been involved and staff had established a model of co-operative working that respected both the learning and support needs of parents, and children's right to high-quality early years education with care. (p. 8)

- using materials and experiences that 'promote opportunities for children to work and think together' (Balaban 2003, p. 85) and that encourage co-operation between children. New technologies offer possibilities for this work. For instance, O'Hara (2004) described several case studies from the UK in which Information and Communication Technologies (ICT) were used to support children working and thinking together. Examples included children using a CD player, amplifier, video camera and television monitor to produce a whole-of-class Karaoke concert; and a group of children using computers, telephones and an audio station to role-play booking and going on an overseas holiday
- developing clear and simple rules that encourage sharing and helping between children. In an American Head Start project, Medvin et al. (2003) used simple rules to encourage sharing and helping behaviours in a computer peer-led learning centre. Those rules were 'find a friend', 'help a friend' and 'share the mouse'. Each prompts children to work together, share and support each other while using the computer in the classroom, thus building a more co-operative learning environment between children
- using group and classroom meetings to celebrate learning (Sterling 1998). The following extract from Sterling (1998, p. 68) provides insights into the active skill development teachers can focus on in order to ensure that classroom meetings support rather than undermine community building within a service:

We teach directly the skill of being an audience: quiet listening, still bodies, patience when a presenter has an awkward moment, and applause at an appropriate time . . . Our students' abilities to keep still, to watch with an attentive attitude, and to refrain from chatting with neighbors are important to guarantee every current and future presenter a respectful and caring audience.

Ramsey (2004) offered useful guidelines about how to incorporate co-operative learning into everyday activities with young children:

- Select experiences that require the group to work together so that they build the skills of working as a group rather than learning to work as individuals.
- Include experiences that enable children to learn to focus on other people's actions, words and feelings so that they become interested in what others do, say and feel.
- Focus on finishing activities together so that children don't attempt to be the first to finish.
- Avoid games in which children eliminate each other till only one person is left as this leads to competition to be the last rather than co-operation.
- Organise the environment so that children can work in groups easily.

Whalley et al. (2001, p. 8) also highlighted the need within a learning community to build the capacity of 'children, parents and staff . . . to be good decision-makers, able to question, challenge and make choices'.

Some writers see the deepening of democratic practices as central to building communities in which reciprocal and meaningful learning can flourish. To deepen democracy in learning requires that the teacher 'practise "democratically wise" professional judgements' (Henderson 2001, p. 19). Henderson described the principles upon which these practices are based in the following ways:

> (1) they work in the inquiry spirit of 'not knowing', (2) they approach their work as a democratic 'calling', and (3) they embrace the artistry of their challenge. (Henderson 2001, p. 19)

To work in the inquiry spirit of not knowing, a teacher must be open to new ways of thinking and understanding in the world and relinquish their role as the expert who knows all. To approach work with a democratic calling the teacher must work as a morally engaged teacher and act 'out of a deep sense of integrity or conscience' (Henderson 2001, p. 19). To embrace the artistry in this work the teacher must seek to work with imagination, creativity, sensitivity and intelligence.

For Goldstein (1997), commitment to teaching with love is central to building community within early childhood settings. She characterised building community as 'the development of intimacy, a critical component of teaching with love' (p. 80) and saw the development of deep connections with children as core to community building.

So, in summary, building learning communities involves:

- making a commitment to community building
- developing learning processes and materials that are democratic and that centre on co-operation, real-life problem-solving, and the use of flexible and open learning resources
- using dialogue to explore diverse ideas and feelings within the group
- building learning processes that are inclusive of all children
- building deep, caring, responsive and meaningful relationships with children
- working with the whole group for periods of time
- celebrating achievements within the group
- honouring a spirit of inquiry.

These processes take time and a community doesn't just build itself overnight. Cuffaro emphasised this point vividly in her exploration of building community within early childhood classrooms from within a Deweyian perspective:

> For a spirit of unity to exist within an ensemble we must add the factor of time—time to define purpose, to share activity, to experiment and to risk, to learn from success and failure, to open up each other's possibilities. The unity created by an ensemble grows out of its history. (Cuffaro 1995, p. 28)

THEORETICAL BACKGROUND

LEARNING COMMUNITIES AND DEWEY'S DEMOCRATIC SCHOOLING

John Dewey (1859–1952) was a philosopher whose work became widely known in educational circles because he used philosophy to study education. His work was important to the Progressive movement in education.

In the United States in the 1920s and 1930s the Progressive education movement challenged the then dominant approach to education (that was based on principles of scientific management theory and social efficiency) with a call for democratic, child-centred, and social reform-oriented education. Dewey's ideas were core to this challenge (Henniger 1999). Two of Dewey's texts that were key to the Progressive movement were *School and Society* (1899), in which he linked schooling with social change, and *Democracy and Education* (1916), in which he outlined in detail how he understood the relationship between schooling, democracy and social change. He linked social change with social improvement. Dewey argued strongly that education and democracy are intimately linked and that education should be used to change society (Pinar et al. 1995). More specifically, Dewey argued for a shift from the mental restrictions he saw within classical approaches to curriculum to a more meaningful and enriching curriculum drawn from the child's own experiences. Pinar et al. (1995, p. 105) described Dewey's arguments against classical curriculum as 'insightful and unrelenting' in the following summary of his position on curriculum:

> Routinization, memorization, and recitation charac-terized the classical curriculum for mental discipline. Dewey's criticism of the classical curriculum was insightful and unrelenting. He insisted that the child's experience must form the basis for the curriculum, and in so doing synthesize the apparent antagonism between the two.

In 1896 Dewey had established a laboratory school at the University of Chicago (USA) in which the development of a democratic social community in the school was core. Longstreet and Shane (1993, p. 71) characterised the curriculum of the school as follows:

> The curriculum was to be based on life itself, on such fundamental human characteristics as socializing, constructing, inquiring, and creating. The school tried to replicate a miniature society including occupational activities typically found in

the real world . . . It was the teachers' responsibility to harmonize adult ends and values with the individuality of each child.

Dewey's work offers a rich basis for exploring the idea that community building is important to children's learning and for exploring how to build a learning community with young children. Dewey believed that learning grows through social interaction (Osterman 2000) and, consequently, high-quality education rests on the extent to which a community forms within the classroom and within the school. Community is 'realized in the degree in which individuals form a group' (Dewey 1958, p. 65). This group included the teacher and the children and it was at the heart of building democracy in and through education:

> When the school introduces and trains each child of society into membership within such a little community, saturating him with the spirit of service, we shall have the deepest and best guarantee of a larger society which is worthy, lovely and harmonious. (Dewey 1958, p. 49)

For Dewey, central to the capacity to build a democratic community of learners was communication (Cuffaro 1995). Communication was the mechanism through which meaning was created and shared. Without communication it was not possible to understand how others thought or understood the world and therefore it was not possible to build a shared understanding of what is valued and valuable for a group (community) of learners. He linked communication and community in the following way:

> To be a recipient of a communication is to have an enlarged and changed experience. One shares in what another has thought and felt and in so far, meagerly or amply, has his own attitude modified. (Dewey 1916, pp. 5–6)

When and why?

GOAL RELEVANCE

Community building can be usefully employed by staff to assist children's learning in many ways. Osterman (2000) reviewed research on the links between children's sense of belonging in a school community and learning. She highlighted the following links between children's learning and children's sense of belonging in a school:

- Being part of a community in which children have a sense of belongingness can reduce stress and help produce a sense of wellbeing.
- Children's sense of community is linked to their motivation to learn. Intrinsic motivation to learn can be greater in children who have a sense of belonging.
- Pro-social behaviour is more likely when children have a sense of belongingness.
- Children's sense of identity is stronger when they are accepted as part of a community.
- Children are more able to regulate their own behaviours when they feel a sense of belongingness.
- Children are more likely to be actively engaged with the curriculum when they are accepted by peers and have a sense of being part of the community.

Osterman (2000, p. 343) concluded:

Children who experience a sense of relatedness have a stronger supply of inner resources. They perceive themselves to be more competent and more autonomous and have higher levels of intrinsic motivation. They have a stronger sense of identity but are also willing to conform to and adopt established norms and values. These inner resources in turn predict engagement and performance.

There is also considerable research evidence that the pro-social skills required for co-operative learning will benefit children's long-term learning and wellbeing. In particular, if children have positive social relationships with others in the early years it can enhance their long-term academic achievement and cognitive development (Bowman et al. 2001).

DEVELOPMENTAL CONSIDERATIONS

Children of all ages thrive when they have a sense of belonging, when they and their ideas are valued and when they have reciprocal relationships with others around them. The foundation for children's sense of belongingness in an early childhood setting and thus for building community is that babies and toddlers have time with responsive and sensitive adults and opportunities for play that comes from the children's interests and pleasures. Babies and toddlers are learning about the 'needs, rights and feelings of others' (Stonehouse 1999, p. 160) through their play and through their relationships with the adults in their lives. They can learn what it means to be part of a respectful and caring community if staff '[respond] to their interests and explorations, play with them, support them and enjoy them' (Stonehouse 1999, p. 160).

Research strongly suggests (Bråtan 1996; Brune and Woodward 2007) that children have pro-social capacities from their first year of life. It is therefore possible for staff to actively include the youngest of children in building a learning community. Adult behaviours that will help to support the development of caring and co-operative relationships in babies and toddlers are those that show babies and toddlers that adults care and respond to others, and they include:

- being encouraging of children's interests
- being nurturing by responding to the needs and interests of individual babies and toddlers
- showing immediate sensitivity to children's distress
- being immediately responsive to children in distress
- demonstrating concern for children's feelings (Bråtan 1996).

These adult behaviours can help in building an emotional memory in babies and toddlers that forms the basis for their own pro-social behaviours towards each other in the present and in the future.

Preschoolers also learn about social relationships through their play with each other. Children's capacity for complex socio-dramatic play, in which relationships are formed and negotiated, grows through their preschool years. It is through this play that they explore what it means to be part of a social group, and how it is possible to build groups in which sharing and learning is possible. Socio-dramatic play therefore offers staff an important vehicle through which to build communities of learners with preschool children. It is through play that preschool children can:

> . . . problem-solve, put ideas together to form new meanings and develop symbolic capacities…practise being grown-up, exercise judgement, develop new and more complex physical skills and increase their strength, balance, speed, endurance and control. (Glover 1999, p. 14)

They also learn about rights, rules and the negotiation of relationships that are fundamental to the development of a democratic learning community:

> In staging these play episodes, the children explore their rights and duties and practise the skills necessary for good citizenship. They enact negotiations and various arguments and formulations. In doing so, they reconsider their place in the world, they work out the points of view which count in their 'real' discussions with adults. They give evidence of an attitude which Dewey deemed of great importance for citizenship and a democratic society: 'a personal interest in social relationships and control, and the habits of mind which secure social changes without introducing disorder'. (Dewey 1916, p. 115, cited in Elbers 1996, p. 512–513)

Children from a very early age can also engage in co-operative learning. For instance, Ramsey (2004) highlighted the capacity of toddlers to physically co-operate with each other in games that require physical co-ordination:

> . . . 'Turtle' is played by having several children lie on the ground under a large blanket or mat. The 'turtle' has to move in a co-ordinated fashion so that the 'shell' (blanket) stays on everyone. (Ramsey 2004, p. 135)

Hasan is alert to toddlers' capacity to physically co-operate with each other and draws on this knowledge in his work with them:

> Hasan works in the Bradley Park Family Centre with toddlers and preschool children. He is keen to build co-operative learning skills within his group but has noticed that the preschool children don't seem to invite the toddlers into their games in their outside play area. Hasan and his co-workers talk about this and decide to introduce the children to some new games which require the children to physically co-operate with each other. One of the games is called 'Snails'. It requires several children to hold onto a cardboard snail's shell that one of Hasan's co-workers has made as a line of children 'slither' like a snail around the silver snail's trail. Hasan has found some old silver cloth for the snail's trail and laid it out in a complex pattern in an underused part of the outside play area.

As children's language capacity grows they can also engage in more complex co-operative learning experiences such as putting on plays, writing group stories and making puppet shows. For children in the early years of schooling, video production, taking oral histories of their families and taking photographs of things that interest them can offer a powerful vehicle through which children can co-operate with each other in bringing diverse perspectives into the classroom and thus build a sense of shared meaning and understanding with the group (MacCleod 2004):

> Once in the classroom each narrative surrounding each item collected becomes part of a shared curriculum and as such becomes the means whereby children learn from each other about one another. (p. 250)

Similarly, Grace and Tobin (1997) described in detail a three-year research project tracking how elementary school children make videos in their classroom and the issues and dilemmas for teachers involved in the project. It powerfully highlights the capacity of children in these early years of school to be video producers and to bring their meanings forward in the classroom through video-making:

Video production in the Waiau classrooms provided an opportunity for students to incorporate their own interests, experiences, and desires into the school world. A space was allocated in which they could explore the limits of speech, behaviour, and humor allowed in the classroom. (Grace and Tobin 1997, p. 160)

Equity considerations

Equitable learning communities rest on equitable processes and equitable participation. Staff can assess equity in their learning community processes and participation by using some simple questions that explore whose ideas drive the understandings and knowledge generated within a specific community. For instance:

- Whose voice is heard in this community?
- What is this voice inviting us to do, think and feel?
- Who benefits from this voice being heard?
- Who else may have a voice on this issue that we are not currently hearing?

'RACE' AND CULTURE

Strategies such as co-operative learning open up larger questions about how groups relate to each other (Sleeter and Grant 1994, p. 105). There is a close relationship between community-building strategies in an early childhood classroom and multicultural and anti-racist education (Kaltsounis 1997). They are linked by a commitment to democracy where there is equity of participation for all in their community and where all children have 'the right to dream' (Nieto 1995, p. 160).

It is important for children from diverse cultural, 'racial' and linguistic backgrounds to find 'safe places' where they can 'discover and develop commonalities across difference' (Lankshear et al. 1995, p. 176) and where there are continuities between home and the early childhood setting (Espinosa 2005). When there are strong continuities between home languages and values and those of the early childhood setting children are more likely to feel positive about themselves as learners (Espinosa 2005).

Tijerina Revilla (1998) offered six basic concepts for building communities in areas where children traverse more than one culture. They represent a 'whole school' approach to community building. These concepts are taken directly from her paper and they are:

1 Vision. There is a clear, compelling, shared image of what should, must and can be provided to promote learning at the highest levels for students.

2 Leadership and governance. Highly creative and imaginative decisions are encouraged. Co-ordinated efforts from school board to parents, teachers and students exist with optimum level of involvement of all concerned.

3 Responsive pedagogy. Creative and imaginative classroom teaching programs and practices effectively utilise relevant curriculum, state-of-the art instructional methods, and materials and assessments that clearly support a positive learning environment that meets the needs of individuals, builds upon the culture and past experiences, and addresses the development and 'readiness' stages of students.

4 Family and community. Parents, businesses and community agencies are actively involved with school affairs, providing support and special services and networking to assure co-ordination.

5 Capacity building. Ongoing utilisation of knowledge bases and unique cultural contexts guide staff development, aggressive program design and appropriate resource allocation.

6 Schooling practice. There is concerted, orchestrated use of only the most effective programs and classroom practices supported by research, professional wisdom, and unified campus and district commitments.

The principles can be used as a checklist for those staff working at community building with children from culturally and linguistically diverse backgrounds. For instance, in my community-building efforts with this group of children have I:

- developed a clear vision of what needs to be provided to support all children to excel?
- co-ordinated my efforts with all adults involved with this group of children?
- developed a responsive teaching and learning environment that is building on all children's strengths and using the very best resources and knowledge available to me at this time?
- created continuities between routines, values and daily life at home and in the early-years setting?
- included families and communities in my vision-making and efforts?
- actively attempted to build the capacity of all staff to be involved in the process?
- attempted to act wisely at all times?

Staff working with young children who are learning English as an additional language need to be alert to the ways in which they can proactively support their sense of belonging and inclusion in co-operative learning. Key dimensions to this work include:

- supporting the maintenance of children's first language to support children's sense of belonging, self-worth and connection with their family and wider cultural contexts
- introducing the second language using models of best practice that include the infusion of bilingual staff, resources and learning experiences throughout the curriculum (Siraj-Blatchford and Clarke 2000; Espinosa 2005).

GENDER

Communities of learners require reciprocal and respectful relations between children and between children and adults. To achieve reciprocity and respect between all children in a group staff will need to be alert to the prevailing gender dynamics and relations in their group and/or classroom. Research shows that disrespectful behaviours between girls and boys, such as bullying and teasing, are often missed or ignored by early childhood staff (Gropper and Froschl 2000). These behaviours can be strongly gendered, with one study of 231 children in early years classrooms showing that boys initiated bullying behaviours three times more often than girls in the study did (Gropper and Froschl 2000). Children in this study were keen for staff to intervene and to set rules that established that bullying and teasing were not acceptable within the classroom. The researchers highlighted the importance of adult vigilance of and intervention in children's gender relations to build a positive climate for learning within early childhood classrooms and concluded:

> . . . when teachers do not intervene, which is true of the majority of incidents we observed, it is conceivable that children perceive that this is condoning the behaviour. Since boys are the predominant initiators of these incidents, children may also see teachers' lack of response as giving boys a license to behave in these ways. (Gropper and Froschl 2000, p. 55)

For staff who wish to build communities of learners in which gender equity flourishes, it is critical that they pay close attention to setting rules and limits that make bullying and teasing unacceptable. Given that children's gender identity construction is linked to the cultural ideas about gender that they encounter, it is important that staff offer boys and girls diverse ways to think about and respond to the idea that 'boys can bully' and 'girls can put up with it':

Brani was a teacher working with six- to eight-year-old children in small country school. She was concerned that three of the girls in her classroom were resistant to working with the boys on any of the co-operative learning tasks she had planned. She had heard from one of the boys in the group that some older boys had been heard teasing the girls in the playground at break time. Brani decided to work with the children to set rules and limits that would make teasing unacceptable in the playground and in doing so strengthen the sense of a safe community in her classroom. To do this she walked the girls around the playground and asked them to talk about the places where it was nice to play and the places they didn't like playing. She then talked to the girls about why they didn't like playing in particular places. The girls talked about the 'rude names' they had been called by the boys. Brani held a classroom meeting where she shared what she had learnt and her concerns about it. She asked the children what they could do to make the playground a nicer place for everyone. This question became the focus of a project in which the children developed rules for a nicer playground. They made posters of their rules and the reasons for them that they shared with the rest of the school.

Research exploring the learning skills of boys and girls in mathematics and technology tasks also provides insights into how gender may influence children's co-operative learning in the classroom. Yelland (1998) found that girl pairs had more success in completing novel tasks on computers than did boy/girl pairs and boy pairs. Yelland linked these difference to the fact that girls:

- were 'planful' in how they approached the task before and after it began
- took time to reflect on their progress
- predicted outcomes before acting
- engaged in dialogue as they worked co-operatively on the tasks (Yelland 1998).

Encouraging boys and girls to use these skills as they engage in co-operative learning tasks can help to support their success in these tasks and help to build a positive sense of community for children within the group.

DISABILITY AND ADDITIONAL NEEDS

Community building rests on staff fostering a climate of co-operative learning. Co-operative learning strategies can be particularly powerful in improving the learning experiences and outcomes for many children with diverse disabilities (Sleeter and Grant 1994). However, some staff may inadvertently undermine the capacity of children with disabilities to learn from co-operative learning. Research has suggested that some early childhood teachers are more likely to interrupt the activities of children with disabilities than children who do not have identified disabilities, to offer them more information and directives and to be more generous with praise (Creaser 1999, p. 127). In this context, it is important to note that self-determination for children with disabilities may be supported if children are able to make choices and to do this within social contexts (Algozzine et al. 2001). Co-operative learning strategies could provide these opportunities.

In addition, children with disabilities in inclusive classrooms are less often included in social play by children without disabilities. To help build more inclusive communities staff can make some simple changes to their environment. Steps such as ensuring that seating arrangements are inclusive of all children and activities that help children see what they share in common and can do together are important. Teacher presence also can increase interactions between children with and without disabilities. Finally, modifying activities so that children with disabilities can be part of them is an important part of community building in inclusive classrooms (Diamond and Huang 2005).

Reflecting on community-building techniques

1 What does research suggest are the keys to successful use of community building to optimise children's learning?
2 How would you define a learning community?
3 To what extent do you agree with the statement, 'In a truly dynamic learning environment, the process of inquiry is lived both by children and adults' (Harada et al. 2002/03, p. 71)?

4　Are there any times when you think community building is inappropriate with young children?

5　What do you think the 'practice of democratically wise professional judgements' (Henderson 2001, p. 19) means? How might such practice support the possibility of community building with children and families?

6　Develop a plan for a learning experience for four- to five-year-old children in which you wanted to support a sense of belongingness for each child.

7　Imagine you were working with a four-year-old child who was having difficulty completing a puzzle. How might community building help you help the child to learn skills for completing this and other puzzles?

8　Design a new game you could use to encourage toddlers to physically co-operate with each other.

9　What do you see as the hardest part of improving your community-building techniques?

Improving teaching in practice

1　Record (using a tape-recorder or written notes) small-group learning with children during several half-hour teaching periods.

2　What was your approach to developing a sense of belongingness for individual children? Did you:
- emphasise co-operative learning rather than competition between children?
- use dialogue as a tool for learning?
- support children to share different ideas and feelings with each other in the group?
- show care for each child in a proactive way?
- take care to include each child in positive social exchanges with their peers and with you?

3　How and how well did you take account of developmental and anti-bias considerations?

4　What are your areas of strength and weakness in facilitating learning communities in your teaching and learning?

5　How can you improve your community-building techniques in practice?

FURTHER READING

Fidler, M. 1995, 'Building a learning community', *Association Management,* 47(5), pp. 40–47.

Harada, V., Lum, D. and Souza, K. 2002/03, 'Building a learning community: students and adults as inquirers', *Childhood Education*, 79(2), pp. 66–71.

Lubeck, S. and Post, J. 2000, 'Creating a Head Start community of practice', in L. Diaz Soto, ed., *The Politics of Early Childhood Education* (pp. 33–58), Peter Lang Publishing, New York.

Osterman, K. 2000, 'Students' need for belonging in the school community', *Review of Educational Research*, 70(3), pp. 323–368.

REFERENCES

Algozzine, B., Browder, D., Karvonen, M., Test, D. and Wood, W. 2001, 'Effects of interventions to promote self-determination for individuals with disabilities', *Review of Educational Research*, 71(2), pp. 219–278.

Anderman, E. and Maehr, M. 1994, 'Motivation and schooling in the middle grades', *Review of Educational Research*, 64(2), pp. 287–309.

Balaban, N. 2003, 'Creating a caring, democratic classroom community for and with young children', in J. Silin and C. Lippman, eds, *Putting the Children First: The Changing Face of Newark's Public Schools* (pp. 82–90), Teachers College Press, New York.

Bowman, B., Donovan, M. and Burns, S. 2001, eds, *Eager to Learn: Educating our Preschoolers*, National Academy Press, Washington, DC.

Bråtan, M. 1996, 'When toddlers provide care: infants' companion space', *Childhood*, 3(4), pp. 449–466.

Brune, C. and Woodward, A. 2007, 'Social cognition and social responsiveness in 10-month old infants', *Journal of Cognition and Development*, 8(2), pp. 133–158.

Campbell, S., Coady, M., Lawrence, H., Smith, K., Totta, J., Saitta, S. and Rolfe, S. 2002, *Our Part in Peace*, Australian Early Childhood Association, Watson, ACT.

Casswell, S. 2001, 'Community capacity building and social policy—what can be achieved?' *Social Policy Journal of New Zealand*, December, pp. 22–36.

Creaser, B. 1999, 'The place of play for young children with disabilities in mainstream education', in E. Dau, ed., *Child's Play: Revisiting Play in Early Childhood Settings* (pp. 111–130), MacLennan and Petty, Sydney, Philadelphia and London.

Cuffaro, H. 1995, *Experimenting with the World: John Dewey and the Early Childhood Classroom*, Teachers College Press, New York.

Dewey, J. 1916, *Democracy and Education*, Macmillan Company, New York [reprinted 1966, the Free Press].

——1958, *Experience and Education*, Macmillan, New York.

Diamond, K. and Huang, H. 2005, 'Preschoolers' ideas about disabilities', *Infants and Young Children*, 18(1), pp. 37–46.

Elbers, E. 1996, 'Citizenship in the making: themes of citizenship in children's pretend play', *Childhood*, 3(4), pp. 499–514.

Espinosa, L. 2005, 'Curriculum and assessment considerations for young children from culturally, linguistically and economically diverse backgrounds', *Psychology in the Schools*, 42(8), p. 837–854.

Fidler, M. 1995, 'Building a learning community', *Association Management*, 47(5), pp. 40–47.

Glover, A. 1999, 'The role of play in development and learning', in E. Dau, ed., *Child's Play: Revisiting Play in Early Childhood Settings* (pp. 4–15), MacLennan and Petty, Sydney, Philadelphia and London.

Goldstein, L. 1997, *Teaching with Love: A Feminist Approach to Early Childhood Education*, Peter Lang Publishing, New York.

Grace, D. and Tobin, J. 1997, 'Carnival in the classroom: elementary students making videos', in J. Tobin, ed., *Making a Place for Pleasure in Early Childhood Education* (pp. 159–87), Yale University Press, New Haven and London.

Graves, L. 1992, 'Cooperative learning communities: context for a new vision of education and society', *Journal of Education*, 174(2), pp. 57–59.

Gropper, N. and Froschl, M. 2000, 'The role of gender in young children's teasing and bullying behaviour', *Equity and Excellence in Education*, 33(1), pp. 48–56.

Gross, C. 2005, 'Promoting problem solving with young children: an approach to community building and classroom management in one classroom', Unpublished dissertation, Columbia University, <http://digitalcommons.libraries.columbia.edu/dissertations/AAI3175690>

Harada, V., Lum, D. and Souza, K. 2002/03, 'Building a learning community: students and adults as inquirers', *Childhood Education* 79(2), pp. 66–71.

Henderson, J. 2001, 'Deepening democratic curriculum work', *Educational Researcher*, 30(9), pp. 18–21.

Henniger, M. 1999, *Teaching young children: an introduction*, Merrill Prentice Hall, New Jersey.

Hong, Y. 2004, 'Cultural meaning of groups discussions on problematic moral situations in Korean kindergarten classrooms', *Journal of Research in Childhood Education*, 18(3), pp. 179–193.

Jilk, B. A. 1999, 'Schools in the new millennium', *American School & University*, 71(5), pp. 46–7.

Kaltsounis, T. 1997, 'Multicultural education and citizenship education at the crossroads: searching for common ground', *Journal of Social Studies*, 88(1), pp. 18–25.

Kim, I., Anderson, R., Nguyen-Jahiel, K. and Archodidou, A. 2007, 'Discourse patterns during children's collaborative online discussions', *The Journal of the Learning Sciences*, 16(3), pp. 330–370.

Konzal, J. 2001, 'Collaborative inquiry: a means of creating a learning community', *Early Childhood Research Quarterly*, 16, pp. 95–115.

Lankshear, C., Peters, M. and Knobel, M. 1995, 'Critical pedagogy and cyberspace', in H. Giroux, C. Lankshear, P. McClaren and M. Peters, eds, *Counternarratives: cultural studies and critical pedagogies in postmodern spaces* (pp. 149–188), Peter Lang Publishing, New York.

Longstreet, W. and Shane, H. 1993, *Curriculum for a New Millennium*, Allyn & Bacon, Needham Heights, MA.

MacCleod, F. 2004, 'Literacy, identity and agency: linking classrooms to communities', *Early Childhood Development and Care,* 174(3), pp. 243–252.

Mattai, R.P. 2002, 'A teacher educator responds', in N. Quisenberry and G. Duhon, eds, *Racism in the Classroom: Case Studies*, Association of Teacher Educators and Association for Childhood Education International, Olney, MD.

Medvin, M., Reed, D., Behr, D. and Spargo, E. 2003, 'Using technology to encourage social problem solving in preschoolers', in G. Marshall and Y. Katz, eds, *Learning in School, Home and Community. ICT for Early and Elementary Education* (pp. 13–20), Kluwer Academic Publishers, Boston.

Nieto, S. 1995, 'From brown heroes and holidays to assimilationist agendas: reconsidering the critiques of multicultural education', in C. Sleeter and P. McLaren, eds, *Multicultural Education, Critical Pedagogy and the Politics of Difference* (pp. 191–220), State University of New York Press, Albany.

O'Hara, M. 2004, *ICT in the Early Years*, Continuum, London.

Osterman, K. 2000, 'Students' need for belonging in the school community', *Review of Educational Research*, 70(3), pp. 323–368.

Pascarella, P. 1998, 'Cultivating the power of community', *Management Review*, 87(4), pp. 52–54.

Pinar, W., Reynolds, W., Slattery, P. and Taubman, P. 1995, *Understanding Curriculum*, Peter Lang Publishing, New York.

Ramsey, P. 2004, *Teaching and Learning in a Diverse World: Multicultural Education for Young Children*, 3rd edn, Teachers College Press, New York.

Schertz, M. 2007, Avoiding 'passive empathy' with philosophy for children, *Journal of Moral Education*, 36(2), pp. 185–198.

Siraj-Blatchford, I. and Clarke, P. 2000, *Supporting Identity, Diversity and Language in the Early Years*, Open University Press, Buckingham and Philadelphia.

Sleeter, C. and Grant, C.A. 1994, *Making choices for multicultural education*, Merrill/Macmillan Publishing, New York.

Sterling, M. 1998, 'Building a community week by week', *Educational Leadership*, 56(1), pp. 65–69.

Stonehouse, A. 1999, 'Play: a way of being for babies and toddlers', in E. Dau, ed., *Child's Play: Revisiting Play in Early Childhood Settings* (pp. 152–163), MacLennan and Petty, Sydney, Philadelphia and London.

Swadner Blue, B. 2000, '"At risk" or "at promise"? From deficit constructions of the "other childhood" to possibilities for authentic alliances with children and families', in L. Diaz Soto, ed., *The Politics of Early Childhood Education* (pp. 117–134), Peter Lang Publishing, New York.

Tijerina Revilla, A. 1998, 'Schools as communities of learners: an initiative toward creating democratic education', *IDRA Newsletter by the Intercultural Development Research Association*, February.

Whalley, M. and the Pen Green Team, 2001, *Involving Parents in their Children's Learning*, Sage Publications, London.

Yelland, N. 1998, 'Gender issues in mathematics and technology', in N. Yelland, ed., *Gender in Early Childhood* (pp. 249–273), Routledge, London.

Chapter 21

Decolonising

 Colonise: To form or establish a colony or colonies in. 2. To migrate to and settle in; occupy as a colony. 3. To resettle or confine (persons) in or as if in a colony. 4. To subjugate (a population) to or as if to a colonial government.

(*The Free Online Dictionary*,
<http://www.thefreedictionary.com/colonize>)

De: prefix, removal of or from something specified. Reversal of something.

(*Collins Dictionary of the English Language*, p. 381)

The central objective in decolonising the African mind is to overthrow the authority that alien traditions exercise over the African. This demands the dismantling of white supremacist beliefs, and the structures which uphold them, in every area of African life. It must be stressed, however, that decolonisation does not mean ignorance of foreign traditions; it simply means denial of their authority and withdrawal of allegiance from them.

(Chinweizu 1987, cited in Hotep 2003)

Decolonization is a journey of self-discovery culminating in a reawakening and a reorientation . . . Like all transforming, liberatory states, decolonization is actually a protracted process demanding constant vigilance and intense dedication to task.

(Hotep 2003, online)

What?

In everyday language to colonise something is to move into a new space and change it to make it yours without permission from its inhabitants to do so. When bees colonise an area they change it by building a new hive for their home. They don't ask permission to build their hive. Bees build hives because they create new sources of food and expand their colonies overall. Once a new hive is established the bees will work together to defend it against removal by stinging those who come near it. This is a powerful way to subdue and control those who attempt to resist the colonisers' arrival and continued presence.

Similar processes are at work when people colonise. People move into a new area and change it by introducing new institutions, languages, practices and values without permission from the original inhabitants. People take over and defend an area forcefully to establish it as theirs by taking land, institutions and minds (Hotep 2003). People as colonisers subdue and control resistance through more complex and long-lasting mechanisms than a sting. They control it though institutions, ideas and practices (discourses) that make the original inhabitants feel less worthy, less capable and less powerful than the colonisers. Discourses are the frameworks we use to make sense of the world. Within this, the position of language is important. As Viruru (2001) noted:

> . . . language has been used as a tool to distinguish between 'civilization and barbarism. (p. 8)

> . . . those civilizations that use written languages are considered superior to those who do not. (p. 36)

To decolonise something is to remove the capacity of colonisers to subdue and control the land, institutions and minds of the colonised. As a teaching strategy, decolonising refers to staff and children removing colonial ways of thinking, being, talking and doing (the colonial discourses) that make the colonised feel that they are less worthy, less capable and less powerful than the colonisers. To do this staff and children decolonise their institutions, relationships, meanings and their knowledge. In this chapter, we focus on decolonising relationships, meanings and knowledge of 'race'.

Issues and debates

CAN WE ALL DO DECOLONISING? WHITE PEOPLE, WHITENESS AND COLONIAL DISCOURSES OF 'RACE'

Colonial discourses of 'race' made colonialism possible. Those discourses of 'race' rested upon creating 'racial' distinctions between white people and black people in which white was seen as superior and normal. Through colonialism, discourses of whiteness were created and used by white people to gain and maintain power over their black colonial subjects. It is important to understand the distinction between whiteness as a discourse and white people in this context, as Leonardo explained:

> 'Whiteness' is a racial discourse, whereas the category 'white people' represents a socially constructed identity, usually based on skin color. (Leonardo 2002, p. 31)

Decolonisation involves challenging whiteness rather than white people *per se*, as not all white people reinforce whiteness and the colonial ideas of 'race' that it implies. Some white people work to challenge and to change colonial discourses in the same way that some men work to challenge and to change sexist discourses. However, as colonisation had and continues to produce different legacies for the colonisers and the colonised there are different tasks for each in the process of decolonising relationships, meanings and knowledge of 'race' in current times.

Borrowing from Kaomea (2001), the decolonising task for indigenous people should involve:

> . . . healing and empowerment. It should involve the return of dignity and the restoration of sovereignty, and it should ultimately bring formerly colonized communities one step further along the path to self-determination. (p. 81)

In contrast, the decolonising task for white educators is to explore how whiteness impacts on their curriculum to racially exclude an 'other' so that they can work against this. As Davis puts it:

> White early childhood educators need to consider and explore how their white constructs and understandings of the world, and of others, influences their curricula practice in ways that excludes and discriminates against these

'others'. Within this, the constructions and influences of hierarchically organized dichotomies used to categorise and position white and non-white needs to be identified, deconstructed and reconstructed in equitable and different ways. (Davis 2006, p. 28)

THEORETICAL BACKGROUND

THE COLONIAL, POSTCOLONIAL AND ANTI-COLONIAL

Gandhi (1998) defined colonialism as the 'historical process whereby the "West" attempts systematically to cancel or negate the cultural difference and value of the "non-West"' (p. 16), relying on distinctions between the 'civilized' and the 'non-civilized'. European colonists saw the original inhabitants of European colonies as non-civilised and 'genetically pre-determined to inferiority' (Ashcroft, Griffiths and Tiffin 1989, p. 47). Colonial views of the world rest on a deficit view of the colonised:

Deficit theory has been used throughout history to justify imperial or colonial pursuits. For example, European colonialists justified Native American genocide and slavery in the U.S. in part by painting native peoples and African slaves as 'savages' who required taming and civilizing—the white man's burden. Deficit theory is used in similar ways today, such as to justify imperial U.S. intervention in the Middle East. (Gorski 2007, p. 6)

New language was invented to help with this process. For instance, the British invented the term 'aborigine' in the mid-1660s to distinguish indigenous inhabitants of its colonies from their 'colonists'. The point of those distinctions was to racialise Indigenous Australians as the primitive savage who was inferior… and yet to be feared. Similar processes of racialisation were and still are at work in other colonised countries, with similar effects—colonisers always seemed superior to the colonised. It is a process that began over 400 years ago but its effects and processes remain with us today. As Merlyne Cruz explains through her own biography as a Filipino woman:

Well, the Philippines is my country of origin and the Philippines suffered from dual colonisations. What happened was that as a result of these colonisations we have lost partly our language because English is used more now, it's more prevalent. It is our medium of instruction, it is the language of business conversations and it is the language of our textbooks. It is not only about losing our identity and cultural roots it is also about taking in values and it's about how people think. For example, from the Spaniards we learnt about 'colourism'—white is beautiful, white is intelligent, white is powerful. And when the Americans came to colonise they thought that it was important for us to be educated and to copy their education. The sad thing for us is that we have taken that as a gift. It is just a natural course of things and in a way we began to act as little brown Americans. Being born in a colonised family means that you inherit these values—it's like you breathe it, it's in the air, and it's normal for me to think this way—very Western and having all these values. (Cruz, 2006, interview transcript)

Colonial discourse emphasises the importance of civilising the inferior primitive through 'trade, administration, cultural, and moral improvement' (Ashcroft, Griffiths and Tiffin 1998, p. 43). Education was key to this. Colonial discourse subdues and controls through promoting the ideas of an inferior 'other' but also through silencing the benefits of colonisation for the coloniser and the brutality and exploitation involved in taking another's land, mind and institutions. The scale of that brutality is briefly described by Viruru (2007, pp. 38–39) in this way:

This occupation was violently imposed over a 500-year period and has a history of slavery, unimaginable and often unrecognized deaths, oppression, and forced displacements and migrations. According to Mohanram (1999), by 1800 fifty-five percent of the earth's land surface had been claimed by the imperial powers of Western and Southern Europe. Further, in the 19th century, Europe acquired new territories at the rate of 210,000 square kilometers a year.

Postcolonial theorists study the effects of colonisation on people. More specifically, they study colonial discourses in the past and present and their effects on colonisers and colonised to reverse and/or disrupt their effects in the present. Two key postcolonial theorists are Edward Said (1936–2003) and Homi Bhabha (1949–).

Edward Said's book *Orientialism* (1978) is often said to mark the beginnings of postcolonial theory. Said studied how 'colonial discourse operated as an instrument of power' (Ashcroft, Griffiths and Tiffin, 1989, p. 46) in the 'Orient'. The term 'Orient' comes from the Latin word *oriens* meaning 'east'. The West used it, especially during the 19th century, to refer to the Middle East, Egypt and Arabian-influenced North Africa, and more recently has included Southeast Asia. People from the Orient were called Orientals. Said writes of how colonial discourses created a place called the 'Orient' and became an instrument of power against those living in the Orient, especially Arabs, Muslims and the Middle East. Of discourses on the Orient and the study by the West of the East (Orientalism), he wrote:

> My contention is that Orientalism is fundamentally a political doctrine willed over the Orient because the Orient was weaker than the West, which elided the Orient's difference with its weakness…As a cultural apparatus Orientalism is all aggression, activity, judgment, will-to-truth, and knowledge. (*Orientalism* 1978, p. 204)

Homi Bhabha (1994) explored how colonial discourse is vulnerable to disruption and resistance. In *Nation and Narration* (1990) Bhabha argued that postcolonial countries are different to each other and do not have a shared identity. From this difference comes the possibility of a 'third space' (Bhabha 1994, p. 37) in which we can integrate and expand our ways of knowing and seeing. In the third space 'negotiation of incommensurable differences creates a tension peculiar to borderline existences' (Bhabha 1994, p. 218) to create new possibilities. The third space 'initiates new signs of identity, and innovative sites of collaboration and contestation' (Bhabha 1994, p. 1)

Bhabha and Said focused on the importance of analysing the complex ideas and values that made colonialism, and the racism on which it was founded, possible. They also help us to understand its changing effects in the present. In analysing colonising processes they point to what needs to happen to reverse them. In particular, they challenge us to understand that decolonising is a political act of making new meanings about differences between each other, and of creating new identities that resist seeing difference as inferior and that rewrite the power dynamics within institutions, ideas and practices to make collaboration possible through our differences from each other. While this chapter will focus on decolonising racialised identities and practices, there is also a strong call to decolonise relations between children and adults (see Viruru 2007) that is of direct relevance to early childhood.

How?

Decolonising is a complex process because colonisation and its effects continue into the present in powerful and shifting ways. As Merlyne Cruz told us, colonising processes seem normal. It is always complex and challenging to challenge what is normal, and no simple decolonising recipe exists. However, many educators have engaged with the project of decolonisation and have begun to describe what decolonising pedagogies are and do. What follows draws on their work as pointers to the strategies that can be engaged to decolonise racialised relationships and knowledge. It requires teachers to:

- build a decolonising mind-set
- build principles for action
- open up new knowledges
- open up new relationships and new identities.

BUILDING A DECOLONISING MIND-SET

This involves practising:

- recognising the presence of power in our relationships and our knowledge (Viruru 2007) by learning about the workings of colonialism and its effects. In work with young children this means introducing children to simple stories about the ways in which unfair treatment of people in the past impacts on the present
- practising 'intellectual disobedience '(Hotep and Hotep 2003; Hotep 2003). This refers to the process of refusing to accept as common sense, discourses that contribute to stereotypes and colonial ideas about ethnic and racial inferiority and superiority. In work with young children this means questioning (Chapter 13) and deconstructing (Chapter 22) stereotypes and colonial ideas about ethnic and racial inferiority
- re-questioning the aims of education by asking questions such as, 'Who is benefiting from this educational experience?' and 'How is it creating the possibilities of a third space?' (Thésése 2006). In work with children this involves engaging children with multiple perspectives on daily experiences and asking, 'Who is kindergarten, child care, etc. fair for?' and 'Who is it not fair for?'
- redefining whose knowledge counts in education and how diverse knowledges can enter the classroom, especially the knowledges of those who have been colonised and struggle against colonisation (Thésése 2006). In work with children this means ensuring the stories and experiences of those who have experienced and continue to experience colonisation are shared and explored
- reflecting on how to build decolonising relationships within the classroom. This is especially important for teachers whose first language is English and who are working with children whose first language is not English. Fumoto, Hargreaves and Maxwell (2007), in their study of relationships between teachers whose first language was English and children whose first language was not English, highlighted that the children with the least experience of English were the least close to their teachers. Again, in work with children this means exploring issues of what feels fair and what doesn't for different children.

BUILDING PRINCIPLES FOR ACTION

Some principles to consider are:

- building the courage to name racial discrimination when you see it (DeLeon 2007)
- self- identifying with a 'racial' group to disrupt the idea that only the colonised 'non-white' are ethnic or have a 'race'. Gillborn explained why this matters:

> . . . whiteness draws much of its power from 'Othering' the very idea of ethnicity. A central characteristic of whiteness is a process of 'naturalization' such that white becomes the norm from which other 'races' stand apart and in relation to which they are defined. When white-identified groups do make a claim for a white ethnic identity alongside other officially recognized ethnic groups (e.g., as has been tried by the Ku Klux Klan in the US and the British National Party in England) it is the very exceptionality of such claims that points to the commonsense naturalization of whiteness at the heart of contemporary political discourse. (Gillborn 2005, pp. 488–489)

- making whiteness the problem and open to questioning. Whiteness has been increasingly recognised as one of the most powerful discourses of privilege that holds racial injustice in place. As Lillian Holt, an Australian Indigenous leader and educator, puts it:

> I'm interested in the topic of whiteness because for too long Aborigines have always been considered "the problem". We have invariably been the ones who are endlessly researched, studied and labeled. (Holt 2007, p. 7)

OPENING UP NEW KNOWLEDGES IN THE CLASSROOM

Ways to do this include:

- creating spaces in which all children have a 'sense of right or entitlement' to shape and manage them (Skattebol 2003, 2005) and thus to contribute to the knowledges of the classroom or group
- using Aboriginal 'cultural practices knowledge' (Orr, Paul and Paul 2002) within the curriculum. It is important to ensure that this cultural practices knowledge enters the classroom via Aboriginal people so that it is relevant to contemporary ways of being Aboriginal in your local context and is culturally meaningful and respectful. Writing of the importance of this within the Canadian context, Orr, Paul and Paul (2002) quoted from the National Indian Brotherhood statement on education that said:

We want education to provide the setting in which our children can develop the fundamental attitudes and values which have an honored place in Indian tradition and culture. We want the behavior of our children to be shaped by those values which are most esteemed in our culture. (National Indian Brotherhood, 1972, p. 2)

Elizabeth, an early childhood teacher in a kindergarten in Northcote, an inner suburb of Melbourne, asked her friend's mother Sal to come and volunteer and to participate with the children in the program each week. Sal is a woman of Aboriginal descent and was keen to help the children to understand and know about Aboriginal ways of living and being in Northcote and to learn about the things that matter to her now.

Reflection point: How do you think that the children got to understand more about Indigenous values and cultures by having Sal in the classroom?

- using narrative life history as a decolonising methodology to 'allow the teller's voice to be heard' and to 'provide a contextual understanding to complex events and phenomena that help academics and policy workers to more accurately represent and give legitimacy to the knowledge of people who have often been silenced and marginalised in academic and professional discourse' (Orr, Paul and Paul 2002, p. 4)

Sal tells the children stories about her childhood in central Australia where she lived and grew up. As the children get to know Sal they ask her more and more questions about her childhood and what kinds of things she did when she was little.

Reflection point: Using stories is a good way to tell others about yourself. Why is this?

- reversing the power relations of who speaks and whose ideas create a majority view. In work with young children this means analysing the voices and stories of children and families in daily practices such as group time (circle time). Wohlwend (2006) describes how an Arab girl in a post-September 11 early childhood classroom in the USA struggled to have her knowledge heard in daily practices, such as classroom meetings where the more powerful and popular speakers were heard. This created a set of majority views within the classroom
- repositioning different languages within the classroom by enabling children to draw on their first languages within the classroom. Srinivassan discusses why this is needed within the Australian context:

The Australian government has declared English as Australia's national language, ascribing unique power and status to one language. Such 'linguicism' is a form of oppression—like racism or sexism—that attributes power and superiority to native speakers of the dominant language, creating unequal distribution of resources and feelings of inferiority among speakers of other Languages. (Srinivassan 2006, p. 109)

> It is a policy at the Richmond Children's centre that each staff member speaks a second language that is relevant to the cultural groups that attend the centre. These staff members are asked to speak to the children and parents in their first language.
>
> *Reflective task:* Describe how this policy would affect the families attending the centre.

When and why?

Decolonising meanings and relationships with adults helps children to learn how to build respectful relationships with each other. Hence, decolonising is a teaching technique that impacts on children's sense of self and wellbeing and their capacity to build relationships with others.

GOAL RELEVANCE

Decolonising can help children to understand the politics of their day-to-day relations with each other and in the world about them. The aim in building this understanding is to reverse those politics that colonise and racially other. Decolonising can be used to reverse colonial relations of 'race' and power that exist and persist within the group. It can be used to open up new relationships and new identities within the group that celebrate otherness rather than repress it, and that engage proactively and positively with difference across and within diverse ethnicities.

Opening up new relationships and new identities that challenge whiteness, linguicism and racism
Ways to do this include:

- critically exposing children's discourses of 'race'. 'This type of teaching may critically explore how and why communities name themselves (or others) in particular ways.' (Skattebol 2003, p. 161)

> Kylie, a child in Year 2 at Wye River Primary School, came to the class on a Monday morning having been to a community fete on the weekend. She shared about her experience of tasting 'wog' food for the first time.
>
> *Reflection point:* What discussion do you think you could have with the children about Kylie's statement?

- challenging colonial stereotypes and discourses of 'race' where racialised identities 'are black/dark skinned, the "other", to the unnamed, unmarked, uncoloured "white race"' (Skattebol 2003, p. 164). The internet is a good source of images that can be used to explore and challenge colonial stereotypes and images relevant to your specific context

> Children are using mirrors to draw their faces with pastels. One child asks another child to pass the 'skin-coloured' pastel. This was an opportunity for the teacher to have a discussion with the children about the different colours of skin.
>
> *Reflection point:* What questions could you ask the children to encourage them to think about their stereotypes of typical skin colour?

- encouraging children to see identities as something they have the power to change rather than something that they are 'stuck' with (Skattebol 2003)
- avoiding homogenising Indigenous people into a collective 'they' and positioning being Indigenous as different to the centre (MacNaughton and Davis 2001)

- developing identities that do not rely on the binary of black/white (MacNaughton and Davis 2001).

These efforts can have a positive effect on more specific learning area goals and intentions within the program. Children's learning across all domains gains when they are free from discrimination and able to be part of positive peer relationships and in respectful relationships with adults (e.g. Sanacore 2004; Colombo 2005).

DEVELOPMENTAL CONSIDERATIONS

Decolonising will involve different aims and processes, depending on the age group of the children. However, it should be remembered that attitudes to themselves and to others begin from the moment a child is born. Children learn about the values placed on who they are from their first interactions with the world. Children can learn both fair and unfair perceptions about themselves and others (Heale and O'Brien 2007). In a decolonising approach to working with young children the emphasis is firmly on helping children to build fair perceptions about differences and similarities between themselves and others. It is important to remember in this work that just as children can learn bias and unfairness, they can unlearn it:

> The South West teachers' group is having its monthly meeting where teachers share ideas, celebrate successes and explore problems about their teaching practice. Justine tells the other teachers about her struggle to constantly challenge the children when they display values that do not accord with hers, such as discriminating against the Vietnamese children in the class. She describes to the group how she tells the children off for using discriminatory language and for excluding the Vietnamese children in their play. She says that it doesn't seem to make a difference.
>
> *Reflection point:* Can you think of some ways that Justine could help the children in her group to be inclusive?

Babies in the first few months of life can notice facial differences between people from 'racial' backgrounds other than their own. This ability appears to reduce over time, with adults finding it harder to notice facial differences between people from 'racial' backgrounds other than their own (Nelson 2001). This can lead to a form of colonial thinking where 'others' all look the same. In postcolonial theory the word 'homogenising' describes this form of thinking (see MacNaughton and Davis 2001). It is important to build on the babies' ability, thereby laying a strong foundation for children to avoid homogenising others later on. Some questions to prompt staff thinking about this in their work with babies are:

- What experience are babies having of different types of faces?
- How do they respond to these differences?
- Are babies associating differences in facial features with pleasurable experiences?
- Are you actively expanding babies' experiences of diverse faces in pleasurable ways?
- Are babies seeing images of people who look like them and their parents as part of the everyday world of the centre? (CEIEC 2006)

Children between 9 and 14 months of age can distinguish and use 'racial' cues when looking at adult faces (Madole and Roth 2000). Some questions to prompt reflection on what is happening with babies in your own context are:

- What evidence do babies show of noticing differences in faces of people with different colour skins, eye shapes, noses, hair, etc?
- How can you expand children's positive experiences with physical differences?
- How can you begin to build their vocabulary for talking about these differences?
- What opportunities are you creating to actively expand babies' knowledge and enjoyment of physical differences? (CEIEC 2006)

The use of Information and Communication Technologies (ICT) can support this work. It is possible to download images from the internet and print them to create your own posters that can help you to explore babies' growing sense of 'racial' differences. The *Cultural Diversity Resource* (CEIEC 2006) is a CD-ROM that can also help with this work. It has a virtual resource room that can be used to build posters for work with young children in this area.

Preschool children's acceptance of 'racial' differences is increased when you deliberately discuss those differences with them. Studies in the USA and the UK show that preschool children are capable of understanding overt discussions of 'race', and their acceptance of 'racial' differences can be increased through these discussions (Bernstein et al. 2000; Rutland et al. 2005). When staff use decolonising as a strategy this overt discussion is important. As discussed above, silencing discussions of 'race' supports a colonial and racist status quo. Some questions to prompt reflection on what is happening with babies in your own context are:

- What do children in your group know and understand about 'racial' differences?
- How are their friendship patterns and preferences influenced by this knowledge?
- What language do children have to describe physical differences in hair texture and colour, eyes, noses and skin tone?
- What opportunities are you creating to actively discuss with children their knowledge, experience and enjoyment of physical differences between themselves and other children? (CEIEC 2006).

Once again, the use of ICT can support this work. Children can search and download images from the internet and print them or use The *Cultural Diversity Resource* (CEIEC 2006) virtual resource room to build posters and books that help them to learn respectful language for talking about differences.

The effects of colonisation will be different in different contexts. Within the Australian context, some white Australian children demonstrated negative 'racial' attitudes towards Aboriginal Australians in their preschool years (see MacNaughton and Davis 2001). Some questions to help staff reflect on the extent to which colonial images and understandings of Indigenous Australians is present among preschool children in their group are:

- Do children know the words 'Aboriginal' and/or 'Indigenous'?
- What meanings do they give to these words?
- What other knowledge do the children you work with have of Indigenous Australians?
- How are you actively introducing them to positive and contemporary images and knowledge of Indigenous Australia?
- How are you actively involving your local Indigenous communities in the teaching and learning about Indigenous Australia in your program? (CEIEC 2006).

Children in the early years of schooling can begin to reflect historically on their world. This offers staff the opportunity to explore with students the extent to which they hold 'old', inaccurate and unfair ideas at a young age about specific groups of people. This is an important strategy for decolonising children's understandings of themselves and others. As DeLeon argued:

> Most students do not have the opportunity to look at historical records of different time periods, but many of the classic stereotypes and representations endure. Whether it is a Native American represented as the noble savage, the sexualized African, or the exotic Asian, representation has a powerful effect on how we view others and how we construct our identity on the basis of the supposed difference of the Other. (DeLeon 2007, p. 266)

Doing this work can make a difference to how white children see black children. For instance, in a US study in which children in the early years of school had history lessons that included information about racism that had been experienced by African-Americans, European-American children become less biased towards African-Americans (Hughes, Bigler and Levy 2007).

In the early years of schooling, talk with children about 'race' can also decrease their racial prejudices when they talk to peers who are less prejudiced than they are (Aboud and Doyle 1996). This means it is important for staff to explore the understandings of racial difference that circulate within their classroom. Some questions to prompt this exploration include:

- What are the different views and values that children in your group have towards racial differences?
- Are you actively talking with children about what's wrong with bias?
- Do you link children who are less biased with children who are more biased in these discussions?
- Are children who are biased regularly hearing non-biased views from you, their peers, and in learning resources such as stories, to counter their own biases? (CEIEC 2006).

Equity considerations

'RACE' AND CULTURE

The emphasis in this chapter has been on decolonising as a teaching strategy to rethink and re-imagine relations of 'race' within early childhood classrooms. As the chapter has focused on issues of 'race' and culture we will not add any specific additional issues at this point.

GENDER

Children's understandings of themselves and others are mediated by their gender. Children are building 'racial' identities as they build gender identities and these processes intersect and mingle in complex ways. The complexity arises because a child's 'racial' identity is gendered and vice-versa. So while it is important to understand there are different ways to be 'normal' boys and girls in different cultural and 'racial' contexts, there are also shared cultural expectations across many different ethnic groups that boys and girls should be different. Hence, the 'right' way to be a boy in Vietnamese-Australian families may differ from the 'right' way to be a boy in Sudanese-Australian families, but there also may be shared ways to be a boy because while their ethnicity differs, they are each living within Australia where broader cultural norms exist about the best way to be a boy. This means that it is important for staff to avoid building 'racially-informed' gender stereotypes about young children (for instance, all Asian girls are quiet and all African-American boys are good at sport).

However, it is also important to recognise that one of the effects of colonisation is that white ways of being male or female are often seen as more desirable and superior to other ways of being male or female. This brings challenges for children. In Pyke and Johnson's (2003) study of Asian-American women's and girls' identities, they found that the Asian-American girls struggled with what was expected of them. When Asian-American girls were assertive they were seen as not being 'real Asians' by their white peers and were rejected by Asian men for their assertiveness.

DISABILITY AND ADDITIONAL NEEDS

It is important that children with disabilities have culturally appropriate and respectful support. Work in New Zealand has shown that Māori children with disabilities can be overlooked and are sometimes excluded from special education provisions (Bevan-Brown 2006). Exclusion from decision-making was a feature of colonisation of Indigenous peoples in countries such as Australia and New Zealand. Therefore, an important part of a decolonising strategy for Indigenous children with disabilities is their strong inclusion in decision-making about what is culturally appropriate for them.

Just as children's understandings of themselves and others are mediated by their gender, they are also mediated by their sense of their own capacities and abilities and how others see these. So the process of children building 'racial' gender identities mingles in complex ways with their sense of their own abilities and how others see these. Again, this means it is important for staff to recognise that one of the key discourses of colonisation was to see those who were colonised as inferior and less capable than their white European colonisers. This is important because current research shows an overrepresentation of ethnic minority groups in special education services in several countries, including Australia and the USA (O'Conner and Ferdandez 2006). According to Chamberlain (2005), misreading the behaviour of ethnic minority children and mis-assessing their abilities is problematic for many reasons. However, within the context of this chapter it is problematic because of the ways in which it reinforces colonial stereotypes about specific ethnic groups. As Chamberlain (2005) argues:

> Overrepresentation is not only problematic for individual students but also for cultural groups, in that it maintains stereotypes about specific groups' educational abilities. (p. 195)

Reflecting on decolonising techniques

1 Define decolonisation in your own words.
2 What are the connections between colonisation and decolonisation?
3 What is the third space?
5 Identify five ways in which you could encourage children to uncover their understandings about 'racial' diversity. Would these be appropriate for children of all ages?
6 Identify five ways in which you could encourage children to share their understandings of power relationships in the use and management of space in your setting. Would these be appropriate for children of all ages?
7 What do you see as the main gender equity issues in decolonising relationships and meanings with children?
8 What do you see as the main 'race' equality issues in decolonising relationships and meanings with children?
9 How might decolonising concepts be used to support anti-discriminatory perspectives on disability?

Improving teaching in practice

1 Record (using a tape-recorder or written notes) several occasions on which you decolonise meaning with a small group of children.
2 What was your current style of decolonising? How and how well did you encourage children to find a third space in making their identities in the classroom?
3 How and how well did you take account of developmental and equity considerations?
4 What are your areas of strength and weakness in using decolonising to promote children's learning?
5 How can you improve your decolonising techniques in practice?
6 What do you see as the hardest part of improving your decolonising techniques?

FURTHER READING
Theoretical background

Cannella, G.S. and Viruru, R. 2004, *Childhood and Postcolonization: Power, Education, and Contemporary Practice*, Routledge Taylor and Francis Group, New York.

Gupta, A. 2006, *Early Childhood Education, Postcolonial Theory and Teaching Practices in India: Balancing Vygotsky and the Veda*, Palgrave Macmillan, New York.

MacNaughton, G. 2005, *Doing Foucault in Early Childhood Studies,* Routledge, London and New York [refer to Chapter 5].

Smith, L.T. 1999, *Decolonizing Methodologies: Research and Indigenous Peoples,* University of Otago Press, Dunedin, New Zealand.

Viruru, R. 2001, *Early Childhood Education: Postcolonial Perspectives from India,* Sage, New Delhi.

Children and pedagogy

Asher, T. 2005, 'At the interstices: engaging postcolonial and feminist perspectives for a multicultural education pedagogy in the South', *Teachers College Record,* 107(5), pp. 1079–1106.

Cave, L., King, S. and Guigni, M. 2005, 'Chromatics: a whiter shade of pink', *International Journal of Equity and Innovation in Early Childhood,* 3(1), pp. 31–49.

Skattebol, J. 2003, 'Dark, darker and darker: negotiations of identity in an early childhood setting', *Contemporary Issues in Early Childhood,* 4(2), pp. 149–166.

——2005, 'Insider/outside belongings: traversing the borders of whiteness in early childhood', *Contemporary Issues in Early Childhood,* 6(2), pp. 189–203.

ONLINE AND MULTIMEDIA RESOURCES

Text

Colombo, M. 2005, 'Reflections from teachers of culturally diverse children', *Young Children—Beyond the Journal,* online PDF: **http://www.journal.naeyc.org/btj/200511/ColomboBTJ1105.pdf**

Hotep, U. 2003, *Decolonizing the African Mind: Further Analysis and Strategy,* Kwame Ture Youth Leadership Institute:

http://www.nbufront.org/html/FRONTalView/ArticlesPapers/Hotep_DecolonizingAfricanMind.html

Noon, D., 'Decolonising education: borderland'. Active blog by a teacher exploring on how to decolonise his classroom: **http://borderland.northernattitude.org/2006/05/08/decolonizing-education**

Online centre for the study of migrant education and labour. Good resources on decolonising pedagogies: **http://www.decolonizing.com**

Multimedia

Centre for Equity and Innovation in Early Childhood (CEIEC) 2006, *Cultural Diversity Resource* (DVD), University of Melbourne. Several video clips and exercises exploring decolonising ideas and practices available from: **http://www.edfac.unimelb.edu.au/CEIEC** (or email **education-ceiec@unimelb.edu.au**)

'Homi K. Bhabha: discussing the potentials of cultural heritage in Austria' (video), scope II, interview before the *Sites & Subjects: Narrating Heritage* conference, 12 July, 2006, Austria. A pre-conference interview in which he focused on what is meant by cultural heritage: **http://www.youtube.com/watch?v=8AhDyvl08_Q**

Several video clips and exercises exploring decolonising ideas and practices available from: **http://www.edfac.unimelb.edu.au/CEIEC**

REFERENCES

Aboud, F.E. and Doyle, A.B. 1996, 'Does talk of race foster prejudice or tolerance in children?', <http://www.cpa.ca/cjbsnew/1996/ful_aboud.html> (accessed 1 December 1997).

Ashcroft, W., Griffiths, G. and Tiffin, H. (eds.) 1989, *The Empire Writes Back: Theory And Practice in Post-Colonial Literatures, New Accents,* Routledge, London.

Baker-Sperry, L. and Grauerholz, L. 2003, 'The pervasiveness and persistence of the feminine beauty ideal in children's fairy stories', *Gender and Society,* 17(5), 711–726.

Bernstein, J., Zimmerman, T., Werner-Wilson, R. and Vosberg, J. 2000, 'Preschool children's classification skills and a multicultural education intervention to promote acceptance of ethnic diversity', *Journal of Research in Childhood Education*, 14(2), pp. 181–193.

Bevan-Brown, J. 2006, 'Beyond policy and good intentions', *International Journal of Inclusive Education*, 10(2/3), pp. 221–234.

Bhabha, H. 1994, *The Location of Culture*, Routledge, New York.

Bhabha, H. 1990, 'Introduction: narrating the nation', in H. Bhabha, ed., *Nation and Narration*, Routledge and Keegan Paul, New York.

Centre for Equity and Innovation in Early Childhood (CEIEC) 2007, *Cultural Diversity Resource: A CD ROM*, University of Melbourne, <http://www.edfac.unimelb.edu.au/CEIEC>

Chamberlain, S. 2005, 'Recognizing and responding to cultural differences in the education of culturally and linguistically diverse learners', *Intervention in School and Clinic*, 40(4), pp. 195–211.

Chinweizu 1987, *Decolonising the African Mind*, Pero Publishers, Lagos.

Colombo, M. 2005, 'Reflections from teachers of culturally diverse children', *Young Children—Beyond the Journal*, online PDF: <http://www.journal.naeyc.org/btj/200511/ColomboBTJ1105.pdf>

Cruz, M. 2006, Transcript from Centre for Equity and Innovation in Early Childhood (CEIEC), *Cultural Diversity Resource* (DVD), University of Melbourne.

Davis, K. 2006, 'Troubling practice: exploring white dichotomies in early childhood practices', *International Journal of Equity and Innovation in Early Childhood*, 3(1), pp. 18–29.

DeLeon, A. 2007, 'Beware of 'Black' the Ripper: racism, representation, and building an antiracist pedagogy', *Journal of Social Studies*, November/December, pp. 263–267.

Fumoto, H., Hargreaves, D. and Maxwell, S. 2007, 'Teachers' perceptions of their relationships with children who speak English as an additional language in early childhood settings', *Journal of Early Childhood Research*, 5(2), pp. 135–153.

Gandhi, L. 1998, *Postcolonial Theory: A Critical Introduction*, Allen & Unwin, Sydney.

Gillborn, D. 2005, 'Education policy as an act of white supremacy: whiteness, critical race theory and education reform', *Journal of Education Policy*, 20(4), pp. 485–505.

Gorski, P. 2007, 'Good intentions are not enough: a decolonizing intercultural education', <http://www.EdChange.org> (accessed 13 September 2007).

Heale, J. and O'Brien, E. 2007, *Race, Ethnicity, and Gender: Selected Readings*, Sage Publications, New York, London and New Delhi.

Holt, L. 2007, '"Be the change you want to see" (Mahatma Gandhi)', *International Journal of Equity and Innovation in Early Childhood*, 5(1), pp. 4–11.

Hotep, U. 2003, *Decolonizing the African Mind: Further Analysis and Strategy*, Kwame Ture Youth Leadership Institute, <http://www.nbufront.org/html/FRONTalView/ArticlesPapers/Hotep_DecolonizingAfricanMind.html>

Hotep, U. and Hotep, T. (eds) 2003, *Dictionary of African-centered Knowledge*, KTYLI, Pittsburgh, PA.

Hughes, J., Bigler, S. and Levy, S. 2007, 'Consequences of learning about historical racism among European American and African American children', *Child Development*, 78(6), pp. 1689–1705.

Kaomea, J. 2001, 'Dilemmas of an Indigenous academic: a Native Hawaiian story', *Contemporary Issues in Early Childhood*, 2(1), pp. 67–82.

Leonardo, Z. 2002, 'The souls of white folk: critical pedagogy, whiteness studies, and globalization discourse', *Race Ethnicity and Education*, 5(1), pp. 29–50.

MacNaughton, G. and Davis, K. 2001, 'Beyond "othering": rethinking approaches to teaching young Anglo-Australian children about Indigenous Australians', *Contemporary Issues in Early Childhood*, 2(1), pp. 83–93.

Madole, K.L. and Roth, M.A. 2000, 'Cross-racial identification and categorization in infancy', Paper presented at the *International Conference of Infant Studies*, 16–19 July, Brighton, UK.

Nelson, C.A. 2001, 'The development and neural bases of face recognition', *Infant and Child Development*, 10, March–June, pp. 3–18.

O'Conner, C. and Ferdandez, S. 2006, 'Race, class, and disproportionality: reevaluating the relationship between poverty and special education placement', *Educational Researcher*, 35(6), pp. 6–11.

Orr, J., Paul, J. and Paul, S. 2002, 'Decolonizing Mi'kmaw education through cultural practical knowledge', *McGill Journal of Education*, 37(3), pp. 331–353.

Pyke, K. and Johnson, D. 2003, 'Asian American women and racialised femininities: "doing" gender across cultural worlds', *Gender and Society*, 17(1), pp. 33–53.

Rutland, A., Cameron, L. Bennett, L. and Ferrell, J. 2005, 'Interracial contact and racial constancy: a multi-site study of racial intergroup bias in 3–5 year old Anglo-British children', *Journal of Applied Developmental Psychology*, 26(6), pp. 699–713.

Said, E. 1978, *Orientalism*, Vintage Books, New York.

Sanacore, J. 2004, 'Genuine caring and literacy learning for African American Children: educators who provide a caring environment that fosters literacy learning also increase the chances for African American children to lead successful academic and personal lives', *The Reading Teacher*, 57, pp. 774–753.

Skattebol, J. 2003, 'Dark, darker and darker: negotiations of identity in an early childhood setting', *Contemporary Issues in Early Childhood*, 4(2), pp. 149–166.

——2005, 'Insider/outside belongings: traversing the borders of whiteness in early childhood', *Contemporary Issues in Early Childhood*, 6(2), pp. 189–203.

Srinivassan, P. 2006, 'The inclusion of linguistic diversity in early childhood', *International Journal of Equity and Innovation in Early Childhood*, 4(2), pp. 104–114.

Thésése, G. 2006, 'A tool of massive erosion: scientific knowledge in the neo colonial enterprise', in G.S. Dei, and A. Kempf, eds, *Anti-Colonialism and Education: The Politics of Resistance,* Sense Publishers, Rotterdam.

Viruru, R. 2001, 'Colonised through language: the case of early childhood education', *Contemporary Issues in Early Childhood*, 2(1), pp. 31–47.

——2007, 'Resisting resistance in postcolonial theory: implications for the study of childhood', *International Journal of Equity and Innovation in Early Childhood*, 5(1), pp. 37–57.

Wohlwend, K. 2006, 'I am not an American girl: resisting discourses of agency, innocence and patriotism', *International Journal of Equity and Innovation in Early Childhood*, 4(1), pp. 48–62.

Chapter 22

Deconstructing

Construct: to put together substances or parts, assemble.
(*Collins Dictionary of the English Language*, p. 323)

De: prefix, removal of or from something specified. Reversal of something.
(*Collins Dictionary of the English Language*, p. 381)

To a deconstructionist, meaning includes what is left out of the text or ignored or silenced by it.
(*Columbia Electronic Encyclopedia* 2003, online)

Deconstruction, or putting a concept or a word under erasure, is a political act. It reveals the generally invisible but repressive politics of any particular forms of representation.
(Davies 1993, p. 8)

What?

Deconstruction is a specialist term that has not entered into everyday language to any large extent. However, we can understand the broad meaning of the term by looking at its two parts—'de-' (implies reversal or removal) and '-construct' (meaning to put something together). To *de*-construct something is to take it apart, to 'unconstruct' it. In social theory deconstruction refers to the process of taking apart concepts and meanings.

More specifically, deconstruction is a form of critical thinking about social relations that involves questioning the meanings of words or concepts that normally go unquestioned. According to Alloway (1995, p. 106) it is '. . . a form of analysis which exposes the multiplicity of possible meanings, contradictions and assumptions underlying our understandings and ways of knowing'. Deconstructionism exposes the internal contradictions in particular systems of thought (Weiner 1994), and in doing so helps us question who benefits, and how, from particular taken-for-granted understandings of our social world. As such, it helps us examine the power relations that can be created and maintained through our ways of thinking and knowing. In other words, it can be used to help us understand the politics of the daily world. It also serves to remind us of those politics and our part in creating and re-creating them through the decisions we choose to take or not to take:

Every decision involves potentially endless levels of choice which we can contrive to forget or conceal but which deconstruction is always ready to uncloak. We are responsible for those decisions in a most extreme way. We have a responsibility for our decisions that the world cannot excuse since the world is, itself, an outcome of our deciding so to take it. (Parker 1997, p. 144)

As a teaching strategy, deconstruction can be used to help children take apart what is fair or not fair in the world and to understand the politics of their day-to-day relations with each other and in the world around them. It is, therefore, a teaching strategy that is suitable for those early childhood staff wishing to implement anti-discriminatory or anti-bias perspectives in their work with children.

Issues and debates

THEORETICAL BACKGROUND

JACQUES DERRIDA AND THE THEORY OF DECONSTRUCTIONISM

The process of deconstruction derives from the work of a French poststructuralist language theorist called Jacques Derrida (1930–). For Derrida, meaning in language is ruled by the principle of 'differance'. This principle declares that meaning in language can never be finally fixed, that there is no final meaning we can give to any one word. Meaning depends on differences between words and images (signifiers), and so can only be relational, not essential or inherent. Meaning is constantly in a process of deferral (differance) to the moment when new meanings are constructed. These new meanings are constructed through changing relations of difference between signifiers that are de/ reconstructed.

Within much modernist thought, notions of differences between signifiers rely on dichotomies (sharp divisions into two) and binary (paired) oppositions. To illustrate, the meaning of gender is constructed through dichotomies such as male and female, or boy and girl. There are seen to be sharp divisions between male and female. The difference in meaning between girl and boy relies on this sharp division. We know a girl is a girl because a girl cannot be a boy. In addition, meaning is constructed through pairing girl and boy and seeing them as opposite to each other. They form, in Derrida's terms, a binary opposition. We cannot understand what a girl is without the concept of a boy. Boy and girl are binary opposites, and each side of the opposition depends on the other for its meaning.

In other words, 'binary opposites' are 'binary intimates': without 'wrong', 'right' has no meaning, and the same is the case for 'male' and 'female', 'good' and 'bad', 'rich' and 'poor'. Modernism tends to seek final, fixed meanings for words (images etc.) through these oppositions. We can finally fix the meaning of male because it is paired with female, it is the opposite of female and there are clearly known sharp divisions between them. Everything male is obviously so because it is not female.

By fixing the meaning of words in this way Derrida argued that an equally fixed and equally final 'Other' is created. A pair always has two, one part of the pair therefore always has an 'Other'. You cannot have meaning without having the opposite or the 'Other'. The 'Other' for female is always male and the 'Other' for good is always bad. *For Derrida, binary oppositions always contain within themselves the impossibility of a definitive 'Other'*. The meaning of the 'Other' is always capable of deconstruction and therefore is never finally fixed.

The importance of understanding binary oppositions and their 'Other' is that they are often organised hierarchically. The pairs are not equal. The 'Other' is not equal to the main part of the pair. The pairs are always ranked in some way that gives one part of the pair a higher order or place in the ranking. In other words, within the binary opposition, some meanings are privileged (given advantages and status) and some meanings are given the lesser status of 'Otherness'.

In other words, using binary oppositions places some meanings in a secondary and subordinate position. Think of the following pairs of words:

- man/woman
- white/black
- straight/gay
- slim/fat.

In each of these pairs we know what each part of the pair means because it is opposite to the other. Slim people are not fat. Slim is the opposite of fat. In each of these pairs the first word is often given more status or advantage in our society. For instance, being a man holds more status than being a woman. However, this status is not inherent in the word and thus not inevitable or accidental. It is socially determined and constructed. The part of a binary opposition that assigned the secondary and subordinate position of 'Other' is also socially constructed. For example, in our society in the binary opposition of man and woman the secondary and subordinate position is given to 'woman'. Woman is not inherently secondary and subordinate to man; we socially determine and construct this subordination.

Deconstruction is about showing how pairs gain their meanings from each other, how one word (meaning) has more advantage and status than the other and how this advantage is not inevitable but socially decided. So, the aim in deconstructing meanings is to show the relations of power between the binary oppositions and to show '. . . that the privileged term derives its position from a suppression or curtailment of its opposite or other' (Grosz 1990, p. 95). Deconstructing (taking apart) binary oppositions is done by showing that each side depends on the other ('Other') for its meaning. Binary oppositions create hierarchical polarities (Derrida 2004).

For example, the meaning of the word beauty comes from the way in which it is paired with ugly (in binary opposition to ugly). It is only possible to have a meaning for beauty if we have a meaning for not beautiful (ugly). Once we identify the word that is paired with beauty to give its meaning we know its 'Other'. Once we know a word's 'Other' we understand what is seen as secondary and subordinate in our social world. When we understand that the 'Other' to beautiful is ugly we can see that being ugly will be secondary and subordinate to being beautiful if this opposition is maintained. By doing away with binary oppositions, new meanings and new desires become possible. Hence, if we see woman and man as linked rather than opposite, a third gender of woman/man becomes possible and thus desirable. Or, if we turn the binary opposition on its head, we could make woman a more advantaged meaning than man.

Derrida believed that finding the 'Other' involves taking a particular word or concept and using reversal or displacement to create a new term, a double-edged word which Derrida calls a 'hinge word' (Derrida 2004). Thus, reversing the binary opposition between beautiful and ugly involves giving ugly the privileged position, and creating a new term involves hinging them to show their links rather than their opposition. The hinge word becomes ugly/beauty. A new word, such as a hinge word, makes new meanings possible.

The aim in deconstruction is '. . . not so much to demonstrate the errors, flaws, and contradictions in texts, but...to reveal the necessity with which what a text says is bound up with what it cannot say' (Grosz 1990, p. 97). Identifying what is not said involves looking at what knowledge is privileged within the text/discourse using two Derridian concepts: of difference/'differance' and the notion of 'Otherness'. Through this process we come to create new meanings that can challenge the current relations of power within our ways of understanding the world. Deconstruction is tied to a politics of possibilities as it offers us ways to imagine new ways and to 'continuously wonder other forms of knowledge' (Hyun 2001, p. 24) and build an 'ethics of resistance' (Lenz Taguchi 2007, p. 275) to what oppresses, constrains and creates injustices.

How?

Deconstruction is a complex and sophisticated process based on critical thinking about our language and the ways in which it constructs and constricts meaning for us. Language not only makes it possible to give meaning to our world, it also limits how we give meaning to it. The aim with deconstruction is to show how language limits meaning, explore in whose interests these limits are and open up the possibility of new meanings. For example, the aim is to show how the ways in which pairs of words are linked, in particular how their linking privileges one word, limits how we understand the world. By making new pairs and changing the ranking within pairs we can make new meanings.

It is possible at a very simple level to begin to help children grasp the idea that language both creates and constricts meaning. They can begin to think about how words are paired and how the ranking of words within pairs gives some meanings more power or status.

Staff can begin to deconstruct social meaning in language with young children through encouraging them to put their current meanings under question, to explore how these meanings limit their desires and understandings, to expand the meanings they have, to imagine new language and hence new meanings, and to think about the political implications of their meanings. The following points identify some of the specific developmental abilities of babies, toddlers and preschoolers that relate to their capacity for self-expression and indicate how staff can take account of these capabilities in their teaching:

- Question children's meanings of words or concepts that are key to their understandings of social relationships. Get children to identify pairs and ranking within pairs of words that are important to their understanding of social relationships. These words or concepts might be present in their everyday language, in the stories they read or in the popular media they watch. How do the children understand what it means to be poor, rich, male or Vietnamese? Zammit (1994) suggests asking children what words make them see and feel.

> Despina works with a group of four-year-old children at a centre in Footscray, a suburb in Melbourne with a high immigrant population. She is having a discussion with the children about what it means to be rich and poor. Despina asks the children a series of questions such as: 'What does being rich mean?'; 'What does being poor mean?'; 'Who is rich?'; 'If you're rich, how are you different?'; 'What other words could we use to describe poor?'. She listens carefully to the children's answers and uses these to extend children's thinking and to help the children begin to deconstruct their notions of poor and rich.
>
> ---
>
> *Reflection point:* What other meanings might it be relevant for Despina to deconstruct with children in her specific context?

- Question if children's meanings are the only meanings possible. Are there other ways of understanding what it means to be, for example, poor, rich, male, Vietnamese? Turning the ranking in pairs upside down or linking a word in the pair in new ways can help this process. Staff can present children with images, ideas and stories that show them ways of understanding that are different to their own: 'What happens when poor is seen as having more status than rich?'; 'When and why might it be good to be poor?'; 'What things do poor people do better than rich people?'. Such questions help children to begin to understand the idea of what Jacques Derrida (see above) called the 'Other'—that is, the marginalised or silenced meanings that are possible within a word or concept.
- Expand the meanings that children are prepared to consider. Staff can use children's playful approach to language to encourage them to make up their own hinge words and think about what they might mean. For example, staff wanting to talk with children about being male and female could encourage them to think of a word for someone who is like a girl and like a boy. What could they call this person? What would they be like?
- Explore with the children how different meanings lead to taken-for-granted assumptions about each other, especially how they limit what children consider possible for themselves and for others. Talk with the children about the meaning of how we act and how we expect others to act if we talk about

good people. How does being good limit what we do? What does it mean about how we expect stories to end, what games we expect to play with each other, who we expect to be friends with, what we think other people can do and enjoy doing? How different would it be if we talked about good/bad people? What would a good/bad person be like? What could we call them? Would a bad person be limited in the same ways as a good person? What could they do differently?

Three-year-old children at the Lupin Centre are concerned with fairness. Their teacher Hisham has noticed the frequent cry of 'it's not fair' when a group of children dominate the home corner and get to play with the new equipment. Hisham has a discussion with the children about fairness. She asks them to say what they think fairness is and leads them through a series of questions which challenge their notion that fair means everyone gets the same all the time.

Reflection point: What are three questions could Hisham use to help the children begin to deconstruct fairness?

- Look with the children at who benefits from specific taken-for-granted assumptions. This involves getting them to think about who might feel sad, hurt or angry by the understandings we have. Who might feel sad if we expect all good people to do certain things? Which children might be happy with this? What does it mean for children who are not good? Who will be their friends?
- Talk with the children about who has the power to decide who is good and what good means. Children can think about who creates word pairs, who can change them and what would happen if they tried to change the meanings within a pair. For example, what would happen if they tried to make a new dictionary or a new language? Who would listen to them? Where could they go? What would they be stopped from doing? Talk to the children about the extent to which it is fair, or not fair, that some people control meaning-making. Work with the children to think about who gets their way because of the assumptions we have about others, and who does not? Is this fair? Is it unfair? Which meanings seem fair, which seem unfair? Would it be fairer if they used their new words to describe people rather than the usual words?

By way of illustration, if staff wanted to work with children to deconstruct (take apart) the class politics of their relations with each other they would need to develop ways of:

- uncovering children's meanings of being rich or being poor
- talking with the children about how the words are paired and how they rank things that happen within this pairing
- offering children alternative meanings of being rich or being poor
- encouraging children to think about new words that include rich and poor in describing people
- examining with the children the assumptions they have about what it means to be rich or poor
- exploring with the children who benefits from assumptions they have about being rich and being poor
- talking with the children about the extent to which their understandings mean that rich people have most power and the extent to which this is fair, or not fair. Would alternative meanings be fairer?

To accomplish these tasks with children staff will need to use a variety of general teaching techniques such as questioning (Chapter 13) and specialist teaching techniques such as co-constructing (Chapter 19), problem-solving (Chapter 27) and task analysis (Chapter 30).

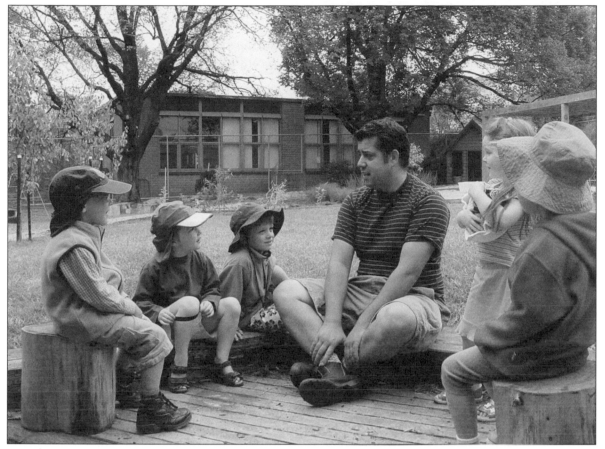

Dom and the children discuss fairness.

When and why?

GOAL RELEVANCE

Deconstruction can be used to help children understand the politics of their day-to-day relations with each other and in the world about them. This may include the gender, 'race', class and disability politics of their daily life and the world about them. Deconstruction can be used to:

- examine the politics (power relationships) present in children's relationships with each other to imagine other possibilities
- examine the politics in the stories they read to imagine other possibilities
- examine the politics in the images about them to imagine other possibilities
- examine the politics of the knowledge in the world about them and imagine other ways to understand and value different forms of knowledge
- examine the politics in current events in their local community to imagine other possibilities
- examine the politics in television programs and videos they watch to imagine other possibilities.

This helps children to think more critically about their relationships and the world around them, and helps them imagine a fairer world in which there is respect for diversity. Some specific strategies staff could use follow.

Examine the politics (power relationships) present in children's relationships with each other to imagine other possibilities

Staff could use the following questions to decide if relationships between the children and between the children and the curriculum offered might be in need of deconstruction:

- Who has access to specific areas of the curriculum because of what they know or the language they have?
- Whose voices do you listen to most?
- Whose voices do you seem to not hear?
- Who is engaged in specific areas of the curriculum?
- How do the children show respect for each other?
- Who co-operates with each other? What are the effects of their co-operation for other children? (adapted from McMillan 2001; MacNaughton 2000)

These questions can be re-formed and put to the children to begin discussions with them about what happens currently, what is fair or not fair in that, and what else might be possible:

- What things do you like to do most?
- What things are hardest for you?
- What things are tricky to do?
- Who listens to you most?
- Who doesn't listen to you?
- Who has special places?
- Who do you play with?
- Who would you like to play with?
- Are there any places you can't play?

Using questions to begin talking with children about what's fair or not fair about what they share with you and how else you might do things can help staff to begin to deconstruct with children.

Examine the politics in the stories they read to imagine other possibilities

To engage children in a critical examination of the politics of the stories they read, they will need to have access to books that present different perspectives and contradictory perspectives on a particular topic or issue (Swindler Boutte 2002). For instance, to explore gender expectations and possibilities with children around the topic of what boys do and don't like, it would be helpful to have books that show boys who do and don't like to play with dolls, dress-ups, etc. These books should be read to the children more than once so that they can become familiar with the story and its messages and then staff can begin to analyse these critically with children. Swindler Boutte (2002) offers helpful guidance on how to approach critical discussions about books with children. She suggests:

- using probing questions to explore with children what they liked and didn't like about it, what sounded the same as they thought and what was different
- reading different versions of the same story by changing endings, feelings, etc. of the characters. Children can be encouraged to do this and to take different roles in the story and imagine different ways for the story to develop.

These strategies open children up to multiple perspectives on the same topic, and enable them to play with different approaches and ideas and to experiment with changing meanings and narratives. As they do this they can begin to imagine other possibilities and become critical meaning-makers in their own lives:

Zeta, a teacher in a prep grade class in a middle-class suburb of Melbourne, searches the library for books that show men and women in stereotypical roles. She uses these books as a starting point for discussions about the politics of gender with the children. She challenges the assumptions portrayed in the books with the children and encourages them to think of different ways of presenting roles of men and women.

Reflective task: Find three books that you could use with young children to deconstruct gender role stereotypes in your context.

Examine the politics in the images about them to imagine other possibilities

Staff can also use other tools such as digital cameras to begin a process of deconstruction with children. Children can be asked to take photographs of when they think children are enjoying playing/working and/ or having a hard time, or photos of things that happen that are not fair. These can then be used to talk with individual children and small groups of children about why these photos are not fair and how they would like to see things change. Photos can highlight diverse perspectives on classroom life and begin to engage children with the idea of multiple perspectives. This knowledge is central to a child's capacity to deconstruct and reconstruct the world and its meanings. As Whitin and Whitin (1998, p. 125) explained:

> One of the ways that learners can appreciate multiple perspectives is to understand that information can change in different contexts.

Using photos can also begin a discussion with children about what's fair or not fair about what they share with you and how else you might do things, and can help staff to begin to deconstruct with children.

Examine the politics in current events in their local community to imagine other possibilities

To act for fairness in the world we need to critically engage with the world. Young children have a capacity to act for fairness, and deconstruction can help them to engage critically with their world. Current events such as war, terrorism, violence, working for peace, standing up against racism, fighting for jobs and working for a sustainable environment offer staff events through which children can critically engage with their world. Campbell et al. (2002) described how an early childhood service engaged young children in critically examining what peace means as a way of building a peaceful and respectful community. It was a centre in which bullying and aggression between the children had become an issue. They decided to start by asking children what they thought a peaceful community looked like. Here is what some of the children had to say:

A peaceful world

There would be peace, grass, sea, birds, whales, lots of people, big birds, seeds around. The world for all the trees and plants, the sun and yellow seeds all around sprinkled for peace. (Ashika, age 5, November 2000)

If other people take your things you have to say peace, and other people will give it back. The house has windows to look out the house at grass or flowers and others playing peacefully. (Lily, age 5, September 2000)

The peace town

The world would look nice if there were only goodies in it and there wouldn't be any Hurt or any killing or anything Broken. There would be lots of pretty colours and everyone will feel happy and safe. They will laugh. Well sometimes. They try to be friendly and the world looks pretty and peaceful. There will be cats and dogs and little parrots and grass and sky and flowers and people. That's my favourite things if it's peaceful because it feels nice. (Lauren, age 4, February 2001)

A peaceful world
Our world would have people. I like all people. I like animals and I like butterflies too and giraffes and elephants. There will be schools and kinders and creches. (Gabriel, age 3, March 2001)

Children, staff and parents discussed and represented their understandings of peace to each other and in doing so brought forth multiple and diverse perspectives on peace that enabled those involved to imagine what a peaceful world might look like in their own service and how aggression and bullying got in the way of peace.

Examine the politics in television programs and videos they watch to imagine other possibilities
Popular culture is rich with examples of the politics of relationships in children's worlds. Children's understandings of and responses to popular culture can offer staff and children a pleasurable starting point for deconstructing cultural meanings with young children. Grace and Tobin (1997) highlight how the exploration of popular culture in primary school classrooms can disrupt the privileging of teacher knowledge in the classroom and in doing so expand the range of meanings and forms of pleasure that are articulated and circulate within a classroom. This is particularly so if the children control the conditions under which the meanings are produced and circulated. Grace and Tobin (1997, pp 165–166) described how student video production can achieve this:

> When popular culture is brought into the curriculum, lines are crossed between high and low (culture), the official and unofficial (curriculum), the authoritative discourses of the school and the internally persuasive discourses of children…Our goal, therefore, should be to validate the popular culture interests of children without appropriating them. Student video production provides an arena for this to occur.

Student videos could provide a rich and extensive source of discussion about how they and other children and adults see what is fair and not fair in their lives and why.

DEVELOPMENTAL CONSIDERATIONS
Deconstruction is a teaching technique that relies on symbolic language, so it is suitable to use with children who have reached this stage in their language development and who have the ability to talk about what words mean. Deconstruction is therefore most likely to be suitable to use with older preschool children and children in the early years of school who are able to use the language(s) spoken by adults in the classroom. However, it is important to note that deconstruction is about critical meaning-making and that all children have the capacity and the desire to make meaning about their world and themselves.

Equity considerations

'RACE' AND CULTURE
Staff can teach children to deconstruct (take apart) their understanding of 'racial' and cultural stereotypes. To do this staff need to:

- uncover children's 'racial' meanings. For example, what meanings do the children give to being black or white?
- offer children alternative 'racial' meanings
- examine with children their 'racial' assumptions and who benefits from these. For example, what assumptions do they have about what it means to be black or white and who benefits?
- talk with children about the extent to which their understandings mean that some people have more power than other people. For example, do their understandings mean that black people or white

people have more power? Encourage the children to think about the extent to which this is fair, not fair and whether alternative understandings are fairer.

Tiger Woods, a young black golf pro, has won several prestigious golf tournaments. This is significant for many black people in the United States, who are still excluded from some golf courses. Several of the children have been talking about Tiger Woods and how 'cool' he is. David brings the newspaper to his second grade class and uses the headline as a starting point for the children to discuss what it means for a young black person in America to win a well-known tournament. David extends the discussion from the particular to a general talk about power and privilege in the USA. He talks with the children about how fair life is there for black people and if all black people live the same sorts of lives. He also talks about what is common in the lives of black people in the USA. He plans to use this to extend children's understandings about 'race', power and privilege in Australia.

Reflection point: What contemporary black celebrities do your children know?

To illustrate how staff can approach these tasks we will look at how they might encourage children to deconstruct their ideas about Native Americans. We have chosen this topic because stereotypes about Native Americans still abound in the Australian context. They can still be seen in children's games of 'Cowboys and Indians' as well as in children's literature (often in alphabet books where 'I' is for 'Indian'), and there are also several centres that have 'Indian' dress-up clothes available for the children. While Australian children have been playing this game for many decades, the release of the Disney film *Pocahontas* revived this. In this revival many negative stereotypes about Native Americans were re-created and reinforced. These stereotypes that still exist were summarised by York (1991, p. 170) in the following way:

Native Americans: take scalps, have red skin, use tepees as houses, speak in grunts, wear feathers and costumes, ride horses, don't live now.

These stereotypes are often created and re-created through children's literature. Common stereotypes include the idea that male Native Americans are 'savage, hostile warriors; drunken thieves; evil medicine men; loyal brave followers; lazy unemployed loafers' (Smardo Dowd 1992, p. 221) and female Native Americans are 'either heavyset, workhorse squaws or Indian princesses' (Smardo Dowd 1992, p. 221). Such stereotypes ignore the current and historical diversity and richness of the lives and lifestyles of Native Americans. As Reese (1996, p. 2) reminds us:

The term 'Native American' includes over 500 different groups and reflects great diversity of geographic location, language, socioeconomic conditions, school experience, and retention of traditional spiritual and cultural practices.

To begin to deconstruct stereotypes about Native Americans with young children, staff could:

- Question children's meanings of words or concepts that are key to their understandings of Native Americans. Ask the children what the following words make them see and feel: Indian, Red Indian, cowboys, savages. What words do they pair with them? One four-year-old child was asked by her mother who Indians are and the responses included the following:

'Indians eat animals like elephants and deer.'
'Indians don't wear any clothes and they don't wear underwear. They just wear cloths over their butts.'
'Indians wear feathers and they kill people.'
'Indians live in stick houses.' (Brady and Bisson 1995, p. 19)

The four-year-old told her mother she had learned these things about Native Americans from the film *Pocahontas*. Realising how children make sense of the words they know helps staff to see what meanings they need to explore further to challenge them.

- Offer children alternative understandings of what it means to be Native American. To do this, staff need to build their own knowledge base of the historical and contemporary ways of Native Americans. Reese (1996) offers some ways of doing this.
- Explore with children how their meanings about being Native American lead to taken-for-granted assumptions. For example, talk with them about how people react if they think that Native Americans 'wear feathers and kill people'. Do we want to be with people who wear feathers and kill people? Do we think that all people who wear feathers kill people? How would you feel if you met a Native American Indian wearing feathers? Would you want to be friends? What else might we expect a Native American to wear or to do?
- Explore with children how their ideas about Native Americans influence how we expect stories to end, what games we expect to play with each other, who we expect to be friends with, what we think other people can do and enjoy doing. The following extract from Brady and Bisson (1995, p. 19) shows how children's games can be influenced by the meanings they give to the word 'Indian' and how these meanings are influenced by films such as *Pocahontas*. Chris had seen the movie three times:

> One morning two-and-a-half-year-old (European American) Chris came in wearing a headband with a feather in the back. One of the teachers greeted Chris at the door with a 'Hi Chris!'. Chris' response was to furrow his brow, cross his arms, and in an angry, loud voice shout 'No! I'm an Indian', and run away 'growling'. . . Later, when a teacher asked Chris about who Indians are, he replied 'They shoot bows and arrows and they shoot people.' The teacher . . . asked, 'What else?' to which he replied, 'That's all.' Then the teacher asked, 'Well, do Indians go to the grocery store?' Chris answered, 'No' . . . 'Do they go to school?' Chris emphatically responded, 'No! It's too expensive'. (Brady and Bisson 1995, p. 19)

To deconstruct Chris' understandings of being a Native American would involve taking the discussion further to explore the implications of his views. His teacher could ask him to think about what games he expects to play with other children about being Indian, who might want to be his friends and play these games, what he thinks Indian people can do and enjoy doing. These questions need to encourage Chris to think about the implications of his assertions about Indians. Questions such as: 'If Indians only shoot bows and arrows and shoot people, then is that the only game you can play if you are an Indian?'; 'Are there any other games you could play if you were an Indian?'; 'Who will be your friend if that is the only game you play as an Indian?'. Books that could help Chris' teacher extend his thinking about being Indian can be found in Jones and Moomaw 2002.

- Look with the children at who benefits from their specific taken-for-granted assumptions about Native Americans. This involves asking children: 'Who might feel sad, hurt or angry by the expectations we have?'; 'Who might feel sad if we expect all Native Americans to shoot bows and arrows and not wear clothes?'; 'Which Native Americans might be happy with this?'; 'What does it mean for the Native Americans who wear suits, jeans etc. and who go to the supermarket for their food?'; 'How would you feel about the idea that Indians shoot people if you were a Native American who went to school and shopped at the grocery store?'
- Talk with the children about who has power, and the extent to which this is fair or not fair. Staff need first to do their own research. They need to learn about what is fair or not fair about how Native American Indians are portrayed in books and films such as *Pocahontas*. There were many inaccuracies in the film that staff would need to know about to show how unfair the representations of Native Americans were. For example, *Pocahontas* was 11 years old at the time of the events in the movie, never kissed John Smith and did not look like the person in the film (Brady and Bisson 1995). Armed with accurate information, staff can encourage children to think about whether it is fair to have films made about people when they are not true and to think about who made the film. Did they make the film to tell the truth or to make money? Is it fair that people make money from films about Native Americans when they are not true?

Deconstructing children's ideas about Native Americans can take time. Children will need time to express and think about their own ideas. They will also need time to think about alternative ideas staff may present them with. The aim in deconstructing meanings with children is not to tell them what to think but to help them understand that the meanings they give to words such as 'Indian' have implications for their own play and how they feel about others, and that these implications may be unfair to other people.

GENDER

Staff can also work with children to deconstruct the gender politics of their relations with each other by:

- uncovering children's meanings of being a girl or boy
- offering children alternative meanings of being a girl or boy
- examining with children the assumptions they have about what it means to be a boy or girl
- exploring with children who benefits from assumptions they have about being boys and/or being girls
- talking with children about the extent to which their understandings mean that boys or girls have more power and the extent to which this is fair or not fair.

Davies (1989; 2003) argues that deconstructing gender relations with young children frees them from the constraints that current dominant understandings of gender place on children. She believes that children need to:

. . . have access to imagery in which new metaphors, new forms of social relations, and new patterns of power and desire are explored . . . and wonder how the social world could ever have been reduced to two types of people related to relatively minor pieces of anatomy. (Davies 1989, p. 141)

Teaching children to deconstruct their gender understandings and to thus imagine new ways of being male and female involves the same processes as teaching them to deconstruct their 'racial' understandings. To show what this might mean in practice we will draw on questions from Dally and Lindstrom (1996, p. 83) about how to help children deconstruct the gender meanings in toys. To do this staff can use the following questions:

- Question children's meanings of gender words or concepts associated with toys. Questions that might do this are: 'What are girls' toys and what are boys' toys?'; 'What toys do people buy for girls?'; 'What toys do people buy for boys?'
- Encourage children to think of other ways of thinking about toys for boys and girls. Questions that might do this are: 'Would people always buy the same types of toys for all girls?'; 'Would people always buy the same types of toys for all boys?'; 'What other types of toys might they buy?'
- Encourage children to find a name for toys that both boys and girls might enjoy. What would such toys be? What would they look like?
- Explore with children how the gender meanings around toys lead to taken-for-granted assumptions about boys and girls. For example, talk with the children about what it means for how we act and how we expect others to act if we think that all girls love dolls and all boys love train sets. What does it mean about what games we expect to play with each other, who we expect to be friends with, what we think other people can do and enjoy doing when people buy toys especially for girls or especially for boys?
- Look with the children at who benefits from their specific taken-for-granted assumptions about gender and toys. This involves getting children to think about who might feel sad, hurt or angry by the toys they are given. Who might feel sad if all boys are given a football to play with? Which boys might be happy with this? What does it mean for the boys who hate playing football? What will the girls or boys learn from the toys they are given? What can they do with them? What can't they do with them? What might boys miss

out on playing with and learning from their toys? What might girls miss out on playing with and learning from their toys?

- Talk with the children about who has power to choose toys and the extent to which this is fair, or not fair. Make the children think about who gets their way because of the assumptions we have about gender and toys, and who does not? Is this fair? Is it unfair? Who decides that boys should play with certain toys and girls with different toys? Is it fair that boys miss out on some toys? Is it fair that girls miss out on some toys?

There are a host of gender concepts that children can be encouraged to deconstruct in this way and through such deconstruction begin to imagine different ways of being a girl and being a boy. Dally and Lindstrom's (1996) suggestions about concepts and issues that children can deconstruct include rhymes and chants that give very 'gendered' messages about children (for example, 'Firecracker, firecracker' and 'King Kong'), dolls, advertisements for toys, stories about men and women in the news, and caring for babies.

DISABILITY AND ADDITIONAL NEEDS

Discriminatory and offensive ideas about disability can also be deconstructed. Staff can teach children to deconstruct their understanding of disability by:

- uncovering children's meanings of being disabled and not being disabled
- offering children alternative meanings of being disabled and not being disabled
- examining with children the assumptions they have about disability and ability
- exploring with children who benefits from their assumptions about disability
- talking with children about the extent to which their understandings of disability mean that people without disabilities have more power than those with disabilities, and the extent to which this is fair or not fair.

We will focus on the issue of beauty to explore how this might happen in practice. Images of beauty powerfully influence what we see as the best way to look. Children learn about what is beautiful from a variety of sources. From an early age children are entered into baby shows and 'Little Miss . . .' shows. These shows judge children against prevailing norms about what is a desirable way to look and so enforce these norms. Children learn that princesses are beautiful in traditional tales such as *Snow White* and *Sleeping Beauty* and that to be beautiful involves looking a particular way. Children also learn that models are beautiful and that real princesses are judged to be beautiful, as Princess Diana was.

In our society the dominant image of being beautiful to which young children are introduced totally excludes images of people with visible disabilities. Children with visible disabilities learn that they are not included in society's dominant concepts of beauty. This makes it hard for them to develop a positive sense of their own body. Children without visible disabilities construct their understanding of beauty in ways that exclude people with visible disabilities. Children who have parents who have a visible disability find their parents are not considered by the rest of society to be beautiful. This constructs for children an overall concept of people with disabilities as different, less valued and less valuable. As Hall (n.d., p. 73) reminds us:

> Prejudice and discrimination are based on appearance. People are judged not on their ability but on the way they look. Disabled people [often] look different from other people. The difference is caused by disability. Discrimination results when this difference triggers off the negative attitudes towards disability that are held by the other person.

One of the alternatives to being considered beautiful is to be considered ugly. This is a label that many people with visible disabilities have experienced.

He had called me ugly. There was more to beauty than wearing makeup and stockings, or the right clothes. I was ugly and not because my legs were too skinny, my bust undeveloped, or my face too plain. I was ugly because I was a disabled person. I was ugly and I would get uglier as my disability progressed. (Hall n.d., p. 68)

Deconstructing children's understandings of beauty and ugliness can contribute to reducing the experience that Lesley Hall described above. To deconstruct children's understandings of beauty and ugliness, staff would need to do the following:

- Question children's meanings of words or concepts associated with being beautiful and ugly. Questions that might do this are: 'Who do you see when you think about beautiful people?'; 'Who do you see when you think about ugly people?'
- Encourage children to think of other ways of thinking about beauty and ugliness. Questions that might do this are: 'What makes you like a person?'; 'Does a person have to look a certain way for you to like them?'; 'What sort of person makes a good friend?'; 'Can people with no legs be beautiful?'; 'Would people with no legs think people with legs are beautiful?'; 'Does beauty come from inside a person and how they feel and act or does it come from outside and how they look?'
- Explore with children how the meanings around being beautiful and being ugly lead to taken-for-granted assumptions about people. For example, talk with the children about what it means for how we act and how we expect others to act if we think that some people are ugly and some people are beautiful. What does it mean about those with whom we expect to be friends? What do we think other people can do and enjoy doing? Can we be friends with people we call ugly?
- Look with children at who benefits from their specific taken-for-granted assumptions about beauty and ugliness. This involves getting children to think about who might feel sad, hurt or angry by being called ugly. What do we miss out on if we make friends only with people who are beautiful? Why would we want to call people ugly?
- Talk with children about who has the power to decide who is beautiful and who is ugly, and the extent to which this is fair or not fair. Where do the children's ideas about being beautiful come from? Do you have to have a crown and lots of money to be beautiful?

There is a host of body image concepts that children can be encouraged to deconstruct in this way and through such deconstruction begin to imagine different ways of judging people. Concepts of body size, body shape, body weight and body style can all be explored in anti-discriminatory ways through deconstruction. Such explorations help children learn to respect physical diversity and to feel pride in their own body. Images from popular culture and advertising can also be used to engage children with multiple perspectives on body image as young children can understand the intentions underlying advertising by around seven to eight years of age (Moses and Baldwin 2005).

Reflecting on deconstructing techniques

1 Define deconstruction.
2 What does research suggest are the keys to using deconstruction to optimise children's learning?
3 When do you think deconstruction should be used in your teaching?
4 Are there any times when you think the use of deconstruction is inappropriate with young children?
5 Find one historical poster and one contemporary poster of Aboriginal and Torres Strait Islander people. How could you use these posters to deconstruct non-Aboriginal and Torres Strait Islander children's understandings of Aboriginal and Torres Strait Islander people? What questions might you ask? What research would you need to do to challenge any stereotypes that emerged?
6 What are some topics/ideas/concepts you could use to deconstruct negative stereotypes of people with disabilities?

7 'The fact is that while people, including young children, are thought of as fat by our society, the word fat is used only in disgust' (Whitney 1995, p. 8). How might you teach children to deconstruct the idea of fatness?

8 Find one television advertisement you could use with young children to deconstruct the idea that only mothers should care for babies.

9 Find one storybook about diverse family lifestyles you could use with young children to deconstruct the idea that all families have one mum and one dad.

Improving teaching in practice

1 Record (using a tape-recorder or written notes) an occasion on which you were deconstructing a social issue or idea with a small group of children.

2 What was your current style of deconstruction? Did you:

- question children's meanings of words or concepts that were the key to their understandings of social relationships?
- explore with the children how these meanings led to taken-for-granted assumptions about each other?
- look with the children at who benefited from specific taken-for-granted assumptions?
- talk with the children about who had power and the extent to which this was fair or not fair?

3 How and how well did you take account of developmental and equity considerations?

4 What are your areas of strength and weakness in using deconstruction to promote children's learning?

5 How can you improve your deconstruction techniques in practice?

6 What do you see as the hardest part of improving your deconstruction techniques?

FURTHER READING

Davies, B. 1993, *Shards of Glass: Children Reading and Writing beyond Gendered Identities*, Allen & Unwin, Sydney.

Lenz Taguchi, H. 2007, 'Deconstructing and transgressing the theory-practice dichotomy in early childhood education', *Educational Philosophy and Theory*, 39(3), pp. 275–290.

MacNaughton, G. 2005, *Doing Foucault in Early Childhood Studies*, Routledge, London and New York.

Nass, M. 2003, *Taking on the Tradition: Jacques Derrida and the Legacies of Deconstruction*, Stanford University Press, Stanford.

Rogers, R. and Christian, J. 2007, '"What could I say" A critical discourse analysis of the construction of race in children's literature', *Race, Ethnicity and Education*, 10(1), pp. 21–46.

Swindler Boutte, G. 2002, 'The critical literacy process: guidelines for examining books', *Childhood Education*, 78(3), pp. 147–152.

ONLINE AND MULTI-MEDIA RESOURCES

Text

Killen, M., 'Early Deliberations'. A developmental psychologist investigates how children think about fairness and exclusion. 'Teaching Tolerance' website: **http://www.tolerance.org/teach/printar.jsp?p=0&ar=322&pi=ttm**

'One family's fight against the binary system'. This webposting discusses ways in which a family is trying to deconstruct gender binaries with their child. It includes responses by others to this. Posted on *Babble: the magazine and community for a new generation of parents*: **http://www.babble.com/CS/blogs/strollerderby/archive/2007/04/11/gender-stereotypes-one-family-s-fight-against-the-binary-system.aspx**

Multi-media

'Presence Is Always Divided'—Derrida on deconstruction. YouTube video clip, 3 minutes: **http://www.youtube.com/watch?v=J1IScOonGMQ** (accessed 27 January 2007).

Jacques Derrida on the problematics of deconstruction, YouTube video clip, 4 minutes: **http://www.youtube.com/watch?v=w9YaNW7Q0c8** (accessed 27 January 2007).

REFERENCES

Alloway, N. 1995, *Foundation Stones: The Construction of Gender in Early Childhood*, Curriculum Corporation, Melbourne.

Brady, P. and Bisson, J. 1995, 'Disney's *Pocahontas* will haunt us: impact on young children and anti-bias opportunities', *The Web Journal: The Culturally Relevant Anti-Bias Early Childhood Educators Network*, 2(3), pp. 16–24.

Campbell, S., Coady, M., Castilino, T., Lawrence, H., MacNaughton, G., Page, J. and Rolfe, S. 2002, *Our Part in Peace*, Australian Early Childhood Association, Watson, ACT.

Columbia Encyclopedia 2003, *The Columbia Electronic Encyclopedia*, 6th edn, Columbia University Press. Licensed from Columbia University Press. All rights reserved. <http//:www.cc.columbia.edu/cu/cup>

Dally, S. and Lindstrom, H. 1996, *Girls and Boys Come Out to Play: Teaching about Gender Construction and Sexual Harassment in English and Studies of Society and Environment*, Department for Education and Children's Services, Adelaide, South Australia.

Davies, B. 1989, *Frogs and Snails and Feminist Tales: Preschool Children and Gender*, Allen & Unwin, Sydney.

——1993, *Shards of Glass: Children Reading and Writing beyond Gendered Identities*, Allen & Unwin, Sydney.

——2003, *Frogs and snails and feminist tales. Preschool children and children* (revised edn), Hampton Press, New Jersey.

Derrida, J. 2004, *Dissemination*, Continuum International Publishing Group, London and New York.

Grace, D. and Tobin, J. 1997, 'Carnival in the classroom: elementary students making videos', in J. Tobin, ed., *Making a Place for Pleasure in Early Childhood Education*, Yale University Press, New Haven and London.

Grosz, E. 1990, 'Contemporary theories of power and subjectivity', in S. Gunew, ed., *Feminist Knowledge: Critique and Construct* (pp. 59–120), Routledge, London.

Hall, L. n.d., 'Beauty quests: a double disservice', in Women with Disabilities Feminist Collective, eds, *Women and Disability: An Issue* (pp. 68–74), Women with Disabilities Feminist Collective, Melbourne.

Hyun, E. 2001, 'Cultural complexity that affects young children's contemporary growth, change and learning', Paper presented at the *Annual Meeting of the Educational Research Association*, 10–14 April, Seattle, WA, ED451941.

Jones, G. and Moomaw, S. 2002, *Lessons from Turtle Island: Native Curriculum in Early Childhood Classrooms*, Redleaf Press, St Paul, MN.

Lenz Taguchi, H. 2007, 'Deconstructing and transgressing the theory-practice dichotomy in early childhood education', *Educational Philosophy and Theory*, 39(3), pp. 275–290.

MacNaughton, G. 2000, *Rethinking Gender in Early Childhood*, Allen & Unwin, Sydney; Sage Publications, New York; Paul Chapman Publishing, London.

McMillan, A. 2001, *Deconstructing Social and Cultural Meanings: a Model for Education Research Using Postmodern Construct*, Common Ground Publishing, Australia.

Moses, L. and Baldwin, D. 2005, 'What can the study of cognitive development reveal about children's ability to appreciate and cope with advertising?', *Journal of Public Policy and Marketing*, 24(2), pp. 186–201.

Parker, S. 1997, *Reflective Teaching in the Postmodern World: A Manifesto for Education in Postmodernity*, London, Routledge.

Reese, D. 1996, 'Teaching young children about Native Americans', *ERIC Digest,* May, *EDO-PS-96-3*, pp. 1–4.

Smardo Dowd, F. 1992, 'Evaluating children's books portraying Native American and Asian cultures', *Childhood Education*, 68(4), pp. 219–224.

Swindler Boutte, G. 2002, 'The critical literacy process: guidelines for examining books', *Childhood Education*, 78(3), pp. 147–152.

Weiner, G. 1994, *Feminism in Education: An Introduction*, Open University Press, Buckingham.

Whitin, D. and Whitin, P. 1998, 'Learning is born of doubting: cultivating a skeptical stance', *Language Arts*, 76(2), pp. 123–129.

Whitney, T. 1995, 'Respecting body size: differences in the classroom', *The Web Journal: The Culturally Relevant Anti-Bias Early Childhood Educators Network*, 2(2), pp. 8–9, 20.

Wilkes, G. (ed.) 1979, *Collins Dictionary of the English Language*, Middlesex, Penguin Books.

York, S. 1991, *Roots and Wings: Affirming Culture in Early Childhood Programs*, Toys'n Things Press, Minnesota.

Zammit, K. 1994, 'Strictly stories: teaching narrative', *EQ Australia*, Autumn, (1), pp. 27–30.

Chapter 23

Democratising

Democracy: The word democracy literally means "rule by the people." It is derived from a Greek word coined from the words demos ("people") and kratos ("rule") in the middle of the 5th century BC as a name for the political system that existed at the time in some of the cities of Greece, notably Athens.

(*Encyclopaedia Britannica*, online student edition, <http://student.britannica.com/comptons/article-9273962/democracy>)

A democratic person is someone who ponders the decisions that he/she is involved in and someone who is even prepared to go against democratically made decisions in order to show solidarity with the less fortunate members of society.

(Lindahl 2005, p. 3)

. . . democracy creates the possibility for diversity to flourish.

(Moss 2007, p. 3)

What?

Democracy in everyday language is about 'people power' and 'majority rule'. To democratise something is to give power to the people involved to decide what happens. As a teaching strategy, democratising refers to staff and children sharing power over what happens in the early childhood centre. It is a teaching strategy that focuses particularly on children's right to participate in decisions and experiences that affect them and to build the skills needed for democratic living.

Issues and debates

ARE CHILDREN COMPETENT TO SHARE POWER AND DECISION-MAKING?

Critics of democratising education argue that children do not have the intellectual capacity for self-governance and that they should not have the responsibility for it (Burgh, Field and Freakley 2006). This argument rests on an image of the child as less able and competent than adults. In contrast, more recent understandings of childhood see children as experts in their own life and capable of expressing views and having preferences about their world (Smith 2007).

IS MAJORITY RULE FAIR FOR ALL?

In working for democratic relationships in the early curriculum it is important to reflect on how culture, 'race', class, gender, sexuality and ability relationships affect how children's voices are encouraged, listened to and enacted—for instance, which children can express their views and preferences with confidence and which children are disempowered within the group. Questions of voice, silence and participation cannot be separated from the dynamics and experiences of discrimination that specific groups of children and individual children may have experiences. Children who have experienced discrimination will not necessarily feel able to express their views and values confidently if they are not in the majority in the classroom or group (For further discussion of these issues see Chapter 21 on decolonising and Chapter 25 on empowering).

THEORETICAL BACKGROUND

A.S. NEILL, DEMOCRACY AND CHILDREN'S RIGHTS

The call for greater democratisation of early childhood spaces is part of a long history of calls for democratising education in several countries. John Dewey's movement for progressive education forms part of that history (see Chapter 20 for more details about Dewey and this movement). A.S Neill's (1883–1973) democratic school movement also forms an important part of it. A.S Neill put his ideas about democratic schooling into practice by forming the Summerhill School in the UK in 1924. Summerhill is still operating, making it the oldest existing democratic school in the UK.

From Neill's perspective governance was core to democratic schooling. The school structures were created to ensure that children and staff have the power for self-rule. This form of democratic schooling involves equal participation by students and staff in all aspects of its operation and is self-governing (Vaughn 2006; Darling 1992; Neill 1960). At Summerhill regular school meetings of staff and students plan the learning and construct school rules to meet the changing needs and ideas of the school community. These processes are described on the school's website as follows:

Summerhill is first and foremost a place where children can discover who they are and where their interests lie in the safety of a self-governing, democratic community.

There are two features of the school which people usually single out as being particularly unusual. The first is that all lessons are optional. Teachers and classes are available at timetabled times, but the children can decide whether to attend or not. This gives them the freedom to make choices about their own lives and means that those children attending lessons are motivated to learn.

Many people suppose that no children would ever go to lessons if they were not forced to. At Summerhill, it is rare for a child to attend no lessons at all—at least, after the initial shock of freedom has worn off.

The second particularly unusual feature of the school is the school Meeting, at which the school Laws are made or changed.

These laws are the rules of the school, made by majority vote in the community meetings; pupils and staff alike having equal votes (<http://www.summerhillschool.co.uk/pages/index.html>).

ALTERNATIVE APPROACHES TO DEMOCRATISING

There is another approach to democratising education that gives more emphasis to building children's skills in articulating views and living in what Lipman (1991) called a community of inquiry (see Chapter 20 on community building and Chapter 26 on philosophising; see also Burgh, Field and Freakley 2006). In more recent times the call for democratisation of early childhood spaces has emphasised elements of each of these ways of conceptualising democracy in education. There is a call for greater child participation in early childhood spaces that has been strongly inspired by international children's rights instruments and documents that give children a right to have a say in issues of governance. For example, the 1989 United Nations Convention on the Rights of the Child (CRoC) contains a series of 'participation articles' that emphasise children's rights and capacities to be involved in decisions that affect them (for example, see Articles 12–15, 17).

More recently, in November 2005, the United Nations Committee on the Rights of the Child released a General Comment (No. 7) on implementing child rights in early childhood. It aimed to 'encourage recognition that young children are holders of all rights enshrined in the Convention and that early childhood is a critical period for the realisation of these rights' (Office of the High Commissioner for Human Rights [OHCHR], 2005, p. 1). The General Comment specifically addressed young children's right to have their views and ideas respected (pp. 6–7 of the General Comment), giving weight to the growing belief that children have a right to be listened to and consulted on issues that affect them (e.g. Moss 2007; Clark 2005; Hughes, MacNaughton and Smith 2007). This belief has resulted in a call for greater participation by children in democratically conceived early childhood spaces in which children are in a community of inquiry based on an ethic of democratic listening. Dahlberg, Moss and Pence (1999) express this call in the following way:

> The children are seen as human beings in their own right, as worth listening to, where we do not impose our own knowledge and categorizations before children have posed their questions and made their own hypotheses. (p. 137)

The children's rights agenda has combined with new images of the young child to give a contemporary theoretical basis to democratising as a teaching technique. Hughes, MacNaughton and Smith (2007) summarised those new images of the child thus:

> Recent developments in developmental psychology and in sociology have generated a fourth model—the young child as a **social actor** who shapes her/his identities, creates and communicates valid views about the social world and has a right to participate in it. As Christensen and James (2000) argue, to regard children as social actors is to treat them as active participants in, 'contexts where, traditionally, they have been denied those rights of participation and their voices have remained unheard'. (p. 2)

In this model of the child the child is seen as an expert on their life (Smith 2007).

How?

Staff democratise teaching and learning by centring children's voice in their daily work and increasing children's participation in decision-making. They do this through seeking their ideas, listening to them and responding to them respectfully. It is, therefore, a teaching process that is empowering (see Chapter 25), relies strongly on listening to children (see Chapter 10 for more discussion on this) and building respectful communities (Chapter 20). It relies on everyday listening to children and not one-off consultations with children about specific topics, issues or events. Borrowing from Clark (2005) to explain, democratising involves:

> . . . everyday listening undertaken by those who regularly work with young children to enable engagement in routines and activities together with one-off consultation about a particular issue, event or opportunity. This twin focus may allow both children's and adults' agenda to emerge. (p. 491)

However, democratising is more than listening. It requires that staff actively ensure that all children experience:

- dignity and security
- the right to participation
- respect for their identities
- freedom
- access to information
- privacy (Osler and Starkey 2006).

Staff can use a variety of strategies to support children's participation and increase their experiences of dignity, security, respect, freedom, access to information and privacy in early childhood spaces. In overview, they are:

- building a mind-set and set of values that open staff to children's rights
- using specific tools to extend children's possibilities of expressing their views and perspectives, and to share information with children
- investing in democratising as a never-ending process
- supporting children so that they will learn to balance their rights and responsibilities (that is, the responsibility to respect the rights of others).

BUILDING A MIND-SET AND SET OF VALUES THAT OPEN STAFF TO CHILDREN'S RIGHTS

Moss (2007) identified four mind-sets that democratic practice in early childhood spaces require:

- respect for diversity built on welcoming 'the other' to who we are
- appreciation of multiple ways of thinking about and seeing the world
- openness to uncertainty and curiosity
- critical thinking about the status quo.

Participants in an Australian project on increasing children's participation in curriculum talked of the need to change their mind-set on what listening means:

Meredith and Brooke describe listening as involving all the senses (Meredith, journal entry), 'to listen with eyes as well as ears'—to body language as well as the spoken language. (Brooke, personal research journal, CEIEC, p. 45)

USING SPECIFIC TOOLS AND PROCESSES TO EXTEND CHILDREN'S POSSIBILITIES OF EXPRESSING THEIR VIEWS AND PERSPECTIVES

When children are seen as citizens in an early childhood space they help to set the agenda in it. Some of the tools and processes that can support children in this process are:

- allowing time for engagement with children's ideas and experiences. Several writers (e.g. Moss 2007; Smith 2007) argue that democratising early childhood spaces requires the reorganisation of time and how it is used to enable meaningful and respectful participation practices for adults and children
- creating structured opportunities for children to set the agenda—for example, by establishing curriculum committees with children, allowing children to chair group meetings and decide their content and/or creating classroom rules with children
- using diverse tools with children so that they have different ways to express their views and perspectives. Some of the techniques that have been used include:
  —individual structured and semi-structured interviews
  —group structured and semi-structured interviews

—annotated drawings

—digital photographs—for example, identifying children's favourite places to play

—taped interviews, later transcribed

—puppet plays followed by discussion groups

—stories followed by discussion groups

—informal conversations

—sorting games in which children explore things they like, don't like, etc.

—Y-chart activities – what does 'X' look like, feel like, sound like?

—observations of informal play

—drawings and paintings.

The ways in which a mind-set, specific tools and processes and time come together in practice are described in a case study of an Australian early childhood professional (Eleanor) who participated in an action research project focusing on democratising the curriculum. This case study is taken from MacNaughton et al. (2006, pp. 26–27):

Child centred practice was part of Eleanor's teaching philosophy. She talked about the fact that there were already many ways that she consulted with children about the room's program. She wrote:

We will often give children materials they ask for in areas that we have put out. We ask children if they prefer to play inside in the morning or go outside. Often we will make a judgement between ourselves [the two teachers in the room]. (Eleanor's journal, 18/04/05)

The project was a way to continue to support the children's participation in the program so that it would reflect their needs and interests.

Initial question
How will I include the children's interests in the program through their voices?
How will their interests be established/implemented?

Reflection—why things need to change

I have to lose the anxiety I feel and learn to trust the children more.

Change in practice
Eleanor set up a planning committee with children. She asked two children at a time what they would like set up in the room. Initially the children were given one space that they could develop with their own ideas and choose the materials that would be used. Michelle wrote:

Today we chose the first two children who were going to be in the committee and help decide the program. Today Jay and Trent will assist in the planning of the program (area 1). Jay and Trent and I sat in a quiet area where I asked them what they would like to have in the room. (Eleanor's journal, 2/06/04)

From the question, 'What would you like in the program?', a conversation unfolded with Eleanor, Jay and Trent. This conversation began:

Jay: I want a jungle.
Trent: Yeah! That would be good, we could have elephants, hippos and gorillas.
Jay: I want lions and tigers.

Eleanor: Where would you like to set up this area? How many children do you want to play in the jungle?

Jay: (points to where he wants the area) I want it here. I think six children.

Trent: I want three children.

Eleanor: This area is very small (usually only for two children); do you think six children will fit?

Jay: No.

Trent: No.

Eleanor: Maybe we could choose another area?

Trent: We could have it there (pointing to a larger area).

Jay: Yeah, more children will fit there.

Eleanor: If Trent wants three and Jay wants six then you need to compromise.

Jay: Ok. Is five children ok with you Trent?

Trent: Yes, five is ok.

Eleanor: What sort of animals do you want? Small (plastic) jungle animals, puppets?

Jay: We want to be the animals.

Trent: Yeah we want to be the animals.

Eleanor: Do you think we could make costumes?

Jay: Yeah. And we can have some other toy animals too.

On 3 June 2004 Trent explained to the children in his room that on Friday they would be setting up a jungle area and explained the rule of five children in the space.

Today my stress levels rose with the setting up of this one area! I think that my stress came from not wanting to disappoint Trent and Jay. (Eleanor's journal, 4/06/04)

Today is Friday and the jungle area has been extremely popular for the entire week. The children have been both using the animals in the area and pretending to be animals. Trent and Jay have done a good job developing negotiation skills and leadership roles. (Eleanor's journal, 11/06/04)

Eleanor's significant learning and change:
The children displaying ownership and a sense of pride in being heard and the involvement of other members of the group eager to assist their peers to achieve their goal (the jungle). I realised I need to let go of my expectations and really look at how the children respond and then judge whether an experience is working. Balance the power! (Eleanor's journal, 11/06/04)

INVESTING IN DEMOCRATISING AS A NEVER-ENDING PROCESS

Democratising is not a technique that can be used once and then put away. It is about establishing an ongoing ethic and practice of participation. Ayers (2005) captured this idea well:

> . . . democracy, like education, is an aspiration that requires continual nourishment, something to be engaged and exercised, a dynamic, expansive experiment that must be achieved over and over again by every individual and each successive generation if it is to live at all. (p. 321)

SUPPORTING CHILDREN TO BALANCE THEIR RIGHTS AND RESPONSIBILITIES RESPECTFULLY

Any democratic endeavour that supports and promotes children's rights needs to help children learn that rights come with the responsibility of being respectful of other people's rights. It is important that staff help children to learn about their responsibilities to listen and care for others as a basis of respecting everyone's rights.

When and why?

Democratising relationships in teaching and learning is about honouring children's rights and building ethical relationships with them (Moss 2007). Hence, democratising is a relevant teaching technique for extending children's rights to citizenship and, in doing so, building their capacity to express their views and perspectives and to negotiate and co-operate with others. These skills directly affect children's learning across all areas and domains of development as they give young children greater power over and in their daily world.

GOAL RELEVANCE

In democratic education the goals are jointly negotiated between staff and children. Hence, the relevance of democratising to specific learning areas and domains will shift and change as the intentions of children and staff shift and change.

DEVELOPMENTAL CONSIDERATIONS

Democratising is relevant to children of all ages. From the moment of their birth children are struggling to participate in the world about them. They actively engage with those around them and seek to influence what happens to them. Infant crying is a prime example of how babies try to participate in and influence their world. To democratise relationships with babies adults need to listen to, watch and interact with them as they struggle to say what they want or don't want, like or dislike, enjoy or are fearful of in their daily worlds.

Young children have preferences and they can express their preferences to others. The forms of expression children can use to express their views and preferences will vary from child to child and within each child as they grow and develop. A baby or a toddler cannot speak in the ways that older children can. However, babies and toddlers can express themselves through gesture, movement and sound. Staff need to offer children media to share their views and preferences that are relevant to the current and emerging capacities of the child.

Babies can express fear, distress and anger, generally through crying. They can also express positive feelings through smiles, being attentive and vocalising using cooing and other sounds (Frank, Stolarski and Scher 2006). Staff can use these expressions to help them to understand babies' views and preferences and use them as a guide to what babies want and need.

Toddlers grow rapidly in their capacity to explore and express their meanings through language, images and constructions. They can express their meanings and discoveries to others through language and gestures, and they can make use of the symbolic languages of music, drama, story, image-making and movement to discover other people's meanings and to share their own. If staff provide opportunities and time for toddlers to build their capacities in using symbolic languages they can strengthen their capacity to express their views and preferences.

In democratising teaching and learning relationships it is also important that toddlers have the opportunity not only to share their views and perspectives but also to have their right to privacy during routine and other times respected (Jones 2003). Private moments can be supported through ensuring access for toddlers to some secluded spaces or corners (Wellhousen and Crowther 2003).

In preschool and the early years of school, children's capacity for meaning-making and meaning-negotiation becomes increasingly complex and well-developed. They develop a growing competence in using the symbolic languages of music, drama, story, image-making and movement to discover other people's meanings and to share their own. They have strong preferences and views about diverse topics and experiences in their world and they are able to express and share those if given the time, space and opportunity to do so. They can also contribute to rule-making within a group and begin to understand their rights and responsibilities within a group.

Children's rights to privacy and information within a democratic endeavour are two rights that staff can help children to understand at this age. They can do this by talking with children about what is happening and why, inviting their comments and enabling children to say no to sharing things with others that they don't want to.

Equity considerations

'RACE' AND CULTURE

Democratising daily practices in early childhood spaces brings children's voices and perspectives more powerfully into the curriculum (Moss 2007). As discussed in Chapter 19 (on co-constructing) there are also equity alerts with using children's voices as a source of curriculum. Those alerts arise from diverse sources (for example, MacNaughton 2003; Viruru and Cannella 2001) but have focused on the ways in which groups who face 'racial' discrimination and marginalisation use silence as a way of speaking and asserting themselves. Staff need to reflect carefully on how silence might be a language of choice and power for ethnic minority groups in their classrooms (see MacNaughton 2005).

In democratising the classroom it is also important to open up space for discussions of 'race' and 'racial' differences to surface and be explored. Children's experiences, views and peer preferences offer insights into how democratised a space is. Polite and Saenger (2003) argue strongly that democratic communities cannot grow when the subject of 'race' is silenced:

Teachers often speak about creating classroom communities. Indeed, constructive, developmentally appropriate communities of learning are essential if solid learning is to happen. And, of course, everyone needs to feel comfortable in order to take risks, and learning is built on risk-taking. But teachers may also unwittingly create communities of silence.

Communities of silence cannot be moral communities. And the most pernicious and pervasive silence in primary school classrooms is the silence surrounding the subject of race. (Polite and Saenger 2003, p. 274)

GENDER

Ensuring children's access to secluded spaces is a simple way to support children's right to privacy in democratic early childhood spaces. There is some research evidence that there are gender differences in children's desire and need for privacy. In research in early childhood classrooms, researchers have found that girls tend to be more attracted to small-scale secluded spaces than do boys, but that boys react negatively, often aggressively, to large overcrowded spaces. However, both boys and girls benefit from having access to small-scale spaces (Lowry 1993; Evans 2006). Room dividers and soft furnishings such as curtains can create small-scale spaces within a larger space. This research offers a point of reflection for staff on how gender may influence children's preferences for privacy in an early childhood space. To ensure both boys and girls have spaces for privacy it is important to have a diversity of small-scale spaces, several of which offer more seclusion for girls. It is also important that boys and girls learn to respect each other's privacy. There is some evidence that boys react more aggressively to their personal space being encroached upon than do girls (Lowry 1993; Brown 2007), so it will be important for staff to work with children on how to express their feelings when others encroach on their personal space, as part of building a democratic community.

DISABILITY AND ADDITIONAL NEEDS

Children with disabilities who have difficulty communicating via spoken language should be supported to express their views and preferences in other ways. They need the opportunity to experiment with many media to find the best and most powerful ways to express their views and preferences and to influence what happens in the early childhood spaces. As has been discussed previously (see Chapter 19 on co-constructing) some children may find clay, paint, chalk, blocks, movement, dance or music most helpful. For other children, computer-enhanced communication might be best. The challenge for staff who want to increase the participation of all children in their settings is to learn to read and to support the diverse languages that different children can use to communicate and express their views and preferences, including their desire for privacy and for information.

Reflecting on democratising techniques

1 Define democratising.
2 What does child participation mean in an early years setting?
4 How does listening to children differ from democratising relationships?
5 Identify five ways in which you could encourage children to learn their rights to privacy in your setting. Would these be appropriate for children of all ages?
7 What do you see as the main gender equity issues in democratising teaching and learning with young children?
8 What do you see as the main 'race' equality issues in democratising teaching and learning with children?
9 How might democratising be used to support anti-discriminatory perspectives on disability?
10 To what extent do you believe that democratising relies too heavily on forms of expression that devalue a child's silence?

Improving teaching in practice

1 Record (using a tape-recorder or written notes) several occasions on which you are democratising relationships with a small group of children.
2 What is your current style of democratising? How well did you encourage all children to:
   • uncover, express and share their meanings with others?
   • uncover, read and acknowledge the meanings of others?
   • negotiate their meanings with others?
3 How well did you take account of developmental and equity considerations?
4 What are your areas of strength and weakness in democratising practices?
5 How can you improve your democratising techniques?
6 What do you see as the hardest part of improving your democratising techniques?

FURTHER READING

Apple, M., and Beane, J. (eds) 1995, *Democratic Schools,* Association for Supervision and Curriculum Development (ASCD), Alexandria, VA.

Clark, A. 2005, 'Listening to and involving young children: a review of research and practice', *Early Childhood Development and Care,* 175(6), pp. 489–505.

Clark, A. and Moss, P. 2001, *Listening to Young Children: the Mosaic Approach,* National Children's Bureau, London.

——2005, *Spaces to Play: More Listening to Young Children Using the Mosaic Approach,* National Children's Bureau, London.

MacNaughton, G., Hughes, P. and Smith, K. (eds) 2008, *Young Children as Citizens,* Cambridge Scholars Press, Cambridge.

Neill, A.S., *1960 Summerhill School: A Radical Approach to Child Rearing,* Hart Publishing Co, UK.

Smith, A. 2007, 'Children and young people's participation rights in education', *International Journal of Children's Rights*, 15(1), pp. 147–164.

Vaughn, M. (ed.) 2006, *Summerhill and A.S. Neill*, Open University Press, Milton Keynes.

Westheimer, J. and Kahne, J. (eds) 2003, 'Democracy and civic engagement', Special Issue, *Phi Delta Kappan*, 85(1).

Woodrow, C. and Press, F. 2007, '(Re)Positioning the child in the policy/politics of early childhood', *Educational Philosophy and Theory*, 39 (3), June, pp. 312–332.

ONLINE AND MULTI-MEDIA RESOURCES

Text

Summerhill school: http://en.wikipedia.org/wiki/Summerhill_School

United Nations Convention on the Rights of the Child: **http://www.unicef.org/crc**

Multimedia

'The Alternative Education Resource Organization. This is a website for democratic schools and the International Democratic Education Conference (IDEC): **http://www.educationrevolution.org/demschool.html**

Summerhill School website: **http://www.summerhillschool.co.uk**

Gabbert, J. 2005, 'Democratic Schools', KRÄTZÄ, Berlin: **http://www.democratic-schools.com**. A short trailer can be accessed at YouTube: **http://www.youtube.com/watch?v=V0zx5YVcpGc**

'Summerhill School vs. Conventional Schools' (video clip about Summerhill School): **http://www.youtube.com/watch?v=abzUqdh6yKY**

REFERENCES

Ayers, W. 2005, 'Teaching toward freedom: early childhood education and the challenges ahead', *Journal of Early Childhood Teacher Education*, 26(3), pp. 321–325.

Brown, J. 2007, 'Time, space and gender: understanding "problem" behaviour in young children', *Children and Society*, 21(2), pp. 98–110.

Burgh, G., Field, T. and Freakley, M. 2006, *Ethics and the Community of Inquiry: Education for Deliberative Democracy*, Nelson Thompson Learning, Melbourne.

CEIEC 2006, 'Children's voices and diversity in the early childhood curriculum', *A Report to the City of Melbourne*, Centre for Equity and Innovation in Early Childhood, The University of Melbourne, Melbourne.

Clark, A. 2005, 'Listening to and involving young children: a review of research and practice', *Early Childhood Development and Care*, 175(6), pp. 489–505.

Clark, A., Moss, P. and Kjørholt, A. 2005, *Beyond Listening: Children's Perspectives on Early Childhood*, The Policy Press, London.

Dahlberg, G., Moss, P. and Pence, A. 1999, *Beyond Quality in Early Childhood Education and Care*, Falmer Press, London.

Darling, J. 1992, 'A.S. Neill on democratic authority: a lesson from Summerhill?', *Oxford Review of Education*, 18(1), pp. 45–57.

Evans, G. 2006, 'Child development and the physical environment', *Annual Review of Psychology*, 57, pp. 423–451.

Frank, I., Stolarski, E. and Scher, A. 2006, 'Caregivers' mediation and toddlers' emotional responses in the child care context', *Early Childhood Development and Care*, 176(3), pp. 239–251.

Hughes, P., MacNaughton, G. and Smith, K. 2007, 'The United Nations General Comment (No. 7) on children's rights in their early childhood years: tensions and possibilities', *International Journal of Early Years Education*, 15(2), pp. 161–170.

Jones, A. 2003, 'The monster in the room: safety, pleasure and early childhood education', *Contemporary Issues in Early Childhood*, 4(3), pp. 235–250.

Lindahl, M. 2005, 'Children's rights to democratic upbringings', *International Journal of Early Childhood*, 37(3), pp. 33–125.

Lipman, M. 1991, *Thinking in Education*, Cambridge University Press, New York.

Lowry, P. 1993, 'Privacy in the preschool environment: gender differences in relation to crowding', *Children's Environments*, 10(2), pp. 47–59.

MacNaughton, G. 2001, 'Silences and subtexts in immigrant and non-immigrant children's understandings of diversity', *Childhood Education*, 78 (1), pp. 30–36.

——2003, *Shaping early childhood: learners, contexts and curriculum*, Open University Press, Berkshire, UK.

——2005, *Doing Foucault in early childhood studies*, Routledge, London.

MacNaughton, G., Smith, K., Hughes, P., Lawrence, H. and Olcay, M. 2006, 'Listening to children—new insights, challenges and possibilities', a report for the Children's Services Branch—Melbourne City Council, Centre for Equity and Innovation in Early Childhood, The University of Melbourne, Melbourne.

Moss, P. 2007, *Bringing politics into the nursery: early childhood education as a democratic practice*, Bernard van Leer Foundation, The Hague, The Netherlands.

Neill, A.S., 1960, *Summerhill School: A Radical Approach to Child Rearing*, Hart Publishing Co, UK.

Office of the High Commissioner for Human Rights [OHCHR], 2005, *Implementing Child Rights in Early Childhood*, General Comment no. 7, p. 1.

Osler, A. and Starkey, H. 2006, 'Education for democratic citizenship: a review of research, policy and practice, 1995–2005', *Research Papers in Education*, 21(4), pp. 433–466.

Polite, L. and Saenger, E. 2003, 'A pernicious silence: confronting race in the elementary classroom', *Phi Delta Kappan*, 85(4), pp. 274–278.

Smith, A. 2007, 'Children and young people's participation rights in education', *International Journal of Children's Rights*, 15(1), pp. 147–164.

Vaughn, M. (ed.) 2006, *Summerhill and A.S. Neill*, Open University Press, Milton Keynes.

Wellhousen, K. and Crowther, I. 2003, *Creating Effective Learning Environments*, Thompson Delmar Learning, Albany, NY.

Chapter 24

Documenting

Document: a piece of paper, booklet, etc. . . . providing information.
(*Collins Dictionary of the English Language*, p. 433)

Quality documentation makes visible the interweaving of adult and child thought and action, providing the possibility of improving the quality of communication and interaction to make learning reciprocal.

(Kroeger and Cardy 2006, p. 391)

. . . documentation—the written descriptions, transcriptions of children's words, photographs, and now the videotapes—becomes an indispensable source of materials that we use everyday to be able to 'read' and reflect critically on . . . the project we are exploring.

(Vecchi 1993, p. 122)

What?

In everyday language, to document a process or event is to gather and organise information about it. Documenting something provides a written or pictorial record of what has occurred. As a teaching technique, documentation refers to gathering and organising information to provide a written or pictorial record of children's learning.

Documentation has been a practice used in many early childhood programs for some time. As part of the overall planning process, all early childhood staff are familiar with written record-taking and observation of children's development in order to help them to plan techniques and learning experiences for a particular child or group of children. This kind of documentation is a support or adjunct to teaching; that is, it gives staff important information from which they devise goals, techniques and learning experiences for the children.

However, in recent years pedagogical documentation as a teaching technique has become strongly associated with, and given particular meaning through, the pre-primary schools of the northern Italian city of Reggio Emilia. For this reason some refer to it as the Reggio Emilia 'Approach' to documentation, and the work that has developed from it will provide the focal point for the discussion in this chapter. This tradition of pedagogical documentation '. . . allows individuals to revisit and reflect on learning experiences' (Kroeger and Cardy 2006, p. 391).

Issues and debates

DOCUMENTATION AS COLONISATION

The widespread use of methods of pedagogical documentation associated with Reggio Emilia is drawing some critical interest within the early childhood field. Johnson (1999) argued that Reggio Emilia has become a well-marketed global product that has had colonising effects within the field. Grieshaber and Hatch (2003, p. 95) further this critique, linking it directly to documentation thus:

> . . . the mass acceptance of Reggio Emilia (and the method of documentation) can also be interpreted within the U.S. and Australia through models of consumption and desire that are often associated with American institutions like McDonald's, Hollywood and CNN—instead of ensuring that you 'Mac your day', teachers passionately set about to 'Reggio their program'.

Staff can use these comments to reflect on how they might develop contextually relevant approaches to documentation within their local context and to consider the pros and cons of using pedagogical documentation within their specific setting.

How?

Documentation requires staff to make decisions about when, why and how to document children's learning. In taking these decisions Katz and Chard (1996, p. 3) argued that staff should document children's learning when '. . . children are engaged in absorbing, complex interesting projects worthy of documentation'. The decision about what to document should arise from consultation between staff over what they deem to be worthwhile learning projects. Increasingly there is an interest in children being consulted as part of this decision-making process (Dixon 2001).

Once staff (and/or children) decide what specific project work will be documented, they need to set aside time for careful observation of children's learning throughout the project. Alongside this they need to develop techniques for recording, organising and displaying their observations. There are many techniques staff can use to record their observations of children's learning, including:

- photographing children's work, including the use of digital camera photographs of children's drawings, sculptures, paintings, buildings and other constructional work. Children can assist in this process (Dixon 2001)
- making written observations of children's work, including recording children's language
- audio-recording children's comments and conversations
- making overhead transparencies of children's representations
- video-recording the processes and products of children's learning. Using digital video-recording equipment means that staff and children can instantly revisit their recordings and take decisions about what they would like to keep for further reflection (Hong and Broderick 2003)
- transcribing children's comments and observations
- collecting a portfolio of children's work (Trepanier-Street 2000; Dixon 2001).

Access to tools such as photocopiers, digital cameras or tape-recorders is important for this work.

> At a kindergarten in Brisbane's outer western suburbs the children are involved in a project about snakes. It is summer and the children have all seen snakes in the grasslands adjacent to the suburb. They have become interested in these animals and have decided with the teacher to explore them through a project that is progressing and evolving.

Mardie, the teacher, sits with a group of children as they reflect on and recall their knowledge of snakes. She asks stimulus questions and provides children with time to speculate about aspects of snakes. She records the conversation on audiotape.

At the end of the day Mardie transcribes the tape onto paper. She interprets and analyses the transcript in order to increase her knowledge of what the children have said. Mardie then makes notes and uses them the next day when she is with the children to deepen and further their knowledge and interest in the subject.

Reflective task: Take an inventory of the equipment you have for documenting children's learning and meaning in your context. What else would be helpful to this endeavour?

New technologies are making the process of documentation easier and speedier for many staff. Trepanier-Street et al. (2001, p. 182) highlighted a number of advantages of using a digital camera to document children's project work and the learning they gained from it. They point to the many ways in which a digital camera and the photographs it produces can be used in project work. They include the following:

- Immediately printing photos taken of children's work in a specific area or on a specific day allows staff and children to discuss what has happened almost as it happens.
- Printing digital photos is cheaper than conventional photographs and so it is possible to build a store of photos of a project that children can revisit and use in their project work.

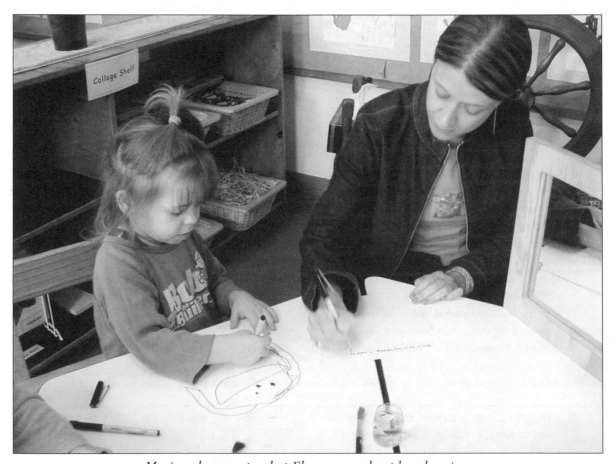

Marissa documents what Elenor says about her drawing.

Diana records aspects of social play during a session.

- Transparencies can be made of digital photographs and, using an overhead projector, projected to all children to revisit work and discuss progress.
- A classroom book is easily made via A4 prints of the photos that can be used to help children sequence the learning that has occurred during the project and support emergent literacy learning.
- Videotaping children's learning offers a rich source of information about their language and interactions. However, revisiting videotape can be time-consuming and staff should bear this in mind if they choose to use it as part of their documentation process. Videotaping can also be used to revisit moments with parents and children.

Videotapes and digital video-recordings serve a purpose not only for the teacher but also for the children and parents. Children can revisit with the teacher the section of the videotape that contains a significant advancement in their learning. Such revisiting can help children to connect their previous learning with current project exploration (Trepanier-Street et al. 2001, p. 183) and support learning being shared with their families (Bers, New and Boudreau 2004; Walters 2006).

After the information on children's learning has been recorded, staff must interpret and organise it in ways that explain children's learning (Forman 1996). Interpreting children's learning is a collaborative process within the Reggio Centres. As Millikan et al. (1996, p. 211) explained:

> . . . collaboration is essential to interpretation because observation is never neutral, never objective, and is only partial. Therefore, the collaboration provides the opportunity for considering different points of view, and the possibility to move closer to reality.

Once staff have identified significant moments in a given project and explored ways of interpreting these, they can organise the documents for display to others. At this point captions often need to be added to pictures or transcripts of children's learning that:

- provide a commentary on what has occurred. This commentary often highlights the activities children have been involved in and how their learning has developed through the activities (Gandini 1993a)
- raise questions about children's learning and how they are being taught (Forman 1996)
- interpret what children have been learning (Forman and Hall 2005)
- provide a basis for 'further inquiry, discussion, and analysis' (Forman 1996, p. 95).
- motivate and sustain children's interest (Walters 2006).

The intention in this phase of the documentation process is to produce documents (photographs, captions, etc.) that enable staff, children and parents to reflect on the processes and issues associated with children's learning around a particular event and to '. . . pursue what is important to the child in constructing meaning' (Hertzberg 1995, p. 8). Such reflection is prompted by public display of the 'documents' in the centre. To excite the interest and reflection of children, staff and parents the display should be easily accessible, well-designed, aesthetically pleasing, and displayed with flair and care (Gandini 1993a).

Campbell et al. (2002) detailed a project in which children, staff and parents used documentation and children's artwork to explore what a peaceful community looks and feels like. Central to their processes of reflecting on the meanings of peace was a gallery space that enabled families, children, teachers and others to make sense of shared concerns and differences about how a peaceful and respectful community looks and feels to them and to:

- spontaneously discuss and reflect upon how hurtful behaviours have occurred, and how they imagined peace and respect would be practised in the centre
- share, admire and provoke different ways of understanding issues of peace and respect in conversations with each other
- encourage and support visitors to share and reflect on how their ideas and understandings of peaceful and respectful communities could be used in their own communities and their own lives
- revisit how their understandings, questions, concerns, and ideas about peaceful and respectful communities change, and why (Campbell et al. 2002).

Staff will need to set aside time to develop effective techniques for gathering information, to organise the information into meaningful documents and to display these with care. While such time can be hard to find, the effort involved will be rewarded as documenting produces information that enables staff to assess individual learning, plan the curriculum and assess their own teaching (Forman et al. 1996, Ratcliffe 2001/02). The reasons for this are outlined by Ratcliffe (2001/02, p. 68) within the context of documenting children's emergent literacy skills:

> For an authentic assessment approach to be successful, a teacher must take time to think about what children already know and are able to do, and about what skills they will need to develop further...Regularly scheduling a time to review and reflect will allow teachers to achieve the insight they need to develop a clear understanding of the progress each child is making, and to plan appropriate experiences . . .

The process of review and reflection can occur with staff and between staff and children. The aim may not always be to find the most accurate assessment of children's learning, but to explore multiple perspectives on children's learning and project work as a provocation and invitation to further work and exploration of a topic. Review and reflection in this instance is not a final point in the documentation process but embedded in it as a driver for further learning. Some questions that can assist in this process include:

- Whose ideas and actions have we documented?
- Whose ideas and actions are missing from our documentation?
- What is similar and what is different in what we learn from different learners?
- What are the differences in how we each see what is significant? This question is especially important to ask if children and adults are sharing the review and reflection cycle and when there is social, cultural and linguistic diversity within the group of reviewers and reflectors.
- What of significance to me is not captured in what has been documented?
- What learning seems worth exploring further?
- What actions do we want to take as a result of this review and reflection?

Some staff document children's learning to support their assessment of children's learning and organise the documentation into portfolios (for example, Shores and Grace 1998; Beeth et al. 2001; Walters 2006).

THEORETICAL BACKGROUND

LORIS MALAGUZZI AND THE PRE-PRIMARY SCHOOLS OF REGGIO EMILIA

Loris Malaguzzi (1920–1994) was an Italian educator who founded and for many years directed the Reggio Emilia system of early childhood education in the northern region of Italy known as Emilia-Romagna. Malaguzzi worked with parents, children and colleagues to develop an approach to educating young children that has been acclaimed internationally and that has become known as the Reggio Emilia Approach. In this approach to early childhood education, children's learning is supported and enriched through in-depth, short- and long-term project work in which 'responding, recording, playing, exploring, hypothesis-building and testing, and provoking occurs' (New 1990, p. 3).

One of the features of the pre-primary schools in Reggio Emilia is the care that is taken to document and display the project work of the children in the schools. Malaguzzi saw this documentation and its display as central to the educational culture of the schools because it tells the school community what has happened and provokes further learning and exploration—for instance, walls and other spaces are used to exhibit the children's work to others.

The documentation is seen as integral to the children's learning and provides them with a reference source of what they have done and a source of information to provoke additional learning (Edwards et al. 1993).

More discussion of the philosophy and practices of Reggio Emilia pre-primary schools is presented in Chapter 31.

When and why?

GOAL RELEVANCE

Documentation can be used as a teaching technique to support and enrich children's learning in a variety of ways. Specifically, documentation can be used by staff to:

- develop and deepen children's interest and curiosity in a project (Goldhaber 2007)
- deepen children's understanding about their own learning (Malaguzzi 1993)
- support children's meta-cognitive learning by enabling them to revisit their ideas and view them from different perspectives (Doverborg and Pramling Samuelsson 1999)
- explore silences in children's worlds (Kroeger and Cardy 2006)

- stimulate children's interest and curiosity in each other's interests, techniques, learning and achievements (Katz and Chard 1996)
- explore and provoke interactions between children as they contribute to the documentation process (Kroeger and Cardy 2006)
- enable children to revisit their own learning (Forman 1996)
- encourage collaboration between parents, staff and children (Gandini 1994) and partnerships with parents (Tayler et al. 2006)
- help build communities of learners (Dixon 2001)
- make visible to the children their own learning journey (Wilson Gillespie 2000)
- enable children to 'examine their own thinking and the thinking of others on a project' (Trepanier-Street et al. 2001)
- encourage children to shape their own learning environment (Gandini 1994)
- help children gain a sense of history and evoke children's memories of past experiences (LeeKeenan and Nimmo 1994).

A documentation/display of photos has been put up in the foyer of the Panay children's centre. The photos trace the evolution of a project the children have completed about dinosaurs which has culminated with a large sculpture of a brontosaurus. The first photo shows a teacher–child discussion about the project. The following photographs show the remaining stages of the project and, in particular, children researching and making the sculpture. The children are looking at the photos with delight and talking animatedly. They recall the different aspects of the project and point out which parts of the project involved them. A teacher sits quietly and takes notes of what the children are saying. These notes will be used at a later time in a discussion with them.

Reflection point: What would be the challenges and possibilities of doing this in your context?

Documentation can also help staff and parents reflect on teaching and learning in their centre, as it provides them with a detailed record of what has been accomplished by children over time. It also shows how children's learning has unfolded and provides adults with an awareness of what children are learning and how the centre supports their learning (Bers, New and Boudreau 2004).

DEVELOPMENTAL CONSIDERATIONS

Documentation of children's learning is relevant for children of all age groups and for learning across all developmental domains. However, children's ability to make sense of different forms of pictorial and written documentation will vary. The younger the child the more important it is to present information to them in a concrete way. For example, LeeKeenan and Nimmo (1994) argue that photographic documentation is particularly useful with two- and three-year-old children as photographs act as a more effective memory trigger with this age group than written representations of events:

Staff at the Millgrove Children's Centre take photographs of all the children in their toddler group at the beginning of the year and put these up on the wall at the children's height. The staff then take care to play games with the children using the photos so that the children get to know each other and remember each other's names more easily. They also take photographs of the work of each child and add this to the display during the year. This acts as a point of conversation for the toddlers and helps them begin to reflect on their changing interests and accomplishments as the year progresses.

Reflection point: What questions might you ask to help you listen to children's understandings of the photos in the centre?

Angela uses photos to record the children at work.

In their work with toddlers, LeeKeenan and Nimmo (1994) also found that involving the children in taking the photographs was important to gain a sense of the children's perspective on the world. By contrast, many preschool children and children in the early years of school will be at a point where their own words, drawings and sketches may trigger memories and comments and further interest in a particular project. For example, in a project on housing in the United States involving children in the early years of schooling, models and written reports made by children played a major role in the documentation process (Abramson, Robinson and Ankenman 1995).

Staff can judge which forms of pictorial and written documentation most effectively stimulate children's thinking and help them revisit their own learning by documenting children's reactions to documentation and by taking the symbolic and expressive language abilities of the children into account. In the project on families described below, the children relied strongly on the visual arts to express what they knew about families:

> In the foyer of the Waikia Children's Centre, the staff have documented the children's project on families. Several of the five-year-olds used photographs of their families and photographs from magazines to help them think about what it means to be a family. Six of the children have made a large collage of families that forms part of the foyer documentation. The collage has several family portraits within it that represent all the different types of families they know. There is a family with a dad, two dogs and one son; a family with one mum and two children; a family with an aunt, a dad, three children and a cat; a family with a mum and a dad and a step-dad and six children; a family with two mums and two children; and a family with a mum and a dad, a grandma, a new baby, a daughter and a parrot.

> Two children painted a frame for the collage and each family portrait they made. One of the children who is able to write has written the title they gave their collage on the top and the names of the families on each of the portraits. The other three children have selected the images that go inside each of the portrait frames to reflect all the families they know. The children are now getting ready to draw what they like most about their families.
>
> _Reflection point:_ What possibilities would there be for this work in your context?

It is important that staff develop criteria for assessing their documentation to assist their decision-making about which projects or learning experiences might be most valuable and meaningful within their specific context. These criteria could address the specific characteristics of the children they work with, including the age of children, children's prior experience of the topic, its cultural relevance and the availability of appropriate resources to support and extend children's learning on the topic.

As children become older they become more able to collaborate with staff in documenting projects. Dixon (2001) described how children were actively involved in documenting their learning about water. The children produced drawings, diagrams, writing, photographs and models of their understandings of water as they researched in their classroom. Their research questions included:

- Where does water come from?
- Where does water go?
- What can water do?
- How does water support life?

Pedagogical documentation has also been used in the early years of schooling to provoke and support literacy learning and to enable parents and teachers to gain deeper insights into what children's literacy strengths are (MacDonald 2007).

Equity considerations

Documentation develops from staff decisions about what they believe to be important to convey to others about children and their learning. It therefore conveys powerful messages about who and what is valued by the staff. In deciding what to document, how to document it and how to interpret what is documented, staff need to be alert to the ways in which bias can enter their work and how this can be challenged.

'RACE' AND CULTURE
'Racial' and cultural bias can enter into several phases of the documentation process. Staff can check against such bias in their own work on documentation by ensuring that:

- all children in the group have an opportunity to have their work valued through documentation
- the projects (themes or topics) chosen for documentation challenge rather than reinforce 'racial' and cultural stereotypes
- the techniques chosen to record observations are culturally inclusive and culturally sensitive
- the interpretations of children's learning display cultural awareness and sensitivity
- the displays of children's projects and learning are accessible to parents, staff and children from a variety of language backgrounds.

Staff should ensure that the black and ethnic minority children have the same opportunities for documentation as the ethnic majority children in the group. This means that the words and thoughts of all children in the group need to be represented and that all children's ideas and traditions should be valued.

To achieve this goal, staff may need to find people who can translate the words and thoughts of children from language backgrounds other than their own.

Staff need to think carefully about which projects they choose to document. Some projects can overtly or covertly reinforce or challenge racism. For example, if several children in the group became interested in golliwogs it would be important to ensure that any project work arising from this interest involved the children in exploring how and why golliwogs are offensive to people of African descent. Offence arises because golliwogs 'reinforce a negative stereotype of black people—childlike, happy-go-lucky, with fuzzy hair, huge round eyes and thickened lips' (Brown 1995, p. 15). Images and text of children thinking about golliwogs should not merely represent any stereotypes the children have, but show how staff and children are working to challenge these stereotypes.

Projects that build children's understanding of and respect for cultural and 'racial' diversity will be those that:

- develop and deepen children's interest and curiosity in cultural and 'racial' differences and similarities. For example, projects that develop from children's questions such as, 'Where do people get their colour from?' or 'Why are her eyes different to mine?' offer lots of opportunity to build respect for 'racial' diversity
- encourage children from different 'racial' and cultural backgrounds to plan and work together
- encourage collaboration between parents, staff and children from different 'racial' and cultural backgrounds
- encourage children from a variety of 'racial' and cultural backgrounds to shape their own learning environment
- help children from different 'racial' and cultural backgrounds to gain a sense of history of working positively together.

Parents should be involved in discussions about the techniques staff wish to use to record children's learning, and staff should not proceed without parental approval. Staff discussion with parents will enable any cultural reservations parents may have about the proposed documenting to surface and for alternative techniques to be explored. It is also important that staff check that parents are happy for their children's images, words, thoughts and actions to be shared publicly. Cultural beliefs and traditions may influence parents' feelings about this.

Interpretation is a very subjective process that is strongly influenced by our cultural values and beliefs, and by those cultural values and beliefs that are dominant in our society. Our cultural values and beliefs can influence how we interpret children's body language, their accomplishments, their knowledge and their relationships. To counter the possibility of cultural misinterpretation or prejudice, staff can check their interpretations of children's learning with people from cultures other than their own and from other than the dominant culture. This collaborative interpretation can lead to better-informed and more flexible ways of thinking about children and their learning as it can bring forth multiple and contrasting perspectives.

If parents are not literate in English, accessibility of the project display can be increased in several ways. Staff can ensure all written text is translated into the languages spoken by parents and use bilingual staff and parents for face-to-face interpretation of the text. In addition, staff can use pictures that reduce the need for textual translation and interpretation.

Children can benefit from seeing scripts of languages other than English. This can support or awaken their interest in such languages (Brown 1995) and add to the cultural richness of the centre.

In the foyer of the Topkapi Child Care Centre, the staff have documented the children's project on spaceships in English and in Turkish. The bilingual staff read this to the children in both languages. The Turkish parents are also able to read this documentation in their first language. Children who are not familiar with the Turkish language have begun to take an interest in the Turkish script and the sounds of the words when they are read out. Several of the five-year-old children are now beginning to incorporate different writing scripts in their spaceship representations. Staff have just found some photographs of spacecrafts from the former Soviet Union and the USA which clearly show the different scripts on each craft. They now plan to talk with the children about the photographs and the words that are often written on spacecraft.

Reflection point: Where could you go to find out what was written on the spacecraft if you were working with the children? How would you support their further exploration of language scripts?

In centres where children are learning English as an additional language, bilingual documentation is especially beneficial. It shows children their first language is respected and it offers them ways of maintaining proficiency in it.

GENDER

Gender bias can also enter into several phases of the documentation process. Staff can check against such bias in their own work by ensuring that:

- boys and girls in the group have an equal opportunity to have their work valued through documentation
- the projects (themes or topics) chosen for documentation challenge rather than reinforce gender stereotypes
- the interpretations of children's learning display gender awareness and sensitivity.

Staff will need to monitor the gender balance in their projects and take steps to counter any imbalances that develop over time. For example, gender can influence whether or not a particular child's interest becomes a group project (Tinworth 1996) and thus influence what staff might consider worthwhile to document over time. In the research reported by Tinworth (1996) boys' interests dominated over those of the girls' and led to a group project on reptiles and eagles. Other research suggests that the power relations between boys and girls often influence what children learn, how they approach their learning and how they express themselves (MacNaughton 2000), with boys often being more dominant than the girls. Given this, it is important that staff work particularly hard to develop and document the interests of girls as well as boys. This means staff need to value the traditional female domains of play, such as domestic play, as much as they value the traditional male domains of play, such as adventure play.

Developing and documenting projects with children that build their understanding of and respect for gender equity can:

- develop and deepen children's interest and curiosity in gender differences and similarities
- encourage boys and girls to plan and work together
- encourage collaboration between male and female parents, staff and children
- encourage girls and boys to shape their own learning environment
- help boys and girls to gain a sense of history of working positively together.

As staff construct the messages they want to convey to children, parents and other staff about children's learning, they need to be sensitive to the potential for gender bias in their interpretations. Staff should be alert to the fact that adults often interpret similar behaviours in boys and girls differently (Thompson, Arsenault and Williams 2006). For example, research has shown that teachers interpret boys' and girls' help-seeking behaviour during problem-solving tasks differently. These research results suggest that staff should critically evaluate their interpretations of children's learning for gender bias and make any adjustments as appropriate.

DISABILITY AND ADDITIONAL NEEDS

Staff can check against disability bias in their documentation work by ensuring that:

- children with and without disabilities in the group have an equal opportunity to have their work valued through documentation
- the projects (themes or topics) chosen for documentation challenge rather than reinforce disability stereotypes
- the techniques chosen to record observations are inclusive and sensitive to children with varying abilities
- the interpretations of children's learning display disability awareness and sensitivity
- the presentations of children's projects and learning are accessible to parents, staff and children of varying abilities and disabilities.

Children with and without disabilities should have an equal opportunity to have their work valued through documentation. If staff regularly monitor whose work is being documented they can identify any inequalities. If any inequalities do exist, staff can take steps to ensure that children with disabilities are represented in future documentation. Equal representation is much easier to manage when a child attends a centre regularly. However, regular centre attendance may not be possible for children whose health is impaired in some way. Conditions such as asthma, severe allergies, heart problems, cancer, epilepsy and juvenile diabetes may affect children's ability to attend regularly, and when children do attend they may need regular periods of rest. Depending on the severity of the condition, a child may need to be hospitalised for periods of time. Staff need to ensure that irregular attendance at the centre, periods of absence and the need for rest does not lead to children's absence from any documentation. To guard against such exclusion, staff will need to record children's learning at times and on occasions when any children with health impairments are present. Staff may also be able to involve parents and other carers, such as hospital staff, in the process of recording a child's learning away from the centre to supplement the documentation that occurs there.

Developing and documenting projects with children that build their understanding of and respect for people with different abilities can:

- stimulate and deepen children's interest and curiosity in ability differences and similarities
- encourage children of different abilities to plan and work together
- encourage collaboration between parents, staff and children of different abilities
- encourage children of different abilities to shape their own learning environment
- help children of different abilities gain a sense of history of working positively together.

The techniques chosen to record observations need to be inclusive and sensitive to children with varying abilities. For example, if children have a disability that makes sharing their ideas, thoughts and feelings through speech difficult, they may communicate via sign language, body language or communication aids that enhance their speech. In such instances, recording children's learning through tape-recording is likely to be less valuable than a video-camera. The tape-recorder may miss most of what a child communicates and thus make revisiting it difficult. On the other hand, video-recording can capture the complex and varied non-verbal ways in which a child may express themselves through dance, movement, facial expression, sign language and the visual arts such as painting and collage.

As mentioned above, interpreting children's learning is a value-based process. Judging what is a significant moment in children's learning or what is intended by children's actions or words is highly subjective. When staff are working with children with disabilities they need to be aware of and sensitive to the complexities of making judgments about what is significant learning. What staff believe to be significant will depend on their own values about what is important to learn, what they believe learning is and how they believe learning can be recognised. It will also depend on their understanding of a specific child and how a child's learning may be enhanced or limited by their particular level and form of disability. Getting to know each child will assist staff in making their judgments about what to document. However, the process of getting to know children can be difficult when children's ability to communicate is limited by their disability. In such instances, staff need to allow children many different ways of expressing themselves; for example, through painting, drawing, collage, dance, music, movement, drama, story or construction. Such opportunities will enhance the possibility of each child finding a 'language' to learn with and communicate through. If children can find such a 'language' it will enhance their staff's ability to sensitively interpret what and how they are learning.

When a child or a parent has a disability that may influence their ability to access the display, staff need to communicate with them about what they can do to ensure accessibility. For example, if a child or parent has a sight impairment, then adding sound, texture and Braille to the display could make the display more accessible to them.

Reflecting on documenting techniques

1   What is documenting?
2   What do you see as the main differences between observation and documenting?
3   What does Katz suggest are the keys to successfully using documenting to optimise children's learning?
4   What do you think are the pros and cons of using documenting in your teaching?
5   What do you see as the key equity issues in using documenting in your teaching?

Improving teaching in practice

1   Use three different techniques to record children's learning during several half-hour teaching periods. Examine the information you have collected and answer the following questions:
    • What themes or issues about children's learning would you like to document?
    • Which technique provided the most useful material on children's learning during this time?
    • How could you display the material you have collected to provide a commentary on what has occurred, to raise questions and to interpret children's learning and how they are being taught?
2   To what extent did equity issues emerge in the process of documenting children's learning?
3   What are your areas of strength and weakness in using documenting to promote children's learning?
4   How can you improve your documenting techniques in practice?

FURTHER READING

Dixon, B. 2001, 'Purposeful learning: a study of water', *Early Childhood Research and Practice*, 3(2), pp. 1–18.

Gandini, L. 1993, 'Educational caring spaces', in C. Edwards, L. Gandini and G. Forman, eds, *The Hundred Languages of Children: The Reggio Emilia Approach to Early Childhood Education*, pp. 135–149, Ablex Publishing Company, New Jersey [refer to p. 146].

Ratcliffe, N. 2001/02, 'Using authentic assessment to document the emerging literacy skills of young children', *Childhood Education*, 78(2), pp. 66–69.

ON-LINE AND MULTI-MEDIA RESOURCES

Explore examples of projects with young children and their documentation at:
http://www.ualberta.ca/~schard/projects.htm

Read a detailed account of a project about water and its documentation by young children at:

http://www.ecrp.uiuc.edu./v3n2/dixon.html

REFERENCES

Abramson, A., Robinson, R. and Ankenman, K. 1995, 'Project work with diverse students: adapting curriculum based on the Reggio Emilia Approach', *Childhood Education*, 71(4), pp. 197–202.

Beeth, M., Cross, L., Pearl, C., Pirro, J., Yagnesak, K. and Kennedy, J. 2001, 'A continuum for assessing science process knowledge in grades K–6', *Electronic Journal of Science Education*, 5(3), pp. 1–17.

Bers, M., New, R. and Boudreau, L. 2004, 'Teaching and learning when no one is expert: children and parents explore technology', *Early Childhood Research and Practice*, 6(2), <http://www.ecrp.uiuc.edu/v6n2/bers.html>

Brown, B. 1995, *All Our Children: A Guide for Those who Care*, 3rd edn, British Broadcasting Commission Education, London.

Campbell, S., Coady, M., Castilino, T., Lawrence, H., MacNaughton, G., Page, J. and Rolfe, S. 2002, *Our Part in Peace*, Australian Early Childhood Association, Watson, ACT.

Dixon, B. 2001, 'Purposeful learning: a study of water', *Early Childhood Research and Practice*, 3(2), pp. 1–18.

Doverborg, E. and Pramling Samuelsson, I. 1999, 'Apple cutting and creativity as a mathematical beginning', *Kindergarten Education*, 4(2), pp. 87–103.

Edwards, C., Gandini, L. and Forman, G. (eds) 1993, *The Hundred Languages of Children: The Reggio Emilia Approach to Early Childhood Education*, Ablex Publishing Corporation, New Jersey.

Forman, G. 1996, 'Design, documentation and discourse: cornerstones of negotiated curriculum', Keynote address presented to the *Weaving Webs: Collaborative Teaching and Learning in the Early Years Curriculum Conference*, July, Melbourne.

Forman, G. and Hall, E. 2005, 'Wondering with children: the importance of observation in early childhood', *Early Childhood Research and Practice*, 7(2), <http://www.ecrp.uiuc.edu/v7n2/forman.html>

Forman, G., Lee, M., Wrisley, L. and Langley, J. 1996, 'The city in the snow: applying the multisymbolic approach in Massachusetts', in C. Edwards, L. Gandini and G. Forman, eds, *The Hundred Languages of Children: The Reggio Emilia Approach to Early Childhood Education* (pp. 233–50), Ablex Publishing Company, New Jersey.

France, P. 1986, 'The beginnings of sex stereotyping', in N. Browne and P. France, eds, *Untying the Apron Strings: Anti-Sexist Provision for the Under Fives* (pp. 49–67), Open University Press, Milton Keynes.

Gandini, L. 1993a, 'Fundamentals of the Reggio Emilia Approach to early childhood education', *Young Children*, 49(1), pp. 4–8.

——1993b, 'Educational caring spaces', in C. Edwards, L. Gandini and G. Forman, eds, *The Hundred Languages of Children: The Reggio Emilia Approach to Early Childhood Education* (pp. 135–149), Ablex Publishing Company, New Jersey.

——1994, 'What can we learn from Reggio Emilia?: an Italian–American collaboration', *Child Care Information Exchange*, (3), pp. 62–66.

Goldhaber, J. 2007, 'The development of an early childhood teacher research collaboration', *Theory into Practice*, 46(1), pp. 74–80.

Grieshaber, S. and Hatch, A. 2003, 'Pedagogical documentation as an effect of globalization', *Journal of Curriculum Theorising*, 19(1), pp. 89–102.

Hertzberg, C. 1995, 'The image of the child', *The Challenge*, June, pp. 7–9.

Hong, S. and Broderick, J. 2003, 'Instant video: revisiting for reflection: extending the learning of children and teachers', *Early Childhood Research and Practice*, 5(1), <http://www.ecrp.uiuc.edu/v5n1/hong.html>

Johnson, R. 1999, 'Colonialism and cargo cults in early childhood education: does Reggio Emilia really exist?', *Contemporary Issues in Early Childhood*, 1(1), pp. 61–78.

Katz, L. and Chard, S. 1996, 'The contribution of documentation to the quality of early childhood education', *ERIC Digest*, April, EDO-PS-96-2.

Kroeger, J. and Cardy, T. 2006, 'Documentation: a hard place to reach', *Early Childhood Education Journal*, 33(6), pp. 389–398.

LeeKeenan, D. and Nimmo, J. 1994, 'Connections: using the project approach with 2- and 3-year-olds in a university laboratory school', in C. Edwards, L. Gandini and G. Forman, eds, *The Hundred Languages of Children: The Reggio Emilia Approach to Early Childhood Education* (pp. 251–267), Ablex Publishing Corporation, New Jersey.

MacNaughton, C. 2000, *Rethinking Gender in Early Childhood*, Allen & Unwin, Sydney; Sage, New York; Paul Chapman Publishing, London.

Malaguzzi, L. 1993, 'History, ideas and basic philosophy', in C. Edwards, L. Gandini and G. Forman, eds, *The Hundred Languages of Children: The Reggio Emilia Approach to Early Childhood* (pp. 41–90), Ablex Publishing Corporation, New Jersey.

MacDonald, M. 2007, 'Toward formative assessment: the use of pedagogical documentation in early elementary classrooms', *Early Childhood Research Quarterly*, 22(2), pp. 232–242.

Millikan, J., Mauger, M., Thompson, J. and Hobba, M. 1996, 'A collaboration in reconceptualising the roles of children and adults in children's learning and development', Paper presented at the *Weaving Webs: Collaborative Teaching and Learning in the Early Years Curriculum Conference*, July, Melbourne.

New, R. 1990, 'Projects and provocations: preschool curriculum ideas from Reggio Emilia, Italy', *Eric Digest,* ED318565.

Ratcliffe, N. 2001/02, 'Using authentic assessment to document emerging literacy skills of young children', *Childhood Education*, 78(2), pp. 66–69.

Shores, E. and Grace, C. 1998, *The Portfolio Book: A Step-by-Step Guide for Teachers*, Gryphon House, Beltsville, MD.

Sloane, M. 1999, 'All kinds of projects for your classroom', *Young Children*, 54(4), pp. 17–20.

Tayler, C., McArdle, F., Richer, S., Brennan, C. and Weier, K. 2006, 'Learning partnerships with parents of young children: studying the impact of a major Festival of Early Childhood in Australia', *European Early Childhood Education Research Journal*, 14(2), pp. 7–19.

Thompson, R., Arsenault, S. and Williams, D. 2006, 'The effects of preschool girls' and boys' help seeking on adult evaluations of dyadic problem solving', *Journal of Language and Social Psychology*, 25(2), pp. 146–166.

Tinworth, S. 1996, 'Octopus tales: perspectives on learning and teaching at the DECS Children's Centre', Paper presented to *Weaving Webs: Collaborative Teaching and Learning in the Early Years Curriculum Conference*, July, Melbourne.

Trepanier-Street, M. 2000, 'Multiple forms of representation in long-term projects: the garden project', *Childhood Education*, 77(1), pp. 18–25.

Trepanier-Street, M., Hong, S. and Bauer, J. 2001, 'Using technology in Reggio-inspired long-term projects', *Early Childhood Education Journal*, 28(2), pp. 181–188.

Vecchi, V. 1993, 'The role of the *atelierista*: an interview with Lella Gandini', in C. Edwards, L. Gandini and G. Forman, eds, *The Hundred Languages of Children: The Reggio Emilia Approach to Early Childhood* (pp. 119–131), Ablex Publishing Corporation, New Jersey.

Walters, K. 2006, 'Capture the moment: using digital photography in early childhood settings', *Research in Practice Series*, Early Childhood Australia, Watson, ACT.

Wilkes, G. (ed.) 1979, *Collins Dictionary of the English Language*, Penguin Books, Middlesex.

Wilson Gillespie, C. 2000, 'Six Head Start classrooms begin to explore the Reggio Emilia Approach', *Young Children*, 55(1), pp. 21–27.

Chapter 25

Empowering

Empower: to give ability to, to enable or permit. To give or delegate power or authority.

(Collins Dictionary of the English Language, p. 408)

In effect, empowerment provides the subject with the skills and knowledge to make sociopolitical critiques about her or his surroundings and to take action (or not) against the oppressive elements of those surroundings.

(Stinson 2004, p. 12)

Empowerment rests on the belief that we should all be able to…participate in the practice of freedom . . . and discover how to participate in the transformation of . . . [our] world.

(Freire 1972, p. 15)

What?

To empower means to give others the power (or ability) to do something. In everyday usage, empowering is often used to describe the process of giving someone the power to do something on our behalf. For example, we might empower someone to sign cheques in our place or empower someone to take decisions about what to do if our dog becomes ill when we are away on holidays.

Empowerment always involves people who have the power to do something giving up or giving over their power to someone who does not have it. In the case of signing cheques, you give up or give over the power to sign your cheques to someone who would not normally have this authority. Empowerment always involves such a transfer between the powerful and powerless in a particular situation. As such, empowerment can occur only when one person or a group of people has more power than others. It is only necessary when there is an unequal distribution of power between people.

While empowerment can be used to describe any transfer of power it most often refers to the transfer of cultural, political, economic and social power between people. In this usage, empowerment is the process of giving greater cultural, economic, social and political power to those who have little access to such opportunities because of injustices and inequalities in a particular society. By giving people who have been treated unequally and unjustly more power (ability) they can take greater control over their lives and participate more equally in the cultural, social, political and economic life of their society. They have more freedom to choose in their daily lives (Wasserman 1991; Darder 2002). The aim of empowerment is to create greater social justice through people participating in the transformation of their lives.

Put simply, people are empowered when they have the resources and the independence to direct their own lives in ways that they are free from discrimination and oppression.

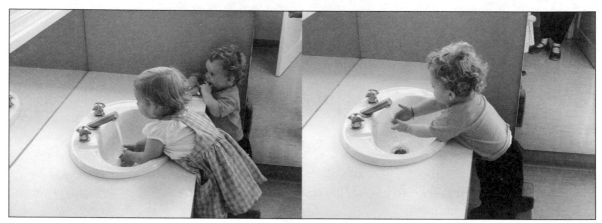

Mimi and Fergus take turns at washing their own hands.

As a teaching technique, empowerment has both a general and a specialist usage. In general usage, empowerment as a teaching technique involves giving children the power (or ability) to do things. For example, giving children the ability to (power to) decide which experiences they want to participate in or when they have milk and fruit.

> Riverbrook Kindergarten uses the High Scope Curriculum. One aspect of this allows the children to decide what they will do. The teacher holds a meeting with the children each morning and asks them what they'll play with first, second, third . . . The teacher has a magnet board where she writes the children's names and then the children stick symbols under their names for the activities that they have chosen each day.

The staff transfer their power to decide what and when the children will do daily tasks. For instance, the New Zealand Ministry of Education believes that empowering children means staff will provide them with the following power (abilities):

The knowledge, skills, and attitudes fostered by the curriculum . . . to:

- take increasing responsibility for their own learning and care;
- continue learning with an enhanced sense of self-worth, identity, confidence, and enjoyment;
- contribute their own special strengths and interests;
- learn useful and appropriate ways to find out what they want to know;
- understand their own individual ways of learning and being creative. (Ministry of Education (NZ) 1996, p. 26)

Issues and debates

WHO IS THE EMPOWERER?

There is considerable debate about the extent to which one person or group can empower another. Writing about empowerment often focuses on the role of one person empowering another person. It is something one person does for another. This is a very individualistic view of empowerment that focuses on changing interpersonal relationships from one individual to the next, and it assumes power is something that can be given from one person to another (Gore 2003).

However, there is another view of empowerment that focuses on empowerment as something that one does for oneself (Lather 1991; Stinson 2004) and that is linked to changing wider socio-political structures that cause oppression. From within this perspective, 'empowerment begins from within' (Kaber 2005, p. 14) and it refers to the level of control a person has over their daily lives that determines whether or not they are empowered. Empowerment is a measure of a person's agency over their lives (Ibrahim and Alkire 2007). Building on this idea Kaber (2005) sees empowerment as 'the processes by which those who have been denied the ability to make choices acquire such ability' (p. 13) and have the capacity to create change in their daily lives.

Gore (2003) argues for a more postmodernist conception of empowerment that recognises that power is not owned by individuals but is exercised by them in actions that they take or do not take. These actions are constrained by wider structural and discursive dynamics but occur in very specific contexts, such as classrooms. It is in these very specific contexts that we can critically explore the possibilities for taking action and exercising our power to help others exercise their power. Drawing on Michel Foucault's conceptions of power as action, Gore (2003) argued:

> Foucault's rejection of conceptions of power as property points to a rethinking of empowerment as the exercise of power in an attempt to help others to exercise their power. (p. 346)

THEORETICAL BACKGROUND

FREIRE: CRITICAL CURRICULUM AND EMPOWERMENT

Paulo Freire (1921–1997) was a Brazilian educator who strongly believed that all education has social and political consequences. He also believed that educators have a moral, social and political responsibility to be involved in education for social transformation which creates a more just and equal social world. These beliefs underpin current anti-discriminatory (or 'anti-bias') approaches in early childhood education and care.

It was Freire's work to eradicate adult illiteracy in Brazil that led him to these beliefs and to develop what has become known as a critical approach to literacy. In Brazil he was Secretary of Education and Co-ordinator of the National Plan of Adult Literacy. After this he spent time as a Visiting Professor at Harvard's Center for Studies in Education and Development, and served as a consultant to UNESCO (Freire 1972).

Freire's first book, *Cultural Action for Freedom*, was published in Brazil in 1967 and first appeared in English translation in 1970. Since the 1970s his view of literacy education has provided a powerful framework for understanding the relationship between teaching and learning, and his work has deeply influenced the development of what is known as critical or transformatory education (Carger 2003; Apple, Gandin and Hypolito 2001).

Critical approaches to education start from the assumption that the world as it is now involves inequalities and injustices. They rest on the assumption that education must explore these inequalities and injustices in order to challenge and then change them. This is a view of education that sees:

> . . . educational issues in a social-political context and attempts to identify the political-economic structures which shape educational provision and practices. (Carr and Kemmis 1986, p. 24)

In particular, the factors that create inequalities and injustices need to be identified and worked against to create a more just and wise social future. Teachers work for empowerment of the oppressed by reflecting critically on the social consequences of what they teach. This requires recognition that all education, including early childhood education, is a social and political act and that knowledge is socially constructed. To do this, staff need to understand how particular knowledge is unjust and oppressive and use this understanding to guide teaching decisions. They need to think and act in ways that help solve injustices confronted in the daily life of students (Daniels and Bizar 2005).

Freire believed that teachers can do this through praxis. Praxis is a perpetual process through which people take informed action for social justice and human liberation through developing a critical, self-reflective stance on the world. Smith and Lovat referred to this knowledge as 'knowing from the inside':

> Self-reflective, or critical knowledge, would then cause us to ask whether the information we have received is reliable, whether we are in a position to learn or not to learn through it, or whether we might not be controlled somehow by the forces of propaganda which surround us: this is helping to satisfy our interest to be free.
>
> For Habermas, it is only when we have reached [critical knowledge]…that we are guaranteed true knowledge because true knowledge demands that we be free…the information which comes from any subject can become a means of bondage, rather than emancipation, a way of oppressing people or keeping them in straitjackets. (Smith and Lovat 1990, pp. 69–70)

Praxis involves linking teaching actions with critical knowledge of and reflection on these actions, producing a critical evaluation of teaching that informs what is done next. It represents how staff process information critically and reflectively about their daily actions of teaching, try to solve problems encountered in teaching and then decide the best way forward with a social justice intent. To do this they need to:

- explore the gap between just intent in their teaching and what happens in reality
- make explicit and deliberate choices for justice after examining their options
- recognise the conflicts and contradictions in their teaching and resolve them in ways that aim to empower children to produce greater equity within the group and for specific children.

Ideally, in critical approaches to education, curriculum content is developed in collaboration with students. According to Freire, such collaboration should arise in and through students and teachers confronting real problems in their daily lives. He called this a 'problem-posing' approach to education and contrasted it with traditional education that uses a 'banking' approach to education. He explained the differences this way:

> Education thus becomes an act of depositing, in which the students are the depositories and the teacher is the depositor. Instead of communicating, the teacher issues communiqués and makes deposits which the students patiently receive, memorize, and repeat. This is the 'banking' concept of education, in which the scope of action allowed to the students extends only as far as receiving, filing, and storing the deposits. They do, it is true, have the opportunity to become collectors or cataloguers of the things they store. But in the last analysis, it is the people themselves who are filed away through the lack of creativity, transformation, and knowledge in this (at best) misguided system. In the banking concept of education, knowledge is a gift bestowed by those who consider themselves knowledgeable upon those whom they consider to know nothing. (Freire 1970, pp. 67–68)

While children and teachers interact to choose the curriculum content, their content selection should contribute to the overall goals of greater social justice and equity. When this occurs a critical, collaborative and problem-posing approach to teaching and learning is seen to be empowering for both children and staff.

The more specialised usage of empowerment as a teaching technique is associated with what are known as 'critical', 'transformative' or 'emancipatory' approaches to education. In early childhood education these are also known as anti-discriminatory or anti-bias approaches.

Critical education theorists drawing on the work of Freire see educators as 'cultural workers' (Darder 2002, p. 171) who can be actively involved in the transformation of their society to a more just society by challenging discrimination and its effects on learners and by opening up multiple possibilities for learners (MacNaughton 2003). As Darder (2002, p. 171) explained:

As teachers we are cultural workers, whether we are aware of it or not. If teachers don't question the culture and values being promoted in the classroom, we socialize our students to accept the inequalities of our society along lines of race, class, gender, and ability.

How?

Empowerment involves transferring power from one group to another in order to create greater social justice and equity between groups in a particular society. This transference of power should give the less powerful a greater ability to control and participate in decisions about their lives. To achieve this transference of power with young children, staff need to:

- decide what skills children need to experience greater control and participation in their learning

> At the Potts Child Care Centre, when each child arrives at the centre a staff member carefully observes the self-help skill level of each child. They then develop a program that will help the child to learn how to feed, dress, toilet themselves and play independently of an adult. This is so that they do not have to rely on others. Once children are able to do this, staff plan lots of opportunities for the children to make choices about what they will do and how they will do it.
>
> *Reflection point:* What opportunities do you currently provide for children to make choices in your context?

- choose teaching and learning techniques that enable children to experience greater control and participation in their learning
- choose content that is compatible with the goals of greater equity and justice underpinning empowerment.

SKILLS FOR EMPOWERMENT

The aim when transferring power to children within a critical approach to education is to enable them to learn how to challenge and speak out against injustices in their own lives and the lives of others (Derman-Sparks et al. 1989; Killoran et al. 2004; Zygmunt-Fillwalk et al. 2007). Young children can gain these abilities when staff:

- help children to feel good about themselves
- build children's capacity to participate in the program to their fullest potential
- build children's ability to have positive relationships with others
- teach children to problem-solve what is fair or not fair in their day-to-day relationships with each other
- help children learn to stand up for themselves and others who are treated unfairly
- build children's capacity to think critically.

STRATEGIES FOR EMPOWERMENT

While there is no specific group of teaching techniques that will automatically develop children's skills for their own empowerment, staff can draw on the critical educational teaching principles shown in the table following to guide their choice of teaching strategies.

Skill development for children's empowerment	Critical education principles	Teaching techniques discussed in other chapters
Help children to feel good about themselves.	Value children's answers and knowledge. Enable children and adults to interact to decide how and when something is to be learned.	Open questioning. Active listening. Scaffolding.
Build ability to have positive relationships with others.	Emphasise the adult's role as facilitator. Encourage self-reflective knowledge.	Careful positioning of adults. Modelling. Open questions about feelings. Co-constructing.
Build capacity to participate to their fullest potential. Teach to problem-solve what is fair or not fair.	Use open-ended materials ensuring bias is not inherent in them. Emphasise open, problem-posing questioning. Encourage self-reflective knowledge.	Organising the environment. Co-constructing. Prolem solving. Task-analysis. Open questions about feelings. Philosophising.
Help to stand up for themselves and others when unfairly treated.	Emphasise open, problem-posing questioning. Encourage self-reflective knowledge.	Problem-solving—social issues. Open questions about feelings. Recalling and revising.
Build capacity to think critically.	Emphasise open, problem-posing questioning. Emphasise the process of learning rather than its product. Emphasise doing rather than knowing facts.	Deconstructing. Open questions. Co-constructing. Documenting.

CONTENT COMPATIBLE WITH EQUITY, JUSTICE AND EMPOWERMENT

Much of the traditional curriculum content for young children has developed over time to serve the interests of particular groups of people. There are, therefore, biases built into this content and staff need to learn to recognise them. These biases will be evident in the children's literature, music, dance, maths and science resources (Siraj-Blatchford and Siraj-Blatchford 1995; Ramsey 2004).

In working to empower children, staff should choose curriculum content that ensures that what is learned and taught is as fair and just as possible. This involves integrating equity issues into the content of what is taught through the topics, themes, stories and songs that staff use to introduce children to contemporary issues, such as issues of environmental sustainability and intergenerational justice (Davis 2005). Staff also can evaluate the information about their social world contained in the formal and informal discussions between children and themselves. These discussions can contain information about various forms of inequalities and injustices in the daily lives of the children and they could otherwise be ignored.

Questions to help staff reflect critically on the content of their teaching are:

- Have you checked the stories, poems and songs used with the children to ensure that they promote positive attitudes to human diversity?
- How do you use your curriculum content to ensure that children learn about and value the various family lifestyles and experiences in the group?
- How do you develop curriculum content to ensure that children learn that gender, 'race', ability, age and class stereotypes exist and that these are inaccurate and hurtful?
- How do you use your curriculum content to ensure that children learn how to be 'fair' to others?
- How do you ensure that your curriculum content assists children to learn how to stand up for themselves when injustices occur?

EVALUATING FOR EMPOWERMENT

Critical education theory emphasises staff collaboration with the children in judging progress towards empowerment. Staff can become involved in collaborative evaluation with children by checking if:

- the learning was comprehensible for all children
- everyone shared the same understandings
- everyone shared equally in developing understandings of the situation
- the staff's actions were appropriate given the differing needs and interests of children in the group
- power was shared in appropriate ways.

These reflections will highlight the:

- gap between intention and actuality in your work with children. Did you actually empower them?
- conflicts and contradictions in your work with the children. For example, what conflicts did you encounter between the need to empower boys and girls? Were their empowerment needs in conflict?

When and why?

To empower children, staff must be committed to creating a more just social world through transferring power from more powerful groups to less powerful groups. This commitment should build from an understanding of how power is currently distributed in a given society at specific points in time and an understanding of the connections between the wider social and political contexts of their work and their daily lives with the children in specific centres.

COMMITMENT TO PROGRESSIVE SOCIAL CHANGE

To use empowerment as a teaching technique, staff must want to change the current distribution of power between different groups in society. They must have a belief that unequal and unjust power relationships currently exist between specific groups of people in their society, and want to change this. Some questions to prompt staff's thinking about their commitment to social change are:

- What groups do you currently belong to?
- What groups currently make up society?
- Do you believe that there should be a fair distribution of resources and experiences between all these groups in society? Do you think that there is? What examples do you have to support your views?
- Do you believe that there should be fair, respectful and non-exploitative relationships between all these groups in society? Do you think that there are? What examples do you have to support your views?
- Do you believe that there should be full participation by all these groups in society in social, economic, cultural and educational life? Do you think that there is? What examples do you have to support your views?
- Do you believe that all these groups in society should have the ability for self-expression and experience self-esteem? Do you think that they do currently? What examples do you have to support your views?

Answering these questions should give staff a sense of their level of commitment to progressive social change and of their understanding about the distribution of power in their society.

UNDERSTANDING THE SOCIAL AND POLITICAL CONTEXTS

Commitment to social change builds from an understanding of the current distribution of power between different groups in a society. Staff, therefore, must be able to identify what is unfair and unjust about the distribution of power. For example, they need to understand who has the ability to actively contribute to, access and transform the cultural, economic, social and political life of their society, and who does and does not benefit from this.

UNDERSTANDING HOW INEQUITIES AND INJUSTICES IMPACT ON CHILDREN

Once staff understand how power is distributed within their society they have a basis from which to think about which groups of children are most likely to have less power than others. From these understandings staff can work with children to enable them to challenge the unfair and unequal as it touches their daily lives and the lives of those about them. Staff need to develop strategies to ensure that the groups of children with less power gain more. They also need to ensure that the children in the group with greater power learn to share their power with others. In early childhood settings this means:

- ensuring a fair distribution of resources and experiences

> Jane noticed that Sarah, a timid, shy child, was looking longingly at the blocks. She attempted to help Sarah join in the block play that was dominated by the boys in the group, but Sarah was reluctant to stay. After several sessions, when Jane encouraged Sarah to play with the blocks with or alongside the others, she decided to use a different approach. She told the children that the blocks would be off-limits to the girls and boys respectively on alternate days. In this way she was able to help Sarah play alongside the other girls in the block area.
>
> *Reflection point:* What do you see as the pros and cons of this strategy?

- ensuring fair, respectful and non-exploitative relationships
- ensuring full participation by all
- ensuring children have the ability for self-expression and experience self-esteem.

GOAL RELEVANCE

Historically, it is possible to identify five different approaches to issues of equity and social justice in teaching young children (MacNaughton 2004). To appreciate when and why to use empowerment teaching techniques, staff should understand the differences between these approaches; these differences are discussed below. Empowerment is used as a teaching technique when staff are committed to the goals of the fifth approach.

1 Laissez-faire approaches. Staff ignore the social, cultural, 'racial', ability and gender differences between children and assume that treating children the same will lead to similarities. While this approach has been prevalent historically, it is not so now.

2 Special provisions education approach. Specialist education is provided for the groups identified as different. The aim is to help equalise educational opportunity for children/groups who are seen as different from the 'norm'. Examples of education for the groups identified as different would include special educational provision for children with disabilities and for non-English-speaking background children. Such approaches tend to segregate the children identified as different from the norm. This segregation can reinforce notions of rejection and create a continued sense that the children being segregated are less valued than others by reinforcing the idea that only 'normal' children can participate in particular activities.

Girls-only in block play today.

3 Cultural understanding approaches (Tourist approaches). The aim of these approaches to equity and diversity is to create understanding between diverse groups of children. Children are made aware of the fact that people dress, eat and live differently. Equality is assumed to come about through increased understandings of our similarities and differences as people by 'visiting' a disability or a cultural group for a day. This approach often leads to special experiences—such as pretending to be blind for the day, having Chinese food for lunch or adding chopsticks to the home corner for a day.

While it is important to educate children about difference, it is important to avoid some of the difficulties that have been identified when teachers rely solely on cultural understanding approaches. First, cultural understanding approaches can lead to simplistic and stereotyped understanding of other cultures, and teaching children about disabilities often focuses on the negative aspects of disabilities, not on the positive aspects of the child as a whole. Second, there can often be a lack of understanding about the fact that there are differences within the abilities of people with specific disabilities or from specific cultural groupings. For example, people who cannot see do not all think, feel and act in the same way, just as all people who can see do not share the same values. Finally, often there is seen to be a need to deal with diversity only if there is social, cultural, 'racial' or ability diversity in the children attending the centre.

4 Human rights approaches. The focus here is to teach children 'living together skills' such as sharing and caring. It is assumed that this will lead to an environment in which each individual is valued and treated with respect. This is a critical first step in building respectful relationships between children, but is not sufficient in and of itself.

5 Anti-discriminatory approaches. Anti-discriminatory approaches to diversity and equity address more than individual people's differences and similarities. They also address the negative impact of discrimination on the lives of people and challenge this discrimination via the experiences and materials they offer. They aim to:
- make the different abilities, cultures and genders of the children visible via the curriculum
- enable all children to experience the richness and diversity of different parts of the curriculum

- develop non-discriminatory attitudes and understandings within the children towards disability, culture, social differences, 'race' and gender
- encourage children to value each other equally
- provide opportunities for children to express their own individuality and life experiences via a variety of curriculum experiences.

Empowerment is also used as a teaching technique when staff are committed to education for progressive social change in other areas of our social, economic, cultural and political life. This would include, for example, peace education, environmental education and education against homophobia, ageism and classism.

DEVELOPMENTAL CONSIDERATIONS

Empowerment will involve different aims and processes, depending on the age group of the children. The table below illustrates how children's age and developmental abilities may influence staff's work towards empowering children.

It should be remembered that attitudes to others and the formation of social values begin from the moment a child is born. Children learn about the world about them and the values placed on who they are from their first interactions with the world. Children can learn both fair and unfair perceptions about themselves and others. In an empowering approach to working with young children the emphasis is firmly on helping children to build fair perceptions about themselves and others. It is important to remember in this work that just as children can learn bias and unfairness they can unlearn it:

Even when children seem to hold unfair social perceptions of others…they have an intellectual capacity for un-doing their pre-existing unfair perceptions through personally meaningful experiences with others. (Hyun 2001, p. 11)

Skills underpinning empowerment	Age group			Concepts children can learn* [Will depend on developmental abilities.]
	Babies	Toddlers	3–8 years	
Help children feel good about themselves.	✓	✓	✓	I'm me. I'm special. Each of us is special. My family is special.
Build children's capacity to participate in the program.	✓	✓	✓	I'm capable; I can do things. I can use sounds, looks and words to express feelings and thoughts. If I try very hard I can do lots of things.
Build children's ability to have positive relationships with others.	✓	✓	✓	I have lots of different feelings. There are lots of ways I can show and tell how I feel. I can take care of others. Friends like to be called by their names. Friends are people we especially like to be with. I can have friends. Friends share things and play together. Friends do special things for each other.
Teach children to problem-solve whether fair or not fair.		✓	✓	It's not fair . . . when someone takes my toy without asking, when someone calls people names, when you laugh and make people cry, when you use words to hurt people, when you say things about people that are not true. It's fair . . . when we all share, when we learn what's special about others, when we can all have a turn, when we can all have special times. People need to have food to eat, somewhere to live, clothes to wear, ways to travel from one place to another, and they need to love and be loved. Not everybody has the same amount of these things. Is that fair?

| Skills underpinning empowerment | Age group | | | Concepts children can learn* [Will depend on developmental abilities.] |
	Babies	Toddlers	3–8 years	
Help children learn to stand up for themselves and others who are treated unfairly.	Model to lay foundations	✓	✓	I can use my words to say how I feel. It's not fair to hurt others. It's not fair for others to hurt me. When my friend is sad I can try to help. When I'm sad my friends can help. We can join together to help each other. There is always something we can do to help.
Build children's capacity to think critically.			✓	Is this true? Is this untrue? Is this fair? Is this unfair? How could we find out? Stereotypes are unfair because they are untrue. Can we always believe what we read in books? Can we always believe what we see on television? How might this picture/story/song hurt someone? What is this picture/story/song saying about people who look like this or dress like this or have skin this colour etc.? How might we find out more? Who could we talk to? What could we look at? What might we need to ask?

Source: Derman-Sparks, L., *Anti-bias Curriculum: Tools for Empowering Young Children*, 1989, 69–71, NAEYC, Washington

Equity considerations

To empower children who face discrimination in their daily lives it is important that staff consciously work with children to support them to:

- take increasing responsibility for their own learning and care
- continue learning with an enhanced sense of self-worth, identity, confidence and enjoyment
- contribute their own special strengths and interests to the group
- learn useful and appropriate ways to find out what they want to know
- understand their own individual ways of learning and being creative.

The challenges and opportunities for doing this will differ according to the inequity and injustice staff are working on with children. The issues in relation to 'racial' inequalities, gender inequalities and inequalities for children with disabilities are different from each other and thus require different approaches to empowering children. For the children who experience discrimination because of their 'race', gender or disability, empowerment involves addressing the negative impact of discrimination on their lives and providing them with the skills to challenge unfair treatment of themselves and others in the future. However, staff cannot work towards empowering these children unless they understand how inequity and injustice is shaping children's lives.

'RACE' AND CULTURE

Racial discrimination influences the lives of all children: those who are the victims of racial discrimination and those who perpetrate it. Children who have been the victims of racial discrimination need special support and encouragement to overcome the racially negative images they may develop about their own 'race'. Some black children may learn to value their skin colour and hair texture negatively. Children who have experienced racism will gain more power over their lives if staff:

- ensure that black children feel proud and confident about who they are. This involves building a strong group and personal identity (Derman-Sparks et al. 1991; Derman-Sparks 1998). Simple measures can be used to help children feel that their skin colour and physical characteristics are valued. For example, staff can ensure that children have access to paints which allow them to represent their own skin or hair colour. It is also important to think carefully about how colours are used and discussed within the curriculum. Is black always associated with negative or fearful images, for example, Halloween, witches, thunderstorms and monsters? Think of creative ways of helping children to rethink these associations, keeping in mind the following:

Help them to see that there is beauty in people of all physical types; develop language which expresses appreciation for people seemingly very different from themselves. Explore with even the youngest children similarities and differences. Use children's natural curiosity about their own peers and others they see around them, to challenge ideas of what's normal. (Brown et al. 1991, p. 5)

- ensure that the children's group and personal identities are strengthened by a program in which their cultural heritage is celebrated on a regular basis
- regularly discuss and challenge 'racial' stereotypes
- provide children who have experienced racial discrimination with the skills and confidence needed to challenge any act of racism against themselves and others. They need to recognise what is fair and what is not, and to work with others for fairness. Games that help children practise telling others that what they are doing or saying is hurtful and stories that provide models of how to stop people hurting others can be useful. Derman-Sparks et al. (1991, pp. 75–76) provide ideas for how these might be structured.

GENDER

Traditional gender stereotypes can limit how boys and girls understand what they are capable of, and how they should think, feel and behave, and also limit how they view other people's capabilities. These gender stereotypes can lead to power imbalances in how boys and girls experience the early childhood program. How these power imbalances impact on the lives of particular boys and girls will differ from child to child.

Not all boys will be powerful and not all girls powerless. For instance, a boy who practises being male in very non-traditional, non-sexist ways may not be very powerful within a group of traditionally gendered boys and girls (Renold 2004). He may face teasing and rejection when he wants to play with dolls or dress in pink. For girls who are non-traditionally gendered there may be similar difficulties in gaining acceptance within the group.

Children who are different to the gender norms of a particular group of children will gain more power over their lives if staff:

- make the different ways of being male and female visible via the curriculum. Stories, songs and images of boys and girls and men and women doing, dressing and trying out lots of different tasks can make children feel that traditional ways of being male and female are just one of many ways, and that their ways are equally valued in the centre
- enable boys and girls to experience the richness and diversity of different parts of the curriculum. Encourage all children to explore all aspects of the curriculum and ensure that the non-traditionally gendered children are supported when they try out new experiences. Being present to prevent and/or step in when teasing or exclusion is happening offers a simple way of ensuring that other children do not use their power to exclude non-traditionally gendered children from their play
- provide opportunities for girls and boys to express their own individuality and life experiences via a variety of curriculum experiences. Talking with children about gender stereotypes and encouraging

them to act in non-stereotypical ways can help children feel more able to be 'different' to the norm and also to feel powerful in their differences. There are some excellent examples of how to do this in Dally and Lindstrom (1996).

DISABILITY AND ADDITIONAL NEEDS

Empowering children with additional needs involves addressing the negative impact of discrimination and providing them with the skills to challenge this in their daily experiences (Yaoying 2007). Children with disabilities will gain more power over their lives if staff:

- make the different abilities of the children visible via the curriculum. Music and movement can be used to make people with disabilities audible and visible. For example, the words 'walking' and 'running' can be changed to 'moving' in songs such as 'Run, Sister, Run'
- enable all children to experience the richness and diversity of different parts of the curriculum. Movement can be used to ensure that constructive, open and sensitive attitudes develop about the children's own bodies and those of others. All children move in their own way, so don't feel that dance is an elitist art
- provide opportunities for children to express their own individuality and life experiences via a variety of curriculum experiences. For example, painting and drawing offer an opportunity to draw and paint images of oneself. It is important that children with disabilities, or children who have parents with disabilities, are encouraged and feel able to depict their bodies as they are and not feel that they need to reproduce images of able-bodied people.

> Con's father has had a serious car accident, and has lost the use of his lower limbs. Con's teacher, Lisa, has helped Con to learn how to draw wheelchairs so that Con is able to represent his family just as the other children do. She has done this by suggesting, describing and presenting Con with images of people in wheelchairs.
>
> *Reflection point:* How else might Lisa help Con to explore what it means to be in a wheelchair?

For children with disabilities to be empowered to participate to their maximum potential in the program it is also important that the children and adults around them actively display non-discriminatory attitudes and understandings towards disability. Stories, images and puppets offer very powerful opportunities for developing positive images and ideas about children with disabilities. Literature also conveys very powerful messages about people and the ways in which they are valued. It would be essential for children to have access to literature in which the heroine has a disability (for example, uses a wheelchair) and in which that disability is not presented as an overwhelming handicap. Unfortunately, children's books can often contain powerful negative images of people with disabilities—think of Captain Hook and the one-legged pirates. Often people with disabilities are portrayed as being naughty or frightening. The checklist in Chapter 14 is designed to help early childhood practitioners critically evaluate the disability content of books from an anti-discriminatory perspective.

An image can say a thousand words. Visual images in posters, photographs and books can relay very powerful messages to young children. Within a disability equity curriculum those images should be positive—avoid images that encourage others to feel sorry for people with disabilities. Focus on the positive aspects of their lives.

Alongside this it is important that staff encourage children to value each other equally. Dramatic play is often the venue that children choose to gain an understanding of others—often by projecting and identifying with them. This must be handled sensitively so that tolerance and empathy develops. It can be developed in ways that show how different places can be geared to the needs of people with disabilities. Equipment such as walking sticks, wheelchairs and dolls with disabilities can be included as a matter of course so that children can use them in their play. This should be accompanied by open and clear discussion. By restricting and banning play of this type the early childhood educator can widen the gap between people with different abilities.

Reflecting on empowering techniques

1   How would you define empowerment?
2   What is the relationship between general teaching techniques, such as questioning, and empowering?
3   Identify five general teaching techniques you will need to be familiar with in order to empower children.
4   Read the following extracts from Derman-Sparks et al. (1989, pp. 69–70).

A four-year-old White child asks a visitor to her day care center, 'What is your name?' The visitor answers, 'Rayko.' 'Yuck, yuck, yucky', responds the child. Her teacher admonishes, 'Be nice to our visitor'.

As their teacher begins reading a story in Spanish to an English-speaking group, a few children begin to giggle. The teacher stops reading and tells the children, 'I am stopping because some children are giggling while I am reading. That is not OK—it is rude. I know Spanish is a new language to some of you. Sometimes we are not comfortable with something we do not know and we laugh to make ourselves feel better, but laughing at how people talk is hurtful and unfair. Laughing is not OK, but it is OK to raise your hand and ask me questions about what I am reading'.

What differences were there between how the teacher acted in each situation? Do you think the teacher's actions were empowering for the children? How else might the teacher have acted to empower the children in each situation?

5   Read the following extracts from Derman-Sparks (1989, pp. 70–71).

Billy, a White child, refuses to sit next to George, a Cherokee child. Billy cries to his teacher, 'I'm afraid that George is going to kill me.' To learn about the source of this fear, the teacher asks, 'Why do you feel that way?'. Billy says, 'Because Indians kill White people. I saw it on TV last night.' Teacher: 'Billy, most TV programs are just make-believe, so there is no reason to be afraid of Indian people. The cowboy and Indian movies you see on TV do not tell the truth about Indian people. Many White people did mean things to Indian people, like taking away their land and their homes. That is why the Indian people fought back, to protect their homes and families. George is a member of our class. He and his family live in our neighbourhood, just like you and your family do. We will not insult him and his family by saying things about Indian people that are not true. Whenever I hear anyone saying untrue things about Indian people, I tell them to stop. I'd like you to help me do that.'

After building a house in the block area, Barbara and Lisa, two Black girls, have a disagreement about where to put the furniture. Unable to reach a compromise, Lisa screams at Barbara, 'Well, I don't like you anyway because you've got short nappy hair. My hair is good'. Teacher: 'Lisa, you are upset because Barbara wants to put the furniture one place and you want to put it some other place. However, you must not hurt Barbara's feelings by saying something that is mean and disrespectful. All hair grows differently. Many Black people's hair grows slowly. It is usually short and springy. How your hair grows depends on the kind of hair your family has. Lisa, in this classroom you may not call your hair better than anyone else's. Barbara, if some people say mean things about your hair, you just tell them that your hair is pretty just as it is. Now let's figure out a way to solve the problem of where to place the doll furniture. By learning to co-operate, you won't say mean things that hurt feelings.'

Which goals do you believe informed the teacher's action in each instance?

Improving teaching in practice

1   Identify a child in your group who you believe is facing unjust or unequal treatment. Observe the child and identify a problem that you can work with the child to solve. Plan at least three periods of time in which you work closely with the child on this problem. Implement and record these sessions.

2   After each session evaluate your own empowering skills by reviewing the extent to which you were able to promote the child's self-esteem and their ability to challenge unfairness.

3   What additional skills and knowledge do you need to consolidate and improve your empowering skills?

4   How and how well did you take account of the following considerations when empowering the child: the child's gender, ability levels, cultural and 'racial' background, and developmental age and stage?

5   Smith and Lovat (1990, p. 8) argued that practising critical reflection with 'critical friends' who can 'listen, clarify, challenge and confront within a trusting, acceptant but risking relationship' can improve our teaching for empowerment. Try the above tasks with a 'critical friend'.

FURTHER READING

Critical curriculum and empowerment

Apple, M., Gandin, L. and Hypolito, M. 2001, 'Paulo Freire, 1921–97', in J. Palmer, ed., *Fifty Modern Thinkers on Education: From Piaget to the Present Day*, Routledge, Taylor and Francis Group, New York, pp. 128–132.

Darder, A. (ed.) 2002, *Reinventing Paulo Freire: A Pedagogy of Love*, Westview Press, Boulder, CO.

Freire, P. 1972, *Pedagogy of the Oppressed* (Myra Bergman Ramos, trans.), Penguin Books, Middlesex.

——1985, *The Politics of Education: Culture, Power and Liberation* (Donaldo Macedo, trans.), Bergin Garvey Publishers Inc., Massachusetts.

Sleeter, C. and Grant, C. 1999, *Making Choices for Multicultural Education. Five Approaches to Race, Class and Gender*, 3rd edn, Prentice Hall, New Jersey [Chapter 6 is of particular relevance].

Empowering young children

Dau, E. (ed.) 2001, *The Anti-Bias Approach in Early Childhood*, Pearson Education Australia, French's Forest, NSW.

Derman-Sparks, L. and the Anti-Bias Task Force 1989, *Anti-Bias Curriculum: Tools for Empowering Young Children*, NAEYC, Washington, DC [refer to pp. 69–81].

Jones, K. and Mules, R. 2001, 'Developing critical thinking and activism' in E. Dau, ed., *The Anti-Bias Approach in Early Childhood*, pp. 192–209, Pearson Education Australia, French's Forest, NSW.

MacNaughton, G. 2003, *Shaping Early Childhood: Learners, Contexts and Curriculum*, Open University Press, Milton Keynes [refer to Chapter 9].

Ramsey, P. 2004, *Teaching and Learning in a Diverse World: Multicultural Education for Young Children*, 3rd edn, Teachers College Press, New York.

ONLINE AND MULTI-MEDIA RESOURCES

Text

Institute of Anti-bias Education Study Guide, which describes the aims of anti-bias education. Full text reading at: **http://www.adl.org/tools_teachers/tip_antibias_ed.html**

Access to practical resources for implementing social justice and anti-bias curriculum with young children at: **http://californiatomorrow.org**

Multi-media – video

Anti-Bias Curriculum, Pacific Oaks College, Extension Services, 714 West California Bvd, Pasadena, CA 91105.

Children Without Prejudice, BBC, London.

Empowered to Learn: Te Whariki for Infants and Toddlers, published for the Ministry of Education by Learning Media, New Zealand, 2001.

MacNaughton, G., Campbell, S., Smith, K. and Lawrence, H. 2002, *Equity Adventures in Early Childhood*, Centre for Equity and Innovation in Early Childhood, The University of Melbourne, available at:
http://www.mup.unimelb.edu.au/e-showcase/0-734-02679-X.html

What's the Difference?, Free Kindergarten Association, Melbourne.

REFERENCES

Apple, M., Gandin, L. and Hypolito, M. 2001, 'Paulo Freire, 1921–97', in J. Palmer, ed., *Fifty Modern Thinkers on Education: From Piaget to the Present Day*, Routledge, Taylor and Francis Group, New York, pp. 128–132.

Brown, C., Barnfield, J. and Stone, M. 1991, *Spanner in the Works: Education for Racial Equality and Social Justice in White Schools*, Trentham Books, Staffordshire, England.

Carger, C. 2003, 'Reflections on compassionate and transformative education', in P. Miller, *Narratives from the Classroom: An Introduction to Teaching*, Sage Publications, London, Thousand Oaks and New Delhi. pp. 108–124.

Carr, W. and Kemmis, S. 1986, *Becoming Critical: Knowing through Action Research*, Deakin University, Geelong.

Dally, S. and Lindstrom, H. 1996, *Girls and Boys Come Out to Play: Teaching about Gender Construction and Sexual Harassment in English and Studies of Society and Environment*, Department for Education and Children's Services, Adelaide.

Daniels, H. and Bizar, M. 2005, *Teaching the Best Practice Way: Methods that Matter*, Stenhouse Publishers, Portland, ME.

Darder, A (ed.) 2002, *Reinventing Paulo Freire: A Pedagogy of Love*, Westview Press, Boulder, CO.

Davis, J. 2005, 'Educating for sustainability in the early years: creating cultural change in a child care setting', *Australian Journal of Environmental Education* 21, pp. 47–55.

Derman-Sparks, L. 1998 (published 2001), 'Education without prejudice: goals, principles and practices', Paper presented at *Respect: Education without Prejudice, a Challenge for Early Years Educators in Ireland* conference, 16 October, Dublin, Ireland, (pub. Pavee Point Travellors Centre, pp. 22–31).

Derman-Sparks, L. and the Anti-Bias Task Force 1989, *Anti-Bias Curriculum: Tools for Empowering Young Children*, NAEYC, Washington, DC, pp. 69–81.

Derman-Sparks, L., Gutierrez, M. and Phillips, C. 1991, *Teaching Young Children to Resist Bias: What Parents Can Do*, NAEYC, Washington, DC.

Freire, P. 1970, *Pedagogy of the Oppressed*, Continuum Publishing Company, London and New York.

——1972, *Pedagogy of the Oppressed* (Myra Bergman Ramos, trans.), Penguin Books, Middlesex.

Gore, J. 2003, '"What can we do for you? What can 'we' do for 'you'?" Struggling over empowerment in critical and feminist pedagogy', in A. Darder, M. Baltodano and D. Rodolfo, eds, *The Critical Pedagogy Reader*, Routledge Taylor and Francis Group, new York, pp. 331–348.

Hyun, E. 2001, 'Cultural complexity that affects young children's contemporary growth, change and learning', Paper presented at the *Annual Meeting of the Educational Research Association*, 10–14 April, Seattle, WA, ED451941.

Ibrahim, S. and Alkire, S. 2007, 'Agency and empowerment: a proposal for internationally comparable indicators', *Oxford Development Studies*, 35(4), pp. 379–403.

Kaber, N. 2005, 'Gender equality and women's empowerment: a critical analysis of the third Millennium Development Goal', in C. Sweetman, ed., *Gender and the Millennium Development Goals*, Oxfam, London, pp. 13–24.

Killoran, I., Panaroni, M., Rivers, S., Razack,Y., Vetter, D. and Tymon, D. 2004, 'Rethink, Revise, React: using an anti-bias curriculum to move beyond the usual', *Childhood Education*, 80(3), pp. 149–156.

Lather, P. 1991, *Getting Smart Feminist Research and Pedagogy With/in the Postmodern*, Routledge, New York.

MacNaughton, G. 2003, *Shaping Early Childhood: Learners, Contexts and Curriculum,* Open University Press, Milton Keynes.

——2004, 'Exploring critical constructivist perspectives on children's learning', in A. Anning, J. Cullen & M. Fleer (eds), *Early Childhood Education: Society and Culture*, Sage Publications, London, pp. 43–56.

Ministry of Education (NZ), 1996, *Te Whariki: Early Childhood Curriculum,* Ministry of Education, New Zealand, <http://www.minedu.govt.nz>

Ramsey, P. 2004, *Teaching and Learning in a Diverse World: Multicultural Education for Young Children*, 3rd edn, Teachers' College Press, New York.

Rees, S. 1991, *Achieving Power: Practice and Policy in Social Welfare*, Allen & Unwin, Sydney.

Renold, E. 2004, '"Other" boys: negotiating non-hegemonic masculinities in the primary school', *Gender and Education*, 16(2), pp. 247–265.

Siraj-Blatchford, I. and Siraj-Blatchford, J. (eds) 1995, *Educating the Whole Child: Cross Curriculum Skills: Themes and Dimensions*, Open University Press, Milton Keynes.

Smith, D. and Lovat, T. 1990, *Curriculum: Action on Reflection*, Social Science Press, Sydney.

Stinson, D. 2004, 'Mathematics as "gate keeper"(?): three theoretical perspectives that aim toward empowering all children with a key to the gate', *The Mathematics Educator,* 14(1), pp. 8–18.

Wasserman, S. 1991, 'Louis E. Raths: theories of empowerment', *Childhood Education*, 67(4), pp. 225–239.

Wilkes, G. (ed.) 1979, *Collins Dictionary of the English Language*, Penguin Books, Middlesex.

Yaoying, X. 2007, 'Empowering culturally diverse families of young children with disabilities: the Double ABCX Model', *Early Childhood Education Journal*, 34(6), pp. 431–437.

Zygmunt-Fillwalk, E., Staley, L., Kumar, R., Lin, C., Moore, C., Salakaya, M. and Szecsi, T. 2007, 'Kids speaking up for kids: advocacy by children, for children', *Childhood Education*, 83(4), pp. 199–206.

Chapter 26

Philosophising

Philosophy: the rational investigation of being, knowledge and right conduct.

(*Collins Dictionary of the English Language*, p. 1101)

Philosophising: to make philosophising speculations.
(*Collins Dictionary of the English Language*, p. 1101)

Philosophy for Children emphasises a conversation and dialogue based process of inquiry. As all participants share their own ideas so each individual must consider many different perspectives.
(Philosophy for Children website, New Zealand, <http://www.p4c.org.nz>)

Philosophy begins in wonder and in the capacity for curiosity. Curiosity is more important than knowledge since it is needed to generate knowledge.

(Fisher 2007, p. 619)

What?

Broadly speaking, philosophy is the study of truth. In studying truth, philosophers seek answers to questions such as, 'What do we know to be true?'; 'What is truth?'; 'How do we know this is true?'; 'How can we prove this is true?'. To answer these questions philosophers study, and try to understand and evaluate, what we claim to be true about our world. They examine critically and take apart our truth claims to see if they are indeed true. For example, when scientists claim that the earth is round, the philosopher of science examines this truth claim critically and asks, 'How do we know that the earth is round?'; 'How can we prove that this is true?'; 'Are the methods we use to prove that the earth is round the right methods to get to the truth?'. Philosophers ask such questions of all areas of knowledge about our social world. For example, philosophers can and do study the truths of medicine, geography, religion, psychology, mathematics, education, law, history and ethics.

In searching for what we know about our world (what we can claim to be true) philosophy uncovers problems in what we claim to be true that often have an ethical and moral dimension to them. This is because what we claim as truth comes to be seen as the right and proper way to conduct ourselves; that is, when we ask philosophical questions about education, we question what we know to be the truth about how we should educate young children. We might find that there is no single truth about how to educate children, but that many different versions of what is the best or 'truest' arise. Parents may have one truth, politicians another and educators yet another. When philosophers probe our claims to truth they may find that we can't prove what we claim to be true.

As such, philosophy is a form of critical reflection about the world. It can improve our ability to think carefully about what we do and say whether it is right and true, and the ethical and moral implications of this. There is good evidence that young children can do this (Murris 2000).

As a teaching technique, 'doing philosophy' or philosophising with children involves studying children's everyday truths and the truths of others in the world about them. In doing this children learn to be curious by learning to ask 'deep and interesting questions' (Fisher 2007, p. 619) and learning to give reasons and evidence for what they think (Fisher 2007).

Philosophising with young children improves their ability to think carefully about what they and others claim to be right and true.

Maria works as child care worker in an upper-class suburb in Melbourne. She cares for a group of four- and five-year-old children who will soon be going to school. Maria decides to use a current issue for discussion with them: the refugee camps in Africa. One of the children has described what he has seen on the TV news. Maria shows the children a photo of a crowded refugee camp.

Maria: 'Has anyone seen pictures like this on TV or in a newspaper? What questions do you have about these people?'

She takes notes of the ensuing questions:

- Who are these people?
- What are they doing there?
- Why are there so many of them?
- How did they get there?
- What do they eat?
- Where do they sleep?
- Are they families?

Maria then encourages the children to reflect on their questions and to make connections between them. She then begins to explore some answers with the children.

Maria: 'What do you think they're doing there? Where might the food come from?'

Maria listens carefully to the children's suggestions, taking care to show them that she values all answers.

At the end of the session Maria feeds back to the children their initial questions and they all discuss how much they have found out about the refugees. Maria praises the children for being so curious and for sticking to the topic at hand.

Issues and debates

CAN YOUNG CHILDREN 'DO' PHILOSOPHY?

There is a longstanding debate about whether or not young children can 'do' philosophy. As Murris (2000) explained:

Philosophers since as long ago as Plato have had plenty to say on the subject—most of it negative. The debate continues unabated, but is often complicated by the confusion between 'doing' philosophy as a subject—i.e., studying the ideas of the world's great thinkers since the Greeks—and 'philosophising', i.e., thinking about any question in a philosophical way. The debate is complicated further by disagreement over what the term 'philosophy' actually means. (p. 261)

The debate about children's capacity to engage or not in philosophy is rooted in different images of the child and their capacities. Opponents of philosophy for children argue that young children cannot learn to do abstract philosophy. Some opponents have drawn from Piagetian theories of children's stages of cognitive development to argue that young children do not have the capacity for formal abstract thought. Other opponents often see the child as innocent of the world and too inexperienced in it to have valuable insights into its complexities. Its proponents answer by giving examples of children talking about abstract concepts such as death, dreaming, bravery and time-travel and note that children can use analogies to engage in complex thinking (Murris 2000).

How?

DeHaan, MacColl and McCutcheon (1995a, 1995b) detailed a 15-point plan for initiating and guiding philosophical discussion in groups with young children. Their guidance builds from the work of Matthew Lipman (1989) and the following points draw heavily on this guidance:

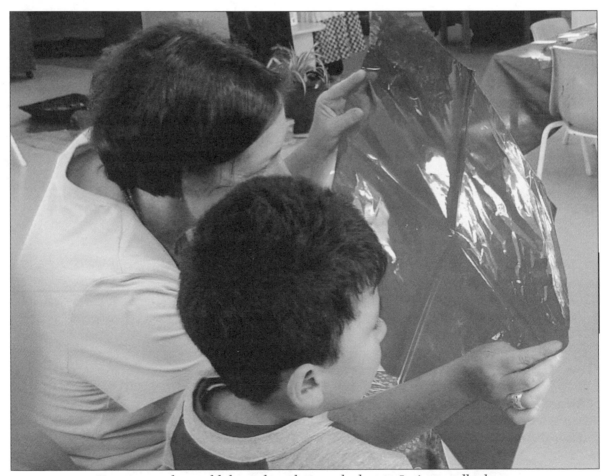

How we see the world depends on how we look at it. Let's try cellophane.

Preparation
- Select materials to stimulate discussion. These could include a storybook, song, poem or image.
- Form small groups and organise them so that everyone can hear each other. Listening is an important part of learning about how others think.

Engaging the children
- Present the materials to the children.
- Ask them what questions they have about what they have heard or seen.
- Makes notes about the questions raised.
- Model careful listening.
- Keep the children focused on the questions and the topic.

Deepening the discussion
- Make connections between the questions by asking if any of the questions are linked.
- Encourage discussion by asking one of the children to explain why they asked a particular question and encourage others to join in. The children should decide which question to explore first.
- Make distinctions between different answers so that children learn about the different ways in which questions can be answered.
- Encourage different points of view on a question.
- Ask children why they have the point of view they have.
- Point out inconsistencies in their answers.
- Talk about any disagreements and try to work out why they occurred.

Concluding the discussion
- Evaluate with the children how they feel at the end. Were they happy with the answers to their questions? What else do they want to know about the topic?

Fisher (2007) offers an alternative format also built from Lipman's work:

- Use a focusing exercise to gain the children's attention and help them to relax.
- Share a stimulus for thinking.
- Allow thinking time for children where they share their ideas with a partner.
- Encourage children to share their questions with each other and the group, and then ask them to select one to start the enquiry.
- Encourage children to discuss each other's ideas.
- Summarise what has been said and reflect on what has been learnt using graphic means to do this.

THEORETICAL BACKGROUND

PHILOSOPHY WITH CHILDREN AND THE WORK OF MATTHEW LIPMAN

Matthew Lipman is an American educator who has developed an approach called 'Philosophy for Children'. Through this work Lipman has generated international interest (see, for example, Robinson 1995). The hall marks of Lipman's approach are:

- Philosophical issues and discussion are generated with young children through narrative forms such as picture books, poems and stories.
- Workbooks with practical resources and exercises help guide teachers and children through their philosophical inquiries.

- The key aim of doing philosophy with children is to help them to become critical thinkers.
- Children learn critical thinking by inquiring, reasoning, forming concepts and communicating meanings to others in what Lipman calls a 'community of inquiry' (Lipman 1995, p. 69).
- A community of inquiry operates on democractic principles (based on Lipman 1995; Fields 1995).

Lipman (1989) pointed out that there are several misconceptions about what constitutes critical thinking and argued that critical thinking is not:

- about drilling children in how to think
- the same as logical thinking.

Critical thinking is a form of thinking that evolves over time through building a community of thinkers.

Successful group philosophy sessions require a climate in which children can enjoy sharing their theories of the world with others. This involves a careful selection of stimulus materials and asking appropriate questions. Fisher (2007, p. 624) details the type of questions that can help build philosophical thinking as follows:

1 Literal (or factual) questions ask for information: 'What is this about?'; 'Can you remember what happened?'; 'What do you have to do?'

2 Analytic questions call for critical and creative thinking: 'What question(s) do you have?'; 'What reasons can you give?'; 'What are the problems/possible solutions here?'

3 Conceptual questions call for abstract thinking: 'What is the key concept (strategy or rule) here and what does it mean?' 'What criteria are we using to judge this (or test if it is true)?'; 'How might we further investigate this concept (strategy or hypothesis)?'

Good stimulus materials to generate philosophical discussion are those in which children have an active interest and in which there are puzzles, issues, dilemmas and problems to be solved (Sprod 1995). The websites listed at the end of this chapter have suggestions for children's books, poems, songs and posters to use. When choosing stimulus material consider the following questions:

- Will the materials encourage the children to wonder about the issue or dilemma? For example, are there surprises in the storyline or image, or is more than one solution to the problem shown?
- Will the materials extend or challenge children's current understandings of the issue?

When deciding which questions to use to help children learn to think philosophically, questions that ask why, how and if generate dialogue that helps to challenge children's thinking (Fisher 2007). More informal opportunities for discussing children's theories of how the world works should also be sought. Children will share their theories with adults if their ideas are valued, if they have lots to wonder about in their daily world and if they have the time and opportunity to share their thoughts with others in a caring relationship. It is also important to be watchful for moments where children can be encouraged to explore different viewpoints on the same issue. Everyday problems between children offer many opportunities for this. When staff encounter differences of opinion between children they can help them learn about different viewpoints by saying, 'We have a problem. It seems that both Jane and Clara want to use the red spade. Does anyone have ideas about what we could do?'

Involving children in public reasoning of the problem will help them see that there is more than one way to understand a situation, generating the possibility of children accessing and exploring multiple subjectivities. This possibility is strengthened in a process of philosophical inquiry in which children's questions and concerns form the basis of dialogue and in which they are exposed to others' belief systems and moral truths (Schertz 2007).

There are many informal opportunities to explore moral questions with young children in the daily life of a centre or classroom and to engage in problem-solving what should happen when we do not all agree.

This form of dialogue supports the growth of relationships and the development of empathy (Hoffman 2000; Schertz 2007).

> Dia, a teacher of three-year-olds, helps two children to sort out who will use the wheelbarrow first. She asks questions about how they might resolve their dispute: 'What can we do when two people want the same thing at the same time? What are the different ways that we can share?'
>
> Jon is having a discussion with his Grade 2 class about taking other people's lunches. He begins by telling the children that he has a problem. He explains it and invites them to help him solve it.
>
> _Reflection point:_ What should Jon's and Dia's next steps be?

USING NEW TECHNOLOGIES TO SUPPORT CHILDREN'S PHILOSOPHISING

Software programs can offer some ways in which to build these skills in young children. However, it is important to choose programs that support the principles underpinning philosophising with young children. As philosophising supports children's empowerment it is important to choose software that encourages children in groups to make a discovery and to construct meanings as they use the software.

New technologies can also be used to link children with others as a way of growing their capacity to think critically and philosophically. An example of this is reported by Ligorio, Talamo and Pontecorvo (2005). They studied two Grade 5 classes from two European countries (Italy and Greece) who 'collaborated in writing fairytales inspired by philosophically relevant issues. The software supporting the task is an asynchronous virtual environment. Videos recorded in the Italian class and materials posted on the platform were analysed using qualitative approaches and discourse analysis.' (p. 357). Similar work could be undertaken with younger children as a way of extending group thinking and questioning around shared interests across geographical and cultural boundaries.

When and why?

GOAL RELEVANCE

Philosophising with children enriches and extends their cognitive skills, and helps to build a strong disposition for curiosity and multiple perspective-taking (Schertz 2007). Such dispositions are important across all areas of learning and across all disciplines. Specifically, philosophising with young children is appropriate when staff want them to learn to be curious about:

- who they are and their place in the world
- how the world works
- how we relate to each other
- what is fair, good and just, or not, in the world (Schertz 2007; DeHaan, MacColl and McCutcheon 1995a, 1995b).

By applying philosophical thinking to the world children will learn to:

- think creatively (Wegerif 2005)
- understand multiple viewpoints in the world (Schertz 2007; Daniel, Doudin and Pons 2006)
- ask questions (Fisher 2007)
- search for answers (Fisher 2007)
- improve social and thinking skills (Stanley 2007)
- use other people's ideas (DeHaan, MacColl and McCutcheon 1995a, 1995b).

'What do you think?'

Philosophising with children also strengthens a sense of community within a classroom and builds strong ethical values in young children and higher order thinking skills. More specifically, researchers (Daniel, Doudin and Pons 2006) argue that it can build children's pro-social skills at the cognitive level from the preschool years. They found a significant difference in primary classroom children's social representations of violence in classrooms where philosophy for children was used and those where it was not. They argued that philosophy for children helps build a mind-set for peace by helping children to better understand the reasons for others' violence and the effects of violence on others.

The New Zealand Philosophy for Children group identifies the following skills that are built through 'doing' philosophy with children:

- cognitive skills
- evaluating reasons and arguments
- exploring and analysing concepts
- drawing inferences
- identifying underlying suppositions and assumptions
- making distinctions
- seeing connections
- identifying fallacies
- testing generalisations
- formulating questions
- clarifying ideas
- constructing arguments
- refining and modifying arguments in response to criticism
- recognising implications: theoretical and practical
- finding examples and counter examples

- finding analogies and disanalogies
- seeing broader perspectives
- formulating and testing criteria
- being consistent
- sticking to the point
- self-correction
- co-operative skills
- listening to others
- open mindedness
- treating others' views with respect
- building on others' ideas
- confident self-expression
- being willing to offer criticism
- being willing to accept and respond to criticism
- becoming committed to inquiry
- valuing reasonableness
- developing intellectual courage (<http://www.p4c.org.nz>).

There is a growing body of research that is establishing these and other benefits accruing in classrooms where philosophy for children is formally structured into the curriculum (e.g. Schertz 2007; Daniel, Doudin and Pons 2006; Fisher 2007; Stanley 2007).

DEVELOPMENTAL CONSIDERATIONS

To share philosophical thinking with others requires language and abstract thought. For young children to share their philosophical thinking with others they need to have the cognitive and communicative capacity to use language to represent thought, the ability to engage in conversation with others and the ability to concentrate. This means that philosophising, as discussed in this chapter, is a teaching technique that will be most appropriately used with older preschool children and children in the early years of school.

However, it is important to remember that babies are struggling to make sense of their world from the moment they enter it. While babies cannot 'talk' of this struggle, staff can encourage and preserve this 'sense of wonder' by allowing them to play with their voices and their environment, and by showing interest and respect for their babbles (Honig 2007). Such encouragement can help build in younger children the 'disposition' to wonder and to be curious, and can act as a spur for them to think philosophically in their preschool years.

Between 18 months of age and two years of age there is an increase in children's ability to use language to talk about feelings. It is also a time when they can 'fast-map' (Honig 2007) learning new vocabulary, so it's a great time to talk with toddlers about feelings—their own and those of other people—and so expand both their vocabulary for talking about feelings and their understandings that different people have different feelings at different times. Learning to communicate feelings at this age is an important part of learning to problem-solve and build constructive social relationships (Hemmeter, Ostrosky and Fox 2006).

> Eighteen-month-old Turc is finding life a little difficult as he wants things 'now' and he often has to wait his turn at the child care centre. He responds to this frustration by flinging himself on the floor and screaming. Shona, his designated child care worker, understands his frustration and helps by verbalising his feelings for him.
> 'I guess that you're a bit cross just now.'
> 'It's hard when you can't have what you want.'
> 'You're pretty angry at the moment.'

'Remember yesterday when you were cross and you waited and got the car after Jon had a turn?'
'Let's think about a way to wait.'

Reflection point: How is Shona helping Turc to problem-solve and reflect on social relationships at an early age?

It is also a time to ask children open-ended questions (refer to Chapter 13 on questioning). Open-ended questions generate a sense of curiosity, wonder and competence in toddlers, yet US research has found that over 80 per cent of the time teachers ask toddlers closed-ended questions (Honig 2007).

Suitable philosophical projects for preschool children will be those that interest them. Children's conversations, artwork and imaginative play will offer many clues as to what they have questions about and what they enjoy thinking about. You can encourage 'possibility thinking' (Burnard et al. 2006, p. 240) by posing questions with children and allowing them to take risks in their creative work.

Children's self-portraits generated though drawing, painting or photography can be used to provoke the question, 'Who am I?'. Children can be encouraged to think about the questions: 'How do I know this is me?'; 'What other things (apart from how I look) make me?'; 'What is the same about me and other children?'; 'What is different about me that makes me who I am?'. Questions of identity and how we know who our 'true' selves are form the heart of much philosophical inquiry. Children can be encouraged to think about these questions in a concrete way that builds on the things they are already working with and thinking about each day.

Examples of questions preschool children ask and comments they make that staff can use to help them learn basic philosophical thinking processes are shown below.

Comments by preschool childen	Source	Issues echoed in 'adult' philosophy	Possible questions to further children's thinking (based on DeHaan et al. 1995a, b)
'I wonder who the first people were?'	Latham 1996, p. 13.	How did life on earth begin?	Why did you say that? How could we find out? What do other people know about that?
'You shouldn't smoke, you might die, it's naughty.'	Collins 1992, p. 12.	What is the relationship between life and death?	How do you know that? Can you think of a time when that wouldn't happen?
'We knocked down the leaves . . . we're trying to find out how many. How many down. How many on the tree.'	Mousley 1993, p. 4.	How is mathematical knowledge of the world verified?	What is it that puzzles you? How could we work that out?
'Being black is hard work.'	Brown 1995, p. 13.	What is the nature of racism?	What do you mean by that? What do others think? How do you know that?

Children in the early years of schooling can be supported in their critical reasoning skills through language arts programs that have the following features:

- a strong relationship between what children are talking about and what they are reading
- a stress on the meaning in children's reading and writing rather than on its form
- a link between children's language experiences and the folklore of their culture. This helps them learn what has been said with language and how language can be used to convey ideas
- they stimulate the children to think about what they are reading
- they make children very familiar with everyday words (Lipman 1988).

In addition, children's critical thinking skills will be improved by learning that everyday words have more than one meaning (Lipman 2003). Word games, puns and nonsense books help with this. Wing Han Lamb (2002, p. 9) identified 10 philosophical questions that could be explored with young children. They were as follows:

1 Why do we exist?
2 How can we be sure that everything is not a dream?
3 Can we make time stand still?
4 What makes us human?
5 What does it mean to be alive?
6 Am I the same person as when I was a baby?
7 Why should I be kind to animals?
8 Should I be good when no-one is watching?
9 What is a friend?
10 What is art?

Fisher (1999) offers the following philosophical questions that are used with children in primary schools in the UK to help them engage in philosophical thinking:

- How do you know you are not dreaming at this moment?
- How do you know when something is true or not?
- Is an apple dead or alive?
- Is it right to eat animals?
- What is the difference between pretending and lying?
- What is the difference between a real person and a robot?
- Is there a difference between your mind and your brain?
- Can animals think?
- Is it ever right to tell lies?
- What are the most valuable things in your life? (Fisher 1999, p. 60)

Equity considerations

Preschool children and children in the early years of school can understand what is fair and what is not fair in their daily world. This ability to understand fairness can be used to explore what rules need to be developed in the centre to ensure fairness around issues of culture, 'race', gender, disability and class. The ideas of fairness and people's rights can be explored using the techniques and processes above to target some of the specific ways in which unfairness can manifest itself in relationships between children and to build young children's awareness of social issues (Chafel et al. 2007).

'RACE' AND CULTURE

Children's friendships can be very flexible and can quickly change from one day to the next. Also, there are many different factors that impact on whom children form friendships with. However, we do know that children can form friendships based on 'race' from their toddler years and can be racist in their friendship choices (MacNaughton 2001). Philosophical questions concerning how we think about what and who a friend is can help children reflect critically on and rethink these decisions. Questions that can prompt this rethinking include: 'How do you know someone is a friend?'; 'Can someone be a friend when they are different from you?'; 'How do we choose our friends?'; 'How do we feel when people are not friends with us?'; 'How would it feel to not have your friend talk to you because your skin was a different colour to theirs?'.

Preschool children's thinking about 'racial' difference is often inconsistent, based on how things look rather than logical reasoning, and they often make incorrect generalisations. This means that young children can be very susceptible to believing the 'racial' stereotypes they see in the world about them (Davis, MacNaughton and Smith 2007). If children see images of Aboriginal Australians with boomerangs hunting kangaroos and wearing loin cloths they can quickly generalise that all Aboriginal Australians do this. Some of the 'racial' stereotypes they see and read, and thus become susceptible to, include the following:

- Native Americans all ride on horseback and shoot bows and arrows.
- All people from China eat with chopsticks.
- All Italo-Australians love pasta.
- All Vietnamese people came to Australia in boats.
- All Anglo-Australians live in big houses and love barbecues.

Philosophising with children can be used to help them rethink their stereotyped 'racial' beliefs. Questions such as the following can help children become critical thinkers about 'racial' truths: 'How do you know Italo-Australians love pasta?'; 'Is someone who loves pasta an Italo-Australian?'; 'Can you be an Italo-Australian if you hate pasta?'.

Some children's books that question 'racial' stereotypes include:

- *All the Colors We Are* by K. Kissinger (1994, Redleaf Press, Minnesota) prompts children's thinking about how people get their skin colour.
- *The Real Story of Stone Soup* by Ying Chang Compestine (2007, Dutton Juvenile,) raises issues of 'ageism, classism, and child labor'.
- *If a Bus Could Talk: The Story of Rosa Parks* by Faith Ringgold (1999, Simon & Schuster Children's Publishing) 'shares a story with young children about a powerful civil rights leader'.
- *Calling the Doves (El Canto de las Palomas)* by Juan Felipe Herrer (2001, Children's Book Press) explores what it means to be an immigrant in a new country.

When children are learning a language in addition to their mother tongue, developing philosophical thinking in the second language will take time. It is important to remember that fairness does not mean that everyone should have the same treatment all of the time. Maintaining mother tongue language is important for a child's identity and cultural heritage. When children are maintaining their mother tongue and learning a second language, fairness will involve giving them attention to ensure that they can contribute effectively to the group. It is important that children learning a new language see its value as a tool that can help them to solve new problems and engage with the world in different ways to their first language (Mushi 2002). Using language to generate philosophical thinking can support this work.

GENDER

There is research that shows that boys and girls often contribute differently to packing away time in early childhood programs. Boys tend to do less of it and girls tend to do more of it. Often the girls tend to do it with fewer reminders from adults than do the boys. One way to encourage children to think about this and work out solutions to it is to engage children in a discussion about whether they think this is fair and how they might make it fairer. For example, children could be asked to think about the following questions: 'Who packs away every day?'; 'Can you tell me who packed up with you yesterday?'; 'How could we find out if everyone shared in packing away?'; 'How would you decide who should help with packing away?'; 'Do you think it is fair that some people pack away more than others?'.

Children have often developed strong and persistent traditional gender stereotypes by the time they are three years of age (MacNaughton 2007). These stereotypes embed clear rules about what boys and girls will, won't, can and can't do into children's thinking, and include:

- Only boys play with trains, blocks and bicycles.

- Only girls play with dolls and in the home corner.
- There are boys' drinks and girls' drinks.
- Girls can't have short hair.

Philosophising with children can be used to help them rethink their stereotyped gender beliefs. Questions such as the following can help children become critical thinkers about their 'gender truths': 'How do you know boys are stronger than girls?'; 'Is someone who is strong always a boy?'; 'Can you be a boy if you are not very strong?'.

Some children's books that challenge gender stereotypes include:

- *Meggie Moon* by Elizabeth Baguley, illustrated by Gregoire Mabire (2005, Good Books) explores what happens when two boys who don't want to play with girls learn that girls have brilliant ideas.
- *Sally Jean, the Bicycle Queen* by Cari Best, illustrated by Christine Davenier (2006, Melanie Kroupa books/ Farrar Straus Giroux) about a girl who builds a new bicycle.
- *The Best Bee-Keeper of Lalibela* by Christina Kessler, illustrated by Leonard Jenkins (2006, unp., distributed by Holiday House) about a girl who challenges the idea that making honey is men's work.

DISABILITY AND ADDITIONAL NEEDS

All children approach and complete tasks such as painting or building in different ways. However, when a child with a disability is in a group with children without disabilities they can often be disadvantaged by how the task is presented. When staff are rethinking how activities offered in the centre can be made more appropriate for children with disabilities, they can involve all the children in the group. Children can explore the idea that there is no right way to complete most tasks and be encouraged to think about finding other ways of doing things that a child with a disability might find difficult. Staff can encourage children to think about what other ways things could be done, how activities could be adapted to suit a particular child's needs and what assistance might be offered. They can also be encouraged to think about how to find out if their suggestions are workable and would be welcomed by a particular child. For example, imagine there is a child in the group (let's call her Beth) with insufficient strength in her hands to hold a paint brush. All the children, including Beth, could be asked to think about how she could participate in painting. They could also be encouraged to think about how they could find out if Beth liked the agreed change.

More general discussion about the nature of hearing, seeing, moving, feeling and tasting things can also help children appreciate the different abilities and disabilities of people. The following questions about hearing and listening, taken from DeHaan, MacColl and McCutcheon (1995a, pp. 72–73), provide some starting points for such discussions. They can readily be adapted to talk about other sensory-motor abilities with preschool children.

- Is it hard to listen?
- Is listening the same as hearing?
- Can we hear without seeing?
- Can we see without hearing?
- Do we all hear the same things?
- How do we know what other people hear?

Reflecting on philosophising techniques

1 Briefly define philosophy.
2 Develop five philosophical questions you could ask if you were a philosopher of early childhood education.

3　What are the main things that early childhood staff need to do to ensure that children do 'remain active and curious philosophers' in the early childhood program?

4　To what extent have you been encouraged to be an 'active and curious philosopher' during your education?

5　Select a poem you could use with young children to engage them in philosophical thinking. What are some of the questions you think children might ask about the poem?

6　Read one of the following picture books. What questions might the book prompt from children?
- Gay, M.L. 2002, *Stella: Fairy of the Forest*, Groundwood Books, Toronto, Canada.
- Ziefart, H. and Doherty, R. 2002, *Toes have Wiggles, Kids have Giggles*, G.P. Putnam and Sons, New York.
- Baylor, B. 1998, *The Table where Posh People Sit*, Aladdin Publishing Company, New York.
- Cole, B. 1986, *Princess Smartypants*, Hamish Hamilton, London.

7　If a child remarked to you, 'I wonder how the sky stays up?', how would you respond?

8　How might you use a photograph of a child's family to prompt philosophical discussion between yourself and the child? How might this be used to stimulate a group discussion session?

Improving teaching in practice

1　Plan, implement and record (using a tape-recorder or written notes) a group discussion with children.

2　What was your style of philosophising with young children? Did you:
- stimulate discussion through your choice and presentation of materials?
- question the children in ways that promoted philosophical thinking?
- help children learn about different ways in which questions can be answered?
- encourage children to share their ideas and respect other children's viewpoints?
- encourage children to listen to a variety of viewpoints and reflect on differences between these viewpoints?

3　Plan, implement and evaluate a group philosophy session in which you talk with children about what a stereotype is. Focus on either 'race', gender or disability stereotypes.

4　What are your areas of strength and weakness in using philosophising to promote children's learning?

5　How can you improve your philosophising techniques in practice?

FURTHER READING

Cam, P. 2006, *Twenty Thinking Tools*, ACER Press, Melbourne.

Davey Zeece, P. 1996, 'Just think of that: concept books in early childhood', *Early Childhood Education Journal*, 23(4), pp. 221–225.

Fisher, R. 2006, 'Thinking about me: me-cognition', *Teaching Thinking*, 20(1), pp. 50–55.

Haynes, J. 2003, *Children as Philosophers: Learning Through Enquiry and Dialogue in the Classroom*, Routledge, London.

Law, K. 2002, *Philosophy Rocks! Find out what it means*, Volo Publishing, New York.

Murris, K. 1992, *Teaching Philosophy with Picture Books*, Infonet Publications, London.

Trickey, S. and Topping, K. J. 2004, 'Philosophy for children: a systematic review', *Research Papers in Education*, 19(3), pp. 365–380.

White, D. 2000, *Philosophy for Kids: 40 Fun Questions That Help You Wonder...About Everything!* Prufrock Press, Austin, TX.

Yaynes, J. 2002, *Children as Philosophers*, Routledge Falmer, London

ONLINE AND MULTI-MEDIA RESOURCES

Text

'Children and Philosophy', *Standford Encyclopedia of Philosophy*. An excellent overview of the Philosophy for Children movement and its practices, with hyper links to key organisations and websites: **http://plato.stanford.edu/entries/children**

Multi-media

'Reason and Imagination: philosophy with children' (video), ACER Press, available from the Australian Council for Education Research, Prospect Hill Road, Camberwell, VIC.

'Teaching Children Philosophy' (DVD). You can access an extract from the DVD where primary school children are philosophising about taste and sight, and judging art: **http://www.mtholyoke.edu/omc/kidsphil/video.html**

'Stillthinking/Harry Potter'. A video of a philosophy session with children aged 5-12. Stillthinking, 25 Prince's Street, Ulverston, Cumbria LA12 7NQ, UK.

'Children's books helping children learn to think about and discuss issues of philosophy, politics and social justice'. A free podcast interview with Professor Thomas Wartenberg, an advocate of philosophy for children: **http://www.justonemorebook. com/2007/02/05/interview-with-thomas-wartenberg**

Regularly updated lists of children's picture books in diverse categories by the National Child Care Information Center, USA: **http://www.nccic.org/poptopics/booklists.html**

Philosophy for Children—websites with links, lesson plans and resources

Australia: Creative and critical thinking journal: **http://www.fapsa.org.au**
Denmark: Extensive links section in several languages: **http://home12.inet.tele.dk/fil**
Germany: A philosophy project for children: **http://www.kinder-philosophieren.de** (German language)
New Zealand: Sample lesson plans: **http://www.p4c.org.nz**
Philosophy for kids: Stories to use in doing philosophy with children: **http://www.philosophyforkids.com**
Thinking skills website: **http://www.standarss.dfee.gov.uk/guidance/thinking**
USA: **http://cehs.montclair.edu/academic/iapc**

REFERENCES

Burnard, P., Craft, A. and Cremin, T. with Duffy, B., Hanson, R., Keene, J., Haynes, L and Burns, D. 2006, 'Documenting "possibility" thinking: a journey of collaborative enquiry', *International Journal of Early Years Education*, 14(30), pp. 243–262.

Chafel, J.A., Flint, A.S., Hamel, J. and Pomeroy, A.H. 2007, 'Young children, social issues, and critical literacy', *Young Children*, 62(1), pp. 73–80.

Daniel, M., Doudin, P. and Pons, F. 2006, 'Children's representations of violence: impacts of cognitive stimulation of a philosophical nature', *Journal of Peace Education*, 3(2), pp. 209–234.

Davis, K. MacNaughton, G. and Smith, K. 2007, 'Researching with children: The challenges and possibilities for building "child friendly" research', in A. Hatch (ed.), *Handbook on Qualitative Research in Early Childhood*, USA.

DeHaan, C., MacColl, S. and McCutcheon, L. 1995a, *Philosophy with Kids, Book 1*, Longman, Melbourne.

——1995b, *Philosophy with Kids. More Ideas and Activities*, Longman, Melbourne.

Fisher, R. 1999, 'Thinking skills to thinking schools: ways to develop children's thinking and learning', *Early Childhood Development and Care*, 153, pp. 51–63.

——2007, 'Dialogic teaching: developing thinking and metacognition through philosophical discussion', *Early Child Development and Care*, 177(6/7), pp. 615–663.

Hemmeter, M, Ostrosky, M. and Fox, L. 2006, 'Social and emotional foundations for early learning: a conceptual model for intervention', *School Psychology Review*, 35(4), pp. 583–601.

Hoffman, M.L. 2000, *Empathy and Moral Development: Implications for Caring and Justice*, Cambridge University Press, Cambridge.

Honig, A. 2007, 'Oral language development', *Early Child Development and Care*, 177 (6/7), pp. 581–613.

Ligorio, B., Talamo, A. and Pontecorvo, C. 2005, 'Building intersubjectivity at a distance during the collaborative writing of fairytales', *Computers & Education* 45(3), pp, 357–374.

Lipman, M. 1989, *Philosophy Goes to School*, Temple University Press, Philadelphia.

——1995, 'Moral education, higher-order thinking and philosophy for children', *Early Child Development and Care,* 107, pp. 61–70.

——2003, *Thinking in Education* (2nd edn), Cambridge University Press, New York.

MacNaughton, G. 2001, 'Silences and subtexts in immigrant and non-immigrant's children's understandings of diversity', *Childhood Education*, 78 (1), pp. 30–36.

—— 2007, 'Constructing gender in early years education', in. C. Skelton, B. Francis and L. Smulyan, eds, *The Sage Handbook of Gender and Education*, Sage Publications, London, Thousand Oaks and New Delhi, pp. 127–138.

Murris, K. 2000, 'Can children do philosophy'? *Journal of Philosophy of Education* 34(2), 261–279.

Mushi, S. 2002, 'Simultaneous and successive second language learning: integral ingredients of the human development process', *Early Child Development and Care,* 172(4), pp. 349–358 .

Schertz, M. 2007, 'Avoiding "passive empathy" with philosophy for children', *Journal of Moral Education*, 36(2), pp. 185–198.

Sprod, T. 1995, 'Cognitive development, philosophy and children's literature', *Early Childhood Development and Care*, 107, pp. 23–33.

Stanley, S. 2007, 'A skills based approach to P4C—philosophy: fairy tales and the foundation stage', *Gifted Education International*, 22(2/3), pp. 172–181.

Wegerif, R. 2005, 'Reason and creativity in classroom dialogues', *Language and Education*, 19(3), pp. 223–237.

Wilkes, G. (ed.) 1979, *Collins Dictionary of the English Language*, Penguin Books, Middlesex.

Wing Han Lamb, W. 2002, 'Philosophy for children and the philosophy of childhood', *Every Child*, 8(4), pp. 8–9.

Chapter 27

Problem-solving

Problem: any thing, matter, person that is difficult to deal with, solve or overcome.

(Collins Dictionary of the English Language, p. 1165)

Solve: to find the explanation for or solution to (mystery, problem etc. . . .).

(Collins Dictionary of the English Language, p. 1386)

Problem-solving is the foundation of a young child's learning. It must be valued, promoted, provided for, and sustained in the early childhood classroom.

(Britz 1993, p. 2)

. . . the social regulation of problem solving is an important component in both the ZPD and in scaffolding.

(Garton 2004, p. 70)

What?

As a teaching technique problem-solving involves helping children learn how to find answers to puzzles, questions, dilemmas, issues, predicaments and quandaries they face in their daily world. It is the foundation for learning in and about the world.

Issues and debates

IT'S MORE THAN COGNITION

Problem-solving is widely recognised as a cognitive skill that supports the development of learning in areas such as literacy, technology, mathematics and science. However, there is a growing research base on the role that problem-solving can have in building young children's social competence and pro-social behaviours (see Gross 2005; Reynolds 2008). This form of interpersonal and social problem-solving is being used more widely with children who struggle to build peaceable relationships with their peers, and it is important for staff to remember that social as well as academic learning can grow through learning how to problem-solve. It allows children to self-evaluate their own behaviours and that of their peers and to brainstorm alternatives that might work for all.

How?

Children need to learn how to problem-solve. To learn this, Britz (1993) suggests children need staff who:

- facilitate a problem-solving climate
- create time to problem-solve
- create space to problem-solve
- use materials to encourage problem-solving
- show familiarity with how to problem-solve
- choose appropriate problems to solve.

We shall now look at each of these in more detail.

FACILITATING A PROBLEM-SOLVING CLIMATE

Staff can facilitate a climate in which children want to solve problems by valuing children's problems and valuing their solutions to them. Within this, staff should ensure that children feel psychologically safe

Pondering on a problem together.

(Tegano, Sawyers and Moran 1989). To feel psychologically safe, children need to know that it's 'OK', that being 'wrong' is not going to be punished and that their judgments are as valued as those of the adults. Children's judgments and solutions should never be ridiculed.

Their interest in problem-solving will be increased if staff pay attention to children's answers and encourage them to try out their ideas in practice (Poole, Miller and Church 2004). These processes act as positive reinforcers (see Chapter 28) for children's problem-solving. Helping children to 'learn to listen, understand other perspectives, recognise problems, and look for alternative solutions' (Browning et al. 2000, p. 233) is the key to facilitating a problem-solving climate.

CREATING TIME TO PROBLEM-SOLVE

Problem-solving takes time. Children need to think about how to solve a problem and to test their solutions in practice. Trial and error is an essential part of learning to solve problems (Poole, Miller and Church 2004). It is, therefore, important to plan large blocks of time for children to fully investigate problems and to give children opportunities to practise their problem-solving skills (Browning, Davis and Resta 2000). Time for problem-solving also enables children to deepen their understandings and construct more complex knowledge about the problem they are attempting to solve (Lambert 2000).

CREATING SPACE TO PROBLEM-SOLVE

Testing out solutions to problems can take space. It is important that children have a suitable and safe space within which to experiment with solutions to problems. If several children are trying to solve a problem co-operatively it is especially important to set aside space that allows for social interaction between them as they try to solve their joint problem.

USING MATERIALS TO ENCOURAGE PROBLEM-SOLVING

From a Piagetian perspective, development of problem-solving skills is associated with the opportunity to play in a wide variety of ways with a wide variety of materials. The flexibility of open-ended materials such as sand, water, blocks and art materials creates more opportunities for children to problem-solve than closed-ended materials. Children can test out solutions readily and shape the open-ended materials in lots of different ways as they explore their solutions and attempt to resolve difficulties in their immediate physical environment (Goffin and Tull 1985; Poole, Miller and Church 2004). Staff can stimulate children's interest in problem-solving with open-ended materials by collecting materials together that are unfamiliar to children in areas such as special interest tables (Hendrick 1990; Kelley 2004) and by allowing children lots of opportunity to be involved in child-directed play. In a study of 48 Grade 4 children's mathematical problem-solving skills in Taiwan, researchers found that children spent less time and performed better on problems where the context of the problem was unfamiliar to the children (Kelley 2004).

New technologies can also promote problem-solving in diverse ways (Haugland 2000). For instance, preschool teachers have used instant video revisiting (IVR) to help children reflect on ways to solve their peer conflicts (Hong and Broderick 2003). Computer software that is open-ended and allows children to explore and test the impact of what they do can build their capacity to hypothesise and wonder, and thus build their problem-solving skills more effectively than drill-based software (Charlesworth 2003).

FAMILIARITY WITH HOW TO PROBLEM-SOLVE

Children can be introduced to a logical sequence for problem-solving. The steps in the process recommended by Britz (1993) echo those of Dewey but are simpler:

- identify the problem

- brainstorm possible solutions
- test out one solution
- evaluate what happened.

Tan, a member of staff in an early learning centre, is very enthusiastic about using art as a medium for children to represent the world around them. The children have been discussing totem poles and have decided to make one that represents their group.

They are using papier maché and have built the base of the pole, but are having difficulty with making the base stand up—it keeps collapsing into itself.

Tan: 'I wonder what you could do to help it stand?'
Susie: 'We could make it solid with paper in the middle.'
Tan: 'That's one idea.'
Sam: 'We could use chicken wire and put the papier maché on the outside like we did when we built Lulu' (Lulu was a full-sized 'person' that the children had constructed last term).
Tan: 'That could be a good way.'
Sulu: 'What about putting wood into the middle to make it strong?'
Tan: 'You're all getting some ideas together here.'
Simon: 'I wonder if we could use strips of paper to hold it all together.'
Tan: 'You've all come up with useful suggestions'—he reminds them of the ones they have just made—'Which one will you try first?'

The children elect to use the chicken wire; they know how to do this and they remember their previous experience of success. After a while Tan approaches the children and encourages them to evaluate what they have done.

Reflection point: To what extent did Tan follow Britz's process for problem-solving?

Understanding the processes of thinking involved in problem-solving helps improve children's problem-solving skills (Browning, Davis and Resta 2000). Staff can help children learn this process of thinking by talking aloud as they themselves solve problems. This should include telling children about the things they thought about when trying to solve problems and why a solution did or did not work (Lambert 2001). Questions which will help stimulate creative problem-solving are those that are open-ended (see Chapter 13). Hendrick (1990) suggests questions similar to the following:

- How could this be made to work again?
- What else could you do?
- What might happen if…?
- How could we find out?
- How could we do this?

Children's capacity to problem-solve is also helped when teachers focus on the process of problem-solving—doing, thinking, and talking—not just the outcomes (West 2007).

APPROPRIATE PROBLEMS TO SOLVE

Finding appropriate problems to solve should not be difficult as children's daily lives are full of puzzles, dilemmas, issues and questions. Problems may be related to how the physical world works or how the social world works. The physical and social worlds generate problems of movement, discussion, skill and strategy (Goffin and Tull 1985). Problems from the physical world could be:

- How to keep a balance scale level while adding weights to it?

- How to fill a bottle with water when there is a hole in the bottom?
- How to tie a shoelace?
- How to reach the top of the painting easel?
- How to make a tunnel in the sandpit without the castle falling down?

Problems from the social world could be:

- How to join in a chasing game that looks fun?
- How to help a friend stop crying?
- How to talk to a friend whose hearing is impaired?
- How to stop the boys knocking over your blocks?
- How to decide who comes to your party?
- How to stop a fight between children?

The problems will be appropriate if they come from the puzzles, dilemmas and issues that children are confronting and trying to find answers to. Using the everyday life experiences of children is important to their motivation to problem-solve. Children are more likely to problem-solve when they can define their own problems and their own goals for solving the problem (Lambert 2000). These turn into good opportunities for problem-solving when staff encourage the children to '. . . plan, predict possible outcomes, make decisions, and observe the results of their actions' (Goffin and Tull 1985, p. 30).

Several children at the Protea Downs Early Learning Centre were puzzled by a comment made by one of their peers, Sabrina, when she was telling them about her birthday party:

Sabrina: 'The best present I got was a puppy. My mums helped me name her. She's called Daxina.'
Toby: 'How many mums do you have?'
Nida: 'One mum, you only ever have one mum, silly.'
Sabrina: 'No, Nida, you can have two mums. I have two mums.'
Petra: 'I have two mums because daddy divorced one. I never see her now 'cos she lives in Coffy. I talk on the phone with her though. When you have two mums one lives a long way away.'
Toby: (to Sabrina) 'Are your mums divorced too? Which one do you speak to on the phone?'
Sabrina: 'My mums live together with me. We don't need the phone, I talk to them all the time.'
Petra: 'Where's your dad live then? Do you speak on the phone with him?'
Sabrina: 'I don't have any dad. My mums had me without a dad.'
Toby: 'No they didn't.'
Sabrina: 'Yes they did.'
Toby: 'You're silly, you can't have a mum without a dad.'

The argument continued until the children asked the teacher to arbitrate. The teacher, Cheryl, decided to help the children find the answer to their puzzle over how many mums you can have by acknowledging their problem and getting them to think about how to solve their puzzle. She asked the children how they might find out how many mums you can have and if you can have a mum without a dad. They had lots of ideas so they agreed that she would help test out their ideas. They decided to ask their own parents and come and tell everybody the next day, and to bring in photos of their parents and count how many mums and dads were in them, and how many had mums and no dads. Cheryl then provided them with:

- time to problem-solve. Each day they were able to spend time on sharing information about their research into families and thinking about new ways to solve their puzzle
- space to problem-solve. Cheryl set up special interest areas on families. The first thing they put on the wall near the interest table were pictures of their parents
- materials to encourage problem-solving. Cheryl found several books and images of different types of families to share with the children.

THEORETICAL BACKGROUND

LEV VYGOTSKY'S SOCIAL MEDIATION AND JEAN PIAGET'S COGNITIVE CONFLICT

Diverse theoretical perspectives have been taken to explore and explain problem-solving in young children. Several researchers in the field have been strongly influenced by the theories of developmental biologist Jean Piaget (1963), others by the theories of Lev Vygotsky (refer to Chapter 29 on scaffolding), and a third group draw from both Piaget and Vygotsky to explore the processes of cognitive change that enable a problem to be solved.

Piagetian theories of problem-solving focus on the role of cognitive conflict in learning to solve problems and the process of the child reaching a state of what Piaget referred to as 'disequilibrium'. Conflict is produced through interaction with the physical and social world, trying things out and finding that they do not work. It is through this process of exploration, mistake-making and struggling to make sense of the world that problem-solving occurs. Britz (1993, p. 1) explains it this way:

> Constructing knowledge by making mistakes is part of the natural process of problem solving. Through exploring, then experimenting, trying out a hypothesis, and finally, solving problems, children make learning personal and meaningful. Piaget states that children understand only what they discover or invent themselves (1963). It is this

discovery within the problem solving process that is the vehicle for children's learning.

Theories of social problem solving have focused on problem-solving between peers and/or in groups and the role of social and cultural contexts in problem-solving. Theories of social problem-solving often draw on the theories of Vygotsky and focus on the role of scaffolding and peer tutors in the process of problem-solving. Children's private speech (or self-talk) during problem-solving is also seen as an important way in which young children problem-solve from within this perspective (Robbins 2007).

The specific mechanisms that trigger the cognitive changes that produce problem-solving are unclear within each of these theoretical perspectives. Research has been more successful at describing the context (cognitive conflict or peer tutoring) that has produced the outcome of a problem being solved (Garton 2004). However, it seems clear that irrespective of the theoretical perspective used, children go through multiple cycles of testing out the solutions to a problem trying to 'remove or create doubts about the truth' (Lesh and Doerr 2003, p. 361) of what they are doing or experiencing before a problem is solved. Harel and Sowder (1998) use the conceptual framework of 'Proof Schemes' to describe this process.

When and why?

GOAL RELEVANCE

Problem-solving skills are the foundation of all areas of knowledge including mathematics, the sciences and the arts. It is through learning to problem-solve that children build their intellectual skills in these areas. Hence, using problem-solving to help children learn is relevant to teaching and learning goals across all curriculum content areas. While problem-solving is an intellectual skill, staff may want to teach children to problem-solve to enhance children's emotional, social, physical, aesthetic and moral development. More specifically, learning to problem-solve has been shown to help children to:

- develop initiative (Marxen 1995)
- enhance their manipulative skills (Marxen 1995)
- develop their creativity (Moyles 1989)
- gain confidence in their ability to work things out for themselves (Marxen 1995)

- become resilient and cope successfully with their world (Mayr and Ulich 1999)
- take responsibility for conflict resolution (Browning et al. 2000). However, this works on only a temporary basis if the teacher does not help the children to solve the problems (Ahn 2005)
- enhance their mathematical thinking when they are paired with a peer who is more competent in mathematics than they are (Shamir, Tzuriel and Rozen 2006) or when they can use gestures as well as words to express their thinking (Domìnguez 2003; Kelley 2004)
- increase their social leadership skills (Hensel 1991).

DEVELOPMENTAL CONSIDERATIONS

As soon as young children begin to ask, 'Why?' and 'How?' they show an interest in learning through problem-solving. However, staff need to match the use of problem-solving to enhance children's learning with their developmental abilities and interests in two ways.

First, staff need to match their expectations of how long children can focus on a problem with their developmental abilities. The older the children the more they are likely to have sustained, focused attention on the problems they encounter. This is particularly the case in 'free' play. However, babies do engage in 'future orientated intentional problem solving' (Romine and Reynolds 2004, p. 49) and staff can engage babies in lots of problem-solving in and about their world from an early age. Babies will be puzzled by many things in the world about them. However, the problems (puzzles) they can learn to solve for themselves are going to be simple puzzles about how the world works and how to make their body work in the world. By about four months of age, babies reach a stage in their cognitive development where they can intentionally begin to make things happen (Seefeldt and Barbour 1986; Poole, Miller and Church 2004). For example, they will use their hands to hit a mobile, or cry for a caregiver. It is the point at which intentionality begins that babies can learn to solve very simple, immediate, short-term problems about how to make things work and how to make things happen. Once babies reach this stage of cognitive development, staff can present babies with simple puzzles that they can solve—for example, moving a mobile that a baby can reach to a slightly different location so that baby has to work out anew how to use their hands to reach it. Or, offering a new toy to a baby requires that they work out what it does or what can be done with it. Remember, babies' concentration span is likely to be short and their frustration and distress levels can rocket quickly. Staff need to choose puzzles that are within the baby's grasp and do not cause distress or frustration. Learning to enjoy problem-solving at this age relies on having problems that are fun and of interest to the baby.

Suitable problems will depend on the particular interests and temperament of each baby. Some examples of the problems they can be encouraged to solve are presented in the following anecdotes:

Andrew, four months old, has rolled over several times but now seems to forget how to do it. His carer, Andrea, gently encourages him by assisting him to get his arm out of the way, and physically prompting him. All the while she is talking to him about how he can manage to roll over.

Hannah, five months old, is lying on her tummy and trying to reach a toy that is on the floor in front of her. Stephanie, the child care worker, comes over and says: 'Hannah, are you trying to get that rattle? You need to move forward, let me help you.' She gently prompts Hannah to move forward by putting her hands on Hannah's feet and pushing.

Mario, nine months old, is trying to transfer a small doll from one hand to the other (by crossing the mid-line). He seems to be having trouble, so his carer, Clare, gently guides his hand across the middle of his body to meet his other hand. She also talks to him and gives praise when he succeeds.

Anthony, 10 months old, wants to reach a biscuit that he can see on the floor under a chair. He can't reach it by himself and screams for attention. His caregiver, Elly, comes over and talks him through a solution. She shows him how to go around the other side of the chair where he is able to reach the biscuit.

Reflection point: Do you consider these appropriate problems to work on with young children? Why? Why not?

Toddlers encounter many puzzles and dilemmas in their constant exploration of the world about them. It is puzzling how shoelaces can be tied into bows, or why someone cries when you borrow their toy; and there are constant dilemmas about what to play with, how to play with it and what happens when you stop playing with it. Toddlers' 'hunting, gathering, building up and knocking down activities' (Kowalski 1996, p. 8) will provide staff with repeated opportunities to encourage a disposition towards problem-solving. Toddlers can learn to enjoy solving problems as they 'hunt, gather, build and knock down' if adults show interest in what they find puzzling and show enjoyment in their attempts to find answers to the puzzles they confront. Poole, Miller and Church (2004, pp. 29–30) advise:

> Let toddlers choose from a wide variety of sensory activities involving different textures, sounds, shapes, and colors. Like all of us, toddlers are more motivated to stick with a problem when they have chosen it.

Open-ended materials that toddlers can manipulate and explore help to promote their problem-solving skills (Segatti, Brown-DuPaul and Keyes 2003). It is, therefore, important to ensure that the environment is toddler-safe (see Chapter 1) and full of open-ended materials for them to explore. Staff interest in and enjoyment of toddlers' own attempts to solve problems will encourage persistent exploration and enjoyment in the business of looking for solutions.

The problems toddlers encounter in social relationships with each other are likely to be disputes over objects, such as who should have the new doll to play with or who should be able to push the trolley. Teaching children physical techniques for solving these problems, such as finding another doll or another trolley to push, are more likely to be successful than teaching verbal techniques at this stage.

Preschool children are likely to encounter many problems in their increasingly complex social relationships with each other. Problems are likely to occur over possession of objects, name-calling, play decisions and facts about what has occurred or should occur. Preschool children can generalise from one situation to another and they quickly learn to use the solutions they reached to solve a problem in one situation to solve a similar problem elsewhere. In social situations this means that preschoolers can learn to generalise about what to do if there is a disagreement over a storyline or if they have a fight over a piece of equipment. For example, a preschooler can learn that whenever another child takes their toy the best way to get the toy back is to name-call until the toy is returned, or to negotiate so each child has a turn with it. Children can generalise positive or negative problem-solving techniques.

To help preschool children learn constructive ways to solve social problems, staff need to encourage them to explain their actions to each other and to encourage children to come up with their own 'fair' solutions. Children who learn to 'use their words' to explain what they want and what they are doing to others are more likely to find solutions to their social problems. Children who reach their own solutions are more likely to abide by what has been agreed to than with solutions adults create for them (Wheeler 1994). However, it can be helpful if staff offer solutions when the children seem stuck. Solutions to disagreements in play and over materials such as changing the activity, creating new rules, forgetting the problem or changing the storyline can all lead to positive and workable outcomes for preschool children, and they often like to co-operatively solve problems (Poole, Miller and Church 2004).

Navaz is an early childhood teacher who believes it is important to encourage children to reach their own solutions to play disagreements through their own problem-solving:

A group of four-year-old girls playing in the home corner have developed a rule called 'no boys allowed'. Their teacher, Navaz, suggested that this might not be fair and helped the girls to think of other rules. After a lengthy discussion they came up with some new rules: 'No pushing, no taking other people's things'; 'Let the boss decide who will play what role'; 'No being silly'.

Reflective task: Discuss with the children you work with what rules they think would work to create fair play in the room.

Preschool children can also learn to generalise about solutions to problems in the physical world around them. They encounter many problems about the physical world that fascinate them and that need solutions for their play to continue. For example, preschoolers encounter problems about how to construct block buildings that stay standing as they build higher and more complex buildings, problems about how to get water from one place to another, problems about how to move objects from one place to another and problems about how to join objects together. Many of these problems can be solved readily by preschoolers, but to do so the children must have plenty of time and opportunity to explore the materials they are working with (Poole, Miller and Church 2004). Unless children thoroughly explore the materials they will experience frustration in their attempts to independently solve problems about how to make the physical world work for them in their play with each other.

Preschoolers often use five strategies to solve problems successfully: recognising the problem, restructuring the problem, monitoring their own efforts at solving the problem, persistence and being planned in their approach to it (Lambert 2001). Staff can support preschoolers in their problem-solving by encouraging children to 'think aloud and verbalise their actions as they explore materials' (Lambert 2001, p. 27) and by modelling thinking aloud to children (Lambert 2001). A US study of 2156 children's problem-solving skills between the ages of 5 and 17 found that this 'self-talk' or private speech during problem-solving is associated with competent younger problem-solvers, but this is not the case for older children (Winsler and Naglieri 2003).

As children become older they become more able to solve problems that involve people having different points of view. By about six to seven years of age children are able to learn, remember and impose rules about how to play with each other. They are, therefore, likely to become involved in conflicts over who is obeying or not obeying the rules they have developed. Staff can use these conflicts as opportunities to encourage the children to problem-solve solutions. Many six- and seven-year-old children will be able to develop workable solutions to their disagreements over rules with some help from teachers. Questions that act as suggestions or encourage them to think of ways to modify the rules of their games are most likely to be successful in prompting them to problem-solve for themselves. Browning, Davis and Resta (2000) reported on action research they conducted in a primary school classroom in which they successfully introduced a 'Wheel of Choice' that enabled the children to make choices about how best to solve conflicts between them in the classroom. This research highlighted how the children were able to choose between several possible solutions to conflict resolution in the classroom and to learn to follow a simple step-by-step approach to problem-solving.

In the early years of school, children also become much more strategic and systematic in their approach to problem-solving (Romine and Reynolds 2004), and they can search for clues to help them problem-solve (Poole, Miller and Church 2004). This provides the opportunity for teachers to talk with children about their problem-solving strategies to support them to understand how best to problem solve in different contexts.

Equity considerations

'RACE' AND CULTURE

Inter-cultural and inter-racial relationships between children offer many opportunities for problem-solving. As children encounter each other's diversity they often flounder. We know that children can reject, ostracise, silence and hurt each other because of 'racial' difference. York (1991) offers a range of problem-solving activities to help children learn to respect and accept each other's diversity that still have relevance. These activities help children explore how they might respond to situations in which they or other children are treated unfairly. One such activity is called, 'What would you do if…?'. In this activity, children are shown a range of pictures of children from different 'racial' backgrounds involved in everyday tasks in the early childhood centre. Children are told a story about the picture and asked what they would do if they were the person in the story. The stories are simple situations in which a child is rejected and hurt. For example,

'This is a picture of a little girl called Khan Tho who is from Vietnam. She was very upset when Sally didn't want to sit with her yesterday at milk and fruit time. Sally said she had funny eyes. What would you do if you were Khan Tho?'

The effectiveness of using a story for social problem-solving may depend on the emotional stance of those involved in the story. In a study of the social problem-solving skills of 402 primary school children of diverse backgrounds, researchers found that the emotions of the provocateur in the story affected what the children would do. The researchers told children stories in which one child provoked another through actions such as spilling water on a painting and asked the children what should happen. When the provocateur was angry or sad a majority of the children saw revenge as the best way to solve the problem. When the provocateur was happy this was not the case (Lemerise et al. 2006). This suggests that how the protagonists in the stories are portrayed emotionally may be important to the success of story-telling as a strategy for problem-solving ways to build respectful relations between young children.

For bilingual children it is especially important to remember that children's self-talk and gesturing during problem-solving supports successful problem-solving. Bilingual children's self-talk and gestures during mathematical problem-solving were found in one US research study to be a better predictor of their performance on mathematical tasks than standardised tests were (Domínguez 2003).

GENDER

Research has revealed that preschool girls tend to perform less well at problem-solving tasks when they are in mixed-gender groupings (Parkin 1991; Holmes-Lonergan 2003). The reasons for this were centred on boys' assertiveness. This intimidated the girls, causing their concentration to waver and their preparedness to become involved in group discussion to reduce. On the other hand, in girls-only problem-solving sessions the girls concentrated better and contributed more to discussion. Research (Browne and Ross 1991) has also shown that boys can quickly undermine girls' persistence and confidence in solving problems, as the following extract highlights:

> . . . a four-year-old girl was in the process of grappling with a problem with a construction toy when a boy approached. He watched for a moment and then said, 'That's not how you make a car. I know how.' He then began to tell her what to do. The girl responded by adopting a helpless demeanour and made no comment. Following the boy's intervention the adult tried to encourage her to continue but she refused, saying 'I can't do it'. (Browne and Ross 1991, p. 44)

Staff need to be alert to the potential difficulties in mixed-group problem-solving and plan for it by positioning themselves close to such groups to monitor relationships within the group. This will enable staff to intervene quickly if and when the gender dynamics prove problematic. However, staff also need to reflect on how they view children's help-seeking behaviour during problem-solving. One US study found that while teachers saw boys as highly motivated when they sought teacher help during problem-solving, they saw help-seeking girls as less motivated and less capable and confident than other children (Thompson, Arsenault and Williams 2006).

Girls have been found in several countries to be less confident in their abilities to solve mathematical problems than are boys. Dutch researchers (Timmermansa, Van Lieshoutb and Verhoevena 2007) found that girls' low performance in subtraction problems was linked to a lack of confidence, rather than a lack of ability. Boys' and girls' confidence in problem-solving may begin to be shaped in infancy. Leipzig (1992) noted that when boys were distressed staff would often direct them into doing activities, while staff would often cuddle and talk to girls who were distressed. This provided boys with strong messages that they are doers and solvers of problems and girls that they should be passive rather than active. Staff should actively plan to avoid such gender differences in how they deal with children's distress. They should also ensure that both girl and boy infants and toddlers have lots of simple problem-solving opportunities.

Observing who has had the opportunity to successfully solve problems each day and noting any gender imbalances in this can provide important information about the extent to which there is gender equity in problem-solving opportunities in the group. Once any inequalities have been identified, staff can plan to overcome them. In this process it is important to focus problem-solving on everyday problems. It has been found that girls tend to improve their problem-solving skills in mathematics and science when they understand that they are being given tools to help them solve everyday problems (Chira 1992) and when they are in constructivist classrooms where teachers guide their problem-solving rather than use direct instruction (Timmermansa, Van Lieshoutb and Verhoevena, 2007). Research in Belgium with 749 children in the early years of school also showed that girls' mathematical problem-solving skills lagged behind those of boys in the first years of school but that they caught up with the boys in the latter years of elementary school (Grades 3 and 4) (Desoete and Roeyers 2006).

DISABILITY AND ADDITIONAL NEEDS

There are two dimensions to anti-discriminatory approaches to disability to consider when using problem-solving as a teaching technique. First, problem-solving can be used to build, enrich and extend the cognitive development of children with disabilities in the group. To do this it is important to focus on problems of interest and relevance to individual children and to provide the time, opportunity and support for individuals to solve problems in their own ways. For some children, such as those who have sensory impairments, the ways in which they solve a problem might be quite different to someone without a sensory impairment. Taking care to respect different ways of solving problems helps build children's confidence in their own ability to be active problem-solvers. Part of learning such confidence is gained through support for developing autonomy and independence as learners. A balance needs to be struck between allowing children with disabilities the time to explore different solutions and take risks, and allowing them to experience enough frustration in this process that they are reluctant to try again.

Second, problem-solving can be used to build positive, respectful relationships between children with and children without disabilities in the group. Stories and books with a child who has a disability as the main character can be used to engage children in problem-solving ways to build inclusive classrooms with preschool children and children in the early years of schooling (Iaquinta and Hipskey 2006). For instance, children can be told a story about the picture and asked what they would do if they were the person in the story. Stories are simple situations in which a child is rejected and hurt or where the strengths and possibilities of a child with disabilities can be explored.

The following anecdotes show how everyday situations offer opportunities for children to practise anti-discriminatory problem-solving:

This picture is of a little girl called Jane who has Down's syndrome. She was very upset when Sam didn't want to play with her this morning. Sam said she looked funny. What would you do and how would you feel if you were Jane?

At a child care centre in Brighton, a bayside suburb in Melbourne, the children are getting excited about a forthcoming excursion to the zoo. Their teacher, Penny, has had several discussions with the children about what they might see.

Osker: 'Steve can't come.' (Osker is referring to a child who is blind.)
Penny: 'Of course Steve can come. Why do you think he can't?'
Osker: 'He can't see!'
Penny: 'That's right, he can't see but he can do other things—what does he use instead of his eyes?'
The group of children come up with a variety of answers such as: 'He uses his ears to hear different sounds'; 'He uses his nose to smell'; 'He can touch things'.

Reflection point: What specific aspects of this conversation promote anti-discriminatory thinking?

It can be particularly useful to initiate discussions about what children believe that those with particular disabilities can and cannot do. Young children can develop very stereotyped and mistaken ideas about what it means to have a disability. Derman-Sparks et al. (1989) described some of these misconceptions that persist today. They include the belief that people in wheelchairs can't be parents and that people who are sight-impaired can't move because they can't see where to go. Problem-solving can be used to work through with children about how people in wheelchairs can be parents, and how you might find out where to go and how you might get there if you have a sight impairment.

Reflecting on problem-solving techniques

1 What is a problem?
2 How would you define problem-solving?
3 What is the relationship between problem-solving and discovery learning?
4 What are the key factors that contribute to good problem-solving with children?
5 What is the relationship between general teaching techniques, such as questioning, and problem-solving?
6 Identify five general teaching techniques you will need to be familiar with in order to practise problem-solving with children.
7 What problems have you solved over the past week? To what extent did you follow the process of problem-solving outlined above? Are there any suggestions from this chapter that might have improved your problem-solving skills?
8 'Children take responsibility for their interactions and generate their own solutions more often when an adult is absent' (Wheeler 1994, p. 3). What implications does this research finding reported by Wheeler have for your role in teaching children appropriate social problem-solving skills?
9 Design a problem-solving activity you could use with four-year-old children to help them learn how to stand up for themselves when they are bullied by another child.
10 Observe one baby, one toddler and one preschool child for 10 minutes each. What problems (puzzles, dilemmas, etc.) did they encounter in this time? To what extent did the children successfully solve the problems they encountered? To what extent did the children need adult assistance to solve the problems? What form of adult assistance were they offered? Is there anything you could have done to improve the children's ability to solve the problems they encountered?
11 Observe staff in an early childhood centre working with a small group of three-year-old children for a period of 30 minutes. To what extent did staff members:

- encourage children to problem-solve issues of interest to them?
- organise time, space and materials to help children problem-solve?
- use clear steps to help children problem-solve?

Improving teaching in practice

1 Identify a child you could involve in your problem-solving techniques. Observe the child closely and identify a problem of interest to them that you can work together to solve. Plan at least three periods of time in which you work closely with the child on this problem. Implement and record these sessions.
2 After each session evaluate your own problem-solving skills by reviewing the extent to which you were able to:
    - recognise problems
    - think of different solutions to these problems
    - choose your preferred solution to a problem and try it out

- reflect on what happened
- work with the children at each step in the problem-solving process.

3   What additional skills and knowledge do you need to consolidate and/or improve your problem-solving skills?

4   How and how well did you take account of the following considerations when problem-solving?
  - developmental
  - culture and 'race'
  - gender
  - disability.

FURTHER READING

Jung, M., Kloosterman, P. and McMullen, M.B. 2007, 'Research in review. Young children's intuition for solving problems in mathematics', *Young Children*, 62(5), pp. 50–57.

Lambert, B. 2000, 'Problem-solving in the first years of school', *Australian Journal of Early Childhood*, 25(2), pp. 32–38.

Poole, C., Miller, S. and Church, E. 2004, 'Development: ages and stages—how children learn to problem-solve', *Early Childhood Today*, 19(2), pp. 29–30.

Reynolds, E. 2008, *Guiding young children: a problem-solving approach*, 4th edn, McGraw-Hill, New York.

Segatti, L., Brown-DuPaul, J. and Keyes, T.L. 2003, 'Using everyday materials to promote problem solving in toddlers', *Young Children*, 58(5), pp. 12–18.

Wallace, A.H., Abbott, D. and Blary, R.M. 2007, 'The classroom that math built: encouraging young mathematicians to pose problems', *Young Children*, 62(5), pp. 42–48.

West, M. 2007, 'Problem solving: a sensible approach to children's science and social studies learning-and beyond', *Young Children*, 62(5), pp. 34–41.

ONLINE AND MULTI-MEDIA RESOURCES

Text

Dinwindle, S., 'I want it my way: problem-solving techniques with children 2 – 8': **http://www.kidsource.com/kidsource/products/I.want.my.way/I.Want.It.My.Way.html** (accessed 12 December 2007).

National Association for the Education of Young Children. Helping toddlers become problem-solvers: **http://www.naeyc.org/ece/2003/12.asp** (accessed 12 December 2007).

Multi-media

Problem-solving video—free access at: **http://www.learningmaterialswork.com/video_holeproblemsolved.html**

REFERENCES

Ahn, H. 2005, 'Child care teachers' strategies in children's socialization of emotion', *Early Child Development and Care*, 175(1), pp. 49–61.

Arthur, L., Beecher, B., Dockett, S., Farmer, S. and Death, E. 1996, *Programming and Planning in Early Childhood Settings*, 2nd edn, Harcourt Brace and Company, Sydney.

Britz, J. 1993, 'Problem-solving in early childhood classrooms', *ERIC Digest*, ED355040.

Browne, N. and Ross, C. 1991, '"Girls' stuff, boys' stuff": young children talking and playing', in N. Browne, ed., *Science and Technology in the Early Years* (pp. 37–51), Open University Press, Milton Keynes.

Browning, L., Davis, B. and Resta, V. 2000, 'What do you mean "think before I act?": conflict resolution with choices', *Journal of Research in Childhood Education*, 14(2), pp. 232–238.

Charlesworth, R. 2003, *Understanding Child Development for Adults who Work with Young Children*, Thompson Delmar Learning, Clifton Park, NY.

Chira, S. 1992, 'How boys and girls learn differently', *Redbook*, September, pp. 191–192, 194–195.

Derman-Sparks, L. and the Anti-Bias Task Force 1989, *The Anti-Bias Curriculum: Tools for Empowering Young Children*, National Association for the Education of Young Children, Washington, DC.

Desoete, A. and Roeyers, H. 2006, 'Metacognitive macroevaluations in mathematical problem solving', *Learning and Instruction*, 16, pp. 12–25.

Domínguez, H. 2003, 'Bilingual students' articulation and gesticulation of mathematical knowledge during problem-solving', *Bilingual Research Journal*, 29(2), pp. 269–293.

Garton, A. 2004, *The child as a Social Problem Solver*, Blackwell Publishing, Oxford.

Goffin, S. and Tull, C. 1985, 'Problem-solving: encouraging active learning', *Young Children*, 40(3), pp. 28–32.

Gross, C. 2005, 'Promoting problem solving with young children: an approach to community building and classroom management in one classroom', Doctoral dissertation, Teachers College Press, New York.

Harel, G. and Sowder, L. 1998, 'Students' proof schemes: results from exploratory studies', in A.H. Schoenfeld, J. Kaput and E. Dubinsky, eds, *CBMS Issues in Mathematics Education* (vol. 3, pp. 234–283), American Mathematical Society, Providence, RI.

Haugland, S. 2000, 'Computers and young children', *ERIC Digest*, EDO-PS-00-4.

Hendrick, J. 1990, *Total Learning: Developmental Curriculum for the Young Child*, 3rd edn, Merrill Publishing Company, Toronto.

Hensel, N. 1991, 'Social leadership skills in young children', *Roper Review*, 14(1), pp. 4–6.

Holmes-Lonergan, H. 2003, 'Preschool children's collaborative problem-solving interactions: the role of gender, pair type, and task', *Sex Roles: A Journal of Research*, 48, pp. 505–517.

Hong, S. and Broderick, J. 2003, 'Instant video revisiting for reflection: extending the learning of children and teachers', *Early Childhood Research in Practice*, 5(1), <http://ecrp.uiuc.edu/v5n1/hong.html>

Iaquinta, A. and Hipskey, S. 2006, 'Practical bibliotherapy strategies for the inclusive elementary classroom', *Early Childhood Education Journal*, 34(3), pp. 209–213.

Kelley, M. 2004, 'The impact of context on children's performance in solving everyday mathematical problems with real-world settings', *Childhood Education*, 81(1), pp. 62–64.

Kowalski, H. 1996, 'What should we do with toddlers?', *Every Child*, 2(1), pp. 8–9.

Lambert, B. 2000, 'Problem-solving in the first years of school', *Australian Journal of Early Childhood*, 25(2), pp. 32–38.

——2001, 'Metacognitive problem solving in preschoolers', *Australian Journal of Early Childhood*, 26(3), pp. 24–29.

Leipzig, J. 1992, 'Helping whole children grow: non-sexist childrearing for infants and toddlers', in B. Neugebauer, ed., *Alike and Different: Exploring our Humanity with Young Children* (pp. 32–41), National Association for the Education of Young Children, Washington, DC.

Lemerise, E., Fredstrom, B., Kelley, B., Bowersox, A. and Waford, R. 2006, 'Do provocateurs' emotion displays influence children's social goals and problem solving?', *Journal of Abnormal Child Psychology*, 34, pp. 559–571.

Lesh, R. and Doerr, H. 2003, *Beyond constructivism: models and modeling perspectives*, Lawrence Erlbaum Associates, New Jersey.

Marxen, C. 1995, 'Push, pull, toll, tilt, swing: physics for young children', *Childhood Education*, 71(4), pp. 212–216.

Mayr, T. and Ulich, M. 1999, 'Children's well-being in day care centres: an exploratory empirical study', *International Journal of Early Years Education*, 7(3), pp. 229–240.

Moyles, J. 1989, *Just Playing: The Role and Status of Play in Early Childhood Education*, Open University Press, Milton Keynes.

Parkin, R. 1991, 'Fair play: children's mathematical experiences in the infant classroom', in N. Browne, ed., *Science and Technology in the Early Years* (pp. 52–64), Open University Press, Milton Keynes.

Piaget, J. 1963, *The Origins of Intelligence in Children*, W.W. Norton, New York.

Poole, C., Miller, S. and Church, E. 2004, 'Development: ages and stages—how children learn to problem-solve', *Early Childhood Today*, 19(2), pp. 29–30.

Reynolds, E. 2008, *Guiding Young Children: A Problem-Solving Approach*, 4th edn, McGraw-Hill, New York.

Robbins, J. 2007, 'Young children thinking and talking: using socialcultural theory for multilayered analysis', Proceedings from *Learning and Socio-cultural Theory: Exploring Modern Vygotskian Perspectives Workshop*, Wollongong University.

Romine, C. and Reynolds, C. 2004, 'Sequential memory: a developmental perspective on its relation to frontal lobe functioning', *Neuropsychology Review*, 14(1), pp. 43–64.

Seefeldt, C. and Barbour, N. 1986, *Early Childhood Education: An Introduction*, Merrill, Toronto.

Segatti, L., Brown-DuPaul, J. and Keyes, T.L. 2003, 'Using everyday materials to promote problem solving in toddlers', *Young Children*, 58(5), pp. 12–18.

Shamir, A., Tzuriel, D. and Rozen, M. 2006, 'Peer mediation: the effects of program intervention, maths level, and verbal ability on mediation style and improvement in maths problem solving', *School Psychology International*, 27, pp. 209–231.

Tegano, D., Sawyers, J. and Moran, J. 1989, 'Problem-finding and solving in play: the teacher's role', *Childhood Education*, 66(2), pp. 92–97.

Thompson, R., Arsenault, S. and Williams, D. 2006, 'The effects of preschool girls' and boys' help seeking on adult evaluations of dyadic problem solving', *Journal of Language and Social Psychology*, 25(2), pp. 146–166.

Timmermansa, R., Van Lieshoutb, E. and Verhoevena, L. 2007, 'The combined effects of contemporary math instruction for low performers on problem-solving behavior', *Learning and Instruction*, 17(1), pp. 42–54.

West, M. 2007, 'Problem solving: a sensible approach to children's science and social studies learning-and beyond', *Young Children*, 62(5), pp. 34–41.

Wheeler, J. 1994, 'Peer conflicts in the classroom', *ERIC Digest*, EDO PS 94-13.

Wilkes, G. (ed.) 1979, *Collins Dictionary of the English Language*, Penguin Books, Middlesex.

Winsler, A. and Naglieri, J. 2003, 'Overt and covert verbal problem-solving strategies: developmental trends in use, awareness, and relations with task performance in children aged 5 to 17', *Child Development*, 74(3), pp. 659–678.

York, S. 1991, *Roots and Wings: Affirming Culture in Early Childhood Programs*, Toys'n Things Press, Minnesota

Chapter 28

Reinforcing

 Reinforce: to give added strength or support.
(*Collins Dictionary of the English Language*, p. 1231)

The most common classroom management design used in primary schools still focuses on rewards and punishments.

(Lake 2004, p. 567)

Whilst most teachers do not think of themselves as behaviourists, they use reinforcers to ensure that desired behaviours will recur or to make the child feel good about himself or herself.

(Robison and Schwartz 1982, p. 47)

What?

In everyday language, to reinforce something is to make it stronger. For example, when concrete is reinforced it is made stronger through the addition of steel mesh or steel rods. This positively reinforces the concrete. In educational language, to positively reinforce a child is to make particular behaviours stronger or more likely to occur. When a child's behaviour is reinforced it is made stronger or more likely to occur through the use of rewards (or reinforcers). Rewards can be social, such as praise, or material, such as food (Kazdin 2005). It is also possible to negatively reinforce a child's behaviour to make it less strong or less likely to occur. As a teaching technique, reinforcement is, therefore, used to increase or decrease the likelihood of a child displaying a particular behaviour.

Issues and debates

Reinforcement as a teaching technique has its advocates and its opponents. Its advocates argue that it is an effective strategy for modifying children's behaviour, particularly that of children who have behaviours that challenge adults, and of children with disabilities who need support to learn specific skills, especially pro-social skills (Kazdin 2005). There is an extensive and recent research literature on the therapeutic use of reinforcement as a strategy for shaping the behaviour of children who are seen to have behaviour disorders (e.g. Choate et al. 2005; Luman, Oosterlaan and Sergeant 2005). However, research on the more general use of reinforcement in educational settings and other settings was conducted in the 1960s–1980s and is drawn on heavily in more recent publications (see for example, Sigler and Aamidor 2005; Bandura 2006).

Its opponents argue that it is ineffective and oppressive.

REINFORCEMENT AS INEFFECTIVE AND COUNTERPRODUCTIVE

Reinforcement has been shown to be a consistently powerful teaching technique that modifies children's behaviour in the short term, rather than the long term. There is now considerable evidence to suggest that behaviour modification programs based on rewards and praise rarely produce any lasting changes in children's attitudes or behaviours (Kohn 1994; Henderlong, College and Lepper 2002). However, because reinforcement can be so effective in changing children's behaviour in the short term it can be tempting to use.

Proponents of reinforcement argue that there are several reasons why reinforcement may be unsuccessful in modifying children's behaviour. Robison and Schwartz (1982, p. 51) cited the following reasons:

- The reinforcement was not appropriate or adequate.
- The reinforcement occurred too often or too infrequently.

Over time it has been argued that reinforcement is counterproductive for the following reasons:

- Children can quickly learn which behaviours are being reinforced by staff and they can come to resent being manipulated. Seefeldt and Barbour (1986) cite an instance where a child who learned that desirable behaviour was rewarded with a sweet crushed hers underfoot when she was given one for finishing a painting.

Adam, a kindergarten teacher in a private boys-only school in Melbourne, was shocked to hear Jasper say, 'What will you give me if I help you pack up the blocks?'. He decided to rethink his approach to encouraging children to pack away, as he had relied on rewards to date.

Reflection point: To what extent do you rely on rewards in your daily conversations with children?

- Praising children's pro-social behaviour can actually reduce it, possibly because it reduces their internal motivation to perform it (Arbeau and Coplan 2007).
- Children can become motivated via reinforcement to learn to get rewards, rather than be motivated to learn (Kohn 1994; Deci, Koestner and Ryan 2001; Bronson 2007).
- When children are not rewarded they can learn to feel they are failures. Children can wonder about what is wrong with them that they never get the rewards that others do.
- Children's feelings and the reasons for their behaviours are ignored. Hence surface change occurs only in behaviours, not feelings (Robison and Schwartz 1982).
- Children can learn to become dependent on adult rewards for learning rather than independent learners (O'Brien 1990).
- Children who are encouraged to work for rewards become 'less inclined to explore ideas, think creatively, and take chances' (Kohn 1994, p. 2).
- When praise is used as a reinforcer of children's behaviour it can lower children's confidence in themselves (Hitz and Driscoll 1988).
- Young children do not always understand negative reinforcement, such as time out, in the ways that adults intend. Children can feel hurt and anxious when they experience time out and these feelings can lead to an increase in negative behaviours (Readdick and Chapman 2000).
- Rewards can undermine children's motivation to learn rather than increase it (Deci, Koestner and Ryan 2001).

REINFORCEMENT AS OPPRESSIVE

Several authors argue that reinforcement can deny children's rights, humiliate them and undermine their self-confidence. As Lake (2004) explained:

> Under this approach, adults must control children's behavior because children are not capable of controlling themselves; adults must decide what is right and wrong for children because children are not capable of deciding right and wrong for themselves. However, controlling young children hinders their development of self-esteem and self-identity. Controlling young children may also reinforce the powerlessness they feel in adult environments and could stunt their growth toward equality. The act of controlling children is the act of oppressing children. (p. 571)

Caution is advised for these reasons. We believe that reinforcement should be used very cautiously and only in very unusual circumstances.

How?

Reinforcement as a teaching technique is based on the theories of behaviourist psychologists. Behaviourists believe that we can change people's behaviour by rewarding it and hence reinforcing it. Those rewards can be given by an adult or built into the physical environment.

To change children's behaviour using reinforcement techniques, the following steps are consistently recommended in the literature.

1 *Identify the antecedents of the behaviour*
- Observe children to identify the specific behaviour (or behaviours) that you want to increase or decrease. In this way staff can target their reinforcement more specifically.

> Habous, a child care worker, was keen to find out why one of the babies in her care was 'fussing' such a lot. After a discussion with a co-worker she decided to look more carefully at what the baby was doing when he was fussing. After several observations at different times of the day she distinguished three types of fussing behaviours; namely, crying loudly, head-banging and moaning to himself. She decided to target the head-banging behaviour first—when this was extinguished she looked at the other two behaviours.
>
> *Reflection point:* How might Habous extinguish the head-banging behaviour?

- Note down the context, setting or prompts that produced the desired or undesired behaviours so you have a clear picture of when, why and how often it occurs. Antecedents might include looks, gestures, instructions, events or a specific experience.

2 *Plan your approach to shaping behaviour*
- Develop clear goals for what you want to have happen. This should specify the behaviours desired (or not), the context in which you expect them to happen (or not) and when you expect them to happen (or not). This should be specific and limited to very few behaviours in the first instance.
- Decide on rewards that can be used to reinforce desired behaviours. They should be something valued by the child. These might be simple, such as a smile or a pat on the back, or more complex, such as reading a favourite book with a child (refer below for more detail).
- Develop a plan of action that rewards desired behaviours and ignores undesired behaviours. Reinforcing a behaviour intermittently is a very effective way to ensure it continues.

Rewards or reinforcers need to vary according to the age, abilities and interests of the child. Research (Turney 1985) has shown that the following reinforcers can be used to successfully change behaviour:

- Verbal—telling a child that you are pleased with what they have done. This is easily administered but needs to be consistent to be effective. These reinforcers can be very simple:

> Gracie always shows the children in her care that she is pleased with their achievements. She often says 'Well done!' and combines this with a smile, and some sort of physical reinforcement such as a pat, a rub or a hug.
>
> _Reflection point:_ To what extent do you think that Gracie's reinforcers are appropriate? Why? Why not?

- Gesture and facial expression—showing a child you are pleased with what they have done through non-verbal signs such as smiles, nods or other culturally appropriate ways to express pleasure to a child.
- Proximity—showing a child you are pleased with what they have done by moving closer to them if this is deemed pleasing within the child's specific cultural context.
- Contact—showing a child you are pleased with what they have done through contact such as a gentle touch on the arm or other forms of contact that would be deemed pleasing within the child's specific cultural context.
- Activity privileges—showing a child you are pleased with what they have done through allowing them to be involved in an activity they enjoy, such as bike-riding or helping with story time. It is important to choose activities that you believe are valuable for the child to be engaged in rather than those that the child themself might prefer.
- Tokens—showing a child you are pleased with what they have done by giving them a special token such as a star or a stamp. Tokens have been found to be highly reinforcing but you need to plan to eliminate them over time so children can perform the desired behaviour without specialist tokens.

3 Implement and evaluate the program
- Observe again and evaluate the success or otherwise of your program. Modifications to the reward may be necessary if the program has not worked.

(This list is adapted from Wearmouth 2004; Kazdin 2005.)

Research shows that rewards work best when they are given as soon as the behaviour is seen, when the child likes the reward, when the child is clear why they are being rewarded and when there are a variety of rewards used (Turney 1985; Kadzin 2005). It is also worth noting that young children generally display more on-task behaviour when they have had a rest and less on-task behaviour after vigorous activity (Wearmouth 2004).

> Erica comes into the kindergarten and shows her teacher her star chart. Her mother has set up a token reward program for Erica. She has a new star on her chart every time she has a dry bed. When she has seven stars she will be going for a special tea to her grandfather's. Erica loves having tea with her grandfather but as he lives out of town she can't visit him very often. Erica has not wet the bed for a week and is proud of her achievements. She excitedly tells her teacher that tomorrow she is going to her grandfather's for tea because she has seven stars on her chart.
>
> _Reflection point:_ What do you see as the pros and cons of star charts?

Generally most classroom reward systems have clearly stated rules and consequences, as Lake (2004) explains:

> The most common version of consequences in such a system includes some variation of these levels: (1) warning; (2) last in line for recess or lunch; (3) time out of perhaps 5, 10, or 15 minutes; (4) time out in another room or an increased time out in the present room; (5) a call or note home; and, finally, (6) being sent to the principal. (p. 568)

When and why?

Goal relevance

Reinforcement can be used to enhance children's learning in several ways:

- Reinforcement can be used to increase children's engagement in a particular activity or experience (Kazdin 2005), especially when they have an initial interest in the task (Cameron 2001).
- Reinforcement can be used to enhance pro-social behaviour (Bandura 2006). Generally, this would be done to increase a desirable behaviour such as sharing and to decrease an undesirable behaviour such as hitting.
- Reinforcement can be used as part of programmed learning instruction. In such programs children's learning is stepped progressively through a task or set of skills by the use of reinforcers. Shimizu and McDonough (2006) describe a three-step programmed learning instruction to teach preschool children with developmental disabilities how to use a computer mouse:

> Stage 1 was designed to teach participants to move the mouse. Stage 2 was designed to teach participants to move the on-screen cursor onto specific items on the screen. Stage 3 was designed to teach participants to click on specific items on the screen. Experimenter-provided prompts were used to facilitate skill acquisition at each stage. The post-assessment showed that all participants learned pointing after intervention. The intervention package consisting of Programmed Instruction and experimenter-provided prompts was effective for teaching the hand–eye coordination required for pointing. (p. 175)

- Reinforcement can be used as part of scripted reading programs in the early years of school to improve basic literacy skills. In scripted reading programs teachers follow a very specific script and reinforce children when they produce responses or behaviours that are expected from the program (Johnston-Parsons et al. 2005).

Reinforcement is a useful technique to use for short-term changes in children's behaviour. Staff should remember that long-term changes in children's learning are unlikely to occur if reinforcement is the sole teaching technique employed.

DEVELOPMENTAL CONSIDERATIONS

Behaviourists studied learning and how it occurs, and then applied the general principles of learning they developed to explain the process of development. They did not propose a stage theory of development and argued that all the basic principles of learning are equally applicable to children irrespective of their developmental abilities. However, they did recognise that children's ability to learn will vary, depending on their level of maturity and their existing skill base.

Hence, reinforcement can be used effectively to develop many of the skills babies and toddlers are striving towards in the early years, such as self-help skills, problem-solving, autonomy and independence, and to help teach preschool children more complex pro-social and cognitive skills.

From a developmental perspective it is important to consider two things when using reinforcement as a teaching technique. First, it is important to try to reinforce only those skills and dispositions relevant to the child's developmental age and stage. The following discussion between a teacher and a parent shows how important this can be:

A teacher–parent discussion is taking place in a child care centre. Trish is talking with Sara, the mother, an intelligent high achiever who works in business. Trish is a very experienced child care worker. They are discussing Sara's daughter, Isobel, who is three years old.

Sara: 'Isobel has started wetting the bed again. I've tried telling her that she's a big girl now and that she'll get a present when she stops completely, but this has been going on for months and it doesn't seem to make any difference. She doesn't seem to care.'

Trish: 'When she wets the bed what do you do?'

Sara: 'I'm usually very cross with her and I remind her that big girls don't wet beds. I also tell her that if she's good until Easter she can have a Barbie Doll.'

Trish: 'Easter is a long way away for a three-year-old [four weeks]. Perhaps you could reward Isobel for being dry more frequently and not make such a fuss when she wets the bed. I know it's hard sometimes when it's the middle of the night not to react crossly. What rewards does Isobel respond to?'

Sara: 'She loves praise, and she likes having breakfast in bed with me on the weekends.'

Trish: 'I wonder if you could reward her for dry nights by praising her and on Saturday morning by making a big fuss of her and allowing her to have breakfast with you in bed? When she does wet, the best thing to do is to simply acknowledge that she has wet the bed, then change the bed and put her back to sleep in a matter-of-fact way. She'll look forward to praise and to the treat on the weekend.'

Reflection point: What do you see as the issues in this conversation? What would you do and say in a similar situation?

Second, it is important to choose rewards appropriate to children's differing developmental abilities and interests and their cultural contexts. For example, while proximity rewards might be suitable across all age groups, tokens are likely to be of interest only to those older children who have reached an appropriate level of symbolic thought. Similarly, the activity rewards that might be enjoyed by babies are likely to be different to those enjoyed by preschoolers and children in the early years of school. Research suggests that intrinsic motivation in school-aged children can be undermined by tangible rewards so it is especially important to reflect carefully on when and how to use reinforcement as a teaching technique in the early years of schooling (Deci, Koestner and Ryan 2001). Additionally, Canadian researchers (Lemmon and Moore 2007), in a study of preschool children's ability to make decisions about actions in the present and their future outcomes, found that three-year-olds preferred small immediate rewards rather than larger rewards delayed to some time in the future. Four-year-olds often chose to wait for larger rewards.

It is also important to bear in mind the concerns raised above about using reinforcement as a teaching technique. It should be used selectively and with great care with all age groups. This will ensure that children's learning does not become dependent on external rewards at the expense of intrinsic pleasure from success and striving to achieve.

Equity considerations

'RACE' AND CULTURE

As mentioned above, reinforcement can be an effective teaching technique for increasing and decreasing specific targeted behaviours. It can be used to decrease children's negative comments and reactions to each other based on 'racial' bias and to increase children's respectful behaviours. For example, staff may have a white child in the group who has refused to play with one of the black children in the group. Staff may have told the white child they find this unacceptable and find as a result that very occasionally he is beginning to play with the black child. Staff may be looking for ways to increase this play and decide that reinforcement might assist. Positive reinforcement can also be used by staff if a child is being rejected by others because of her 'racial' or ethnic background. Staff can increase inter-group contact by reinforcing the positive behaviours of the rejected child in front of other children (Ramsey 2004). However, once again caution should be exercised in relying on this teaching technique. There is some older research evidence that children whose social behaviour is shaped regularly by adults through rewards tend to be less generous to others than children whose behaviour has not been shaped in this way (Kohn 1994).

When deciding on rewards for children for specific behaviours it is important to consider the cultural relevance of the rewards being chosen. Special care should be given to using proximity and gesture as rewards when the children are from a cultural group different to that of the staff, because non-verbal signals such as eye contact and touching can be understood differently. For example, for some Indigenous Australian children eye contact is highly problematic culturally. It can be read as shameful or threatening rather than as supportive (Howard 2006). The level of comfort people feel standing or sitting next to each other can also differ between cultural groups. In some cultures it can be considered extremely impolite to be very near someone and, therefore, children from these cultures may see this as a negative reward. In other cultures, the opposite can be true. It is important for staff to take time to learn from the children and their families how body language might be read by the children. This can prevent rewards and praise being misread and can help staff to choose rewards that are culturally sensitive and appropriate.

Additionally, if verbal reinforcement is not given in a child's first language it may be ineffective (Rhodes and Pufahl 2004).

It is important for staff to seek relevant and up-to-date information on appropriate patterns of non-verbal interaction among the cultural groups that they are working with. Speaking with members of the relevant communities can be an important part of gaining this information as traditions and expectations within communities can change over time and depending on contexts.

It is important that staff do not rely strongly on reinforcement as a teaching technique for increasing pro-social behaviour between children from different 'racial' groups. Research (Krebs 1983) suggests that there are only a very few pro-social behaviours that are learned effectively via reinforcement.

It may also be the case that what is considered anti-social behaviour by adults is, in effect, a child resisting what they believe to be unfair expectations or cultural requirements placed on them. Sleeter and Grant (1999, p. 195) make this point well:

> Most people, often as part of a group, oppose on a daily basis what they see as unfair authority or restrictions imposed by someone else. In school, this may take countless forms, such as girls resisting being viewed as sex objects, students in wheelchairs ganging up against those who tease them, or students living below the poverty line who refuse to obey middle-class teachers with low expectations of them.

Positive reinforcement has been used in a CD-ROM resource to support learning English and Māori languages in New Zealand. When using the multi-media resource with children, adults are encouraged to give children positive reinforcement messages in English and Māori (Bolstad 2004).

GENDER

There is considerable research to suggest that girls and boys partly learn their gender through adult reinforcement of their gender behaviours. Research in 18 US early childhood classrooms and seven child care centres with 50 teachers (Dobbs, Arnold and Doctoroff 2004) found that teachers rewarded the girls more than they did the boys. While the reasons for this were not clear, it does indicate that teachers need to be alert to how they use reinforcing as a teaching strategy with boys and with girls.

One reason posited for gender differences in adult reinforcement is that boys are likely to be more involved in aggressive behaviour than girls (Dobbs, Arnold and Doctoroff 2004). It is also likely that some of boys' physically aggressive behaviour will be directed towards the harassment of girls and be destructive for girls (Keddie 2003; Ostrov et al. 2004). Harassment may take the form of hitting girls, knocking over their blocks, pinching their bottoms and pulling their hair. When such harassment occurs girls will often shy away from the harassment and relinquish any play areas in which the harassment occurs (MacNaughton 2000). Staff can use negative reinforcement to reduce the boys' aggression towards the girls and to increase the girls' determination to challenge the harassment and maintain involvement in their chosen play areas. In planning to use reinforcement for these goals, staff need to remember that there may be differences in what boys and girls will find rewarding and when they will find it rewarding. A meta-analysis of delayed gratification in boys and girls and men and women found that, overall, girls and women are more able and willing to delay receiving a larger and more preferred reward in the future than are boys and men (Silverman 2003).

Researchers have argued over time that young children learn gender stereotypes in part through adults' direct reinforcement (Patterson and Bigler 2006). There is some evidence (see Browne and Ross 1991) that the converse is also true, but the research base is scant. Adults can increase non-traditional gender behaviours through using proximity rewards. For instance, if boys are playing in a caring and enjoyable way with dolls, having an adult nearby makes it more likely that the behaviour will be strengthened and then recur. This research also indicates that rewarding preschool girls with praise for their involvement in non-traditional areas such as play with construction materials can be counter-productive. Girls quickly learn that producing a construction with minimal effort and complexity can produce considerable praise from staff. This can teach them that not much is expected of them in the area of construction. The girls also learn that once they have received praise for their efforts nothing much else is expected and they move quickly on to other learning areas.

It is important to remember that reinforcement may change behaviours but not change how children feel. Moreover, reinforcement does not enable children to understand why staff see some behaviours as more acceptable than others. It is, therefore, not prudent for staff to rely heavily on it as a teaching technique in implementing gender equity programs.

DISABILITY AND ADDITIONAL NEEDS

When children with and without disabilities first meet there will be a lot to learn about each other and about how to build relationships. Careful use of simple reinforcement techniques can help them build positive relationships. Simple rewards for children without disabilities appropriately helping those children with disabilities can strengthen such behaviours. In a review of pro-social programs for children with disabilities over a 25-year period (1975–1999), researchers found that reinforcement was one of the most effective strategies to build pro-social skills in children with disabilities. They also found that the rewards used most often with preschool children with disabilities were edible reinforcements, such as raisins, and social reinforcements, such as hugs (Vaughn et al. 2003).

Reflecting on reinforcement techniques

1 Consider the following concerns about the use of reinforcement as a teaching technique raised by Spodek and Saracho (1994, pp. 192–193):

Some feel that the focus on behaviour leads to a concern for symptoms rather than causes. Others object to the use of rewards, equating it with bribery. Still others feel that this technique places the control of behaviour outside the individual and does not help the children learn to judge what is proper behaviour, thus limiting autonomy.

To what extent do you agree with the comments? Why? To what extent do you disagree with the comments? Why?

2 Kohn (1994, p. 1) writes:

A child promised a treat for learning or acting responsibly has been given every reason to stop doing so when there is no longer a reward to be gained.

To what extent do you agree with the comments? Why? To what extent do you disagree with the comments? Why?

3 Imagine you are working with a four-year-old boy who always tries to be the leader when he is playing with other children. If he isn't allowed to be the leader he often hurts the other children verbally or physically. His favourite places to play are in the outside play area and he loves all types of water play. What else would you need to know about this child before deciding to use reinforcement to change his behaviour in group settings?

4 Review an 'educational' software program for children under five years of age. To what extent is the program based on learning through reinforcement? Would you use the program with young children? Why? Why not?

5 Choosing appropriate reinforcers is an important part of using reinforcement as a teaching technique. Consider what might be some appropriate reinforcers to use for children of different ages by completing the following table.

Reinforcer	Babies	Toddlers	Preschoolers
Verbal Gesture Proximity Activity Token			

Improving teaching in practice

1 Identify a child for whom reinforcement techniques may be appropriate in the short term. Observe the child closely and identify a behaviour that you would like to positively reinforce. Plan at least five periods of time in which you work closely to reinforce this behaviour. Implement and record these sessions.

2 At the end of the fifth session evaluate your own reinforcing skills by reviewing the extent to which you were able to increase the desired behaviour.

3 What additional skills and knowledge do you need to consolidate and improve your reinforcing skills?

4 How and how well did you take account of the following considerations when reinforcing the desired behaviour with the child you selected?
- developmental
- cultural and 'race'
- gender; and
- disability.

FURTHER READING

Duncan, T., Kemple, K.M. and Smith, T. 2000, 'Developmentally appropriate practice and the use of reinforcement in inclusive early childhood classrooms', *Childhood Education*, 76, pp. 194–203.

Dunlap, G. and Carr, E. 2007, 'Positive behaviour support and developmental disabilities: a summary and analysis of research', in S. Odom, ed., *Handbook of Developmental Disabilities*, Guildford Press, New York [refer to Chapter 23].

Kazdin, A. 2005, *Parent Management Training*, Oxford University Press, Oxford [refer to Chapters 2 and 3].

Kohn, A. 2001, 'Five reasons to stop saying "Good Job"', *Young Children* 56(5), pp. 24–28.

O'Brien, S. 1990, 'Praising children: five myths', *Childhood Education*, 66(4), pp. 248–249.

Readdick, C. and Chapman, P. 2000, 'Young children's perception of time out', *Journal of Research in Childhood Education*, 15(1), pp. 81–87.

Wolfgang, C. 2000, 'Another view on "reinforcement in developmentally appropriate early childhood classrooms"', *Childhood Education* 77(2), Winter, pp. 64–67.

ONLINE AND MULTI-MEDIA RESOURCES

Text

Home page of the B.F. Skinner Foundation. This has extensive links to publications and summaries of his work: **http://www.bfskinner.org**

Duncan, T. K., Kemple, M. and Smith, T. 2000, 'Reinforcement in developmentally appropriate early childhood classrooms', *Childhood Education*, 77(2), pp. 194–205: **http://findarticles.com/p/articles/mi_qa3614/is_200007/ai_n8890770**

REFERENCES

Arbeau, A. and Coplan, R. 2007, 'Kindergarten teachers' beliefs and responses to hypothetical prosocial, asocial, and antisocial children', *Merrill-Palmer Quarterly*, 53(2), pp. 291–318.

Bandura, A. 2006, *Psychological Modeling: Conflicting Theories*, Adline Transaction Publishers, Edison, NJ.

Bolstad, R. 2004, *The Role and Potential of ICT in Early Childhood Education: A Review of New Zealand and International Literature*, Ministry of Education, Wellington, New Zealand.

Bronson, P. 2007, 'How not to talk to your kids: the inverse power of praise', *New York Magazine*, 40(6), pp. 24–31.

Browne, N. and Ross, C. 1991, '"Girls' stuff, boys' stuff": young children talking and playing', in N. Browne, ed., *Science and Technology in the Early Years* (pp. 37–51), Open University Press, Milton Keynes.

Cameron, J. 2001, 'Negative effects of reward on intrinsic motivation—a limited phenomenon: comment on Deci, Koestner, and Ryan (2001)', *Review of Educational Research*, 71(1), pp. 29–42.

Choate, M., Pincus, D., Eyberg, S. and Barlow, D. 2005, 'Parent-child interaction therapy for treatment of separation anxiety disorder in young children: a pilot study', *Cognitive and Behavioral Practice*, 12(1), pp. 126–135.

Deci, E., Koestner, R. and Ryan, M. 2001, 'Extrinsic rewards and intrinsic motivation in education: reconsidered once again', *Review of Educational Research*, 7(1), pp. 1–29.

Dobbs, J., Arnold, D. and Doctoroff, G. 2004, 'Attention in the preschool classroom: the relationships among child gender, child misbehavior, and types of teacher attention', *Early Child Development and Care*, 174(3), pp. 281–295.

Henderlong, J., College, R. and Lepper, M. 2002, 'The effects of praise on children's intrinsic motivation: a review and synthesis', *Psychological Bulletin*, 12(5), pp. 774–795.

Hitz, R. and Driscoll, A. 1988, 'Praise or encouragement? New insights into praise: implications for early childhood teachers', *Young Children*, July, pp. 6–13.

Howard, D. 2006, 'Classroom case study: cross cultural obstacles to the referral of Aboriginal children for hearing tests', *Australian and New Zealand Journal of Audiology*, 28(1), pp. 41–46

Johnston-Parsons, M., Wilson, M., McManamon, G. and Karl, M. 2005, 'Living in the land of a scripted reading program', in M. Johnston-Parsons, ed., *Success Stories from a Failing School: Teachers Living Under the Shadow of NCLB*, Information Age Publishing Inc., New York, pp. 69–86.

Kazdin, A. 2005, *Parent Management Training*, Oxford University Press, Oxford.

Keddie, A. 2003, 'Little boys, tomorrow's macho lads', *Discourse: Studies in the Politics of Education*, 24(3), pp. 289–306.

Kohn, A. 1994, 'The risks of rewards', *ERIC Digest*, EDO-PS-94-14.

Krebs, D. 1983, 'Commentary and critique: psychological and philosophical approaches to prosocial development', in D. Bridgeman, ed., *The Nature of Prosocial Development: Interdisciplinary Theories and Strategies* (pp. 205–217), Academic Press, New York.

Lake, V. 2004, 'Ante up: reconsidering classroom management philosophies so every child is a winner', *Early Child Development and Care*, 174(6), pp. 565–574.

Lemmon, K. and Moore, C. 2007, 'The development of prudence in the face of varying future rewards', *Developmental Science*, 10(4), pp. 502–511.

Luman, M., Oosterlaan, J. and Sergeant, J. 2005, 'The impact of reinforcement contingencies on AD/HD: a review and theoretical appraisal', *Clinical Psychology Review*, 25(2), pp. 183–214.

MacNaughton, G. 2000, *Rethinking Gender in Early Childhood Education*, Allen & Unwin, Sydney; Sage Publications, New York; Paul Chapman Publishing, London.

——2003, 'Eclipsing voice in research with young children', *Australian Journal of Early Childhood*, 28(1), 36–43.

Martens, B. and Ardoin, S. with Hilt, A., Lannie, A., Pahahon, C. and Wolfe, L. 2002, 'Sensitivity of children's behaviour to probalistitic reward: effects of a decreasing-ration lottery system on math performance', *Journal Of Applied Behavior Analysis*, 35(4), pp. 403–406.

O'Brien, S. 1990, 'Praising children: five myths', *Childhood Education*, 66(4), pp. 248–249.

Ostrov, J., Woods, K., Jansen, E., Casas, J. and Crick, N. 2004, 'An observational study of delivered and received aggression, gender, and social-psychological adjustment in preschool: "This White Crayon Doesn't Work . . .'", *Early Childhood Research Quarterly*, 19(2), pp. 355–371.

Patterson, M. and Bigler, R. 2006, 'Preschool children's attention to environmental messages about groups: social categorization and the origins of intergroup bias', *Child Development*, 77(4), pp. 847–860.

Ramsey, P. 2004, *Teaching and Learning in a Diverse World: Multicultural Education for Young Children*, 2nd edn, Teachers College Press, New York.

Readdick, C. and Chapman, P. 2000, 'Young children's perception of time out', *Journal of Research in Childhood Education*, 15(1), pp. 81–87.

Rhodes, N. and Pufahl, I. 2004, 'Teaching foreign languages to children through video', *Online Digest*, December 2003, EDO-FL-03-10, updated October 2004, <http://www.cal.org/resources/Digest/0310pufahl.html> (accessed 30 October 2007).

Robison, H. and Schwartz, S. 1982, *Designing Curriculum for Early Childhood*, Allyn & Bacon Inc., Boston.

Seefeldt, C. and Barbour, N. 1986, *Early Childhood Education: An Introduction*, Merrill, Toronto.

Shimizu, H. and McDonough, C. 2006, 'Programmed Instruction to teach pointing with a computer mouse in preschoolers with developmental disabilities', *Research in Developmental Disabilities*, 27(2), pp. 175–189.

Sigler, E. and Aamidor, S. 2005, 'From positive reinforcement to positive behaviors: an everyday guide for the practitioner', *Early Childhood Education Journal*, 32(4), pp. 249–253.

Silverman, I. 2003, 'Gender differences in delay of gratification: a meta-analysis', *Behavioural Science*, 49(9/10), pp. 451–463.

Sleeter, C. and Grant, C. 1999, *Making Choices for Multicultural Education: Five Approaches to Race, Class and Gender*, Merrill, Columbus, OH.

Spodek, B. 1987, 'The knowledge base of kindergarten education', Paper presented at *Five-Year-Olds in School Conference*, East Lansing, MI, 9 January.

Spodek, B. and Saracho, O. 1994, *Right from the Start: Teaching Children Ages Three to Eight*, Allyn & Bacon Inc., Boston.

Turney, C. 1985, *Anatomy of Teaching*, Sydney, Novak Publishing.

Vaughn, S., Kim, A., Sloan Claire V., Tejero Hughes, M., Elbaum, B. and Sridhar, D. 2003, 'Social skills interventions for young children with disabilities: a synthesis of group design studies', *Remedial and Special Education*, 24(1), pp. 2–26.

Wearmouth, J. 2004, *Understanding Pupil Behaviour in School: A Diversity of Approaches*, David Fulton Publishing Ltd, DUV, Wiesbaden, Germany.

Wilkes, G. (ed.) 1979, *Collins Dictionary of the English Language*, Penguin Books, Middlesex.

Chapter 29

Scaffolding

 Scaffold: a temporary structure or framework that is used to support (people) during erection, a repair of a building or other construction.

(*Collins Dictionary of the English Language*, p. 1300)

Teachers should . . . be sensitively attuned to children's abilities, interests and strengths, and remain accessible enough to provide appropriate scaffolding.

(Smith 1996, p. 332)

Another important component of scaffolding is the eventual independence of the child. Support is gradually lessoned, allowing the child to take ownership of the situation.

(Fair et al. 2005, p. 230)

What?

In everyday usage scaffolding describes a temporary structure of support that is used by construction workers to assist with constructing or with repairing buildings. Jerome Bruner developed the metaphor of 'scaffolding' children's learning to describe the process through which a more competent peer or adult helps a less competent child to become more competent and eventually function independently of the original person's help (Burman 2008; Fair et al. 2005).

As a teaching technique, scaffolding describes the process of providing temporary guidance and support to children moving from one level of competence to another. The guidance may be verbal or non-verbal (Vandermaas-Peeler, Way and Umpleby 2002). 'Scaffolds' (or the support of more competent adults or peers) can help increase children's level of competence in all areas of development. The 'scaffolds' in education are the adults and peers who tutor others (Fair et al. 2005). Adult and peer tutors support the child's exploration of new meanings, relationships and knowledges, and this consolidates what is nearly known by the child. Scaffolding is a teaching technique that has been developed from the work of Leo S. Vygotsky and Jerome Bruner.

Issues and debates

LIMITATIONS OF SCAFFOLDING AS A METAPHOR FOR TEACHING

There has been concern raised by some researchers that teachers may interpret the metaphor of scaffolding too narrowly and overemphasise the role of the teacher in children's learning. This could and can lead to teachers emphasising the role of adult direct instruction in children's learning and position the child as a passive recipient of this instruction (Verenikina 2003).

BROADENING CONCEPTIONS OF SCAFFOLDING POTENTIALLY UNDERMINING ITS MEANING

Concern has been raised about the extent to which scaffolding is becoming a meaningless term as its use has broadened to include anything an adult or competent peer does to support children's learning. Turner and Berkowitz (2006, p. 175) express this concern as follows:

> The concept's theoretical origins have been diluted to the extent that even the idea of self-scaffolding is often raised. Bickhard (1992) has been a strong proponent of the value of self-scaffolding.

They, along with others (e.g. Gauvain 2006), argue further that the concept of scaffolding is becoming meaningless because it has lost its connection to its socio-cultural theoretical roots that emphasise the socially and culturally mediated and negotiated nature of meaning-making and learning.

THEORETICAL BACKGROUND

VYGOTSKY AND SCAFFOLDING

Leo Semenovich Vygotsky (1886–1934) was a Russian academic whose theory of cognitive development in the 1920s and 1930s provided a powerful framework for understanding the relationship between teaching and learning. It also provided a '. . . fresh perspective on children's development . . .' (Berk and Winsler 1995, p. 3).

Vygotsky's work reached Western, English-speaking scholars only recently. His work was banned in the Soviet Union until 1953, and the Cold War between the USA, its allies (including Australia) and the Soviet Union limited the possibility of the academic exchange of his ideas (Berk 1994a).

The following beliefs about learning and development held in Vygotsky's work provide the theoretical rationale for scaffolding as a teaching technique. He believed:

- child development occurs as a result of natural *and* cultural activity. Natural activity refers to the biological growth and maturation of the person. Cultural activity refers to the social processes through which we learn to use cultural tools and to think

- thought processes occur on a lower and a higher plane. The lower plane we share with other mammals. The higher plane involves the use of language and cultural knowledge, and its existence distinguishes us from other animals
- each plane of learning requires the assistance of a more experienced learner to maximise learning
- higher plane thought processes (cognition) are highly dependent on language
- 'Education leads development' (Berk and Winsler 1995, p. 17) and thus learning on the higher plane of thinking.

More specifically, Vygotsky believed that learning occurred most effectively on the higher plane of thinking through competent adults interacting with a child in a theoretical zone of development called the Zone of Proximal Development (ZPD). The ZPD referred to a region in which a child could work at higher levels of competence in relation to a particular skill, understanding or disposition when working with more competent peers or adults than when working by herself (Meadows and Cashdan 1988, p. 53). In the ZPD there is a transfer of ability from a more competent person to the child.

Vygotsky defined the ZPD as the '... distance between the actual developmental level as determined by independent problem-solving and the level of potential development as determined through problem-solving under adult guidance or in collaboration with more capable peers ...' (Vygotsky 1978, cited in Berk and Winsler 1995, p. 38). Once children develop cognitive competencies in a social context they are internalised by the child. At this point a child no longer needs adult guidance and support for their newly acquired competency. However, there will be new competencies that now can be practised in the ZPD and will, through adult support and guidance, be internalised.

Vygotsky's work supports a play-based early childhood curriculum because he strongly believed that imaginative play was important in building young children's intellectual and social competencies. He saw play as a '... leading activity which determines the child's development ...' (Vygotsky 1932, p. 552). Vygotsky believed that imaginative play expresses children's zone of proximal development as it allows the child to perform tasks, experience feelings and test competencies not possible in non-imaginative play (Jones and Reynolds 1992).

In imaginative play children can imagine themselves beyond what they can accomplish in ordinary interactions with themselves and others (Fimreite, Flem and Gudmundsdottir 1999). This idea gains support through research showing that children involved in child-directed fantasy play produce more varied and alternative uses for objects than children who have not had this experience (Moyles 1989). In addition, while involved in imaginative play, children regulate their behaviour according to the rules of the play and thus learn to regulate their impulsive actions (Berk 1994b). Vygotsky believed each of these attributes of imaginative play supports the emergence of a wide range of competencies and thus it should be fostered.

Vygotsky's beliefs on imaginative play have been supported by research which shows that it enhances children's imagination and creativity, improves their ability to reason about the impossible or absurd, extends all aspects of children's conversational competence, and promotes children's story-telling and story-memory abilities (Berk 1994b; Fimreite, Flem and Gudmundsdottir 1999).

In recent years there has been considerable conceptual advancement and refinement of the processes and nature of scaffolding (see Marsh 2006). For example, Granott (2006) has focused on the changing nature of the child's performance during the scaffolding transaction. She has developed the idea of the ZCD— the Zone of Current Development—to explain how children perform in a bounded way over time through negotiating meaning with others. Miller (2006, p. 209) explains the significance of this work as follows:

> Her conceptualization thus adds an important focus on social context to the study of variability. Also useful is her notion that variability can be both vertical (the scaffolder's band of variability in level of performance corresponds to but is higher than that of the scaffoldee) and horizontal (changes in the nature of the scaffolding activity itself, such as changing strategies or activities).

How?

The role of staff in scaffolding children's learning is threefold:

1   First, staff need to be sensitive to children's ability levels and judge when children are ready to move from one level of competence to another (Fair et al. 2005). Staff can carefully observe and note the social, cognitive and communicative competencies of the child. This may mean joining in children's imaginative play and intervening in children's other learning experiences to find out what they can or cannot currently do without assistance (Meadows and Cashdan 1988). Staff need to ask themselves: 'Have I seen . . . do this before?'; 'How easily can . . . do this?'; 'What would present the child with a challenge in this situation?'; 'What is the next level for the child in this situation?'.

2 Second, staff need time to support, guide and assist children's moving from one level of competence to another using explicit guidance that may include hints, questions, modelling, instructions and descriptions (Anghileri 2006; Marsh 2006). Successful scaffolding rests on staff spending time with children on a one-to-one basis or in small groups (Fleer 1996).

3 Third, staff need to judge how best to assist children's movement to increased competence. This involves using a variety of verbal and non-verbal general teaching techniques to extend children's understandings and skills. Staff may use a single technique or a combination of techniques. Teaching techniques that support scaffolding include several of the general teaching techniques discussed in previous parts of this book. For example, questioning, prompting, praising, confirming, pointing out things to children and modelling are involved in scaffolding (Madsen and Gudmundsdottir 2000):

Maria has drawn on general techniques such as questioning, encouraging, praising and non-verbal suggesting as part of her scaffolding process with Adrian:

Adrian: 'How do you draw a person?'

Maria: 'Can you make a shape for the head?' She makes a round motion around her head. Adrian makes a roundish shape.

Maria: 'That's good—now what shape is the body?' She indicates length in front of her body. Adrian makes a long oval shape below the head.

Maria: 'Well done—now what else does a person have?' She holds out her arms. Adrian draws lines off the body.

Maria: 'And . . .' She holds up her legs.

Adrian draws the legs off the body. They have a further discussion about body parts and Adrian adds hands and hair. Maria enthusiastically praises him.

Reflection point: Which specific techniques is Maria using at each point of the conversation?

According to Berk and Winsler (1995) good quality scaffolding involves the following features:

- joint problem-solving
- inter-subjectivity
- warmth and responsiveness
- keeping the child in the ZPD
- promoting self-regulation.

We shall now look at each of these in turn.

JOINT PROBLEM-SOLVING

The first feature in quality scaffolding is that two or more people (child–child or child–adult) try to solve a problem together. They must each be interested in the problem and the problem must be culturally meaningful to them (Gauvain 2006).

INTER-SUBJECTIVITY

The meaning of inter-subjectivity can be easily understood by splitting the word into two: 'inter' and 'subjectivity'. Inter means mutual or reciprocal. Subjectivity means a person's consciousness (thoughts) or perception (feelings/senses). Hence, inter-subjectivity involves trying to reach shared (mutual) understandings between adult and child or child and child of how each thinks and feels. Inter-subjectivity 'creates a common ground for communication as each partner adjusts to the perspective of the other' (Berk 1994a, p. 256). This means interacting to find out what the other thinks and feels, and negotiating a common understanding—sometimes through compromise. This common understanding must be within the child's ZPD (Gauvain 2006).

Zone of Actual Development (ZAD) is the term that can be used to describe the level of competence a child has reached in relation to a particular skill, understanding or disposition when working by her or himself.

Zone of Proximal Development (ZPD) is the term Vygotsky used to describe the level of competence a child can potentially reach in relation to a particular skill, understanding or disposition. This potential is reached when working with more competent peers or adults. It is easy to think of the ZPD as the zone of 'next development' (Meadows and Cashdan 1988, p. 53).

WARMTH AND RESPONSIVENESS

Scaffolding involves social collaboration between child and adult to enhance children's learning. Its effectiveness as a teaching technique is, therefore, strongly dependent on the 'emotional tone' (Berk and Winsler 1995, p. 41) of the relationship between learner and teacher. A positive 'emotional tone' is more likely when staff acknowledge children's efforts and understandings. Staff need to take notice of what children are doing and saying, comment positively on children's work and stay closely attuned to children's need for additional support:

> Pia works with Leo, a four-year-old, in the block area. She sits close to him and makes several suggestions as to how he can make the structure he is building stronger. She has observed Leo in the blocks over time and has noticed that he gives up easily when his structures fall over. She continues to support his learning in this way until he has completed the structure. As she sits next to him she takes care to encourage his efforts.
>
> ———————
>
> *Reflection point:* In what ways does Pia stay closely attuned in this episode?

KEEPING THE CHILD IN THE ZPD

Learning for the child will be at its most intense and most effective when she is regularly working within her ZPD. In other words, children's learning is maximised when they are regularly working at the upper level of their competence. To enable this to happen, staff need to ensure that children's learning experiences and their learning environment challenge them to 'do' and think beyond their current abilities when unaided by others. This involves staff encouraging children to try new tasks and skills and use equipment in novel ways, and it requires that staff be close by to adjust their level of support accordingly. Successful scaffolding leads to children being independent of their tutor and moving into the Zone of Current Development (ZCD) (Granott 2006).

Once a child is able to verbalise his thoughts, staff can judge if a task is within a child's ZPD by listening to the child's private speech. Private speech is the chatting children do with themselves when working on a task. Private speech generally happens when a task is challenging enough for a child to need to talk his way through it. If a child is using clear, task-related private speech then it is likely that the task being attempted is within the child's ZPD (Berk and Winsler 1995).

PROMOTING SELF-REGULATION

When children self-regulate they control their learning. In successful scaffolding, staff are actively involved in promoting this via the distancing techniques they use. In low-level distancing, staff pose questions and comment on the immediate problem at hand. In medium-level distancing, staff compare and contrast what is happening currently. In high-level distancing, staff encourage children to think hypothetically about what might happen in a particular task or situation (Berk and Winsler 1995).

To decide how much assistance to offer children during play with each other, Berk and Winsler (1995) suggested that staff ask themselves what they have seen children do before, how much help children need to successfully achieve their goals and what staff–child interactions will keep the children focused on each other.

The children in Year 1 are cooking Easter buns. They have written out the recipe, shopped for the ingredients and are now in the process of mixing the dough. Jo, their teacher, leaves them alone to do this because she knows from previous cooking sessions that they are capable. Once mixed, the dough must be kneaded for 10 minutes. Jo knows that the children have little experience of kneading or of timing their work. She stays near where they are working and comments occasionally on what they are doing to keep them focused on their task with each other. She is also watching for the time when they will need assistance with kneading the dough and when they may need suggestions about how best to time this process.

Reflection point: What specific techniques is Jo using to scaffold learning in this experience?

Successful scaffolding involves a changing relationship between the scaffolder (tutor) and the scaffoldee (tutee) that involves calibrating and recalibrating the input from the tutor to match the changing capacities of the tutee and increasing activity levels for the tutee, with a positive and changing effect for each (Granott 2006).

In summary, scaffolding involves staff using a variety of verbal and non-verbal general teaching techniques to identify children's current levels of competence in specific developmental domains and to challenge the children to move beyond their original level of competence.

When and why?

The staff's aim when scaffolding is to move children to a point where they can do something without help from a more competent adult. The role of the adult or peer is to support the child and challenge the child to build new knowledge or skills but to not frustrate the child through over-challenging or extending the child (Vandermaas-Peeler, Way and Umpleby 2002). Hence, scaffolding is a relevant teaching technique to use whenever staff plan to extend children's current level of understanding and skill in any area of development. It is particularly pertinent when staff plan to lead development rather than allow children to discover something for or by themselves.

Klaus has chosen to lead the children's physical co-ordination skills as he feels that the older preschool children in his group are ready for some new physical skill challenges:

Klaus is keen to teach the children to do somersaults. He guides them by verbal instruction and physical prompting. He also demonstrates the different steps involved in doing somersaults as each child attempts them.

Reflection point: What evidence is there that Klaus is leading development and why is he doing this?

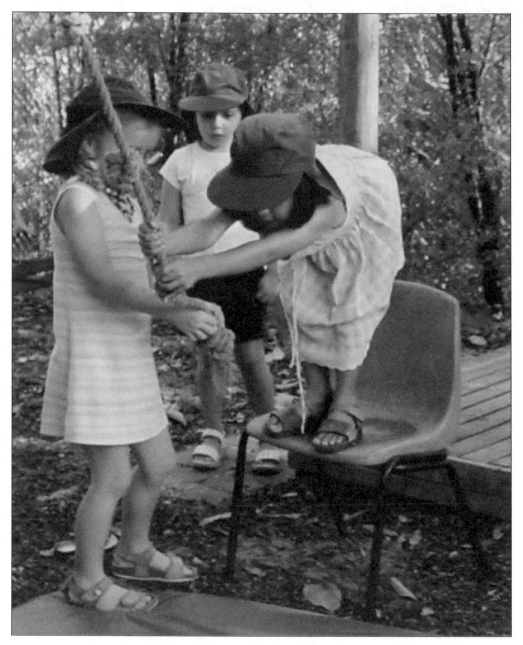

One child scaffolds another as she learns a new skill.

Scaffolding is, therefore, a teaching technique that is strongly mediated by others and therefore is highly interventionist in children's learning.

GOAL RELEVANCE

Scaffolding can be used for a wide range of diverse teaching goals or intentions across diverse learning areas and specific areas of skill development. A range of research that has shown the relevance of scaffolding to specific skill development follows, to capture some of the ways scaffolding has been used deliberately as a teaching technique to support children's learning:

Teaching aim	Scaffolding process
Shaping a child's understandings.	Giving verbal feedback which affirms, negates, recasts, models or hints at what has been said or should be said to be accurate.
Reinforcing a child's proposition.	Restating or expanding what the child has said.
Maintaining joint attention and involvement between child and adult.	Requesting clarification of what the child has said, reflecting on what has been said or done, or asking the child questions.
Linking thoughts and actions through using language.	Commenting on the present, on what the child or the adult remembers about the situation, or on what the adult thinks about what is happening, and comparing and contrasting thoughts and actions.
Extending understanding beyond the current situation.	Questioning through closed and open questions, modelling new understandings, expanding what is said by the child, talking about the implications of what is said, comparing and contrasting thoughts and actions.

Specific skill development

- Cooking skills were taught to 14 preschool children in the USA by their parents during a cooking experience (Vandermaas-Peeler, Way and Umpleby 2002).
- Craft activities were successfully taught to 24 children in the early years of school in the USA by older children scaffolding younger children (Fair et al 2005).
- Multi-media literacy in film-making was built using new technologies in a culturally and linguistically diverse group of 53 nursery school children in the UK.
- Problem-solving skills. The emphasis within Vygotsky's work on the relationship between thought and language means that scaffolding is a particularly pertinent technique to use when extending children's cognitive and linguistic competencies. Scaffolding can stimulate children to chat to themselves as they work on problems or play. Vygotsky called this their 'private speech' (Berk and Winsler 1995). Private speech contributes to children's ability to solve problems. When children talk to themselves during a task, they are more able to solve problems related to it than when they don't (Berk and Winsler 1995).
- Scaffolding can also be used to build children's literacy skills. Boyd Ingram (2000) described a literacy program in a home-based child care setting in which the carer scaffolded children's literacy learning by reading to the children and allowing them to complete words that were missing.
- Technology skills. Fleer (1996) described three case studies in which teachers used scaffolding with preschool and school-age children to develop their ability to think technologically about the space in which they were learning and living. For example, one teacher set up the play area as an architect's studio and the children used this space to investigate what architects do and how to build. The relationship between scaffolding and the development of technological thinking involved:
  — the provision by the adult of a meaningful context in which children could solve technological problems and develop an extensive technological vocabulary through conversation with adults and each other
  — the encouragement by the adult of children to orally report, evaluate and, hence, learn to reflect on what had happened as they solved their technological problems.

DEVELOPMENTAL CONSIDERATIONS

The existence of inter-subjectivity between adults and young babies is evident in babies' ability to finely tune themselves to each other through such activities as jointly gazing at the same objects. Babies' play is more advanced in joint attention episodes where adults scaffold their play (Bigelow, MacLean and Proctor 2004). By the second year of life, inter-subjectivity is possible in relation to play, language and problem-solving skills (Berk 1994a). As Pellegrini and Boyd (1993, p. 110) reported:

> Infants, it seems, can attend to those parental suggestions relevant to tasks that they are in the process of mastering and ignore comments relevant to skills already mastered or beyond their capabilities.

This suggests that staff can scaffold with young babies and toddlers by presenting them with objects and experiences that challenge them. Good scaffolding with babies involves the same five factors mentioned earlier. However, as the following discussion illustrates, the process will be of a shorter duration, maybe only a few minutes, and will be focused on less complex 'problems' than with other children:

- Joint problem-solving—find a problem that interests you and the baby. For example, 'How can a particular toy be taken apart?'; 'Where do the pictures go when the book is closed?'; 'Where does the sound come from when you drop the keys on the floor?'
- Inter-subjectivity—establish joint interest by taking note of a child's reactions. Are you both looking and listening for the same thing or is the baby interested in something else?
- Warmth and responsiveness—establishing a positive relationship is as important to babies' learning as it is to that of older children. Pelligrini and Boyd (1993) argued that secure attachment to the adult involved in scaffolding a baby's learning is an important precursor to successful scaffolding. This is because secure attachment is an important factor in infants' disposition to explore and gather information about their environment.
- Keeping the child in the ZPD—do you know the child's current level of development in various developmental domains? Staff need to know this in order to challenge baby beyond what is known or understood. Simple scaffolding can occur when staff have this knowledge.

> April is 12 months old; she is attempting to climb up the steps to the slide. Dominic, her carer, comes over and holds her hand so that she won't overbalance.

- Promoting self-regulation—staff can do this once a baby can successfully drop the keys on the floor and anticipate the sound they will make. Babies will show that they can do this by being attentive to the floor and showing delight when the sound happens. Staff can then watch for the child's desire to continue with this or test out new understandings. Take the cue from the child. Do they want you to make the sound? Do they want to try something else out with the keys? Are they checking your reaction to the noise the keys make when they fall?

Infants and toddlers can also benefit from the support and guidance of more competent peers. Staff can scaffold infants' and toddlers' growing language and cognitive abilities through providing opportunities for pretend play in mixed-age groupings. The complexity of toddlers' pretend play is significantly greater when they have opportunities for play with preschool children (Kowalski et al. 2005).

Adding novel and surprising items to the imaginative play of toddlers is another important way in which adults can challenge children to move to their ZPD during socio-symbolic play. Studies have also shown that the acquisition of syntax and vocabulary in the first two years of life is facilitated through the use of scaffolding (Bowman, Donovan and Burns 2001).

Scaffolding is also a useful technique for developing older children's skills as written-language users. Staff–child discussions about the processes and outcomes of children's efforts at writing can be used to scaffold these skills. It seems that when staff ask children questions about how they write, and comment to children about their own writing processes, children begin to internalise these questions and comments (Hass Dyson and Genishi 1993; Bowman, Donovan and Burns 2001). As children internalise staff questions and comments about writing processes, they begin to use these questions and comments to reflect on these processes. This reflection helps the children become more competent in using written language. Children in their early years of schooling can successfully scaffold each other's writing skills. Positive and collaborative peer interactions and peer tutoring can improve the quality and quantity of children's writing (Ferguson-Patrick 2007).

Scaffolding can also be used with older children to support friendship-building in classrooms where there are children with disabilities. Specifically, teachers can create a structured environment in which they scaffold children's friendship-building skills such as joining in group activities, negotiating roles in play, exchanging ideas, offering to help each other and sharing (McCay and Keyes 2001/02).

As more competent peers can act as effective scaffolders of learning for children of any age, it is important to group children to allow opportunities for peer scaffolding to occur (Fimreite, Flem and Gudmundsdottir 1999; Bowman, Donovan and Burns 2001) (see Chapter 9 for further discussion of this point).

Equity considerations

'RACE' AND CULTURE

There is a growing research base exploring how culture and teaching techniques interact. For instance, US research exploring the similarities and differences in how mothers of preschool children from an Anglo-American background and from an Iranian immigrant background scaffolded children's learning suggested minimal cross-cultural differences in their scaffolding strategies in relation to their sensitivity to children's competence. The researchers found that each group of mothers scaffolded children's learning by adapting their interactions with children to the demands of the task and the competence of the child. However, Iranian mothers were often more directive in their teaching than the Anglo-American mothers when specific goals had to be achieved (Kermani and Brenner 2000). However, how to teach and what is considered valuable for children to learn, do and know is culturally constructed and mediated, so it is important to reflect on if, when and how formal scaffolding of children's learning should progress in culturally diverse settings (Sternberg 2007). For instance, cultural differences have been found in how mothers speak to their children and gesture to their children as they scaffold their learning (e.g. O'Neill et al. 2005; Fildalgo and Pereira 2005). As always it is important to think carefully about cross-cultural use of scaffolding and to remember that different cultural groups may scaffold children's learning in different ways.

There is some evidence that scaffolding can be useful in promoting co-operative play between children in multicultural settings (Doolittle 1995) and build more collaborative and democratic relationships in multicultural settings (DeWitt 2003).

Scaffolding can also be used to promote anti-discriminatory 'racial' attitudes through adapting the general process of scaffolding to this work:

Teaching aim	Scaffolding process
To increase children's vocabulary for talking about different hair texture.	Activity in which children are pretending to be hairdressers. They are brushing the hair of dolls that represent children from a variety of 'racial' backgrounds.
Shaping a child's understandings of hair texture. Give children words for different hair texture: silky, springy, smooth, flat, crinkly, bristly, spiky.	Giving verbal feedback as children comment on the hair texture which affirms, negates, recasts, models or hints at what has been said or should be said to be accurate.

379

Reinforcing a child's proposition that the hair they are brushing is hard to brush because it is very springy.	Restating or expanding what the child has said. For example, 'Yes, I can see that it's hard to brush the doll's lovely curly hair because it's so springy.'
Maintaining joint attention and involvement between child and adult about the different hair textures the child is experiencing and the implements he or she is using to care for the doll's hair.	Requesting clarification of what the child has said, reflecting on what has been said or done or asking the child questions. For example, 'Do you think that it might be easier to care for the doll's springy hair using an "Afro"-comb?'
Linking thoughts and actions by using language to describe them. As the child puzzles over how to tie long, straight, slippery hair into a pony-tail, staff can comment on how the child is attempting the task and describe the sequence of actions.	Commenting on the present, on what the child or the adult remembers about the situation, or on what the adult thinks about what is happening and comparing and contrasting thoughts and actions. For example, 'It's hard to make a pony-tail when the doll's hair is so shiny and slippery. Asking Patrick to open the scrunchy for you while you hold the hair together seems to have worked.'
Extending understandings beyond the current situation. Staff can talk with the children about scientific explanations for differences in hair texture, such as the role of hair shape in determining hair texture and the role of melanin in determining hair colour. Children can learn that hairs grow up from the skin and melanocytes (the cells that produce melanin) in the root of the hair produce more or less melanin, making the hair darker or lighter. Carotene helps give red hair its redness.	Questioning using closed and open questions, modelling new understandings, expanding what is said by the child, talking about the implications of what is said, and comparing and contrasting thoughts and actions. For example, staff can encourage children to make a chart of the differences in hair colour they have in their group. They can talk about whose hair has lots of melanin and whose hair has less melanin.

GENDER

There is very little published research that we have found that specifically examines the gender implications of scaffolding as a teaching technique. However, there is some evidence that gender influences how teachers see children's help-seeking behaviours during problem-solving that could influence how teachers approach scaffolding with young children. Researchers in the USA (Thompson, Arsenault and Williams 2006) found that teachers see girls with high help-seeking behaviours as less competent and confident than other girls and than boys. The reverse was the case for boys. This offers a point of reflection for teachers about how their own perceptions of children's competence levels during scaffolding might differentially affect their approach to scaffolding with boys and girls.

General research about gender relations in early childhood settings offers some pointers as to how gender might influence some parts of the process of scaffolding in mixed-gender groups of children:

- Joint problem-solving—finding a problem that interests adults and the children is the beginning part of scaffolding. It is important that staff monitor which children are taking the lead in defining problems to be investigated and ensuring that there is an opportunity for both boys and girls to lead such decisions.
- Inter-subjectivity—establishing joint interest in and understandings of the problem offers the potential for the more vocal or assertive children in the group to establish their meanings and interest as paramount. If there are more boisterous boys in the group this could lead to many of the girls losing interest in the task at hand. It is important that staff monitor the gender implications of any children who leave such group work.
- Promoting self-regulation—in learning to take the cue about what has been learned from the children it is important to check once again who is taking the lead. What room has there been for boys and girls to self-regulate?

Good scaffolding begins with a shared problem that needs solving. There are many areas of gender relationships between children that offer fruitful ground for problem-solving between children and teachers.

Think of the often-discussed problem of boys and girls not playing together or defining particular learning areas as 'no-go' areas for the 'other' gender. This could include:

- the boys always rushing for the bicycles and the girls missing out
- the boys being bored with playing dad whenever they go into the home corner with the girls
- the boys and the girls laughing at one of the boys who loves dressing in pink
- one of the girls being upset because none of the girls will play superhero games with her
- the boys and girls always wanting to sit apart at snack time.

The emphasis in scaffolding is not for the adult to tell the children how to solve the problem (for example, by establishing girls-only days in the block area), but to build on children's interests to help them solve the problem for themselves. What do the girls want to do about the fact that the boys won't let them in the block area? What do the boys want to do about the fact that the girls won't let them play in the sandpit? The following conversation provides some flavour about how this might happen. It is an adaptation of a teacher–child discourse reported in Berk and Winsler (1995):

Problem: A group of four-year-old girls has just talked to an early childhood staff member about the fact that the boys have barricaded the block corner and said that they don't want the girls playing in it. The girls are cross and want the adult to do something about it. The adult is also concerned.

Adult: 'I can see that you want to play with the blocks and that you are cross about what the boys have done. I am upset too. What would you like to do about it?'

Sally: 'You tell them that they can't do it.'

Adult: 'I'd like you to think about what we could do together.'

Sally: 'Too hard.'

Adult: 'Well, how about we talk about some different things we could do. I could tell the boys to leave but I'm not sure they would be happy. Is there anything else we could do with all of us helping?'

Mei Thu: 'We [pointing to the girls] could tell them?'

Adult: 'How could you tell them?'

Sally: 'We could all tell them together, you [to the adult] could help?'

Adult: 'I could be with you when you tell the boys but you could do the talking. Would you all like to talk at the same time? Would that mean you were telling them together?'

Clara: 'We could sing all at once, that would be together.'

Adult: 'What do you think? Do you want to try?'

Girls in unison: 'Yeah, let's try.'

Adult: 'What would you want to tell them in your song?'

Reflection point: What are the key scaffolding strategies being used in this conversation?

The conversation continues until the children and the adult have a song worked out. They then try out their technique and reflect on what happens. The cycle of learning starts again at this point with the girls having learned to tell the boys how they feel without total reliance on the adult. The aim would be to move them to a point in their relationships with the boys that they felt able to try out different ways of telling them how they felt. This process could be used to build fairer gender relations between the children in many areas of daily life.

DISABILITY AND ADDITIONAL NEEDS

The development of competence and self-regulation of learning is just as important for children with disabilities as it is for children without them. However, McCollom and Blair (1994) caution that scaffolding is likely to be a more complex and difficult process with many children with disabilities. One of the main reasons given for this is that establishing mutuality with some children with disabilities (inter-subjectivity) and assuming that children can be the major initiators in their own learning may be less appropriate in some instances. As they explained:

> For children who may initiate interactions less frequently, such as those with Down's Syndrome or visual impairment, the adult's role may require more aggressive recruitment ... Thus, for the child with a disability, the appropriate balance of support and challenge may look quite different from that which is appropriate to a child who frequently initiates and independently pursues encounters with objects or events in his environment. (McCollom and Blair 1994, pp. 98–9)

However, this does not mean that scaffolding is inappropriate to use with children with disabilities. For instance, research on use by teachers of different forms of scaffolding strategies with seven-year-old children with Down's syndrome shows that the children were more responsive to strategies that involved the use of gestures than they were to those using words (Wang, Bernas and Eberhard 2001).

In promoting positive attitudes to children with disabilities, scaffolding offers an interesting way forward. The adult can act as a strong lead in teaching children without disabilities how best to interact with children with disabilities. The Burns-Hoffman (1993) framework for using verbal scaffolding (see above) to enhance children's factual knowledge of the world could provide a guide to this. In particular, it is important that staff take a lead in scaffolding friendship-building skills with all children in a group to help build an inclusive climate within the group (McCay and Keyes 2001/02).

Reflecting on scaffolding techniques

1 How would you define scaffolding?
2 What is the relationship between scaffolding and Vygotsky's idea of the ZPD?
3 What are the key factors that contribute to good scaffolding by adults concerned with children's learning?
4 What is the relationship between general teaching techniques (such as questioning) and scaffolding?
5 Identify five general teaching techniques you will need to be familiar with in order to practise scaffolding with children.
6 Clements and Nastasi (1993) argued that computers provide an important scaffolding tool for early childhood staff. They can allow children to perform a variety tasks that they are unable to perform by themselves. What do you see as the pros and cons of using computers as a scaffolding tool in early childhood settings? In what ways could computers achieve the requirements for good scaffolding outlined by Berk and Winsler (1995)? What, if any, of these requirements are not met by computers?
7 Read the following conversation between a two-year-old child and her mother. How is the mother scaffolding Melinda's learning? What else might she have said or done to scaffold Melinda's learning on this occasion?

McDonald's is the family's favourite restaurant.

Mother: 'You're going to McDonald's.'

Melinda: 'Yeah!'

Mother: 'Is Andrew the cook?' (Andrew is a four-year-old friend who is playing with Melinda's sister.)

Melinda: 'Yep…My cook.'

Mother: 'You're the cook? You can cook with your dishes, right? Do you have some pots and pans?'
(Extract based on Berk and Winsler 1995, p. 74.)

Improving teaching in practice

1 Identify a child you could practise your scaffolding techniques with. Observe the child and identify a problem that you could work together to solve. Plan at least three occasions in which you work closely on this problem. Implement and record these sessions.
2 After each session evaluate your own scaffolding skills by reviewing the extent to which you were able to:
   * jointly problem-solve with the child
   * achieve inter-subjectivity between yourself and the child
   * establish warmth and responsiveness in your relationship with the child
   * keep the child in her ZPD
   * promote the child's self-regulation of the problem-solving.
3 What additional skills and knowledge do you need to consolidate and improve your scaffolding skills?
4 How and how well did you take account of the following considerations when scaffolding?
   * developmental
   * cultural
   * gender
   * disability and additional needs.

FURTHER READING

Anghileri, J. 2006, 'Scaffolding practices that enhance mathematics learning', *Journal of Mathematics Teacher Education*, 9, pp. 33–52.

Berk, L. and Winsler, A. 1995, *Scaffolding Children's Learning: Vygotsky and Early Childhood Education*, National Association for the Education of Young Children, Washington, DC.

Pea, R. 2004, 'The social and technological dimensions of scaffolding and related theoretical concepts for learning, education, and human activity', *The Journal of the Learning Sciences*, 13(3), pp. 423–451.

ONLINE AND MULTI-MEDIA RESOURCES

Text

Bodrova, E. and Leong. D. 2001, *Tools of the Mind. A Case Study of Implementing the Vygotskian Approach in American Early Childhood and Primary Classrooms*, International Bureau of Education, Geneva, Switzerland. Full text: **http://www.ibe.unesco.org/publications/innodata/inno07.pdf**

Scaffolding website. Links to research and full text articles: **http://condor.admin.ccny.cuny.edu/~group4/**

Verenikina, I. 2003, 'Understanding scaffolding and the ZPD in Educational Research', full text: **http://www.aare.edu.au/03pap/ver03682.pdf**

Multi-media
Play: A Vygotskian Approach, 1996, Davidson Films Inc., 231 E. Street, Davis, California, available in DVD format from: **http://www.davidsonfilms.com**

Scaffolding: Self Directed Learning in the Primary Grades, 1996, Davidson Films, distributed by Educational Media Australia or available from: **http://www.davidsonfilms.com**

Scaffolding website. Short demonstration video on scaffolding in mathematics teaching: **http://condor.admin.ccny.cuny.edu/~group4/**

REFERENCES

Anghileri, J. 2006, 'Scaffolding practices that enhance mathematics learning', *Journal of Mathematics Teacher Education*, 9, pp. 33–52.

Berk, L. 1994a, *Child Development*, 3rd edn, Allyn & Bacon, Boston.

——1994b, 'Vygotsky's theory: the importance of make-believe play', *Young Children*, 50(5), pp. 30–39.

Berk, L. and Spuhl, S. 1995, 'Maternal interaction, private speech and task performance in preschool children', *Early Childhood Research Quarterly*, 10, pp. 145–169.

Berk, L. and Winsler, A. 1995, *Scaffolding Children's Learning: Vygotsky and Early Childhood Education*, National Association for the Education of Young Children, Washington, DC.

Bigelow, A., MacLean, K. and Proctor, J. 2004, 'The role of joint attention in the development of infants' play with objects', *Developmental Science*, 7(5), pp. 518–526.

Bowman, B., Donovan, M. and Burns, S. 2001, *Eager to Learn: Educating Our Preschoolers*, National Academy Press, Washington, DC.

Boyd Ingram, H. 2000, 'Literacy contexts in family day care', *Australian Journal of Early Childhood*, 25(3), pp. 19–24.

Burman, E. 2008, *Deconstructing Developmental Psychology*, 2nd edn, Routledge, East Sussex and New York.

Burns-Hoffman, R. 1993, 'Scaffolding children's informal expository discourse skills', Paper presented at the *Biennial Meeting of the Society for Research in Child Development*, New Orleans, LA, ED362292.

Clements, D. and Nastasi, B. 1993, 'Electronic media and early childhood education', in B. Spodek, ed., *Handbook of Research on Early Childhood Education* (pp. 251–75), Macmillan Publishing Company, New York.

DeWitt, S. 2003, 'Multicultural democracy and inquiry pedagogy', *Intercultural Education*, 14(3), pp. 279–290.

Doolittle, P. 1995, 'Understanding cooperative learning through Vygotsky's Zone of Proximal Development', Paper presented to the *Lilly National Conference on Excellence in College Teaching*, Columbia, SC,, ED36055.

Fair, C., Vandermaas-Peeler, M., Beaudry, R. and Dew, J. 2005, '"I learned how little kids think": third-graders' scaffolding of craft activities with preschoolers', *Early Childhood Development and Care*, 175(3), pp. 229–241.

Ferguson-Patrick, K. 2007, 'Writers develop skills through collaboration: an action research approach', *Educational Action Research*, 15(2), pp. 159–180.

Fildalgo, Z. and Pereira, F. 2005, 'Socio-cultural differences and the adjustment of mothers' speech to their children's cognitive and language comprehension skills', *Learning and Instruction*, 15(1), pp. 1–21.

Fimreite, H., Flem, A. and Gudmundsdottir, S. 1999, 'Peer interactions among preschool children in play', Paper presented at the *8th European Conference for Research on Learning and Instruction*, 24–28 August, Goteborg, Sweden.

Fleer, M. 1996, 'Talking technologically in preschool and school: three case examples', *Australian Journal of Early Childhood*, 21(2), pp. 1–6.

Gauvain, M. 2006, 'Scaffolding in socialization', *New Ideas in Psychology*, 23(3), pp. 129–139.

Granott, N. 2006, 'Scaffolding dynamically toward change: previous and new perspectives', *New Ideas in Psychology*, 23(3), pp. 140–151.

Hass Dyson, A. and Genishi, C. 1993, 'Visions of children as language users: language and language education in early childhood', in B. Spodek, ed., *Handbook of Research on the Education of Young Children* (pp. 122–36), Macmillan Publishing Company, New York.

Jones, E. and Reynolds, G. 1992, *The Play's the Thing: Teachers' Roles in Children's Play*, Teachers College Press, New York.

Kermani, H. and Brenner, M. 2000, 'Maternal scaffolding in the child's Zone of Proximal Development across tasks: cross-cultural perspectives', *Journal of Research in Childhood Education*, 15(1), pp. 30–52.

Kowalski, H., Wyver, S., Masselos, G. and de Lacey, P. 2005, 'The long-day childcare context: implications for toddlers' pretend play', *Early Years: Journal of International Research and Development*, 25(1), pp. 55–65.

Madsen, J. and Gudmundsdottir, S. 2000, 'Scaffolding children's learning in the Zone of Proximal Development: a classroom study', Paper presented at the *Annual Meeting of the European Conference on Educational Research*, 19–21 September, Norway.

Marsh, J. 2006, 'Emergent media literacy: digital animation in early childhood', *Language and Education*, 20(6), pp. 493–506.

McCay, L. and Keyes, D. 2001/02, 'Developing social competence in the inclusive primary classroom', *Childhood Education*, 78(2), pp. 70–78.

McCollum, J. and Blair, H. 1994, 'Research in parent–child interaction: guidance to developmentally appropriate practice for young children with disabilities', in B. Mallory and R. New, eds, *Diversity and Developmentally Appropriate Practices: Challenges for Early Childhood Education* (pp. 84–106), Teachers College Press, New York.

Meadows, S. and Cashdan, A. 1988, *Helping Children Learn: Contributions to a Cognitive Curriculum*, David Fulton Publishers, London.

Miller, P. 2006, 'Commentary on scaffolding: constructing and deconstructing development', *New Ideas in Psychology*, 23(3), pp. 207–211.

Moyles, J. 1989, *Just Playing: The Role and Status of Play in Early Childhood Education*, Open University Press, Milton Keynes.

O'Neill, K., Bard, M., Linnell, M. and Fluck, M. 2005, 'Maternal gestures with 20 month-old infants in two contexts', *Developmental Science*, 8(4), pp. 352–359.

Pellegrini, A. and Boyd, B. 1993, 'The role of play in early childhood development and education: issues in definition and function', in B. Spodek, ed., *Handbook of Research on the Education of Young Children* (pp. 105–121), Macmillan Publishing Company, New York.

Smith, A. 1996, 'Quality programs that care and educate', *Childhood Education*, 72(6), pp. 330–335.

Sternberg, R. 2007, 'Who are the bright children? The cultural context of being and acting intelligent', *Educational Researcher*, 36(3), pp. 148–155.

Thompson, R. B., Arsenault, S. and Williams, D. 2006, 'The effects of preschool girls' and boys' help-seeking on adult evaluations of dyadic problem-solving', *Journal of Language and Social Psychology*, 25, pp. 146–166.

Turner, V. and Berkowitz, M. 2006, 'Scaffolding morality: positioning a socio-cultural construct', *New Ideas in Psychology*, 23(3), pp. 174–184.

Vandermaas-Peeler, M., Way, E. and Umpleby, J. 2002, 'Guided participation in a cooking activity over time', *Early Childhood Development and Care*, 172(6), pp. 547–554.

Verenikina, I. 2003, 'Understanding scaffolding and the ZPD in Educational Research', <http://www.aare.edu.au/03pap/ver03682.pdf>

Vygotsky, L. 1932, *Thought and Language*, MIT Press, Massachusetts.

Wang, X., Bernas, R. and Eberhard, P. 2001, 'Effects of teachers' verbal and non-verbal scaffolding on everyday classroom performances of students with Down's Syndrome', *International Journal of Early Years Education*, 9(1) pp. 71–80.

Wilkes, G. (ed.) 1979, *Collins Dictionary of the English Language*, Penguin Books, Middlesex.

Chapter 30

Task analysis

Task analysis: to analyse: to break down into component features.
(Collins Dictionary of the English Language, p. 50)

If teachers are to plan for each child on the basis of his or her needs they must…understand task analysis, how to break a task down into its component parts and present the steps in an orderly sequence.

(Allen 1982, p. 3)

Task analysis. A procedure through which learning tasks are broken down into smaller steps for children with learning disabilities.

(Charlesworth 2003, p. 85)

What?

A task is a piece of work that needs to be carried out to achieve something. A task may refer to a small job such as picking up a piece of paper or a large job such as building a house. Analysis is the detailed study of the key elements or processes in something or someone. Task analysis is the detailed study of the key elements or processes involved in a particular piece of work that needs to be done. As a teaching technique, task analysis is used to help children understand the key steps involved in a particular task they are about to tackle—for example, to help them understand the key steps involved in tying shoelaces. Task analysis may be used to help children learn skills and knowledge. It allows children to have early success in learning certain things.

Issues and debates

DISCOVERY LEARNING VERSUS GUIDED INSTRUCTION

Task analysis is an adult-directed and structured approach to learning a specific task that positions the adult as expert and the child as novice. As such, it generates debates about its place in early childhood teaching and learning. Its opponents believe that children learn best through discovery and that meaningful learning occurs through children being able to construct their own meanings and make their own discoveries.

Its proponents argue that direct guidance of children's skill-based learning is efficient and effective:

> Although unguided or minimally guided instructional approaches are very popular and intuitively appealing, the point is made that these approaches ignore both the structures that constitute human cognitive architecture and evidence from empirical studies over the past half-century that consistently indicate that minimally guided instruction is less effective and less efficient than instructional approaches that place a strong emphasis on guidance of the student learning process. (Kirschner, Sweller and Clark 2006, p. 75)

Task analysis can also act as a diagnostic strategy for teachers. When they understand the specific steps involved in learning a new skill or new knowledge they can more readily identify when a child is struggling with a skill or new knowledge and why (Li and Klahr 2006).

There has been recent debate in the USA about the role of forms of direction instruction, using techniques such as task analysis, in children learning science. In exploring this debate and the research evidence for specific pedagogies within science education Li and Klahr (2006) argued:

> We disagree with the perception that instructional approaches such as hands-on science, discovery learning, and direct instruction are mutually exclusive rather than intersecting and complementary. (p. 18)

How?

There are two main dimensions to task analysis. The first dimension involves analysing the child's abilities in relation to a given task. Staff need to ask: 'What can the child do currently?'; 'What does the child need to learn to successfully complete the task?' The second dimension involves analysing the task itself. Staff need to ask: 'What are the steps involved in this task and how are they sequenced?' The following points summarise the key steps involved in task analysis and suggest a sequence in looking at these steps:

- Identify the task that you wish a child to learn.
- Identify the sub steps involved in the task.
- Sequence the key steps in a logical way.
  An example:

> Snack time.
> *Key steps*:
> Child to get plate and mug from trolley.
> Take plate and mug to table.
> Sit at table.
> Pour drink.
> Select fruit or other snack and put on plate.
> Eat and drink.
> Take empty plate and mug to trolley.

- Sequence the key steps developmentally to minimise the difficulty of successfully learning and completing the task.
- Check what the child can currently do and not do in relation to the task.
- Present the steps to the child through direct instruction.
- Teach the child one step at a time until the task is successfully mastered.
- Offer extra guidance if the child has difficulty with the task. This guidance could involve child or adult modelling and verbal guidance.
- Restructure the task, if necessary, to assist with successful completion. (Based on Lerner et al. 1987; Cole and Chan 1990; Petriwskyj 1992; Jerome, Frantino and Sturmey 2007.)

Some of the more lengthy and complex tasks that a child may need to or may wish to learn can be taught through backward chaining (Lerner et al. 1987; Jerome, Frantino and Sturmey 2007). In backward chaining, staff complete each of the steps involved for the child until the last step in the task is reached. The child completes the last step. When the child has learned the last step the child can then be taught the second-last step. The teaching of the steps continues 'backwards' until the skill or knowledge has been learned. To work successfully, backward chaining should be accompanied by direct positive reinforcement as each step in the chain is learned.

An example:

Tying a shoelace. *Steps:* Hold one lace in each hand. Cross one lace over the other. Tie a granny knot. Form a bow with each lace. Knot bows. Pull tight.

In backward chaining, the child would be taught each of the steps separately and then taught to put the steps together backwards. The teacher would perform all of the steps for the child except the last one (pull tight). The child would then be encouraged to carry out the last, the second-last step and so forth until all of the steps have been achieved.

An example: (from Jerome, Frantino, and Sturmey 2007).

Accessing a website *Steps:* Press the computer power button. Press the monitor power button. Place hand on the mouse. Move the cursor with the mouse until it points to the Internet Explorer® icon. Double click the Internet Explorer® icon. Move the cursor with the mouse to the Google® search box. Left click in the box. Type in the search topic of interest. Place hand back on mouse. Move cursor to the box labelled 'search'. Single click the box. Move the cursor with the mouse down to the website of choice. Single click the website of choice.

THEORETICAL BACKGROUND

TASK ANALYSIS AND GAGNE'S CLASSES OF BEHAVIOUR

Robert Mills Gagne (1916–2002) graduated with a major in psychology from Yale University in 1937. From that time he held various research and academic posts as a psychologist, including eight years with the US Air Force, a professorship in psychology at Princeton University and a professorship in education psychology at the University of California.

Gagne's best-known book, *The Conditions of Learning* (1985), has been translated into most major languages. In this book, Gagne outlined a detailed range of behaviours that can be observed as people learn. These behaviours can be used to help analyse the different levels of learning that children may engage in. The behaviours described by Gagne are as follows:

1 Signal learning—refers to the learning that occurs when a person produces a particular behaviour when a particular signal is produced.
2 Stimulus response learning—refers to the learning that occurs when a person learns to reproduce a clear and specific physical response to a specific stimulus.
3 Chaining—refers to the learning that occurs when a person links two or more steps that have been learned via stimulus response learning to perform a more complex task.
4 Verbal association—refers to the learning that occurs when a person can associate several words with the one object and can link them in a phrase or a sentence.
5 Multiple discrimination—refers to the learning that occurs when a person is able to accurately distinguish what makes a specific object different from others that are similar to it. For example, what makes one car a station wagon and another a four-wheel drive? The person can discriminate between the multiple characteristics of a car (it has tyres, four wheels, etc.) and isolate those that discriminate one type of car from another.
6 Concept learning—refers to the learning that occurs when a person uses abstract properties of objects (for example, shape, size or position) to distinguish between things, people and events.
7 Principle learning—refers to when a person learns how to use several concepts to develop principles about how things work.
8 Problem-solving—refers to the learning that occurs when a person uses principles to achieve a particular goal. It always involves internal thinking processes. (based on De Cecco 1968)

Gagne's work in *The Conditions of Learning* emphasised the hierarchical nature of learning. He stressed that more complex learning behaviours such as problem-solving built from simple learning behaviours such as chaining. Gagne's particular understanding of how learning behaviours were organised hierarchically underpins the sequencing of learning in task analysis. His theory details nine instructional events and corresponding cognitive processes that can be used to teach a task or concept:

1 Gain the learner's attention (reception).
2 Inform learners of the objective of the experience (expectancy).
3 Stimulate recall of prior learning (retrieval).
4 Present the stimulus for the learning (selective perception).
5 Provide learning guidance by showing how to complete the task or experience (semantic encoding).
6 Elicit performance by asking the learner to undertake specific tasks (responding).
7 Provide feedback on the extent to which the learner has performed the task or understood it correctly (reinforcement).
8 Assess the learner's performance and give them feedback on their level of performance (retrieval).
9 Enhance retention and transfer by introducing material and experiences that support and reinforce the learning (generalisation). (Gagne et al. 1992)

More recently, there has been a growing interest in using Ecological Task Analysis in working with young children with disabilities. This approach to task analysis assumes that:

- variation in how a child performs a task is essential, rather than a problem
- the relationships between parts of a task are as important to learn as the specific discrete elements of a task
- the views and experiences of the child learning the task should form part of the evaluation of its success (Van Emmerick 2007).

When and why?

GOAL RELEVANCE

Task analysis can be usefully employed by staff to assist children's learning across all developmental domains. Recent research on the value of task analysis has primarily been focused on children with disabilities (e.g. Lovaas 2003; Wilson 2005; McElrath and Axelrod 2006), including babies (Chen, Klein and Haney 2007).

Teachers have used task analysis to support the development of specific skills in a wide range of domains for children, including:

- building children's skill in entering play with peers
- building children's self-care skills such as dressing, putting on shoes, etc.
- developing children's skills in using equipment such as scissors and staplers
- improving children's physical skills such as climbing and balancing
- improving children's language learning skills (Wenden 1998; De Jong 2006).

DEVELOPMENTAL CONSIDERATIONS

Children's ability to successfully learn complex tasks is related to their developmental skills and abilities. It is, therefore, important to ensure that the skills children are being encouraged to learn are appropriate to their developmental abilities and skills. Observing the children closely will provide information about the developmental abilities they have currently and what new skills they may be interested in acquiring. Remember, the key questions are: 'What can the child do now?'; 'What do I want them to do?'; 'What are the steps involved in getting her to the desired point?' Often task analysis can be used with younger children to build simple motor skills and capacities (Douville-Watson, Watson and Wilson 2002). Consider the following examples:

Paula is 14 months old. She is keen to do everything by herself. Tiziana, her caregiver, wants to help Paula achieve maximum independence at this stage of life. Tiziana task analyses 'eating with a spoon' and teaches this to Paula with backwards chaining—in that way Paula has success every time she feeds herself. Very soon she is able to eat with a spoon by herself. Both Paula and Tiziana are pleased with the results.

Patrick is learning to crawl, he has just begun to push himself on to his knees and he rocks back and forth, then collapses again. His caregiver watches his struggle and through task analysis of creeping, she is able to assist him to propel himself forwards, moving each leg in turn.

Sophie is sewing around a shape that she has cut out of material. She wants to add sequins to her creation. She finds it difficult to hold the sequin in one hand and to fasten it with the thread to the material. Her teacher analyses what Sophie is doing and helps her to hold the sequin in one hand as she manoeuvres the thread in the other.

Reflection point: What steps is the teacher using in each example? To what extent does she follow the advice of Douville-Watson, Watson and Wilson (2002) in each case?

Task analysis can also be useful with children in the early years of schooling as they learn new games and new skills. It can be especially helpful in teaching children new games (Schwartz 2005). Staff may find it helpful to teach them the basic steps involved in a new game or in an activity in which they will be developing new skills. Bohning and Williams (1996/97) discuss how such instruction in the steps involved in quilting and using tangrams helped the children feel confident in using the materials. They were, with task analysis, able to quickly move to a point where they could use and create very complex mathematical shapes.

Equity considerations

'RACE' AND CULTURE

Learning about similarities and differences between people's cultures and learning to recognise stereotypes is a complex task. Task analysis can be used by staff to help sequence this learning into small, logical steps for the children. For example, teaching children about stereotypical images of different cultural and 'racial' groups involves them learning that:

- pictures can make people feel happy or sad
- pictures can be fair or unfair
- pictures can give us true or false images of people
- pictures that show unfair and false images of people can make them feel sad. These pictures are called stereotyped pictures.

York (1991) provides many ideas for how to introduce these ideas to children using pictures from magazines. The process can begin with children being asked to find pictures that make them feel happy or sad and pictures that might make other people feel happy or sad. From this base, children begin to learn that images carry important messages and can influence how we feel. Once this concept has been understood, staff can move to the next step of talking about pictures that are fair or unfair. In this process it will be important for staff to talk about why they think particular pictures are unfair and encourage children to do the same. For example, staff may say that a picture of an Asian person that shows him looking silly is unfair and talk about why before moving on from this point to other groups. By breaking down the process of learning about 'racial' and cultural stereotypes into discrete steps, teachers with practical activities can help children learn abstract and complex concepts.

GENDER

There are gender differences in the ease with which girls and boys learn particular physical, social and linguistic skills. For example, preschool girls sometimes take longer than preschool boys to learn to throw and catch balls, and the reverse is the case with sewing skills. There is strong evidence to suggest that these skill differences are due to different expectations of boys and girls rather than a genetic difference between the two sexes. Task analysis can be used to help children gain competence and confidence in skill areas that they might otherwise miss out on. For example, if staff want girls who lack ball-handling skills to gain these skills and boys who lack sewing skills to gain these skills, then breaking skills into smaller components and working on these in a logical, sequential way can assist.

Task analysis can also be used to challenge preschool children's gender stereotypes about what men and women, boys and girls can do. If children in the group believe only men can change tyres, be doctors, etc. staff can analyse with the children the tasks involved in these jobs. Changing tyres might involve getting the spare tyre and the jack from the car boot, undoing the tyre bolts, jacking up the car, etc. Children can think about what skills are needed and if a woman can do it. The children may think a woman is not strong enough to lift the tyre from the car boot. This can be countered with the idea that women lift groceries out of the car boot and whether a tyre would be any heavier. Such detailed analysis of tasks that children believe can only be done by one gender is a good way to help them rethink their ideas.

DISABILITY AND ADDITIONAL NEEDS

Task analysis has been widely used to help teach children with a variety of additional needs new skills. It is, therefore, an important teaching technique to help build the self-esteem of children with additional needs in the group through increasing their sense of competence and confidence. However, as much of this work is highly specific, we will not focus on how to do this in this section. Books and articles in the further reading list provide specialist information on skill-building with children with a variety of additional needs (for example, Whinnery and Whinnery 2007).

Task analysis can be a positive support for teaching children in the group without specific disabilities how to assist and support those with them. Staff can observe what the children currently know about the specific needs of the child(ren) with a disability, think about what else they need to know and then sequence this into manageable steps. For example, if a child in the group (we will call him Saul) has a communication disorder because his speech is impaired by a very husky voice, then Saul will need particular support and assistance from the other children to ensure that his needs and thoughts are understood. Children will need to learn to listen carefully when Saul speaks, to be particularly quiet when Saul is speaking, to have games with Saul that don't always involve talking and to let Saul have rests from speaking. Breaking each of these skills into smaller sub-skills and carefully planning experiences through which the children can learn them will help provide a strong supportive environment for Saul.

Reflecting on task analysis techniques

1   What does research suggest are the keys to successfully using task analysis to optimise children's learning?
2   How would you define backward chaining?
3   When do you think task analysis should be used in your teaching?
4   Are there any times when you think that task analysis is inappropriate with young children?
5   Imagine you wanted to teach a toddler to pour her own drink at snack time. What are the sub-skills involved in this task? Would it be appropriate to teach a toddler these sub-skills? Why? Why not? Would backward chaining assist in teaching the toddler this task? How would this work?
6   Develop a plan for a learning experience for four- to five-year-old children in which you wanted to increase their balancing skills. How could you use task analysis as a teaching technique to do this?
7   Imagine you were working with a four-year-old child who was having difficulty completing a puzzle. How might task analysis help you help the child to learn skills for completing this and other puzzles? What sub-skills for completing puzzles could help you answer this question?
8   What do you see as the hardest part of improving your task analysis techniques?

Improving teaching in practice

1   Record (using a tape-recorder or written notes) a task analysis session with children during several half-hour teaching periods.
2   What is your current style of task analysis? Did you:
    - decide on a specific task you wanted the children to learn?
    - make a written or mental list of the sub-tasks involved?
    - plan a logical sequence to introduce the sub-tasks to the children?
    - take account of the children's current ability and developmental levels in planning the sub-task sequence?
    - demonstrate the sub-tasks to the children one step at a time until each was mastered?

- support the children's attempts at task mastery through using appropriate reinforcement and restructuring of the task when necessary?
3   How and how well did you take account of developmental and anti-bias considerations?
4   What are your areas of strength and weakness in using task analysis to promote children's learning?
5   How can you improve your task analysis techniques in practice?

FURTHER READING

Dick, W., Carey, L. and Carey, J.O. 2005, 'The systematic design of instruction', 6th edn, Allyn & Bacon, Boston [refer to Chapter 3].

Gagne, R., Briggs, L. and Wager, W. 1992, *Principles of Instructional Design,* 4th edn, HBJ College Publishers, Fort Worth, TX.

Gargiulo, R. 2006, *Special Education in Contemporary Society: An Introduction to Exceptionality*, Thompson Wadworth, Belmont, California [refer to pp. 180–181].

Morrison, G.R., Ross, S.M. and Kemp, J.E. 2006, *Designing effective instruction*, 5th edn, John Wiley & Sons, Hoboken, NJ [refer to Chapter 4: Task analysis].

Whinnery, K and Whinnery, S. 2007, 'MOVE: systematic programming for early motor intervention', *Infants & Young Children*, 20(2), pp. 102–108.

ONLINE AND MULTI-MEDIA RESOURCES

Text

The following websites provide further information about Gagne and his work: **http://www.psy.pdx.edu/PsiCafe/KeyTheorists/Gagne.htm http://www.ittheory.com/gagne1.htm**

Multi-media

'Text Comprehension: Students Take Charge'. In this video clip a teacher helps children to analyse and enact the task of leading a book reading discussion. Free access podcast or video streaming available from: **http://www.readingrockets.org/podcasts/classroom#sounds**

Two examples of task analysis (tying shoes (long and short versions) and toilet training of a child with autism) can be found on the following website: **http://maxweber.hunter.cuny.edu/pub/eres/EDSPC715_MCINTYRE/TaskAnalysis.html**

Practising task analysis: Rieber, L. 2006, 'In Search of Lost Wisdom: An Online Game Teaching Task Analysis' (PDF download): **http://it.coe.uga.edu/~lrieber/aect2006/ISO_Lost_Wisdom_description.pdf** and related activity website: **http://www.nowhereroad.com/instructionaldesign/asp/activity/index.asp?ID_activity_admin=2**

REFERENCES

Allen, K. 1982, 'The preschool program: adaptation to the individual child', *Eric Digest,* ED015407.

Bohning, G. and Williams, R. 1996/97, 'Quilts and tangrams: linking literature and geometry', *Childhood Education*, 73(2), pp. 83–87.

Charlesworth, R. 2003, *Understanding Child Development*. Thompson Delmar Learning, New York.

Chen, D., Klein, D. and Haney, M. 2007, 'Promoting interactions with infants who have complex multiple disabilities: development and field-testing of the PLAI curriculum', *Infants & Young Children*, 20(2), pp. 149–162.

Cole, P. and Chan, L. 1990, *Methods and Strategies for Special Education*, Prentice Hall Inc., New Jersey.

De Cecco, J. 1968, *The Psychology of Learning and Instruction: Educational Psychology*, Prentice Hall Inc., New Jersey.

De Jong, P. 2006, 'Understanding normal and impaired reading development: a working memory perspective', in S. Pickering, ed., *Working Memory and Education*, Academic Press, Oxford, pp. 34–61.

Douville-Watson, L., Watson, M. and Cam Wilson, L. 2002, *Infants & Toddlers: Curriculum and Teaching*, 5th edn, Thompson Delmar Learning, New York.

Gagne, R. 1985, *The Conditions of Learning*, 4th edn, Holt, Rinehart and Winston, New York.

Gagne, R., Briggs, L. and Wager, W. 1992, *Principles of Instructional Design*, 4th edn, HBJ College Publishers, Fort Worth, TX.

Jerome, J., Frantino, E., and Sturmey, P. 2007, 'The effects of errorless learning and backward chaining on the acquisition of internet skills in adults with developmental disabilities', *Applied Behavior Analysis*, 40(1), pp. 185–189.

Kirschner, P. Sweller, J. and Clark, R. 2006, 'Why minimal guidance during instruction does not work: an analysis of the failure of constructivist, discovery, problem-based, experiential, and inquiry-based teaching', *Educational Psychologist*, 41(2), pp. 75–86.

Lerner, J., Mardell-Czudnowski, C. and Goldenberg, D. 1987, *Special Education for the Early Childhood Years*, 2nd edn, Prentice Hall Inc., New Jersey, pp. 140–142.

Li, J. and Klahr, D. 2006, 'The psychology of scientific thinking: implications for science teaching and learning', in J. Rhoton and P. Shane, eds, *Teaching Science in the 21st Century*, National Science Teachers Association and National Science Education Leadership Association, NSTA Press, Arlington, VA.

Lovaas, O.I. 2003, *Teaching Individuals with Developmental Delays: Basic Intervention Techniques*, Pro-Ed, Inc., Austin, TX.

McElrath, K. and Axelrod, S. 2006, 'Behavioral intervention for autism: a distinction between two behavior analytic approaches', *The Behaviour Analyst Today*, 7(2), pp. 242–252.

Petriwskyj, A. 1992, 'Integrating children with special needs into early childhood centres', *Australian Early Childhood Resource Booklets*, AECA, Canberra, pp. 1–16.

Schwartz, S. 2005, *Teaching Young Children Mathematics*, Greenwood Publishing Inc., Sydney.

Van Emmerick, R. 2007, 'Functional role of variability in movement coordination and disability', in W. Davis and G. Broadhead, eds, 'Ecological Task Analysis and Movement, Human Kinetics', *Human Movement Science*, 15(2), pp. 25–52.

Wenden, A. 1998, 'Metacognitive learning and language learning', *Applied Linguistics*, 19(4), pp. 515–537.

Whinnery, K. and Whinnery, S. 2007, 'MOVE: systematic programming for early motor intervention', *Infants & Young Children*, 20(2), pp. 102–108.

Wilkes, G. (ed.) 1979, *Collins Dictionary of the English Language*, Penguin Books, Middlesex.

Wilson, P. 2005, 'Practitioner review: approaches to assessment and treatment of children with DCD: an evaluative review', *Journal of Child Psychology and Psychiatry*, 46 (8), pp. 806–823.

York, S. 1991, *Roots and Wings: Affirming Culture in Early Childhood Programs*, Toys N Things Press, Minnesota.

PART FOUR
Educational Philosophies, Goals and Teaching Techniques

Chapter 31

Building a strategic approach to teaching techniques

> *Strategic:* of, relating to, or characteristic of strategy.
> (*Collins Dictionary of the English Language*, p. 1437)

> *Strategy is the determination of basic long-term goals and objectives together with the adoption of courses of action and the allocation of resources for carrying out those goals.*
> (Pugh et al. 1983, p. 50)

> *. . . strategy is concerned with those decisions which determine the direction which an enterprise is taking. The formulation of strategy is thus a primary determinant of the character of an organization.*
> (Minkes 1987, p. 132)

Strategies and strategic decisions

A strategy is a broad plan of action for achieving a goal. Strategic decisions are those in which people decide the general approach they will need to take to gain something they want. In other words, strategic decisions determine how a person will achieve their organisational goals.

Strategic decisions provide organisations with purpose and direction because they require the people within them to be clear about what they want to achieve (their goals) and how they might successfully achieve what they want (their general approach). To take a strategic approach to decision-making, people in organisations need to have several things in place. They need:

- a clear vision of what they want to do. Organisations often have different names for their vision. Some organisations talk of their mission statement, others their philosophy and others their organisational goals, objectives or purposes
- a general approach (or strategy) for putting their vision into practice. This involves deciding what is permissible or not (policies), and how people and resources will be organised to achieve the goals (resource management)
- a match between their vision and their general approach to making it a reality.

Therefore, when people in an organisation are being strategic they are being deliberate about what they want to do and how they will get there. They are being purposeful in making plans to ensure that their vision becomes a reality.

Not all organisations are strategic. Some organisations do not have a clear sense of what they want to do and how they will do it. Some organisations have a clear vision of their work but do not have a set of tactics they can use to make their vision a reality. These organisations tend to take decisions in an ad hoc rather than a strategic way. Ad hoc decision-making makes it harder to turn an organisational vision into a reality.

Strategies and strategic teaching

Applied to teaching and learning, strategic decisions are those in which staff decide the general approach they will use to help children learn. They then draw on this general approach to choose the specific teaching techniques that best reflect their educational vision.

Strategic teaching decisions in an early childhood setting give staff purpose and direction because they require staff to be clear about what they want to achieve with children (their educational vision) and how they might successfully achieve what they want (their educational approach or strategy). To take a strategic approach to teaching, staff need to have several things in place. They need:

- a clear educational vision
- a general approach (or strategy) for making their vision a reality
- a match between their vision, their general approach (or strategy) and their specific teaching techniques.

We shall now consider the first two points (the following section considers the third point in some detail).

A CLEAR EDUCATIONAL VISION

EDUCATIONAL VISION
A statement about your broad, long-term educational goals for the children. Goals are based on your vision of the child as a learner and your vision of what it is valuable for children to learn.

A coherent educational vision embraces a vision of who the child is, how the child learns, what the child should learn and what the adult's role in children's learning should be. This vision is described in various ways, including a mission statement, an educational philosophy or educational goals, objectives or purposes. Staff generally name their vision according to their personal preference and/or their centre's preference.

Staff's vision of the child as learner, their role in the child's learning and their beliefs about what the child should be learning will be influenced by their personal and professional knowledge base and their value systems. Staff's knowledge and values will influence how they view:

- the role of the child's developmental achievements and challenges in learning
- the role of the individual child's cultural, personal and political characteristics in learning
- what is educationally, culturally, socially, morally, politically and ethically appropriate for young children to learn.

Developing an educational vision involves grappling with these issues in order to decide:

- what is to be learned by the child
- when it is to be learned
- how it is to be learned (Katz 1995).

In addition, staff need to have some sense of how they will know when a child has learned what they believe she can and should learn. They therefore need to also ask: 'How will I know when the child has learned what is to be learned?'

Answering this question will result in clear goals about how staff can and should support the child as a learner.

A GENERAL APPROACH (OR STRATEGY)

A GENERAL APPROACH TO TEACHING

A general or strategic approach to teaching is a broad description of how your vision will be made to happen, which can guide your choices about:

- how you organise the learning environment
- which specific range of teaching techniques you use to support children's learning
- how you will evaluate children's learning.

Making an educational vision a reality involves developing a general approach to teaching to ensure that:

- children learn what staff believe needs to learned
- children learn what is to be learned when it is appropriate to be learned
- children learn what is to be learned in the ways staff believe are appropriate
- staff can assess what has been learned and how they have assisted or not in that learning.

Staff can use the following questions to determine an overall approach to teaching that reflects their educational vision.

DEVELOPING A GENERAL APPROACH TO TEACHING

What should children learn?

Who should determine the learning goals?

Central government, local community, local centre, individual staff, parents, children.

Which educational theory reflects your vision?

Content driven—traditional versus non-traditional knowledge.

Process driven—dispositions, values, skills, attitude.

Which educational values reflect your vision?

Transforming values—education for equity and social justice.

Reforming values—education for individual growth.

Conforming values—education for the status quo.

When should children learn?

Who should determine how children learn?

Central government, local community, local centre, parents, individual staff, parents, children.

Which educational theory reflects your vision?

Age driven—all children learn the same at a given age.

Developmentally driven—individual differences: what is learned when.

How do children learn?

Which learning theory reflects your vision?

Maturationist, behaviourist, interactionist, psychodynamic, constructivist.

Which general teaching strategy bests suits your vision?

Child-directed via free play and self-discovery.

Adult-directed via formal learning experiences and adult instruction.

Which general teaching environment best suits your vision?

Open-ended or closed-ended materials.

Highly structured or flexible use of time, people, materials and space.

How can children's learning be evaluated?

Who should evaluate children's learning?

Central government, local community, parents, local centre, individual staff, children.

Which general evaluation strategy bests suits your vision?

Highly structured observation or flexible individualised observation.

Highly structured standardised testing or flexible individualised assessment.

Answering these questions will enable staff to develop an overall approach to teaching young children that reflects their educational vision. This overall approach to teaching young children can then be used by staff to choose the specific teaching techniques that are in theoretical and practical harmony with their vision.

To illustrate: an early childhood practitioner who has a vision of the child as an active learner may decide that constructivist learning theory best suits their educational vision. Drawing on constructivist theory the practitioner would want to develop an overall approach to teaching young children in which there was a balance between adult-directed and child-directed learning. The teaching techniques that would be most in harmony with their theory of learning and general approach to teaching would need to allow for this balance between adult- and child-directed learning. The specialist teaching techniques of scaffolding and co-constructing and the general strategies of open-ended questioning, demonstration and suggestion could provide this balance. To use these techniques, the practitioner would need to develop a schedule and an approach to positioning people that allowed lots of opportunities for staff–child interaction. There would also need to be an environment that allowed the child to actively explore and hence construct their own knowledge. This would require the practitioner to emphasise open-ended materials and to develop scheduling which allowed for long periods of time for child exploration and for in-depth staff–child interactions. As the practitioner believes that children are active in constructing their own meanings, the general approach he takes to evaluation will need to be strongly individualised and flexible. Teaching techniques that would allow him to evaluate a child's learning in a flexible way include documenting, listening and open-ended questioning.

A match between an educational vision and a general approach to teaching and learning increases the possibility that a vision may become a reality. The next part of the chapter shows how this match can work in theory and in practice. We will look at the theoretical match between the educational visions and teaching techniques underpinning five well-known approaches in early childhood education and care:

- the High/Scope Preschool Curriculum
- Montessori education
- the Reggio Emilia Approach
- Rudolf Steiner and Waldorf schooling
- the Anti-Bias Curriculum.

Matching educational visions and teaching techniques

THE HIGH/SCOPE PRESCHOOL CURRICULUM

. . . High/Scope curriculum . . . is an approach to education and not a specific curriculum. Thus, it is a method that helps organise the day, frames teacher–child relationships and interaction, encourages use of child development principles . . . (Morrison 1995, p. 149)

The High/Scope Preschool Curriculum (formerly known as the High/Scope Cognitively Orientated Curriculum) was first developed in 1962 by the staff at the High/Scope Educational Research Foundation based in Michigan, USA. The curriculum model is widely used within the United States and it has been the most widely used curriculum model to emerge from the Head Start program in the USA (Bowman et al. 2001). There is also growing international interest in the High/Scope Curriculum model with High/Scope programs being formally developed in 15 other countries. These include the UK, the Netherlands, Singapore, Finland and Mexico (Weikart 1995/96).

Overview of educational vision

The High/Scope Curriculum is strongly based on Piagetian theories of development and learning. The Piagetian base to the Curriculum is evident in three major ways. First, the Curriculum goals focus on the development of children's cognitive skills. Second, the cognitive skills that are prioritised (language, experiencing and representing, classification, seriation, number, spatial relations and time) directly reflect Piaget's understandings of cognition. Specifically the Curriculum is designed to:

> . . . allow children to develop meaningful representational abilities and to see relationships between objects and events. (Spodek and Saracho 1994, p. 106)

These cognitive skills are nurtured through key learning experiences in which children learn to be active learners; to use language; to represent experiences and ideas; to classify objects; and to use number, space and time concepts. These skills help children become problem-solvers and independent thinkers (Schweinhart and Hohmann 1992; Henniger 1999; Samuelsson, Sheridan and Williams 2006).

Third, the teaching techniques encouraged in High/Scope are based on Piaget's assumption that children are active learners who need direct personal interaction with the world to learn from it and that children need to reflect on this experience and to use their reflections to increase their understanding of the world about them. Hence, the philosophy of learning that underpins High/Scope is that children learn best when they have time to experience and explore their world for themselves and time to reflect on what they have learned from this. As such, children's learning can best be supported by allowing them to plan and implement and reflect on their concrete experiences of the world about them (Weikart and Schweinhart 1987; Ryan, 2004; Samuelsson, Sheridan and Williams 2006).

Teaching techniques

In the High/Scope Curriculum, staff support children's active learning in several ways:

- Positioning equipment and materials: staff select and arrange materials and experiences to encourage children's active exploration and reflection.
- Scheduling: staff develop a daily schedule based on what is known as the 'Plan–Do–Review' cycle of learning. The schedule generally includes a planning time for children to decide who and what they will work with; a work time in which these plans can be implemented and represented in some way (for example, via a model, photograph, collage or story); a time to pack away; and a time to recall and reflect on the plans, experiences and representations of the day. This recall and reflection may occur in small and/or large group times. The aim is to create a schedule that allows children to initiate, plan, carry out, reflect on and discuss their experiences and ideas.
- Verbal interaction: Staff develop content around key learning experiences (refer above) that help children develop rational thought. To develop rational thought via the key learning experiences, staff need to be actively involved in open-ended questioning of the children, listening to the children's responses to these questions and problem-solving with them. Using these teaching strategies throughout each part of the 'Plan–Do–Review' learning cycle in each of the key learning experience areas, the teacher builds rational thought by helping the '. . . children learn to place things in categories, to rank things in order, [and] to predict consequences . . .'. (Weikart and Schweinhart 1987, p. 253)

Sample plans of small-group and large-group experiences within a High/Scope preschool from Hohmann and Weikart (2002) show the following sequencing of learning for the children:

- Staff identify an idea or concept to explore with the children that originates from their interests—known as the originating idea—and this is what begins a 'Plan-Do-Review' sequence.
- Staff gather suitable learning materials that will allow children to physically explore the idea or concept.
- Staff set up classrooms that are divided into interest sections or areas (Walsh and Petty 2007).
- Staff establish consistent routines and provide children with advanced notice if these routines are altered (Roopnarine and Johnson 2005; Walsh and Petty 2007).
- Staff identify potential key learning experiences for the children.
- Staff plan a way to begin the experience—samples offered by Hohmann and Weikart (2002) illustrate a strong use of staff questioning to begin the experience. For instance, in a sample small-group plan in which staff wish to help clarify children's understandings of coconuts, staff offer children a coconut and various materials with which to explore it, such as a hammer, and then begin with the question, 'What can you find out about your coconut?'
- Staff then allow children to explore the materials with staff listening and observing children's explorations.
- The experience ends with staff asking children to review what they have learnt and plan what they might do to extend their experiences. For instance, in the small-group experience in which coconuts were explored, it was suggested that staff end with the question, 'What could we do with these pieces tomorrow at work time?' The aim is to motivate children 'to reach higher levels of understanding' (Henniger 1999, p. 64).
- The staff then plan how to extend the experience with the children on the following day.

Evaluation of children's learning focuses on staff observation in which they track children's learning by using the key learning experiences areas. Observational checklists which detail the developmental steps involved in progressing through each of the key learning experiences are used to record children's progress. These checklists are specific and detailed. For example, the Number Concepts observation checklist includes the following:

The child compares continuous quantities in terms of more versus less (or fewer).
The child judges that continuous quantities are the same...
The child can recite the number series by rote from '1' to '3'. (Weikart and Schweinhart 1987, p. 261)

A CD-ROM is available from the High/Scope Foundation (see end of chapter) that supports staff as they build their skills in tracking children's learning.

In summary, teachers in the High/Scope Curriculum support children's active learning by identifying children's developmental level, by providing a physical environment relevant to their developmental level, by scheduling the day in ways that respect children as active learners and by interacting with children in ways that enable them to become decision-makers and problem-solvers. Interactions centre on staff:

- collecting together appropriate materials
- asking questions of children that prompt them to problem-solve
- observing children's problem-solving and concept development
- listening to and evaluating children's explorations so that they can be extended further.

MONTESSORI EDUCATION

> With my methods . . . the teacher teaches little and observes much; it is her function to direct the psychic activity of the children and their physiological development. For this reason I have changed the name of the teacher into that of directress. (Montessori 1936, pp. 96–97)

Overview of educational vision

Maria Montessori (1870–1952) was an Italian doctor who initially developed her educational goals and methods when working with children with intellectual disabilities (Catron and Allen 1993) who at the time were considered mentally 'deficient' and were living in the Rome asylum. Her main educational goals in this and her later work were to improve the individual child's practical daily living skills and to develop each child's intellectual potential to the full.

Current Montessori programs have a wide range of goals aimed at developing the individual child's practical daily living skills and intellectual potential. Such goals include encouraging the child's independence and problem-solving skills, developing children's concentration skills, encouraging children to respect themselves and others, and helping children to become responsible group members (Morrison 1995; Cossentino, 2006) through work experiences in the classroom (Henniger 1999).

Montessori's ways of achieving her educational goals derived from three interrelated beliefs she held about children's growth and development. First, she believed that from birth children are active, self-motivated learners who have moments in their development when they are able to learn some concepts more easily than at other times. Montessori called these moments sensitive periods. In this belief, Montessori differed from several of her contemporaries who believed that children do not learn during infancy (Brewer 1992).

Second, Montessori believed that children learn best through active involvement in their physical and sensory environment because, in her view, sensory learning was the foundation of all other learning. This idea is captured powerfully in the following statement:

> Set the children free, let them have fair play, let them run out when it is raining, take off their shoes when they find pools of water, and when the grass of the meadows is damp with dew let them run about with bare feet and trample on it; let them rest quietly when the tree invites them to sleep in its shade... (Montessori 1948/1962, p. 100)

In forming this belief she drew on the ideas of two Parisian doctors, Jean-Marc-Gaspard Itard and Edouard Seguin, whose work with children considered to be 'mentally defective' emphasised the success of sensory training in developing the children's intellectual skills (Kramer 1988).

Third, Montessori believed that children learn best when they are free to self-educate. Such beliefs earned her the title in the USA of '. . . the Italian apostle of a new libertarian education . . .' (Kramer 1988, p. 227).

Using her understandings about children's growth and development and her own experiences of working with children with intellectual disabilities, Montessori developed her program of education for young children. It strongly emphasised the educational potential of allowing children's sensory and physical exploration of self-correcting materials and using carefully sequenced exercises appropriate to each of their sensitive periods. To support her program Montessori used a range of self-correcting materials which provided children with physical and sensory feedback about whether or not they had used the materials correctly, and she developed a number of exercises targeted at maximising children's learning during their sensitive periods. Seguin and Itard first developed the materials Montessori used, but she modified them in the light of her experiences in Rome. These initial materials borrowed from the work of Seguin and Itard included: '. . . three-dimensional shapes and letters to be felt, matched, set into holes of corresponding shapes . . . [and] a whole series of objects of differing sizes, shapes, colours, [and] textures . . .' (Kramer 1988, p. 86) that children sorted, matched and joined together. Many of the materials Montessori used, such as the three-dimensional shapes and letters, were the forerunners of current educational materials for young children such as inset puzzle boards.

Teaching techniques

The Montessori approach to curriculum design relies strongly on structured skill-acquisition activities in which staff model the skills to be acquired (Robison and Schwartz 1982; Edwards 2002; Cossentino, 2006) using the prescribed exercises and materials developed by Montessori in the early 1900s. However, children can choose which of these materials they use and when they use them. To optimise children's capacity to self-educate, staff draw strongly on the following teaching techniques:

- Positioning equipment and materials: as Montessori believed strongly in the child's ability to self-educate, staff need to position equipment and materials to maximise the child's choice and independence. This involves arranging equipment and materials in a highly ordered way so that children can readily access and choose the equipment and materials they wish to work with, and easily identify where the materials should be returned. Equipment and materials should be positioned neatly, in an orderly manner and respectfully (Jackson 1997). The materials should be chosen with 'careful attention to concept development…graduated difficulty/complexity…[be] self-correcting… [and] sensory-oriented (Henniger 1999, p. 55).
- Scheduling: the child's self-paced, self-directed learning is also supported within a Montessori program by staff scheduling large blocks of uninterrupted time for the children to explore the learning materials and exercises at their own pace (Morrison 1995; Kahn 1997). There need to be opportunities for repetition so that children are able to master concepts and tasks (Cossentino 2006).
- Non-verbal interaction: staff involvement in children's activities is minimal because Montessori believed that children self-educate if the environment is appropriately prepared. When staff do interact with children there is often a strong emphasis on indirect, non-verbal teaching techniques such as modelling and redirecting. Montessori emphasised that modelling should be provided only when children need assistance with a skill or new piece of equipment, and that redirection is needed only when children are behaving inappropriately (Brewer 1992).
- Verbal interaction: once staff have selected developmentally appropriate self-educating materials, Montessori suggested that they should 'leave [their]…little scholars in liberty' (Montessori, cited in DeCecco 1968, p. 139). Hence, in a Montessori program, verbal interaction between staff and children is kept to a minimum. However, recent research suggests that Montessori teachers are likely to intervene when children make errors in their understandings of mathematical concepts and when they use incorrect language. (Chattin-McNichols 1991)

Montessori's belief that there are key periods when children's readiness to learn a particular skill is at its height means that staff need to look for the emergence of these periods and provide materials appropriate to them. It is through this observation that children's learning is evaluated. As Kahn (1997, p. 1) puts it:

> . . . the child can only be free when the adult becomes an acute observer. Any action of the adult that is not a response to the children's observed behaviour limits the child's freedom.

THE REGGIO EMILIA APPROACH

> One of the most challenging aspects of the Reggio Emilia approach is the solicitation of multiple points of view regarding children's needs, interests, and abilities, and the concurrent faith in parents, teachers, and children to contribute in meaningful ways to the determination of school experiences. (New 1993, p. 2)

As mentioned in Chapter 24, Loris Malaguzzi (1920–1994) founded and for many years directed the Reggio Emilia system of early childhood education in the northern Italian region of Emilia-Romagna. The approach he developed to educating young children has been acclaimed internationally and is known as the Reggio Emilia Approach. In recent years there has been considerable international interest in the Reggio Emilia Approach to early childhood education and its influence can be seen in early childhood programs in the USA, the UK and Australia.

Overview of educational vision

The educational vision underpinning the schools of Reggio Emilia is not fixed. It constantly evolves as staff, parents and children reflect on how best to promote children's learning. However, Malaguzzi (1993) identified wide and disparate sources of inspiration for the vision that has evolved to date. They included names familiar to early childhood educators in Australia, such as Vygotsky, Erikson, Piaget, Brofenbrenner, Montessori and Dewey. There were also many European theorists less well known in Australia such as Decroly, Freinet and Chaperade. Of the multiple and diverse sources of inspiration for the educational vision underpinning the schools of Reggio Emilia, Malaguzzi said that staff have learnt how versatile research and theory can be (Malaguzzi 1993).

This versatility has led to a complex and changing vision of the child as a competent learner and of the way in which the child can best be supported in her learning. There is a strong vision of the child as an active constructor of knowledge:

> What children learn does not follow as an automatic result from what is taught. Rather, it is in large part due to the children's own doing as a consequence of their activities and our resources. (Malaguzzi 1993, p. 59)

The child is seen to learn through being actively engaged in a rich and complex set of relationships and interactions with the adults around them, the peer group and an 'amiable' learning environment.

The vision of the child as a competent learner strongly influences how curriculum is decided. The child's ability to construct knowledge positions the child as a person who has the right and capability to direct his own learning. A strong child-directed curriculum model which places the child in the centre of curriculum negotiations has evolved. However, negotiation is a critical word within the Reggio Emilia Approach to curriculum, as there is a strong belief that children learn through relationships with others, including parents and staff. This belief in part derives from the work of Vygotsky (see Chapter 29) and his belief that children learn through interaction, modelling and support from competent others at critical periods in the acquisition of new skills and knowledge.

While Vygotsky's ideas on children's learning and the role of social relationships in this learning have influenced the vision of the child as competent learner, they have also been modified through the experiences and theory building of staff in the schools of Reggio Emilia. The relationship between adult and child in the child's learning is seen as highly complex and Vygotsky's ideas as somewhat problematic. The idea that an adult can help a child gain competence when the child is not yet competent is seen as problematic and the idea that there is just the right moment to offer help is also seen as problematic. However, the need for adults to carefully time their interventions in children's learning is seen as a critical issue to grapple with.

The shape, style, tone, focus and content of the curriculum evolves from the day-to-day happenings in the lives, experience and interests of children and adults in the centre. The emphasis is on communication and interaction to deepen children's inquiry and theory building about the world around them and on building a community of inquiry between adults and children through which this can happen (Knowles Kennedy 1996; Rinaldi 2006). Children's learning is supported and enriched through in-depth, short- and long-term project work in which 'responding, recording, playing, exploring, hypothesis-building and testing, and provoking occurs' (New 1993, p. 3). Within the project work, the arts play a powerful role. The children are encouraged to use many forms of symbolic language to express their ideas and further their understandings in their project work, and the aesthetics of the schools have led to the claim by Malaguzzi (1993, p. 57) that the 'walls speak and document'.

Teaching techniques

One of the key techniques used in the pre-primary schools in Reggio Emilia is the documentation and display of children's project work. The specialist technique of documentation is seen as essential to the process of children being able to express, revisit, construct and reconstruct their feelings, ideas and understandings (Moran, Desrochers and Cavicchi 2007). Community building is also critical to the teaching and learning experiences within Reggio Emilia pre-primary schools.

Documenting is discussed further in Chapter 24 and community building is discussed further in Chapter 20. However, alongside the technique of documentation, several other general and specialist techniques support staff in implementing their educational vision of the child as a competent learner. These techniques include:

- Positioning equipment and materials: staff select and organise equipment and materials in ways that invite children's discovery, that enable children to express their ideas in multiple ways and that enable children to revisit their work. Equipment and materials are also positioned to enable children's long-term project work to take place. It is also important that the physical space 'foster communication and relationships' (Henniger 1999, p. 70) and be alive with children's representations of the world around them. A workshop area in which children can engage in project work is often present:

One special space found in Reggio classrooms is called the atelier. The teacher sets aside this special workshop as an area for recording in visual form what students learn as they engage in projects of their own choosing...The atelier contains a wealth of tools and resource materials that children can use for their documentations. (Henniger 1999, p. 71)

- Scheduling: children's learning is supported and enriched through scheduling time for in-depth project work. There is also a minimum of six hours per week provided for staff to engage in planning, in-service training and reflection on their work with children and their families (Henniger 1999; Rinaldi 2006).
- Verbal and non-verbal interaction: staff actively interact with children to encourage expression of their ideas and theory construction. The role of the adult is in part a participant-observer in children's learning and in part it is to be an agent provocateur. To a large extent Vygotsky's view of the child learning through scaffolding with competent others informs this sense of the role of the teacher (Malaguzzi 1993). Open-ended questioning, problem-solving, recalling, feedback, demonstrating and describing help staff participate in and provoke children's learning. Dialogue is central to the teaching and learning experience within Reggio Emilia:

Reggio Emilia educators commonly study conversations among children and between children and adults . . . They believe such conversations allow children to reflect on their ideas and extend their thinking . . . (Hughes 2002, p. 137)

Robertson (1995) describes a project she observed at the Diana school in Emilia-Romagna and how staff's organisation of the environment and their interaction with the children respected the vision of the child as a competent learner:

. . . a group of three five-year-old children had been given a bucket, a Plexiglas mirror and asked if they could make a rainbow. Eventually, after sorting out they needed water and light, and a great deal of trial and error they achieved the result . . . In the Reggio Emilia tradition the whole event is documented closely with photographs. (Robertson 1995, p. 14)

RUDOLF STEINER AND WALDORF SCHOOLING

> When the Waldorf curriculum is carried through successfully, the whole human being—head, heart, and hand—has been truly educated. (Barnes 1991, p. 54)

Rudolf Steiner (1861–1925) was an Austrian intellectual who widely researched and wrote on the scientific and philosophical thinking of his time. As part of his writing and research he developed a spiritual science called Anthroposophy. Steiner became involved in education in 1919 when he was asked by a German factory owner, Emil Molt, to create an educational program for Molt's Waldorf-Astoria cigarette factory workers and their families based on Steiner's anthroposophical views. By the 1990s approximately 550 schools in over 30 countries had been established using Waldorf educational principles established by Steiner in 1919 (Barnes 1991). Several of these schools have a preschool component.

Overview of educational vision
Steiner's educational philosophy was derived from humanistic philosophy and emphasised the importance of education for life and education for the whole being. For Steiner, the spiritual, physical and intellectual being were equally the concern and responsibility of education. This meant that Steiner was a strong advocate of an integrated and a holistic approach to education.

Steiner also believed that each person attains their spiritual, intellectual and physical potential as an adult by passing through three developmental stages: early childhood, middle childhood and adolescence (Barnes 1991). Writing about his approach to curriculum in 1919, this developmental approach is clear:

> Knowledge of the special needs of each life period provides a basis for drawing up a suitable curriculum. This knowledge also can be a basis for dealing with instructional subjects in successive periods. By the end of the 9th year, one must have brought the child to a certain level in all that has come into human life through the growth of civilization. (Steiner 1919, p. 3)

In each developmental stage the concerns, interests, capacities and ways of knowing of a person differ. Accordingly, Steiner argued that the nature of the educational content and methods should differ in each developmental stage. For example, in the phase of early childhood it is the physical being that is pre-eminent. Children are absorbing the world through their senses and their major way of learning and knowing is through imitation. The responsibility of adults educating children in their early childhood years is to nurture the positive development of the physical being by ensuring that the child has a sensory world of sounds, sights, gestures, actions, aesthetics and feelings that are worthy of imitation (Barnes 1991).

Each developmental stage lays the foundations for the concerns and ways of knowing in the next phase. Hence, inappropriate educational content or methods in the early childhood stage can harm the later development of the child. As Barnes (1991, p. 52) explains:

> Drawing the child's energies away from this fundamental task [their physical development] to meet premature intellectual demands robs the child of the health and vitality he or she will need for later life.

Conversely, the experience of Waldorf teachers is that matching curriculum content with the developmental stage enhances children's enjoyment in and capacity for learning across a range of content areas including mathematics (Mollet 1991).

While many of Steiner's beliefs paralleled those of several other educationalists influenced by humanistic philosophy, his anthroposophical views provided his pedagogy with a distinctive philosophical, educational and spiritual coherence lacking in the writings of other educationalists:

> Steiner's emphasis on the development of the normal child's inner capacities at the proper times has much in common with Montessori, Neill, Ashton-Warner, even Dewey, but Steiner is unique in that this emphasis is

underpinned by an entire cosmology so that students sense their interconnection with everything: earth and planets, body and spirit, past and present, life and death. (Reinsmith 1989, p. 82)

His approach to education was linked powerfully to spirituality:

Steiner Education is an explicitly spiritual approach. The teacher nourishes the soul of the child through story, art, music, and movement. The kindergarten class remains together through to the eighth grade with the same teacher from 1–8. A strong set of relationships and sense of community is formed. (Lawrence and Coady 2002, p. 18)

The foundation of the spiritual approach to teaching and learning in Steiner schools is Anthroposophy:

The term 'Anthroposophy' comes from the Greek '*anthropos-sophia*' or 'human wisdom'. Steiner expanded an exacting scientific method by which one could do research for her/himself into the spiritual worlds. The investigation, known also as Spiritual Science, is an obvious complement to the Natural Sciences we have come to accept. Through study and practiced observation, one awakens to his/her own inner nature and the spiritual realities of outer nature and the cosmos. The awareness of those relationships brings a greater reverence for all of life. (Steiner Schools in Australia: <http://www.steiner-australia.org/other/Wald_faq.html>)

Steiner's philosophies of spirituality, humanity and education are not without their controversies. In particular, there is debate over the extent to which his view of humanity rested on colonial perspectives of 'race' (see Chapter 21). Myers (2006) articulates this concern as follows:

Though Steiner was certainly a well-meaning humanist and would-be humanitarian, his Orientalism selectively interprets and recontextualizes cultural meaning with biased discursive purposes and thus naturalizes a colonialist world-vision in a more subtle way than assumed for Western, and more specifically German, forms of colonialism. (p. 389)

Teaching techniques

Steiner formed his views on the nature of development and learning into five principles which guided the curriculum content and teaching methods of the Waldorf schools. The curriculum, that was integrated, developmental and spiritual, drew strongly on artistic method and processes, and taught students the art of eurhythmy. Eurhythmy was described by Steiner (1970) as a form of language based on gesture and movement. While individual Waldorf schools may now differ in the detailed content of their curriculum, these five principles still exemplify the essential components of the Waldorf approach to education (Reinsmith 1989; Lim 2004).

Waldorf teaching involves learning specialist teaching methods (for example, for teaching eurhythmy). However, it also draws on several generalist teaching techniques to support its distinctive approach to education in the early childhood years. These techniques include:

- Positioning equipment and materials: staff select and arrange materials and experiences to encourage children's sensory exploration of their environment and to stimulate their artistic sense of being. Natural materials are used as these are seen to '. . . breathe and enhance the life forces' (Linden Steiner Kindergarten, no date, p. 8).
- Scheduling: activities requiring mental concentration are scheduled early in the day. There is also a strong rhythm to the scheduling of activities for the week and of the year. At the Linden Steiner Kindergarten they describe their schedule as follows:

All the children participate in a mixed-age, play-centred curriculum with a strong emphasis on rhythm...Each day the children participate in a rhythmic circle time, often seasonally based, which includes songs, verses and movement. At the end of each morning session the children are told a story, most often a fairy story. Eurhythmy and various artistic activities and crafts are offered during the week. (Linden Steiner Kindergarten, no date, p. 8)

In addition, there is strong emphasis on providing long blocks of time for children's free play to allow children to fully explore their environment and express themselves.

- Non-verbal interaction: as imitation is seen to be the young child's main form of learning, teachers must think carefully about the physical, spiritual and intellectual model they provide for the children. As Steiner believed strongly that children are affected by their teacher's inner being, it is important that teachers are positively committed to learning and personal growth (Reinsmith 1989). Staff need to model social skills such as sharing and co-operation and work hard to model '. . . positive, quiet and calm behaviour' (Linden Steiner Kindergarten, no date, p. 6). Facilitation of opportunities for the child's self-expression is also emphasised, with particular stress placed on encouraging and nourishing children's imaginative play (Linden Steiner Kindergarten, no date).

- Verbal interaction: as children's learning is seen to occur through imitation, direct instruction is kept to a minimum. When staff need to tell children to do something for reasons of their own or for other people's safety the direction is given in short, simple sentences. Staff are involved in daily story-telling and singing with the children as a way of enhancing children's sense of wonder and connection with the spiritual world.

Evaluation of children's learning happens via observation. Daily observation of the child based on the teacher's knowledge of Anthroposophy builds a deep spiritual knowledge of each child which the teacher uses to individualise her teaching and alter her teaching methods and content as appropriate. Steiner refers to this process as 'learning to observe in the most intimate way . . .' (Steiner 1970, p. 28) the young child's '. . . gift of imitation'. (Steiner 1970, p. 31)

THE ANTI-BIAS CURRICULUM

The Anti-Bias Curriculum embraces an educational philosophy as well as specific techniques and content. It is value-based: differences are good, oppressive ideas are not. It sets up a creative tension between respecting differences and not accepting unfair beliefs and acts (Derman-Sparks et al. 1989, p. x).

The Anti-Bias Curriculum was first developed in the late 1980s by a task force of early childhood educators from Pasadena and Los Angeles in California, USA. The task force wanted to develop a curriculum for working on issues of diversity with young children. They met for two years, shared their ideas and experiences, and eventually developed an approach to diversity which they named the Anti-Bias Curriculum. The philosophy, goals and techniques of their approach to diversity were first published by the National Association for the Education of Young Children (NAEYC) in 1989 as the *Anti-Bias Curriculum: Tools for Empowering Young Children*. This publication has since sold over 100 000 copies.

Overview of educational vision

The educational philosophy underpinning the Anti-Bias Curriculum has much in common with other approaches to early childhood education. It is premised on the beliefs that early childhood education should be developmentally appropriate and that its goal should be 'the development of each child to her or his fullest potential' (Derman-Sparks et al. 1989, p.x).

However, the Anti-Bias Task Force also argues that early childhood education should be culturally and socially appropriate and that much early childhood education is not. This is because much mainstream early childhood education fails to acknowledge the real and continuing ways in which children's development is constrained by the inequalities and oppression they notice and experience in their daily lives.

Specifically, children's development is constrained by racism, sexism, handicappism, classism and heterosexism from an early age. In support of this claim the Anti-Bias Task Force cite their own experiences and research about young children's awareness that specific forms of difference, such as 'racial' difference and physical abilities, are connected with status, privilege and power in their society (see Dau 2001). They believe that children come to understand the way different groups are privileged in their society through observing the spoken and unspoken messages that adults and other children provide about differences between people. Drawing on their work, they argue that children need:

- a future free from the constraints of racism, sexism, classism and handicappism
- early childhood education which directly addresses equity issues in, and through, the early childhood curriculum.

To build a curriculum that met these goals the task force drew on their own educational experiences as early childhood educators and on the philosophy, goals and techniques of critical or transformative education (see the section on Freire and empowerment in Chapter 25; also refer to MacNaughton 2003). Derman-Sparks (1989, p. 22) describes how the Anti-Bias Curriculum began:

> The term 'anti-bias' has a similar meaning to 'education without prejudice'. We chose it because we wanted to say that this work requires a very active stance in relationship to challenging racism, sexism and all other forms of systematic oppression ... We also need to look at the power relationships that interfere with the possibility of true diversity—the institutional structures and beliefs that systematically result in less resources, power and status for large numbers of people because of their racial and ethnic group membership, their gender, their class, their sexual orientation.

The aim of critical curriculum is to develop educational processes which create a more just and wise social world. Within this there are two broad goals: challenging discrimination and empowering children. Translating and developing these goals for within early childhood education led the task force to argue that early childhood education needs to help children to:

- take increasing responsibility for their own learning and care
- continue learning with an enhanced sense of self worth, identity, confidence and enjoyment
- contribute their own special strengths and interests to the group
- learn useful and appropriate ways to find out what they want to know
- understand their own individual ways of learning and being creative
- be active in confronting and challenging inequality and injustice.

The challenges and opportunities for doing this differ according to the inequity and injustice staff are working on with children. The issues in relation to 'racial' inequalities, gender inequalities and inequalities for children with disabilities are different from each other and thus require different approaches to empowering children. For children who experience discrimination because of their 'race', gender or disability, empowerment involves addressing the negative impact of this discrimination on their lives and in providing them with the skills to challenge unfair treatment of themselves and others in future. More detailed discussion of these issues and practical strategies related to them can be found in Dau (2001).

The Anti-Bias Task Force named their approach to tackle social inequality and discrimination with young children an anti-bias approach for the following reasons:

> In a society in which institutional structures create and maintain sexism, racism, and handicappism, it is not sufficient to be non-biased (and also highly unlikely), nor is it sufficient to be an observer. It is necessary for each individual to actively intervene, to challenge and counter the personal and institutional behaviours that perpetuate oppression. (Derman-Sparks et al. 1989, p. 3)

The Anti-Bias Curriculum is, therefore, a political, activist approach to the education of young children.

Teaching techniques

While empowerment is the prime technique used in the Anti-Bias Curriculum, staff also draw on several generalist and specialist teaching techniques to support this distinctive approach to education in the early childhood years. These techniques include:

- Positioning equipment and materials: while there is no specific direction given to staff about how to position equipment and materials in an Anti-Bias Curriculum, there are clear guidelines for the creation of an anti-bias learning environment in which selection of equipment and materials are the key (see Jones and Derman-Sparks 1992). Equipment and materials should be anti-discriminatory, culturally inclusive and relevant, and they should enable children to explore issues of human diversity and anti-discriminatory (anti-bias) ways of being. Collecting equipment that supports this work is an important part of anti-bias teaching.
- Non-verbal interaction: staff are actively involved in children's activities because children's biased ideas and behaviours need to be challenged and confronted. However, there is also a strong emphasis on staff modelling anti-biased ways—children are seen to learn many of their biased and anti-biased attitudes from the adults around them.
- Verbal interaction: staff develop anti-bias content around the children's daily experiences (see Derman-Sparks and Ramsey 2006). As Derman-Sparks (1993/94), p. 71) explains:

Critical thinking and activism activities should rise out of real-life situations that are of interest to the children.

Staff use a variety of verbal teaching techniques to build this content and to enable the children to engage with it and with each other in anti-biased ways. Staff need to be actively involved in open-ended questioning of the children around issues of diversity and equity, listening to the children's responses to these questions, problem-solving with the children what is fair and unfair, and empowering the children to think critically about their social world and to take action against inequalities and injustices. Story-telling and story-reading are seen as powerful ways to raise issues of equity and diversity with young children. A specialist story-telling technique using dolls has also been developed to support the development of children's critical thinking and problem-solving abilities around issues of diversity and equity. This was developed by Kay Taus, a member of the Anti-Bias Task Force, and is known as the 'Persona Doll' technique. A key element of the Persona Doll technique involves introducing children to 'personalised' storylines about equity and diversity that extend, enrich and challenge their current knowledge and attitudes. Examples of this technique can be found in van Keulen (2004), Dau (2001), Brown (2001) and MacNaughton and Hughes (2001).

Evaluation of children's learning is through observation of their interactions with each other and with educational materials, and through staff discussing with the children their values and attitudes towards diversity.

Conclusion

When early childhood staff take a strategic approach to their teaching and children's learning they are being educationally purposeful and making plans to ensure that their educational vision becomes a reality.

Not all early childhood staff are strategic about teaching and learning. Some staff do not have a clear sense of what they want to do and how they will do it. Some staff have a clear vision of their work but do not have a coherent approach to their teaching that harmonises with their vision. When staff are not being strategic they tend to take ad hoc educational decisions that may not achieve what is best for children. Program-planning on a daily, weekly or fortnightly basis can be an ad hoc approach to teaching when it is not based on an overall approach that reflects an educational vision.

There are clearly many different educational visions that influence curriculum for young children. Staff must choose between a staggering array of competing philosophies, educational goals and processes when deciding what and how they will teach. Sometimes staff have to make their choices in isolation, sometimes in consultation with parents and other staff. Irrespective of who is involved in these decisions, the decision about what and how to teach is strongly value-based. As Elliot and Hatton (1994, p. 55) stated:

> Teaching is not a value-neutral activity. It is premised on certain values and promotes certain, although not always the same, values.

Understanding the values that underpin teaching decisions is an important component of excellence in teaching (Elliot and Hatton 1994). However, it is equally important for staff to know how to build their own educational and professional values into a strategic approach to teaching and learning. We borrow from the writing of Lillian Katz to summarise our argument:

> The main argument in this chapter is that consideration of what young children should learn, and when and how they should do so, have to be addressed together in order to formulate an appropriate pedagogical approach for any of them. (Katz 1995, p. 115)

By staff being strategic in this way, it is more likely that the educational vision of excellence in teaching for all young children, as outlined in this book, can become a reality.

Reflecting on being strategic

1　What is the difference between strategic decision-making and ad hoc decision-making?
2　How can strategic decision-making help you achieve your teaching and learning goals with young children?
3　Do you have a clear educational vision? What are your current beliefs and values about:
   - how children's development influences their learning?
   - how children's learning is influenced by their cultural, social and political background?
   - what cultural, social, moral, political and ethical goals should underpin an educational program for young children?
4　What are your current ideas about:
   - what children should learn?
   - when children should learn?
   - how children should learn?
5　Which of the following general teaching techniques do you feel are best suited to your own educational vision for young children?
   - demonstrating
   - describing
   - encouraging, praising and helping
   - facilitating
   - feedback
   - grouping
   - listening
   - modelling
   - positioning people
   - questioning
   - reading
   - recalling
   - singing
   - suggesting
   - telling.

6 Which of the following specialist teaching techniques do you feel are best suited to making your own educational vision for young children a reality?

- co-constructing
- community building
- deconstructing
- documenting
- empowering
- philosophising
- problem-solving
- reinforcing
- scaffolding
- task analysis.

7 Visit one of the following websites and answer the following questions:

- To what extent is there a clear philosophy underpinning teaching and learning practices in the service?
- In which ways do the teaching techniques discussed link with the service's philosophy?
- How strategic is this service in its approach to teaching and learning?

Sheridan College Early Childhood Centres: <http://www.sheridan.on.ca/academic/edserv/miss.htm>

Education Review Office: <http://www.ero.govt.nz/Publications/pubs2002/Montessori.htm>

I Live and Learn Private Preschool and Day Care Centres: <http://www.preschoolnz.co.nz> (this site leads to several specific centres whose philosophy you can analyse).

FURTHER READING AND RESOURCES

The High/Scope Preschool Curriculum (USA and Singapore)

Bredekamp, S. 1996, '25 years of educating young children: the High/Scope Approach to preschool', *Young Children*, 51(4), pp. 57–61.

Extensions (newsletter of the High/Scope Curriculum), available from the High/Scope Educational Research Foundation, 600 North River St, Ypsilanti, MI 48198-2898, USA, tel. 1 (313) 4850704.

High/Scope Resource: A Magazine for Educators, available from the High/Scope Educational Research Foundation, 600 North River St, Ypsilanti, MI 48198-2898, USA, tel. 1 (313) 4850704.

Hohmann, M. and Weikart, D. 1995, *Educating Young Children: Active Learning Practices for Preschool and Child Care Programs*, High/Scope Education Research Foundation, Ypsilanti, MI.

Montie, J., Xiang, Z. and Schweinhart, L. 2006, 'Preschool experience in 10 countries: Cognitive and language performance at age 7', *Early Childhood Research Quarterly*, 21, pp. 313–331.

Morrison, G. 1995, *Early Childhood Education Today*, 6th edn, Merrill, New Jersey [refer to pp. 136–153].

Post, J. and Hohmann, M. 1995, 'Planning the day in infant and toddler programs', *Extensions*, 10(3), pp. 1–3.

Weikart, D. 1995/96, 'High/Scope in action: the milestones', *High/Scope Resource, Special Edition* [refer to pp. 4–6].

Weikart, D. and Schweinart, L. 1987, 'The High/Scope cognitively orientated curriculum in early childhood', in J. Roopnarine, ed., *Approaches to Early Childhood Curriculum* (pp. 253–67), Merrill Publishing Company, Ohio.

Online resources

Extensive information and resources are available from the High/Scope Educational Research Foundation, 600 North River St, Ypsilanti, MI 48198-2898, USA. The website for the Foundation contains detailed links to reading lists, videos (listed below), research, sample plans and newsletter updates: **htp://www.highscope.org**

High/Scope COR Self-Study Guide on CD-ROM, High/Scope Foundation, 0-57379-084-9.

Videos (available from **http://www.highscope.org**)
High/Scope Curriculum. Its Implementation in Family Child Care Homes.
The High/Scope Curriculum. The Daily Routine.
The High/Scope Curriculum. The Plan-Do-Review Process.
Setting up the Learning Environment.
Supporting Children's Active Learning. Teaching Strategies for Diverse Settings.

Montessori Education

Albanseia, F. 1990, *Montessori Classroom Management*, Crown Books, New York.

Brewer, J. 1992, *Introduction to Early Childhood Education: Preschool through Primary Grades*, Allyn & Bacon, Boston [refer pp. 38–45].

Association Montessori International (AMI). This association was founded by Maria Montessori in 1929. AMI, 170 West Scholfield Road, Rochestor, New York, 14617, USA.

Hainstock, E. 1986, *The Essential Montessori*, New American Library, New York.

Jones Jensen, S. 2004, 'One individual at a time: instruction in the Montessori classroom', *Montessori Life*, Fall.

Kramer, R. 1988, *Maria Montessori*, Hamish Hamilton Paperback, London.

Montessori Life is a journal which publishes current international research on Montessori education.

Moll, I. 2004, Towards a constructivist Montessori education, *Perspectives in Education*, 22(2), pp. 37–49.

Morrison, G. 1995, *Early Childhood Education Today*, sixth edn, New Jersey, Merrill [refer pp. 91–119].

Reed, M. and Smith, J. 2005, Counting the Pinecones: Children's Addition and Subtraction Strategies, *Montessori Life* (Spring).

Online resources

Montessori Connections. A website developed by the IntelleQuest Education Company that has links to other websites concerned with Montessori education, journals, teacher resources and details of Montessori schools: **http://www.montessoriconnections.com**

Montessori Foundation. Email: timseldon@montessori.org or see **http://www.montessori.org**

Montessori International Index with details about teacher training, environments and materials, lectures and conferences and online resources: **http://www.montessori.edu**

Videos

Maria Montessori: Follow the Child, 1994, Douglas Clark Associates, California.
Montessori: Freedom in a Structured Environment, *Reggio Emilia*, 1991, University of Melbourne.
Practical Teaching Excerpts: Montessori Method, *Sister Christine's Class*, 1991, University of Melbourne.
'Spontaneous Concentration in the Montessori Prepared Environment', available at **http://www.montessori-namta.org**

Reggio Emilia

Ardzejewska, K. and Coutts, P. 2004, 'Teachers who support Reggio—exploring their understandings of the philosophy', *Australian Journal of Early Childhood*, 29(4), pp. 17–25.

Edwards, C. 1993, 'Partner, nurturer and guide: the roles of the Reggio teacher in action', in C. Edwards, L. Gandini and G. Forman, eds, *The Hundred Languages of Children: The Reggio Emilia Approach to Early Childhood Education* (pp. 151–169), Ablex Publishing Company, New Jersey.

Firlik, R. 1996, 'Can we adapt the philosophies and practices of Reggio Emilia, Italy, for use in American schools?', *Early Childhood Education Journal*, 23(4), pp. 217–220.

Fraser, S. 2007, 'Play in other languages', *Theory into Practice*, 46(1), pp. 14–22.

Gandini, L. 1993a, 'Educational caring spaces', in C. Edwards, L. Gandini and G. Forman, eds, *The Hundred Languages of Children: The Reggio Emilia Approach to Early Childhood Education* (pp. 135–149), Ablex Publishing Company, New Jersey.

——1993b, 'Fundamentals of the Reggio Emilia approach to early childhood education', *Young Children*, 49(1), pp. 4–8.

Hendricks, J. (ed.) 1997, *First Steps Towards Teaching the Reggio Way*, Merrill/Prentice Hall, Columbus, OH.

Hughes, E. 2002, 'Planning meaningful curriculum: a mini story of children and teachers learning together', *Childhood Education*, 78(3), pp. 134–139.

Innovations in Early Education: The International Reggio Exchange is a journal through which subscribers can keep up to date with developments in the Italian programs and hear about how these programs are being adapted in other countries. Available from The Merrill-Palmer Institute, Wayne State University, 71-A E. Ferry Ave, Detroit MI 48202, USA.

Katz, L. 1995, 'Lessons from Reggio Emilia: an American perspective', *ERIC Digest*, ED388425.

Kang, J. 2007, 'How many languages can Reggio children speak?: many more than a hundred!', *Gifted Child Today*, 30(3), pp. 45–65.

Mercilliott Hewett, V. 2001, 'Examining the Reggio Emilia Approach to early childhood education', *Early Childhood Education Journal*, 29(2), pp. 95–100.

New, R. 2007, 'Reggio Emilia as cultural activity theory in practice', *Theory into Practice*, 46(1), pp. 5–13.

New, R. 2003, 'Reggio Emilia: new ways to think about schooling', *Educational Leadership*, 60(7), pp. 34–39.

New, R. 2000, 'Reggio Emilia: catalyst for change and conversation', *ERIC Digest*, ED447971.

Rinaldi, C. 2006, *In Dialogue with Reggio Emilia: Listening, researching and learning*, Routledge, New York.

Strong-Wilson, T. and Ellis, J. 2007, 'Children and place: Reggio Emilia's environment as third teacher', *Theory into Practice*, 46(1), pp. 40–47.

Trepanier-Street, M., Hong, S. and Bauer, J, 2001, 'Using technology in Reggio-inspired long-term projects', *Early Childhood Journal*, 28(3), pp. 181–188.

Online resources

Selected resources about Reggio Emilia and its influences in early childhood education can be found at: **http://www.members.aol.com/ouidameier/reggio/cavallo_bib.htm**

Reggio Emilia LIST SERV: email REGGIO-L **listserv@postoffice.cso.uiuc.edu**

Reggio Emilia Information Exchange: **http://reggio-oz.dd.com.au**

Reggio Emilia Australia Information Exchange: **http://www.reaie.org.au**

This site provides information about the Municipal Infant-Toddler Centres as well as Preschools of Reggio Emilia: **http://zerosei.comune.re.it/inter/index.htm**

Reggio Emilia Provocations explores the philosophy of the Reggio Emilia infant and toddler centres and preschools within the cultural context of Aotearoa/New Zealand: **http://www.reggioemilia.org.nz/index.php?option=com_frontpage&Itemid=1**

Videos

An Amusement Park for Birds, 1994, Perfomanetics, USA.

Lyon, M.S., *The Hundred Languages of Children*, 1995. A visit to the Reggio Emilia Exhibit, USA, fax USA (415) 3978211.

The Long Jump, 1992, Perfomanetics, USA.

Rudolf Steiner and Waldorf Schooling

Barnes, H. 1985, *An Introduction to Waldorf Education*, Mercury Press, Spring Valley, NY.

——1991, 'Learning that grows with the learner: an introduction to Waldorf Education', *Educational Leadership*, October, pp. 52–54.

Blackwood, R. 1992, 'Alternative early childhood education: the Steiner way', *Journal of the Australian Early Childhood Association*, Victorian Branch, 10(3), pp. 25–26.

Masters, B. (ed.) 1989, *Rudolf Steiner: Waldorf Education*, The Robinswood Press, Stourbridge, UK.

Mollet, D. 1991, 'How the Waldorf Approach changed a difficult class', *Educational Leadership*, October, pp. 55–56.

Petrash, J. 2002, *Understanding Waldorf Education: Teaching from the Inside Out*, Gryphon House, Beltsville, MD.

Reinsmith, W. 1989, 'The whole in every part: Steiner and Waldorf schooling', *The Educational Forum*, 54(1), pp. 81–91.

Steiner, R. 1919, 'An introduction to Waldorf Education', an essay by Rudolf Steiner, downloadable from **http://wn.elib.com/ Steiner/Articles/IntWal_index.html**

——1970, 'Education and the Science of Spirit (Lecture, 1921)', in P. Allen, ed., *Education as an Art* (pp. 19–49), Rudolf Steiner Publications, New York.

——1982, *The Roots of Education*, Rudolf Steiner Press, London.

Online resources

Useful links to a variety of sites associated with Steiner's educational philosophy: **http://www.awsna.org**

Steiner Waldorf Schools for Curriculum Choice in Scotland: **http://www.steinerweb.org.uk**

Video

Candle on the Hill, 1990, BBC TV.

Anti-Bias Curriculum

Byrnes, D. and Kiger, G. 1992, *Common Bonds: Anti-Bias Teaching in a Diverse Society*, Association for Childhood Education International, Wheaton, MD.

Dau, E. (ed.) 2001, *The Anti-Bias Approach in Early Childhood*, 2nd edn, Harper Educational, Sydney.

Derman-Sparks, L. 1992, '"It isn't fair!". Anti-bias curriculum for young children', in B. Neugebauer, ed., *Alike and Different: Exploring our Humanity with Young Children* (pp. 2–10), National Association for the Education of Young Children, Washington, DC.

——1993/94, 'Empowering children to create a caring culture in a world of differences', *Childhood Education*, 70(2), pp. 66–71.

——2003, Understanding differences age by age, *Scholastic Early Childhood Today*, 18(3), p. 45.

Derman-Sparks, L. and the Anti-Bias Task Force 1989, *The Anti-Bias Curriculum*, National Association for the Education of Young Children, Washington, DC.

Derman-Sparks, L. and Ramsey, P. 2006, *What if all the kids are white?: anti-bias multicultural education with young children and families*, Teachers College Press, New York.

Jones, E. and Derman-Sparks, L. 1992, 'Meeting the challenge of diversity', *Young Children*, January, pp. 12–16.

Jones, K. and Mules, R. 2001, 'Developing critical thinking and activism', in E. Dau ed., *The Anti-Bias Approach in Early Childhood*, (pp. 192–209), Pearson Education Australia, French's Forest, NSW.

Killoran, I., Panaroni, M., Rivers, S., Vetter, D. and Tymon, D. 2004, 'Rethink. Revise. React. Using an anti-bias curriculum to move beyond the usual', *Childhood Education*, Spring, pp. 149–156.

LGCC, 1996, *Caring for Every Child: Ideas to Meet Diverse Needs in Child Care*, Lady Gowrie Child Centre, Sydney.

Neugebauer, B. (ed.) 1992, *Alike and Different: Exploring our Humanity with Young Children*, National Association for the Education of Young Children, Washington, DC.

van Keulen, A. (ed.) 2004, 'Young children aren't biased, are they?!', Van Leer Foundation, Amsterdam.

Online resources

A child care centre in the USA with an anti-bias philosophy: email address cshrc@stuaf.umass.edu

Equity Alliance: **http://www.RootsforChange.net**

MacNaughton, G., Campbell, S., Smith, K. and Lawrence, H. 2002, *Equity Adventures in Early Childhood* (CD-ROM), Centre for Equity and Innovation in Early Childhood, University of Melbourne: **http://www.edfac.unimelb.edu.au/LED/ CEIEC**

Web pages with extensive resources on anti-bias perspectives:

Access to practical resources for implementing social justice and the Anti-Bias Curriculum with young children: **http://californiatomorrow.org**

A journal on projects that foster equity, respect and understanding available at: **http://www.splcenter.org/teachingtolerance/tt-index.html**

A great list of resources on equity and diversity available at: **http://www.ali.apple.com/naeyc/06.shtml**

Institute of Anti-bias Education Study Guide, which describes the aims of anti-bias education. Full text available at: **http://www.adl.org/tools_teachers/tip_antibias_ed.html**

A list of the articles on Diversity produced by the National Network for Child Care: **http://www.nncc.org/Diversity/divers.page.html**

A journal related to equity issues and education available at: **http://www.rethinkingschools.org**

Resources for building social justice in the classroom available at: **http://www.teachingforchange.org**

Videos

Anti-Bias Curriculum, Pacific Oaks College, Extension Services, 714 West California Bvd, Pasadena, CA91105.

Fair Play: Anti-Bias in Action. A Training Kit, 1997, Lady Gowrie Children's Centre, Sydney.

REFERENCES

Barnes, H. 1991, 'Learning that grows with the learner: an introduction to Waldorf Education', *Educational Leadership*, October, pp. 52–54.

Bowman, B., Donovan, S. and Burns, S. 2001, *Eager to Learn: Educating Our Preschoolers*, National Academy Press, Washington, DC.

Brewer, J. 1992, *Introduction to Early Childhood Education: Preschool through Primary Grades*, Allyn & Bacon, Boston, pp. 38–45.

Brown, B. 2001, *Combating Discrimination: Persona Dolls in Action*, reprinted 2005, Trentham Books, London.

Catron, C. and Allen, J. 1993, *Early Childhood Curriculum*, Macmillan Publishing Company, New York.

Chattin-McNichols, J. 1991, 'Montessori teachers' intervention: preliminary findings from an international study', *Eric Digest*, ED341499.

Cossentino, J. 2006, 'Big work: vocation, and engagement in the Montessori method', *Curriculum Inquiry*, 36(1), pp. 63–92.

Dau, E. (ed.) 2001, *The Anti-Bias Approach in Early Childhood*, 2nd edn, Pearson Education Australia, Sydney.

DeCecco, J. 1968, *The Psychology of Learning and Instruction: Educational Psychology*, Prentice Hall Inc., New Jersey.

Derman-Sparks, L. 1993/94, 'Empowering children to create a caring culture in a world of differences', *Childhood Education*, 70(2), pp. 66–71.

Derman-Sparks, L. and the Anti-Bias Task Force 1989, *The Anti-Bias Curriculum: Tools for Empowering Young Children*, National Association for the Education of Young Children, Washington, DC.

Derman-Sparks, L. and Ramsey, P. 2006, *What if all the kids are white?: anti-bias multicultural education with young children and families*, Teachers College Press, New York.

Edwards, C.P. 2002, 'Three approaches from Europe: Waldorf, Montessori, and Reggio Emilia', *Early Childhood Research and Practice,* 4(1), <http://ecrp.uiuc.edu/v4n1/edwards.html>.

Elliot, R. and Hatton, E. 1994, 'Neutrality and the value-ladenness of teaching', in E. Hatton, ed., *Understanding Teaching: Curriculum and the Social Context of Schooling*, Harcourt Brace, Sydney.

Henniger, M. 1999, *Teaching Young Children: An Introduction*, Merrill, Colombus, OH.

Hohmann, M. and Weikart, D. 2002, *Educating Young Children: Active Learning Practices for Preschool and Child Care Programs*, High/Scope Press, Ypsilanti, MI.

Hughes, E. 2002, 'Planning meaningful curriculum: a mini story of children and teachers learning together, *Childhood Education*, 78(3), pp. 134–140.

Jackson, P. 1997, 'Orient express: intercontinental destinations for Montessori Education?', Paper presented at the *1997 Montessori Congress*, downloaded from <http://www.ilu.uu.se/ilu/montessori/MOrient.htm>

Jones, E. and Derman-Sparks, L. 1992, 'Meeting the challenge of diversity', *Young Children*, January, pp. 12–16.

Kahn, D. 1997, 'The child and nature: "set the child free"', in P. Jackson, *Orient express: intercontinental destinations for Montessori Education?*, Paper presented at the 1997 Montessori Congress, <http://www.ilu.uu.se/ilu/montessori/MSettech.htm>.

Katz, L. 1995, *Talks with Young Children: A Collection*, Ablex Publishing Corporation, New Jersey.

Knowles Kennedy, D. 1996, 'After Reggio Emilia: may the conversation begin!', *Young Children*, July, pp. 24–27.

Kramer, R. 1988, *Maria Montessori*, Hamish Hamilton Paperback, London.

Lawrence, H. and Coady, M. 2002, 'Development of spirituality acknowledgement in education and early childhood thinking', *Every Child*, 8(4), pp. 18–19.

Lim, B. 2004, 'Aesthetic discourses in early childhood settings: Dewey, Steiner, and Vygotsky', *Early Child Development and Care,* 174(5), pp. 473–486.

Linden Steiner Kindergarten, no date, *Welcome to Linden*, Linden Steiner Kindergarten, Melbourne.

MacNaughton, G. 2003, *Shaping Early Childhood: A Learners, Curriculum and Context*, Open University Press, Milton Keynes.

MacNaughton, G. and Hughes, P. 2001, 'Creating interpretive communities through staff parent communication', Research paper presentation to the *Association for Childhood Education International Conference*, 4–7 April, Toronto, Ontario, Canada.

Malaguzzi, L. 1993, 'History, ideas and basic philosophy', in C. Edwards, L. Gandini and G. Forman, eds, *The Hundred Languages of Children: The Reggio Emilia Approach to Early Childhood* (pp. 41–90), Ablex, Norwood, NJ.

Minkes, A. 1987, *The Entrepreneurial Manager: Decisions, Goals and Business Ideas*, Penguin Books, New York.

Mollet, D. 1991, 'How the Waldorf Approach changed a difficult class', *Educational Leadership*, October, pp. 55–56.

Montessori, M. 1936, *The Secret of Childhood*, Ballantine Books, London.

——1948/1962, *The Discovery of the Child*, Ballantine Books, London.

Moran, M., Desrochers, L. and Cavicchi, N. 2007, 'Progettazione and documentation as sociocultural activities changing communities of practice', *Theory into Practice*, 46(1), pp. 81–90.

Morrison, G. 1995, *Early Childhood Education Today*, 6th edn, Merrill, New Jersey.

Myers, P. 2006, 'Colonial consciousness', *Journal of European Studies,* 36(4), pp. 389–417.

New, R. 1993, 'Reggio Emilia: some lessons for US educators', *ERIC Digest,* EDO-PS-93-3.

Pugh, D., Hickson, D. and Hinings, C. 1983, *Writers on Organisations*, 3rd edn, Penguin Books, New York.

Reinsmith, W. 1989, 'The whole in every part: Steiner and Waldorf schooling', *The Educational Forum*, 54(1), pp. 81–91.

Rinaldi, C. 2006, *In dialogue with Reggio Emilia: listening, researching and learning.* Routledge, London/New York.

Robertson, J. 1995, 'Projects', *The Challenge*, June, pp. 12–15.

Robison, H. and Schwartz, S. 1982, *Designing Curriculum for Early Childhood*, Allyn & Bacon Inc., Boston.

Roopnarine, J.L., and Johnson, J.E. 2005, *Approaches to early childhood education*, 4th edn, Pearson, Upper Saddle River, NJ.

Ryan, S. 2004, 'Message in a model: teachers' responses to a court-ordered mandate for curriculum reform, educational policy', 18(5), pp. 661–685.

Samuelsson, I., Sheridan, S. and Williams, P. 2006, 'Five Preschool Curricula—Comparative Perspectives', *International Journal of Early Childhood*, 38(1), pp. 11–30.

Schweinhart, L. and Hohmann, C. 1992, 'The High/Scope K–3 curriculum: a new approach', *Principal*, 71(5), pp. 16, 18–19.

Spodek, B. and Saracho, O. 1994, *Right from the Start: Teaching Children Ages Three to Eight*, Allyn & Bacon Inc., Boston.

Steiner, R. 1919, 'An introduction to Waldorf Education', an essay by Rudolf Steiner, downloadable from <http://wn.elib.com/Steiner/Articles/IntWal_index.html>

——1970, 'Education and the Science of Spirit', lecture 1921, in P. Allen, ed., *Education as an Art* (pp. 19–49), Rudolf Steiner Publications, New York.

van Keulen, A. 2004, 'Persona Dolls are play friends in a group: about dolls with their own character and their own story', in A. van Keulen, ed., *Young children aren't biased, are they?!* (pp. 125–136), van Leer Foundation, Amsterdam.

Walsh, B. and Petty, K. 2007, 'Frequency of six early childhood education approaches: a 10-year content analysis of Early Childhood Educational Journal', *Early Childhood Education Journal*, 34(5), 301–305.

Weikart, D. 1995/96, 'High/Scope in action: the milestones', *High/Scope Resource, Special Edition*, pp. 4–6.

Weikart, D. and Schweinhart, L. 1987, 'The High/Scope cognitively orientated curriculum in early childhood', in J. Roopnarine, ed., *Approaches to Early Childhood Curriculum* (pp. 253–267), Merrill Publishing Company, Ohio.

Wilkes, G. (ed.) 1979, *Collins Dictionary of the English Language*, Penguin Books, Middlesex.

Index

Van Emmerick, R. 390
van Keulen, A. 410
van Kleeck, A. et al. 132
Van Scoter, J. and Boss, S. 73, 75, 76, 86
Vandermaas, M., Way, E. and Umpleby, J. 370
Vandermaas-Peeler, M., Way, E. and Umpleby, J. 375, 377
Vaughn, M. 286
Vaughn, S. et al. 222, 365
Vecchi, V. 296
verbal interaction 131–2
verbal techniques 68–73, 93–5, 364, 370, 400, 403, 405, 408, 410
Verdugo, D., Belmonte, V. and Alonso, I. 124
Verenikina, I. 371
Vermette, P., Harper, L. and Dimillo, S. 234
Vincent, J. 86
Viruru, G. and Cannella, G. 228, 292
Viruru, R. 255, 256, 257, 258
visual aids 35, 37, 41, 47, 59, 217
vocabulary 59–60, 62, 121, 131, 171, 172, 196
Vorderer, P. 118
Vygotsky, Leo Semenovich (1886–1934) 11–12, 122, 229, 348, 370, 371–2, 374, 377, 404

W
Waldorf Schooling 406–8
Walsh, B. and Blewitt, P. 171, 172
Walsh, B. and Petty, K. 401
Walters, K. 299, 300, 301
Wang, X., Berna, R. and Eberhard, P. 382
Ward, C. 73
Wardle, F. 105
Warger, C. 77
Warner, L. and Lynch, S. 72
Wasserman, S. 312
Wearmouth, J. 361
Wegerif, R. 154, 333
Weikart, D. 400
Weikart, D. and Schweinhart, L. 400, 401
Weincr, G. 268
Welch, G. 196
wellbeing, sense of 34, 53, 72, 95–6, 108, 120, 131, 194, 208
Wellhousen, K. and Crowther, I. 291
Wenden, A. 390
Wertsch, J. 229
West, B. 76
West, M. 346
Westwood, P. 49
Whaley, K. and Swadener, B. 187
Whalley, M. et al. 243, 244
Wheeler, J. 350, 354

Whinnery, K. and Whinnery, S. 392
Whitehead, M. 33, 220, 221
Whitehurst, G. et al. 171
Whiteman, P. 196
Whitin, D. and Whitin, P. 275
Whitney, T. 282
Wieder, S. and Greenspan, S. 95
Wilburne et al. 172
Williams, L. 228
Williamson, R. and Markman, E. 130
Willis, S. 25
Wilson Gillespie, C. 302
Wilson, P. 390
Wing Han Lamb, W. 337
Wing, L. 164
Winsler, A. and Naglieri, J. 351
Winter, P. 120
Winter, S. 136
Witt, S. and Kimble, L. 172
Wohlwend, K. 259
wonder, sense of 159–60, 172
Wood, K. and Frid, S. 108, 109, 110
Woolley, G. 74
Wright, J. and Cleary, K. 123
writing skills 48, 74, 86, 96, 162–3, 210, 378–9

Y
Yaoying, X. 323
Yelland, N. 250
Yelland, N., Rubin, A. and McWilliam, E. 87
York, S. 98, 198, 351, 391
Young, S. 192–3, 194
Youngquist, J. 48
Yuzawaa, M. et al. 82

Z
Zafranas, N. 218
Zammit, K. 271
Zhang, H. and Zhou, Y. 96
Zone of Proximal Development (ZPD) 371–2, 374, 378
Zygmunt-Fillwalk, E. et al. 315